ch 3-6

LAWYERS AS COUNSELORS:
A Client-Centered Approach

Second Edition

By

David A. Binder

Professor of Law, University of California, Los Angeles

Paul Bergman

Professor of Law, University of California, Los Angeles

Susan C. Price, Ph.D.

Paul R. Tremblay

Clinical Professor of Law, Boston College

AMERICAN CASEBOOK SERIES®

Mat #16366846

 *TEXT IS PRINTED ON 10% POST
CONSUMER RECYCLED PAPER*

Preface

This edition of <u>Lawyers As Counselors</u> builds on the client-centered approach that its predecessor editions have helped establish as the predominant hallmark of effective lawyer-client conversations devoted to problem-solving. We want to briefly highlight some of the principal additions and revisions that characterize this new edition.

The United States is increasingly a multi-cultural country, meaning that lawyers are more likely than ever to represent clients who identify with cultural backgrounds that lawyers are unfamiliar with. We have tried to address that trend in this edition with several discussions of "inter-cultural communication." You will find the most detailed coverage in Chapter 2, which sets forth dimensions of culture difference that cultural anthropologists, psychologists and sociologists have identified. Here and in other chapters, we discuss and illustrate how you might respond when you believe that cultural differences might be affecting the effectiveness of interviewing or counseling. At the same time, discussions of cultural difference can all too often lead to embarrassing and misleading reliance on stereotypes. Thus, we stress throughout the likely presence of variations within seemingly narrow cultures, and the reality that clients who share a common cultural background do not necessarily reflect that culture's values and traditions.

The counseling model that this book continues to set forth attempts to assure that clients have the opportunity to make sensible decisions that are satisfactory and in their best interests. At the same time, research continues to demonstrate that people's decision-making capacities are often influenced by a variety of "irrational" reasoning methods that collectively are often called "Cognitive Illusions." For example, the "Availability Heuristic" may lead clients to rely on single episodes that stick out in their minds, even though those episodes have little relevance to the clients' problems. Chapters 17 and 18 discuss how Cognitive Illusions such as these may affect decision-making, and how you might respond when you detect a Cognitive Illusion at work.

This edition refines and we think improves on the earlier books' discussions of interviewing strategies and techniques. For example, we no longer try to portray rather artificially what might happen during a single initial interview, and instead recognize that information-gathering may continue though a series of initial meetings. Moreover, we eliminate the suggestion that you should almost always temporarily terminate initial meetings in order to prepare for "theory development" questioning. We sincerely doubt whether that suggestion would have been popular with clients, or whether attorneys were likely to follow it. Also, this new edition provides a more complete picture of effective interviewing, describing strategies and techniques for uncovering and combating harmful information. (See Chapters 7 and 8.)

This new edition is in many other ways a richer book than its predecessors. We have not simply added and subtracted, but rather have revised the original text to improve its organization, readability and timeliness. We hope that while remaining true to our original conception of client-centered lawyering we have produced a much-improved text. To the extent that we have not succeeded in our aims, we encourage you to let us know.

PREFACE TO THE FIRST EDITION

Like the earlier *Legal Interviewing and Counseling: A Client-Centered Approach*, this book also adopts a client-centered approach. More than a set of techniques, the client-centered approach is an attitude of looking at problems from clients' perspectives, of seeing problems' diverse natures, and of making clients true partners in the resolution of their problems.

Clients often complain that, "My lawyer doesn't listen to me." Behind this complaint lies the reality that clients' problems typically embrace both legal and non-legal aspects-e.g., economic, social and psychological aspects. But lawyers, trained to focus on problems' legal aspects, tend to pigeonhole problems along substantive law lines such as a "medical malpractice case" or a "real property subdivision matter." As a result, lawyers tend to miss much of what clients are trying to explain and accomplish. Our hope is that the client-centered approach can help produce decisions that take account of all aspects of clients' problems and thereby make the world a bit better for both you and your clients.

While retaining many of the earlier work's client-centered themes, we have tried in this book to move beyond it in several ways.

First, we have tried to be more explicit about the principles that constitute a client-centered approach. Set forth in Chapter 2 [now Chapter 1], these principles underlie many of the book's concepts and techniques.

Second, we examine interviewing (information-gathering) not as a separate task, but as an integral part of the counseling process. Because we see lawyers' principal role as helping clients solve problems, we approach interviewing as an opportunity to learn about problems from clients' perspectives as well as to gather legally salient data.

Third, in an effort to write a book that will be useful in nearly all attorney-client relationships, we examine counseling principles and techniques in both litigation and transactional contexts. Thus, some chapters focus primarily on litigation matters (e.g., Chapters 8, 9, 10 and 21) [now Chapters 6, 7, 8 and 18]; others on proposed business deals (e.g., Chapters 11, 12 and 22) [now Chapters 9 and 19]; while the remaining chapters illustrate concepts and techniques with examples drawn from both litigation and transactional matters.

Fourth, we set forth and explore an explicit counseling standard. Most notably, the standard (described in Chapter 15) [now Chapter 12] is process-based rather than content-based. That is, we do not attempt to define how much "actual awareness" of relevant factors a client should have before making a decision. Rather, our standard encourages lawyers to engage clients in counseling dialogues during which clients' decisions, are preceded by joint examination of objectives, options and likely consequences. Since the state of clients' "actual awareness" is' unknowable, and the extent of counseling typically varies according to each client's unique circumstances, we think that our process standard is best suited to helping clients become active and knowledgeable participants in the resolution of their problems.

Finally, we recognize that in some circumstances, it is both proper and desirable for lawyers to give advice about what clients ought to do. Moreover, lawyers may even intervene in decisions when clients mis-predict their likely outcomes or when decisions are likely to have "immoral" consequences. The earlier book, perhaps in over-reaction to the tendency of many lawyers to tell their clients what to do, gave little comfort to those who thought that clients often expected and benefited from their lawyers' opinions. Taking what we now believe is a more realistic approach to advice-giving enables us to discuss how to give advice in a way that preserves client autonomy.

*

Acknowledgments

Numerous people helped to illuminate the way on our return visit to the complex subject of counseling. At the UCLA School of Law, many colleagues provided substantial help. Ken Klee, Steve Bainbridge and Iman Anabtawi provided special expertise with respect to the "deals counseling" chapters. Russell Korobkin gave often and willingly whenever we sought his advice with respect to the subject of "cognitive illusions." And Scott Cummings and Pat Sekaquaptewa provided us with many helpful insights into the subject of cross-cultural communication, Pat particularly with respect to Native Americans. Lastly, Tim Malloy provided helpful advice with examples of counseling conversations about environmental law issues.

At Boston College Law School, Leslie Espinoza Garvey, Alan Minuskin, Mark Spiegel, and Carwina Weng provided valuable suggestions across a range of counseling topics. Thanks also and especially to Lynn Barenberg.

Susan Gillig, the Director of the UCLA School of Law Clinical Program, provided even more assistance with this edition than she did with the previous one. Sue, you'll no doubt persevere until we get it right.

To all of these colleagues, we express our gratitude for your friendship, support, professionalism and genuine respect for and interest in the work of lawyers. And in the event of a future edition, should you want to do some of the actual writing, that will be fine too.

Randy Even, Esq., thank you for the insight about insurance—retained counsel and confidentiality.

As proof that we can maintain friendships outside the legal academy, we thank Dr. Felice Miller, Ph.D., for advice about cross-cultural communication.

Susan Price gratefully thanks Stephen Feldman, Andy Benjamin, Peter Klika, Timothy Coy, and Richard Reinking for their suggestions for coping with difficult clients and especially lawyers (co-authors excepted!) and referring the lot of them to mental health professionals.

As this edition of the book progressed at somewhat less than the speed of light from tentative outline to nearly-finished book (the Completely Finished Book being the Holy Grail that has eluded authors from time immemorial), a few wonderful law students went through puberty, graduated from college and entered and in some cases graduated from law school just so they could spend hours in various libraries doing research and providing helpful perspectives on our ideas. At UCLA, special thanks to Katy Klinedinst for cheerfully pretending that we had clearly delineated the type of research help we needed and likely sources of information; your assistance was invaluable in bringing the work to fruition. Our sincere gratitude as well to Pitter Hogan, Kal Shobaki and Mathew Sngilek. At Boston College, special thanks to Jason Bryan, Peter Durning, Rocky Pilgrim, Miguel Flores and Tatum Pritchard.

Tal Grietzer, thank you for your masterful help with word processing. Every time one of our sneaky computers tried to play tricks with our ideas, Tal taught it a lesson it will never forget.

Kenney Hegland, it is fair to say that your contributions to this book matched those for the previous edition.

Our gratitude to the UCLA Academic Senate, the UCLA Dean's Fund, the Boston College Law School Dean's Fund, and Hale and Dorr, LLP for your generous financial support. We did our best to spend your money wisely.

Finally, Paul Tremblay thanks Linda, Chris and Jen, for their endless support, encouragement and patience. As a result, David Binder and Paul Bergman have to say something nice about Melinda and Andrea, respectively.

DAVID A. BINDER
PAUL BERGMAN
SUSAN C. PRICE
PAUL R. TREMBLAY

February, 2004

Summary of Contents

Page

PREFACE iii
ACKNOWLEDGMENTS vii

PART ONE. INTRODUCTION TO CLIENT–CENTERED COUNSELING

Chapter 1. Client–Centered Lawyering 2
1. Introduction 2
2. Why Should You Adopt a Client–Centered Approach? 4
3. Hallmarks of Client–Centered Counseling 8
4. Integrating Client–Centered Hallmarks Into the Interviewing
   & Counseling Process 11

PART TWO. FUNDAMENTAL COUNSELING SKILLS

Chapter 2. Motivation 16
1. Introduction 16
2. A General Description of Motivation 16
3. Motivation in Lawyer–Client Dialogues 18
4. Inhibitors 19
5. Facilitators 27
6. Summary 31
7. Personality Conflicts 31
8. Motivation in Inter–Cultural Contexts 32

Chapter 3. Active Listening 41
1. Introduction 41
2. Identifying Content and Feelings 42
3. Obstacles to Good Listening 44
4. Passive Listening Techniques 44
5. Active Listening 48
6. Difficulties in Mastering Active Listening 57
7. How Much Active Listening? 63

Chapter 4. Forms of Questions 64
1. Introduction 64
2. Forms of Questions 65
3. Common Advantages and Disadvantages of the Different
   Forms of Questions 68
4. Conclusion 77

Page

PART THREE. INFORMATION–GATHERING

Chapter 5. Beginning Client Conferences ---------------------------- **80**
1. Introduction --- 80
2. Pre–Initial Meeting Communications---------------------------------- 81
3. Greeting Clients --- 82
4. Icebreaking-- 83
5. Preliminary Problem Identification ---------------------------------- 86
6. Preparatory Explanations -- 103
7. Beginning Follow–Up Meetings ------------------------------------- 108

Chapter 6. Eliciting Time Lines --------------------------------------- **112**
1. Introduction --- 112
2. How Two Phase Interviews Help Develop Persuasive Stories ---- 113
3. Time Line Story Features -- 114
4. Advantages of Eliciting Time Line Stories -------------------------- 116
5. The Tentativeness of Time Line Stories ----------------------------- 119
6. Time Line Preparatory Explanations-------------------------------- 120
7. "Start at the Beginning" -- 126
8. Expanding "Quickie" Time Line Stories ---------------------------- 127
9. Time Line Questioning Techniques --------------------------------- 128
10. Taking Probe Notes -- 135
11. Examples and Analyses of Time Line Stories ---------------------- 137
12. Special Time Line Issues-- 141
13. Prepare and Update Chronologies --------------------------------- 148

Chapter 7. Theory Development Questioning—Pursuing Helpful Evidence -- **149**
1. Introduction --- 149
2. The Process of Theory Development Questioning----------------- 150
3. Identifying Material Facts-- 151
4. Identifying Emotive (Non–Material) Factual Propositions -------- 158
5. Identifying Helpful Evidence -- 159
6. Theory Development Questioning Techniques --------------------- 166
7. Bolstering Credibility -- 186

Chapter 8. Theory Development Questioning— Undermining Adversaries' Likely Contentions ----------- **194**
1. Introduction --- 194
2. Uncovering Evidence Tending to Rebut Harmful Disclosures---- 194
3. Uncovering Adversaries' Likely Contentions---------------------- 196
4. Probing Clumped and Conclusory Responses --------------------- 199
5. Probing Clumped Events and Behavior Over Time Responses --- 200
6. Filling Gaps in Stories--- 200
7. Preserving Information --- 201
8. Example: Integrating the Four Theory Development Tasks ------ 202

Page

Chapter 9. Gathering Information for Business Transactions _____ **208**
1. Introduction _____ 208
2. Do Not a "Deal–Killer" Be _____ 209
3. The Typical Process of Completing Business Transactions _____ 209
4. Information Gathering Similarities Between Deals and Litigation _____ 211
5. Gathering Legal and Non–Legal Information _____ 211
6. Topics That Commonly Arise In Proposed Business Transactions _____ 213
7. Transaction–Specific Topics _____ 219
8. Preparing Draft Agreements _____ 221

Chapter 10. Techniques for Gathering Information About Proposed Business Transactions _____ **223**
1. Introduction _____ 223
2. Preliminary Problem Identification _____ 224
3. Preparatory Explanations _____ 225
4. Topical Inquiries _____ 226
5. Order of Inquiry _____ 226
6. Using T–Funnels _____ 227
7. Eliciting Chronologies _____ 229
8. Conclusion _____ 233

Chapter 11. Concluding Client Conferences _____ **234**
1. Introduction _____ 235
2. Specifying "The Next Steps" _____ 235
3. Concluding Initial Meetings: Establishing a Professional Relationship _____ 236
4. Concluding Initial Meetings: Giving a Tentative Assessment _____ 238

Chapter 12. Gathering Information From Atypical and Difficult Clients _____ **247**
1. Introduction _____ 247
2. Reluctance to Discuss Particular Topics _____ 247
3. Reluctance to Commence an Initial Interview _____ 253
4. Communicating With Aged and Infirm Clients _____ 255
5. Rambling Clients _____ 256
6. Clients Who Are Hostile, Angry and Explosive _____ 260
7. Fabrication _____ 262

PART FOUR. DECISION–MAKING

Chapter 13. Principles Underlying Effective Counseling _____ **270**
1. Introduction _____ 271
2. Clients Are Primary Decision–Makers _____ 272
3. A Standard for Client Decision–Making: "Substantial Legal or Non–Legal Impacts" _____ 275
4. The "Substantial Impact" Standard and Lawyering Tactics _____ 280
5. Your Role in the Counseling and Advising Process _____ 281

                                                                    Page
Chapter 14. Implementing an Effective Counseling Process ------ **299**
1. Introduction -- 299
2. The Importance of Neutrality ------------------------------- 300
3. Counseling Plans --- 301
4. Provide Preparatory Explanations -------------------------- 301
5. Clarifying Clients' Objectives ---------------------------- 302
6. Identifying Alternatives ----------------------------------- 304
7. Identifying Consequences ---------------------------------- 306
8. Making Decisions -- 322

Chapter 15.   Clarifying Clients' Objectives --------------- **323**
1. Introduction -- 323
2. Vague or Uncertain Objectives ----------------------------- 323
3. Incomplete Objectives ------------------------------------- 325
4. Updating Clients' Objectives ------------------------------ 326
5. Illegal or "Immoral" Objectives --------------------------- 328

Chapter 16.   Identifying Alternatives --------------------- **331**
1. Introduction -- 331
2. Two Bases of Expertise ------------------------------------ 332
3. Identify "Pivotal" Alternatives --------------------------- 332
4. Professional Satisfaction --------------------------------- 333
5. Develop Familiarity With Relevant "Industries" ----------- 334
6. Briefly Describe Alternatives and Outcomes That Are Likely to Be Unfamiliar to Clients ------------------------------------ 338
7. Frame Options Neutrally ----------------------------------- 340
8. Evaluate Clients' Immediate Rejection of Alternatives ---- 342
9. Recast Clients' Inadequate Alternatives ------------------ 343
10. Adding Additional Options as the Counseling Process Continues -- 345
11. The Impact of Changed Circumstances --------------------- 346

Chapter 17.   Identifying Consequences --------------------- **347**
1. Introduction -- 348
2. Responding to Consequences That Clients Foresee ---------- 348
3. Probe the Adequacy of clients' Data Bases ---------------- 349
4. Respond to Data Bases Emanating From Cognitive Illusions - 351
5. Helping Clients Recognize Non–Legal Consequences --------- 356
6. Articulating Legal Consequences You Foresee -------------- 358

Chapter 18.   Final Decision–Making ------------------------ **367**
1. Introduction -- 367
2. Clients Request Your Opinion ------------------------------ 368
3. Responding to Clients Who Are Unable to Decide ----------- 371
4. Intervening in Clients' Decisions ------------------------- 379
5. Accepting Differences in Risk Aversion & Values ---------- 393
6. The Borderland of Intervention --------------------------- 395
7. Counseling "My Mind Is Made Up" Clients ------------------ 397

Page

Chapter 19. The Counseling Model and Litigation **400**
1. Introduction 400
2. A Case Study: Vitissian v. Linus Hauling Co. and Industrial
   Resources Corp. 400
3. "Snapshot 1": Whether to File Suit 401
4. "Snapshot 2": Whether to Take A Deposition 406
5. "Snapshot 3": Whether to Settle 409

Chapter 20. Counseling "Deals" Clients **415**
1. The Scope of This Chapter 415
2. Case Study No. 1: PSD Corporation 416
3. Preparing to Review an Agreement 417
4. Topics to Explore When Counseling About Deals' Individual
   Provisions 422
5. Counseling Clients About Deals' Overall Wisdom 437

**Chapter 21. Referring Clients to Mental Health
   Professionals** **445**
1. Introduction 445
2. Strategies for Making Referrals 445
3. Archetypal Situations Involving Case–Related Referrals 452
4. Archetypal Situations Involving Client–Related Referrals 454
5. Conclusion 455

INDEX 457

*

Table of Contents

                                                                    Page

PREFACE -- iii

ACKNOWLEDGMENTS -- vii

PART ONE. INTRODUCTION TO CLIENT–CENTERED COUNSELING

Chapter 1. Client–Centered Lawyering ------------------------- 2

1. Introduction --- 2
2. Why Should You Adopt a Client–Centered Approach? -------------- 4
   A. Clients Are Autonomous "Owners" of Their Problems-------- 4
   B. Clients Are Generally in a Better Position Than Lawyers to Identify and Assess the Importance of Solutions' Non-Legal Consequences --- 5
   C. Clients Are Normally in a Better Position Than Lawyers to Determine What Risks Are Worth Taking --------------------- 7
   D. Clients Are Capable of and Interested in Participating in the Counseling Process and Making Important Decisions 8
   E. Active Lawyer–Client Collaboration Promotes Effective Implementation of Decisions ----------------------------------- 8
3. Hallmarks of Client–Centered Counseling ---------------------- 8
   A. Seek Out Potential Non–Legal Consequences ---------------- 9
   B. Ask Clients to Suggest Potential Solutions --------------- 9
   C. Encourage Clients to Make Important Decisions ----------- 10
   D. Provide Advice Based on Clients' Values ----------------- 10
   E. Acknowledge Clients' Feelings and Recognize Their Importance -- 11
4. Integrating Client–Centered Hallmarks Into the Interviewing & Counseling Process --- 11
   A. The Remaining Three Parts of the Book ------------------- 11
   B. The Unpredictability of the Counseling Process --------- 12

PART TWO. FUNDAMENTAL COUNSELING SKILLS

Chapter 2. Motivation -- 16

1. Introduction -- 16
2. A General Description of Motivation--------------------------- 16
   A. The Nature of Human Need------------------------------- 16
   B. Conflicting Needs -------------------------------------- 17
3. Motivation in Lawyer–Client Dialogues----------------------- 18

Page

4. Inhibitors 19
   A. Ego Threat 19
   B. Case Threat 20
   C. Role Expectations 21
   D. Etiquette Barrier 23
   E. Trauma 24
   F. Perceived Irrelevancy 25
   G. Greater Need 26
5. Facilitators 27
   A. Empathic Understanding 27
   B. Fulfilling Expectations 29
   C. Recognition 30
   D. Altruistic Appeals 30
   E. Extrinsic Reward 31
6. Summary 31
7. Personality Conflicts 31
8. Motivation in Inter–Cultural Contexts 32
   A. The Risk of Stereotyping 32
   B. Dimensions of Potential Cultural Differences 34
   C. Strategies for Responding to Inter–Cultural Communications Difficulties 38
   D. Example for Analysis 40

Chapter 3. Active Listening **41**
1. Introduction 41
2. Identifying Content and Feelings 42
3. Obstacles to Good Listening 44
4. Passive Listening Techniques 44
   A. Silence 45
   B. Minimal Prompts 46
   C. Open–Ended Questions 47
5. Active Listening 48
   A. Generally 48
   B. Responding to Vaguely Expressed Feelings 49
   C. Responding to Unstated Feelings 50
   D. Responding to Non–Verbal Expressions of Feelings 52
   E. Responding to Clearly–Articulated Feelings 55
   F. Non–Empathic (Judgmental) Responses 55
6. Difficulties in Mastering Active Listening 57
   A. "Feelings Are for 'Shrinks,' Not Lawyers" 57
   B. "I Feel Empathic, But I Just Can't Find the Right Words" 58
   C. "There's No Way I Can Empathize With That Client" 59
   D. "Using Active Listening Will Make a Client Too Emotional" 60
   E. "Talking About Feelings Makes It Difficult for Me to Get Back on Track" 60
   F. "The Client Is So Confused That I Don't Know Which Feelings to Reflect" 61

Page

6. Difficulties in Mastering Active Listening—Continued
   G. "Active Listening Is Manipulative" --------------------------- 62
7. How Much Active Listening? ----------------------------------- 63

Chapter 4. Forms of Questions ------------------------------ **64**
1. Introduction --- 64
2. Forms of Questions --- 65
   A. Generally --- 65
   B. Open Questions -- 66
   C. Closed Questions -- 67
   D. Yes–No Questions -- 67
   E. Leading Questions --------------------------------------- 67
3. Common Advantages and Disadvantages of the Different
   Forms of Questions -- 68
   A. Open Questions -- 68
      1. Open Questions Often Motivate Full Client Partic-
         ipation -- 68
      2. Open Questions Often Enhance the Amount of Informa-
         tion You Uncover ------------------------------------- 69
      3. Open Questions May Inhibit Full Client Participation ---- 70
      4. Open Questions Do Not Thoroughly Mine Clients' Mem-
         ories -- 70
      5. Open Questions May Be Inefficient --------------------- 70
   B. Closed Questions -- 71
      1. Closed Questions Elicit Details ---------------------- 71
      2. Closed Questions May Provide Motivation -------------- 71
      3. Too Many Closed Questions May Harm Rapport ---------- 72
      4. Closed Questions May Prevent You from Learning Im-
         portant Information ---------------------------------- 73
      5. Closed Questions Can Create Inaccurate Responses ------ 73
   C. Leading Questions --------------------------------------- 74
      1. Leading Questions May Overcome Potential Inhibitors -- 74
      2. Leading Questions May Enhance the Possibility of Elic-
         iting Incorrect Information -------------------------- 75
      3. Leading Questions May Be Ethically Improper ---------- 75
   D. Factors Tending to Result in Over–Reliance on Narrow
      Questions --- 75
      1. The "Filling in" Phenomenon ------------------------- 75
      2. Premature Diagnosis --------------------------------- 76
4. Conclusion --- 77

PART THREE. INFORMATION–GATHERING

Chapter 5. Beginning Client Conferences -------------------- **80**
1. Introduction --- 80
2. Pre–Initial Meeting Communications ------------------------- 81
3. Greeting Clients --- 82
4. Icebreaking -- 83

Page

5. Preliminary Problem Identification ----------------------------------- 86
   A. The Four Main Topics-- 87
      1. Problem Description--- 87
      2. Desired Outcome --- 87
      3. Means of Achieving Desired Outcome ---------------------- 88
      4. Legal and Non–Legal Concerns ----------------------------- 88
   B. Why Begin With Preliminary Problem Identification? -------- 89
   C. Carrying Out the Process of Preliminary Problem Identifi-
      cation --- 91
   D. Examples for Analysis -- 94
   E. Responding to Clients' Volcanic Descriptions----------------- 99
   F. Responding to Early Requests for Your Opinion--------------- 101
6. Preparatory Explanations --- 103
   A. Benefits of Preparatory Explanations ------------------------ 104
   B. Contents of Preparatory Explanations ------------------------ 104
   C. Confidentiality --- 106
   D. Risks of Excessive Length ------------------------------------- 107
7. Beginning Follow–Up Meetings -------------------------------------- 108
   A. Clients' Changed Concerns and Objectives ----------------- 108
   B. Clients' New Information -------------------------------------- 109
   C. Your Interim Activity-- 109
   D. Your New Information --- 110
   E. Order of Discussion --- 111

Chapter 6. Eliciting Time Lines------------------------------------ **112**
1. Introduction --- 112
2. How Two Phase Interviews Help Develop Persuasive Stories ---- 113
3. Time Line Story Features -- 114
4. Advantages of Eliciting Time Line Stories ------------------------- 116
5. The Tentativeness of Time Line Stories --------------------------- 119
6. Time Line Preparatory Explanations------------------------------- 120
7. "Start at the Beginning" -- 126
8. Expanding "Quickie" Time Line Stories --------------------------- 127
9. Time Line Questioning Techniques --------------------------------- 128
   A. Open Questions--- 128
   B. Closed Questions --- 130
   C. Summary Technique-- 131
   D. Avoid Creating Gaps --- 132
   E. Events vs. Details -- 133
   F. Referring Clients to Documents----------------------------- 134
   G. Using Active Listening --------------------------------------- 135
10. Taking Probe Notes --- 135
11. Examples and Analyses of Time Line Stories --------------------- 137
12. Special Time Line Issues-- 141
   A. The Travels of Odysseus------------------------------------- 141
   B. Co–Authored Time Lines ------------------------------------- 141
   C. Multiple Time Lines--- 142
   D. Clients Who Can't Provide Time Lines ---------------------- 143
13. Prepare and Update Chronologies ---------------------------------- 148

Page

Chapter 7. Theory Development Questioning—Pursuing Helpful Evidence 149
1. Introduction 149
2. The Process of Theory Development Questioning 150
3. Identifying Material Facts 151
   A. Identifying Legal Theories 152
   B. Parsing Legal Theories Into Constituent Elements 153
      1. Legal Theories Are Abstract Shells 153
      2. Elements Themselves Are Legal Abstractions 153
      3. Restating Elements As Factual Propositions 154
         a. Multiple Factual Propositions 156
         b. Plaintiffs' and Defendants' Factual Propositions 157
4. Identifying Emotive (Non–Material) Factual Propositions 158
5. Identifying Helpful Evidence 159
   A. The Role of Experience 159
   B. Circumstantial Evidence 161
   C. Historical Reconstruction 163
      1. In General 163
      2. Chronology: Before, During and After 164
      3. Multiple Perspectives 165
   D. Strengthening Generalizations 165
6. Theory Development Questioning Techniques 166
   A. Direct Inquiries 167
   B. The T-funnel Questioning Pattern 167
   C. T-funnel Questioning Techniques 168
      1. T-funneling Events 168
      2. T-funneling Topics 170
      3. Using "Partial" T-funnels 172
   D. Additional T-funnel Techniques 173
      1. "Park" Information to Avoid Becoming Sidetracked 173
      2. Use T-funnels Cyclically as You Unpark Data 174
      3. "Kick Start" Clients' Memories through Visualization 175
      4. Press Clients to Search Their Memories 177
      5. Summarize Clients' Responses 178
      6. Use Judgment 178
      7. The Ethics of T-funnel Questioning 178
   E. Break General Descriptions Into Sub–Events 180
      1. Techniques for Probing Clumped Events 181
      2. Techniques for Probing Conditions and Behaviors over Time 183
   F. Probe Conclusions for Details 184
   G. Probe Gaps to Uncover Additional Events 185
7. Bolstering Credibility 186
   A. Credibility Enhancers 187
      1. Ability to Perceive 187
      2. Reasons to Recall 188

Page

7. Bolstering Credibility—Continued
   3. Ability to Provide Surrounding Details 189
   4. Consistent Actions 189
   5. Reasons/Motive to Engage in Conduct 190
   6. Corroboration 191
   7. Neutrality/Bias 191
   B. Exploring the Credibility of Hearsay Evidence 191
   C. Preserving Rapport 192

Chapter 8. Theory Development Questioning— Undermining Adversaries' Likely Contentions 194
1. Introduction 194
2. Uncovering Evidence Tending to Rebut Harmful Disclosures 194
3. Uncovering Adversaries' Likely Contentions 196
   A. Preparatory Explanations 197
   B. Questioning Clients About Adversaries' Contentions 198
4. Probing Clumped and Conclusory Responses 199
5. Probing Clumped Events and Behavior Over Time Responses 200
6. Filling Gaps in Stories 200
7. Preserving Information 201
8. Example: Integrating the Four Theory Development Tasks 202

Chapter 9. Gathering Information for Business Transactions 208
1. Introduction 208
2. Do Not a "Deal–Killer" Be 209
3. The Typical Process of Completing Business Transactions 209
4. Information Gathering Similarities Between Deals and Litigation 211
5. Gathering Legal and Non–Legal Information 211
6. Topics That Commonly Arise In Proposed Business Transactions 213
   A. Clients' Objectives 213
   B. Proposed Deals' Current Terms and Prior History 214
   C. Timetables for Finalizing Deals 215
   D. Other Parties 216
   E. Business Operations 217
   F. How Deals Will Function 218
   G. Deals' Economics 219
7. Transaction–Specific Topics 219
8. Preparing Draft Agreements 221

Chapter 10. Techniques for Gathering Information About Proposed Business Transactions 223
1. Introduction 223
2. Preliminary Problem Identification 224
3. Preparatory Explanations 225
4. Topical Inquiries 226
5. Order of Inquiry 226

Page

6. Using T-funnels 227
7. Eliciting Chronologies 229
   A. The Terms of Proposed Deals 229
   B. How Deals Will Function 231
   C. "Quasi" Time Lines 232
      1. Business Operations 232
      2. Parties' Past Dealings 232
8. Conclusion 233

Chapter 11. Concluding Client Conferences **234**
1. Introduction 235
2. Specifying "The Next Steps" 235
3. Concluding Initial Meetings: Establishing a Professional Relationship 236
   A. Formalize an Attorney–Client Relationship 236
   B. Establish a Relationship's Parameters 236
   C. Establish a Fee Arrangement 237
4. Concluding Initial Meetings: Giving a Tentative Assessment 238
   A. Adjourning Without Assessing Rights 239
   B. Adjourning After Providing a Tentative Assessment of Rights 241
   C. Adjourning in the Face of Uncertainty About Potential Options 242
   D. Good News, Bad News 243
   E. Rookie Naiveté and Tentative Assessments 246

Chapter 12. Gathering Information From Atypical and Difficult Clients **247**
1. Introduction 247
2. Reluctance to Discuss Particular Topics 247
   A. Sources and Indicia of Reluctance 247
   B. Techniques for Responding to Client Reluctance 248
      1. Motivational Statements 249
      2. Confidentiality 251
      3. Changing the Pattern of Questions 251
3. Reluctance to Commence an Initial Interview 253
   A. Motivational Statements and Closed Questions 254
   B. Asking Clients to Question You 254
4. Communicating With Aged and Infirm Clients 255
5. Rambling Clients 256
6. Clients Who Are Hostile, Angry and Explosive 260
7. Fabrication 262
   A. Common Causes and Indicia of Fabrication 262
   B. Responding to Suspected Fabrication 263
      1. Prevention 263
      2. Confrontation 265
         a. Request Clarification 265
         b. The Omniscient Third Party 266

Page

7. Fabrication—Continued
   3. Silence 267
   4. Direct Verbal Confrontation 268

PART FOUR. DECISION–MAKING

Chapter 13. Principles Underlying Effective Counseling 270
1. Introduction 271
2. Clients Are Primary Decision–Makers 272
3. A Standard for Client Decision–Making: "Substantial Legal or
   Non–Legal Impacts" 275
4. The "Substantial Impact" Standard and Lawyering Tactics...... 280
5. Your Role in the Counseling and Advising Process 281
   A. Explore Alternatives and Consequences 282
      1. Information to Elicit from Clients 282
        a. Clients' Objectives 283
        b. Potential Solutions 283
        c. Potential Consequences 283
        d. Bases for Clients' Predictions 283
        e. Questions and Concerns 284
      2. Information to Provide to Clients 284
        a. Potential Solutions 284
        b. Potential Consequences 285
        c. Advice 285
   B. Provide an Opportunity to Evaluate Options and Conse-
      quences 285
   C. Afford Clients a Reasonable Opportunity to Evaluate Alter-
      natives and Consequences 286
      1. "Pivotal Alternatives and Consequences" 286
      2. "Similarly–Situated Clients" 287
      3. "Reasonable Opportunity to Understand and Evaluate" 287
   D. Providing Advice 289
   E. Intervening in Clients' Decisions 292
      1. Decisions That Substantially Contravene Clients' Stated
        Objectives 292
      2. Decisions That Contravene Your Moral Beliefs 293
      3. Other Lawyer–Client Value Conflicts 296
        a. Risk–Aversion 296
        b. Interference with Professional Skills 297
   F. Refusing to Implement Clients' Choices 298

**Chapter 14. Implementing an Effective Counseling
   Process 299**
1. Introduction 299
2. The Importance of Neutrality 300
3. Counseling Plans 301
4. Provide Preparatory Explanations 301
5. Clarifying Clients' Objectives 302
6. Identifying Alternatives 304

Page

7. Identifying Consequences ------------------------------------ 306
   A. The Necessity to Predict ------------------------------- 306
   B. Predicting Legal Consequences ------------------------- 307
   C. Predicting Non–Legal Consequences -------------------- 308
   D. Organizing the Discussion of Consequences ----------- 308
      1. Review Options Separately -------------------------- 309
      2. Ask Clients to Choose a Starting Place ------------ 309
      3. Adopt the Role of Information Seeker -------------- 309
      4. The Cross over Phenomenon ------------------------ 311
      5. Discuss Consequences You Foresee ---------------- 317
      6. Identify Downstream Consequences --------------- 320
      7. Chart Alternatives and Consequences ------------- 320
8. Making Decisions -- 322

Chapter 15. Clarifying Clients' Objectives ------------- **323**
1. Introduction -- 323
2. Vague or Uncertain Objectives ------------------------- 323
3. Incomplete Objectives -------------------------------- 325
4. Updating Clients' Objectives -------------------------- 326
5. Illegal or "Immoral" Objectives ---------------------- 328

Chapter 16. Identifying Alternatives -------------------- **331**
1. Introduction -- 331
2. Two Bases of Expertise ------------------------------- 332
3. Identify "Pivotal" Alternatives ---------------------- 332
4. Professional Satisfaction ----------------------------- 333
5. Develop Familiarity With Relevant "Industries" ------- 334
6. Briefly Describe Alternatives and Outcomes That Are Likely to Be Unfamiliar to Clients ------------------------------ 338
7. Frame Options Neutrally ------------------------------ 340
8. Evaluate Clients' Immediate Rejection of Alternatives --- 342
9. Recast Clients' Inadequate Alternatives --------------- 343
10. Adding Additional Options as the Counseling Process Continues --- 345
11. The Impact of Changed Circumstances ----------------- 346

Chapter 17. Identifying Consequences ------------------- **347**
1. Introduction -- 348
2. Responding to Consequences That Clients Foresee ------ 348
   A. Convert Consequences Into Pros or Cons ----------- 348
   B. Inquire Into Clients' Data Bases ------------------ 349
3. Probe the Adequacy of clients' Data Bases ------------ 349
4. Respond to Data Bases Emanating From Cognitive Illusions ----- 351
5. Helping Clients Recognize Non–Legal Consequences ----- 356
   A. "Industry Knowledge" ----------------------------- 356
   B. Everyday Experience ------------------------------ 357
   C. Effects on Other Persons ------------------------- 358

Page

6. Articulating Legal Consequences You Foresee ----------- 358
    A. Describe Sub–Predictions ------------------------- 358
    B. State Predictions as Numerical Probabilities When Prac-
        tical --- 360
    C. Identify Ranges of Outcomes ---------------------- 362
    D. Characterize Legal Predictions as Advantages and Disad-
        vantages -- 362

Chapter 18. Final Decision–Making ------------------ **367**
1. Introduction --- 367
2. Clients Request Your Opinion ------------------------- 368
    A. Giving Advice Based on Clients' Values ----------- 368
    B. Giving Advice Based on Your Personal Values ------ 369
    C. Responding to Clients' Premature Requests for Your Opin-
        ion --- 370
3. Responding to Clients Who Are Unable to Decide ------ 371
    A. Acknowledge Conflicting Feelings ----------------- 371
    B. "Value–Rate" Consequences ----------------------- 373
    C. Involve Clients' Trusted Associates in Decision–Making --- 376
    D. Offering Unsolicited Advice ---------------------- 378
4. Intervening in Clients' Decisions -------------------- 379
    A. Misprediction ----------------------------------- 380
        1. Potentially Insufficient Data Bases --------- 380
        2. Mispredictions and "Cognitive Illusions" ---- 382
            a. The Sunk Costs Phenomenon -------------- 383
            b. The Gambler's Fallacy ------------------ 383
            c. The Endowment Effect ------------------- 384
            d. The Overconfidence Phenomenon ---------- 384
            e. Self–Serving Bias ---------------------- 385
            f. The Anchoring Effect ------------------- 385
        3. De–Biasing Strategies ---------------------- 386
            a. Lawyer as Educator --------------------- 386
            b. Consider the Other Side ---------------- 388
    B. "Immoral" Decisions ----------------------------- 391
5. Accepting Differences in Risk Aversion & Values ----- 393
    A. Risk Aversion ----------------------------------- 393
    B. Value Differences ------------------------------- 394
    C. Cultural Differences ---------------------------- 395
6. The Borderland of Intervention ---------------------- 395
7. Counseling "My Mind Is Made Up" Clients ------------- 397

Chapter 19. The Counseling Model and Litigation ---- **400**
1. Introduction -- 400
2. A Case Study: Vitissian v. Linus Hauling Co. and Industrial
    Resources Corp. ------------------------------------- 400
3. "Snapshot 1": Whether to File Suit ------------------ 401
4. "Snapshot 2": Whether to Take A Deposition --------- 406
5. "Snapshot 3": Whether to Settle -------------------- 409

Page

Chapter 20. Counseling "Deals" Clients ------------------- **415**
  1. The Scope of This Chapter ------------------------ 415
  2. Case Study No. 1: PSD Corporation ----------------- 416
  3. Preparing to Review an Agreement ------------------ 417
    A. Deciding Which Provisions to Discuss -------------- 418
    B. Alerting Clients to Omitted or Alternative Versions of Provisions ------------------------------------ 420
    C. Order of Review of Provisions -------------------- 421
    D. Use "Term Sheets" ------------------------------ 421
  4. Topics to Explore When Counseling About Deals' Individual Provisions --------------------------------------- 422
    A. Provisions' Meaning ----------------------------- 422
    B. Provisions' Adequacy From Clients' Perspectives ------- 423
    C. Provisions' Adequacy From Other Parties' Perspectives ------ 426
    D. An Illustrative "Deals Counseling" Conversation ------ 428
  5. Counseling Clients About Deals' Overall Wisdom ------ 437
    A. Case Study No. 2: Snacks Sixth Avenue ----------- 437
    B. Should Josef Enter Into The Lease?: "Go/No Go" ------ 438

Chapter 21. Referring Clients to Mental Health Professionals ------------------------------- **445**
  1. Introduction -------------------------------------- 445
  2. Strategies for Making Referrals ------------------- 445
    A. Pre–Referral Processes -------------------------- 445
    B. Discussing Referrals With Clients ---------------- 446
      1. Client–Related Referrals --------------------- 447
      2. Case–Related Referrals ---------------------- 451
  3. Archetypal Situations Involving Case–Related Referrals ---------- 452
  4. Archetypal Situations Involving Client–Related Referrals -------- 454
  5. Conclusion --------------------------------------- 455

INDEX --- 457

*

LAWYERS AS COUNSELORS:
A Client-Centered Approach

Second Edition

*

Part One

INTRODUCTION TO CLIENT-CENTERED COUNSELING

Consisting solely of a single chapter, Part One explores the general nature of clients' problems and identifies the central components of client-centered interviewing and counseling processes for resolving them.

Chapter 1

CLIENT–CENTERED LAWYERING

* * *

John Crampton of Mid–Marine Insurance enthusiastically describes Mid–Marine's potential acquisition of Entcrprises Inc., a small aluminum manufacturer. Gary Swartz of the Crestwood Home Owners Association frantically wants to enjoin a Crestwood property owner who, despite deed restrictions, wants to split his lot. Stephanie Belandis, Jacquie Bowman, and Jennifer Van Campen, representatives of the Brighton Tenants Union, cautiously describe their plans to purchase and renovate an abandoned building for use as low-income housing. Alex Combs sadly wonders how his arrest for burglary will affect his job and children. Louise Harris, manager of Blake County Water District, discusses the District's need to raise capital through a new bond issue. Marlene Fox excitedly describes a new record deal that Columbia wants her to sign. Phil Bondchefski, the CEO of Apex Steel, is furious that Apex has been sued for price fixing. Arlene Wagner, executive director of the local NAACP chapter, is concerned about renewing the chapter's lease. Helen Reston angrily relates that she was fired for reporting the company's practice of overcharging on government contracts. Charles Winnegar quietly states that he wants to make a will leaving nothing to his son. Grace Parker dispassionately expresses her desire to sell her $750,000 lakeside vacation house without capital gains liability.

* * *

1. INTRODUCTION

Clients come to lawyers seeking help in solving problems. And as the opening examples suggest, the range of people and problems that you are likely to encounter as a lawyer is enormous. The array embraces differences in size, complexity, emotional content and legal status.[1] Some

---

1. By size, lawyers typically mean the amount at stake. Cf. Mark Galanter, *Mega–Law & Mega–Lawyering in the Contemporary United States*, in THE SOCIOLOGY OF THE PROFESSIONS, 156–57 (1983). Complexity, on the other hand, usually has no single meaning. Cases are seen as factually, procedurally and/or legally complex. Factual complexity typically refers to matters involving a number of factual disputes, a large number of witnesses and a substantial amount of evidence. When terming a case legally com-

problems involve disputes over past events and others focus on planning for the future. Nonetheless, all of the problems have something in common—the clients hope that satisfactory solutions can be achieved with the aid of your lawyerly knowledge, skills and judgment.

Thus, no matter who your client, what the substantive legal issues or whether a situation involves litigation or planning, your principal role as a lawyer will almost always be the same—to help clients achieve satisfactory and effective solutions to problems. The process by which you facilitate the resolution of clients' problems—that is, the process of counseling—is the subject of this book.

This book sets forth a "client-centered" approach to counseling. The client-centered conception has its source in a perspective that legal problems typically raise both legal and non-legal concerns for clients, that collaboration between attorneys and clients is likely to enhance the effectiveness of problem-solving, and that clients ordinarily are in the best position to make important decisions. The book describes, analyzes and illustrates a variety of strategies and techniques that will enable you to carry out client-centered counseling.

Since the original precursor of this edition was first published over 25 years ago, client-centered counseling has become among the most broadly shared conceptions of lawyering in the country. You can use a client-centered counseling approach "across the board" to facilitate solutions in all legal counseling situations. For example, you can follow client-centered principles:

- In both transactional and litigation matters;

- In complex cases (e.g., securities fraud) and straightforward ones (e.g., collection on a promissory note);

- No matter what substantive legal issues a matter involves (e.g., wrongful termination case, construction defect litigation or stock purchase agreement);

- Regardless of a client's identity (e.g., individual, corporation, representatives of a loosely-knit community group); and

- When you and a client have a prior professional relationship as well as when you represent a client for the first time.

plex, lawyers use different criteria. Sometimes legal complexity encompasses the notion that the subject matter is intellectually demanding. (For a discussion of the substantive subject areas lawyers in the Chicago, Illinois area perceive as intellectually demanding, see Edward Laumann & John Heinz, *Specialization and Prestige in the Legal Profession: The Structure of Deference*, 1977 Am.B.Found.Res.J. 155, 166–68. Or, the term may mean that the matter involves legal issues for which the substantive law is unclear or in a state of continual flux (see id.) or needs to be modified or perhaps even reversed in order to protect the client. Or, legal complexity may mean that the substantive law involves a number of rules that are unfamiliar to all but those who are specialists in the particular substantive area. For example, even lawyers who have some experience in areas such as securities fraud, anti-trust or murder prosecutions, might well describe such areas as complex because of the number of rules with which one must be familiar in order to handle such cases.

In sum, the strategies and techniques represented by a client-centered approach allow you to fulfill your ethical responsibility to "explain a matter to the extent reasonably necessary to permit the client to make informed decisions regarding the representation."[2]

2. WHY SHOULD YOU ADOPT A CLIENT–CENTERED APPROACH?

One traditional image of lawyers portrays them as professionals who control the choices that clients make by convincing clients as to what is in their best interests.[3] Underlying this image is an attitude that objectively "best" solutions to legal problems exist and that by dint of training, experience and superior judgment, a lawyer's role is to develop these solutions. The traditional image generally regards clients as unsuited to the task of legal problem-solving, and usually satisfied to leave decision-making to lawyers.

Client-centeredness challenges the traditional image's attitude towards both legal problems and clients. The subsections below elaborate briefly on the client-centered conception of clients, legal problems and their solutions and in so doing provide the primary justifications for the client-centered approach.

A. CLIENTS ARE AUTONOMOUS "OWNERS" OF THEIR PROBLEMS

Underlying client-centeredness is the philosophy that clients are autonomous and therefore deserving of making important decisions that lead to resolution of their legal problems. Whether a client is a labor organization involved in negotiations for a new contract, a parent with an abusive spouse, a young couple who want an estate plan that will protect their young children or a developer seeking permission to demolish an existing building, clients do not give up the right to shape their destinies simply because they seek the help of lawyers. As unique social actors, they deserve to be made aware of relevant concerns and potential solutions and to determine for themselves which solutions best respond to the financial, social, psychological, moral and other ramifications that may arise from adopting particular solutions to legal problems. After all, clients and not lawyers live with decisions' consequences. For example, if a plaintiff in a wrongful termination matter decides to accept a sum of money in settlement rather than pursue reinstatement through trial, it is the plaintiff and not the lawyer whose future life the decision helps to shape. Thus, the starting point of client-centeredness is that respect for clients' autonomy means that decisions about solutions to clients' legal problems are for clients to make.

---

2. Rule 1.4 (b), ABA MODEL RULES OF PROFESSIONAL CONDUCT.

3. For a well-analyzed description and critique of this traditional image, see DOUG-

LAS ROSENTHAL, LAWYER AND CLIENT: WHO'S IN CHARGE? (1974)

As you undoubtedly know, both litigation and transactional matters typically require the making of numerous decisions as the matters progress from beginning to end. Your lawyer-client relationships would quickly become unwieldy if you had to consult with clients every time a decision had to be made. Therefore as a client-centered lawyer you'll need to exercise judgment about when to involve clients in decision-making, and a later chapter furnishes a guide to that judgment.[4]

B. CLIENTS ARE GENERALLY IN A BETTER POSITION THAN LAWYERS TO IDENTIFY AND ASSESS THE IMPORTANCE OF SOLUTIONS' NON–LEGAL CONSEQUENCES

Clients consult lawyers rather than other helping professionals when they recognize that problems have important legal dimensions. For example, people who want to leave property to relatives and friends while minimizing the impact of taxes and other expenses will go to a lawyer because they realize that if their wishes are to be carried out, their estate planning documents must comply with legal requirements. Similarly, manufacturers who want to sell merchandise to retailers will go to a lawyer because they want the protection of legally enforceable contracts should the retailers fail to meet their obligations. And of course, people whose disputes cannot be otherwise resolved will consult a lawyer who can draft the pleadings and motions and carry out the other tasks that protect their legal rights. Ordinarily, lawyers are no doubt in a better position than clients to evaluate legal consequences such as the ramifications of estate planning documents, contracts and litigation processes.

However, a second justification for client-centeredness emanates from the reality that the satisfactoriness of solutions often depends on how well they respond to clients' concerns about non-legal consequences. Significant non-legal ramifications are typically embedded in solutions to legal problems.[5] The following examples illustrate how concerns about non-legal consequences are apt to be part and parcel of deciding what course of action should be followed to resolve legal problems:

> Your client who is considering a settlement offer may not only be concerned about the value of the settlement compared to the likely outcome of trial, but also may worry that accepting the offer will result in a lost opportunity to pursue future financial goals; a loss of face among friends and relatives to whom the client had repeatedly made promises to "see this case all the way through to trial" or create feelings akin to "buyer's remorse."

> Your client may be a business executive who is considering sacking a long-time and popular employee. The executive's legal concerns may

---

4. See Chapter 13.

5. Indeed, so common are non-legal concerns that had Sir Isaac Newton been a lawyer rather than a physicist, his Third Law would probably have read, "For every solution, there are both legal and non-legal consequences."

center on the likelihood that the "waiver of claims" document that the employee will be asked to sign in order to receive a severance package will be effective for barring an age discrimination lawsuit that the employee might want to institute. At the same time, the executive may fear that firing the employee will hurt company morale and cut into overall productivity.

Your client may be a developer whose plans to build a new housing subdivision will require the moving of a grove of old trees. The developer's legal concerns may center on the conditions that the developer may have to satisfy to comply with environmental regulations. However, your client may also be concerned about financial costs that will result from the conditions that the county may impose before approving the subdivision. Additionally, your client may be worried about the negative publicity that removal of the trees is likely to create, the economic impact of the publicity about the project on the value of the client's company, and the client's own reluctance to destroy the trees.

The significance and frequency of non-legal ramifications that necessarily attach to potential solutions to legal problems affects your approach to counseling because clients are almost always in a better position than you to identify non-legal consequences. This is especially likely to be true because clients with similar legal problems may have very different non-legal concerns. That is, two clients' matters may concern the same legal *issues*, but their legal *problems* may be very different because of differences in the clients' circumstances, personalities and values.

For example, you may represent two different manufacturers who allegedly provided non-conforming goods to retailers and thereby materially breached contracts. However, these clients' legal problems may be very different. One manufacturer may be a modestly capitalized "start up" making "niche market" products that is anxious to do future business with the retailer while the other manufacturer is a long-established company that is phasing out of the product line in question and does not anticipate further business with the retailer. These clients are apt to evaluate potential solutions to their problems very differently. Such variations from one matter to another are common, with the consequence that objectively "best" or "one size fits all" solutions rarely exist.

Moreover, clients are typically in a better position than lawyers to assess the importance of the potential non-legal consequences of proposed solutions. For instance, the business executive faced with the decision to fire an employee will undoubtedly be in a better position than you to assess the importance of the harm to company morale and the effect of that harm on the company's operations when it comes time to decide whether to actually fire the employee.

In sum, clients are typically in the best position to identify non-legal consequences and assess their importance. Because such consequences significantly affect the determination of what solutions are most satisfactory, it makes sense for clients to play an active role in developing and analyzing potential solutions and to have the final say in deciding what course(s) of action to choose when trying to resolve legal problems.

C. CLIENTS ARE NORMALLY IN A BETTER POSITION THAN LAWYERS TO DETERMINE WHAT RISKS ARE WORTH TAKING

A third primary justification for client-centered counseling emanates from the fact that decisions in legal matters (as in most other aspects of life) are almost always made under conditions of uncertainty. That is, decisions almost always give rise to risks that potential consequences will not occur as predicted and that unforeseen consequences will instead result. Like decisions about which team will win the Super Bowl or whether to take a raincoat on a trip to Chicago, deciding what course of action to follow to resolve legal matters almost always entails taking a risk. For example, neither you nor clients can know for certain whether a client who settles a lawsuit will suffer "buyer's remorse," what the costs of complying with environmental requirements will be, or the extent to which firing a popular employee will harm employee morale.

However, as a few minutes observing the action at a Las Vegas blackjack table will verify, people vary enormously in their willingness to take risks. Some people are by dint of their personalities more willing to take risks than are other people. Moreover, risk-taking is often situational; people may take risks in some situations that they would be unwilling to take in others. For example, clients' readiness to take risks may be influenced by the importance they attach to the gains they foresee if their predictions are correct or to the losses they fear will ensue if their predictions are wrong.

Hence when it comes to making decisions about what solutions are most likely to be satisfactory, it makes sense to conclude that as "owners" of legal problems, clients deserve the right to determine how great a risk they are willing to run with respect to possible outcomes. Hence, clients should ordinarily be the primary decision-makers with respect to important matters.

For example, assume that your client is a computer company that plans to hire a highly experienced programmer to lead the development of a new line of software products. The company wants the programmer to agree to a highly restrictive non-competition clause, predicting that it will prevent the programmer from going elsewhere before the project is completed. The risks of insisting on such a restrictive form of non-competition clause include (a) the programmer may walk away from the deal and (b) the programmer may agree to the deal but go elsewhere without penalty because a court will regard the non-competition clause as too restrictive to enforce. You may regard these risks as not worth taking and therefore opt for a milder form of non-competition clause. The client, by contrast, may be a risk taker who thinks that the restrictive form of clause will not be a deal-breaker and will prevent the programmer from quitting in mid-stream.

D. CLIENTS ARE CAPABLE OF AND INTERESTED IN PARTICIPATING IN THE COUNSELING PROCESS AND MAKING IMPORTANT DECISIONS

Other justifications for client-centeredness would mean little if clients typically were incapable of making important decisions or rarely were willing to participate in the counseling process. However, quite the opposite is likely to be true. That is, most clients are quite capable of actively participating in the effort to resolve important problems. Moreover, clients typically want to participate in counseling, though of course their level of interest is likely to vary according to such factors as the relative importance of decisions and the time available to decide. At least, it makes sense for the "default" position to be that clients are capable of and desirous of participating in the counseling process until you have information to the contrary.

Of course, not all clients conform to this perspective. Even with respect to important decisions, some clients may not want to participate in the counseling process and others may be unable to "pull the trigger." Suggestions for responding to such situations in a way that is consistent with client-centeredness are in a later chapter.[6]

E. ACTIVE LAWYER–CLIENT COLLABORATION PROMOTES EFFECTIVE IMPLEMENTATION OF DECISIONS

Once decisions are made, clients often have to implement them. In such situations, clients' active participation in the counseling process enhances the likelihood that they will effectively carry out the tasks necessary to implement decisions.

For example, assume that your client is involved in a dispute that the client hopes to resolve through mediation. You will not participate in the mediation, and the client has consulted you so as to go into mediation with an understanding of potential legal rights, solutions and pitfalls. Surely the client's ability to achieve a satisfactory outcome through mediation is enhanced if you and the client have collaborated in an analysis of potential outcomes and their likely consequences.

3. HALLMARKS OF CLIENT–CENTERED COUNSELING

Lawyer-client conversations are extremely idiosyncratic. Thus, how you approach counseling conversations and the courses those discussions take inevitably vary greatly from one client to another, depending on such factors as the nature of a client's problems, a client's prior legal experiences and level of sophistication, the types of and the importance of non-legal concerns, and the decision that has to be made. Neverthe-

6. See Chapter 18.

less, even as you adjust your style according to individual clients' needs and concerns, your counseling conversations can exhibit characteristics that you might regard as "hallmarks" of a client-centered approach. The subsections below describe these hallmarks. Ensuing chapters explore strategies and techniques for carrying out counseling in ways that are consistent with these hallmarks.[7]

A. SEEK OUT POTENTIAL NON–LEGAL CONSEQUENCES

Helping clients develop satisfactory solutions requires you not only to uncover information that is relevant to legal *issues*, but also to help clients identify non-legal ramifications that are embedded in solutions to their legal *problems*. Hence, one hallmark of your counseling conversations is to actively encourage clients to identify potential non-legal consequences. With potential non-legal consequences on the table, you can assist clients in evaluating their likely impact on potential solutions. Actively encouraging clients to talk about non-legal concerns is often necessary because clients may not on their own identify and evaluate the non-legal ramifications that may legitimately bear on the problem-solving process. For example, assume that your client is the CEO of a small company that wants to obtain a zoning variance so that the company can expand its operations. The CEO will no doubt understand the importance of providing information that justifies the need for a variance. However, the CEO may not without inquiry on your part talk about such non-legal concerns as the CEO's need to obtain the variance in order to maintain the confidence of the company's Board of Directors.

With experience, you will no doubt anticipate possible non-legal ramifications that tend to accompany particular types of legal problems. You may certainly raise such non-legal possibilities in the course of counseling conversations. At the same time, you will also need to encourage clients to identify non-legal concerns that may not be on your "radar screen" because no amount of experience and legal expertise can enable you to fully recognize or evaluate all the non-legal consequences that may attend a given client's situation.

B. ASK CLIENTS TO SUGGEST POTENTIAL SOLUTIONS

Clients reasonably expect you to develop potential solutions to their legal problems, and client-centered counseling is certainly consistent with your doing so. However, a second hallmark of client-centered counseling is that you encourage clients to identify potential solutions as well. Clients' backgrounds and experiences may lead them to suggest sensible options that you might have overlooked. At the very least, clients' suggested solutions may suggest concerns that you can account for in solutions that you devise.

---

7. The "hallmarks" described above do not of course constitute the entire range of features of an effective attorney-client relationship. For example, your professional responsibilities include keeping clients reasonably informed about the status of their matters and responding promptly to clients' requests for information. See Rule 1.4, ABA Model Rules of Professional Conduct.

By way of illustration, consider a situation in which you represent a building contractor who has been sued by a residents' association for alleged construction defects in a large apartment complex. The residents contend among other things that a basement laundry facility floods as a result of the contractor's failure to properly seal the foundation walls. The contractor is probably more likely than you to identify a solution that includes a repair process that will cure the flooding. Thus, asking the contractor to suggest possible solutions promotes the likelihood that the contractor is satisfied with the eventual outcome.

C. ENCOURAGE CLIENTS TO MAKE IMPORTANT DECISIONS

A third hallmark of client-centered counseling is that you encourage clients to make important decisions. The strategies and techniques that constitute a client-centered approach put clients in a position to make knowledgeable decisions by facilitating identification of possible outcomes and their likely consequences. At the end of the day, however, the factors described above, such as the inevitable presence of non-legal ramifications and variations in values and risk-aversion, suggest that important decisions are for clients to make.

Depending on such factors as clients' readiness to make decisions and the time available for decision-making, you may play a more or less active role in the decision-making process. For example, you may recommend a course of action to an indecisive client or suggest that a client who has made a too-hasty decision may want to reconsider. However, across a broad spectrum of client conversations your basic task is to provide clients with a reasonable opportunity to evaluate options and likely consequences, and leave to clients the choices that they believe are in their best interests.[8]

D. PROVIDE ADVICE BASED ON CLIENTS' VALUES

Within the universe of decision-makers are clients who may require that you take a more active role in decision-making. For example, even experienced and sophisticated clients may not want to make decisions until hearing your advice. Other clients may be "socially disempowered" from decision-making. That is, because of mental impairment or social, economic or cultural disadvantage, some clients may need your advice as to the solution that you think is in their best interests.[9] Your ethical obligation is to maintain a normal attorney-client relationship "as far as is reasonably possible."[10] Thus, even if a client is not so disabled as to require appointment of a guardian or other formal rights-holder, provid-

---

8. Of course, if your client is a minor or suffers from some sort of mental impairment, you may need to undertake more of the decision making than when such factors are not present. See Rule 1.14, ABA MODEL RULES OF PROFESSIONAL CONDUCT.

9. See WILLIAM H. SIMON, THE PRACTICE OF JUSTICE: A THEORY OF LAWYERS' ETHICS (1998).

10. See Rule 1.14, ABA MODEL RULES OF PROFESSIONAL CONDUCT.

ing effective representation to socially disempowered clients may require you to take an expanded role in the decision-making process.

In all such situations, provide advice according to your understanding of clients' circumstances, values and non-legal concerns. Giving advice based on the consequences you personally think important would impose your values and sense of appropriate risk taking on clients and would be antithetical to client-centeredness.

E. ACKNOWLEDGE CLIENTS' FEELINGS AND RECOGNIZE THEIR IMPORTANCE

Another hallmark of client-centeredness is that you understand and respond to clients' feelings. Legal problems do not exist in emotionless vacuums. Clients' emotional reactions to problems and their possible solutions are often as significant as the facts which generate the problems. Thus, clients often want and need to talk about their feelings. Later chapters introduce you to techniques for talking about and acknowledging clients' emotions. Use of those techniques enables you to recognize implicit feelings, to reflect them back to your clients, and to include those emotions in a search for appropriate solutions. By responding to clients' feelings as well as to the substance of their problems, you can build rapport, promote clients' motivation and recall, and help fashion solutions that meet clients' needs.

At the same time nothing about these techniques requires you to play "amateur psychologist." Your legal training and experience do not equip you to counsel clients with respect to psychological problems, and the client-centered approach does not require you to try to help clients overcome not only their legal but also their psychological problems. A client-centered approach simply acknowledges the reality that legal problems often give rise to emotional feelings and concerns and seeks to incorporate a consideration of those feelings and concerns into searches for satisfactory solutions.

4. INTEGRATING CLIENT–CENTERED HALLMARKS INTO THE INTERVIEWING & COUNSELING PROCESS

This book focuses on the lawyer-client relationship, and on strategies and techniques for establishing and maintaining an effective relationship, gathering information from clients, and helping clients reach satisfactory solutions to their problems.

A. THE REMAINING THREE PARTS OF THE BOOK

The remainder of the book consists of three parts:

Part Two sets forth the "building blocks" of client-centered lawyering. The chapters in this part examine a variety of listening and questioning skills that you may usefully employ throughout the counseling process.

Part Three focuses on the information-gathering process. In these chapters you will find strategies and techniques for identifying clients' problems, eliciting information relevant to assessing clients' likely legal positions and providing tentative advice.

Part Four explores the process of decision-making. The first chapter in this part suggests a standard to help you exercise judgment as to which decisions you should encourage clients to make, and sets out a process you may follow to help insure that clients have adequate bases to make those decisions. Succeeding chapters explore a variety of counseling options and also discuss when and how you may effectively intervene in the decision-making process, such as when clients make seemingly illogical choices or make decisions that you believe to be immoral.

B. THE UNPREDICTABILITY OF THE COUNSELING PROCESS

The above summary may suggest that counseling is usually a linear process that starts with information gathering and proceeds smoothly to decision-making. Seemingly, all that remains is to implement clients' choices: "sue the jerks;" "form a limited liability corporation."

Certainly, some degree of linearity is inherent in helping clients reach decisions about solutions that will best solve their legal problems. For example, some data-gathering almost always precedes the giving of tentative advice or the identification of potential solutions.[11] However, a number of factors typically cause the road from identifying clients' problems to final problem resolution to be anything but smooth and straight. For one thing, evaluating the likely consequences of various options often makes you and clients realize the need for additional data. By way of example, assume that your client Marshall wants to go into business with Moore and that you and Marshall are discussing the option, "form a partnership with Moore." You point out that a consequence of this option is that Moore's creditors, if any, will be able to reach the partnership assets. As a result, before finally evaluating the option, you may ask Marshall to gather more data about Moore's financial condition.

Second, while "choosing a course of action" may sound like the end of the counseling process with respect to individual decisions, often it is not. In the course of implementing decisions, factors such as changed circumstances, a client's change of heart, or unforeseen hurdles may result in the decision's revision or abandonment. That, in turn, may require additional data-gathering as part of a search for a new solution.

---

11. For example, in litigation, you typically do need to elicit rule-specific evidence before beginning to assess a client's legal rights. See JEROME FRANK, COURTS ON TRIAL 14–16 (1949); DAVID A. BINDER & PAUL BERGMAN, FACT INVESTIGATION 58 (1984). See also FED.R.CIV.P. 11, which concerns require- ments that plaintiffs must satisfy before filing suit. By contrast, in the initial phases of transactional matters, you are rarely concerned with identifying evidence before discussing potential alternatives. See Chapter 11.

For example, assume that Marshall's and Moore's decision was to form a limited liability corporation in order to include outside investors. Before you could fully implement this decision, interest rates fell. As a result, the pair decide to borrow the necessary capital instead of taking in additional partners. This decision may result in more meetings with Marshall, in which you engage in further data-gathering in pursuit of other options such as a sub-chapter S corporation.

Similarly, assume that your client, a Ms. Santiago, had come to see you because the company holding a mortgage on her home had threatened her with foreclosure. Her initial decision was to sue to enjoin the sale, and to pursue the suit aggressively. Shortly thereafter, she tells you that she and her husband are moving out of state, and that she does not want to put a lot of money or effort into the suit. This information will lead you both to revisit and perhaps revise Ms. Santiago's initial decision.

Finally, counseling tends to be non-linear because clients typically confront a number of important decisions as their matters proceed. For example, during an initial interview a client may describe a central problem:

> "I found out that the house I bought has a cracked foundation, and that it'll cost me about $75,000 to repair it. What can I do?"

> "I'm here to see about avoiding probate. What can you suggest?"

And clients often ultimately decide which option is most likely to best resolve the central problem:

> "I'd like to sue the seller;"

> "I'll establish a revocable living trust."

But inevitably, intertwined with the choice of basic solutions to central problems are important auxiliary issues that clients also need to resolve. For example, after deciding to sue the seller, the buyer of the defective house may have to make decisions about whether to hire an expert and how many depositions to take. Similarly, the client who chose the living trust may thereafter have to decide who to name as successor trustee and whether family members should be told of the trust's terms. In turn, each of these decisions may require you to repeat the processes of gathering data and identifying and evaluating options.

*

Part Two

FUNDAMENTAL COUNSELING SKILLS

Part Two (Chapters 2 through 4) explores basic skills that underline all aspects of client-centered counseling, from initial meetings with clients to decision-making.

Chapter 2

MOTIVATION

1. INTRODUCTION

A hallmark of client-centered counseling is that clients are active participants in the counseling process. For example, clients' roles commonly include disclosing non-legal concerns and identifying and evaluating potential solutions. However, the extent to which you achieve active client participation may well depend in part on the presence or absence of the psychological factors that this chapter explores. One group of factors tends to inhibit clients' willingness to participate, while a second group of factors tends to motivate participation. This chapter offers strategies for limiting the impact of the inhibitors and expanding the impact of the motivators. Using such strategies increases the likelihood that clients will actively participate in interviewing and counseling. The chapter concludes by examining inhibitions that may arise when your clients have cultural backgrounds that differ significantly from yours.[1]

2. A GENERAL DESCRIPTION OF MOTIVATION

A. THE NATURE OF HUMAN NEED

Human beings have a variety of needs. However, precise agreement about their exact nature or number is non-existent.[2] In general, psychologists divide needs into two broad categories: (1) physical needs and (2) psychosocial needs. Physical needs are often called primary and include the need for food, shelter, sex, and the like. These needs are innate and common to all people, although the particular ways in which they are

---

1. This chapter in no way relies on or adopts a particular theory of psychology or motivation that may be a subject of contention in the scientific community. Rather, the chapter sets forth broadly accepted ideas about human behavior.

2. For a description of some of the various theories regarding the nature of human needs see DENYS A. DeCATANZARO, MOTIVATION AND EMOTION: EVOLUTIONARY, PHYSIOLOGICAL, DEVELOPMENTAL, AND SOCIAL PERSPECTIVES (1999); EDWARD L. DECI & RICHARD FLASTE, WHY WE DO WHAT WE DO: THE DYNAMICS OF PERSONAL AUTONOMY (1995); RUSSELL G. GEEN, HUMAN MOTIVATION: A SOCIAL PSYCHOLOGICAL APPROACH (1995); PAUL L. LAWRENCE & NITIN NOHRIA, DRIVEN: HOW HUMAN NATURE SHAPES OUR CHOICES (2002); BERNARD WEINER, HUMAN MOTIVATION: METAPHORS, THEORIES & RESEARCH (1992).

satisfied are learned behaviors and consequently tend to show tremendous variation.

Psychosocial needs are often referred to as secondary. These needs are learned through individuals' associations or affiliations with particular societies or cultures. Included among these secondary needs are the desire for love, status, recognition, a winning basketball team, and so on. Attempts to enumerate all psychosocial needs and to arrange them in a hierarchy of importance have produced little consensus. Secondary needs vary greatly from one culture to another. In addition, they find unique organization and expression within each individual.

Although little agreement may exist as to the precise nature of psychosocial needs, there tends to be universal agreement that these needs, in combination with the primary ones, profoundly influence patterns of thought, attitude, and behavior. In general, individuals act (or refrain from acting) primarily to fulfill one or more primary or secondary needs. Thus, motivation to act exists principally when people perceive (either at a conscious or intuitive level) that their conduct will satisfy one or more of their needs.

Though these needs serve to energize and direct (motivate) human behavior, individuals may not be aware of their presence or the influence they exert. The needs are usually experienced in the form of feelings. Typically, the feelings involve some sort of longing or discomfort accompanied by a desire to find relief.[3]

B. CONFLICTING NEEDS

Needs of different types typically exist contemporaneously and are often in conflict. For example, assume that a client named John Bridgeport has consulted you regarding a potential divorce and bankruptcy. He is an aerospace engineer who has been unable to find employment for the past six months. His house and car are about to be foreclosed upon, and his wife is threatening to leave him because of their frequent disputes about debts. The local high school district has offered him a janitorial job on the swing shift. The job pays fairly well, but Mr. Bridgeport is in doubt as to whether or not to accept it. Though the income may indeed be sufficient to save his material possessions and his marriage, his needs for self-respect and esteem may not enable him to accept working as a janitor.

When needs are in conflict, motivation to act likely exists only when individuals feel that a course of action will satisfy one or more needs without unduly interfering with others. Thus, only when individuals perceive overall gain in terms of need satisfaction will there be sufficient motivation to act.

---

3. There are theories of motivation which postulate that not all behavior is motivated by a desire for relief from discomfort. *See* ABRAHAM H. MASLOW, MOTIVATION AND PERSONALITY 56–61 (3d ed. 1987).

As in Mr. Bridgeport's situation, some of the strongest needs that individuals experience have to do with feelings of self-esteem and self-regard.[4] Individuals may even choose courses of action that produce little material satisfaction over those that provide greater material benefits if their perceived need for self-respect is of greater importance than whatever needs material gain might satisfy.

3. MOTIVATION IN LAWYER–CLIENT DIALOGUES

If people generally act (or refrain from acting) in order to satisfy needs, what needs might motivate clients to participate in, or withdraw from, the counseling process? Of course, clients are usually motivated to participate in interviews. After all, clients presumably seek you out because they believe that you can help them resolve their problems.[5] However, even though clients may be generally motivated to talk with you, the interviewing and counseling process is typically fraught with motivational difficulties. Frequently, full participation is contrary to certain client needs. From a psychological perspective, clients often have psychological needs that disclosure of relevant information will undermine. For example, clients' needs to protect their self-esteem and to avoid marital stress and embarrassment may lead them to conceal that they were engaged in a romantic tryst with a paramour at the time of crucial events, even though revelation of the tryst would further the client's legal claims (for example, by showing that the client was not drinking in a bar shortly before getting behind the wheel of a car). Similarly, clients may not be motivated to share information that they perceive to be irrelevant to their legal claims.

Since psychological factors can affect the level of clients' participation in the interviewing and counseling process, it makes sense to examine common factors that may impact the effectiveness of your counseling conversations. These factors fall into one of two groups. "Interfering" or "inhibiting" factors tend to prevent clients from fully participating in counseling conversations, whereas "positive" or "facilitating" factors tend to assist full client participation.[6] You can help

---

4. Robert L. Kahn & Charles F. Cannell, The Dynamics of Interviewing 40 (1957); Russell G. Geen, Human Motivation 93–94 (1995); Abraham Tesser, *Toward A Self-Evaluation Model of Social Behavior*, in 21 Advances in Experimental Psychology 181–227 (Leonard Berkowitz ed. 1998). How individuals view themselves and how they might act to in order to maintain or achieve self-esteem varies from culture to culture. *See, e.g.*, Richard E. Nisbett, The Geography of Thought: How Asians and Westerners Think Differently 53–56 (2003); Marieke de Mooij, Global Marketing and Advertising 149–153 (1998).

5. This is not always the case, however. A client who comes to see a lawyer about a will may be doing so simply to please a

spouse. A businessperson about to enter into an agreement may want nothing more than for the lawyer simply to document terms the parties have already agreed upon rather than to provide any counsel. In each of these situations, the client may well not be particularly motivated to participate in a full and thorough discussion.

6. These factors have been described in different ways. *See* Raymond L. Gorden, Interviewing: Strategy, Techniques, and Tactics 70–95 (1998); Kahn & Cannell, *supra* note 4, at 45–53; Gay Gellhorn, *Law and Language: An Empirically–Based Model for the Opening Moments of Client Interviews*, 4 Clinical L. Rev. 321, 344 (1997); Thomas L. Shaffer & James R. Elkins, Legal Interviewing and Counseling (3d ed. 1997)

clients to participate actively in describing and resolving their problems by minimizing inhibiting factors and maximizing motivating factors.

Taking advantage of elementary psychological principles in no way requires that you undergo psychological training or learn to develop complex profiles of each client's unique configuration of needs. Your professional task is to help clients resolve legal problems, not to provide psychological counseling. Unless you have specialized training you cannot expect to identify and remove deep psychological needs blocking clients' full participation. The process of uncovering unmet needs and conflicts is most appropriately undertaken by a trained mental health specialist.[7] The following example illustrates the distinction between a lawyer's level of psychological understanding and that of a trained psychologist. As a lawyer, you may recognize that an unusually high degree of risk-aversion is at the root of a client's reluctance to file a lawsuit. However, only a trained psychologist is capable of delving into the reasons why your client is so abnormally risk-averse, and to help the client become more willing to take reasonable risks.[8]

4. INHIBITORS

The seven inhibitors that this section describes are common in lawyer-client dialogues. While other phenomena may also inhibit active client participation, these seven operate across a wide range of client personality types. Though the discussion treats each inhibitor as a separate phenomenon, in practice each often intertwines with others.

Of the seven inhibitors, the first two—ego threat and case threat—probably play the most pervasive role in blocking full communication.

A. EGO THREAT

Clients tend to withhold information that they perceive as threatening to their self-esteem. The requested information may relate either to past or anticipated behavior, and the feelings that a question may arouse can range from mild embarrassment to a strong sense of guilt or shame. If clients believe that a truthful response will lead you to evaluate them negatively, such a response threatens their self-esteem; the response is "ego threatening." Rather than risk your negative evaluation, clients may answer falsely or evasively, or become reluctant to participate in that part of the conversation.

Consider two examples of how "ego threat" may arise during an interview. First, assume that you are consulted by Al, an experienced businessperson. Al claims that he was fraudulently induced to invest in a large real estate venture. Despite his business experience, Al had ne-

---

7. Certainly, this book's brief discussion does not provide you with the training to uncover and resolve an individual's deep psychological needs and conflicts. However, some authors believe lawyers can be trained to engage in a fair degree of psychosocial analysis. *See* Andrew S. Watson, The Lawyer in the Interviewing and Counselling Process 153–54 (1976).

8. Chapter 21 discusses techniques for referring clients to mental health professionals.

glected to make even a cursory investigation of the venture before parting with his money. He had simply relied upon the smooth talk of the scam artist who presented him with "the deal." When you inquire about Al's knowledge of the venture at the time the investment was made, Al is reluctant to admit that he knew nothing. He believes that he was stupid and naïve. Additionally, he is afraid that you will think him stupid and a poor businessperson if he admits to knowing nothing about the venture before investing. The "ego threat" posed by your inquiry thereby inhibits Al's full and open disclosure of the events leading up to his making the investment.

Next, assume that you have asked your client Barbara about what she sees as the advantages of proceeding to trial. Barbara may be reluctant to reveal that in her mind a major advantage of proceeding to trial is that it will cause the adversary great financial and emotional discomfort. Barbara is ashamed to admit that revenge is a principal motive. She believes that revealing her true motive will lead you to view her behavior as unconscionable.[9]

Countering the potential effects of "ego threat" depends in part on establishing an atmosphere of trust and confidence in the attorney-client relationship. For example, clients may reveal portions of ego-threatening information to gauge your reactions. By remaining non-judgmental, you may encourage clients to reveal further information. Another strategy that you can sometimes use is to mention ego-threatening information yourself. For example, you might say to Al something along these lines: "Even experienced and quite astute businesspeople can get involved in deals without checking them out adequately." Opening up the subject yourself may make it easier for Al to provide information he would have otherwise tried to conceal.

B. CASE THREAT

A second major factor tending to inhibit client communication is "case threat." As the term suggests, "case threat" may arise when clients believe that revealing information will hurt their case. For example, Susan may not want to reveal to you that she was near the scene of a crime because she fears that if the judge and jurors were to find out she will be convicted even though she is not guilty. Alternatively, Susan may fear that revealing the information will cause you to believe that the case is a loser and therefore fail to pursue it zealously.[10] In either event, "case threat" is present. Similarly, assume that in a civil matter you ask Ernesto about the whereabouts of a business document.

9. Which, depending on her degree of her vindictiveness, very well may be true,. The powerful truth about ego threat is that it is often grounded in reliable predictions about the perceptions and opinions of others. GORDEN, *supra* note 6, at 72–73.

10. In such situations, ego threat may be present as well. If the client believes that revealing that she was at the scene of the crime will cause the lawyer to disbelieve her claim of innocence, the potential loss of self-esteem may well inhibit a truthful response.

If Ernesto fears that information on the document contains damaging information, case threat may lead him not to reveal its whereabouts.

"Case threat" may also inhibit clients who have transactional matters. Assume that Jean consults you in connection with a proposal to lease space in an office building. During a conversation about negotiation strategy, you inquire about the maximum length lease that Jean will accept. Jean is willing to accept a ten year lease, but she hopes the owner will agree to a five year term. Jean may be unwilling to reveal her willingness to accept a ten year deal, fearing that once you know her "bottom line," you will not press as hard as you otherwise might for a shorter lease term.

Overcoming the "case threat" inhibitor typically involves helping clients to understand that sharing all information is generally in their bests interests, regardless of whether the information is helpful or harmful.[11] One potential strategy is to suggest that information that clients perceive as harmful often turns out to be helpful. (A "war story" drawn from your experience can be a helpful way of making the abstract principle more concrete and vivid.) A second strategy is to advise clients that the earlier you know about harmful information, the better prepared you will be to counter it if and when your adversary seeks to capitalize on it.

C. ROLE EXPECTATIONS

Role expectations often affect communication between lawyers and clients. Most of us have sets of beliefs about what kind of behavior is appropriate within the confines of particular roles and relationships.[12] For example, most people think that there are certain ways that one should (or should not) behave when interacting with parents. Similarly, most people have beliefs about how employers should relate to employees. We may each have different sets of beliefs regarding proper behavior, but most of us do approach many relationships with preset viewpoints on what constitutes correct conduct in given relationships.[13]

Beliefs about what constitutes proper behavior are "expectations." Since the expectations under discussion here pertain to what people

---

11. Contemporaneously reminding the client of your general duty of confidentiality can be helpful in this regard. For a more complete discussion of what you may say to clients regarding confidentiality, see Chapter 5.

12. For a powerful example of how one's assigned role scan direct one's actions, see GEORGE ORWELL, SHOOTING AN ELEPHANT AND OTHER ESSAYS 3–12 (1945). In this true account, Orwell, serving as a British police officer in Lower Burma, describes his killing an elephant which had escaped from its chains. By Orwell's account, no good reason existed to kill the elephant, but the eyes of the Burmese peasants, and his understanding of how a British officer was expected to act, led inevitably to his shooting the animal.

13. Galen V. Bodenhausen et al., *Social Cognition*, in 5 HANDBOOK OF PSYCHOLOGY 257, 271–77 (Theodore Millon & Melvin J. Lerner eds., 2003); *see also* RICHARD NISBETT & LEE ROSS, HUMAN INFERENCE: STRATEGIES AND SHORTCOMINGS OF SOCIAL JUDGMENT 7 (1980); RUDOLPH F. VERDERBER & KATHLEEN S. VERDERBER, INTER-ACT: USING INTERPERSONAL COMMUNICATION SKILLS 34 (5th ed. 1989). *See generally* JANE S. HALONEN & JOHN W. SANTROCK, PSYCHOLOGY: CONTEXTS OF BEHAVIOR 657–88 (1996) (offering a general explanation of social psychology).

believe constitutes proper behavior in a particular relationship, the entire phenomenon may be labeled "role expectations." The effect of role expectations is that when people have preset expectations about others with whom they interact, those beliefs may (if only unconsciously) come into play and cause people to modify their behavior to conform to the beliefs.

Our role expectations are shaped by our life experiences, both actual and vicarious. For example, from our actual experiences of going to school, most of us develop patterns of how to interact with teachers. In addition, family, friends, associates, news media, popular culture and the like constantly deliver messages about what constitutes appropriate behavior. For instance, probably few of us have met England's reigning monarch, but we probably have a good idea of how we should behave should our paths cross.

In most relationships, one person assumes a position of authority or leadership over the other. Therefore, when people initially enter into a particular relationship, they often expect to be in either a dominant or subordinate position.[14] If one is a parent one expects to dominate; if one is a child, one expects to be dominated. Teachers often see their students as occupying subordinate roles. Again, these beliefs develop unconsciously from years of cultural infusion. Undoubtedly, people might be better off if they saw more relationships as involving shared responsibility, but the fact is that frequently they do not. Rather, they tend to see relationships in terms of dominant and subordinate positions.

The "role expectations" phenomenon means that clients will frequently enter your law office with a set of expectations about what constitutes appropriate "client behavior." For some clients, those expectations will be that lawyers occupy positions of authority. Such clients may be somewhat reluctant to communicate fully in the belief that you know what subjects are deserving of inquiry. Thus, if you fail to broach a topic that a client feels is important, the client may assume (again, either consciously or intuitively) that the topic is not a significant one. Similarly, such clients may think it outside their role to suggest potential solutions to their problems.

Strategies that might motivate such clients to participate more actively center on persuading them that you genuinely desire their input and that it is an important part of the counseling process. For example, if you sense that a client's role conception is likely to inhibit communication, you might include a message along these lines in a "preparatory explanation."[15]

---

14. The pattern of domination and submission within social relationships is very culturally determined. For instance, traditional Asian customs based on Confucian ideals place great emphasis on respect for age, social status and occupational status. *See, e.g.,* John N. Hawkins, *Issues of Motivation in Asian Education, in* MOTIVATION: THEORY AND RESEARCH 101 (Harold F. O'Neil, Jr. & Michael Drillings eds., 1994). *Also see, e.g.,* RICHARD E. NISBETT, THE GEOGRAPHY OF THOUGHT: HOW ASIANS AND WESTERNERS THINK DIFFERENTLY 63–64 (2003).

15. See Chapter 5 for a discussion of preparatory explanations.

Interestingly, many clients have an opposite set of beliefs. This second group of clients tends to believe that a lawyer's role is limited to carrying out their wishes and that it is their privilege to speak their minds about any and all topics. In short, these clients see themselves in a dominant position vis a vis legal counsel, and they are often not interested in fully responding to inquiries they perceive as unimportant. For example, many corporate and business clients tend to want to dominate their lawyers.[16]

Strategies for motivating "dominators" to participate generally center on convincing them of the importance of the information you seek. For example, perhaps a client brushes aside your inquiries for more information about what took place during a particular meeting based on the client's belief that she has already told you everything of importance. When you sense this to be the situation you might tell the client something like, "Marie, I want to be sure that we don't run into any surprises down the line. Since this meeting was an important one, I appreciate your telling me everything else you can recall that occurred at the meeting." Of course, the content of your message will necessarily vary depending on what subject a particular "dominator" deems inconsequential.

D. ETIQUETTE BARRIER

A fourth inhibitor is the "etiquette barrier."[17] Often, individuals have information that they will freely provide to persons in a similar peer group but not to "outsiders." For example, women may discuss topics with other women that they will be reluctant to discuss with men. Similarly, students may discuss some subjects with each other students but not generally with teachers or parents. The same phenomenon may affect communication among ethnic groups; for instance, Hispanics may discuss topics with other Hispanics that they'd be reluctant to discuss with Caucasians, African–Americans or other non-Hispanics. The etiquette barrier arises from our desire not to shock, embarrass, offend or discomfort others. It reflects our thinking about the effect of information on listeners, rather than concerns about how listeners will view us. Hence, loss of self-esteem is not a component of the etiquette barrier.

For example, assume that your client seeks recompense for injuries suffered in an automobile accident. You and the client are of different genders. You suspect from the nature of the injuries that they have probably caused your client to experience sexual dysfunction, but the client has said nothing about such problems in response to your questions about the impact of the injuries. The culprit might be the etiquette

---

16. See, e.g., JOHN P. HEINZ & EDWARD O. LAUMANN, CHICAGO LAWYERS: THE SOCIAL STRUCTURE OF THE BAR 160–75 (1982). David B. Wilkins, *Do Clients Have Ethical Obligations to Lawyers? Some Lessons From the* *Diversity Wars*, 11 GEO. J. LEGAL ETHICS 855, 875 (1998).

17. The term is borrowed from Raymond L. Gorden. See GORDEN *supra* note 6, at 76–78.

barrier; the client might be more willing to talk about sexual dysfunction with a person of the same gender.

When you sense that the etiquette barrier may be inhibiting clients' participation in the counseling process, one strategy you may employ is to mention the importance of disclosure to your ability to help clients arrive at satisfactory outcomes. Another strategy, most notably employed by the "Kinsey Report" researchers, is for you to broach the uncomfortable topic.[18] For example, you might have said to the client above that "Based on what I know about these types of injuries, I expect that you may be experiencing sexual dysfunction along with your other problems. That's nothing to be embarrassed about, and it's important to include that in our planning. What can you tell me about the sexual problems you may be experiencing?" When appropriate and a colleague is available, another possibility is to ask a client's permission to include another individual with whom a client may be more comfortable in the discussion. In the above matter, for example, you might suggest that the client might be more comfortable were another lawyer or paralegal in your office who is of the client's gender to sit in on at least the part of the discussion that is causing discomfort.

E. TRAUMA

This phenomenon occurs when you ask clients to recall experiences that evoke unpleasant feelings. Many events (especially those that clients relate to lawyers) cause people to experience negative feelings such as fear, anger, humiliation, and sadness. When you ask clients to recall such events, they may re-experience the negative feelings. Consequently, clients may avoid thinking and talking about the unpleasant events that give rise to those feelings. For example, a parent asked about a severe injury to a child may be reluctant to talk about the incident in an effort to avoid re-experiencing the anger, frustration, and sadness that the incident caused. Likewise, an estate planning client who is considering disinheriting a close relative may for similar reasons be reluctant to talk about the reasons for wanting to disinherit the relative.

When you sense that avoidance of traumatic events may be a source of client reluctance to participate, one strategy is to stress the importance of information to a satisfactory outcome. Another possibility is to postpone discussion of painful events, at least when those events are not so central that a meaningful discussion cannot otherwise take place. Finally, a third strategy is to ask clients to consider that discussion of traumatic events may be cathartic.[19] However, recognize that overcoming

18. ALFRED C. KINSEY ET AL., SEXUAL BEHAVIOR IN THE HUMAN MALE, CH. 2 (1948).

19. An important caveat about your responses to clients who have experienced tragedy and trauma: Not all persons who suffer terrible misfortune wish to avoid talking about it. Quite the contrary—many, and perhaps most, victims of catastrophes benefit and heal by talking to others about their experience, and the more sympathetic ears, the better. *See, e.g.*, John A. Updegraff & Shelley E. Taylor, *From Vulnerability to Growth: Positive and Negative Effects of Stressful Life Events*, in LOSS AND TRAUMA: GENERAL AND CLOSE RELATIONSHIP PERSPECTIVES 3, 12 (John H. Harvey & Eric D. Miller eds.,

trauma may be outside your ability. For example, in extreme cases involving severe trauma, symptoms of post-traumatic stress disorder may leave people with no active memory of the traumatic events.[20] Thus, you may need to consider referring severely-affected clients to a mental health professional.[21]

F. PERCEIVED IRRELEVANCY

This inhibitor is often difficult to recognize, as clients may not signal feelings of discomfort or threat. The attitude involved here is a client's feeling that there exists "no good reason to provide that information." Clients who feel that they have nothing to gain by providing information may be reluctant to provide it.

An interview of a parent accused of child abuse provides an illustration. Although many factors may be present in any abusive situation, parents who maltreat their children often suffer from depression and tend to be individuals who have significant emotional problems of their own and/or were abused or neglected themselves as children.[22] If you represent a parent accused of child abuse, therefore, you may wish to uncover information about the nature and extent of the client's social contacts, emotional state and personal history. However, to a parent accused of child abuse, questions about the general nature of the parent's social activities, well-being and childhood are quite likely to seem irrelevant, if not frivolous. The questions are seemingly not relevant to the relationship between the parent and the child. As a consequence, the client may feel little motivation to provide a detailed response.

"Perceived irrelevancy" is just as likely to arise in transactional contexts. Assume that you represent a partnership that has asked you to negotiate the purchase of a building. You may ask the partners for information about why the owner wants to sell, so that in problem-solving fashion you can structure the deal in such a way that it meets both your clients' and the seller's needs.[23] But the clients, perhaps seeing little importance in exploring the seller's needs, may provide only perfunctory information.

A straightforward strategy you can use when you perceive this phenomenon at work is to point out the reasons for your inquiries. For example, you might tell the partners in the instance above that knowing

2000) (discussing basic coping styles). See generally Leslie S. Greenberg, Robert Elliott, and Germain Lietaer, *Humanistic-Experiential Psychotherapy* in 8 HANDBOOK OF PSYCHOLOGY: CLINICAL PSYCHOLOGY (George Stricker and Thomas A. Widiger, eds., 2003), at 301–325.

20. *See* Diagnostic and Statistical Manual § IV (4th Revised ed. 2000).

21. See Chapter 21.

22. Martha Farrell Erickson & Byron Egeland, *Child Neglect*, in THE APSAC HANDBOOK ON CHILD MALTREATMENT 3, 13–14 (John E.B. Myers et al. eds., 2d ed. 2002).

23. For a discussion of the importance of needs analysis particularly when using a problem solving approach to negotiation, see ROBERT H. MNOOKIN, SCOTT R. PEPPET & ANDREW S. TULUMELLO, BEYOND WINNING: NEGOTIATING TO CREATE VALUE IN DEALS AND DISPUTES, 35–37; 179–181 (2000); CHARLES B. CRAVER, EFFECTIVE LEGAL NEGOTIATION AND SETTLEMENT, 11–15 (4th ed. 2001).

something about the seller's needs can help you negotiate the sale while saving time—and the partnership's money. However, such a strategy can give rise to ethical concerns. Your explanations may well signal to clients your desired answers. For example, your disclosure to the alleged child abuser that you want to know about his background so that you can establish that he was not abused may cause the client to withhold information. On the other hand, simply asking this client to tell you about how his parents treated him may engender responses such as "How I was raised? What does that have to do with anything?" Your sometimes difficult task is to provide enough information to allow clients to understand the relevance of your inquiries, but not such specific information that you unduly influence clients' stories.

G. GREATER NEED

The last of the common inhibitors is "greater need." This situation arises from clients' needs or desires to talk about subjects other than the one that is of immediate interest to you.[24] As a consequence, clients do not concentrate on your questions, and full and accurate information is not forthcoming. For example, an incarcerated defendant concerned primarily with bail or "own recognizance" release will often be unable to turn full attention to questions relating to the underlying charge. Similarly, a tenant threatened with eviction may be more concerned with when and where he can move than with inquiries related to a potential "habitability defense."

In such situations, your questions are not perceived as irrelevant or threatening. Rather, clients are simply concerned with subjects that while perhaps secondary to you are primary to them.

One strategy for overcoming this phenomenon is simply to anticipate clients' likely needs and invite clients to talk about them before addressing topics of greater concern to you. For example, your statement to the tenant might go something like this: "I'll want to ask you some questions about the conditions in your apartment, because they pertain to a legal rule that we lawyers call 'habitability.' But first you may want to talk about problems that the eviction process itself is causing you and your family. Anything you'd like to talk about before we get into habitability?" If you are uncertain about why clients seem distracted, you might ask for explanations: "I've asked you some questions about the conditions in the apartment, but my sense is that you might have other concerns that at the moment are more important. Anything you want to go over with me now? We can talk about conditions in the apartment some other time if necessary."[25]

---

24. Sometimes the phenomenon is present in the form of the interviewee wishing to do anything other than talk. A potential witness busy with his or her work is an obvious example. For a discussion of competing time demands, see GORDEN, *supra* note 6, at 117–18.

25. Delaying inquiries in the service of clients' greater needs may not always be sensible. For instance, if you need information in order to prepare a pleading that you must file by the end of the day, you may need to pursue that information immediately despite the client's perceived greater

5. FACILITATORS

The five facilitators described below encourage clients to participate fully in counseling dialogues. This section describes the facilitators and offers illustrations of how to employ them effectively. You may choose to employ facilitators without waiting for client reluctance to rear its annoying head. That is, you can incorporate facilitators into all counseling conversations as part of your routine style, whether clients are enthusiastic or reluctant participants.

A. EMPATHIC UNDERSTANDING

Empathic understanding may arouse in clients feelings of trust and confidence and thereby motivates clients to participate fully in conversations. Empathy probably cannot be defined or precisely described.[26] Perhaps the following comments by Carl Rogers give some sense of what empathy involves:

> Empathy in its most fundamental sense ... involves understanding the experiences, behaviors, and feelings of others as they experience them. It means that [lawyers] must, to the best of their abilities, put aside their own biases, prejudices, and points of view in order to understand as clearly as possible the points of view of their clients. It means entering into the experience of clients in order to develop a feeling for their inner world and how they view both this inner world and the world of people and [events] around them.[27]

People have limited opportunities in our society to express their thoughts and feelings to someone who is willing to (1) listen, (2) understand, and (3) at the same time, not judge. People on the receiving end of a communication are often too busy to really listen, and too interested in their own ideas to avoid responses that include their own "two cents." The "two cents" can appear in a variety of forms, including:

> (a) Advice on how to handle the situation: "Don't worry. You'll feel less angry as time goes on."

> (b) Analysis of why the feelings have arisen: "You probably feel angry because you feel you should have seen through that smoke screen."

Providing advice or analysis, even if done with a genuine desire to be of help, ironically tends to give individuals little impetus to delve further into a subject. There is little point in expressing your ideas and feelings

need to talk about something else. In such a situation, an empathic response that acknowledges clients' desires may be appropriate: "I understand that you're anxious to talk about how this has affected your working conditions, and we will certainly talk about that. But we need to file a written response with the court by this afternoon, so for the moment I need to ask you about ..."

26. See GERALD GOODMAN, THE TALK BOOK 41 (1988); MARK H. DAVIS, EMPATHY: A SOCIAL PSYCHOLOGICAL APPROACH 5–12 (1994).

27. GERALD EGAN, THE SKILLED HELPER 87 (3d ed. 1986). In general see also DAVIS, supra note 26, at 7–12 .

if all you get in return is lay psychoanalysis or advice on how to change or ignore your feelings.

However, in the presence of someone who exhibits non-judgmental understanding—a listener who provides empathic responses—people often are strongly motivated to continue communicating. Almost without realizing it, people tend to provide an ever-increasing amount of information. Precisely why non-judgmental understanding results in increased inducement to communicate is not known.[28] However, many experts in the field of psychology have stressed the fact that it does have this self-propelling effect.[29]

The opportunities for you to utilize empathic understanding are endless. Clients almost always are emotionally involved in their problems, and thus repeatedly express feelings about what has occurred or is likely to occur. Their recitals of information are likely to be accompanied by and intertwined with feelings about such diverse matters as: (1) how they felt at the time an event occurred; (2) how they feel about people or institutions involved in their problem; (3) why events have unfolded, and why people have behaved as they have; (4) how they feel about an event at present; and (5) how they feel about what is likely to happen in the future. Consider these examples:

(a) "When the policeman told me she was dead, I was stunned. The week before, she told me she had made out a new will, but I didn't attach any significance to it. And now those vicious people want to contest the will; they are the ones that must be crazy."

(b) "Now I have to decide whether to accept the $35,000. If I don't accept it, I may regret my decision for a long time. On the other hand, if I don't go to trial I may always wonder if I could have gotten a lot more."

(c) "My partner and I couldn't believe it when we heard the building was for sale. We had been looking for a site in that area for years."

As Chapter 3's exploration of "active listening" explains in more detail, you can provide empathic understanding by acknowledging the feelings attached to factual descriptions such as these. So doing will enable you to receive information that clients might not otherwise disclose, develop clients' trust, and encourage clients to participate actively in the solutions to their problems. For example, in response to the statements above, your empathic replies might go as follows:

(a) "You can't understand how people can be so cruel."

(b) "You feel torn about which way to go here."

(c) "The two of you must have been on Cloud 9."

---

28. Cf. GOODMAN, *supra* note 26, at 51: "When it comes to professionals . . . There's some debate about how reflections help healing or when they heal, and how often to employ them, but it's unusual to find a practitioner who doesn't use them at all." See also MICHAEL P. NICHOLS, THE LOST ART OF LISTENING Chp. 7 (1995).

29. CARL R. ROGERS, COUNSELING AND PSYCHOTHERAPY 131–51 (1942); LESLIE GREENBERG ET AL. HUMANISTIC-EXPERIMENTAL PSYCHOLOGY, 301, 310–314 (1998).

B. FULFILLING EXPECTATIONS

The phenomenon of "fulfilling expectations" refers to people's tendencies to want to satisfy the perceived expectations of those with whom they interact. As described by a leading psychologist,

> One of the important forces in social interaction is the tendency for one person to communicate, verbally and nonverbally, his expectations to another person. The second person then tends to respond, consciously or unconsciously, to those expectations. This may be viewed as one manifestation of the more general human tendency to conform to the group of peers and to the suggestion of higher status persons in the society.[30]

Thus, you can motivate clients to participate actively by communicating (through verbal or nonverbal means) your expectation that they will do so.

For example, you may verbally communicate your expectations simply by telling clients at the outset of representation that you anticipate that they will tell you everything that concerns them with respect to their problems, regardless of whether they think it has legal significance. You might also explicitly encourage them to put forward ideas of their own, because in your experience clients often contribute to satisfactory resolutions of problems. You might repeat such expectations from time to time as matters progress, particularly when you sense that clients are reluctant to address particular topics.

"Silence" is a common non-verbal strategy you may use to convey expectations. For example, remaining silent after clients have spoken conveys your expectation that they will continue to talk about the same topic. A non-verbal strategy you might use to convey expectation when clients appear reluctant to speak is to lean forward and raise your eyebrows, thus conveying an expectant look.

The strategy of "fulfilling expectations" is one that you can also use to press clients to overcome memory difficulties. For example, assume that a client has indicated that she is having difficulty recalling what occurred at a meeting held two years earlier. You may respond by conveying your expectation that by probing her memory further, the client will be able to recollect more information:

> "I understand how hard it is to recall; I've often had that difficulty myself. Often I find, however, that if I visualize myself back in the setting I am trying to recall, things start to come back. Why don't you take a moment and try to picture yourself sitting at the meeting, and then let's see what you can recall."

30. Gorden, *supra* note 6, at 84.

Your statement employs two facilitators. First, you empathize with the client's difficulty. Also, you tell the client that you expect the visualization exercise to help her recall additional information.

Empathizing with clients' memory difficulties may lead you inadvertently to convey *negative* expectations. For example, assume that in the example above you had said:

> "I understand that it is difficult to remember the details of an event that happened so long ago."

Here, you again empathize with the client's inability to remember. Standing alone, however, the empathic response may convey an implicit message that "I don't expect you to be able to recall any more than you've already been able to." Thus, the more effective response to memory difficulties is to convey both empathy and a positive expectation of additional information.

C. RECOGNITION

Human beings often need attention and recognition from people outside their close circle of family and friends. They enjoy feeling important and seek the attention and esteem of outsiders. As a lawyer, you are likely to be an "outsider" whose statements providing "recognition" may motivate clients to be cooperative and open.[31]

You may supply "recognition" simply by sincerely praising clients' cooperation or help: "Your giving me that information is very helpful." "That was very important information you just gave me." "You're really doing a great job of getting the other employees to find the documents we need."

D. ALTRUISTIC APPEALS

People often need to identify with a "higher value" or cause that is beyond their immediate self-interest. This need may be a form of identification with the objectives of a large social group. Individuals' performance of altruistic deeds usually increases their self-esteem. Thus, you may motivate clients to participate actively in counseling conversations by suggesting that topics have a significance beyond the clients' immediate personal circumstances.[32] For example to motivate a client to try to recall more information, you might ask the client whether "another advantage of pursuing the sexual harassment claim would be protecting the jobs of others who work in that department?" Similarly, you may tell a client who is planning to build a new shopping center that "almost the best part of this is the jobs you'll be providing and the car trips you'll be saving the people who live and work in that area."

---

31. GORDEN, *supra* note 6, at 86–87.

32. Altruism is distinct from recognition, since a person may feel altruistic even if his or her actions never become public knowledge. See GORDEN, *supra* note 6, at 87–88.

E. EXTRINSIC REWARD

You are undoubtedly aware from everyday experience that people tend to act in their self-interest. Thus, you can often motivate clients to participate actively by pointing out how disclosure of information is likely to help them achieve more satisfactory outcomes.[33]

For example, clients who want you to draft estate planning documents may nevertheless be reluctant to provide information about their financial situation. Hence, you may facilitate cooperation by making a statement along the following lines before beginning to explore that topic: "Mr. Bonds, next let's talk about your general financial situation. Now, I don't need chapter and verse at this point about specific bank accounts or investments. But if we can go through them generally, we can talk intelligently about whether we need to draft the trust in such a way as to minimize taxes, assuming that's something you'd like to do."

6. SUMMARY

The book refers to the common inhibitors and facilitators described above frequently. Thus, you may want to refer back to the summary list below as you read through other chapters.

INHIBITORS	**FACILITATORS**
Ego Threat	Empathic Understanding
Case Threat	Fulfilling Expectations
Role Expectations	Recognition
Etiquette Barrier	Altruistic Appeals
Trauma	Extrinsic Reward
Perceived Irrelevancy	
Greater Need	

7. PERSONALITY CONFLICTS

This chapter has explored a number of psychological phenomena without mentioning a factor that all of us recognize as important to the interaction of any two people—their personalities. As the common phrase "we just hit it off" connotes, all of us are more comfortable with some people than we are with others. Thus, personality conflicts can potentially influence clients' willingness to participate actively in counseling conversations. If clients for whatever reason perceive you as someone with whom they are not comfortable, or someone who is too aggressive or too passive to handle a matter effectively, they are likely to be reluctant to participate fully. By the same token, if you perceive clients as too aggressive, passive, unscrupulous, or disorganized, your perceptions may inhibit your interactions.

Luckily for most of us, an ideal personality type necessary to be an effective attorney does not exist. Whatever your personality, you can practice law effectively and competently. Moreover, what may be a

---

33. This approach has been called "persuasive framing" since it motivates individuals to participate more fully by explaining why participation is in their best interests. See Jay Conger, *The Necessary Art of Persuasion*, 76 Harv. Bus. Rev. 84–95 (1998).

pleasing personality to one client may be abrasive to another. With self-examination and specialized training, you may develop greater awareness of how clients are likely to perceive you. However, intensive training is not readily available to most law students and lawyers.[34] Moreover, no amount of personality restructuring or self-awareness will enable you or any other lawyer to work effectively with every client.

Nevertheless, even in the absence of specialized training, you can interact more successfully with most clients by learning to relate to them in an open and supportive manner. Whatever your individual personality, you can undoubtedly employ the elementary facilitators described above. By combining these facilitators with the skills described in subsequent chapters, you can develop the sensitivity and ability necessary to maintain satisfactory rapport with most clients.

8.   MOTIVATION IN INTER–CULTURAL CONTEXTS

The United States is increasingly a multi-ethnic society. In contrast to the older image of the country as a "melting pot" in which people of different backgrounds shed their differences and became "just plain Americans," a newer image envisions the country as a "stew" in which members of ethnic sub-cultures often retain at least aspects of cultural distinctiveness. That is, clients' values, understandings, attitudes and traditions may reflect distinct subcultures with which the clients identify.

The presence of cultural diversity means that it is likely that many of your clients will have their roots in cultural backgrounds that differ from yours. Although most of us interact regularly and successfully with individuals whose cultural backgrounds are different from our own, cultural differences do have the potential to inhibit clients' participation in interviewing and counseling conversations. For example, clients' cultural traditions may inhibit participation by leaving them uncertain about how open they should be when during counseling they are asked to express their concerns. This section examines common dimensions of inter-cultural differences that might inhibit active client participation in the interviewing and counseling process, and offers suggestions for how you might respond should you believe that such differences are inhibiting clients' participation.

A.   THE RISK OF STEREOTYPING

An undeniable aspect of the dominant American culture historically has been a tendency to stereotype members of ethnic minority groups

---

34. There are some authors who believe that intensive training in personality analysis should be the cornerstone of any beginning course in legal interviewing and counseling. See WATSON, *supra* note 7, at 75–93. However, others believe that many of the skills necessary for effectively overcome personality conflicts can be learned in other ways. See DANIEL GOLEMAN, RICHARD BOYATZIS & ANNIE MCKEE, PRIMAL LEADERSHIP: REALIZING THE POWER OF EMOTIONAL INTELLIGENCE (2002); Majorie A. Silver, *Emotional Intelligence and Legal Education*, 5 PSYCHOL. PUB. POL'Y & L. 1173 (1999). See also the courses offered by various executive training programs that can be found through a Google search for "Executive Training." *See, e.g., www.leadership.opm.gov/* (includes course offering on emotional intelligence as a leadership skill).

according to presumed attitudes and behaviors. "Lawyer literature" sometimes reflects this history.[35] Most Americans these days explicitly eschew stereotypical thinking. However, even seemingly benevolent efforts to overcome inter-cultural differences can easily resurrect the stereotypes of bygone days.[36] The reason is that in an effort to develop rapport and empathy with clients whose cultural backgrounds differ from yours, you may make two types of assumptions. One assumption concerns the values and practices associated with a particular cultural heritage. The second assumption is that clients who come from a particular cultural heritage share the values and engage in the practices associated with their culture. Of course, either of your assumptions may be wrong. That is, your knowledge of a culture's values and practices may be faulty.[37] And any two people from the same cultural background may well have divergent levels of understanding, values, and concerns.[38] Another way of saying this is that "communication always takes place between individuals, not cultures."[39]

For example, assume that you are a New York lawyer and that you are about to meet a client who hails from North Carolina. A sophisticated consumer of material on cultural difference, your image of North Carolinians is that they "are very religious; they have developed fierce loyalties to family, their land and church."[40] However, even if the stereotype is generally accurate, it may not apply to your client. Thus, were you to try to develop empathy with the client and motivate the client to participate actively by, for instance, sprinkling the conversation with religious references, you might well end up creating a barrier to full communication if your client is not like the "typical" North Carolinian.

Thus, broad assertions regarding cultural differences are at best tentative. Cultural patterns constantly evolve, especially as countries' populations increasingly consist of people from different cultural back-

---

35. See, for example, JOSEPH KELNER AND FRANCIS E. McGOVERN, SUCCESSFUL LITIGATION TECHNIQUES: STUDENT EDITION 10–10 (1981). ("German, Irish, Swedish and Norwegian jurors are supposed to be conservative, less emotional and hence pro-defendant in their sympathies.")

36. See, e.g., JACK SCARBOROUGH, THE ORIGINS OF CULTURAL DIFFERENCES AND THEIR IMPACT ON MANAGEMENT 255 (1998)("[Keep] in mind the need to avoid stereotyping, the mistake of assuming that every Indian, Filipino, Arab or German we meet conforms to the profiles described in preceding chapters...."); Alex J. Hurder, *The Pursuit of Justice: New Directions in Scholarship About the Practice of Law*, 52 J. LEG. ED. 167, 173 (2002)(referring to the danger that learning general information about communities will produce stereotypical assumptions about individuals).

37. One common reason is that what looks from a distance to be a single culture may be in reality a number of sub-cultures with divergent values and practices.

38. See SCARBOROUGH, *supra* note 36, at 6. ("Any individual, regardless of cultural origin, can fall anywhere on any [cultural] continuum.") It is especially likely for two people from the same non-United States culture to have diverse values if one person has been in this country significantly longer than the other person.

39. TERRI MORRISON, WAYNE A. CONAWAY, GEORGE A. BORDEN, KISS, BOW OR SHAKE HANDS: HOW TO DO BUSINESS IN SIXTY COUNTRIES (1994).

40. Mirja Ilvonen, Diane H. Sonnenwald, Maria Parma & Evelyn Poole–Kober, *Analyzing and Understanding Cultural Differences: Experiences From Education in Library and Information Studies*, http://www.ifla.org/IV/ifla64/o77–155e.htm.

grounds.[41] Moreover, any single culture reflects a continuum of values; core values in essence lie at the mean of a normal distribution of the population of a particular culture.[42] Finally, people vary markedly in the extent to which their values and behavior reflect those of the culture to which they belong.

B. DIMENSIONS OF POTENTIAL CULTURAL DIFFERENCES

If you cannot assume that cultures are stable and that clients' values and practices are consistent with their cultural backgrounds, neither can you be oblivious to the potential for inter-cultural differences to affect clients' thinking and behavior. A sensible middle ground approach is to combine the information that you learn about clients through the interviewing and counseling process with awareness of common dimensions of cultural difference.[43] Your awareness of the ways in which values may differ from one culture to another can sensitize you to possible explanations for clients' lack of active participation in interviewing and counseling conversations. When cultural differences do inhibit clients' participation, use of the strategies described in the next subsection may help you motivate clients to participate more fully. However, to begin thinking about the dimensions of culture that may inhibit clients' participation in the counseling process, consider the following cultural dimensions identified by a prominent cultural researcher, Geert Hofstede.[44] Hofstede's dimensions provide you with a heuristic for thinking about culture differences without requiring that you attribute cultural attitudes or practices to people from specific ethnic, religious or national origins.[45]

"Uncertainty Avoidance" is one dimension that may vary from one culture to another. This dimension refers to people's tolerance of unpredictability. People from high-uncertainty avoidance cultures prefer formal rules and structured situations. They may also have higher levels

41. See for example, Chulwoo Lee, 'Us' and 'Them' In Korean Law, in EAST ASIAN LAW: UNIVERSAL NORMS AND LOCAL CULTURES, (Arthur Rosett, Lucie Cheng & Margaret Y.K. Woo eds., 2003). Similarly, racial categories are increasingly indeterminate. For a personal account of the impact of traditional social categories about race on multiracial individuals, see JUDY SCALES-TRENT, NOTES OF A WHITE BLACK WOMAN (2003).

42. See FONS TROMPENAARS, RIDING THE WAVES OF CULTURE: UNDERSTANDING DIVERSITY IN GLOBAL BUSINESS (2d ed. 1998).

43. The cultural dimensions described in this section grow largely out of the work of Geert Hofstede. Hofstede's book, CULTURE'S CONSEQUENCES: COMPARING VALUES, BEHAVIORS, INSTITUTIONS AND ORGANISATIONS ACROSS NATIONS (1980), "launched what some have called a revolution within the social sciences." Giana Eckhardt, Book Review, 27

AUSTRALIAN J. OF MANAGEMENT 89–94 (June 2002). The second edition of Hofstede's book was published in 2001.

44. See GEERT HOFSTEDE, CULTURE'S CONSEQUENCES: COMPARING VALUES, BEHAVIORS, INSTITUTIONS AND ORGANIZATIONS ACROSS NATIONS (2d ed. 2001). These works by Hofstede have set the agenda for much of the current research into cultural differences. See for example, Eckhardt, supra note 43.

45. In addition to Hofstede's framework, other influential taxonomies relating to cultural dimensions include Alan P. Fiske, The Four Elementary Forms of Sociality: Framework for A Unified Theory of Social Relations, 99 PSYCHOLOGICAL REVIEW 689 (1992); S. H. Schwartz, Universals in the Content and Structure of Values: Theoretical Advances and Empirical Tests in 20 Countries, ADVANCES IN EXPERIMENTAL SOCIAL PSYCHOLOGY 25 (M. Zanna, ed. 1992).

of anxiety and engage in behavior that may seem compulsive. By comparison, people from low-uncertainty avoidance cultures are more flexible and comfortable in situations in which bright line rules don't exist.[46]

"Power Distance" is a second dimension of cultural difference. This dimension refers to people's willingness to accept unequal distribution of power. People from large-power distance cultures tend to be obedient; they feel dependent on authority figures and generally accept their rules. These people tend to believe that those in authority have earned their positions, either by superior expertise or birth. People from low-power distance cultures, by contrast, tend to expect to have more control over their lives and to be included in decision-making.[47]

"Individualism/Collectivism," a third dimension of cultural difference, refers to people's preference to work alone or as a part of groups. Individualists tend to view life as a competitive zero-sum game, and generally seek to maximize their wealth. Collectivists however feel more loyalty to group than to personal interests, and may sacrifice their own interests for the good of others.[48]

"Masculinity/Femininity" is a dimension that refers to the relative importance in a culture of traits generally associated with masculinity and femininity. People from masculine cultures tend to prefer well-defined gender roles, place primary value on work done outside the home, to be task oriented, and competitive and aggressive. People from feminine cultures tend to favor interchangeable gender roles, prefer to settle conflicts through negotiation and compromise, and value teamwork and relationships.[49]

"Long Term/Short Term Orientation" is a fifth dimension of cultural difference. People from long term cultures tend to be less attentive to time considerations and to emphasize tradition. They are also more likely to adopt long-term goals, sacrificing immediate benefits in order to build strength in the future. People from short term cultures are more likely to try to make every moment productive; they are punctual, less interested in relationship-building and tend to insist on immediate returns on investments.[50]

"High Context/High Content Communication" is a sixth dimension of cultural difference. People from high *content* cultures tend to draw meaning from the contents of communications. They are comfortable with written communications, the accuracy of which is crucial for understanding. People from high *context* cultures tend to draw meaning from unspoken cues such as facial expression and posture. People from these cultures may see precise verbiage as insulting or condescending,

---

46. See SCARBOROUGH, *supra* note 36, at 10.

47. *Id.* at 9.

48. *Id.* at 7.

49. *Id.* at 11.

50. *Id.* at 7.

and they prefer to communicate face to face so that the entire context can be understood.[51]

Differences between you and clients with respect to these dimensions can become important in a variety of counseling contexts. For example:

- A client's attitude with respect to what constitutes a satisfactory outcome may differ from yours. For instance, perhaps you have a short term orientation and a client has a long term orientation. If so, you may consider a lawsuit as the best method to force a manufacturer to compensate your client, a wholesaler, for losses your client incurred as a result of receiving damaged goods. However, the client may be hesitant to sue, in view of the negative impact of a lawsuit on future dealings between the client and the manufacturer.[52]

- A client's understanding of language may differ from yours. For instance, if a client's cultural background has conditioned the client to rely heavily on the non-verbal context in which words are used, the client's understanding of the terms of a written agreement may differ from yours. Or a client's having been raised and educated in a different society from yours may prevent a client from understanding common terms such as "corporation," "internet," "web page," or "SEC."

- A client's attitude with respect to appropriate problem-solving processes may differ from yours. For instance, a client who is culturally conditioned to prefer structured situations may not be comfortable negotiating a deal until familiar rituals have been observed.

Part of successfully overcoming problems such as these that may be due to inter-cultural differences is understanding your own core values.[53] Reminding you of the earlier proviso about the difficulty inherent in identifying broad cultural characteristics and in particular the dangers of stereotyping, consider core values that have been linked to the United States as well as to other countries or ethnic groups.[54] The outline of values below again reflects Hofstede's work.[55]

51. *Id.* at 8.

52. See Chapter 18 for further discussion of responding to value conflicts during the decision-making process.

53. See Christine Zuni Cruz, *On the Road Back In: Community in Indigenous Communities*, 5 CLIN. L. REV. 557 (1999).

54. Your values may differ from those generally ascribed to people from your cultural background. If so, that will help you appreciate the need to avoid stereotyping individual clients according to the ascribed values of the cultures from which they come.

55. GEERT HOFSTEDE, CULTURAL CONSEQUENCES: COMPARING VALUES, BEHAVIORS, INSTITUTIONS AND ORGANIZATIONS ACROSS NATIONS, (2d ed. 2001); *Cultural Differences in Teaching and Learning*, 10 INTERNATIONAL JOURNAL OF INTERCULTURAL RELATIONS 301–319 (1986). Not all cultural researchers necessarily agree that cultures can be seen along these dimensions. For example, some researchers argue that difficulties in sampling undermine the accuracy of Hofstede's approach. See e.g. Robert Bontempo, *Blindfolded: Culture Is Not a Useful Independent Variable* (Paper presented at a meeting of the Academy of Management, Atlanta, Ga. 1993). Other scholars argue that taxonomic

COLLECTIVE SOCIETIES	INDIVIDUALISTIC SOCIETIES
Arab and African countries, Mexico, Japan, Portugal	United States, Great Britain, Germany, Spain, France

SMALL POWER DISTANCE SOCIETIES	LARGE POWER DISTANCE SOCIETIES
United States, Sweden, Australia, Canada, Netherlands	France, Japan, Arab and African countries, Korea, South Africa

LONG TERM ORIENTATION	SHORT TERM ORIENTATION
China, Taiwan, Japan, South Korea, Brazil, India	United States, Great Britain, Zimbabwe, Canada, Philippines, Nigeria, Pakistan

HIGH UNCERTAINTY AVOIDANCE SOCIETIES	LOW UNCERTAINTY AVOIDANCE SOCIETIES
Canada, Sweden, India, Hong Kong	Japan, Greece, Austria, Peru

FEMININE SOCIETIES	MASCULINE SOCIETIES
Japan, Spain, Chile, Ireland, Mexico, Austria	Scandinavian countries, France, United States, Australia

HIGH CONTENT COMMUNICATIONS	HIGH CONTEXT COMMUNICATIONS
Germanic, Scandinavian and Anglo Countries	Southern Europe, China, Japan, and Arab Countries

This chart can serve as a reminder that not only are some of your core values and norms likely to differ from people who come from other societies, but also that people from other cultures are quite likely to have stereotypes about Americans, American lawyers and the American legal system.[56]

dimensions are likely to be inaccurate because they represent constructs from the cultures of the creators of the taxonomies. See Kenneth J. Gergen, Aydan Gulerce, Andrew Lock and Girishwar Misra, *Psychological Science In Cultural Context*, 51 AMERICAN PSYCHOLOGIST 496 (1996). Still other researchers generally accept Hofstede's dimensions but argue they do not take sufficient account of the fact that many people (e.g. American born Hispanics, African Americans and American born Chinese) are bi or multi cultural. See Hong, Y., Morris, M. W., Chiu, C., & Benet–Martinez, V., *Multicultural Minds: A Dynamic Constructivist Approach to Culture and Cognition*, 55 American Psychologist, 709–720 (2000). See also M.W. MORRIS, AND H–Y FU, HOW DOES CULTURE INFLUENCE CONFLICT RESOLUTION? A DYNAMIC CONSTRUCTIVE ANALYSIS (2000). These authors argue that assessing the role that culture plays in decision-making also requires taking cognitive biases into account. For more discussion of cognitive biases, see Chapter 17. See also Giana Eckhardt, *supra* note 43 at 89–94.

C. STRATEGIES FOR RESPONDING TO INTER–CULTURAL COMMUNICATIONS DIFFICULTIES

Identifying dimensions of inter-cultural difference is somewhat easier than providing strategies that have a track record of overcoming inhibitions that may be due to such differences. However, some principles seem readily apparent:

- From the perspective of client-centeredness, not all differences are appropriate for you to overcome. For example, if a client's cultural background helps impel the client to an outcome that you personally disfavor, at the end of the day the client's values trump yours.

- If your practice regularly brings you into contact with clients from cultures that differ from yours, you may take explicit steps to familiarize yourself with those cultures. For example, you may study the history of a community and its relations with outsiders.[57] Another possible approach is to accompany clients to community meetings and events where other people who share a client's cultural background will be present.[58]

- When you can reasonably do so, conduct counseling conversations in a way that anticipates the preferences of clients from other cultures. For instance, if you recognize that a client's cultural background inclines the client towards formality, you might sit at your desk even though your usual preference is to talk to clients at an informal table. Similarly if you anticipate that a female client would be uncomfortable discussing a topic with you (a male), you might ask, "would you be more comfortable discussing this with another woman present?"

- When you sense that a client's background and experiences may have left the client unaware of the practices in a legally complex legal system such as exists in the United States, you may need to explain the reason for those practices rather than simply assuming that the client will accept them. Assume for example that a client who was raised in a non-legally complex society consults you in connection with a proposed business deal. The client brings you the lengthy draft agreement proffered by the lawyer for the other party, and is mystified by the assortment of terms and conditions pertaining to possible future occurrences. You may need to explain American lawyers' predilections for anticipating

---

56. See Russell Korobkin, Negotiation Theory and Strategy 270–272 (2002). Recognize also that law-related American movies and TV shows are shown all over the world and tend to shape people's images of American lawyers and the legal system. See Paul Bergman and Michael Asimow, Reel Justice (1996).

57. Michelle S. Jacobs, *People From the Footnotes: The Missing Element in Client–Centered Counseling*, 27 Golden Gate U. L. Rev. 345 (1997).

58. See Anthony V. Alfieri, *Reconstructive Poverty Law Practice: Learning Lessons of Client Narrative*, 100 Yale L. J. 2107 (1991).

and trying to resolve in advance contingencies that may never occur.

- At the same time, do not be so afraid of trampling on a client's cultural preferences that you cease to represent clients effectively. Give clients credit—if they have strong cultural preferences, they are likely to inform you about them. For example, if a female client is strongly disinclined to discuss case-related sexual matters with you, a male, you might reasonably expect the client to ask that another female (perhaps a colleague of yours or a friend of the client) be part of the conversation.

- Similarly, do not abandon your need for pertinent information in an effort to avoid encroaching on a client's cultural preferences. Your ability to help clients arrive at satisfactory outcomes will generally entail their understanding what you have to say about American laws and processes rather than your understanding their cultures' alternatives.

As you know, client-centered counseling suggests that you take reasonable steps to motivate all clients to participate actively in the problem-solving process. In the inter-cultural context, one strategy you can follow is to modify your use of language. For example, you can explain terms that may be unfamiliar to clients, and ask them to explain terms that may be unfamiliar to you. Since visual images are more universal than language, also look for opportunities to illustrate points with charts, diagrams and the like. While you can't draw a picture of "due process," you can use boxes and arrows to illustrate the effect of the provisions in a will.

Another strategy you can pursue is to look upon your clients as resources rather than guessing at the reasons for their seeming reluctance to participate actively or to seek outcomes that strike you as strange or perhaps even improper. As a counselor, you can probably learn more about clients by asking them questions than by making assumptions based on their cultural backgrounds.[59] For example, questions you might ask include:

"Before we talk about what happened in more detail, is there anything you can tell me about your background that will help me represent you more effectively?"

"Is there any reason that you might find it difficult to discuss this problem with me?"

"I realize that I'm having some difficulty explaining what I mean in a way that is clear to you. Would you prefer bringing in a friend who can translate what I'm saying?"

"I realize that you grew up in China and not in the United States and that I cannot speak Chinese. I may from time to time use an

59. See HURDER, *supra* note 36, at 173. See also JAMES W. LEIGH, COMMUNICATING FOR CULTURAL COMPETENCE 42–50 (1998) (exploring how social workers might use clients as cultural guides).

English word that you do not fully understand. If I do use a word that you don't understand , please tell me. I'd really appreciate that because it will help me make myself clear as we talk. Will you feel comfortable letting me know if I use some words you don't know?"

"Can you help me understand why you think it would be best if we first have a preliminary meeting with his lawyer before we start the real negotiations?"

Of course, a risk always exists that clients' cultural backgrounds incline them not to answer such questions directly, perhaps for fear of offending you or fearing that you will think them rude. However, clients are likely to appreciate your efforts to overcome the communication difficulties that cultural differences may create. As the attorney-client relationship continues and rapport grows, clients may develop sufficient confidence in you to override the inhibitions that cultural differences may initially create.

D. EXAMPLE FOR ANALYSIS

Consider the following remark that a client has made. What possible dimensions of culture may be playing a role in the client's thought processes?

"I'm concerned about accepting their offer. I've talked it over with both my wife and with my father. My dad comes from the old school; he ran a successful business for years and he thinks I shouldn't accept. He keeps raising the point, which I tend to agree with, that they have not lived up to the letter of the contract and we should hold them to what they've promised. But my wife sees it differently. She thinks that if I go to trial and lose we'll look bad in the eyes of her relatives. She also thinks that the offer is a sure thing that we ought to take and set aside for the kids' college tuition."

Chapter 3

ACTIVE LISTENING

* Reprinted by permission: Tribune Media Services.

1. INTRODUCTION

This chapter explains and illustrates a variety of effective listening skills. Certainly, core functions during initial client meetings typically include questioning and advice-giving. However, listening too is a crucially important skill. In fact, your ability to engender clients' trust, develop rapport, elicit full descriptions of clients' problems and help clients develop effective solutions may hinge as much on your listening as on your questioning and advice-giving skills. Thus, helping clients find satisfactory solutions to their problems often depends on your effectiveness as a listener.

If you listen carefully what will you hear? Of course, you will hear factual content. But often you will also hear feelings accompanying the content. That is, clients' descriptions of what happened often include the feelings that events aroused at the time they took place.[1] Moreover,

---

* Reprinted by permission: Tribune Media Services.

1. Indeed, it has been suggested that human beings are incapable of viewing facts without emotion. For a general discussion of how emotion affects perception, see H. Egeth, *Emotion and the Eyewitness*, in THE HEART'S EYE: EMOTIONAL INFLUENCES IN ATTEN-

clients' acts of recall may trigger still further emotional reactions. For example, a client may say something like, "At the time I was somewhat upset, but now just talking about it makes me seethe." Finally, clients' discussions of proposed solutions almost inevitably generate emotional reactions. For example, a client may say, "I'm nervous about leaving the terms of the payout provision so uncertain." Accordingly, when you listen carefully you are likely to hear both content and current and past feelings.

Effective listening generally demands more than sitting back and saying nothing. Rather, and perhaps counter-intuitively, the sort of listening that motivates clients and helps to produce effective solutions often relies on what you say and how you say it when responding to clients' statements. In other words, far from being an intuitively simple task, listening is a skill requiring positive action. As with other skills, your ability to listen effectively rests on both awareness and use of specialized techniques. One such technique, "active listening," is this chapter's primary focus.[2]

2. IDENTIFYING CONTENT AND FEELINGS

"Content" consists of information that affects clients' legal interests and the likely effectiveness of potential solutions. "Feelings" are clients' internal reactions to their problems and possible solutions. When describing their feelings, clients may use words such as happy, amused, excited, sad, angry, anxious, disappointed, frightened, irritated, and confused.

Your legal training and experience undoubtedly means that you need no encouragement from this book to attend to the content of clients' problems and possible solutions. Thus this chapter emphasizes how to respond to clients' emotional reactions.[3] To sharpen your ability to distinguish content from feelings, consider the following examples.

Client 1:

"My husband and I sat down shortly after we got married and wrote a will together, but I guess I never really thought we'd use it. Then they called to say my husband had had a heart attack at work. He died two days later. When he died, I was overwhelmed. Lately, I've been worrying about our finances. It's hard to think of money at a time like this, but I feel like I should. I can't sleep at night, and I just sit around all day. Other times, when I think about him, I start crying and it seems like it will never stop. On top of all this, his children from his first marriage

---

TION AND PERCEPTION (P. M. Niedenthal & S. Kitayama eds., 1994). See also PHILIP H. RHINELANDER, IS MAN INCOMPREHENSIBLE TO MAN? 48–50 (1973).

2. Chapter 2 stressed the importance of empathic understanding as a communica-

tion facilitator. Active listening is the technique through which you may most readily communicate empathic understanding.

3. Recall from Chapter 1 that recognizing and responding to clients' feelings is a hallmark of a client-centered approach.

are saying they are going to contest the will. They've already hired a lawyer. I'm really surprised, I never expected this."

What is the content of the client's situation?

What are the client's past and current feelings?

Client 2:

"The chance to be part owner of a restaurant is really the dream of a lifetime. Over the last few years I've gotten increasingly disenchanted with being an aerospace engineer—you're always dependent on government contracts, and having to meet deadlines. When Mike called and said he had found a third investor and a great neighborhood restaurant for sale, it was like a huge weight came off my shoulders. My wife said, 'Do it—it's what you've always wanted.' She's been great. I'm sure it'll work out. The cash flow could be a little tight in the beginning, but according to the books the restaurant has always made money."

What is the content of the client's situation?

What are the client's past and current feelings?

Client 3:

"I think that filing a lawsuit is the best thing to do at this point. I know that the doctor should not have prescribed that medication for me with my history of asthma. He just never took much time with me and by suing I will recover what I can and maybe I can protect other patients. I'll never be the same as I was before—I guess you can't get my health back for me. But at least I'll show the bastard."

What is the content of the client's situation?

What are the client's past and current feelings?

Here is how you might have conceptualized these three matters:

Client 1:

Content: Husband died unexpectedly and wife must assume responsibility for family finances. Children from the husband's first marriage plan to contest the will and have already hired a lawyer.

Feelings: Sad, overwhelmed, depressed, worried, surprised.

Client 2:

Content: Client, an aerospace engineer, has an opportunity to purchase an interest in and operate a restaurant. Two other people will be involved in the venture, and his spouse is supportive.

Feelings: Disenchanted, happy, relieved, optimistic, somewhat anxious.

Client 3:

Content: Client suffered ailments after a doctor who spent little time
                with her prescribed the wrong medication.

Feelings: Satisfied, hopeful, angry, sad, frustrated, revengeful.

3.   OBSTACLES TO GOOD LISTENING

Effective listening requires a number of skills. Of these, perhaps the
hardest to master is clearing your mind of distractors. We all are easily
distracted by our own feelings and needs, and therefore may only "half
listen" to what clients are saying. Consider the following factors that can
easily distract you from fully attending to your clients:

   1.   Performance distractors: You are so eager to display how
competent you are that you focus on what YOU are going to say
next, rather than on what your client is saying now. Or, in contrast,
you are so worried you will not know what to say next that you can
barely focus on a client's concerns.

   2.   Personal distractors: You are preoccupied with your own
personal worries, such as a case that is not going well, a deadline
you forgot, or an argument with your spouse, and therefore are less
attentive to a client.

   3.   Client distractors: This category involves your reactions to
any of a number of client characteristics. Perhaps a client's personality is such that you are more focused on the sort of person a client
is than on what the client is saying. Or, you may be so concerned
about whether a client's goals are consistent with your personal
values that you become distracted. Perhaps you find a client either
very attractive or very unattractive, and you pay more attention to
your feelings about the client's appearance than to what the client is
saying.

   4.   Time and money distractors: Rather than focusing on a
client, you are busy mentally calculating how much time a client's
matter will require and whether your client can afford to have you
continue with the matter.

Keeping your mind clear of common distractors such as these
requires considerable concentration and effort. Even if at the outset of a
discussion you wipe your mind clear of distractors, they commonly creep
back. A conscious effort to identify distractors when they arise may help
you push them aside more successfully.[4]

4.   PASSIVE LISTENING TECHNIQUES

Passive listening techniques are those that encourage clients to talk
with relatively little activity or encouragement on your part. Often,

---

   4. Though this discussion focuses on ob-   such obstacles can block your reception of
stacles to hearing clients' feelings, obviously   content as well.

when clients provide useful information, you simply want them to continue doing so. Yet, you also want clients to know that you are hearing and understanding what they are saying *without running the risk of interrupting their trains of thought*. The following passive listening techniques provide an ideal method for accomplishing these goals.

A. SILENCE

Clients may respond to your questions or comments by remaining silent. Rather than routinely immediately rushing to fill the conversational vacuum with additional questions or statements, often your most effective response is to remain silent yourself. By responding to silence with silence, you may allow clients the space they need to think carefully and to respond in a way that makes them comfortable.

If remaining silent seems awkward, the reason may be that in everyday life we often interpret others' silence as indicating lack of understanding or confusion. However, clients' silence may in fact suggest that they need additional time to consider what to say or how to say it. This is especially likely to be true for clients confronting crucial legal problems and for clients who are unused to talking with lawyers.[5] For example, clients may need time to recall a sequence of events, to decide whether to reveal embarrassing information, or to decide how to word their responses. Or, consider a client whose lawyer reports that an adversary has no interest in settlement. The client may be so surprised by the unexpected rejection or so angered that the client wants to calm down before speaking.[6] In situations such as these, remaining silent and allowing clients to collect their thoughts is often an effective way of motivating clients to provide information.

Of course, clients' silence is not always an indication that they are working towards responding. Silence may well indicate a desire not to respond or confusion or uncertainty about what to say. In such situations, extended silence on your part may make clients uncomfortable and threaten their self-esteem.[7] Thus, you'll have to rely on judgment to decide whether to remain silent and how long to do so before speaking again. In this respect, take account not only of clients' silence but also of non-verbal cues. Non-verbal reactions such as facial expressions can often help you gauge whether clients are befuddled or are working

5. Think about your experiences as a law student. Unfamiliarity with legal issues and uncertainty as to what kinds of responses were appropriate may well have made you hesitant to respond immediately to instructors' questions.

6. For a fuller discussion of the various reasons clients may remain silent and what their silences may mean, see Stefan H. Krieger, *A Time to Keep Silent and a Time to Speak: The Functions of Silence in the Lawyering Process*, 80 OR. L. REV. 199, 202–204, 219–235 (2001). See also James White, *Free Speech and Valuable Speech: Silence,*

Dante and the Marketplace of Ideas, 51 UCLA L. REV. Vol. 3 (2004).

7. This may be especially true for clients whose backgrounds (perhaps rooted in different cultures) tend to inhibit them from disclosing certain kinds of information, for instance facts regarding family background. See e.g. Sungeun Yang & Paul C. Rosenblatt, *Shame In Korean Families*, 32 J. COMP. FAM. STUD. 361 (2001). For a further discussion of silence as a cultural phenomenon, *see* Krieger, *supra* note 6 at 233–235.

towards responding.[8] Moreover, if clients are silent for longer than five seconds, that may indicate that they do not want to respond or fail to understand you or do not know what to say.[9] In that case, you may reconsider continuing to remain silent, and switch to active listening or other questioning techniques.[10]

When you do remain silent, send non-verbal cues of your own that you are remaining silent in order to give clients space to formulate responses. For example, you may maintain eye contact with clients, lean slightly forward, and nod your head as clients begin to speak. Such behavior tends to communicate your expectation that they will respond. Your silence together with your non-verbal behavior thereby takes advantage of the facilitator, "fulfilling expectations."

B. MINIMAL PROMPTS

While silence on your part can motivate clients, your silence may also inhibit them. Particularly if you remain silent for a long period or on repeated occasions, clients may doubt your attentiveness and interest. As a result, they may feel anxious or on the spot and "clam up."

To reassure clients of your attentiveness without interrupting their trains of thought, you may interject brief expressions termed "minimal prompts."[11] These include such brief comments as:

"Oh"

"I see"

"Mm-hmm"

"Interesting"

"Really"

"No fooling"

"You did, eh"

---

8. For a further discussion of the necessity to consider the context in which silence occurs, see Krieger, supra note 6 at 211, 243.

9. Allowing 5 seconds of silence before speaking is meant as a suggestion not as the "correct" amount of time. Counseling literature contains disagreement on how long one should allow clients to remain silent before one speaks. See Krieger supra, note 6 at 342.

10. What you think of as a long pause in a conversation may in reality be a very short one. Goodman notes that most people are uncomfortable with "conversational allowing" because the typical amount of time between when one person in a conversation stops talking and the other person starts is nine-tenths of a second. See GERALD GOODMAN, THE TALK BOOK 147–48 (1988). He gives an example of a conversation between Carl

Rogers, a master of client-centered therapy, and a patient in which Rogers allowed pauses of up to 17 minutes. Id. at 167–68.

11. This term is borrowed from GERARD EGAN, THE SKILLED HELPER 114–15 (7th ed. 2002). This technique is also sometimes referred to as "minimal verbal activity," WILLIAM H. CORMIER & L. SHERILYN CORMIER, INTERVIEWING STRATEGIES FOR HELPERS 74 (4th ed. 1998), and "brief assertions of understanding and interest," ROBERT LOUIS KAHN & CHARLES F. CANNELL, THE DYNAMICS OF INTERVIEWING 205–210 (1957). For further discussion of minimal prompts see Julie Gerhardt & Sandra Beyerle, What if Socrates Had Been a Woman? The Therapist's Use of Acknowledgement Tokens as a Nonreflective Means of Intersubjective Involvement, 33 CONTEMPORARY PSYCHOANALYSIS 378–79 (1997).

Here is an example of this technique in an interview:

C: I can see a lot of problems with this contract.

L: Mm-hmm

C: It really locks me in for five years and I'm not sure I want to do that.

L: I see.

Minimal prompts can be *nonverbal* as well. Consider this example:

C: My partner is very stubborn. He resists every suggestion to computerize our operations. (Pause)

L: [Nods her head.]

C: Maybe it's not so much stubbornness as fear. He's afraid we'll dramatically, and perhaps needlessly, increase our overhead and end up in bankruptcy.

L: Mm-hmm

Minimal prompts are non-committal; they give no indication of how you are evaluating a message. Yet they can be quite effective. Non-committal responses such as those above tend not to interrupt clients' trains of thought. They also tend to serve as re-enforcers that encourage further elaboration. As with silence, try to accompany prompts with body language that communicates your interest and involvement with what clients are saying.

C. OPEN–ENDED QUESTIONS

Open questions ask clients to discuss subjects in their own words.[12] Like minimal prompts, open questions allow you to move stories along without interrupting clients' trains of thought. Examples of open questions include:

"What else happened?"

"What other reasons are there?"

"Can you tell me some more about that?"[13]

"Please continue."

The techniques described in this section—silence, minimal prompts, and open-ended questions—are basically passive. They function primarily to give clients the space to freely communicate their thoughts and feelings. At the same time, these techniques involve little activity on your part. However, they do not communicate empathic understanding. To accomplish that goal, you must employ a technique known as active listening.

---

12. For a more detailed discussion of open questions, see Chapter 4.

13. Often, open-ended questions are used interchangeably with directive probes such as "Tell me more about that" and "Please continue." Clients will generally perceive a directive request in the same way as an open-ended question. In this book, the two are treated as synonymous. See Chapter 6.

5. ACTIVE LISTENING

A. GENERALLY

Active listening is the "most effective talk tool that exists for demonstrating understanding and reducing misunderstanding."[14] It is the process of picking up clients' messages and sending them back in reflective statements that mirror what you have heard.

> Client: "When I asked him for the money, he had the nerve to tell me not to be uptight."

> Lawyer: "Rather than offering to pay you back, he suggested that you were somehow wrong for asking. You were angry."

Your reply is a classic active listening response. It demonstrates that you understand the content of the client's remark. Also, the reply reflects back your understanding of the client's feelings that accompanied the incident. Further, the statement only mirrors the client's statement; it does not in any way "judge" it.[15] And, though your statement reflects the client's feelings, you do not ask the client to explore those feelings in greater detail. Rather, the statement simply indicates your awareness that the client was angry.

As in the example above, active listening does not consist simply of repeating, or "parroting," what clients say. Rather, your reply reflects the *essence* of the content of the client's remark, as well as your perception, based both on the statement and on the client's non-verbal cues that indicate clients' feelings. You distill the information and emotion from the clients statement, and then convey back what you have heard and understood—hence the term, "active listening."

Active and passive listening responses share some similarities. Neither type of response is likely to disrupt clients' trains of thought, or switch clients from one topic to another. The primary difference is that reflective responses explicitly communicate to clients that you have actually heard and understood what they have said; they explicitly demonstrate your comprehension. By contrast, passive responses, such as "Mm-hmm" or "Tell me some more about that," can only imply that you have heard and understood. Active listening responses demonstrate empathy and understanding, and in a way that encourages clients to continue speaking on whatever subject they choose.

Moreover, active listening responses probably fulfill the empathic ideal of "non-judgmental acceptance" more effectively than passive ones. Reflective statements generally imply a greater degree of non-judgmental

---

14. GOODMAN, *supra* note 10, at 38.

15. For a discussion of active listening which contains illustrative samples drawn from actual recorded dialogues, see CORMIER & CORMIER, *supra* note 11 at 87–104. See also

Bruce J. Winick, *Therapeutic and Preventitve Law's Transformative Potential for Particular Areas of Legal Practice*, 5 PSYCH. PUB. POL. AND L. 1075–76 (1999).

acceptance than do passive remarks. Again, it is the explicit mirroring of clients' remarks that suggests a non-judgmental attitude.

While an active listening response may mirror both content and feelings, this chapter primarily emphasizes techniques for using active listening responses to reflect feelings. It does so for two reasons:

> 1. As a general rule, lawyers probably pay too little attention to clients' feelings. Lawyers are prone to seeing themselves as rational fact-gatherers and decision-makers. At either a conscious or intuitive level, lawyers tend to perceive feelings as either irrelevant, or as unwelcome impediments to what should ideally be a completely rational process. This attitude towards the non-importance of feelings in the attorney-client relationship is wrong on at least two grounds. First, empathy is the real mortar of an attorney-client (indeed, *any*[16]) relationship. To be empathic you need to hear, understand and accept clients' feelings, and to find a way to convey this empathic understanding to your clients. Second, as stressed in Chapter 1, clients' problems do not come in nice, neat, rational packages devoid of emotional content. Problems evoke feelings, and feelings in turn shape problems. Lawyers can neither communicate fully with clients nor help fashion satisfactory solutions if they ignore feelings.

> 2. Everyday life and years of schooling have given most of us the skill to understand and respond to content. For example, what do we study more in secondary education—the strategic importance of Civil War battles, or the feelings of the participants? We have little formal training in listening for and articulating the human feelings that accompany events and future plans. And many of us do not intuitively discuss feelings with people with whom we are not close. Therefore, you are likely to need to devote more effort to learning to reflect feelings than to learning to reflect content.

Feelings, however, often do not come tightly packaged, ready to be reflected on. How clients express feelings influences how you reflect them. Hence, the next sections examine the different ways that clients are likely to express feelings, and the manner in which you may respond reflectively.

B. RESPONDING TO VAGUELY EXPRESSED FEELINGS

Clients often express feelings in poorly articulated, rather vague terms. In such situations, you can be empathic by making a reflective response that puts a precise label on the feelings. By specifically labeling feelings, you can help clients understand their own emotions. The labeling helps bring the feelings out into the open, so that the feelings are explicitly included in the counseling process. Examine a few examples of client statements that articulate feelings in a vague, abstract, or

---

16. See Alvin R. Mahrer, Donald B. Boulet & David R. Fairweather, *Beyond Empathy: Advances in the Clinical Theory and Methods of Empathy*, 14 CLINICAL PSY-CHOL. REV. 183–196 (1994).

general way, and responses that attempt to identify and label the feelings:

Client: "I felt bummed out when I found out she was having an affair with him. I thought our marriage meant something. I guess I was wrong."

Lawyer: "You were hurt and disappointed when you learned about the affair."

Client: "I've felt out of it ever since I moved to Minneapolis. I don't have friends here or even neighbors to talk to."

Lawyer: "You've felt lonely and isolated since you came to Minneapolis."

Client: "With Marcia in the business I know we can make it. She knows more about accounting in the fashion industry than anyone."

Lawyer: "You feel happy and confident with Marcia as a partner."

In each example, you restate in more specific terms the feelings that each client expressed only vaguely. Note that reflective responses may begin with phrases such as, "That must have made you very ...''; or, "It sounds like you felt...." However, the simple and direct responses illustrated in the three examples above are just as effective.

Try your own hand at active listening. As the lawyer in the examples below, what precisely-labeled feelings might you reflect back to the client?

Client: "When I told him I was going to a lawyer for a divorce, he just looked at me. He looked for a long time and then he left. It was strange."

Client: "After she told me the loan for the dental equipment had been approved, tears almost came to my eyes. My parents had worked so hard to put me through school, and I wish they could have been there with me."

C. RESPONDING TO UNSTATED FEELINGS

Frequently, without explicitly expressing emotion, clients discuss situations that your everyday experience suggests are emotion-laden. In such situations, the absence of explicitly-expressed emotions need not cause you to overlook clients' real but unstated feelings.

For example, assume that you represent a parent whose young child was injured at a day-care center. The parent is describing what happened after the parent was notified of the child's injury:

Client: It took them about an hour to find me at work to get the message to me that something had happened to Jan. After about 15 minutes Ms. Wyden, the day care director, told me that Jan wasn't hurt too badly, and she told me which emergency room Jan had been taken to. When I got to the emergency room, the nurse in the reception area couldn't give me any details on how Jan was or where Jan was. I had to wait for about 45 minutes for the doctor to come out.

Lawyer: Then what happened?

Here, the client's statement is devoid of expressed emotion. And, perhaps focused only on content, your response was, "Then what happened?"

However, the client has described a situation that, for most people, would be extremely stressful. Therefore, an active listening response would certainly have been appropriate. You might have reflected the emotions that the client did not put into words, but which the client undoubtedly felt: "Despite the director's assurance, you must have been really anxious about Jan and upset that you had to wait so long for information."

Providing empathic responses to clients who neither directly nor indirectly assert any emotions is a two step process. Once you recognize that a situation was probably emotion-laden, the first step is to identify and label the feelings. The second step is to mirror the feelings with a reflective response.[17]

To carry out the first step of identifying and labeling clients' unstated feelings, place yourself "in a client's shoes."[18] If you had been in the client's situation, what emotions would you probably have felt? Even if you have never experienced a client's precise situation, you can almost always hazard an educated guess about how the client felt. Through vicarious (films, books, friends' stories) and analogous experiences, you generally have a reasonably good idea of the emotions a client was feeling. Then, in the second step, incorporate the feelings into a reflective response.

The examples below provide practice in this two-step process. The clients' statements do not overtly state feelings. Formulate an active listening response that you might make in response to each statement.

Client: "When he failed to pay, I sent him two letters. I got no response. I called three times. He was never in. The secretary said he would return the calls; he never did."

17. For a discussion of the steps involved in the empathic response see See Alvin R. Mahrer, Donald B. Boulet & David R. Fairweather, *Beyond Empathy: Advances in the Clinical Theory and Methods of Empathy*, 14 CLINICAL PSYCHOL. REV. 183–196 (1994) and T. Bruneau, *Empathy and Listening, in* PERSPECTIVES OF LISTENING (Andrew D. Wolvin & Carolyn Gwynn Coakely eds.,

1993). For a basic illustration of identifying feelings and providing a reflective response see MICHAEL P. NICHOLS, THE LOST ART OF LISTENING Chp. 7–8 (1995).

18. Researchers have discovered that metaphorically placing oneself in the shoes of another is an important step in making empathic responses. *Id.*

Client: "The bank has been dealing with these builders for over 40 years. We've always provided all their construction financing, and often gone out on a limb to make loans when times were hard. Now they say that if we don't refinance on more favorable terms they will take their business elsewhere."

Client: "We've known each other for over 50 years. I know that people usually appoint their children as executors, but Pat is so familiar with everything and such a trusted friend that I really want Pat to be my executor."

Sometimes, you may be confident that a situation was an emotional one, but less confident about precisely what emotion was aroused. If so, you may doubt whether the feeling you identify in a reflective response will be completely accurate. As a result, you may shy away from verbalizing feelings when a client has not done so first.

However, a reflective response need not be "in the center of the bulls-eye" to provide empathy. For example, assume that in the second situation above, your reflective response was, "You sound pretty aggravated." If you are correct, your client may well validate the accuracy of your statement: "Yeah, I really am; given how we have helped these people for all this time, I can't believe they are doing this." But even if you are somewhat off the mark, a client will usually clarify the inaccuracy—"Well, I'm not aggravated yet, but I certainly am puzzled. What do you think they're up to?"[19] Thus, even if your statement is somewhat inaccurate, in all likelihood it will facilitate communication. The reflective response indicates your desire to understand, and may elicit further clarifying information.

D. RESPONDING TO NON–VERBAL EXPRESSIONS OF FEELINGS

Your everyday knowledge of how people are likely to react to situations is one basis for identifying unstated feelings. A second is clients' non-verbal cues. Non-verbal cues are generally of two types—auditory and visual.[20] Auditory cues include such things as voice intonation, pitch, rate of speech, and pauses in conversation. Visual cues include posture; gestures; facial expressions; body movements such as fidgeting fingers and constantly shifting positions; and autonomic physiological responses such as sweating and blushing. When non-verbal cues indicate the presence of a particular emotion, an active listening response is often appropriate.[21]

19. Therapists and other listening "experts" agree that some distortion in labeling another's feelings is unavoidable and therefore recommend that caution be used when reflecting or identifying an interviewees' emotions or feelings. See CORMIER & CORMIER, *supra* note 11, at 98.

20. For a more detailed discussion of the interpretation of non-verbal behavior,

see CORMIER & CORMIER, *supra* note 11, at 63–85.

21. Recall from Chapter 2 that clients from "high context" cultures may be especially likely to rely on non-verbal methods of communication. When clients identify

Though non-verbal behavior is extremely difficult to illustrate in a book, an attempt may be helpful. Assume that a client's voice cracks and that the client talks rapidly while describing the tentative terms of a proposed partnership deal. The deal is not of the sort that strikes you as laden with emotion. However, the non-verbal cues suggest that this particular client is extremely anxious to conclude the deal. Hence, an active listening response would be appropriate: "You seem anxious to have this deal concluded as quickly as possible."

You may feel somewhat hesitant to identify and respond to feelings evidenced by non-verbal cues, perhaps out of fear that you will make an inaccurate interpretation. After all, both individual and cultural variations in the way people express themselves may leave you uncertain about what inference to draw from non-verbal behavior. For example, is a smile a client's way of showing happiness or anxiety, or is it simply the client's typical facial expression? Do a client's tears signify sadness, relief, or your having left half an onion on your desk? Unless you are confident that you are reading a client's non-verbal behavior correctly, you may be understandably reticent to make a reflective response based on that behavior.

Developing "baseline pictures" of clients' non-verbal behavior is one technique for evaluating the meaning of possibly ambiguous non-verbal behavior. Over the course of representing a client, you may recognize that certain non-verbal behavior is "standard" and thus does not signify significant emotion. But a change of standard behavior may be an emotional clue.

For example, if a client habitually wrings his hands, wringing hands is probably not a sign that a particular topic is producing a significant emotional reaction. However, if a client who does not normally wring his hands suddenly begins to do so when you mention a particular topic, you may be able to infer that the client's emotions have been aroused.

Non-verbal cues tend to appear spontaneously; they are much less subject to conscious control than verbal expressions. Thus, they tend to "leak" information about clients' inner lives. Sometimes, clients try very hard to "maintain composure" by masking non-verbal cues. However, unless they have won an "Oscar" for "Best Actor," most clients are unable to repress all non-verbal expression. For example, an anxious client may avoid facial expressions, but be unable to hide body movements such as drumming fingers or rapid changes in position. Hence, if you are observant, you may detect those feelings that clients try to conceal, and respond empathically.

However, a more difficult question is whether you *ought* to make an active listening response when you sense that clients are *consciously* attempting to leave feelings unstated, perhaps by speaking and behaving

with "high context" cultures, therefore, you may be especially likely to active listen in response to clients' non-verbal behavior.

in a very guarded and restrictive manner.[22] If clients do not want to face the emotional dimensions of a problem, should you attempt to pressure them to do so?

From the standpoint of technique, the question is probably irrelevant. As you recall, active listening responses do not direct clients to talk about their feelings. Rather, they are a method for keeping clients on track in an empathic manner. After active listening responses, clients typically respond by continuing to talk about whatever aspect of situations they feel comfortable discussing.

However, clients who consciously attempt to mask feelings may *perceive* active listening remarks as an attempt to probe feelings. For example, noting a client's clenched fists, you say, "This subject seems to worry you." If the client has been attempting to conceal that emotion from you, the client may interpret your active listening comment as an attempt to probe feelings.

If clients are likely to perceive active listening responses as unwelcome probes into feelings, client-centeredness suggests that you typically respect their wishes and avoid injecting feelings into discussions. For one thing, for some clients, the assumption that a solution should be chosen after several possible options have been examined may be incorrect. For example, a client may be paralyzed and unable to choose an effective solution if too many issues are on the table. Thus, a client's masking of feelings may be an attempt to simplify a problem and keep it manageable. In such a situation, client-centeredness suggests that you accede to a client's implicit wish to focus exclusively on content.

Second, as autonomous individuals, clients are entitled to privacy and should be allowed to decide how much of their emotions and private thoughts to convey to you. Some clients may value their privacy more than they do a solution that is reached only after consideration of all relevant dimensions of a problem. Again, client-centeredness may lead you to respect a client's wishes.

More specifically, then, the question is how to identify those situations in which you are likely to help clients by bringing forth consciously-masked feelings. In the abstract, no answer may be possible. You cannot take refuge in the bromide of "informed consent." Clients cannot give informed consent until they are aware of the extent to which their disclosure of emotions and private thoughts will increase the chances of finding satisfactory solutions. But the very process of making clients fully aware of whether disclosure will provide increased chances for success requires an extensive foray into their privacy! Hence, a conundrum exists. Informed consent about whether to disclose feelings is possible only after an invasion of that which clients may want to keep quiet.[23] In the end, then, you must exercise professional judgment about whether to reflect emotions that clients seem anxious to avoid.

---

22. Please understand that we are not discussing or attempting to deal with subconscious or unconscious repression of feelings.

23. For further discussion of issues related to informed consent, please see Chapter 13.

E. RESPONDING TO CLEARLY–ARTICULATED FEELINGS

When clients clearly state feelings, reflecting back those identical feelings is likely to affect clients negatively. For example, assume that a client mentions that she was disappointed in the reaction of her partner. You mirror the remark by saying, "You were disappointed." The client's internal reaction may well be something like, "Yes, that's what I said, you dummy; I was disappointed." The client's verbal reply, however, will hopefully be more polite: "Yes, I really was." But in terms of the self-generating force usually associated with empathic understanding, parroting responses are minimally effective. Clients usually will do little more than confirm that they were heard correctly.

Hence how do you mirror back the essence of clients' clearly-articulated feelings without parroting? One opportunity arises when situations are so common that clients will readily believe that you have been in the same or similar situation. When a situation is of this type, you can empathize by directly expressing your understanding of the client's reaction:

Client:　　　I was so angry and frustrated when he again refused to go through with the deal.

Lawyer:　　　I can understand how upset you'd be after he did it again.

Verbalizing your understanding often avoids the irritating aspect of "parroting" and is fully empathic at the same time.

Be hesitant, however, to make such a response when clients are likely to realize that a situation is probably quite foreign to you. If you assert your direct understanding of a situation that is obviously outside your world of experience, clients may think you insincere or patronizing. For instance, assume that a client who is unemployed and homeless states, "I really feel humiliated when I have to talk with the welfare worker about finding a place to stay." The client is unlikely to feel empathy from your response, "I know just how humiliating that is." In such a situation, a passive listening response may be more facilitative. Or, if you have had ongoing contact with the client and believe you know the client well, you might say something like, "I know how much you hate situations like this." This response conveys understanding but does not imply that you have been in the same situation.

F. NON–EMPATHIC (JUDGMENTAL) RESPONSES

Consider the following examples of responding to clients' feelings in non-empathic ways:

Client:　　　When the promotion list came out, I was not on it. And I know I had been on the preliminary list. To see such blatant discrimination made me realize it was finally time to do something about it.

Lawyer:

No. 1:   I don't blame you.

No. 2:   But I guess after a while you calmed down.

No. 3:   You finally acknowledged what you probably knew all along. You as well as many others were victims of discrimination, and would probably continue to be.

Lawyer No. 1 has judged the appropriateness of the reaction. Lawyer No. 2 has treated the feeling as irrelevant and shifted the discussion to another time frame. Lawyer No. 3 has played amateur psychologist, by attempting to analyze the reason for the reaction. None has simply mirrored back the client's likely emotions—"You were really furious," or "You feel wronged and want to take action."

Many of us are far more used to giving advice and searching for underlying causes of emotions than we are to simply reflecting others' feelings.[24] And generally we do so out of a genuine desire to be of help. However, judgmental responses may actually reflect our own discomfort in dealing with feelings. None of the lawyers above encourages the client to continue talking about feelings; if anything, the replies divert the clients' attention away from the feelings.

To think a bit more about the difference between empathic and non-empathic responses, consider the following examples, and analyze the lawyers' responses. In which instances, if any, does the lawyer provide an empathic response?

Case #1

Client: We had only been married for three years. She was only 32 and now she is gone. I can't believe it; she had so much to give. I feel like I'm not in this world.

Lawyer:

No. 1:   Don't worry; most people feel that way at first. The feeling will pass with time.

No. 2:   It's probably because her death was so unexpected; you had no time to prepare.

No. 3:   You're feeling lost and abandoned.

24. *See* Cormier & Cormier, *supra* note 11, at 95–99.

No. 4:   It's perfectly proper for you to feel that way. Under the circumstances, no one could expect anything else.

Case #2

Client: We've been working on landing this account for over two years. Our competitors were sure they were going to get it. I've got so many ideas for positioning the whole product line; I can't wait to finalize the contract and get going.

Lawyer:

No. 1:   You have every right to gloat after pulling off a deal like this.

No. 2:   You're enjoying the fruits of two years of hard work and anxious to move forward.

No. 3:   That's great but you have to take your time and go over the contract carefully. If you don't you may regret it.

No. 4:   You're probably happy because you feel you are achieving a potential you always knew you had.

6. DIFFICULTIES IN MASTERING ACTIVE LISTENING

Without doubt, you may find it difficult to become immediately comfortable with, and proficient in the use of, active listening. However, do not use this initial discomfort as an excuse to abandon your efforts to improve your listening skills. With a little practice, you are likely to develop confidence in your ability to incorporate active listening responses in counseling conversations. Therefore, if your initial reaction to active listening is one of discomfort, persevere. Your clients will be much better off for your patience and willingness to learn an unfamiliar technique.

To put your potential personal reactions into perspective, consider the following objections to learning active listening that some lawyers and law students have advanced, and rejoinders to those objections.

A. "FEELINGS ARE FOR 'SHRINKS,' NOT LAWYERS"

1. "I'm afraid we'll get so involved in feelings, I won't properly deal with the legal issues."

2. "Cases are decided on the basis of facts. Lawyers deal in facts; psychiatrists, psychologists, and social workers deal with feelings."

A belief that feelings are largely irrelevant to lawyer-client interactions may come from a number of sources. The word "feelings" may connote irrationality and trigger the idea that feelings must be avoided so that problems can be resolved in a rational and objective manner. Or, feelings may seem irrelevant to the achievement of satisfactory solutions. Finally, thinking about feelings may generate discomfort. An easy way to avoid such discomfort is to deny the existence and importance of feelings. If the rationalization is successful, discomfort can be put to rest.

Remember, however, that your role is not to analyze feelings, but to acknowledge problems' emotional aspects when clients raises them. As one scholar has noted,

> A reflection doesn't try to understand the other person's thoughts or feelings better than he does. It doesn't try to solve the other's problems. It doesn't try to add new meaning or to analyze the message. Reflections simply show that meaning has been registered. They reveal an act of empathy. They tell the listener that he or she has been heard.[25]

B. "I FEEL EMPATHIC, BUT I JUST CAN'T FIND THE RIGHT WORDS"

1. "Reflecting feelings makes me feel awkward."

2. "It feels so mechanical, reflecting back what they feel."

3. "When I listen to myself, it sounds so hollow and forced. I'm sure the client will feel that way, too."

Your comfort with active listening may be enhanced if you recognize that there is no one "right" way to phrase active listening responses. Empathy results from a reflection of feelings, not from a magic combination of words. For example, assume that a client says, "I had always trusted my broker, but then she went and bought shares over-the-counter without any authorization from me at all." Assume further that the emotion you believe that the client is expressing is "disappointment." Any of these reflections, and undoubtedly more that you can think of, would be appropriate:

"You must have been disappointed."

"You felt disappointed."

"You were disappointed."

"It was very disappointing."

"Your broker really disappointed you."

"That must have been disappointing."

"I imagine you were disappointed."

"I can see how that must have disappointed you."

Moreover, recall that reflections do not need to be absolutely correct to be useful. If a client feels that your reflection does not quite "fit," the client may clarify and thereby gain additional insight into his or her feelings. For example, had the client above felt that "disappointment"

25. *Id.*

did not accurately capture her or his feelings, the client might have responded, "It's not just disappointment. I'm pretty angry."

Finally, if you find that reflecting feelings is extremely uncomfortable, you might start the learning process by reflecting only the content of clients' statements. Once you feel comfortable making reflective statements about content, reflections of feelings will come more easily to you.

C. "THERE'S NO WAY I CAN EMPATHIZE WITH THAT CLIENT"

1. "Look, I just feel phony. There is no way I could say, 'So you felt like you just couldn't stop yourself.' I can't say that; people can control themselves."

2. "Even if I try to be empathic, I'm sure my voice will give away the fact that I don't really mean it."

3. "Acknowledging those feelings makes me feel like I'm condoning that behavior."

4. "The guy seems so slick that it makes me feel if I respond to his feelings, he'll think I'm weak or just plain foolish."

5. "She's so aggressive, I feel that if I respond to her feelings, she'll see me as saying it's OK to act out of spite."

You are bound to encounter many individuals who tax your willingness to be empathic and non-judgmental. You may be reluctant to help people who have engaged in behavior you cannot personally abide or who have certain kinds of personalities. For example, some people may find that they do not want to help welfare recipients, bankrupts, tax evaders, child molesters, con artists, or rapists. Others find they are reluctant to assist people they view as having personalities that are extremely passive, dependent, aggressive or manipulative.

When clients or prospective clients are persons who, by dint of personality or past conduct, you are reluctant to help, you may experience a reaction similar to those above. Pursuing your own reactions further, however, you may differentiate between situations in which you totally lack empathy and situations in which you have partial empathy. For example, you may be unable to empathize with the passions that may have consumed an alleged child molester, but able to empathize with the abused childhood that helped produce those passions.

Unless you totally lack empathy for clients, you probably will be able to make some active listening responses to the emotional aspects of their problems. On the other hand, if you feel no empathy at all for clients, recognize that you may not be able to adequately represent them and consider referring them to other lawyers or withdrawing.[26]

26. Your are, of course, not obligated in the first instance to represent any client. However, if you are an associate in a law firm you may not have a choice about representing a particular client. Perhaps the best you can do, apart from leaving the firm, is to ask not to be assigned to work on matters for a client whom you find to be offen-

D. "USING ACTIVE LISTENING WILL MAKE A CLIENT TOO EMOTIONAL"

1. "I really feel uncomfortable when the client starts crying."

2. "I 'active-listened' to his anger and he just seemed to keep on going; I didn't know what to do."

3. "I think it might be a good idea, but I'm afraid the client will get so upset he'll fall apart. What'll I do then?"

Responding to feelings may result in an outpouring of even more intense emotions. If you are a beginner, experiencing such intense feelings may make you uncomfortable and lead you to back away from the use of active listening. You may feel that you are unable to stop the outpouring of emotion; that you inadvertently made the client feel worse; or that you are wrong to elicit all the emotion since there is little that you can do to resolve the feelings.

You usually can overcome concerns about eliciting an excessive amount of emotion if you recognize two propositions. First, although clients may express solely negative feelings, their overall reaction may be quite positive. The clients have had the opportunity to get "feelings off their chests," along with the satisfaction of being heard and understood. Usually this experience will result in a feeling that a discussion was, as a whole, quite beneficial.

Second, often the best way to alleviate clients' distress is to let an outpouring of emotion continue. Continued empathy usually causes an emotional tide to recede. If you can struggle through the initial discomfort, admittedly a difficult task, you will generally find that clients regain their composure. Thus, if you can, on a couple of occasions, continue to be empathic despite your discomfort, you will usually experience the success that comes from allowing clients the opportunity to ride out their emotions. With this success, you will likely experience less anxiety about eliciting and empathizing with intense emotions the next time they arise.

E. "TALKING ABOUT FEELINGS MAKES IT DIFFICULT FOR ME TO GET BACK ON TRACK"

1. "After talking about how angry she was with the Board's decision, and how it had double-crossed the employees, I felt uncomfortable having to return to questions about the specific terms of the deal."

2. "After he poured out his heart about how hurt he was when his wife left, I felt terrible having to start talking about what property they had and how title was held."

Once active listening has put a clients' feelings on the table, you may find it difficult to shift gears to matters of content. It seems

sive in some way. Note also, that ethical rules may constrain your ability to withdraw in certain circumstances. *See* Model Code of Prof'l Responsibility EC 2–32 & DR 2–110 (1980); Model Rules of Prof'l Conduct R. 1.16 (2002).

awkward when clients "pour their hearts out" to suddenly ask questions as if nothing of emotional importance had happened.

To smooth the transition, you may find it helpful first to summarize clients' situations, including their emotional reactions, and then to ask if they feel ready to move to other topics. Consider this example:

Lawyer: You invested your lump sum retirement in various real estate projects with your friend Bill, whom you've known on and off since high school. He didn't follow through on his promises, and as far as you can tell you've lost most of your investment. You're extremely upset, and to make matters worse his family is calling at all hours of the night begging you to help find a way to stop him from squandering even more money. You find it hard to be sympathetic and helpful because you're so angry at Bill. And to top it off, your doctor just told you that you're headed for a heart attack, which isn't surprising given all that you've been through.

Client: That's right. Sometimes I wish I were dead and didn't have to face this mess. It's hard to live with myself, I feel so stupid for ever getting mixed up with him.

Lawyer: I can see how upset and aggravated you are, and I want to start helping as quickly as possible. If you feel ready, I'd like to ask some questions about the deal you had with Bill.

Client: I think I'm ready to get on with this, but I get furious talking about what happened.

Lawyer: That's fine, feel free to express your anger as we go along.

Here, in addition to summarizing the client's situation and feelings, you explicitly state your desire to help and willingness to allow the client to continue to express feelings.

F. "THE CLIENT IS SO CONFUSED THAT I DON'T KNOW WHICH FEELINGS TO REFLECT"

"He says he's eager to go ahead with the deal, yet in the same breath says he's afraid of committing himself."

Sometimes clients express confused and contradictory feelings. You may feel stymied—should you focus on all the feelings, or just on one?

Recognize that contradictory feelings are the norm, not the exception. For example, when buying their first home, people typically have a variety of contradictory feelings such as wanting to put down roots vs. being afraid of feeling trapped; wanting to save money vs. being worried about taking on a big debt. Here, a young woman describes her feelings about buying a house alone:

"I want to put an offer on this house. I've been looking for months and I know this one will be a good investment. Best of all, I like this house. But the mortgage payments scare me and I'll be living there alone and it feels so disappointing. But my accountant says I'd be crazy to go on paying so much rent and taxes...."

When clients have contradictory feelings, your professional role is not to try to decipher and resolve the conflicts. Your most helpful response is to try to reflect the contradictory feelings:

>   1.   "It seems like you feel very torn about buying this house all alone."

>   2.   "Right now you seem to have very mixed feelings. On the one hand it seems like a good investment, but on the other hand living there alone feels disappointing."

G.   "ACTIVE LISTENING IS MANIPULATIVE"

>   1.   "Maybe she's not stating her feelings because she doesn't want to talk about her feelings. I don't think I should do things to try to make her talk about feelings."

>   2.   "I don't think lawyers should manipulate people to expose their feelings. It's an invasion of their privacy."

>   3.   "Look, I can go through the right motions to make the person believe I feel understanding and supportive, but I'm really just doing it to get information."

The use of active listening skills is in part the use of a technique to gain information. However, you do not employ active listening simply out of a voyeuristic interest in clients' private feelings. Rather, active listening is one among many techniques you employ in order to assist clients to find satisfactory solutions to problems. If any technique that produces information that clients might not otherwise reveal is to be denounced as "manipulative," then perhaps such standard practices as putting clients at ease with a bit of chit-chat and a cup of coffee, eliciting information in chronological fashion, probing for details with closed rather than open questions, and showing clients documents to refresh their recollection are all unfairly "manipulative."

Thus, the answer to the claim that active listening is unfairly "manipulative" is this: Clients come to you for assistance and advice, and clients' full participation is necessary if you are to help them find solutions that address all dimensions of problems. Active listening, which provides non-judgmental understanding, is an essential technique for gaining full client participation.[27]

27.   As suggested in section 5 above, you may sometimes limit your use of active listening when you sense that a client is consciously avoiding a discussion of feelings. In the absence of client reluctance to discuss feelings, you need not routinely tell clients what active listening is, and secure permission to use it. Such routine requests are likely to drive a wedge into an attorney-client relationship, as clients do not normally come to attorneys for enlightenment as to lawyer techniques, whether it be active listening, forms of questions, sequencing of questions, or the inclusion or omission of particular topics. Moreover, seeking client permission to employ active listening, or any other "technique," would almost certainly lead to the informed consent dilem-

7. HOW MUCH ACTIVE LISTENING?

Clients typically reveal emotions repeatedly as you gather information about their problems and seek to resolve them. Given this continual emotional presence, how often should you reflect feelings?

There is no single, right, or easy answer to this question.[28] You might think that some kinds of legal matters (say, marriage dissolution and wrongful termination) are inherently more prone to emotion than others (say, antitrust litigation or a simple lease deal), and thus give rise to more active listening. Or, your reaction may be that the extent to which you use active listening typically depends on how open, reticent or emotional clients are. However, none of these categories is a sure guide to how much active listening is appropriate with any individual client.

For example, if a client is talking fully and openly, you may make a number of active listening responses simply to be empathic. But if a client is not participating fully in discussions, you may make a like number of active listening responses in an effort to encourage the client to "open up." Similarly, of two clients involved in antitrust litigation, one may be an eager participant in a discussion, while the other may be the opposite. Hence, despite the subject matter similarity, you may use active listening in the latter matter more than in the former. Finally, whatever a client's general personality, the same client may be quite open in one matter, and rather reticent in another. Hence, in any individual matter, you must ultimately rely upon your judgment when deciding how frequently to reflect clients' feelings.

ma discussed in section 5. Finally, if one could not use any information-gathering technique without warning a client in advance that a response may in some way hurt the client's cause, it would seem that attorneys would have to preface all remarks with warnings. Others may disagree with this view. See Stephen Ellmann, *Lawyers and Clients*, 34 UCLA L. Rev. 717 (1987). But see John K. Morris, *Power and Responsibility Among Lawyers and Clients: Comment on Ellmann's 'Lawyers and Clients,'* 34 UCLA L. Rev. 781 (1987); Stephen Ellmann, *Manipulation By Client and Context: A Response to Professor Morris*, 34 UCLA L. Rev. 1003 (1987).

28. Psychologists have praised helping conversations in which the helper's remarks consisted almost entirely of reflections. *See* CORMIER & CORMIER, *supra* note 11. In lawyer-client dialogues, you probably will not active listen to this extent.

Chapter 4

FORMS OF QUESTIONS

---

1. INTRODUCTION

This chapter examines common forms of questions and their likely advantages and disadvantages. The chapter's goal is to further your ability to adapt questioning consciously according to the circumstances of individual interviews and the type of information you seek. The potential benefits of an effective questioning style include enhancing rapport with clients, motivating them to participate fully, conducting interviews efficiently, and maximizing your opportunity to elicit full descriptions of clients' problems and concerns.

It is probably fair to say that in everyday conversation, few us pay much attention to the types of questions we ask and respond to. Nevertheless, we are likely to react differently according to the kinds of questions we are asked. For example, assume that you are at a restaurant and that a friend asks you either: (1) "What kind of food are you in the mood for?" or (2) "Are you going to have the chicken breast with Dijon mustard sauce?" Or, assume that during one of your favorite law school classes, an instructor asks you either: (1) "Please tell us about *Palsgraf.*" or (2) "In *Palsgraf,* what did the trainman do to bring about the plaintiff's injuries?"

In the restaurant example, would you be likely to respond more expansively to one question than the other? Does one question indicate more interest in your underlying feelings and attitudes than the other? In the law school example, do you have a preference for one question rather than the other? Would one put you more "on the spot" than the other? If your friend or your law school instructor is interested in specific information, which question is more likely to elicit it?

Perhaps not everybody would answer these questions in the same way. But most people would probably, for instance, state that the first restaurant question indicates more interest in them as a person than the second. Moreover, apart from the issue of whether everyone would react in an identical manner, undoubtedly most people would answer *differently* depending on which question in each pair was asked of them.

What is true in everyday life is true in legal interviewing and counseling conversations. The information you get from clients, their motivation to speak and their attitudes towards you are all a product to some degree of the kinds of questions that you ask. Of course, human behavior is too complex to conclude that a particular form of question will always generate the same type of client response. Nonetheless, research and experience demonstrate that different forms of questions are likely to affect the amount, nature and quality of information that you receive. Thus, awareness of different forms of questions and the typical consequences of each can help you make explicit questioning choices so as to motivate clients and further the effectiveness of information-gathering in client meetings.[1]

2. FORMS OF QUESTIONS

A. GENERALLY

The forms of questions range from open to leading. No hard and fast line separates one form from another. But the principal touchstone that distinguishes forms of questions is the degree of freedom that questions allow in responses. For example, consider the following questions:

1. "Tell me about the car."

2. "Tell me about the color of the car."

3. "Tell me whether the car was red."

On the surface, each question seems pretty much like the others; each begins with "Tell me" and asks about a car. Yet the questions differ markedly in the freedom of response they allow. The first question invites discussion of any or all characteristics about the car. The second question restricts the scope of discussion to characteristics pertaining to the car's color. The third question allows no description at all; it restricts the respondent to verifying the car's color.

---

1. This chapter proceeds for the most part on the assumption that clients are generally able to recall and report their observations, experiences, and feelings. In reality, of course, clients are not perfect recording devices. The accuracy with which clients perceive, recall, and report data is subject to a variety of influences. These influences include factors within a client personally (e.g., how much attention a client was paying to an event; whether a client was under stress); and factors within the environment (e.g., light or dark when a client saw something.) For the most part, such factors potentially affect credibility, and are the subject of an extensive literature. *See, e.g.,* Brian L. Cutler, *Strategies for Mitigating the Impact of Eyewitness Experts*, 37 PROSECUTOR 14, 18 (2003), and PE-

TER B. AINSWORTH, PSYCHOLOGY, LAW AND EYEWITNESS TESTIMONY (1998). *See also* ELIZABETH F. LOFTUS & JAMES M. DOYLE, EYEWITNESS TESTIMONY: CIVIL AND CRIMINAL 12–45 (3d ed. 1997); AMINA MEMON, ET. AL., PSYCHOLOGY AND LAW: TRUTHFULNESS ACCURACY AND CREDIBILITY 108–13 (1998) (calling the factors "estimator variables"); JEAN-MARC MONTEIL & PASCAL HUGUET, SOCIAL CONTEXT AND COGNITIVE PERFORMANCE 31 (1999); Deborah Davis & William C. Follette, *Foibles of Witness Memory for Traumatic/High Profile Events*, 66 J. AIR L. & COM. 1421 (2001). The chapter also proceeds on a second assumption—that clients for the most part are capable of tailoring their responses to your questions. Sometimes this is not the case; see Chapter 12 for further discussion of this point.

The freer that respondents are to choose the scope of responses, the more "open" questions are. The more that questions restrict the scope of responses, the more "closed" they are. Neither form of question is necessarily more effective than the other. Given how clients typically react to open and closed questions, each has its purposes.

B. OPEN QUESTIONS

Open questions allow clients substantial latitude to select the content and wording of a response. Open questions generally communicate your expectation that clients will respond at some length and in their own words. At their broadest, open questions even allow clients to choose the subject matter of a response.

Examine the following questions:

1. "Tell me what brought you in here."[2]

2. "Tell me about your family."

3. "What happened after the meeting?"

4. "What took place during the conversation."

5. "How will your employees react if you move the business to a new location?"

Each question is open. Each invites a lengthy response, on a variety of potential topics, and in words of the clients' own choosing. Yet distinctions exist even among open questions. No. 1 imposes no subject matter restriction at all. Granted, a client will probably respond by talking about a legal problem rather than, say, an insight into the poetry of Byron. But the question allows the client to describe the problem in any way that the client sees fit, and to delve into whatever aspects seem most important.

No. 2 imposes a general subject matter limitation—"your family." But its openness allows the client to talk about family heritage; occupations of family members; statistical data such as names, addresses and ages; personality traits of family members, and the like. Also, the client can decide whether the term "family" means "immediate family only" or includes more distant relatives.

No. 3 imposes a chronological limitation—the client is limited to talking about what took place "after the meeting." But which post-meeting events to discuss are entirely up to the client.[3]

---

2. Note that an inquiry in the assertive form can be the equivalent of a question. Psychologists sometimes refer to such inquiries as probes since the comment is in the form of a statement rather than a question. *See* Barbara F. Okun, Effective Helping: Interviewing and Counseling Techniques 75 (6th ed. 2002); Gerard Egan, The Skilled Helper 120–21 (7th ed. 2002) (discussing probes of many varieties).

3. At trial, open questions that ask witnesses to describe events that unfolded over a period of time, often are objected to on the ground that they "call for a narrative response." The basis of the objection, and the reason that the objection is sometimes sustained, is that the question leaves the witness to talk about a series of events in whatever words the witness chooses, and some portions of the response might be

No. 4 imposes a different type of limitation—the client's response is limited to a single conversation. Yet, this question too is open. The client may talk about the parties to the conversation, what they said, and/or what activities took place during the conversation.

Lastly, No. 5 asks the client to discuss possible reactions of employees to a proposed decision. Its openness allows the client to discuss a variety of possible consequences, to differentiate among different groups of employees, and perhaps to talk about the client's long-range business goals.

C. CLOSED QUESTIONS

Closed (narrow) questions typically seek specific information; they select the subject matter of responses and also limit the scope of replies. Examples of closed questions include:

"In which hand was she holding the gun?"

"How fast was the blue car going?"

"Just where did the chicken cross the road?"

"How many employees are likely to quit if you move the business to a new location?"

D. YES–NO QUESTIONS

"Yes–No" questions are a commonly employed form of closed question. Yes–No questions even more severely limit the scope of a client's response by including in the question all the information you seek and asking the client only to confirm or deny it. All closed questions can, of course, be restated in Yes–No form. Thus, the Yes–No versions of the closed questions above are:

1. "Was she holding the gun in her left hand?"

2. "Was the blue car exceeding the speed limit?"

3. "Did the chicken cross the road in the crosswalk?"

4. "Will more than five employees quit if you move the business to a new location?"

E. LEADING QUESTIONS

As you are no doubt aware, leading questions not only provide all the information that you seek but also suggest the desired answer. Leading questions are little more than outright assertions, accompanied either by a tone of voice or language clue that you desire a particular answer. They are closed questions in assertive form. For example, in leading form the closed questions from subsection (C) are as follows:

inadmissible. *See* Paul Bergman, Trial Advocacy in a Nutshell 308 (3d ed. 1997); Thomas A. Mauet, Trial Techniques 481–82 (6th ed. 2002); *see also* Fed.R.Evid. 611(a). Other forms of open questions, which do limit a witness to a particular chronological point in time, are much less likely to be ruled improper.

1. "She was holding the gun in her left hand?"

2. "The blue car was going over 65, correct?"

3. "The chicken crossed the road in the crosswalk, right?"

4. "I take it you'll lose more than five employees if you move the business to a new location?"

The rather dramatic "Isn't it true . . ." phrase that cross-examiners tend to use during trial is certainly not a necessary characteristic of leading questions. Questions two and three have other and less dramatic verbal clues, while the first and fourth rely on voice intonation.

3. COMMON ADVANTAGES AND DISADVANTAGES OF THE DIFFERENT FORMS OF QUESTIONS

In addition to delineating the scope of responses, a question's form can also influence clients' ability and willingness to recall and provide information. This section examines this potential impact.

A. OPEN QUESTIONS

The typical advantages of open questions are as follows:

1. *Open Questions Often Motivate Full Client Participation*

Because they allow clients to decide what information is significant, open questions provide "recognition." Open questions communicate confidence in clients' ability to know what information is significant. Both the recognition and the fact that clients talk about what they see as important tend to provide motivation.

Open questions typically avoid potential inhibitors. The primary inhibitors that open questions avoid are ego threat, case threat, and the etiquette barrier. For example, clients may be embarrassed about certain aspects of their problems and therefore reluctant to talk about those aspects. A closed question seeking information about an embarrassing topic may therefore harm rapport by forcing clients either to talk about the topic or consciously avoid it. Open questions by contrast allow clients to avoid talking about threatening subjects.[4]

Your chosen profession may often require you to ask clients about sensitive subjects. When planning a client's estate, for example, you may raise the possibility that a client's child may predecease the client. Talking to a business client, you may ask about the integrity of the client's partner or office manager. As a criminal defense lawyer, you may explore a client's mental functioning and past criminal record. Clients may be uncomfortable and reluctant to talk if, with closed questions, you directly seek such sensitive information. Open questions allow clients to

---

4. Of course, you may well be unable to allow clients to duck discussion of uncomfortable topics entirely. But open questions may allow you to postpone discussion of such topics until clients are comfortable with you and understand the need to talk about the topics.

discuss sensitive information in their own way and when they are ready to do so.

Similarly, open questions also tend to overcome the inhibitor of "greater need." Since open questions allow clients to talk about what to them seems most important, you avoid any reluctance that might be created were you to ask closed questions about topics that clients regard as being of secondary importance.

2. Open Questions Often Enhance the Amount of Information You Uncover

Because both problems and clients' experiences are unique, you almost never will be able to think of everything that might be important to achieving a satisfactory solution. As one author has put it, "Qualitative answers—feelings, reasons, other experiences—can only come when the question is open-ended, not closed, and when the answer must be a paragraph, not a word."[5] For example, whether the issue is past events giving rise to a lawsuit, or potential consequences of a proposed resolution, you usually cannot think of all the factors that might bear on the issue. Thus, you cannot rely on closed questions to elicit all important information.

Open questions promote clients' recall of information by preserving their trains of thought. When clients are allowed to describe matters in their own words, their paths of association remain intact and they tend to recall data that they might not in response to closed questions.

Open questions also promote the accuracy of information. Psychological research suggests that answers to open questions are more accurate than answers to closed questions.[6]

Open questions also tend to be more efficient than closed questions.[7] Even if you could think of everything that might affect clients' problems, pursuing each and every detail with closed questions would consume an inordinate amount of time. An answer to a single open question will often cover more ground than the answers to a series of closed questions.[8]

However, lest you be ready to award a Nobel Prize to open questions, be warned that they have disadvantages as well.

5. SONYA HAMLIN, WHAT MAKES JURIES LISTEN TODAY 328 (1998); *see also* GERALD GOODMAN, THE TALK BOOK: THE INTIMATE SCIENCE OF COMMUNICATION IN CLOSE RELATIONSHIPS 127 (1988).

6. *See* ELIZABETH F. LOFTUS & JAMES M. DOYLE, EYEWITNESS TESTIMONY: CIVIL AND CRIMINAL 64 (3d ed. 1997); *cf.* AMINA MEMON, ET AL., PSYCHOLOGY AND LAW: TRUTHFULNESS ACCURACY AND CREDIBILITY 158 (1998) ("Indeed recollection of an experience is more likely to be most successful when a retrieval cue reinstates a person's subjective perception of the event, including any thoughts, fantasies and inferences.").

7. *See e.g.,* DAVID A. BINDER & PAUL BERGMAN, FACT INVESTIGATION: FROM HYPOTHESIS TO PROOF 269–70 (1984); SHELLY CORMIER & BILL CORMIER, INTERVIEWING STRATEGIES FOR HELPERS: FUNDAMENTAL SKILLS AND COGNITIVE BEHAVIORAL INTERVENTIONS 121 (4th ed. 1998).

8. Of course, in some situations you may need specific data very quickly. For example, if you are conducting a jailhouse interview of a recently arrested client, you may need bail data quickly. In such situations, you may rely on closed questions.

3. *Open Questions May Inhibit Full Client Participation*

Open questions put much of the burden for recalling and describing information on clients. Many people are not comfortable in the conversational limelight and will prefer you to carry the load. In such situations, open questions may elicit only short, minimal responses.

4. *Open Questions Do Not Thoroughly Mine Clients' Memories*

Open questions do little to stimulate memory. As a noted psychologist suggests, "Compared to other forms of report, narrative reports ... tend to be less complete.... [A] narrative produces much higher accuracy but much lower quantity."[9] As a result, events or other information known to clients typically remain undisclosed in response to open questions. For example, the open question, "What happened next?" might unearth conversations A, B and C. However, it may not uncover conversation D, nor details about A, B and C.

Thus, to get sufficient information you typically have to combine open with closed questions. Because of their ability to call specific data to clients' attention, closed questions are generally more successful than open ones at stimulating their recall.[10] For example, the closed question, "Did you talk about precise geographical limits during conversation A?" may remind a client of details that might not emerge in response to the open question, "What did you talk about during conversation A?" The reason is that in response to closed questions, clients may *recognize* data that they do not *recall* in response to open ones.[11]

Open questions may also fail to elicit information that clients do remember, but that they do not recognize as being legally salient. When clients are mistaken about or unaware of legal requirements, they may well omit information from narrative responses in the belief that the information is without legal significance.

5. *Open Questions May Be Inefficient*

Open questions may not be effective with clients who ramble or are extremely verbose. Certain clients may regard a question such as, "What

---

9. ELIZABETH F. LOFTUS, EYEWITNESS TESTIMONY 91–92 (1979); *see also* RAYMOND GORDEN, BASIC INTERVIEWING SKILLS 35–36 (1998); ELIZABETH F. LOFTUS & JAMES M. DOYLE, EYEWITNESS TESTIMONY: CIVIL AND CRIMINAL 64 (3d. ed. 1997).

10. However, closed questions can be as suggestive as leading ones, and therefore produce inaccurate responses. STEPHEN A. RICHARDSON, BARBARA SNELL DOHRENWEND & DAVID KLEIN, INTERVIEWING: ITS FORMS AND FUNCTIONS 173, 181 (1965). Because closed questions may pressure clients into believing that they *should* answer questions, *id.*

at 180, the risk of inaccurate replies in response to closed questions may be especially high in attorney-client interviews. *See* ROBERT F. COCHRAN, JR. ET AL., THE COUNSELOR AT LAW: A COLLABORATIVE APPROACH TO CLIENT INTERVIEWING AND COUNSELING 50 (1999); CORMIER & CORMIER, *supra* note 7 at 112–114; ALLEN IVEY, INTENTIONAL INTERVIEWING AND COUNSELING (5th ed. 2003).

11. For further discussion of the differences between recall and recollection, *see* GEORGE MANDLER, CONSCIOUSNESS RECOVERED: PSYCHOLOGICAL FUNCTIONS AND ORIGINS OF CONSCIOUS THOUGHT 82–83 (2002).

happened since our last meeting?" as an invitation to describe irrelevant events in great detail, and to vilify all with whom they disagree. Asking open questions of such clients may be the equivalent of pouring gasoline on a fire.

B. CLOSED QUESTIONS

The typical advantages of closed questions are as follows:

1. *Closed Questions Elicit Details*

Perhaps the most important advantage of closed questions is that they allow you to elicit details. For example, assume that Fong consults you concerning problems that have developed with a partner over how to best operate the partnership's business. One of Fong's options is to dissolve the partnership. The following dialogue ensues:

L: And what occurred at the meeting?

C: Well, my partner Miyoko started off by complaining that sales were down, especially in the sports apparel line, and asked us for our ideas. There were a number of suggestions made, ranging from getting out of the line altogether to trying to get the line into bigger retail stores like Sears. Everyone had their own ideas—the meeting went on for almost an hour.

L: Anything else that you can recall?

C: I know that Miyoko got really angry when we went over sales figures.

L: Anything else?

C: Not that I can remember.

Here, you rely only on open questions. In response, Fong quickly provides a picture of what took place at a meeting. But, as is often the case with responses to open questions, the picture is incomplete. It lacks many details that may well be significant. For instance, what specific sales figures did Miyoko report? What were the various suggestions that were presented at the meeting, and how did Miyoko respond to each? What exactly does Fong mean by "really angry?" The answers to such questions are likely to be critical in helping Fong to decide whether staying in business with Miyoko makes sense.

To elicit such details, you would probably need to ask closed questions. Such questions focus on specific topics, thereby stimulating memory and producing details that clients might otherwise omit or not remember.

2. *Closed Questions May Provide Motivation*

Clients may be uncertain of how to respond to open questions. For example, a question such as, "What consequences do you see if we reject the proposal?" may confuse a client. Does the question call for every possible consequence, or only for the most significant ones? How much elaboration do you expect? Does the question somehow "test" the client to see how many consequences the client can identify? Clients for whom open questions create such thoughts will probably be reluctant to answer fully and openly. Such clients may find closed questions "easier" to answer: their topics are readily identifiable, their scope is readily apparent, and a client has only to produce a limited amount of information. Therefore, for such clients, closed questions may provide greater motivation to answer.

Closed questions may provide greater motivation than open questions in other contexts as well. Recall the suggestion that open questions often motivate clients by allowing them to postpone discussion of sensitive topics. You may employ closed questions to delay discussion of sensitive matters as well. Closed questions allow you to "tippy toe" either into or around sensitive topics. When you know or strongly suspect that clients are reluctant to discuss a particular topic, closed questions may allow you to pursue the topic a small bit at a time, and stop at the point that clients become reluctant to proceed further.[12]

For instance, assume that in the partnership example above, Fong's responses lead you to believe that Fong feels foolish for having started the partnership with Miyoko in the first place. However, you want Fong to talk about the reasons for going into business with Miyoko initially. You might ask an open question: "Can you tell me how the partnership came about?" However, Fong may be reluctant to respond fully to this question. Thus, you may try to tippy-toe through the discussion with a series of closed questions that allow Fong to disclose information at a slower and perhaps less threatening pace:

"When did you first meet Miyoko?"

"How many times did you meet before you formally entered into the partnership?"

"Who first suggested a formal partnership?"

"Did you talk about how long the partnership should continue?"

You might continue this type of questioning into Fong's reasons for entering the partnership, or you might stop questioning before arriving at that point. At least, closed questions may motivate specific responses and provide you with insight into how far to pursue the topic.

Alas, as you undoubtedly suspect, closed questions also have disadvantages:

3. Too Many Closed Questions May Harm Rapport

Over-reliance on closed questions may result in clients leaving meetings with the feeling that they never had a chance to say what was really on their minds. The more you ask questions that limit the scope of responses, the less likely are you to learn everything that clients think is

---

12. This discussion assumes that a compelling reason to pursue a topic at once does not exist. In the absence of a compelling reason to pursue a sensitive matter at once, it often makes sense to postpone discussion until a client is comfortable.

important. In turn, clients are likely to be less engaged in identifying problems and actively participating in their resolution.

4. Closed Questions May Prevent You from Learning Important Information

Asking numerous closed questions is likely to cause you to miss both trees and forest. You miss trees, because in any matter there are too many for you to find with closed questions. Moreover, clients tend not to volunteer information when faced with a plethora of closed questions, figuring that if a bit of data is important, surely you will seek it out.

At the same time, your focus on individual trees is likely to obscure your view of the forest. The immersion in bits of detail may undermine your learning clients' overall stories.

5. Closed Questions Can Create Inaccurate Responses

Closed questions tend to produce more erroneous information than open questions.[13] The tendency may be due in part to the influence of the motivator, "fulfilling expectations." That is, your asking closed questions may signal your expectation that clients are able to answer them. Rather than frustrate your expectations (and perhaps damage their own self-esteem), clients may guess or respond with what they think "probably" happened rather than admit that they do not know or do not remember.

Closed questions may distort responses in another way. Because closed questions define topics for clients to a greater extent than do open questions, closed questions are likely to reflect your choice of vocabulary, not that of your clients. For instance, compare the open question, "Describe Jones' behavior" with the closed question, "Was Jones angry?" The closed question identifies a specific emotion and attaches your label to it. If the term "angry" captures at least an aspect of Jones' emotional state, a client may simply answer "yes" in response to the closed question even though the open question would have elicited a different response.

In one study, for example, changing a word in a question from "frequently" to "occasionally" produced markedly different results. In this often-replicated study, one group of random respondents was asked, "Do you get headaches frequently and, if so, how often?" Another group was asked, "Do you get headaches occasionally, and, if so, how often?" The first group reported an average of 2.2 headaches per week; the second group only 0.7 headaches per week.[14] Changing even the word "a" to "the" in a question can affect results. It is not surprising that one

---

13. *See* RAYMOND L. GORDEN, BASIC INTERVIEWING SKILLS 36 (1998).

14. ELIZABETH LOFTUS, EYEWITNESS TESTIMONY 94–95 (1979). *See also* Russell B. Korobkin & Thomas Ulen, *Law and Behav-*

ioral Science: Removing the Rationality Assumption for Law and Economics, 88 CAL. L. REV. 1051 (2000)(accountants influenced in their estimate of management fraud by language of questions from interviewers).

researcher has concluded, "[I]n a variety of situations, the wording of a question about an event can influence the answer that is given."[15]

C. LEADING QUESTIONS

Although the term "leading question" is often accompanied by or greeted with sneers, such questions are sometimes proper and necessary for eliciting an adequate picture of clients' problems. The sub-sections below examine leading questions' common advantages and disadvantages.

1. *Leading Questions May Overcome Potential Inhibitors*

Leading questions may help you to overcome the inhibitors of ego threat, case threat and the etiquette barrier. These inhibitors tend to make clients reluctant to disclose matters they perceive as sensitive. Hence, when discussions touch on sensitive matters, use of leading questions suggests that you already know about the troublesome data, that a client need not fear letting the cat out of the bag, and that you are prepared to talk about it in a forthright manner.[16]

The classic example of this use of leading questions is provided by the Kinsey study of American sexual mores. Rather than asking individuals *if* they had engaged in such potentially embarrassing conduct as oral sex or homosexuality, Kinsey's researchers asked *when* or *how often* they had done so.[17] The leading form of the questions suggested to respondents that the interviewers expected that such activity had taken place, would not condemn the respondents for admitting it, and were prepared to discuss it openly. The examples below illustrate how leading questions may overcome embarrassment in two typical legal situations. Compare the following sets of questions:

"Have you ever been arrested before?"

"I guess you've had some problems with the police before?"

"Do you see any problems in letting them look at your books?"

"The acquiring company's examination of your books will bring to light things like allowing employees to use company cars for personal use. How should we talk to them about these matters?"

Assuming that you strongly suspect that the troublesome conduct has in fact occurred, the use of leading questions may overcome these clients'

15. ELIZABETH F. LOFTUS & JAMES M. DOYLE, EYEWITNESS TESTIMONY: CIVIL AND CRIMINAL 65 (3d ed. 1997).

16. *See* ROBERT F. COCHRAN, JR ET AL., THE COUNSELOR AT LAW: A COLLABORATIVE APPROACH TO CLIENT INTERVIEWING AND COUNSELING 54 (1999); *cf.* HANDBOOK OF THE PSYCHOLOGY OF INTERVIEWING 158 (Amina Memon & Ray Bull eds., 1999) ("By being open and specific about sex, and non-judgmental at the same time, an interviewer can, as to speak, *give permission* to bring up these matters."). See also, RAYMOND L. GORDEN, BASIC INTERVIEWING SKILLS (1998).

17. ALFRED KINSEY, ET AL., SEXUAL BEHAVIOR IN THE HUMAN MALE 53–54 (1948).

fear and embarrassment, and consequent reluctance to talk openly and honestly.

However, as the sneer that often accompanies or greets the term "leading" suggests, leading questions are not without their disadvantages.

2. Leading Questions May Enhance the Possibility of Eliciting Incorrect Information

Leading questions often reflect your ardent desire to have facts come out in a way favorable to your clients. For example, if an appellate case or a statute uses a word, you might want a client to use precisely that word in recounting a past event. Hence, you may incorporate that word in a leading question. Though that word may be an inaccurate label, the leading question may cause a client, consciously or unconsciously, to affirm it. You may thereby introduce inaccuracy into discussions. When you later discover an inaccuracy (or have it pointed out to you by another party), it may be too late to seek solutions that you and a client might have pursued if the true information had come to light earlier.

3. Leading Questions May Be Ethically Improper

Use of leading questions in your office can be even more problematic than it may be at trial. Generally, you cannot ethically suggest "correct" answers to clients. For example, assume that a couple consults you about a new house that they purchased, based in part on their understanding that the roof on the house was brand new. When it later turns out that the roof is old and needs replacing, the clients seek advice about what they should do. Might you ask, "I take it that the seller actually told you that the roof was new?" Such a question does nothing except tell the clients what to say and absent unusual circumstances is surely improper.

D. FACTORS TENDING TO RESULT IN OVER–RELIANCE ON NARROW QUESTIONS

As the discussion above suggests, effective motivation and information-gathering typically involves a mix of open and closed or leading questions. The sub-sections below examine two factors that may influence your questioning choices by inclining you towards over-reliance on narrow questions.

1. The "Filling in" Phenomenon

The "filling in" phenomenon refers to a subconscious tendency we all have to complete (or "fill in") stories with information drawn from everyday experiences. That is, we may fill in clients' stories with information that they haven't mentioned. When this happens, you may picture clients' stories as more complete than they really are. As a result, you may eschew open questions in favor of closed questions seeking those details that your experience doesn't provide.

This phenomenon grows out of the reality that none of us approaches events from a totally neutral perspective. Instead, we carry around mental "schema," or expectations drawn from experience about how events commonly unfold. Schema are valuable; they allow our past experiences to make sense of new ones.[18] Think about how complicated life would be if each trip to a supermarket, say, were a completely new and unique experience. At the same time, schema may cause you to "fill in" by completing clients' stories with information drawn from your experience. To recognize your capacity to fill in, think about the following situations:

     1.   Two cars collided in an intersection.

     2.   A wife suddenly deserted her husband and their two young children.

Take a moment and try to conjure up a picture of each situation. In the first example, can you visualize, if only hazily, a particular intersection, makes of cars, the point of collision, and how the collision came about? In the second, do you have an image of the feelings, desires and concerns of the husband whose wife has left home, and of factors that might have led the wife to abandon her family?

If you do, recognize that these images are not explicitly set forth in the sentences themselves. Rather, you "filled in" the gaps with information furnished by your own schemas. In the same way, you may fill in information as you listen to clients describe past events or concerns. And as a result you may tend to over-rely on narrow questions to elicit the specific details that your general schema cannot provide.

For example, assume that a client seeks your help in negotiating the terms of a long-term lease. Especially if you have had prior experience with such matters, you may have developed schema concerning the "needs and concerns of long-term lessees." If so, you may overlook open questions seeking information about this particular client's goals and concerns in favor of narrow questions focusing on specific terms to include in the final lease agreement.

With schemas such a routine and important part of everyday life, an attitude of "ignore schemas" is impossible. However, cognizance of the advantages of open questions and active listening can help you minimize their influence during information-gathering.[19]

2. *Premature Diagnosis*

"Premature diagnosis" is a second factor tending to produce over-reliance on narrow questions. Premature diagnosis occurs when you

     18. *See* HANDBOOK OF THE PSYCHOLOGY OF INTERVIEWING 294–95 (Amina Memon & Ray Bull eds., 1999); STEFAN H. KRIEGER, ET AL., ESSENTIAL LAWYERING SKILLS 112–14 (1998); GEORGE MANDLER, CONSCIOUSNESS RECOVERED: PSYCHOLOGICAL FUNCTIONS AND ORIGINS OF CONSCIOUS THOUGHT 44–45 (2002).

     19. Because lawyers deal with certain types of situations regularly, it is easy to "fill in" client and witness accounts with personal knowledge and speculation. *See* Deborah Davis & William C. Follette, *Foibles of Witness Memory for Traumatic/High Profile Events*, 66 J. AIR L. & COM. 1421, 1490 (2001). For a discussion of filling in the context of eyewitness identification, see Robert Buckhout, *Eyewitness Testimony*, 231 SCI. AM. 23, 24–27 (1974).

pigeonhole stories around legal claims even before clients finish describing their problems. For example, at the drop of a few facts you may pigeonhole a story as a "products liability" case, an "inter vivos trust" matter, or a "securities issuance" problem. Your diagnosis may well be inaccurate, or at least incomplete. But once you place problems into pigeonholes, you may rely on closed questions in an effort to shoehorn stories into them.

As with "filling," inoculating yourself completely against the tendency to engage in premature diagnosis can be difficult. Early awareness of legal possibilities can in fact help you gather information effectively and efficiently. Thus, be of two minds during initial client meetings. Even as you instinctively riffle through legal claims as clients begin to relate their stories, continue to use open questions that may activate legal theories you otherwise might overlook. For example, even though you may pigeonhole a plaintiff's story as involving a claim for monetary damages, you might nevertheless ask an open-ended question such as, "If you could write your own ticket, what result would you like to see?"

4. CONCLUSION

Even though you may employ the "correct" forms of questions at the "correct" times, you cannot be sure that the result will be motivated clients who provide full, accurate information. Clients vary greatly, and a question that motivates one client may inhibit another. Moreover, one client may respond to a yes-no question as though it were open, while another client may interpret questions quite literally. Lastly, any one client may respond to the same form of question differently at different times. Thus, you need to adapt the forms of questions to the dynamics of individual conversations.

*

Part Three

INFORMATION–GATHERING

Part Three (Chapters 5 through 12) examines a variety of subjects related to information-gathering. Chapter 5 explores approaches and techniques for beginning initial and follow-up meetings. Chapters 6 through 8 explore approaches and techniques for initial data-gathering in litigation matters. Chapters 9 and 10 explore these subjects in the context of proposed business transactions. Chapter 11 concerns methods for concluding initial and follow-up conferences. Finally, Chapter 12 considers approaches and methods of interviewing problematic clients.

Chapter 5

BEGINNING CLIENT CONFERENCES

---

* * *

Nice to see you again, Norma. How's that new plant that Trinomics built working out?

Very well. We've increased production by 50%, and we're still behind in our shipments. So things are going about as well as they can. Actually, having the new plant is the reason we're thinking about the deal I mentioned to you over the phone.

I'm delighted to hear that things are going so well. From what you said on the phone, this new deal sounds like a great opportunity for Trinomics. But before we get into any details, why don't you tell me what Trinomics is trying to accomplish by going into the deal.

* * *

1. INTRODUCTION

Daily life constantly reminds us of the importance of first impressions. Whether evidenced by cliches such as "put your best foot forward," or by advice to trial lawyers to "win your case during voir dire,"[1] everyone understands that relationships' beginnings often strongly influence their future course. Beginnings may even determine whether there *is* a future. Hence, a sensible strategy is to think carefully about how to begin client conferences.[2]

---

1. *See. e.g.,* THOMAS A. MAUET, FUNDAMENTALS OF TRIAL TECHNIQUES 23 (4th ed. 2000); MARILYN J. BERGER, JOHN B. MITCHELL & RONALD H. CLARK, TRIAL ADVOCACY—PLANNING, ANALYSIS & STRATEGY 164 (Little, Brown and Co. 1989).

2. The importance of the beginning phase of interviews is illustrated by the fact that the subject is covered in nearly every work in an extensive interviewing literature

for lawyers. *See, e.g.,* THOMAS L. SHAFFER & JAMES R. ELKINS, LEGAL INTERVIEWING AND COUNSELING IN A NUTSHELL 76 (3d ed. 1997); ROBERT M. BASTRESS & JOSEPH D. HARBAUGH, INTERVIEWING, COUNSELING AND NEGOTIATION: SKILLS FOR EFFECTIVE REPRESENTATION 85–97 (1990); STEFAN H. KRIEGER ET AL., ESSENTIAL LAWYERING SKILLS: INTERVIEWING, COUNSELING, NEGOTIATION, AND PERSUASIVE FACT ANALYSIS 63–70 (1999).

This chapter describes a client-centered approach to beginning initial and follow-up client conferences. Less a set of strict procedures to be slavishly copied than a general guide to professional judgment, the approach is one you may use both in litigation and transactional matters, regardless of a matter's substantive law content. Moreover, you may adapt the approach to all new matters, regardless of whether or not you have previously represented a client.

2.   PRE–INITIAL MEETING COMMUNICATIONS

Before you first meet personally with clients about new matters, you may first talk to them over the phone or perhaps even communicate with them electronically. Unless you have had ongoing relationships with clients, such pre-meeting contacts are generally not a useful setting for trying to elicit significant information about problems. However, informal contacts such as these often do offer you the opportunity to engender client confidence and begin to establish rapport. Strategies that you might follow to enhance rapport during pre-meeting contacts with clients include the following.

- Ask a few general questions about clients' reasons for wanting to meet with you. Demonstrating immediate interest in problems tends to boost clients' confidence in you and helps you prepare for interviews. Moreover, if you specialize, knowing that clients' problems are outside your practice specialty allows you to refer them elsewhere without their having to meet with you. Additionally, what you learn about clients' problems in advance of personal meetings may reveal reasons to expedite them, such as a deadline on a transaction or the rapid approach of a statute of limitations.[3]

- Ask clients to bring to meetings any documents or other materials that they consider pertinent to their legal situations. Among the messages that such requests implicitly convey is your desire help and to make the initial meeting productive.

- Ask clients whether they have any immediate questions. For example, clients may want to know what your legal fees are likely to be, whether they will have to pay for the initial consultation, and whether you have experience with matters such as theirs. Whatever clients' expressed concerns, try to respond briefly and directly even if definite answers are impossible. For example, you might say something like,

   "As you can imagine, I can't at this point do any more than give you a ballpark estimate of what my fees might eventually be. Based on my past experiences in these kinds of matters I'd say that a realistic figure is in the neighborhood of a few thousand dollars. But we can talk about how I determine fees when we

---

3. As discussed later in the chapter, information you learn in this kind of pre-engagement conversation is just as confidential as information you learn within a more established attorney-client relationship. *See* Model Rules of Prof'l Conduct R. 1.18.

get together, and of course if you decide not to go ahead after we've discussed your situation you will have no legal fees whatsoever. Does that sound OK?"[4]

- Assure clients that you are glad that they contacted you and that you will do your very best to help them in as short a time frame as possible.

If you are unavailable when clients contact your office to arrange initial meetings, try to make sure that your assistants know the information that you like to obtain from prospective clients in advance and have them obtain as much of it as they can. When clients talk to your assistant rather than to you, a good practice is to personally return clients' calls in advance of initial meetings, thank them for consulting you, and assure them of your desire to help. [5]

3. GREETING CLIENTS

At initial meetings, the first consideration (chronologically, if not in order of importance) is where to meet clients. Typically your choice will be between your office and a waiting/reception room. Most clients will prefer you to meet them in the waiting area and escort them to your office. Meeting clients in a waiting area immediately demonstrates your personal concern. Also, as you walk to your office you can put clients at ease through casual conversation or by offering them a hot or cold drink. Moreover, you avoid awkward moments such as being on the phone at the moment a client enters your office or trying to shake hands while dodging a sharp corner of your desk.

Generally, where you choose to greet clients remains the same whether clients make initial or follow-up visits. No matter how well you know clients, most people appreciate the extra bit of attention you show them by coming to a waiting area to greet them.

The usual alternative to meeting clients in a reception area is to have a receptionist or other assistant escort clients to your office.[6] You might think that an advantage of this approach is that it stimulates client confidence by implicitly communicating that you are busy and important. However, most clients probably prefer a personal greeting in a reception area. Hopefully, your effective representation will be a more meaningful confidence booster for clients than where you greet them.

Whichever approach you adopt, follow ordinary social niceties. Greet clients by name and be sure that new clients know your name. You may be surprised how often, even if you have spoken by phone to clients

4. If you choose to charge a consultation fee for the initial interview, you will change this answer appropriately.

5. Of course, in some practices lawyers routinely have clients (new and ongoing) talk with secretaries or other assistants to arrange initial meetings regarding new matters. In terms of initially building rapport such procedures seem problematic.

6. In no case should clients have to try to find your office on their own, with such instructions as, "Turn left at the first corridor, then left again at the copy machine." Given the maze-like quality of many law offices, such clients may never be seen again.

before an initial meeting, new clients will not be quite sure what your name is.[7] Conduct interviews in an area of your office that is conducive to personal conversation. For some clients, a desk is off-putting. You might instead sit together with clients at a small table or even in facing chairs with no table in between. For other clients, especially new ones, a more formal venue may prove more comfortable. For example, television and movies may lead clients to expect that meetings with "real lawyers" take place in a conventionally formal environment. Or clients' cultural notions of propriety may cause them to feel that a casual setting brings them into uncomfortably close contact with a stranger. [8]

Smile.

4. ICEBREAKING

* * *

We can sit over here, Mr. Wilson. You can put your coffee right here.

Thanks; say, that's a nice view you have.

It is, and when things get crazy around here I like to stop and spend a few minutes just looking at the view; I like the light that north-facing windows provide. Did you have any trouble parking?

None at all.

Good. The parking situation in this building can be quite horrid at times and it bothers me when clients get delayed by the inefficiency of our parking service. I normally warn new clients that parking may be a problem, and I realized I didn't say anything to you when you called. I'm glad things worked out well.

* * *

As do many social interactions, effective client meetings typically begin with a few moments of "chit-chat." Chit-chat tends to put both

---

7. For this reason, you may want to hand new clients your business card when you first meet them. On the other hand, you may consider this practice to be cold and distancing, and prefer to wait for meetings' conclusions to hand out your card.

8. While substantial literature developed in the 1970s and 1980s regarding how offices should be decorated and arranged in order to put clients at ease, see, e.g., Paul Marcotte, *Was It Something I Said? Office Decor Can Help Determine Whether You Keep Clients*, A.B.A. J. 34 (Aug. 1987); Steven G. Fey and Steven Goldberg, *Legal Interviewing from a Psychological Perspective: An Attorney's Handbook*, 14 WILLAMETTE L. REV. 217, 221–24 (1978), that literature tended to assume that all clients achieve comfort through similar "proxemics." More recent literature shows that cultural background and practices can affect how an individual might feel in certain set-

tings. See SHELLY CORMIER & BILL CORMIER, INTERVIEWING STRATEGIES FOR HELPERS: FUNDAMENTAL SKILLS AND COGNITIVE BEHAVIORAL INTERVENTIONS 85 (4th ed. 1998) (discussing differences in proxemics across different cultures); RAYMOND GORDEN, BASIC INTERVIEWING SKILLS 67 (1998) (explaining that the comfortable distance for "personal space" is a cultural pattern that varies within a country by region, ethnicity, social class, and sex; and may also change depending upon the topic being discussed). A prudent lawyer will try to anticipate some of those cultural differences. See generally Susan Bryant, *The Five Habits: Building Cross–Cultural Competence in Lawyers*, 8 CLINICAL L. REV. 33 (2001); Bill Ong Hing, *Raising Personal Identification Issues of Class, Race, Ethnicity, Gender, Sexual Orientation, Physical Disability, and Age in Lawyering*, 45 STAN. L. REV. 1807 (1993).

you and clients at ease and demonstrates that you are interested in them as people and not simply as sources of legal fees. The preliminary conversation may, as above, involve that ubiquitous enemy, parking. Or, depending on such variables as where you live, how well you know clients, and what you and clients have in common, chit-chat may touch on local news or a sporting event, previous contacts, the person who referred the client to you, and the like.[9]

Recognize, however, that some clients may be annoyed by chit-chat, especially if they are feeling anxious and they find the small talk unduly prolonged. Thus, the soundest client-centered strategy is to try to tailor the amount of chit-chat to each individual client's needs and desires. Of course, deciding upon a satisfactory amount of small talk can be difficult when you have little more to go on than a handshake and perhaps a brief prior telephone conversation. Probably your best "default position" is to begin with a few moments of chit-chat. Small talk is such a common social practice that few clients will take umbrage at a minimal amount of preliminary conversation. These few preliminary moments typically provide a basis for you to size up clients and assess their tolerance for or interest in this social convention.[10]

Clients who appear to be relaxed and ready to discuss their problems often don't need the transitional moments that chit-chat provides. In such situations, you might curtail the pre-interview social repartee. For example, assume that the conversation as you and a new client enter your office goes as follows:

L: Did you have any problems getting here?

C: No, no problems at all. In fact, I arrived early so I could go over my outline. I also made sure that I brought the documents you asked about; I have them right here.

This client's response suggests that the client feels at ease and is ready to get down to business. Following the client's lead, you might move right to the business at hand rather than talk about the parking, the weather or the latest courtroom film.

When clients appear to be distressed and anxious, you will have to assess whether they will appreciate a bit of small talk as a way to calm down so as to better focus on the problem at hand, or will find chit-chat annoying and patronizing. For example, assume that in response to your polite inquiry about whether the client had difficulty getting to your office, the client had responded, "Yes, it was really a hassle. I was stuck in traffic for nearly an hour. It's tough for me to get to this part of

---

9. Expect clients to frequently ask you about the legal scandal of the week from television news or even from popular law-related TV shows. For example, for a few years running much lawyer-client chit-chat ended up having something to do with O.J. Simpson.

10. Icebreaking may be of special importance in cross-cultural situations. For clients from other cultures, jumping too quickly into data gathering "may well be perceived as intrusive and disrespectful." Instead, you might seek to learn about "family and friends." See JAMES W. LEIGH, COMMUNICATING FOR CULTURAL COMPETENCE 40 (1998).

town." Or, perhaps the client responded, "Yes, in fact I barely made it here today. I was up practically all night talking to my partner in New York; it was almost impossible to get back to sleep. I overslept and still don't feel totally awake."

Comments such as these signal that a client has arrived tense or tired. You therefore may want to make a special effort to put the client at ease. You can do this by expressing concern and consideration for the client's distress:

> I'm sorry you had such a difficult time getting here. Perhaps I can get you something to drink; we're not quite as well equipped as the coffee bar down in the lobby but we turn out some nice drinks. In addition, I want you to know that once we start working together, I'm happy to do as much as possible over the phone. I know it's hard to get downtown at this time of day.

or

> I know what those late night calls are like. I always have trouble getting back to sleep when I get a late business call and it can take time to get going the next day. Would you like some coffee before we start?

When clients are distressed, you also may be able to help by saying something like, "Would you like to take a few moments and catch your breath before we start?" If you receive an indication that a client would like more time, engaging in additional chit-chat may help. However, the small talk should not be indiscriminate. An empathic approach is to personalize your chit-chat. That is, try to focus on a topic that is personal to a specific client. If you know a client's business or occupation, talk about that. If a client is wearing a Lion's Club pin, ask or comment about that. If a client's clothing indicates interest in a particular sport or other activity, comment or ask about that. Or, you might consider mentioning something about the person who referred the client:[11]

> "I'm really happy that Charlene referred you to me. She is such a fine person. I've known her for many years...."

On the other hand, if a client is wearing a pin that reads, "Ask me about what's new in term life insurance," you might want to chit-chat about something else.

Finally, how can you effectively respond to clients whose distress grows out of their problem, not traffic woes or a sleepless night? Should you forgo chit-chat and discuss the case immediately? Consider this example:

---

11. When talking about the person who referred the client, be careful. Avoid making the client feel that the referring person disclosed confidences. Avoid making the client feel you "checked the client out" with the referral source. Also, consider whether you may be putting the client on the spot by asking how the client knows the referring person.

L: How are you?

C: I'm furious. Take a look at these papers I was served with. I can't believe what those slimeballs are trying to do.

While on the surface the client appears to want to talk about the case, the client may really just want to vent resentment and agitation. Hence, rather than moving into a structured exploration of the client's problem, you may simply sit back and let the client blow off steam. Ask the client to tell you more. Empathize with the client's feelings, and "park" your efforts at systematic data-gathering until the client begins to calm down.

5. PRELIMINARY PROBLEM IDENTIFICATION

* * *

Mrs. Bishop, perhaps the easiest way to get started is for you to explain how I might be of help.

Well, I'm not exactly sure. My husband and I are having a second story put on our home and our neighbor, a guy named Ken Young, has threatened to sue us if we don't stop.

I'm sure this is very upsetting to both of you and I certainly want to help. Can you tell me a little bit more?

Well, Young lives next door and claims that deed restrictions prevent us from building a second story because it will block his view. But as far as we can tell, no such restrictions exist.

That's helpful; it gives me a sense of where this problem is coming from, and I have had some experience in these sorts of matters. However, before I get into the details, probably it would be useful for you to tell me if there are other concerns on your mind that you've not mentioned. Are there other things besides the threat of a lawsuit that you want to talk about this morning?

* * *

Mr. Falconi, why don't you start by telling me what's on your mind.

Sure. I've been talking to Bob Barton, the president of ABC Realty, a large real estate development company, about exchanging some property I own in Palm Beach for some stock in ABC. Economically, the deal makes sense if there are no taxes; I think ABC has a very good future. But what I want to know about are the likely tax consequences. I want the trade to be tax free if at all possible.

Tax free exchanges is an area I'm familiar with. To determine whether you can arrange such an exchange I'm going to need to get some details from you. However, before I get into those I want to make sure we get to go over everything that is on your mind. Besides the tax situation, are there other things that you'd like to review this afternoon?

* * *

When initial interviews move to the substance of clients' problems, you can usefully begin to elicit information with "preliminary problem identification." Consistent with the goals of client-centered counseling, preliminary problem identification encourages clients to provide personal perspectives on their legal problems. Even if further questioning and investigation reveal that a client's perspective is in whole or in part mistaken or unrealistic, understanding problems from your clients' perspectives can help you establish rapport and achieve satisfactory solutions. The sections below set forth the topics that typically comprise preliminary problem identification inquiries, explain the benefits of beginning interviews in this manner, illustrate questioning techniques and suggest how you might provide tentative advice at the conclusion of this phase of interviews.

A. THE FOUR MAIN TOPICS

Preliminary problem identification consists of asking clients to discuss four topics that together will usually enable you to gain quick understanding of problems' subject matter and scope as well as clients' attitudes and expectations. The topics are relevant to all types of legal problems, whether they involve disputes or transactions. The topics that you may focus on during preliminary problem identification are as follows:

1. Problem Description

This topic refers to the gist of your clients' problems. Why have they come to see you? Whether a problem revolves around a transaction or a dispute, understanding the gravamen of clients' situations enables you to size up quickly the probable contours of the upcoming attorney-client relationship. Of course, clients won't describe problems in the abstract language of law school casebooks: "I've got a unilateral contract problem involving a third party beneficiary." Some clients will provide capsule summaries of the facts that motivated them to seek legal help. For example, a client may say something like, "This jerk ran a red light and ran into my car; he should have to pay for all the damages he's caused," or, "My wife passed away a few months ago and now my children think that I need to change my will." Other clients will be far less concise, melding a summary of their problem with a great deal of factual background and emotion.[12]

Typical questions for eliciting problem descriptions include: "How can I help you?," "What brings you here today?" and "What can I do for you?"

2. Desired Outcome

This topic identifies clients' goals and expectations. For example, a client who claims to have been wrongfully fired from her place of employment might want to be rehired with full back pay and damages

---

12. As you will see, dealing with clients who respond in this more verbose manner may require you to proceed in a somewhat different manner than you might respond when clients' initial descriptions are more succinct.

for lost income and payment for a job retraining program. Of course, clients' goals may change as cases progress. Also, clients' initial goals may also be unrealistic. For example, if the client with the wrongful termination problem states that what she expects is to be rehired at double her previous salary, part of your later counseling will probably have to involve educating her about what she may realistically expect from any lawsuit that you may file on her behalf.[13]

Typical questions for eliciting information about desired outcomes include: "How'd you like to see this come out?" and "If you could write your own ticket, what would you like to see happen?"

3.   *Means of Achieving Desired Outcome*

This topic concerns clients' ideas for achieving their objectives. For instance, one client whose remodeling project has been held up by a neighborhood association may think that the best way to get the project back on track is for you to write a "lawyer letter" to the association; a second client with the same type of problem may think that the best approach is for you to file suit immediately against the association.

Unless they have dealt with lawyers previously, most people are largely unaware of the processes through which lawyers work towards ultimate resolution of problems. Hence, it is hardly surprising that even clients who have firm objectives in mind may be uncertain as to how to go about achieving them. For example, if a client with a remodeling project problem has never previously retained a lawyer in a dispute situation, the client may know that what she wants is to complete the project, but may have no ideas about how to accomplish that goal.

However, asking clients for their ideas about the best means for achieving their desired outcomes can be helpful preliminary information regardless of whether they have any such ideas. You'll either be able to factor clients' ideas into counseling discussions, or you'll gain insight into clients' legal experience and sophistication.

Typical questions for eliciting information about means of achieving desired outcomes include: "What are your thoughts about how best to achieve that goal?" and "Do you have any ideas as to the steps you think we should take to accomplish that?"

4.   *Legal and Non–Legal Concerns*

This final topic pertains to the variety of concerns that clients may consider related to their problems. Clients' legal concerns of course are

---

13. Some clients may not have any solutions in mind. For example, the client who has been terminated from her job may be so upset and inexperienced that her only reply is that "I have no idea what can be done about this." *See* STEFAN H. KRIEGER, ET. AL., ESSENTIAL LAWYERING SKILLS 73 (1998). Other clients may lack thoughts about possible solutions because they lack familiarity with the legal system and what it might accom-plish. *See* PAUL M. LISNEK, EFFECTIVE CLIENT COMMUNICATION: A LAWYER'S HANDBOOK FOR INTERVIEWING AND COUNSELING § 2.2 (1992); Gary Bellow, *Turning Solutions into Problems: The Legal Aid Experience*, 34 NLADA BRIEFCASE 106, 110 (1977). However, knowing that clients have no solutions in mind can itself be valuable information for you to obtain.

intimately tied to the nature of their problems as well as their desired objectives and means of achieving them. For example, the legal concerns of a client whose contractor has abandoned a home remodeling project are likely to include how to deal with mechanics liens filed by sub-contractors (which relates to "desired outcome"), how long the project might be delayed, and the attorney's fees she is likely to incur (which relate to "means of achieving desired outcome").

As you may recall, non-legal concerns result from clients' unique personal circumstances. Thus, two clients with very similar legal problems may have very different non-legal concerns due to the clients' differing backgrounds, cultures and life circumstances. For example, the major non-legal concern of one client who claims to have been wrongfully terminated from employment may be relationships with other employees if the client ultimately returns to the same job, while the primary non-legal concern for a second client with a similar legal problem may be handling the depression caused by the loss of the job. Likewise, two clients may consult you with respect to job-related grievances. One client's non-legal concerns may focus on fear of retaliation by the employer should the client go forward with the grievances, while the second client may relish the idea of retaliation because that will generate an additional arena of combat.

Typical questions for eliciting information about legal and non-legal concerns include: "Do you have any specific concerns that we need to take into account as we go forward?" and "Apart from achieving the goal you've identified, are there any other issues we need to think about?"

The four topics described above are not mutually exclusive. For example, a client who asks, "Can I sue them?" may be expressing a thought about a potential solution, as well as raising legal and non-legal concerns. But the client may have other potential solutions in mind, as well as other concerns. Hence, effectively viewing problems from clients' perspectives generally entails separate inquiry into each of the four topics.

B. WHY BEGIN WITH PRELIMINARY PROBLEM IDENTIFICATION?

Beginning initial interviews with preliminary problem identification primarily helps you to gain a general understanding of clients' circumstances and perspectives before you begin in-depth questioning. Thus, preliminary problem identification can help you avoid "premature diagnosis," to which you might fall prey if you launch into detailed questioning immediately after catching a whiff of clients' problems.[14] For exam-

---

14. Data from the medical field shows that doctors are continually misdiagnosing their patient's problems because they do not allow them to explain their problem fully in the first instance. *See* VINCENT M. RICCARDI & SUZANNE M. KURTZ, COMMUNICATING COUNSELING IN HEALTH CARE 88–91 (1983); Howard B. Beckman & Richard M. Frankel, *The Effect of Physician Behavior on the Collection of Data*, 101 ANN. INTERN. MED. 692, 694 (1984); Frederic W. Platt & J.C. McMath, *Clinical Hypocompetence: The Interview*, 91 ANN. INTERN. MED. 898, 900–1001 (1979); *cf.* Frederic W. Platt, et. al., *"Tell*

ple, assume that a client responds to your initial request for information by handing you an application for a preliminary injunction and saying, "I'm a teacher and the school board is trying to enjoin me from picketing the school with regard to its racist policy of student discipline." You would be engaging in premature diagnosis if you were to jump to the conclusion that the client simply wanted to prevent the school board from obtaining an injunction and immediately asked questions relating to the lawfulness of his conduct in picketing the school. If it turns out that the client really is concerned about being terminated prior to the time he began his picketing, you probably would have frustrated the client by starting out with questions that did not deal with the core of his problem.

Moreover, the preliminary problem identification phase of initial interviews tends to motivate clients to provide full and accurate information as interviews progress. Clients are often more responsive to later inquiries once they've had a chance to describe problems in their own words. Think about your own experiences as a patient in a doctor's office. If a doctor asks numerous questions before you fully explain what is bothering you, you are more likely to be thinking about how to explain your problem than fully responding to the doctor's questions. Similarly, if you start in on questioning before clients have a chance to describe their problems and voice their concerns, they may become reluctant to provide information. For example, if you begin to question a client who hasn't had a chance to express concerns about how much your services might cost, the client may be disinclined to disclose information.

By engaging in preliminary problem identification you also demonstrate empathy, helping to build rapport and confidence. Most people like and trust helping professionals who they believe understand their problems.[15] Establishing rapport usually motivates clients to provide information and to participate actively in the process of formulating and selecting solutions. Given that rapport is such an important element in successful attorney-client relationships, it makes sense to begin to develop rapport as early in relationships as possible.

A last benefit of preliminary problem identification is that it can serve as a metaphorical string around your finger. This stage of the interview reminds you that clients come to you not merely for technical legal advice, but for help in finding solutions that respond to the fullest extent to their unique legal and non-legal concerns. Encouraging clients to discuss the four topics mentioned above at the outset focuses you immediately on what is ultimately important and reminds you of the full range of clients' concerns throughout each attorney-client relationship.

Me About Yourself": The Patient–Centered Interview, 134 ANN. INTERN. MED. 1079, 1080 (2001) ("Inattention to the person of the patient, to the patient's characteristics and concerns, leads to inadequate clinical data-gathering, non-adherence, and poor outcomes.").

15. See GERARD EGAN, THE SKILLED HELPER 97 (7th ed. 2002); PAUL M. LISNEK, EFFECTIVE CLIENT COMMUNICATION: A LAWYER'S HANDBOOK FOR INTERVIEWING AND COUNSELING § 2.6 (1992); THOMAS L. SHAFFER & JAMES R. ELKINS, LEGAL INTERVIEWING AND COUNSELING IN A NUTSHELL 62, 66 (3d. ed 1997).

Of course, clients' initial problem descriptions may be incomplete or erroneous. For example, a client who consults you for help in setting up a partnership may in reality be better off doing business as a corporation. Similarly, it may turn out that the client who ascribes personal injuries to an automobile accident was in all likelihood victimized by medical malpractice. Moreover, clients' non-legal concerns may change as matters progress. Nevertheless, the value of preliminary problem identification is the process itself and the snapshot of clients' circumstances that it provides. The information may be tentative and subject to change, but the benefits are likely to extend throughout your attorney-client relationships.

C. CARRYING OUT THE PROCESS OF PRELIMINARY PROBLEM IDENTIFICATION

The process of preliminary problem identification usually begins with your asking open-ended questions calling for descriptions of clients' problems. As suggested above, open-ended questions such as "How can I help you?," "Let's start with your telling me why you've come to see me?" or "What brings you here today?" allow clients to describe problems in any manner that feels comfortable and in as much detail as they deem appropriate. Such open questions also tend to facilitate rapport by permitting clients to avoid threatening topics and by signaling recognition that what the clients have to say is important. Also, clients' descriptions typically allow you to interject passive or active listening responses, thereby further building rapport and empathy.

Open-ended questions are effective even if, as will often be the case, you already know something about matters based on pre-meeting communication you've had with prospective clients. You can increase rapport by letting clients know that you recall what they've previously said while asking for a fresh description of a problem that is not limited to what you already know. For example, you may say something along these lines: "I know that we spoke on the telephone about your having lost your job recently, and I have some notes here about what you told me then. But just so we're both up to date, why don't you briefly tell me again about your problem and how you might like me to help."[16]

Desired objectives may seem so obvious that inquiring into them seems foolish. For example, when a client has been sued in a civil action, the client's desired outcome seems quite apparent—dismissal of the case in the next 5 minutes without paying a nickel. Surely the client will question your professional judgment if you ask, "How would you like this to turn out?" But your assumption may be wrong. Not every defendant in a civil case wants or expects complete vindication without paying for any injury the plaintiff may have suffered. Defendants sometimes feel partly responsible for harm to plaintiffs and will be willing to

---

16. In some instances, the prior conversation will have been with a partner, a receptionist, or an intake worker, and not with you personally. The suggested approach should work just as well when the prospective client has told some of his story to one of your colleagues.

pay something. If so, their primary objective may be to make sure that any damages that they pay (or are paid on their behalf) are reasonable. Similarly, not every client about to enter into a business deal wants the best possible price. Business people, perhaps to preserve a long term relationship, save legal fees, or for other reasons, often will agree to terms that are less favorable than they might have insisted on. Hence, rather than overlooking entirely a client's desired outcome when it seems obvious, you might at least check out your assumption:

> "I gather from what you've said that you want the suit terminated without paying anything to the plaintiff. Am I correct?"

> "I take it that you do not want the lease to include a rent escalation clause. Am I right?"

Clients may well agree with such assumptions and you can move on to other matters. When your assumptions are wrong, however, you will be glad that you checked out the topic at the preliminary problem identification stage:

> No, I think we should go along with an escalation clause if they ask for one; the clause is so standard in this kind of lease that if we try to avoid it, I'm afraid they'll get the idea that we are going to be hard nosed at every turn. If they get that idea who knows what might happen; it's just not a risk I feel comfortable with.[17]

Better some brief awkwardness than the more formidable embarrassment that would accompany your stumbling out, at the end of your conference, "you mean what you really wanted all along is … ?"

Just as potential embarrassment may cause you to shy away from the topic of seemingly-obvious objectives, so too may it lead you to avoid a discussion of seemingly-obvious concerns. For example, a shop owner whose landlord has refused to extend a shopping center lease obviously is worried about whether she will be able to stay in business. Similarly, a client who seeks a liquor license for his new restaurant obviously is concerned about adequate revenue. Again, a better strategy is to check out your assumptions rather than avoid concerns that seem obvious. If your assumptions are wrong, better to find out during preliminary discussion than to try to solve the wrong problem. Also, clients' descriptions of concerns typically afford opportunities for you to make empathic responses, thereby building rapport.

To check assumptions about concerns, you may again use the "verification" approach illustrated above: "From what you've told me it seems that a major concern you have is making sure the restaurant generates adequate income. Is my understanding correct?"

Somewhat different issues may arise when you attempt to elicit information about what course of action clients have in mind. Remember

---

17. Of course, there is a third possibility: a client may indicate that your assumption is only partially correct. The lease client may state, for example, "I don't feel a rent escalation clause is warranted, but I'll agree to a minor one just to keep the negotiations going smoothly."

that, as mentioned above, clients who know what outcomes they desire and who can articulate their concerns may have no idea about what steps you might take to achieve their objectives. For example, if you ask, "How do you think we ought to go about trying to resolve this matter?," you may get a polite or impolite version of a response such as, "I don't know what to do; that's why I'm coming to you." Such a statement conveys two thoughts: clients do not know what to do, and they expect that you do. Thus, asking clients about how to go about resolving problems may embarrass them and lead them to wonder just why they ought to be paying you.

On the other hand, clients may well have ideas (perhaps overly optimistic ones) about how you might go about resolving their problems. These clients will be more than happy to provide you with their ideas about what ought to be done. If you are uncertain as to whether clients are interested in answering questions about potential solutions, you may wait for clues about what's on their minds.[18] Alternatively, consider making a statement along these lines:

> When I've gotten a fuller picture of what is involved here, I'll go over with you some options that might make the most sense in your situation. However, I frequently find that clients have their own notions about how to resolve a matter and it can be most helpful if I start out knowing them. Did you have some ideas about how we might best approach this situation?

In sum, throughout the process of preliminary problem identification, except when checking "obvious assumptions," use open-ended questions, active listening and structural guides to encourage clients to continue describing problems until you feel you fully understand them from their perspectives.

A useful way to conclude preliminary problem identification is with an active listening response summarizing a client's problem. Your summary may briefly review what you have learned, and refer to each of the four general topics which together constitute the problem:

> So, the situation, if I've got it right, is that the remodeling job is less than half finished, the general contractor has been unavailable and subcontractors have been placing liens against the property. This has caused tremendous disruption in your family's daily life, and a lot of worry for you and your husband. And you feel that as we discuss the situation we should keep in mind your idea of trying to pressure the contractor into finishing the job by contacting the state contractors' licensing board. Is this about right? Is there an angle that I've missed?

* * *

---

18. Clues may include clients' apparent level of intelligence; the extent to which clients' responses indicate that they have invested time thinking about a problem; a client's openness in answering questions; and the like.

OK. I see that you want to acquire control of Soifer Realty if you can do so through a tax free exchange. You're worried not only about the tax aspects but also about tying Avi Zolton, Soifer's president, to the company for at least a year.[19] Is this a fair description of your situation? [20]

* * *

Brief summaries of this sort take early and maximum advantage of the facilitator of empathic understanding. A summary assures clients that you have heard and understood the principal aspects of their problems. The summary completes the groundwork for your more active role in the ensuing data-gathering stage of the relationship.

D. EXAMPLES FOR ANALYSIS

The three preliminary problem identification dialogues that follow will help you apply the principles set forth above to actual situations. In each dialogue, assume that your ice-breaking small talk has concluded. As you read through each dialogue, think about what strikes you as effective or ineffective. Detailed analysis follows the first two dialogues; analysis of the third one is for you.

Case No. 1

1. L: Mr. Cabello, I understand from our previous phone conversation that your problem involves money owed to you by your stepfather. But just so we both have a clear picture of what's going on, why don't you start by telling me about the problem.

2. C: My mother died about four months ago. When she passed away she and my stepfather owed me some money, and now my stepfather won't pay me.

3. L: How much money does he owe you?

4. C: Oh, I guess about $65,000.

5. L: Has he signed a promissory note or anything in writing?

6. C: No.

7. L: How recently have you asked him for the money?

8. C: About a month ago.

9. L: What did he say?

10. C: He said he'd pay me when he could.

11. L: So you want to know if you're entitled to sue him to get the money back?

12. C: I guess so.

---

19. Remember not all clients will have ideas about possible solutions.

20. These active listening responses do more than reflect the *content* of the clients'

descriptions; they also acknowledge the clients' feelings.

13. L: Besides the question of your right to get the money, are there other matters that are of concern to you?

14. C: Not really.

15. L: Are you sure?

16. C: Yes.

17. L: Are you worried about the possibility of a family squabble?

Analysis

In No. 1 you appropriately encourage Mr. Cabello to talk generally. Also, since you knew something about Mr. Cabello's problem from your prior phone conversation, you properly allude to what you already know.

In Nos. 3, 5, 7, and 9, you probe for specific details about the underlying transaction. Given that you will necessarily pursue these specific details later, these questions (except, perhaps, for the question about how much money is at stake) seem unnecessary at this preliminary stage. Moreover, the narrow questions may be distracting to Mr. Cabello, since they may not relate to the problem from his perspective. If you felt the need for more factual description, you could have employed a more open-ended probe such as, "Tell me a little bit more about the situation."

In No. 11, you switch to the issues of objectives and solutions. However, instead of inquiring about what outcome Mr. Cabello desires, or asking whether your assumed objective is correct, through a leading question you virtually decide that his aim is return of the money and that the best course of action is a lawsuit. Perhaps Mr. Cabello had other goals in mind or was thinking about another solution, such as renegotiating the loan and obtaining a security agreement. Not every potential plaintiff wants a lawsuit.

No. 13 is a useful open question that attempts to obtain a general description of Mr. Cabello's concerns. It recognizes that he may have more than one worry. No. 17, on the other hand, seems less appropriate. Rather than being an open inquiry into other concerns, No. 17 is a narrow question that fishes for a very specific concern. Especially during the early stages of an initial conference, before some degree of rapport is established, a client such as Mr. Cabello may be reluctant to talk about a potential family squabble even if that is one of his concerns.

If you review the dialogue as a whole, you'll realize that you do not treat concerns, objectives and solutions as distinct subjects. In No. 11, for example, which of these three topics do you have in mind? While there are no "magic words" to use to identify these topics, you should give clients a chance to address each topic separately if they are to have a useful opportunity to articulate problems from their perspectives.

Case No. 2

1. L: Now, Mr. Montgomery, how might I help you? I have a brief summary of your problem that my receptionist pre-

pared for me, but why don't you tell me in your own words why you came to see me?

2.   C: Well, I've been arrested, and I don't know what to do. Nothing like this has ever happened to me before.

3.   L: I can tell you're quite concerned about the situation. I'd really like to help. Perhaps it would be best if you told me a little bit more about the situation—you know, how the arrest came about.

4.   C: Well, they say I'm guilty of shoplifting over at Sears on 48th Street.

5.   L: Can you tell me a little bit more about that?

6.   C: Well, as I was near a store exit they stopped me and searched my jacket. They took out the calculator I was going to buy, and then they arrested me. I was going to pay for the calculator.

7.   L: Okay, that gives me a good start on what happened. I'll get more details in a little while. I assume that if you could dictate how this would turn out, that you would have the charges against you dismissed as quickly as possible. Am I correct on this point?

8.   C: Absolutely.

9.   L: Are there other results you'd like to obtain besides a dismissal of the charges?

10.   C: Could I get the people who arrested me to pay what it cost me to get out of jail?

11.   L: That is certainly something we can try to accomplish, but I'll need more information before I can give you an answer. However, before I get to my questions, why don't you tell me about any concerns you have that I haven't discussed? Are there other things you are worried about that you'd like to talk about?

12.   C: Well, sort of; I'm worried about keeping my job.

13.   L: No question that's a concern that we'll want to address. Any other concerns I should have in mind?

14.   C: Not really.

15.   L: So the situation is that you've been arrested for shoplifting at Sears, and of course you want the charges dismissed. In addition, you would like to have Sears pay for your costs, and you're also concerned about how all of this may affect your job.

16.   C: Yes, that's it; you've put it quite well.

17.   L: As I said, I'm going to need more information from you before I can answer your questions. But before I turn to my questions, let me go into one other thing that's often worthwhile to talk about before we get into the details. I assume that you'd like me to work out how to proceed to best accomplish what you'd like. But sometimes I find clients have useful ideas about how to approach a case and I was wondering if you have any notions about how we

should proceed so that we can get the charges dismissed and have Sears pay?

Analysis

In No. 1, you begin appropriately with an open question and acknowledge that Mr. Montgomery had prior contact with your staff. When your open question elicits only minimal information, you attempt in No. 3 to elicit further factual information. No. 3's active listening response demonstrates that you understand Mr. Montgomery's feelings. Additionally, you attempt to reassure him by expressing a willingness to help. You then provide a structural guide that asks for elaboration of the triggering events: "Perhaps it would be best if you told me a little more about the situation—you know, how the arrest came about." The request for elaboration does not press for details. Instead, it is quite open, giving Mr. Montgomery leeway to describe in terms that are comfortable to him what in all probability is an ego-threatening event. No. 5 is another appropriately open probe.

After Mr. Montgomery identifies the triggering transaction (No. 6), you turn to his likely objectives. In No. 7, you check out the correctness of your assumption that Mr. Montgomery's goal is to avoid a conviction, but your question assumes that he has been charged with a crime. Better, perhaps, to confirm that fact rather than assume it. Then in No. 9, albeit through a narrow question, you recognize the possibility of other objectives and provide Mr. Montgomery with an opportunity to state them.

In No. 11, after acknowledging Mr. Montgomery's second goal of being recompensed, you use an open question to move to the separate subject of concerns. Both the open question and the separate discussion of objectives and concerns seem appropriate. However, before moving to the topic of concerns, you might have stayed a bit longer with the subject of objectives. Mr. Montgomery might have other objectives besides avoiding a conviction and being reimbursed for the expenses of getting out of jail.

Your treatment of Mr. Montgomery's potential concerns, however, is more thorough. Nos. 11 and 13 are both open questions seeking his concerns, and only after receiving the "not really" answer in No. 14 do you move to a new subject.

No. 13 bears further analysis. You acknowledge that job worries are a concern to be addressed, and ask about possible other concerns. Though you perhaps have never faced the possibility of losing a job because of an arrest, Mr. Montgomery will probably accept your response as sincere and not patronizing. Most people can understand the effects of having their jobs threatened by an arrest for a crime that they believe (sincerely or not) that they did not commit.

No. 15, an active listening summary of Mr. Montgomery's problem, informs him that you have heard and understood his problem.

Finally, No. 17 switches to the topic of solutions. Should you have raised that topic in this case? In any event, what do you think of the approach? Is this a situation where the client's likely reaction might be of the "That's what I'm coming to you for" genre? Is your explanation adequate to minimize the chances of such a reaction?

Case No. 3

1. L: Ms. Rose, why don't you start by telling me what's on your mind?

2. C: Well, I have a small gold plating business. What I think I'd like to do is set up a pension plan of some type for my long-time employees.

3. L: You're considering providing retirement benefits for loyal employees. But it sounds as though you are not sure that's what you should do.

4. C: That's right.

5. L: How many employees are we talking about?

6. C: I have twenty employees but I'm only concerned about five or six.

7. L: How long have these people been with you?

8. C: They've all been with me for over six years.

9. L: How about the other employees; how long have they worked for you?

10. C: There's a real gap. Probably no one else has been there for more than three years.

11. L: Could you tell me why the notion of a pension plan is on your mind at this point? What prompted you to think about it now?

12. C: Well there have been a couple of things. First, it's time I started thinking about my retirement. Also, I recently lost a very good employee because we didn't have a plan; he went to work for a competitor who provided benefits. I don't want my other good employees to do the same thing.

13. L: Are there particular things that concern you in thinking about setting up a pension plan?

14. C: Nothing other than can I afford it.

15. L: So as I understand it what you'd like to do is set up a pension plan for your senior people provided you feel you could afford it. Have I stated the situation correctly?

Analysis

Analyze for yourself the effectiveness of this preliminary problem identification dialogue. The following questions may aid your analysis:

    1. Is No. 1 appropriately open, or is it perhaps too vague?

    2. Assuming that No. 2 was delivered in a tone of voice that indicated uncertainty, in what way, if any, would you alter No. 3?

3.   Nos. 5, 7 and 9 are narrow questions. They ask for specific information rather than calling for an elaboration. Are these inquiries therefore inappropriate at this point?

4.   Assuming that No. 11 represents the beginning of an attempt to identify the triggering transaction, how if at all could you have modified this inquiry?

5.   How adequately did you cover the topic of Ms. Rose's concerns?

6.   What additional questions, if any, could you have asked regarding Ms. Rose's objectives?

7.   How accurate was your summary (No. 15)?

8.   What additional topics, if any, would you have explored with Ms. Rose during the problem identification stage?

E.   RESPONDING TO CLIENTS' VOLCANIC DESCRIPTIONS

Occasionally, open questions seeking overviews of clients' problems produce near-volcanic types of responses. That is, clients may spew out information so quickly and continuously that you have a hard time understanding the gravamen of their problems. For example, assume that in response to your question of "Why don't you start by giving me a thumbnail sketch of your problem and how it came about?" a client replies as follows:

My ex partner, Georgina, is suing me; here are the papers. She claims that I breached our agreement and stole money from her. It's unbelievable because she is the one who drove us out of business. The final straw was when she failed to come through on the audit with our biggest client, Sunrose Enterprises. After that we were kaput. But that came at the end. There were several other semi-disasters along the way. I should have known when I first met her that she was trouble. She was complaining about too much work back at Darlene's house. That's where I met her. We were both working for large accounting firms and we both wanted out. She claimed to have several good clients and I had a few. So we got together and things went to hell right at the start. I came through with my clients but all she brought was crap. Her supposed clients were flakes and they had no business for us. And then she totally dropped the ball with Sunrose. Also, my clients were unhappy with her work from the get go. But since she was my partner I had her work with some of my clients. There is no way I can describe the aggravation she has caused me; it's unbelievable. And I can't tell you how angry my husband is. And that is a real problem, I don't know what to say to him. He is also in this deal and I also need to focus on what I can do to make sure he doesn't get left holding the bag. He signed some guarantees and when he finds out about this lawsuit he is going to go ballistic especially since he didn't want us to take the lease. Moreover, I'm pretty sure Georgina is trying to grab up a couple of clients I'm trying to hold on to. Last week, Henry Workham, whose work I've been doing for years, called and said he was thinking of having me do some projections on a new project of his but he wanted to check out my rates. I told him and he said he would get back to me. It was weird because he had never asked anything like that before. So that's the problem.

Emotional and convoluted responses such as these may frustrate your desire for thumbnail overviews of clients problems and concerns. Nevertheless, your most effective strategy may be to temporarily shelve your desire for structure and accept clients' need to blow off steam. The alternative is for you to interrupt with a series of structural guides that clients are likely to find frustrating and that they may well ignore anyway. As the professional, the burden of frustration is generally yours to bear. Moreover, even disjointed accounts such as the one above do tend to provide useful information, and your willingness to listen may bolster rapport by demonstrating your sincere interest in clients' problems and feelings.

At the same time, client-centeredness does not demand complete abdication of your role as an interviewer. If you are to help clients arrive at satisfactory outcomes, you need to obtain relevant information in a reasonable period of time. Thus, at a point that only your judgment in individual cases can determine, continuance of the attorney-client relationship may depend on clients' willingness to stop venting and start becoming responsive to more focused inquiries. When you do move toward a more structured conversation, you may briefly summarize what clients have told you and then use focused questions to seek information pertaining to remaining preliminary problem identification topics. For example, you might follow up the statement above in this manner:

1. Ms. Bloom, I'm going to jump in here for a minute. What you have been telling me is very useful information and important for me to know, and I can see how this situation has caused you no end of professional and personal concern. What happened is that you've been sued by your ex-partner for breaching an agreement, when in reality you think that she caused your business to fail. I'll need more information from you, but first, let me ask you how you want to see this resolved, if you could write your own ticket?

2. (Ms. Bloom responds.)

3. Okay, that let's me know how you'd like this resolved. In my experience clients often have very good ideas about how to achieve what they want. So tell me about any ideas you have about how we could accomplish this result.

Thus, clients' rambling narratives need not prevent you from pursuing the topics of preliminary problem identification. As with clients who are content to provide brief, capsule problem summaries, you can usually ask more verbose clients about topics they may have neglected to address, such as in this example Ms. Bloom's objectives and thoughts about how to accomplish them.[21]

F. RESPONDING TO EARLY REQUESTS FOR YOUR OPINION

At or near the conclusion of preliminary problem identification, clients may seek assurance that they can achieve their desired outcomes. For example, litigation clients may ask questions such as, "Do I have a good case?" A transactional client concerned with tying a key employee to the company may ask something like, "Do you think we can draft an agreement that will prevent her from working for some one else for at least two years?" Clients may also seek your opinion with sweeping questions such as, "What do you think I should do?"

Preliminary problem identification rarely provides you with sufficient information to respond to such questions by providing opinions about the ultimate outcomes of clients' matters. Your factual information is often skimpy and the same may be true of your legal knowledge when problems raise unfamiliar legal issues. Yet clients' requests for your opinion are understandable and deserving of a response. A brief form of response is to advise clients of your need for additional information and your hope to provide them with a tentative opinion by the end of the interview. This portion of a conversation may go something like this:

1.   C: Do I have a good case?
2.   L: At this point I simply don't have enough information to answer that question. I'd like to find out a little bit more about what happened, and hopefully by the time you leave today I'll be able to give you some idea of where you stand.

This approach is succinct, and your mention of providing tentative advice by the time the interview ends may motivate clients to provide information.[22]

A second possible response to what you consider to be a premature request for your opinion is to indicate not only that you lack enough information to give a meaningful response, but also to indicate the kind of information you will seek in order to give tentative advice. As above, you can again conclude by advising clients of your hope to provide a tentative opinion by the end of the interview. This kind of conversation may go as follows:

1.   C: So do you think it makes sense for me to take Mr. Cummings into the business?
2.   L: Ms. Zasloff, I'll certainly be happy to give you my opinion on that once I know some more about your situation. At

---

21. For a further discussion of dealing with clients who tend to stray from the topic at hand, see Chapter 12.

22. Preliminary problem identification may provide enough information for you to realize that you'll need to do legal research before you can provide even a tentative opinion. If that's the case, you should say so.

this point it would help me to learn more about things such as how you and Mr. Cummings plan to work together, how many employees you are likely to have during the first year, your anticipated profits from the joint venture, and your thoughts on what you might do should this deal with Mr. Cummings not make the profits you anticipate. For instance, knowing more about Mr. Cummings, how active he is likely to be in the day to day operations of the business and the business' likely income stream and expenses will influence whether in my opinion it makes sense for you to take him into your business as a partner. From what you've told me so far it sounds like working out some type of arrangement with Cummings makes a great deal of sense and I'll get back to your question before we leave here today. But at this point, I don't have enough information to give you an informed opinion. Does that make sense?[23]

This approach may be appropriate with clients who you think will appreciate knowing the kind of information you need at an early stage of an interview. Such clients may be put off by the brevity of a simple "I need more information" response to a request for your opinion. Possible downsides are that your response may come across as more of a "lawyer lecture" than a response to what a client may see as a straightforward inquiry, a lecture that may imply that a client's problem is truly complex and therefore likely to result in large legal fees.

Finally, recognize that you may be able to give "partial opinions" even at the conclusion of preliminary problem identification. For example, a portion of an interview of a client whose overview suggests that she may have a claim based on "wrongful termination of employment" may unfold as follows:

1. C: Now that you've gotten a sense of what I've been going through, can you give me any idea of whether I'll be able to get my job back?

2. L: I'm sure that you understand that at this early point, I can't predict what the outcome is likely to be. However, I can tell you that in the circumstances you've described, judges do have the power to order employers to rehire employees who have been wrongfully dismissed. What I'd like to do now is find out a little bit more about what happened, and hopefully by the time you leave today I'll be able to give you some idea of your chances of being rehired. Does this make sense?

By informing the client that her desired objectives are legally possible, this response provides a "partial opinion" that the client may

---

23. This type of response is also duplicative of what you might say during a "preparatory explanation." See Sec. 6 below. Thus, it would generally not make sense for you to provide such a detailed response to a request for your opinion and then also make a preparatory explanation.

find helpful and reassuring. At the same time you do not commit yourself to the outcome of the client's particular case, but instead try to motivate her by indicating your hope to provide a tentative opinion by the end of the interview.

6. PREPARATORY EXPLANATIONS

At the conclusion of preliminary problem identification, unless your clients are "repeat players," they are likely to be unfamiliar with what is going to occur in the remainder of initial meetings. Hence, you may put clients at ease by providing them with a "preparatory explanation" that alerts them to what will happen. Consider the following examples.

Mr. Jagger, am I correct in saying that what you'd like to do today is determine the best way for you and Mr. Richards to organize the insurance agency that the two of you contemplate opening?

That's right. Should we have a corporation or what? That's what I'd like to know.

Before I can fully answer your question, I'll first need to get some more information from you about matters such as your existing operation, Mr. Richard's existing business, and the proposed business the two of you intend to establish. I think we should be able to cover most of what I need to know this afternoon, although I may have to get back to you with some additional questions after we finish today. Before we wrap up our conversation, we can begin exploring the various options that would be available to you in setting up the new business. [24]

* * *

The situation as I understand it, Ms. Gooden, is that you'd like to enjoin Xray Corp. from distributing these Groove software packages and put the issue of damages on the back burner. Is that right?

Exactly. We don't want to become involved in a lengthy trial about the amount of damages we may have suffered. What we want, as quickly as we can get it, is a permanent injunction.

Okay, let me start to get into the facts so that I'll have a basis for letting you know what I think your chances are of obtaining an injunction. The way I find it most helpful to approach the facts is for

---

24. The Jagger interview topic should set off warning flags for you about possible multiple representation and conflicts of interest. If you assist Jagger to establish a business with Richards, is Jagger alone your client? Or might Richards be your client as well. since your work benefits him? Or, alternatively, maybe you represent the business, and neither of the individuals? *Cf.* Jesse v. Danforth, 485 N.W.2d 63 (Wis. 1992) (after a lawyer worked with doctors to set up a medical consulting corporation, the court holds that the lawyer represented the corporation and neither of the individual constituents). *See generally* William H. Simon, *Whom (or What) Does the Organization's Lawyer Represent?: An Anatomy of Intraclient Conflict*, 91 Cal. L. Rev. 57 (2003) (discussing and critiquing situations in which representation is characterized as "joint" representation of an organization's constituents or as "entity" representation).

a client to first take me through the facts chronologically from the beginning right up to the present. When I've gotten the chronology, I'll then go back and ask some more detailed questions. When we've talked about those matters, we can go over some options you have in trying to enjoin Xray. In that connection, I'll get back to your question about fees and try to give you a more accurate estimate of how much it is likely to cost to secure an injunction. Do you have any questions?

A. BENEFITS OF PREPARATORY EXPLANATIONS

Providing clients with preparatory explanations can put them at ease.[25] While this is of value in its own right, increasing new or inexperienced clients' comfort levels is likely to improve their willingness and ability to supply information. One reason is that reducing clients' uncertainty about the interviewing process tends to promote their ability to concentrate. Preparatory explanations can also help you overcome the inhibitor of "role expectations." Left to their own devices, clients may not know whether you expect them to volunteer information, or only to respond to specific inquiries. Preparatory explanations can clarify such uncertainties and thereby help you bolster rapport and gather salient information.

B. CONTENTS OF PREPARATORY EXPLANATIONS

Based on the typical concerns that new and/or inexperienced clients are likely to have, your "default" preparatory explanation may address the following topics:

- *The subjects you intend to inquire about during the remainder of the conference.* Depending on whether clients' problems involve litigation or transactional planning your questioning in initial client conferences is likely to take different paths. In litigation matters, you will typically proceed by asking clients to provide a "time line story," a chronology of the events giving rise to the actual or potential litigation (See Chapter 6). You may follow time line questioning with "theory development" questions. (See Chapters 7 and 8). Thus in a litigation matter you might say something such as: "In a few moments I'll ask you to provide a chronological, step-by-step account of the events that brought you here. I'll try to interrupt you as little as possible, and I want you to talk about any events that you think are important. After that I'll be asking questions that go back through your story in more detail."

   By contrast, in transactional matters, you might start by asking clients for information regarding the history of their dealings

---

25. *See e.g.,* Robert Louis Kahn & Charles F. Cannell, The Dynamics of Interviewing 81 (1957); Noelle C. Nelson, Connecting with Your Client 43 (1996); Allen E. Ivey & W. Matthews, *A Meta–Model for Structuring the Clinical Interview,* 63 J. Counseling & Dev. 237, 238 (1984). In fact, some lawyers believe that clients also have a right to know this information. *See* Paul M. Lisnek, Effective Client Communication: A Lawyer's Handbook for Interviewing and Counseling §§ 5.8, 9.26 (1992).

with the other party and in particular that party's objectives, business experience and financial condition. (See Chapter10) Hence in a transactional matter involving a lease in which you represent the lessor, your preparatory explanation may go in part as follows: "Bob, what I'd like to do now is begin by having you give me a brief history of the interactions you've had with Yellen, and what you know about him and in particular why he wants to lease the space and what you know about his financial condition."

- *Role Expectations.* To familiarize clients with your expectations as to their role in an interview, you might say something as follows: "I don't have any pre-set notion here of what's important. If you think some event or detail is important, please let me know. And I encourage you to tell me as much as you can in your own words. If you start going into more detail than I need to hear at this stage, don't worry, I'll let you know. And if at any time questions occur to you, please feel free to ask them. Does that sound OK?"

- *Confidentiality of Attorney–Client Communications.* Explaining your general obligation to maintain confidentiality tends to encourage clients to talk freely and openly. Section "C" below explores this topic in more detail.

- *The possible need for follow-up meetings.* An "initial" interview may in reality extend over two or three meetings because of your need to gather documents and conduct legal research before concluding initial information-gathering from clients. When you anticipate multiple meetings, you might say something along these lines: "I'll try to get as much information as I can from you today, but I think we'll probably have to get together at least a couple of more times before we start talking about the best way to proceed. In between our meetings I'll be gathering some documents and checking into the language of some recent changes to a statute that could affect your situation."

- *Solutions.* You will return to a discussion of possible solutions.

Beyond these "default" topics, what you say in a preparatory explanation is likely to depend on clients' unique concerns. For example, assume that your custom is to estimate legal fees at the conclusion of initial meetings, and not to address fees at all until that time. However, if a client expresses a concern about fees during preliminary problem identification, you may decide to say something about fees in your preparatory explanation. For example, you may say something like, "A few moments ago you mentioned that you are very concerned about legal fees. I'm not in a position at this point even to give you a ballpark estimate, but I promise we'll talk more about fees at the end of this meeting. Is that OK?"[26] Similarly, assume that a client raises a unique

---

26. In virtually every case, though, you will ensure that your client understands the fees, if any, for that interview meeting. For

concern during preliminary problem identification, such as, "I'm very worried about what to tell my accountant." In that event, you may tell the client that, "Before we're done here today, we'll talk about what you might tell your accountant."[27]

C. CONFIDENTIALITY

Preparatory explanations are typically a useful time to mention confidentiality. As you undoubtedly know, every jurisdiction has ethical rules and/or statutes that protect the confidentiality of attorney-client discussions. Making sure that clients know about confidentiality before you begin to explore their problems in depth is important both because clients deserve to know about confidentiality and because clients who know that what they say is confidential are more likely to be willing to disclose all pertinent information.

However, you may be uncertain about how best to talk about confidentiality. After all, confidentiality is not absolute. Every jurisdiction has rules that to one degree or another strip certain types of client communications of their confidentiality.[28] Thus, it would be simple but misleading to tell clients that "everything you say today will remain confidential, and will not leave this office without your permission."

On the other hand, pontificating at length on the subtleties in and the exceptions to your jurisdiction's confidentiality rules is an equally unacceptable option. As an empirical matter, the probabilities are that you will complete your career as a lawyer without having had a client whose confidences you've had to reveal. Moreover, some clients would strongly and understandably resent being advised that "there's no confidentiality if you tell me of your plans to kill someone or blow up a building."[29]

An effective general strategy is to advise clients in a general way of your obligation to maintain the confidentiality of what they tell you. For example, you might say something along these lines:

> As a general matter, what is said between attorneys and clients is confidential. That means that nothing we talk about will leave the privacy of this office unless you give me express permission to reveal what has been said between us. Now, there are some narrow exceptions to the confidentiality rules. It's unlikely you'll have to be concerned about them, but if at some point I have any worries along those lines I'll let you know. In the meantime, do you have any questions about confidentiality?

discussion of how you might talk about fees with clients, see Chapter 11.

27. Subsequent chapters include a variety of context-specific preparatory explanations. At this point, you need only be aware of reasons for using them, and their potential limitations.

28. In many states you also have an affirmative duty to disclose to a tribunal that a client has lied under oath. *See* MODEL RULES OF PROF'L CONDUCT R. 3.3(a)(2).

29. *See* Purcell v. District Attorney, 424 Mass. 109 (1997). In some states, you will be obligated to call the authorities. *See, e.g.,* Florida Rule 4–1.6(b); Illinois Rule 1.6(b).

A statement such as this provides reassurance and comfort while leaving open the unlikely possibility that you will revisit the matter in the future. In most cases, a simple assurance of general confidentiality is preferable to saying nothing or running through a laundry list of specific exceptions.[30] Of course, in the unlikely event that a client's description of a problem veers into areas where you cannot give assurances of confidentiality, you will have to advise the client more specifically about the limits of confidentiality protection.

Insurance–Retained Counsel

Attorneys who represent defendants in civil actions often have been retained by a defendant's insurance company. For example, assume that a patient sues a physician for allegedly botching a surgery. The physician carries medical malpractice insurance. Typically the insurance policy obligates the insurance company to hire a lawyer for the physician should the physician be sued for malpractice. Pursuant to the policy if the physician is sued, the insurance company retains a lawyer to defend the physician and pays the legal fees. Under this arrangement an attorney-client relationship exists between the lawyer and the physician. Similarly, insurance companies typically retain counsel to represent insured homeowners and car owners who are sued for negligence.

Unquestionably, client-centered strategies are helpful whether clients retain attorneys personally or have them retained by the clients' insurance companies. However, when you act as an insurance-retained counsel, difficult questions of confidentiality may arise. The reason is that while the insured parties may be your clients, the insurance companies who pay your bills want and are entitled to information about the progress and likely outcomes of cases. Thus, you often have to reveal what would otherwise be confidential statements to insurers. In such situations, emphasize to clients that you are their attorney and that your primary loyalty is to them. At the same time, advise clients that you may have to reveal case-related information, including the substance of your discussions with them, with insurance company representatives.

D. RISKS OF EXCESSIVE LENGTH

The content of preparatory explanations can easily expand as you gain experience and encounter client misconceptions that strike you as dandy for coverage in all future preparatory explanations. For example, many clients' understandings of legal rules and processes are shaped by law-related movies and television shows, and you might include in a preparatory statement some warning about the differences between fiction and reality.[31]

30. Not all commentators agree with the position defended here. See, e.g., Clark D. Cunningham, *How to Explain Confidentiality?*, 9 Clin. L. Rev. 579 (2002); Lee A. Pizzimenti, *The Lawyer's Duty to Warn Clients about Limits on Confidentiality*, 29 Cath. U. L. Rev. 441, 478. One state supreme court has implied that clients should not be warned about the exceptions to the confidentiality rules. See Purcell v. District Attorney, 424 Mass. 109 (1997).

31. Lawyer Jan Schlichtmann, whose class action environmental lawsuit was dramatized in the book and film, *A Civil Ac-*

However, recognize that while preparatory explanations are often motivational because they help clients understand how initial interviews will unfold, overly-lengthy explanations are likely to make clients' eyes glaze over, just as yours might have in law school during a lecture on "the ancient origins of diversity jurisdiction." They may tune you out, rendering meaningless much of what you say. Too, clients who already know what to expect during an interview may consider a detailed explanation to be unnecessary and patronizing. Similarly, clients who are anxious to talk about their problems may become annoyed, and clients worried about fees may be upset by how much they are paying for a lecture.

At the end of the day, what to say in a preparatory explanation is a matter of judgment, informed by your past experiences and clients' unique problems, needs and concerns. Pay attention to the non-verbal clues and to clients' attentiveness to your remarks, and when in doubt, err on the side of brevity.

7. BEGINNING FOLLOW–UP MEETINGS

You often cannot complete initial information gathering during a single meeting. Not only may initial information gathering extend over two or three meetings, but in most cases you need to periodically consult with clients by phone and/or in person. As you can undoubtedly imagine, the variety of circumstances giving rise to follow-up meetings makes a "standard" client-centered approach to their beginnings unrealistic.[32] While beginning most initial conferences with preliminary problem identification is sensible, no comparable standard procedure for starting follow-up meetings exists. Nevertheless, in the absence of a dramatic turn of events that demands immediate discussion, you might in the beginning portions of follow up meetings discuss one or more of the topics set forth below.[33]

A. CLIENTS' CHANGED CONCERNS AND OBJECTIVES

Clients' concerns and objectives may change from one meeting to the next. For example, a change in a client's job status may produce new economic difficulties. Or, reading a newspaper account of a jury verdict or hearing about the outcome of a friend's lawsuit in a related situation may lead a client to consider new objectives. You may get into this topic with questions such as:

> "Have any new concerns or worries arisen since the last time we spoke?"

---

tion, devotes a portion of initial client meetings to the differences between art and reality. See Gary M. Stern, *Courtroom Life Imitates Art*, NAT'L L.J., July 22, 2002, Vol. 24, No. 44, at A1 (Col. 2), A9.

32. Perhaps the only feature common to the beginning of perhaps every follow-up meeting is "chit-chat." At least, by the time of a follow-up meeting you have a more informed basis for deciding how much chit-chat a client will appreciate.

33. Chapter 11 examines approaches for concluding initial and subsequent client meetings.

"At our last meeting you said that you were worried about how the time demands of litigation might affect how much time you could devote to your business. Is that still an important concern?"

B.   CLIENTS' NEW INFORMATION

Clients may come to a follow up meeting armed with new information. For example, perhaps a client has gained access to a document you asked the client to read, or a previously-unknown witness contacted a client. Similarly, a client on whose behalf you are negotiating a real estate purchase may learn that the seller is suddenly in desperate need of money. In such situations, the new information may so dramatically affect a client's legal rights, concerns or objectives that proceeding on the basis of "old news" would be a waste of time. Therefore, you might want to explore this topic with an inquiry such as:

"Have you learned anything new since the last time we met?"

Of course, clients may have new information without having new concerns, and vice versa. Therefore, avoid compound questions such as, "Has anything new come up since we last met, or do you have any new concerns?" The question is confusing and thus no more desirable in a law office than in a courtroom. Moreover, combining the inquiries into a single question may send an implicit signal that you are not terribly interested in a client's response. Hence, to encourage clients to think seriously about both changed concerns and new information, make each the subject of a separate question.

C.   YOUR INTERIM ACTIVITY

A common way to end meetings is to describe the tasks that you plan to carry out before you next meet with or talk to your clients. For example, you might have ended a meeting by promising to research a particular legal issue and contact a witness. If so, a useful way to begin follow up meetings is to tell clients what you have done and accomplished since a prior meeting. Such a tactic tends to bolster clients' confidence, because clients usually perceive lawyers who actively work on cases as interested, concerned and competent.[34] Moreover, demonstrating that you are a "person of action" may overcome the common perception popularized by sources ranging from Dickens' *Bleak House* to everyday newspaper and television stories that lawyers unreasonably drag out legal matters.

All well and good, you may say, but what if you have done nothing in the interim, or what you have done has produced little or no concrete gains? Generally, clients appreciate lawyers who keep them informed.[35] Hence, if you have not taken any action since a prior meeting, say so and indicate when the client can expect a new development:

---

34.   See ROBERT F. COCHRAN, JR. ET. AL., THE COUNSELOR AT LAW: A COLLABORATIVE APPROACH TO CLIENT INTERVIEWING AND COUNSELING 106 (1999).

35.   *See* DOUGLAS E. ROSENTHAL, LAWYER AND CLIENT: WHO'S IN CHARGE? 20, 51 (1974); RONALD E. MALLEN & JEFFREY M. SMITH, LEGAL MALPRACTICE 277–79 (5th ed. 2000).

I haven't had a chance to get together with Graham's attorney yet; he's been tied up out of town, apparently. But we've scheduled a meeting for next Wednesday, and I'll call you Wednesday evening and let you know if we've ironed out the remaining disagreements.

Usually, the same policy of disclosure applies when the actions you have taken have gained little:

I did take the deposition of InterState's Vice–President, and as we figured, she claimed not to have seen the audit. But she did mention a couple of things that should prove useful for establishing that the audit was conducted improperly; we can talk about those later. Meanwhile. . . .

For too long, lawyers have not been sufficiently cognizant of the deleterious effect of failing to keep clients up to date on what is happening in the attorney-client relationship.[36] You have an obligation to keep clients informed, and the beginning of a follow-up conference is an excellent time to summarize what you have done since last speaking to a client.

D. YOUR NEW INFORMATION[37]

Another useful topic for follow up meetings is new information that you have uncovered since a prior discussion. Your new information may be important because it alleviates clients' previously expressed concerns or suggests new strategies or legal theories. Disclosing new information also tends to bolster clients' confidence in you because it demonstrates your active commitment to their welfare.[38] Such confidence in turn typically encourages clients to work more closely with you to achieve satisfying results.[39] Don't hesitate to disclose bad news, because such disclosure may lead to a necessary reassessment of objectives.[40]

Though it often makes sense to disclose new information early in follow-up discussions, you may not want to do so when the new information is "bulky." For example, if you've taken a number of depositions or talked to experts in the interim between meetings, you may prefer to begin follow-up meetings with other topics. In such a situation, you may

---

36. See, e.g., Noelle C. Nelson, Connecting with Your Client 41, 64–65 (1996); Scotty P. Krob, *Grievances: Recognizing the Realities and Reducing the Risks*, 24 Colo. Law. 2197, 2198 (1995); *Cf.* Roger S. Haydock, et. al., Lawyering: Practice and Planning 48 (1995) ("There is no substitute for regular communication with a client, and nothing can do more to prevent client dissatisfaction with the lawyer.").

37. Often there will be overlap between the categories of "activity" and "information." That is, activity often produces information. But activity often has no informational aspect: it may consist, for example, of scheduling depositions. And the contrary may also be true; you may garner information without engaging in activity. For example, you may receive a report from an investigator or an accountant.

38. See Center for Professional Responsibility of the ABA, Avoiding Client Grievances 6–9 (1988); Roger S. Haydock, et. al., Lawyering: Practice and Planning 48 (1995); Ronald E. Mallen & Jeffrey M. Smith, Legal Malpractice 278 (5th ed. 2000).

39. *See*, Douglas E. Rosenthal, Lawyer and Client: Who's in Charge? 168–69 (1974); *see generally* Stanley S. Clawar, You and Your Clients 19–31 (2d ed. 1996).

40. For examination of how you might discuss bad news, see Chapter 11.

reassure clients at the outset that you do have new information and that you will get to it after clearing away other beginning matters:

> "Ms. Daar, since our last meeting I've completed the depositions of the assistant manager and the cashier. In a few moments I'd like to go over what they said in detail with you. But before we get to that, have you come up with any new information since we last spoke?"

E. ORDER OF DISCUSSION

The above sections describe four topics that often are appropriate for discussion in the beginning stages of follow up meetings. The upshot is that either you and a client will have to talk very fast and loud, or in any one conversation you will have to give one topic pride of place.

As you might imagine, your judgment about where to begin will depend on the dynamics of individual clients and matters. For example, if you think it unlikely that a client has done any work on a case since a previous meeting, it makes little sense to begin a follow-up meeting by asking for the client's new information. Similarly, if you know that non-legal concerns are paramount to a client, you might begin a new conversation by asking whether those concerns have changed in any way.

In the absence of information that might lead you to prefer one topic to another, the client-centered "default" position is to begin follow-up meetings by asking clients whether any new concerns have arisen since your last conversation. If clients do have new concerns and don't have a chance to voice them, they are likely to pay less attention to what you have to say. Even if they don't have new concerns, they'll probably appreciate your asking.

Chapter 6

ELICITING TIME LINES

* * *

Mr. Hopkins, after Cameron Markey suggested that you contact Bollinger, what is the next thing that happened?

I called Bill Locklear and told him that Markey had suggested changing the records; I was scared and I wanted advice.

It must have been very upsetting. I mean, Cameron Markey is your boss and you didn't want to do anything to jeopardize your job. But on the other hand, changing records to get rid of a federal inspection team is certainly not something you want to do.

It really was a nightmare.

I'll bet. Now, what happened when you talked with Locklear?

He told me to sit tight and do nothing until he called me back.

What happened next?

Patricia Alvarez called me; she's one of the vice presidents. She said she had spoken to Locklear, and that I should make an appointment with her secretary. I did that and I planned to see her the next day. I think that would have been the tenth. But before I could see her, Bollinger called. He said he had talked with Markey and he was expecting me. I panicked.

I can see how you would. What happened then?

* * *

1. INTRODUCTION

Once you have preliminarily identified clients' problems and concerns,[1] a useful follow up in most litigation matters is to obtain more complete information using the two-phased interviewing approach described in this and the next two chapters. The first phase consists of obtaining "time lines," the subject of this chapter. Time lines are chronological accounts of the major events giving rise to clients' problems. You typically take something of a "back seat" role during time line

---

1. See Chapter 5.

questioning, focusing primarily on helping clients to recall events chronologically to the extent they can do so. The ensuing two chapters explore the theory development phase of initial meetings, when you generally play a more active role by probing time line stories in the light of legal principles and clients' desired outcomes.[2]

2. HOW TWO PHASE INTERVIEWS HELP DEVELOP PERSUASIVE STORIES

Time line and theory development questioning represent a strategy for exploring clients' legal rights in dispute matters thoroughly and from a client-centered perspective. The ultimate goal of this strategy is to help you uncover evidence that persuades triers of fact (judges or juries) that your clients' accounts of past events are accurate.

The two phase strategy grows out of the reality that all substantive legal rules are conditional statements of past events that constitute material facts.[3] That is, legal rules provide in essence that "If A and B occurred, then legal consequence X follows." For instance, a rule of contract law provides that if two parties enter into an agreement supported by consideration, an enforceable contract results. Thus, from a plaintiff's perspective, your task in a contracts dispute is to uncover information proving that past events constituting the material facts of contract formation took place. And from a defendant's perspective, you may seek to uncover information suggesting that past events constituting the material fact of contract formation did not unfold as the plaintiff contends or that past events constituting the material facts for an affirmative defense took place.

One common feature of persuasive litigation stories is that they have a narrative structure. This narrative structure is little different from the structure that underlay the stories you began listening to as a child, before you exchanged rattles for textbooks. Think back to "Jack and the Beanstalk." The story tells us, chronologically, of Jack's pitiful social status, his trade of a cow for magic beans, his mother's anger and subsequent chucking of the beans out the window, the growth of the beanstalk, Jack's climb and confrontation with the giant, and Jack's eventual triumph.

Chronological narratives such as "Jack and the Beanstalk" are in fact the typical medium of human communication.[4] And like any other

---

2. If you need to better familiarize yourself with the issues raised by a time line story, you may postpone all or most theory development questioning to a later interview. For further discussion of adjourning information-gathering to consider potentially-applicable legal theories and develop potential evidence pursuant to those theories, see Chapter 9.

3. *See,* JEROME FRANK, COURTS ON TRIAL: MYTH AND REALITY IN AMERICAN JUSTICE 14 (1971).

4. See, W. LANCE BENNETT & MARTHA S. FELDMAN, RECONSTRUCTING REALITY IN THE COURTROOM 7 (2d ed. 1984); see also DAVID B. PILLEMER, MOMENTOUS EVENTS, VIVID MEMORIES 52 (1998). While this assertion may be accurate for the prevailing American culture, it may not apply across all cultural settings. For further discussion of how cultural differences might affect the time line phase of information-gathering, *see* SUSAN BRYANT, *The Five Habits: Building Cross–Cultural Competence in Lawyers,* 8 CLINICAL L. REV.

good story, law stories have narrative meaning and make sense to listeners. Indeed, in the words of a famous historian, "[C]hronological narrative is the spine and the blood stream that brings history closer to 'how it really was' and to a proper understanding of cause and effect."[5] The importance of time line questioning of clients is that it helps you develop understandable and meaningful narrative structures.[6]

At the same time, stories at trial usually differ in important respects from everyday stories. Stories at trial are shaped by your need to satisfy legal principles, counter adversaries' versions of past events, and support your witnesses' credibility while undermining the credibility of adverse witnesses. In other words, persuasive litigation stories typically not only present rhetorical accounts of "what" happened, but also present evidence that explains "why" events happened as your clients contend they did. Theory development questioning of clients helps you to probe clients for information that makes stories persuasive.[7]

3. TIME LINE STORY FEATURES

As suggested above, time line stories provide the narrative structure that typically underlies persuasive litigation stories. Time line stories generally have three essential features:

1. They consist of discrete events.

2. The discrete events are so far as possible chronologically ordered, starting from when problems began and continuing up to the interview.

3. The discrete events are substantially free of specific details.

Without some assistance from you, few clients can steer a conversational course that produces stories with these three attributes. For most clients, a question such as, "Why don't you start by giving me a time line of events" is unlikely to evoke much more than unhappy memories of a high school world history course. Typically, rather than providing a sequential description of discrete events, clients are likely to provide rather terse, partial descriptions of stories couched in conclusory terms.

33, 64–67 (2001); Roland Acevedo, et. al., *Race and Representation: A Study of Legal Aid Attorneys and Their Perceptions of Significance of Race*, 18 Buff. Pub. Int. L. J. 1, 16–17 (2000).

5. Barbara W. Tuchman, Practicing History 9 (1981).

6. "Time line stories" are by no means synonymous with testimony you present at trial, should cases go that far. For example, persuasive trial testimony may include evidence as to *why* events occurred as your clients claim they occurred, yet information about causation may not emerge during time line questioning. Similarly, at trial you may attempt to enhance persuasiveness by presenting evidence non-chronologically. In short, time line stories assist your ability to make persuasive choices, but time line stories do not determine the content and manner of presentation at trial. For further information about presenting stories effectively at trial, *see,* Stefan Krieger and Richard Neumann, Essential Lawyering Skills 155 et seq. (2d ed. 2003); Paul Bergman, Trial Advocacy in a Nutshell 88–91 (3d ed., 1997).

7. Of course, rarely will you gather all the information you need from clients by completing time line and theory development questioning. Rather as cases progress and you gain additional information, you commonly return to clients for more information.

For example, assume that your client is Norma West, who during preliminary questioning indicated that her problems stem from the recent purchase of a house that turned out to have a leaky roof. When you ask Ms. West to go though a chronological, step-by-step account of what happened, starting from the beginning up to the present time, she tells this story:

> My broker and I went through the house in August, we entered into negotiations and my offer was accepted. The sale concluded about September 15th. After I moved in I did some minor remodeling, even replacing all the rain gutters. Then one rainy day in November I came home and found water all over the hall floor. In a second bedroom I saw that the ceiling had collapsed; there was water and plaster everywhere. I went ballistic as you can imagine, but after talking to some contractors I got things fixed up. With the damage to the inside, it cost me $40,000 and I had to take out an expensive second mortgage. I'm sure that the seller knew about the leaks, because one of my neighbors, Mr. Harris, indicated that the seller had had roof problems. But when I talked to the seller, he said he had never done anything to the roof but that's not what the roofer told me.

Here, the sequence of events is unclear. For example, when did Mrs. West talk to the seller about the roof? Was it before she bought the house or after the roof collapsed? Similarly, did Ms. West talk to the neighbor about the roof before or after she replaced the rain gutters? Ms. West's account provides a sense of events and chronology, but not a time line story.

Moreover, everyday experience suggests that Ms. West's account probably omits a number of important events. For example, house buyers typically arrange for pre-purchase inspections. Did Ms. West do so, and if so what did that entail? Also, homeowners in need of major repairs commonly obtain several estimates. Did Ms. West obtain estimates for the roof repair, and if so what were they and why did she select who she did?[8] Also, Ms. West may have noticed evidence of leaks prior to the ceiling's collapse, and if so her earlier observations are likely to be important to any claim for damages based on a fraud claim.

Finally, many seemingly discrete events in Ms. West's initial story are in reality "clumped events." A clumped event is a series of separable occurrences that clients refer to as a single event. For example, Ms. West indicates that "My broker and I went through the house in August." But what she describes as a single event was in reality a series of sub-events consisting of examinations of different rooms, conversations relating to each, etc. Breaking clumps into constituent occurrences is often necessary for important discrete events to emerge.

After reading the above critique of her story, Ms. West has been kind enough to retell a portion of it, as follows:[9]

---

8. The information you obtain might affect the reasonableness of damages.

9. While Ms. West's story appears here in uninterrupted narrative form, in an actu-

After my house flooded, the first thing I did was call a friend and get the name of a roofer. I called the roofer immediately and set up an appointment for two days later; I needed someone who could work quickly because of the threat of continued rain. I also called a handyman who'd done some work for me in the past; he sent somebody over the next day to clean up the mess left by the water and collapsed ceiling. I also called the seller. He denied knowing anything about problems with the roof. But when the roofer came by and was up on the roof my neighbor Mr. Harris walked over and said that the seller had told him about roof problems months before.

Ms. West now has provided a time line of some of the important events. For instance, she indicates that she talked to her neighbor Harris after the house had been damaged. And these events are largely shorn of detail. For example, Ms. West provides only a brief accounts of her conversations with the seller and Harris. While you may want to inquire further into these events during theory development, the details are not crucial to your understanding of the overall narrative.

With respect to "clumped" events, Ms. West now tells you about the individual people she called after the damage occurred: a friend, a roofer, a handyman, and the seller. Yet the retold story does include some clumped events. For example, Ms. West does not describe how the mess in her house was cleaned up. This makes sense, because all of us commonly group incidents into larger conclusions. Any story of past occurrences will necessarily include clumped events, at least if we expect anyone to listen. With clumped events such a common method of communication, as a lawyer you try to break clumps into constituent events only if it seems helpful to do so. By that standard, eliciting a step-by-step account of how the house was cleaned up seems unnecessary. On the other hand, Ms. West earlier referred to her "negotiations" with the seller. Breaking that clump into sub-events might be important for eventually producing a persuasive story of the seller's fraudulent conduct.

In sum, the retold time line story provides a chronological overview of discrete events that would allow you to select for further probing during theory development questioning those events that seem particularly significant.

4. ADVANTAGES OF ELICITING TIME LINE STORIES

You might in the abstract elicit case-related information from clients in any of a number of ways. For example, you might go one by one through the elements of claims or defenses suggested by clients' initial descriptions of problems. Or, without regard to legal theories, you might ask clients to tell you everything that they believe is important.

al counseling conversation a transcript would likely include questions and comments by you that help her stay on a chronological track.

Both of these approaches, however, are seriously flawed. Most fundamentally, neither of these approaches provides a platform for developing narrative structures that are the "spine and blood stream" of persuasive stories. Moreover, while the "tell me everything" approach does place clients in the conversational limelight and thus has client-centered aspects, the approach provides little memory stimulation. Finally, the "pursue legal theories" approach runs the risk of "premature diagnosis," and may prevent you from learning about significant events that are not encompassed by initial theories.

Consider by contrast the primary advantages of beginning to elicit case-related information from clients by obtaining time lines. First, time line stories provide the foundation for the testimony your clients may give at trial. In court, you typically elicit testimony in chronological order. Time lines are thus a preview of testimony.[10] That in turn enables you to start to evaluate stories from the perspective of judges, jurors or opposing counsel and thus to begin to assess clients' legal rights.[11]

Second, time line questioning tends to enhance the accuracy and completeness of the stories you eventually obtain. The reason is that you tend to promote clients' recall ability by asking them to relate events chronologically.[12] To see this for yourself, in a "gestalt" mode try to remember everything you did yesterday. Next, try to remember everything you did yesterday by going through the day step by step, starting from when you woke up and continuing until you went to sleep. If you are like most people, you will recall more of what occurred yesterday when you use the second approach. Moreover, when people relate events in their own words before they are questioned in detail, they generally are more accurate than when they are asked for details before they can give a narrative account.[13]

---

10. See, e.g., ALBERT J. MOORE ET AL., TRIAL ADVOCACY: INFERENCES, ARGUMENTS AND TECHNIQUES 111 (1996); PAUL BERGMAN, TRIAL ADVOCACY IN A NUTSHELL 13 (3rd ed. 1997); DAVID A. BINDER & PAUL BERGMAN, FACT INVESTIGATION: FROM HYPOTHESIS TO PROOF 263–286 (1984). Of course, the content of testimony will usually vary greatly from clients' initial time line narratives. For instance, testimony is likely to include details that you learn through theory development questioning, and may omit events that are not germane to a relevant legal theory or detract from the credibility of a client's story. However, the format both of time lines and trial testimony is generally chronological.

11. For a more expansive discussion of how factfinders evaluate stories told at trial see, DARYL K. BROWN, *Plain Meaning, Practical Reason, and Culpability: Toward a Theory of Jury Interpretation of Criminal Statutes*, 96 MICH. L. R. 1199, 1216–1219 (1998); NANCY PENNINGTON and REID HASTIE, *The Story Model For Jury Decision Making*, *in* INSIDE THE JUROR: THE PSYCHOLOGY OF JUROR

DECISION MAKING 194 et. seq. (REID HASTIE ed., 1993); W. LANCE BENNETT AND MARTHA S. FELDMAN, RECONSTRUCTING REALITY IN THE COURTROOM 7 (Rutgers University Press 1981). *See also* STEFAN H. KRIEGER, RICHARD K. NEUMANN JR., KATHLEEN MCMANUS AND STEVEN D. JAMAR, ESSENTIAL LAWYERING SKILLS: INTERVIEWING, COUNSELING, NEGOTIATION, AND PERSUASIVE FACT ANALYSIS 127–148 (1999).

12. See LAWRENCE W. BARSALOU, *The Content and Organization of Autobiographical Memories*, in REMEMBERING RECONSIDERED: ECOLOGICAL AND TRADITIONAL APPROACHES TO THE STUDY OF MEMORY 213–14, 222–24 (ULRIC NEISSER & EUGENE WINOGRAD eds., 1995). Where a person is asked to recall only a single event a different order may be beneficial. See R. EDWARD GEISELMAN & RONALD P. FISHER, THE COGNITIVE INTERVIEW TECHNIQUE FOR VICTIMS AND WITNESSES OF CRIME 3–6 (1989) [manuscript on file with authors].

13. Given people's limited powers of perception, memory and recall, what time lines probably promote are accurate pic-

Third, time line questioning tends to enhance rapport. Your role at this stage consists primarily of organizing the flow of information that clients think is important. Thus you tend to avoid interfering with clients' trains of thought and implicitly convey the message that what they have to say is important. Moreover, since clients are primarily responsible for content, they can downplay or omit uncomfortable topics, at least for the time being. This factor enhances accuracy, because pointed questions directed at topics that clients are not yet comfortable discussing may impel clients to provide false information.

Fourth, by letting clients take the lead in determining the content of stories you avoid imposing your own sense of relevance on interviews. After listening to clients' preliminary problem descriptions, you may be mistaken in your initial reactions about what legal claims or factual information to pursue.[14] As a consequence you may waste time asking clients about matters that in light of clients' overall stories are of little importance. Thus the time line phase tends to enhance the efficiency and productiveness of later questioning.[15]

Fifth, time line stories can clarify important inferences. That is, the order in which events happen often determines the inferences that can reasonably be drawn from them. For example, compare these two possible series of events:

(a) Marty left his house, got in his car, drove down 42nd Street to Broadway, hit a power pole, went into a bar, and had two beers.

(b) Marty left his house, went into a bar, had two beers, drove down 42nd street to Broadway and hit a power pole.

The stories contain the identical events. However, the inferences that a trier of fact might draw with respect to Marty's responsibility for hitting the power pole are clearly different because of the different order in which the events occurred.

Finally, time line stories tend to enhance the effectiveness of theory development questioning. The discrete events that constitute time line stories can serve as points of reference that enable clients to remember

tures of what clients *believe* happened, which may not necessarily be pictures of "what in fact happened."

14. Assume for example that preliminary problem identification reveals that a client's problem concerns injuries sustained at work while she was using a piece of machinery. Your legal diagnosis may be that her rights are governed by workers' compensation doctrine or products liability law. Armed with this diagnosis, you might be inclined to ask detailed questions pursuant to those theories. However, the client's time line story might indicate that before the accident the machine had been repaired, and also that the client's real difficulties arose after she underwent surgery and began taking a particular medicine.

Such information might alter your diagnosis considerably.

15. Studies of interview techniques in the medical field show that physician-dominated interviews also result in the loss of valuable information. *See* H. Beckman & R. Frankel, *The Effect of Physician Behavior on the Collection of Data*, 101 Ann.In-Tern.Med. 692, 694 (1984); F.W. Platt & J.C. McMath, *Clinical Hypocompetence: The Interview*, 91 Ann.Intern.Med. 898, 900–01 (1979); A.D. Poole and R.W. Sanson–Fisher, *Understanding the Patient: A Neglected Aspect of Medical Education*, 13A Soc.Sci. & Med. 37, 40–41 (1979); H.B. Beckman, M.D. and R.M. Frankel, Ph.D., *The Effect of Physician Behavior on the Collection of Data*, 101(5) Ann. of Intern.Med. 692 (1984).

additional details. For example, assume that in a fraud-in-the-sale-of-a-house case you want to elicit information from the seller indicating that the seller disclosed to the buyer that the city was considering widening a nearby small country lane to accommodate more traffic. You might ask the client, "Did you ever tell the buyer about possible plans to widen the lane?" However, inquiring about discrete events in a time line story may enhance a client's ability to recall:

> "You mentioned earlier that you had a dinner meeting with the buyer on June 27. Did the two of you talk about the lane at that time?"

Specific events tend to enhance memory because "The human mind is not yet like a computer. In response to a "Did you ever" type question, a (client) is unable to systematically search through all relevant time periods and spit out each instance in which the topic arose.... More likely, the (client) will consider the question in some quite unfocused way and respond affirmatively only if for some reason one or two such (instances) stick out in the (client's) mind."[16]

5. THE TENTATIVENESS OF TIME LINE STORIES

Underlying the use of time lines, and indeed the concept of seeking justice through litigation, is a belief that parties (and witnesses) are generally able to recount past events accurately. Yet, extensive research has identified numerous factors that may interfere with your clients' abilities to tell accurate time line stories. Summarizing this research, the leading investigator of the frailties of human perception and memory states that:

> Over a period of decades, a number of investigators have established that when we experience an important event, we do not simply record it in our memory as a videotape recorder would.... First the event is perceived by a witness, and information is entered into the memory. This is called the acquisition stage. Next, some time passes before a witness tries to remember the event, and this is called the retention stage. Finally, the witness tries to recall the stored information, and this is called the retrieval stage. This three-stage analysis is central to the concept of human memory.... Numerous factors at each stage are known to affect the accuracy and completeness of an eyewitness account.[17]

The application of this research to client interviews is uncertain, since most of the research data comes from laboratory experiments with witnesses who know that they are participating in simulated events.[18]

16. David Binder and Paul Bergman, Fact Investigation: From Hypothesis to Proof 294–295 (1984).

17. Elizabeth F. Loftus and James M. Doyle, Eyewitness Testimony: Civil and Criminal 10 (3rd ed.).

18. *Id*. at 319 ("The vast majority of psychological knowledge concerning the process of eyewitness identification is derived from laboratory experiments. These experiments, which attempt to imitate real-life situations, suffer from several disadvantages.")

However, the research suggests that it makes sense for you to regard stories that emerge through time line questioning as tentative. Theory development questioning provides you with an opportunity to seek additional information from clients tending to bolster their stories.[19] Additionally, of course, try to substantiate clients' recollections through the use of documents and information from other witnesses.

Cultural experience is a second factor tending to affect the accuracy of time line stories. Research suggests that "fundamental beliefs about the nature of the world, as well as the ways of perceiving and reasoning about it, differ dramatically among modern peoples."[20] An earlier chapter of the book described common dimensions of inter-cultural differences.[21] Those differences, it turns out, can "produce very different patterns of literally *seeing* the world."[22] For example, Asians tend to attend to context and may have difficulty visually separating objects from environments. Westerners, by contrast, often focus on objects while slighting the field and thus tend to see fewer objects and relationships than do Asians.[23] Moreover, "causal attribution differences mirror the attention differences."[24] That is, Westerners tend to rely on personality traits to explain behavior, while Asians tend to emphasize the importance of situational factors for explaining behavior.[25]

Thus, culture is a separate factor that renders time line stories tentative. The information that clients provide to you during time line questioning may reflect in part not simply "what actually happened" but rather what their cultural backgrounds have "taught" them to perceive and recollect. Again, you may look to theory development questioning and later information-gathering to substantiate and perhaps modify clients' initial accounts of events.

6. TIME LINE PREPARATORY EXPLANATIONS

The subject of time line questioning techniques is unaccountably neglected by most elementary, high school and college curricula. Nor does time line questioning feature prominently in many movies and TV shows about litigators. As a result, clients may be uncertain about how to respond when you ask them to provide a "step by step account of events." Thus, an effective strategy often is to precede time line questioning with a preparatory explanation.

Consider this sample preparatory explanation:

L: O.K., Paul, I think I have a pretty good sense of why you've come to see me. You retained Barbara Snider to file a lawsuit

---

19. See Chapters 7 and 8. Of course, the same factors that affect clients' sensory abilities with respect to the substance of their stories will affect the accuracy of clients' responses to inquiries about the presence of these factors.

20. RICHARD E. NISBETT, THE GEOGRAPHY OF THOUGHT: HOW ASIANS AND WESTERNERS THINK DIFFERENTLY . . . AND WHY xxi (2003).

21. See Chapter 2.

22. NISBETT, *supra* note 20, at 79 (emphasis in original).

23. *Id.* at 109.

24. *Id.* at 114

25. *Id.* at 123.

for you against a stock broker who you feel misled you about the financial condition of a company in which you purchased stock. You're really upset about Snider's failure to file a lawsuit against the broker and want to explore whether or not you may have a good basis for filing a malpractice case against her.

Here's how I suggest we proceed at this point. I'd like you to go through what happened in your dealings with Snider starting from the beginning. As best you can, go event-by-event in chronological order; just tell me in your own words everything that has happened right up to today. Tell me about any event you think matters; don't worry about whether or not you believe it is legally important. I may have a few questions from time to time, usually to make sure I'm understanding what happened, but basically I want you to do the talking. When you finish going over what happened, I'll go back and ask you some questions that seem to me legally important.

I'm planning for us to talk for about an hour today. If that won't work, please let me know. From what you've told me so far, I'm not sure we'll have time to cover all the information I'll need, and if so we can arrange another time to meet. However, before you leave today, I assure you that we'll talk over some ideas about what approach to take that might best resolve this matter. Any questions?

C: No.

L: Good. Why don't you start your story from the beginning, going event-by-event.

This is a "generic" preparatory explanation that you can use to inform clients of what to expect during an initial conference. The explanation gears clients to expect a two-phased discussion that may not be completed at one sitting. It concludes by recognizing explicitly what is likely to be uppermost in most clients' minds—potential solutions.

What else you might add to preparatory explanations is a matter for your judgment. For example, you might routinely mention clients' need to be truthful, though you may choose to omit such remarks out of concern that they indicate mistrust. Another component of a preparatory explanation may be a "war story"—a tale about a different client with a similar problem. But be forewarned. As you garner experience and encounter the difficulties that clients tend to have when attempting to provide time line stories, you may want to head each off in advance during a preparatory explanation. As a result, explanations may become so lengthy that clients doze off in mid-explanation.

But one matter not contained in the sample explanation that you may want to include concerns note-taking. You cannot readily convey empathy and interest in clients' stories if your head is buried in a computer or legal pad. On the other hand, taking notes is necessary lest important data be lost and your theory development questioning be curtailed. Hence, you usually take notes as you listen to a time line narrative, and may want to explain your actions ahead of time in language such as:

> "As we go through the story, I'll be jotting down some notes on what you tell me so that I can go back to the point if it becomes important. The notes are simply to make sure I don't forget. If you have any question about what I'm writing down, feel free to ask me about it."

Of course, preparatory explanations are not always called for. For example, a client may be one you have represented previously in a similar matter, legally sophisticated, or obviously anxious to relate a story at once. The first two types of clients may find a preparatory explanation condescending; a client particularly anxious to talk may find it frustrating.

In other situations, you may want to tailor the "generic" preparatory explanation to a specific client based on early information you have acquired. For example, if during initial discussion a client shows a marked tendency to excessive detail, you may want to include a remark along these lines:

> "Ms. Sossin, I can see that you are anxious to tell me everything. But my experience is that we can proceed more quickly, and I can better advise you, if you can give me a brief description of each of the events you recall; later we can go into the details if necessary. So why don't you start at the beginning and tell me, step-by-step and event-by-event, what has happened with your mortgage difficulty."

Of course, you need not routinely caution clients against excessive detail. The implied criticism is not the best method of fostering rapport. But this example indicates how you may tailor a preparatory explanation to an individual client.

Clients may be so preoccupied with their own problems that they do not fully digest your explanatory comments. Hence, you may find it useful to repeat part of a preparatory explanation as interviews proceed. For example, a client may relate events in a topic-by-topic fashion rather than in chronological order. If so, you may want to repeat a portion of your preparatory explanation during the interview. In this situation, you may make a statement such as:

> You've been doing a fine job so far of telling me what happened. Remember that you can help me by as much as you can going through the events in the order that they took place. So if you don't mind, I'd like to return to the point at which you first received the mortgage and ask you to tell me step-by-step from that point until the meeting you just told me about.

This statement praises the client while repeating part of the preparatory explanation.

To further your understanding of preparatory explanations, and how you might tailor them to specific situations, consider the following three short hypothetical cases.

Case No. 1

Following preliminary problem identification, you regard your client, Pei Huang, as not anxious to tell his story quickly and legally inexperienced. Moreover, you suspect from Pei's cultural background that he probably has little familiarity with the American legal system and therefore is likely to be uncertain about what you expect of him. The dialogue picks up at the conclusion of preliminary problem identification:

1. L: So, Pei, you've suffered a whiplash as the result of an automobile collision and what we need to figure out is whether you have a basis to file suit against the other driver to recover for your injuries.

2. C: Right. Basically, is this the kind of case that I'll be able to collect on? I've been through a hell of a lot.

3. L: When we've had a chance to talk a bit more, I'll try to give you an answer. What I'm going to have to do first is to get your story, including a description of your injuries and how they've affected you. Start in, why don't you, by telling me everything that has happened; just use your own words.

Analysis

This preparatory explanation seems shallow and lacking in adequate detail. Although Pei was not anxious to tell his story at once and may well have been unsure about what to expect, you do not tell him that the discussion will unfold in phases. That is, you do not tell Pei that after he tells his story, you will probe for additional information. Also, you do not provide guidance as to how he should tell his story—e.g., by proceeding in chronological order. You hint at a discussion of solutions (No. 3), but do not estimate when this discussion might occur. Such omissions are likely to leave Pei uncertain about what will occur. Finally, you might have made an active listening response to Pei's comment that "he had been through a hell of a lot," but you needn't slavishly actively listen at every opportunity.

Case No. 2

Your appraisal of the client is the same as in Case No. 1, with one exception. Here, you realize from the client's preliminary problem description that you need to brush up on potentially applicable legal doctrine before conducting theory development. Hence, you intend to ask the client to return for a second interview after completing the time line phase. Again the dialogue picks up at the conclusion of preliminary problem identification:

1. L: As I understand it, your husband mortgaged your home to AA Credit Company without your knowledge, and now they are trying to foreclose. You want to know whether anything can be done to stop the foreclosure, and you are concerned about how all this will affect your relationship with your husband.

2. C: That's it in a nutshell.

3. L: What I've found to be most helpful, Linda, is that we start out by having you tell me in your own words just what happened. I want you to start at the beginning and go step-by-step, telling me in chronological order everything you can recall. Take your time and tell me as much detail as you can. When you've finished, I'll review the notes I'll be making and I'll probably have a number of specific questions for you. At first I won't interrupt too much, because many of my clients find it helps their memory to talk largely without interruption. Then I'll go through your story in detail with additional questions. Do you have a fairly good idea of what we'll be doing?

4. C: Yes, I think I understand.

5. L: Great. Just a couple of other points. In all probability, I'll ask you to return for a second interview after you tell me your story, or maybe we can talk over the phone. This is an important matter, and I want to be sure you have a chance to tell your whole story. Also, that will give me a chance to review the most recent statutes and court decisions concerning mortgage foreclosures before I finish my questioning. Before we finish today, I'll try to give you as good a legal judgment as I can based on your story, but it will have to be somewhat tentative. O.K.—shall we proceed?

6. C: Yes.

7. L: All right, please start at the beginning and tell me, event-by-event, everything that has occurred.

Analysis

Given Linda's uncertainty and lack of a sense of urgency, a preparatory explanation of some detail seems appropriate here. Nos. 3 and 5 tell Linda to expect a two-phased review of the facts. No. 3 also explains how Linda is to proceed while telling the time line story, and prepares her for note-taking. No. 5 explains the likelihood that detailed questioning will take place another day and that more informed legal advice will have to wait until then. You openly inform her of your need to engage in legal research. Hopefully, you do so in such a way that Linda does not fear that you lack legal competence. Finally, you end the explanation by reinforcing Linda's duties during the time line phase.

This explanation would undoubtedly aid Linda's understanding of what to expect. At the same time, you neglect to mention how long the meeting might take, yet clients often appreciate knowing that. No. 3 asks

Linda to "tell me as much detail as you can." If she adheres to that advice, you may end up seeing more leaves than trees. Also, No. 5 talks about making a "legal judgment." This phrase may be confusing, as a legally inexperienced client may not understand that you are using "legal judgment" as a synonym for legal "advice."

Case No. 3

Here, you again believe that the client, who owns a small liquor store, is uncertain about what will take place during the interview, but you also believe that the client is extremely anxious to tell his story and get an immediate answer. After preliminary problem identification, the dialogue goes as follows:

1. L: So what's happened is that the Alcohol Control Board has served you with a Notice of Hearing on its petition to revoke your liquor license. The Board claims that the store is a public nuisance, but you strongly suspect that this is all a political ploy and that once your license is taken away the Board will award a new license to a friend of the mayor. Do I have it right?

2. C: You do. I'm terribly worried; this store is my family's entire means of support.

3. L: I understand your concern and I think we should get started right away. By the way, have you ever been to a lawyer before?

4. C: Well, just in connection with acquiring the property and the liquor license years ago.

5. L: All right, so you'll probably understand that as your lawyer I'll first need to get some additional information from you. I think we can get at this fastest by having you tell me step-by-step everything that has happened. I need a good picture of the facts before I can get some idea of what we can do. Start in now and tell me, event-by-event, everything that has happened with respect to the license since you got wind that the Board intends to revoke it.

Analysis

In reviewing this case please consider the following questions:

1. Many lawyers routinely ask a question such as No. 3 to help them gauge clients' familiarity in dealing with lawyers. If you believe that in general a question such as No. 3 is a useful one to ask, what do you think of its utility in this situation?

2. Looking back at the generic preparatory explanation above, how much of its contents would you have mentioned to this client?

3. Without regard to the contents of the generic preparatory explanation above, what else might you have included in your preparatory explanation?

　　4.　What if anything might you have added to the active listening response in No. 3?

7. "START AT THE BEGINNING"

The sample preparatory explanations above do not instruct the clients just where to start their stories. For example, in Case No. 2 you do not tell the client to, say, "Start in from when you first realized that the bank might foreclose." Many of the same reasons that support the efficacy of time line stories underlie advising clients simply to "start at the beginning." Just as you might prematurely diagnose clients' problems, so too might you incorrectly guess where stories begin. If you tell clients to begin at specific points in time, you may not learn of prior events that are important but which you did not anticipate. For instance, does an automobile mishap commence when a client starts out on a trip, with important personal news the client received the day before, or with a pre-existing medical condition? In the face of such uncertainty, you generally should not impose your sense of "beginning" on clients.

With this in mind, refer to No. 5 in Case No. 3 above. There, you tell the client to describe "everything that has happened with respect to the license since you got wind that the Board intends to revoke it." Since you have only partial information, does this statement run a risk that the client will ignore prior events that may turn out to be important?

Of course, clients may be as uncertain about the "true" beginning as you are. How should you react if clients respond to your request to "start at the beginning" by asking, "Where should I start?" Perhaps your simplest rejoinder is to say something like, "Start wherever you feel the story begins." Such a statement permits clients to begin where they feel comfortable.[26]

Often, when clients begin telling a story, you strongly suspect that they have not begun a narrative at a problem's "true" beginning. Your suspicion may grow out of information that other people have given to you. Or, intuition and your experience as a lawyer may suggest the likelihood of earlier events.[27] For example, often events follow a "normal course"—banks take certain steps before they foreclose; doctors discuss certain matters with patients before they operate; police officers follow a prescribed "booking process," and the like. Finally, apart from any suspicions you may have, as a careful lawyer you may simply want to be sure that clients do not start time line stories somewhere in the middle.

In any of these situations, should you interrupt clients' narratives to inquire about possible earlier events? Generally the answer is "no." Having invited clients to start wherever they choose, you should not lightly interrupt them to suggest better starting points. Interruptions

---

26. If a client persists in asking you where to start a narrative, you may have no choice other than to select a topic. You do not facilitate rapport by forcing a truly puzzled client to guess at where to begin.

27. For example, colleagues who are criminal defense attorneys tell us that their clients commonly start stories at the point of arrest, rather than with any of the events leading up to their arrest.

conflict with client-centeredness, may indicate that you have prematurely diagnosed clients' problems, and may deny clients the opportunity to delay mention of painful or troublesome events. In those situations where you suspect that clients have started their stories somewhere in the middle rather than at the beginning, you normally have the ready alternative of searching for earlier events after they have concluded their time line narratives. Thus when clients have concluded their time line versions, you might gently prod clients to reconsider a story's starting point with a statement such as:

> Donna, you've really given me a great deal of helpful information covering the events from last May right through to the present and that has been very helpful. What I'd like to do now is return you to the previous November, when you received the solicitation letter from the Hagberg Time Share folks. Think carefully for a moment; are there any other events that took place before you got that letter that you think may be a part of what happened?

In some cases, though, you may quickly realize that starting with a "second-half story" is counterproductive, and a result more of client confusion than of an intentional desire to postpone discussion of painful or troublesome events.[28] Some stories require that you understand the beginning in order to make sense of the end. In such situations, if a client begins at a time that obfuscates the significance of what the client is saying, you may have to politely intervene. Accepting responsibility for the intervention when you interrupt a client is a useful approach for building rapport and confidence:

> I'm sorry, Hugh, but can I stop you there for a moment? I apologize for doing this, but I realize that I need more background in order for me to follow along with you about what happened at the special education mediation session that you're describing. If you can start instead a while earlier, maybe when someone first suggested the need for special education services for Tina, and walk me through what happened from that point up to the mediation, that would help me a lot. I know I just told you that you should choose a starting point wherever you want, but I see now that as a newcomer to your case I'll need more background than I thought. Does that make sense?

This explanation tries to avoid insulting or criticizing the client for having chosen an inappropriate beginning point. Most likely, the use of this type of intervention will be rare, but at times necessary.

8. EXPANDING "QUICKIE" TIME LINE STORIES

Clients may fail to understand what you want when you ask for a step-by-step chronological account and provide no more than a brief

---

28. Again, criminal defense cases are a prime example of when you may decide not to interrupt a client who pretty obviously begins a narrative at a point other than at its true beginning.

summary of events. When this happens, you may repeat and amplify on a portion of a preparatory explanation. Consider the following example:

1. L: O.K., Mr. Thomas, please start from the beginning and tell me in your own words, step-by-step, everything that happened.

2. C: Sure. We were headed east on 43rd Street, when all of a sudden this car came out of a driveway. I tried to swerve, but he hit us. I was in the hospital about a week and off work for four. Now he's suing me.

This account does not constitute an adequate time line story. It may be chronological and shorn of detail, but it consists of conclusions, not discrete events. In such a situation, you might respond as follows:

3. L: You were severely injured and you're quite angry. I understand that and want to get as good a picture of what happened as I can. (Pause) What will help me is if you can start again and tell me one step at a time each and every thing that has happened. Try not to leave out anything. I need information about anything that happened before and after the collision that you feel is connected to your injuries. Take your time and go slowly through the story, one event at a time.

You might employ a second approach if, despite a repeat of your explanation, a client continues to talk in conclusory terms. The approach is to tell clients explicitly what you expect, and in what way what they have said differs from what you expect. For example, you might say,

Mr. Thomas, you've told me that after you changed lanes, he hit you. That's fine, it gives me some picture of what happened. But it really doesn't tell me step-by-step how the collision occurred. Can you go one step at a time, and tell me as best you can everything that happened after you changed lanes?

9. TIME LINE QUESTIONING TECHNIQUES

This section illustrates and evaluates effective time line questioning techniques. How you combine these techniques in particular interviews is of course a matter for your judgment.

A. OPEN QUESTIONS

Time line questions are principally open-ended. Open questions typically encourage clients to narrate events in their own words, keep clients' paths of association intact, free clients from preconceived notions of relevancy you may have, allow clients to postpone discussion of troublesome events, and generally are empathic as they cast you primarily in the role of listener. Hence, open questions are ideally suited to the general time line goal of obtaining chronological narratives free from excessive detail.

Three different forms of open questions typically serve to keep clients on a chronological track. As much as possible, limit time line questions to these three forms:

    1.   When clients mention an event, you may want them to move forward in time to the next event they can recall. To accomplish this, ask open questions such as, "What happened next?" or "What was the next thing that occurred?"

    2.   When clients mention an event, you may want them to stay with that event and tell you a bit more about it. Thus, you may ask open questions such as, "Tell me more about that," or "Please describe that for me in a little more detail." Such questions move a client neither forward nor backward; the story figuratively idles in neutral and allows you to obtain more information without subjecting clients to a barrage of closed questions

    3.   When clients mention an event, you may want to move them back in time, to search for possibly-omitted events. For example, if a client has mentioned that "the chicken crossed the road," you might ask, "What was happening before the chicken crossed the road?" When you do want clients to go back in time, you may aid their recall by repeating events they have already mentioned that might "bookend" a possibly-omitted event: "Between the time the chicken left the restaurant and the time the chicken crossed the road, what else happened?"

A brief example in the context of a "wrongful termination" matter demonstrates how you may orchestrate a time line relying principally on these three forms of open questions:

1.   L: George, after you complained to Barbara Epstein about the company's failure to inform its customers that it had switched to Grade 3 metal, what happened next?

2.   C: The next day I got a note telling me to report to the sales office. When I got there, they told me I had no business complaining to Epstein about sales policies.

3.   L: Tell me more about what went on in the sales office meeting.

4.   C: (Response omitted)

5.   L: What's the next thing that happened after the sales office meeting?

6.   C: About a week later I received my annual employee evaluation. After that meeting in the sales office, you can imagine what my supervisor wrote.

7.   L: You must have been really upset—we'll talk more about that very soon. But before we get to the evaluation, think just for a moment. What happened between the time of the sales office meeting and your receiving the evaluation?

Nos. 1 and 5 move the client forward in time; No. 3 asks the client to stay with the just-mentioned event; No. 7 searches for possibly-omitted prior events.

B. CLOSED QUESTIONS

Closed questions (questions seeking specific information) are often effective for clarifying ambiguities in clients' time line stories. Consider the following dialogue with Mr. Kafka:

1. L: O.K., Mr. Kafka, what happened next?

2. C: Well, the seller and I were talking about the electrician. He told me that he would come the next day and see just what the problem was.

3. L: When you say "he" was to come the next day, who are you referring to?

4. C: Oh, sorry. The seller was going to come the next day.

5. L: All right, after the seller said he would come by the next day, what took place?

Inquiry No. 3 is a simple example of using a closed question to clarify a story. As you did not understand which of two people Mr. Kafka referred to, you clarified the reference briefly and immediately returned to the narrative.

Another typical ambiguity that you may want to clarify during time line questioning concerns the chronology of events. A closed question may help you clarify the order in which events happened, or the time gap between events. Consider this dialogue:

1. L: O.K. Ms. Handler, what happened next?

2. C: Well, the Immigration Agency people came to our offices and asked to look at our Employment Eligibility Verifications for the last two years. We showed them our records and they talked to us about our hiring practices and how we checked for immigration status. They told us about our rights to remain silent and to talk to a lawyer, and they said we would probably be charged with some immigration violations.

3. L: I'm sure that was upsetting. I want you to tell more about this incident, but first, can you recall whether the Immigration agents told you about your rights before they started talking to you about your hiring practices or looking at your records?

4. C: Let's see. I'm pretty sure that the lead Immigration agent, Fred something or other, started looking at our files and then talked to us. Then his partner said that we had a right to remain silent and have a lawyer.

In this instance, inquiry No. 3 is closed; it seeks to clarify confusion as to the sequence of events. Similarly, a closed question may clarify confusion about the length of time between events. Just as the order in which events occur can affect the inferences we draw, so too can variations in time gaps. For example, a factfinder will almost certainly draw different inferences about a client's state of sobriety if the client had two martinis forty five minutes before getting behind the wheel of a car or two hours and forty five minutes before getting behind it. Thus, time line questions should not only seek to arrange events chronologically but also should attempt to elicit approximate intervals between events. Closed questions are often useful for uncovering information about intervals. The interview of Ms. Handler continues:

> 5. L: And just one other thing I'd like to clear up. How much time elapsed between the time the agents started looking at your records and they read you your rights?
>
> 6. C: Let me think. It must have been at least 25 minutes, because after we took out our records and showed them to the agents they looked through the records and asked us some questions before they said anything about our rights.
>
> 7. L: Thank you. OK, why don't you continue. I know this is hard, but you're doing a fine job of telling me what happened. What happened next after the Immigration agents left?

The amount of time that elapsed before the Immigration agents warned your clients of their "Miranda" rights may affect an inference as to whether the agents illegally gathered case-related information. No. 5 is a closed question that seeks that specific bit of information.[29]

In all three examples, the closed questions are limited to clarifying the time lines rather than flushing out additional details of events that clients have already identified, and therefore seemingly do not overly divert their attention from the chronological narratives.

C. SUMMARY TECHNIQUE

Summary statements can be a useful strategy for keeping you and clients on the same page while reassuring them that you are listening carefully to what they have to say. For example, assume that when describing a meeting, a client states that "we talked about the problems for our office staff that the expected upsurge in applications might cause and how to deal with the uncertainty caused by one of the secretaries being on extended sick leave." You were uncertain about what the client meant by an upsurge and want to clarify this matter. Before moving on to the next event in the time line, you might provide a brief summary as follows:

29. As you obtain time lines, you may ask clients for specific dates on which events took place. However, people often cannot recall specific dates, at least without the aid of documents. Hence during time line questioning you may settle for approximate dates and/or time intervals between events.

L: So that meeting was devoted primarily to the problems that you expected to be created by an anticipation upsurge in applications combined with one of the secretaries being on extended sick leave, is that right?

C: Yes.

L: And after this meeting, what's the next thing that happened?

When summarizing clients' stories, guard against the tendency (conscious or unconscious) to slightly alter what they have said so as to make their stories more compatible with governing substantive law. As a "zealous advocate," you are at risk for hearing what you want to hear and so might use a summary to try to commit clients to stronger stories than they have given. Consider this example from the interview of a client who with his spouse believes they bought a house from a seller who failed to reveal problems with the house's foundation.

1. L: During this last pre-purchase walk-through of the house, what happened next?

2. C: We looked around the living room and everything seemed fine.

3. L: Did you notice anything that indicated that there might be problems with the foundation?

4. C: Not really. I noticed a slight crack in the wall behind the entertainment center but it was so small that it didn't seem worth mentioning.

5. L: So at that point you looked around the living room and everything looked fine, is that right?

6. C: Yes.

7. L: What happened next after you looked at the living room?

8. C: We went. . . .

No. 5 seems to alter the client's story in a way that strengthens an argument that the client was unaware of potential problems with the foundation prior to purchasing the house. In No. 4 the client notices a "slight crack," yet No. 5 asks the client to agree that "everything looked fine" in the living room. If No. 5 is an artful attempt that succeeds in strengthening the client's story, you would be suborning perjury.[30]

D. AVOID CREATING GAPS

You may inadvertently create gaps in time line stories if you mistakenly assume that subsequent events to which clients allude are the next events in their time lines. Consider this example:

1. L: After you received the notice, what happened next?

2. C: I met with my neighbors to discuss how we should respond.

30. For a further discussion of problems that arise from the type of rephrasing that occurs in No. 5, see Chapter 3.

3.   L: When did that meeting take place?

4.   C: About a week after we got the notice. It came in early June.

5.   L: What happened at that meeting?

6.   C: We discussed the various ways in which we might approach the EPA and decided to visit the landfill ourselves.

7.   L: Okay. What happened during the visit to the landfill?

8.   C: Not much. The owner wouldn't give us access to it.

9.   L: OK, tell me what did happen.

In No. 6, the client refers to a future occurrence, a visit to a landfill. Your question in No. 7 assumes that this visit took place and that it was the next event in the time line. On these assumptions, you ask the client to describe what happened during the visit. However, by moving the client from the meeting with the neighbors to the landfill visit you risk overlooking events that might have taken place in the interim. Hence No. 7 may have created a time line gap. To avoid creating such a gap, you might have phrased No. 7 as follows: "After the neighbors' meeting and before the landfill visit, did anything else happen?"

E. EVENTS vs. DETAILS

This chapter has repeatedly urged you to elicit time line stories primarily through open questions. At the same time, it has recognized that closed questions are often helpful for clarifying ambiguities and time intervals. However, it is a mistake to allow the closed question "exception" to swallow the open question "rule." Permission to ask closed questions should not be the equivalent of allowing an alcoholic one drink. Repeated efforts to clarify stories are likely to result in gluts of details that vitiate the benefits of event-focused time line stories. Of course, at the end of the day the decision as to how often to use closed questions to clarify time line stories is a matter for your judgment.

To illustrate the type of judgment you may often have to make, assume that in a suit for workplace sexual harassment, a client refers to an incident in which her supervisor asked her for a drink after work. You ask, "Tell me more about his asking you for a drink," and the client says, "Well he said you look tired, why don't we go for a drink and relax." At this point should you ask another open question, such as, "What else happened at that time?" Would such an open question be appropriate to clarify what occurred? Or is it a quest for detail that can more properly await theory development questioning? Your judgment, not a reference work, will have to supply the answer. Depending on the circumstances of each individual matter, you might consider such a question a necessary clarification or an unnecessary interruption.

In general, however, when in doubt hold off on asking closed questions until theory development. As a litigator, your instinct when eliciting stories may resemble that of a tiger faced with a hunk of raw meat: tear it apart! Aware of a number of potentially-applicable legal theories, you may find yourself champing at the bit to probe stories for details that might substantiate or vitiate those theories. And once you start down the road of detail pursuit, you will find it difficult to obtain a chronology of events. But do not despair. Even if you consciously confine yourself largely to open questions, you will inevitably elicit a fair amount of detail. On their own, clients often describe some events in detail. When you ask an open question such as, "Can you please tell me more about . . . ?" clients invariably provide details. Hence, time line stories should not and will not be totally free of detail. However, to gain the benefits of beginning information-gathering with complete time lines, you may need to reign in your lawyerly taste for clarification that may quickly descend to repeated probes for detail. For example, in the sexual harassment example above you would probably put aside closed questions such as the following until you get to theory development questioning: "Did he say anything else about how you looked?" "Did he suggest where you might go for a drink?" "Was he suggesting that just the two of you go for a drink?"[31]

F.   REFERRING CLIENTS TO DOCUMENTS

In many instances, clients are unable to tell adequate time line stories by employing only their present recollections. However, clients will often not have to. Increasingly, roads to courthouses are cluttered with an array of documents. Letters, memos, reports, electronic mail trails, receipts and the like memorialize almost every human activity. Thus, if you have a chance to speak with clients prior to an interview, one request you should make as a matter of course is for them to bring along written documents pertaining to the matter they plan to discuss. And if during time line questioning you refer clients to such documents, you will usually enhance their recollection.[32]

For example, assume that a client mentions that a lengthy meeting occurred but can recall almost nothing of what took place during the meeting. Asking the client to refer to a memorandum written after the meeting may well refresh the client's recollection.[33] Consider this brief bit of dialogue from a matter involving an alleged claim wrongful termination of employment:

L: So what happened next?

C: I'm not sure. There was a big meeting at some point involving the head of Jones' department, Jones' immediate supervisor, the director of personnel, the union shop steward, and myself. But I'm not sure exactly what led up to the meeting.

31. For further discussion of the event/detail distinction, see Chapter 7.

32. You may sometimes decide to refer clients to documents before they express any difficulty of recollection. If you can reasonably anticipate that unaided recall will be difficult (say, a series of meetings took place), clients will often appreciate a reminder that they can look at the documents they've brought with them to help answer your questions.

33. This discussion assumes that the client can identify and readily bring to an interview a relatively small number of documents that pertain to a matter.

L: I see you've got your file there. Maybe you can take a moment and look to see whether any documents in there might remind you of what happened before the big meeting.

C: OK. Oh, I can see from this memo that I met with Jones' supervisor before that big meeting.

L: And when was that meeting?

C: My memo is dated July 15 and it refers to the meeting having taken place the day before, so July 14.

L: Having looked over the memo, please tell me what you can recall about the July 14 meeting.

C: . . .

An important proviso concerning the use of documents is that you should not become so engrossed in the contents of documents that you slip into theory development questioning. Documents, not subject to the whims and caprices of memory, are often quite rightfully of particular importance to matters' outcomes. Confronted with a variety of documents, then, you may want to focus your attention on them rather than on clients and their overall stories. Hence, to keep on the time line, refer clients to documents only if necessary to enable them to recall important events. Save detailed questioning about documents and a thorough review of them for theory development.[34]

G.   USING ACTIVE LISTENING

Active listening may be of particular value during time line questioning. Not only does it facilitate rapport, but also it provides questioning variety. After all, you cannot help but sound like a metronome if your questions consist of little more than variations on the theme, "What happened next?"

Assume for example that you want a client to elaborate on a meeting that the client referred to as "when those jerks really showed their true colors." Instead of asking, "Tell me more about the meeting," you might implicitly request additional information about the meeting with an empathic response such as, "I guess that's when their real intentions became clear." Statements such as this are gentler forms of probes than questions. They tend to convey that you are listening and trying to understand clients' thoughts and feelings, and they encourage clients to elaborate on topics.[35]

10.   TAKING PROBE NOTES

If time lines are to serve as bases for theory development questioning, note-taking is essential. Notes enable you both to reconstruct fairly complete time line stories after interviews conclude, and to make intelli-

---

34. *See* Avrom Sherr, Client Care for Lawyers 181–82 (2d ed. 1999).

35. As this example illustrates, your active listening response can focus on content or feelings or both.

gent choices about which events to probe further. But during counseling conversations you cannot take anything like verbatim notes and hope to maintain rapport. On the other hand, writing down only what immediately strikes you as important creates a real danger of omission. Matters that initially seem irrelevant, and that become meaningful only in the light of subsequent information, may be lost.

"Probe notes" are a helpful compromise. As clients mention events or topics, jot down key words as a reminder. If possible, use clients' actual words. During theory development, echoing clients' own words helps you stimulate their recollection. Do not hoard yellow pads or a computer's memory when taking probe notes. You can fill in events from your memory after interviews conclude and prepare "memoranda to the file" that sets out clients' time line stories.

The following example demonstrates how you may memorialize a time line story with probe notes. On the left is a time line dialogue with Jean, who is accused of being an accomplice in a liquor store robbery. The other suspects are Bill, Charlie and Ralph.

Dialogue	**Notes**
L: Tell me, from the beginning, what happened that night.	
C: We were sitting around at Charlie's. I guess I got there around 6 P.M. Bill was already there. We had some beer and Charlie's wife made some dinner, and then we had a few more beers.	Charlie's, 6 P.M. Bill already there. Charlie's wife-dinner Drinking beer
L: I see.	
C: Bill kept asking Charlie whether Ralph had called. Charlie kept saying no, it probably wouldn't be today. I didn't pay much attention. I hardly know Ralph.	Bill asks about call from Ralph. "Not today." Hardly knows Ralph
L: You're doing fine. Tell me more.	
C: We had the TV on, watching the fights. We were talking about playing poker. Charlie's wife came in and said there was a call for Bill. Bill went to the phone and then came back and told Charlie that Ralph wanted to talk with him. Charlie left the room and came back a few minutes later and asked Bill to go with him to pick up Ralph and buy some booze. They then left after Ralph said I should set up for poker. They came back with Ralph and some booze about 45 minutes later and we began to play poker.	TV. Ralph calls, asks for Bill and then Charlie. C & B pick up Ralph, buy some booze and come back in 45 minutes.

While these notes may appear sparse, they are probably adequate for the time line phase. They preserve the essential chronology and story.

Importantly, they retain remarks concerning possible witnesses (Charlie's wife) and a possible intoxication defense.[36]

11. EXAMPLES AND ANALYSES
OF TIME LINE STORIES

The three dialogues below explore many of the considerations addressed in this chapter. In each instance, assume that preliminary problem identification has taken place, and that you have already given a preparatory explanation.

Case No. 1

(During preliminary problem identification, the client's main concern involved a foreclosure of a mortgage on the client's house.)

1.   L: Tell me now step-by-step everything that has occurred. Start at the beginning.

2.   C: Well, about four months ago I lost my job. At first I wasn't worried, but pretty soon my savings started to disappear. I tried to find another job, but I couldn't. Two months ago, in June, I missed the payment on my second mortgage.

3.   L: O.K., what happened next?

4.   C: I got a letter from the mortgage company. It said if I didn't pay, they would foreclose.

5.   L: Do you have the letter?

6.   C: Yes.

7.   L: Can I see it?

8.   C: Sure, here it is.

9.   L: Did you contact them after you got the letter?

10.   C: Yes, a while later.

11.   L: Tell me about that.

12.   C: I called up and told them I'd lost my job, and asked for more time to pay.

13.   L: Who did you talk to?

14.   C: I talked to a Ms. Howl. She said that under the law I had time, and that I had no need to worry.

15.   L: That must have made you feel better. Did Ms. Howl specify the specific law she was referring to?

16.   C: I'm not sure. But a few days ago I got this notice; it says they are foreclosing.

17.   L: When exactly did you get this notice?

18.   C: Last week.

19.   L: What happened when you received it?

---

36. For discussion of considerations relating to mechanically recording interviews, see Chapter 8.

Analysis

This dialogue primarily illustrates how easily chronological gaps can creep into a time line story. Examine No. 9. It is a closed question that is likely to pull the client off a chronological track by moving from the point in time when the client received the letter (No. 4) to what you seemingly assumed was the next event—the client's contacting the company. Even if the client did eventually contact the company, the contact may not have been the next significant event to occur. Other significant events, such as the arrival of other letters, phone calls, or partial payments could have occurred before the client contacted the company. Hence, No. 9 should have been an open question, such as, "After you received this letter, what happened next?"

Examine next No. 16. Here the client may have created a chronological gap by overlooking events between the phone call with Howl and receipt of the notice. Hence, you might have asked in No. 17 a question such as, "Let's go back for a moment to your conversation with the mortgage company. What is the very next thing you can recall happening after this conversation?" Or, you might have asked, "Between the time you talked to Ms. Howl and you received the foreclosure notice, what else happened?"

The dialogue also illustrates how searching for details during the time line phase may draw you "off-side," or cause a client to be drawn off. Nos. 5, 7, 13 and 15 exemplify unnecessary searches for detail (though No. 15 does include an appropriate active listening response reflecting the client's past feelings). While the questions may not call for excessive clarification or elaboration, they do divert the attention of both you and the client from the narrative. The information does not appear necessary for understanding the overall story, and could easily await theory development. By contrast, the detail sought in No. 17 concerns when an event occurred and appropriately seeks to clarify the overall chronology.

Case No. 2

(During preliminary problem identification the client's main concern was that the client had been fired for interceding on behalf of another employee.)

1. L: Start at the beginning and tell me, step-by-step, everything that has happened.

2. C: About six months before I got fired, this friend of mine, Monica, came to me and told me that she was being fired for insubordination.

3. L: Hmm. Please tell me a bit more about that.

4. C: She said she had gotten into an argument with the shift boss who had called her a "psycho." Monica told me that she thought the real reason she was being fired was that she had reported the boss to the manager. Monica was real angry, and she asked me to help her.

5. L: I see.

6. C: Anyhow, I went to the shift boss and asked for an explanation.

7. L: Between the time Monica asked you to help her and your going to the shift boss, what else occurred?

8. C: The only things that happened were that we formed a committee to help Monica, and I was elected representative to see the shift boss. I didn't have contact with anyone from the company that involved Monica.

9. L: What you're telling me is very helpful. After you were elected, what happened next?

10. C: I went to see him. He told me Monica was always demanding too much and not following orders. He said he was sorry for calling her a psycho. I told him that we had a committee and that we were going to protect Monica. He said there was nothing he could do, so I went to see the personnel manager.

11. L: Just to make sure we don't miss anything, after you saw the shift boss but before you saw the personnel manager, did you do anything else?

12. C: No.

13. L: O.K., tell me about your conversation with the personnel manager.

14. C: We just talked a bit about the situation.

15. L: Tell me as much as you can remember.

16. C: All I really remember is she said she'd check with the shift boss and get back to me.

17. L: This conversation must have left you a bit frustrated.

18. C: It really did.

19. L: What happened next?

20. C: A meeting was set up to go over things.

21. L: Who was at the meeting?

22. C: Monica, me, the shift boss, Ms. Dawson from personnel, and Donald Furnish, another employee.

23. L: What happened?

24. C: Monica, Donald and I talked about the good job Monica always did, and that we thought her complaint was proper. The shift boss said that he called her a "psycho" because he had heard Monica using that term herself when she referred to other employees. That really made me angry; I called him a liar.

25. L: I can imagine you were very angry. By the way, has the shift boss ever used the term "psycho" when talking to you?

Analysis

With a couple of exceptions, this conversation represents an effective time line strategy. No. 7 demonstrates the use of known "bookend" events to try to fill a possible gap in chronology. Nos. 9 and 19 illustrate the use of open questions to move a story ahead in time. Nos. 3, 13 and 15 are open questions that keep the story in neutral; you ask the client to elaborate on already-mentioned events. No. 11, however, shows how you must be careful to use open questions even when seeking to fill in possible gaps. There, you ask whether the client *did* anything during the time period in question. You would have been safer to ask, "Did anything else occur during that time period?"

No. 21 is a closed question of the type that runs the risk of leaving the chronological track in favor of unnecessary detail. However, since it asks only for limited detail and you have not to this point sought details, the digression seems to be reasonable. Knowing who attended the meeting also helps to clarify the story.

The beginning of No. 9 illustrates "recognition," and Nos. 17 and 25 are active listening responses. However, the follow-up question in No. 25 may take the client off the chronological track.

Case No. 3

(During preliminary problem identification the client's main concern was to regain custody of her children after they were taken away by the Department of Social Services.)

1. L: Go step-by-step from the beginning, Ms. Jong, and tell me everything that has happened.

2. C: Two police officers came to the door and asked if they could come in. I asked why, and they said they had a report of child neglect. I said I had done nothing wrong, and they could come in and look around.

3. L: Go ahead.

4. C: Well, they looked in all the rooms and asked if they could check the kitchen. I said sure. They went in and asked why there was so little food. I said I'd been sick, but that I was going to the market soon. They said they would have to take the baby and that my daughter Sylvia had already been detained at school.

5. L: You must have been stunned.

6. C: I really was. I was crying and shouting, almost hysterical I guess.

7. L: I can understand how you would be. Tell me, what else happened while the police were there?

8. C: Not much. They told me to come to court in two days.

9. L: O.K., then what happened?

10. C: I ran to my sister's house. We tried to find a lawyer but we couldn't. She took me home, and we found this telegram from the Welfare people.

11. L: Do you have the telegram?

12. C: It's home.

13.   L: What did the telegram say?

14.   C: I don't know, maybe who to call to find out where my kids were.

15.   L: Did you call?

16.   C: Sure, but they said I couldn't see them, just that I should be in court the next day.

17.   L: What happened after this call?

Analysis

Please evaluate this dialogue for yourself. For example, which of Nos. 3, 7, 9, 13, and 17 ask the client to move to the next event, which potentially create or encourage chronological gaps, and which seek details that may be unnecessary? Do Nos. 5 and 7 reflect past or present feelings? Toward the end of the dialogue, how might you have caused a chronological gap?

12. SPECIAL TIME LINE ISSUES

A. THE TRAVELS OF ODYSSEUS

How you might respond when clients' stories, like that of Odysseus, are extremely lengthy or complex? In general, the longer or more complex a story, the more useful an overall chronology. In such circumstances, a narrative of events is particularly helpful for stimulating clients' memories and evaluating stories' inferential impact. Hence, the usual upshot of a long story is simply a long time line, even if you need more than one meeting to complete it.

Assume for example that Sarah Armstrong consults you about a threat by Greatest Second Mortgage to foreclose on her home. Sarah's story starts with a phone call that she received from Greatest offering her a loan. It then covers negotiations about that loan. Thereafter it picks up six months later with the receipt of a notice increasing her loan payment and several phone calls and letters that allegedly resolved that dispute. Then it jumps forward for another four months to a similar dispute and a series of phone calls and letters. Finally her story leaps ahead another six months to an official notice of foreclosure and Armstrong's failure to get anyone at Greatest to talk with her about the foreclosure notice. Even though this situation covers more than a year's time, and you may not be able to obtain a complete time line in one meeting, theory development questioning is likely to be more effective if you first elicit a time line from Sarah.[37]

B. CO–AUTHORED TIME LINES

For the most part, this chapter assumes that time line stories are within the grasp of a single person. However, especially in corporate

---

37. Of course, if the client does not have documents that reflect what happened during this year period, getting anything approximating a complete time line may be almost impossible.

litigation, a client's story may require the input of several contributors. Consider for example a products liability lawsuit in which the client is a manufacturing company whose power saw was allegedly defectively designed. The client's full story probably includes how the company designed, tested and marketed the saw. Hence, putting together a time line story may require that you talk to company executives, engineers and salespeople and get a separate time line from each person you talk to.[38]

Documents may sometimes help you cut down on the number of people you have to contact to put together a time line story. If you can identify an individual or two as the "main contributors," and use documents to remind these individuals of other events, talking to them may enable you to put together a fairly complete time line story.

Recognize that "co-authored" time lines often require you to make compromises with a pure time line approach. For example, it may be unrealistic to try to limit each of several contributors to "time lines only," and then after you have elicited a time line from each and put together a client's overall time line, go back to each for theory development. Instead, you may have to complete both phases with one person before moving on to the next.[39] Similarly, relying on documents to piece together a co-authored story may involve more immersion in documents than if a story were within a single person's grasp.

C. MULTIPLE TIME LINES

Think for a moment about the storyline of a typical hour-long television drama. It probably has two or three separate subplots. If you were asked for a time line of the show, you might find it easier to discuss each subplot separately. Because events pertaining to different subplots often occur concurrently, you might get confused trying to develop a chronology of all events. In like manner, when you can identify separate strands in clients' stories, you may help them recall important events by pursuing each strand separately. After you develop a chronology of one strand, you then pursue another, and so on until you have obtained the entire story.

For example, assume that the chief executive of our power saw manufacturer could, with the aid of documents, recall many events pertaining to the development, testing and marketing of the power saw. Assume further that many of the relevant events took place simultaneously. That is, even as research was in progress, marketing strategies were being planned; as models were tested, additional research took place. In this situation, you might try to obtain a time line of all events relating to research, another time line of events relating to testing, and yet another time line of events pertaining to marketing.

---

38. Indeed a similar need may exist in the Armstrong and Greatest example in the preceding section.

39. Of course, you may not complete both phases during a single meeting.

Similarly assume that at the outset of an initial interview a client tells you that a contractor failed to complete several aspects of a home remodeling contract. You might want to obtain separate time lines for each of the alleged failures.

Again, you cannot rely on rules to guide your judgment as to when to break stories into separate time lines. Ordinarily you look to such factors as a story's complexity, a client's memory ability, and perhaps considerations of time.[40]

D. CLIENTS WHO CAN'T PROVIDE TIME LINES

Clients may for a variety of reasons be unable to provide even rough chronologies of important events. Consider these common circumstances:

- Clients' stories may be embedded in events that happened so long ago that the clients can no longer recall many of them, let alone the order in which they unfolded. For example, assume that you represent a lawyer who has been sued by a former client for giving inadequate advice with respect to a complex agreement that the ex-client entered into many years earlier. At least in the absence of a good paper trail, the lawyer may well have difficulty recalling and ordering events concerning when the lawyer talked with the ex-client.

- Clients' stories may be rooted in numerous, largely fungible occurrences that defy unpacking and ordering. For example, assume that you represent a group of neighbors who have consulted you with respect to health problems caused by noxious fumes emitted by a nearby factory. Your clients may be unable to identify specific instances when toxic fumes caused health problems.[41]

- By dint of personality or injury, some clients may be simply unable to relate matters chronologically. For example, repeated requests for step by step accounts may be met with verbose descriptions that ignore order altogether.

Strategies for responding to chronological shortcomings such as these may differ according to your diagnosis as to their cause. One strategy you may attempt with verbose clients whose stories are as tangled as the limbs of a briar patch is to substitute narrow questions for open-ended ones. That is, instead of asking a client to "go step by step through what happened," try asking the client to tell you "when this

40. Insofar as time is concerned, you may need, for example, to respond to an adversary's request for a preliminary injunction. You may not have time to pursue sub-stories separately.

41. Clients faced with divorce and child custody issues often face this kind of dilemma. Thus a client seeking a divorce and custody of the couple's three children may not be able to produce a chronology of the spouse's abusive behavior, drunkenness, child neglect and monetary parsimony. The individual occurrences that make up the spouse's behavior in each of these four areas are in the client's mind indistinguishable. Moreover the instances in one area, say intoxication, overlap and merge with instances in the other areas, for example abuse and child neglect.

problem first arose." Then you might go one event at a time through the story. Consider this example involving a client who contends that he was discharged from employment without just cause, and who wants to file a lawsuit seeking damages and reinstatement. After your preparatory explanation, the interview proceeds as follows:

1.   L: Mr. Harper, why don't you tell me in your own words step by step everything that led up to your dismissal. Perhaps start with the first time you had any sense that something might be wrong.

2.   C: Well one day I heard Connie, that's my boss, telling her boss, Edward Volokh, that things were not going well in our department because of laziness in some of her groups. This was the kind of thing Connie did all the time. She was always blaming things on other people. I've been at the company for over five years and Connie is notorious for putting the blame elsewhere when she screws up. Anyhow Connie tells Volokh that she just wants to let him know that I was falling behind on his project for B & W Wholesale. What she doesn't say is that despite my repeated requests for more help she has never done anything but load more work on me. That's something she does to everyone, load on more work when she knows you're behind. She's like an evil monster; if you tell her things are going fine she tends to leave you alone but if you indicate you have problems you're going to end up with more work. Anyhow later on when it's pretty clear that I'm not going to finish the B & W Wholesale job on time she really starts to get on my case. She berates me and says she is going to have to consider the situation in my semi-annual evaluation. And, of course, that's not the first time she'd talked about my evaluation. There were a couple of other occasions earlier on where she had done virtually the same thing.

3.   L: You've given me a great deal of helpful information and I want to make sure that I'm understanding just what happened. You said something about overhearing a conversation between Connie and her boss, Volokh. You also mentioned what happened later when you got behind on the B & W project and talked about earlier occasions involving employee evaluations by Connie. To give me a clear picture of what happened, perhaps we can go over what happened in sequential order, one step at a time. So let's start with the next thing that happened after you overheard Connie talking with Volokh. What was the very next thing that you recall happening?

4.   C: Well, I honestly can't be sure that it was the next thing but I do remember going to Connie and asking for more help.

5.   L: Fine, just do the best you can. Can you give me any idea of when it was that you went to Connie to ask for more help?

6.　C:　Sometime in May is about the best I can do. Maybe she has some records that can pinpoint it better.

7.　L:　That's a good idea, we can think of trying to get them if it's necessary. But while we're on that meeting, anything in particular that you recall about that conversation with Connie?

8.　C:　Just that she went into a tirade about my always complaining and asking for help. That wasn't true. Her reaction was no different from what had happened a few months earlier and I should have realized she wouldn't change. At that time . . .

9.　L:　OK, let me stop you there. We can talk about that earlier event later. For now, try to remember what was the very next thing that you recall happening after you met with Connie.

10.　C:　I think I got a memo from her.

11.　L:　From Connie?

12.　C:　Yes.

13.　L:　Good. Do you have a copy of that memo?

14.　C:　Not any more.

15.　L:　Okay. Anything specific you can recall about that memo?

No. 2 makes it apparent that chronology is not Harper's strong suit. In No. 3 you take several steps to try to develop a time line. First, you try to motivate him by providing "recognition." You then summarize part of what Harper told you, repeat your desire for a chronology, and then conclude by starting back through the story with a narrowly focused question, "What is the very next thing that you recall happening?" As is typical, your change of approach does not magically alter Harper's personality, so that in No. 8 he begins to stray once more. Without being critical, however, you "park" the out-of-sequence event and proceed in No. 9 with a similarly focused question. No. 11 clarifies the story; do you think Harper's reference in No. 10 was sufficiently ambiguous to justify the inquiry? Similarly, does your inquiry in No. 13 promote the time line, or might you have waited until later to ask it? Finally, No. 7 asks Harper whether he can recall anything specific about a time line event, a conversation with Connie. While time line questioning is generally not the time to explore events in detail, one or two open questions seeking brief description of events can be helpful and is consistent with overall time line goals.

An alternative strategy for interviewing verbose clients who have difficulty focusing on chronology is to forsake chronology at least temporarily and instead continue to use open-ended "what happened next" type of questions. This approach maintains the customary benefits of open questions: you do not try to swim upstream against clients' familiar speaking styles, nor do you interfere with their paths of association. Also, open questions tend to promote rapport. Ultimately, this strategy may encourage clients to be more cognizant of chronology in their responses. If not, at least you may emerge with a variety of specific events that you can later ask clients to order chronologically so far as possible.

When stories include events that are too numerous and fungible for clients to sort out, an effective strategy is to ask them for specific examples. When clients can identify concrete instances, you may succeed in having them organize at least those instances chronologically. Consider the following example:

1. L: So the situation is that Great Wall, the wallboard subcontractor, claims that you've failed to pay for the work it did in the East Wind housing development.

2. C: Precisely. Olsen and the others are a bunch of thieves and as far as I'm concerned we should be suing them.

3. L: It sounds like this has been pretty stressful. What I'd like you to do at this point is give me is a step by step account of your dealings with Great Wall on this project, starting from the beginning and continuing right up to today. Start with where ever you think the story begins.

4. C: Well, it starts with my conversation with Olsen right after I opened up their bid.

5. L: Okay, why don't you first tell me about the bid.

6. C: The bid was for both labor and material and the per unit price looked pretty good. It wasn't rock bottom but it wasn't out of the question. But we had never dealt with them so I wanted to get some references and that's why I called Olsen.

7. L: Go ahead, tell me about that conversation.

8. C: I introduced myself and said that their bid was attractive but we needed to check references. I said I'd like a bank reference and also to check with three or four firms that Great Wall had done work for. Olsen gave me some information, and later faxed me a written authorization to check with his bank and I did that. He appeared to be in good financial condition. The three references also appeared to check out but I later learned that at least one of them was a brother-in-law.

9. L: What happened next?

10. C: We gave Great Wall the dry wall contract and at first things went quite smoothly. The project had one hundred and thirty five homes but once we hit about fifty homes we started having trouble with them. They were late getting material to the job, they often didn't show and that caused all kinds of delays and their work was frequently poor. We often had to insist that they take out what they had done and start over. When they were late it caused other trades to also fall behind. The painters in particular were having all sorts of problems because of delays and poor workmanship by Great Wall.

11.   L: Sounds like a mess. Can you take me through these problems chronologically, one by one?

12.   C: I'd like to, but I can't. I have a calendar that I carried around with me on the job and it has some of the meetings I had with them on the job about various screw ups but it doesn't have most of them. Also there were dozens of phone calls and I just don't have record of these. All I can say is that whenever they caused a delay I'd call them and the response would almost always be the same. They'd have an excuse and promise to get on it right away. If the problem involved poor workmanship sometimes they'd deny it and we'd have to meet at the job site. At other times they'd admit that a problem existed but blame it on some other trade. For example, they were continually claiming that the framing contractor was using green wood that would bow after they installed the wall board. Then I'd have to get them together with the framing contractor and we'd have to work it out. Green wood was almost never the cause of their poor workmanship.

13.   L: Any way you can recall approximately when these various things happened in relationship to each other?

14.   C: Not really. Don't forget, when I would go out to the job site on any given day I'd also meet with many of the other subs and with the on-site supervisor. My days on the job were just one big blur of meetings.

15.   L: During what period of time were you having these problems with Great Wall?

16.   C: I'd say over a six month period from May through November of last year.

17.   L: Okay let's start with instances of delay, can you give me some specific examples of occasions when they failed to get materials to the project?

18.   C: I remember the time when we were working on ten units near the community center. The units had been framed and wired and we were ready for the wall board. I'd called them and talked to one of their lead men, Hector. I asked if they were ready to go the next day and Hector said yes. But they failed to show up. I called and talked to Olsen himself and he promised they'd be there the next day. But they were a no-show again. I was really upset and tried to reach Olsen again but was told that he and the managers were out of town for a meeting.

19.   L: Can you recall when this happened?

20.   C: I'd say in early June.

21.   L: It's really helpful that you can remember some dates. Can you give me another example of a delay?

22.   C: There was a delay involving the three large houses in the cul-de-sac on the northeast corner of the project. They were some of the few two story houses.

23. L: Tell me about this problem.

24. C: (Response omitted)

25. L: You're giving me just the kind of information I need. When did this problem occur?

26. C: I'm not sure exactly.

27. L: Was it before or after the failure to get material to the 10 houses during June.

28. C: I'd say it was a couple of months after that.

29. L: Fine, let's go on to another example.

30. C: Let's see. . . .

Here, No. 12 expresses the client's understandable inability to separate out and order numerous fungible occurrences. You respond by seeking specific examples (Nos. 17 and 21) and attempt to establish approximately when they occurred (Nos. 19, 25, 27). You might continue to search for examples pertaining to different kinds of problems until you have pieced together an adequate time line.

When disputes grow out of "ancient" events, your ability to develop time lines (or other information) is of course to some extent limited. Clients who claim to recall accurately events that happened years earlier may have little credibility in the eyes of judges and jurors. One approach is to locate documents and other records that may serve as "signposts" that can credibly stimulate clients' memories. Also, if not complete timelines, you may be able to elicit a number of examples that clients may be able to order according to a rough chronology.

13. PREPARE AND UPDATE CHRONOLOGIES

Your litigation files should normally include a document or a computer file consisting of updated versions of case chronologies. Begin memorializing your clients' time line stories when initial meetings take place, and update those stories as case investigation continues. With narrative meaning so crucial to stories' credibility, maintaining running case chronologies is an effective method for evaluating the persuasiveness of your arguments and for identifying gaps and inconsistencies that you may want to pursue. [42]

If you practice in a law firm, case chronologies are also helpful for quickly bringing partners and associates up to speed on the strength of your clients' factual contentions.

Finally, you may also try to maintain chronologies of your adversaries' versions of events. Doing so can help you focus on primary points of dispute.

---

42. For a discussion of the likely content of a case chronology, *See* DAVID A. BINDER, ALBERT J. MOORE & PAUL BERGMAN, DEPOSITION QUESTIONING STRATEGIES AND TECHNIQUES 296–207 (2001). While you don't need a computer to create a case chronology, many popular computer litigation support programs reserve a portion of their databases for chronologies. One computer litigation support program that the authors have found particularly useful in creating case chronologies is "CaseMap."

Chapter 7

THEORY DEVELOPMENT QUESTIONING—PURSUING HELPFUL EVIDENCE

* * *

Bob, you've given me a quite clear picture of how this situation unfolded from the first day you met Ross right up to today. What I need to do now is to flesh out the story so that we can get a better picture of where you stand legally. We can get started on that today, but we may need another meeting before we can decide on the best way to proceed from here. However, before you leave today, we should be able to kick around some ideas about how you might best resolve this matter with Ross. How does that sound?

* * *

1. INTRODUCTION

With clients' time line stories in hand, you can turn your attention to the second major phase of initial information-gathering in litigation matters. This book refers to this phase of interviews as "theory development questioning," because during this phase you seek evidence to bolster your clients' legal contentions and vitiate those of your adversaries.

Theory development questioning generally places you in a more active questioning role than time line questioning. The reason is that like gold ore, nuggets of useful evidence that may be present in clients' recollections often do not lie on the surface, waiting for you to scoop them up with a few open-ended time line questions. Instead, you may have to dig down into clients' recollections with questions that reflect your analytical judgment.[1] Thus, the orientation underlying this and the

---

1. For example, you might ask about a possible additional event that a client did *not* mention during time line questioning because its occurrence would support a helpful legal theory. Similarly, you might seek additional details pertaining to an event that a client *did* mention during time line questioning because those details might unearth evidence supporting a helpful legal

next chapter's approach is that information-gathering is more likely to be productive if you start out with some concrete ideas of what you're looking for.

2. THE PROCESS OF THEORY DEVELOPMENT QUESTIONING

Theory development questioning grows out of a quintessentially legal task, carrying out the analytic process of connecting concrete time line stories to the abstract rules that constitute legal claims and defenses. This analytic process typically leads you to identify legal theories (claims or defenses) that time line stories suggest are relevant. You then work backwards from those legal theories to identify helpful potential evidence; that is, potential evidence tending to substantiate those theories. Sections 3 through 5 of this chapter explain this analytic process.

Typically, you devote a substantial portion of theory development questioning to fleshing out those portions of time line stories that seem most likely to reveal evidence tending to support your clients' legal contentions. Section 6 explains and illustrate techniques for pursuing helpful evidence thoroughly and efficiently.

A second common theory development task is to pursue evidence bolstering clients' credibility. Section 7 sets forth topics that commonly affect credibility, and illustrates techniques for seeking evidence bolstering clients' credibility.

Theory development questioning is also an appropriate time to pay attention to your adversaries' legal contentions. Either time line stories themselves or the information that results from theory development questioning may reveal harmful evidence, that is, evidence tending to undermine your clients' legal contentions. If so, you may try to rebut (diminish the impact of) that evidence. Chapter 8 suggests how you may use the same techniques that you use when pursuing helpful evidence to pursue information that rebuts harmful evidence.[2]

Finally, during theory development you may also explore what your clients know about their adversaries' legal contentions, and seek evidence undermining those contentions. Chapter 8 also addresses this theory development task.

In summary, theory development questioning often incorporates four separate kinds of tasks: pursuing helpful evidence, seeking to bolster the credibility of helpful evidence, seeking to rebut the impact of harmful evidence, and seeking to undermine adversaries' legal contentions. This book devotes separate sections and indeed separate chapters to these tasks solely to promote your understanding of each. In practice, you are unlikely to carry out these tasks separately or in the order just

theory and/or enhance the client's credibility.

2. Inability to rebut harmful evidence may lead you to abandon legal theories that

initially seemed promising and to pursue alternative ones.

listed. Instead, you may jump back and forth among these tasks as questioning unfolds. For example, you may stumble on harmful evidence in the course of seeking helpful evidence. Your response may be to immediately seek to rebut that harmful evidence rather than continue pursuing helpful evidence.

Indeed, pursuing helpful evidence may not always be a primary theory development task. For example, assume that the person initially contacting you on behalf of First Rate Mortgage Inc. is Felicia Korn, a company vice-president. First Rate is a defendant in a wrongful termination case. Korn had no involvement in the events giving rise to the lawsuit. However, prior to the time that the lawsuit was filed, Korn discussed those events briefly with a company employee (the plaintiff's former supervisor) and had a couple of telephone conversations with the plaintiff's lawyer just before the lawsuit was filed. In these circumstances, your questioning of Korn might focus primarily on the plaintiff's likely factual contentions. The discussion of helpful evidence with Korn might be quite cursory, since she wasn't involved in the underlying events and the supervisor and perhaps other employees are likely to be far better sources of such evidence.

Moreover, you may well provide preliminary advice and undertake actions on clients' behalves even before addressing each of the four theory development questioning tasks. For example, if an answer from Korn's company is due the day after Korn comes to see you, you may have to file an Answer or seek an extension of time to do so before fully addressing any of the tasks.

Thus, taken together the two theory development chapters do no more than describe an approach and a group of tasks that generally increase the effectiveness of theory development questioning. While the chapters take up these tasks separately, how you conduct theory development questioning in individual cases depends on your judgment about the dynamics of particular clients and their problems.

3. IDENTIFYING MATERIAL FACTS

The process of effectively and thoroughly probing time line stories for additional helpful evidence usually begins with your identifying the material (ultimate) facts that you seek to prove. The subsections below describe a three step process for doing so. While you may depending on your experience sometimes be able to carry out this process automatically and perhaps subconsciously, this section explicates its component parts in order to aid your ability to gather helpful evidence when you are confronted with legal or factual situations with which you are unfamiliar. The three step process is as follows:

1. Identify applicable legal theories
2. Parse legal theories into constituent elements.
3. Convert legal elements into factual propositions.

A. IDENTIFYING LEGAL THEORIES

The process of identifying the facts you want to prove begins by identifying the potentially-viable legal theories suggested by clients' time line stories. That is, evidence is "helpful" not in the abstract, but to the extent that it furthers a relevant legal claim or defense. For example, when interviewing a tenant in an unlawful detainer (eviction) case, you may seek evidence concerning illnesses suffered by the tenant's children not simply because illnesses would be "part of the story," but because the evidence would tend to show that lack of heating in the apartment rendered it "uninhabitable."[3]

Often, and especially when you have received information about clients' problems before in-person interviews begin, you will have potentially-viable legal theories in mind at the conclusion of (and perhaps even at the start of) time line questioning. If so, then an initial meeting may flow rather seamlessly from time line to theory development questioning.

At times, however, you may be uncertain about the legal theories you can most profitably pursue during theory development questioning. For example, you may want to check on whether an established legal claim or defense applies to a client's time line story. Or, you may be uncertain as to whether a potential theory is legally permissible in your jurisdiction.[4] A third possibility, no doubt the most disquieting, is to simply draw a blank after listening to a time line story.

In most cases, your general legal knowledge will be sufficient for you to probe time line stories at least preliminarily as soon as that phase of interviews concludes. However, thorough theory development questioning may require a temporary adjournment of an initial meeting while you do legal research. The length of the postponement will, apart from other time commitments, typically depend on the amount of time you need to fully acquaint yourself with the applicable law. In all events where you lack full understanding of applicable law, theory development questioning may have to extend over at least two meetings.[5]

The strategies for identifying helpful evidence to pursue during theory development begin with a specific legal claim or defense that you seek to prove or disprove. From this point on, therefore, the discussion assumes that you have identified a viable legal theory pursuant to which you want to identify helpful evidence.

---

3. Evidence may be "helpful" whether or not it is admissible at trial. The reason is that information often has an emotional or "non-legal" value. For example, an adversary may settle to avoid the risk that questionable evidence may be admitted. Similarly, a party's moral attitudes may be affected by inadmissible evidence. See Linda F. Smith, *Interviewing Clients: A Linguistic Comparison of the "Traditional" Interview and the "Client–Centered" Interview*, 1 CLINICAL L. REV. 541, 580 (1995).

4. For example, at one time a landlord's failure to maintain leased premises in a habitable condition was not a theory that would defeat a suit for eviction. In most states, it now is.

5. When theory development questioning does extend over at least two meetings, clients may nevertheless expect a tentative assessment of their legal positions before you conclude theory development questioning. For suggestions about how you might respond to such expectations, see Chapter 11.

B. PARSING LEGAL THEORIES INTO CONSTITUENT ELEMENTS

1. Legal Theories Are Abstract Shells

The earth probably did not move for you when you read that you should probe time line stories pursuant to legal theories. What other source would you use—theories of skeletal structure as set forth in Gray's Anatomy? However, you may feel at least a small tremor when you realize that legal theories are largely ephemeral. Most legal theories, be they criminal or civil, common law or statutory, are abstract shells that are not themselves provable. At a minimum, provable legal theories consist of bundles of elements that constitute the content of legal theories. For example, if you were asked what evidence you would offer to prove breach of contract or securities fraud, you would have to ask first what requirements (elements) you must satisfy to establish each legal theory. The legal theories standing alone are simply housings for elements, not concrete guides to proof.

2. Elements Themselves Are Legal Abstractions

Elements establish the requirements of legal theories. Nevertheless, elements themselves remain legal abstractions. As a result, even elements are not a sufficient guide to case-specific questions.

For example, assume that a client's time line story focuses on his near-decapitation by an exploding kitchen appliance. The story suggests to you a number of potentially-applicable legal theories, such as negligent manufacture of goods, breach of warranty, and strict liability on a theory of defective design. A quick riffle through your memory bank enables you to bring to the fore the following requisite elements of a claim for "strict liability/defective design:"

1. The defendant introduced a product into commerce.
2. The product when introduced contained a design defect.
3. The design defect was the actual cause of damages.
4. The design defect was the proximate cause of damages.
5. The design defect resulted in damages.[6]

As you can see, these elements tell you nothing about what facts you must prove in your client's specific situation to succeed with this legal claim. For example, the elements are silent with respect to such basic facts as the type of product involved, its design, the client's injuries and other damages and what the defendant did to introduce the product into commerce. The elements are so broad that they can apply to an infinite number of stories. Indeed, elements are intentionally broad and abstract, for it is impossible to draft a specific rule for each set of factual circumstances that might arise in the context of a given legal element.[7]

---

6. *See* American Law Institute, Restatement (Second) of Torts § 402A and Comment (1965); 63 Am. Jur. 2d, Products Liability §§ 528–577 (1989).

7. For example, "citizenship" for purposes of diversity jurisdiction is a combina-

Thus, abstract elements alone are not adequate guides to the facts that either you or an adversary may attempt to establish at trial, or to the questions you might ask to develop evidence of such facts.

3. *Restating Elements As Factual Propositions*

Converting abstract legal elements into provable "factual propositions" is the next step for identifying topics for theory development probing. Factual propositions meld abstract elements with legally salient facts in clients' time line stories. That is, factual propositions tailor intangible elements to each client's concrete situation, so that proof of a factual proposition's accuracy establishes an element. Restating elements as factual propositions tells you what facts establish that element in a client's specific case. In turn, delineating factual propositions enables you to think concretely about what evidence in the existing story as well as what potential evidence is likely to establish the facts you need to prove.[8]

To understand the process of converting legal theories into factual propositions, assume that you represent a personal injury client named Wilson. The interview thus far has revealed that Wilson was injured when the brakes in his car failed, causing the car to collide with another vehicle. Wilson's time line story of this misadventure is as follows:

(1) On June 10, Wilson brought his car to a Goodstone Service Center to purchase two new tires.

(2) Goodstone's manager stated that the car needed new brakes and Wilson authorized Goodstone to do a brake job.

(3) The brake job took longer than anticipated, and Wilson was without a car for two days, which caused him hardship, including being late for work, needing friends to pick up children, etc.

(4) On June 12, Wilson picked up his car.

(5) During the following week Wilson noticed that the car pulled to the left whenever he applied the brakes.

(6) On June 20th, Wilson returned to Goodstone and explained his problem to a service representative and the mechanic who had originally worked on his car.

(7) Wilson left his car at Goodstone and picked it up later the same day after receiving a phone call indicating that the problem was with the brakes and that it had been fixed.

(8) The brakes worked fine for two days and then again the car began pulling to the left when Wilson applied the brakes.

tion of geographical residence and intent. Obviously it is impossible to draft rules for every combination of factors that would govern determination of citizenship.

8. In addition to proving the elements of substantive legal theories, you may also have to prove miscellaneous facts such as those related to jurisdiction or a litigant's legal status.

(9) Wilson was returning to Goodstone on June 22nd to have the brakes checked when, approaching a red light at an intersection, Wilson applied the brakes and they failed totally.

(10) Wilson's car collided with the rear end of another car at a speed of about 35 mph.

(11) Wilson was in the hospital with head injuries for three days, incurring medical costs of about $38,000; over $7,300 in damages was done to Wilson's car.

(12) The insurance company for the driver of the car that Wilson collided with contacted Wilson and asked him for a statement. Wilson gave a statement to the insurance company.

(13) Six weeks after the accident, Wilson returned to Goodstone to talk to the mechanic who had worked on the brakes and learned that the mechanic was no longer employed by Goodstone.

Wilson's time line story may suggest to you a number of potentially relevant legal theories by which Wilson might recover damages against Goodstone, including negligence, fraud and breach of warranty. For purposes of this discussion, focus on the negligence theory. In abstract terms, one element of this theory is "breach of the duty of reasonable care." Having heard Wilson's story and looked into how braking systems operate, you believe that Goodstone would have breached the duty of reasonable care if the mechanic had neglected to check the condition of the master brake cylinder.[9] Thus, you might formulate the following factual proposition:

"Goodstone failed to check the master brake cylinder when repairing the brakes on Wilson's car."

As you can see, the factual proposition identifies a concrete fact, proof of which satisfies the element, "breach of the duty of reasonable care." Unlike the abstract element, the factual proposition enables you to identify case-specific topics likely to produce evidence establishing the proposition's accuracy. For example, using the strategies set forth below, you might pursue the following topics during theory development questioning of Wilson:

a. Whether Wilson was billed by Goodstone for inspection of the master brake cylinder.

b. Whether Wilson was billed by Goodstone for replacement of the master brake cylinder.

c. Whether Wilson was given any old parts when he picked up the car.

d. Whether the car's brake warning light came on before the accident.

---

9. "Might have breached" is the correct term because "reasonable care" constitutes a normative standard. The trier of fact must decide whether failure to check the master brake cylinder, even if true, is unreasonable behavior on Goodstone's part. For a discussion of the differences between historical factual propositions and normative ones, see DAVID BINDER & PAUL BERGMAN, FACT INVESTIGATION: FROM HYPOTHESIS TO PROOF 7 (1984).

a. Multiple Factual Propositions

Any single legal element may be satisfied by a virtually unlimited number of factual propositions. Across cases, this assertion is obvious. Two cases involving identical legal theories and elements will almost certainly lead to different factual propositions because of variations in their factual histories. For instance, the factual proposition that you might formulate for the element of "formation of contract" in a case involving breach of an employment contract will in all likelihood be very different from one that you might assert in a case involving breach of a construction contract.

Perhaps less obviously, you may want to formulate and pursue multiple factual propositions even for a single element in a single case. One reason is simply that a time line story may give rise to multiple factual ways of satisfying the same abstract legal element. For instance, assume that you represent a plaintiff in a fraud case, and your client states that the defendant made four different material misstatements. You therefore might formulate four different factual propositions, each one satisfying the element, "misrepresentation." Similarly, if you represent a defendant in an equitable action, a defendant's story may give rise to multiple factual propositions demonstrating the plaintiff's "unclean hands."

A second reason for formulating and pursuing multiple factual propositions for a single element in a single case is that a time line story may leave you uncertain of an element's factual equivalent.[10] For example, in the Wilson/Goodstone matter, Wilson's story may not enable you to pinpoint what Goodstone did wrong that constitutes "breach of the duty of reasonable care." Consider two common factors that often create uncertainty:

- Clients may be unaware of how events actually have transpired. For example, Wilson may have no idea why the brakes failed and may not know what the mechanic did or failed to do to Wilson's car.
- Clients who think they are aware of how events took place may be mistaken. For example, Wilson's story about why the brakes failed may be incorrect.

In such situations, often a sensible strategy is to formulate a number of factual propositions, each based on what seems to you a reasonable possibility. For example, factual propositions you might reasonably formulate on Wilson's behalf that would satisfy the element "breach of the duty of reasonable care" would include:

- Goodstone failed to replace the brake fluid in Wilson's car.
- Goodstone failed to install new brake linings properly.

---

10. By the time of trial, perhaps you will assert only a single factual proposition to prove an element. But prior to trial, and especially when you are in the early stages of eliciting information, you often cannot be confident of the evidence you will uncover to establish a possible factual proposition and hence what story and arguments will be the most persuasive.

• Goodstone installed discs not designed for Wilson's model of car.

When as in Wilson's case a number of propositions might reasonably support a time line story, be reluctant to discard them out of hand before completing initial fact gathering.[11] If you limit questioning to a single factual proposition, you are in trouble if down the road that solo proposition does not pan out with evidence. Searching feverishly for new factual propositions late in the game, you may instead be searching for a new client.

Especially if you are knowledgeable about cars, you might well be able to formulate additional factual propositions. But even the few alternatives above demonstrate how their creation increases the scope of potentially relevant evidence. Propositions about master cylinders, brake fluid, brake linings and discs each may be established by different evidence, and hence each suggests different lines of inquiry. For example, evidence that stepping on the brakes caused Wilson's car to pull to the left or right might suggest a problem with the discs or linings, rather than with the master brake cylinder or the brake fluid. The same might be said about evidence that the brakes were smoking prior to the accident.[12]

Depending on your background and experience, in any given case you may feel that you lack the experience to develop alternative propositions. For example, as the subject probably was not covered in law school, you may know little about the potential causes of brake failure. Or, you might represent landowners who contend that a nearby dump contains illegal toxic wastes, and you may not be aware precisely of how toxic waste problems manifest themselves. In such situations, you may need to develop "industry knowledge" by involving an expert in the process of formulating factual propositions.[13]

One note of caution: Judges and jurors do not award prizes to the side that produces the most factual propositions. Developing propositions to excess may prove the depth and breadth of your "industry knowledge" (e.g., that you are a master mechanic) as it drowns you in a sea of factual propositions. Do not be limited by the factual boundaries contained in a time line story, but be reasonable in your creation of alternative ones.

b. Plaintiffs' and Defendants' Factual Propositions

The process of converting legal elements into one or more factual propositions appears to respond primarily to the way that plaintiffs'

---

11. You need not ritualistically develop alternative factual propositions for every element in every cause of action. But rare will be the case in which you do not need to develop alternative propositions for at least one element. For example, in an action for breach of contract, you may never consider more than one factual proposition for the element of formation of the contract, but may consider a number of possible propositions for the element of breach.

12. As this discussion suggests, your ability to develop factual propositions generally depends on your level of experience with the subject matter of a client's story.

13. An "expert" is not necessarily an individual; books are also sources of expertise. For further discussion of involving experts in the investigatory process, see BINDER & BERGMAN, *supra* note 9, at 172–174.

lawyers view the world. Plaintiffs normally pursue as many legal theories as are reasonably feasible, and they typically have the burden of proving each element of each alleged cause of action or criminal offense. Formulating a variety of provable propositions and trying to uncover evidence pursuant to each therefore well serves plaintiffs' interests.

Perhaps for less obvious reasons, defense counsel often have to identify the factual propositions on which their adversaries are likely to rely (at least for those elements that defense counsel plan to contest). Defense counsel cannot simply rely on the pleadings, because complaints typically do not specify the factual propositions by which plaintiffs may attempt to prove their various theories. For example, in the Wilson/Goodstone matter, Wilson's complaint may well allege little more than that Goodstone negligently serviced Wilson's car. Because Goodstone cannot attempt to negate every possible way in which its service might have been negligent, Goodstone's counsel must try to identify the factual propositions that Wilson will attempt to pursue.

At the same time, defendants often have to formulate their own factual propositions. Defendants may not typically have the burden of proving elements, and they may not contest each and every element. But as to those elements that defendants do contest, they often not only try to disprove plaintiffs' versions of events, but also offer their own affirmative stories.[14] For example, Goodstone is likely to do more than pursue a factual proposition that "Goodstone did indeed check the master brake cylinder." In addition, Goodstone's counsel might formulate and try to identify evidence for the factual proposition "Wilson's driving at an excessive speed was the cause of the accident."

Still less are defense counsel simply naysayers when they allege affirmative defenses as to which they have the burden of proof. For instance, if in a criminal case the defense relies on an alibi, the defense is unlikely to limit itself to denying that the defendant was present at the scene of the crime. The defense will probably also try to prove defendant's actual whereabouts, and may even offer its own evidence as to the identity of the actual culprit. In such an instance, the defense might offer evidence to support at least two factual propositions, such as: (a) "Defendant was actually in Miami Beach at the time of the robbery in Cleveland;" and (b) "The actual robber was Al Moore."

Hence, regardless of the burden of proof, defense attorneys also typically need to develop factual propositions before embarking on theory development questioning.

4. IDENTIFYING EMOTIVE (NON–MATERIAL) FACTUAL PROPOSITIONS

Litigation has both rational and emotive aspects. Hence you may also want to look for evidence tending to prove the accuracy of informa-

---

14. Of course, in criminal cases defendants do occasionally sit silently at trial and argue the burden of proof, but except in criminal matters this tactic is fairly rare.

tion that may lead a judge or juror to believe in the moral justness of your clients' causes. Assume for example that in providing a time line story, Wilson told you that when he picked up his car on June 22nd, the service representative told him, "We've got it this time. You don't have to worry, your brakes are in perfect condition now." Proof that the service representative made this statement does not establish that Goodstone negligently serviced Wilson's brakes. At the same time, establishing that the service representative did make this remark may incline a judge or juror to want to decide the case in Wilson's favor. Thus, you may want to pursue proof of this "non-material" fact to the same extent as material facts.

Consider a second example in which you might want to pursue proof of a non-material fact. Assume that you represent a defendant tenant in an unlawful detainer (eviction) matter and have asserted a defense based on breach of the warranty of habitability because of the landlord's failure to keep the premises free of rodents. During her time line story, the client indicated that when she was absent the landlord often entered her apartment to snoop around. Establishing this emotive fact might strengthen your claims with respect to the material facts.

5. IDENTIFYING HELPFUL EVIDENCE

Factual propositions, the case-specific counterparts of abstract elements, are the foundation for identifying helpful evidence tending to amplify the persuasive impact of time line stories. The subsections below explore strategies for identifying such evidence.

A. THE ROLE OF EXPERIENCE

Law school's emphasis on tools of legal analysis tends to obscure the extent to which the resolution of factual disputes depends on reasoning drawn from everyday experience. In reality, your own personal experience is often your primary source for identifying helpful evidence tending to support factual propositions. In other words, much of the helpful evidence you identify simply results from your use of the experiences you've had in daily life, including observing and reading about how others live. Through your experiences you have undoubtedly internalized understandings about matters such as:

— how people typically behave

— how institutions typically behave

— how transactions commonly unfold

— how mechanical devices operate

— how people typically think

— how people normally react in emotional situations

— the charm of the Rule Against Perpetuities.

How does experience enable you to identify helpful evidence based on factual propositions? Our everyday experiences lead us to expect that events usually unfold primarily according to recognizable patterns. Most of us accept, for example, that bystanders will be frightened when they witness violent crimes, that stockbrokers will stress the safety and growth potential of an investment when soliciting potential purchasers for newly issued stock, that people will be in a rush when late for an important meeting, and that cars with bad brakes may pull to the left or right when the brakes are applied. Because we accept that events occur in recognizable patterns, we can identify a variety of features that are likely to have been part of past events. Thus, when you employ personal experience to identify potential evidence topics, you identify happenings that are consistent with a factual proposition. Proof of those happenings in turn suggests a proposition's accuracy.

For example, assume that you want to identify topics likely to lead to evidence proving the proposition that "Store clerk Jones was afraid that the robber was going to shoot him." (This proposition satisfies a typical element of robbery, taking property "through means of force or fear.") Even knowing nothing about the robbery, you can undoubtedly use everyday personal experience to identify a number of topics that would establish this proposition's accuracy. You might include such topics as the realism of the gun's appearance, the robber's pointing it at Jones, the robber's nervousness, and the robber's use of threatening words. You can identify such evidence not simply because of any experience you have had with Jones or robberies but because your everyday experience provides you with a pattern of factors that are likely to make a robbery victim fearful of being shot.[15]

You are undoubtedly familiar with the process of reasoning from evidence to legal conclusions. Judges and jurors engage in it routinely when weighing evidence pursuant to legal principles. Using experience to identify potential evidence is simply the converse of this familiar process. During theory development questioning you begin with a conclusion (a factual proposition) and from that conclusion you identify topics that are likely to be present if the conclusion is accurate. Instead of piecing together evidence to reach conclusions, you start with a conclusion and reason backwards.[16]

Despite its importance, everyday experience alone may not constitute a sufficient source of helpful topics. You may again need "industry knowledge"—that is, experience in the underlying context of a dispute. If a dispute centers on the language of a shopping center lease, it

---

15. You can readily call on experience even when you lack actual experience because experience can be vicarious. That is, you may never have been involved in a robbery, but you have read about robberies in books and newspapers and seen them depicted (perhaps every day of your adult life) in movies and on television. Experience may also be analogous—you may never have been involved in a robbery, but you probably have experience observing people in other kinds of dangerous situations (like being called on in the first month of law school).

16. Of course, this is the standard mode of reasoning found in many popular detective and mystery novels. *See, e.g.,* Arthur Conan Doyle, The Silver Blaze and a Study In Scarlet (1887). *See generally,* The Sign of Three: Dupin, Holmes, Peirce (Umberto Eco and Thomas A. Sebeok, eds., 1988).

behooves you to know something not just about contracts in general or even about leases in general but specifically about lease agreements for shopping centers. If you represent a stockbroker who allegedly illegally "churned" an individual client's account, you must know not just about the stock market industry but about brokerage practices for non-institutional investors. If a client contends that she was negligently shot by a duck hunter, you must learn about guns and duck hunting. Experience with the underlying circumstances giving rise to clients' problems is critical for identifying helpful evidence topics tied directly to factual propositions. When you lack sufficient experience, you'll generally need to rely on others, often paid experts, to help you identify helpful evidence.

Obviously, one reason that lawyers develop specialized practices is to accumulate experiences in a particular industry or way of life. But even specialization is no guarantee of subject matter experience. For instance, though you may specialize in "wrongful termination" matters, your experience with matters that originate in government offices may be insufficient for a matter that arises in a restaurant. Even specialists, therefore, may need to call on experts.[17]

Experience, then, both in general and in the activity involved in a particular dispute, is the bridge that connects legal principles and real world events. Remember, each and every day you use such experience to identify "evidence," if only subconsciously. Consider this sample dialogue:

Bo: "Why was the teacher smiling when we got to school today?"

Jo: "Probably because we did real well on the test yesterday."

Thus, identifying topics that might uncover helpful evidence pertaining to legal claims or defenses entails using the same thought processes you use in everyday life. Two organized approaches to applying experience to factual propositions are "Historical Reconstruction" and "Strengthening Generalizations." Both of these approaches rely on the importance and characteristics of circumstantial evidence.

B. CIRCUMSTANTIAL EVIDENCE

As you probably know, direct evidence establishes a proposition without the aid of an inference. In the Wilson/Goodstone hypothetical, the mechanic's admission that "I never did look at the master brake cylinder" is direct evidence in support of the factual proposition for breach of duty, "Goodstone failed to check the master brake cylinder." No inference (other than that the testimony is truthful[18]) is required to

---

17. Note that an "expert" you consult to identify potential evidence can simply be a person who has experience that you do not. To learn about "restaurant practices," for instance, you would not need the advice of one who holds a graduate degree in res-

taurant management. You might do quite well consulting with a waitress or a cook.

18. For purposes of defining evidence as "direct," evidentiary principles generally disregard the potential for the trier of fact to disbelieve the evidence. *See* CHARLES ALAN WRIGHT & KENNETH GRAHAM, FEDERAL PRACTICE

go from the mechanic's testimony to the accuracy of the factual proposition.

By contrast, circumstantial evidence establishes a proposition with the aid of one or more inferences. For example, evidence that thick grease covered the master brake cylinder would constitute circumstantial evidence that the mechanic did not inspect it. From the presence of thick grease, one can infer that the cylinder was not touched; from that, one can infer that it was not inspected.[19]

For a variety of reasons, most evidence that you uncover and offer at trial is circumstantial.[20] However, the persuasiveness of circumstantial evidence to prove or disprove a factual proposition rests on the strength of an underlying premise. That is, circumstantial evidence has probative value only according to the strength of the premise that connects the evidence to a proposition. In the vast majority of cases, premises are generalizations about the behavior of people and objects. They are postulates about how people and objects typically behave. The probative value of evidence, then, typically depends on the strength of these underlying generalizations.

For example, assume that a factual proposition you are attempting to prove is, "Snider ran a red light and struck Mantle's car." Seeking to prove the accuracy of this proposition, Mantle's attorney calls Mays, who testifies, "I spoke to Snider 15 minutes before the collision, and he told me that he was very late for an important meeting across town." Mays's testimony is circumstantial evidence. And its probative value depends on the strength of the following two generalizations:

"People who are late for a meeting are often in a hurry."

"People who are in a hurry sometimes run red lights."

In the absence of such premises (generalizations), a trier of fact could make no inference connecting Mays' testimony about "lateness" and Snider's running the red light.

"Historical Reconstruction" and "Strengthening Generalizations" are two strategies for identifying topics that are likely to lead to helpful evidence. Each depends on your recognizing that generalizations connect items of circumstantial evidence to factual propositions. The difference is that you need not explicitly formulate generalizations when you employ the strategy of "historical reconstruction," whereas you do explicitly formulate generalizations when you employ the "strengthening generalizations" approach. Neither approach is necessarily better than the other. You may employ whichever one is more comfortable and helpful to you, and this may vary from one case to another or even from one

AND PROCEDURE: EVIDENCE § 5162 & notes 21–23 (1990).

19. If this inferential chain strikes you as wrong, it may be due to the authors' lack of pertinent "industry knowledge" regarding brake repairs. We intended to obtain better industry knowledge by driving around without brakes, but neither of our deans would permit us to use his car for this educational endeavor, and Dr. Price refused for psychological reasons.

20. For a discussion of the reasons that circumstantial evidence predominates, see BINDER & BERGMAN, *supra* note 9, at 81–82.

proposition to another in the same case. If a case's complexity justifies it, you may even employ both reasoning methods.

C. HISTORICAL RECONSTRUCTION

1. In General

Historical reconstruction is a method of reasoning by which you combine experience with chronology to identify potential evidence. The notion behind historical reconstruction is that most events are neither isolated nor random but are parts of larger sequences of events. For instance, most of us can identify the kinds of problems that the owner of a small retail shop probably experienced when just starting out, and the activities of an apartment seeker who has two small children and who suddenly had to move. Experience can tell us a lot not just about how any discrete event may have unfolded, but how an entire sequence of events is likely to have unfolded.

To use historical reconstruction to identify topics likely to lead to helpful evidence, adopt the attitude that a factual proposition is accurate. Then ask yourself, in essence, "If this proposition is true, what else also would probably have occurred?" The "what else" will be topics consisting of potential evidence that, if confirmed, become circumstantial evidence tending to prove the accuracy of the proposition.

As an illustration of the use of historical reconstruction, assume that as counsel for Wilson, one factual proposition you have tentatively decided to pursue is that, "Goodstone failed to check the master brake cylinder when it repaired the brakes on Wilson's car." Start from the premise that this proposition is accurate. Then, using everyday experience, think about what actions or happenings are consistent with failure to check a master brake cylinder. Probably even the most mechanically inept among us can identify such indicators as:

    a. the mechanic's worksheet did not indicate that the mechanic had inspected the master brake cylinder;

    b. Wilson was not billed for inspection of the master brake cylinder;

    c. When Wilson picked up the car, the mechanic said nothing to Wilson about the condition of the master cylinder;

    d. Goodstone mechanics are paid according to how many cars they repair per day.

Though you need not explicitly formulate generalizations when using historical reconstruction, you can see that the potential evidence this technique identifies is circumstantial. That is, each item implicitly rests on an underlying generalization. For example, the generalization underlying item "c" is something like, "Mechanics who inspect master brake cylinders are likely to tell car owners that they did so." The generalization supporting item "d" is something like, "Mechanics who are paid according to the number of cars they repair are likely not to inspect cars thoroughly for latent problems.''[21] Try formulating generalizations for items ''a'' and ''b'' on your own.

2. *Chronology: Before, During and After*

As you know, events that culminate in litigation typically take place over a period of hours, days, months and even years. An alleged contract may follow lengthy negotiations; a traffic accident may follow a driver's attending a round of parties and engaging in social drinking; prolonged bitterness between a testator and a child may culminate in a will disinheriting the child. However, legal elements, and therefore factual propositions, nearly always bless particular moments in time with substantive importance.[22] For example, a factual proposition asserting that a party breached a contract typically focuses on the specific moment in time that the breach occurred. Similarly, a factual proposition asserting a testator's incompetence to make a will focuses on the testator's state of mind at the moment the will was signed. In a legal contest, then, the parties battle over whose version of substantively critical events is accurate.

However, events that occur ''before'' and ''after'' the substantively critical ones often determine which party's version of substantively critical events is believed. For example, a testator's behavior in the months preceding and following the signing of a will may well be determinative on the issue of testamentary capacity. From a party's conduct before, during and after a long course of negotiations, a trier of fact is likely to infer whether or not the party agreed to enter into a contract. Evidence that a defendant has a lengthy drug habit and left town the day after a robbery may produce an inference that the defendant committed a crime. Thus, circumstantial evidence describing what happened before and after, as well as during, substantively critical moments in time often determines the outcomes of disputes.

Historical reconstruction encourages you to identify events that may have occurred before and after the substantively critical ones. The usual question is, ''If a factual proposition is true, what events are likely to have preceded or followed the substantively critical ones?'' For example, assume that a factual proposition you are trying to prove is, ''Testator P.J. Giddy was competent to make a will in that at the time he signed his will Giddy knew his children's names, ages and occupations.'' Potential ''before'' and ''after'' evidence suggesting that this proposition is true includes evidence that Giddy sent his children birthday and anniversary cards, telephoned them, and made statements to others about them both before and after the execution of the will.

Expanding the temporal scope of an interview through historical reconstruction typically expands the spectrum of potential sources of

---

21. We do not address the tactical question of whether you should, at trial, explicitly identify underlying generalizations for judge or juror.

22. See Chapter 8.

information. One goal of developing potential evidence is to learn of other people (or documents) that might either support your clients' accounts or provide evidence of which your clients are unaware. But often, the only people who can describe what occurred at a moment of substantive importance are the interested parties themselves. For instance, assume that a plaintiff investor seeks to establish that a defendant company knew that its prospectus was false when issued. In that situation, only the company officials who prepared the prospectus may know what knowledge they had concerning the statements in the prospectus. Likewise, no one other than the drivers may claim to know how an accident occurred; and only a lawyer and a couple of strangers who acted as witnesses may have been present when a will was signed. By identifying potential prior and subsequent events you typically uncover potential sources of evidence other than the parties themselves.

3. *Multiple Perspectives*

When using historical reconstruction, you may try to re-create events from the perspectives of the different actors who might have had roles in those events. Sometimes you will find that viewing events from the perspectives of different individuals leads you to think of potential evidence you might have overlooked had you been considering only one point of view. For example, return to the factual proposition, "Goodstone failed to check the master brake cylinder when it repaired the brakes on Wilson's car." The prior subsection briefly identified potential evidence that might support this proposition primarily from the standpoint of actions in which the mechanic might have engaged.

But further perspectives are possible. You might, for instance, think about how Wilson was likely to have behaved during the incident. Is Wilson generally experienced with cars? How do people who do have some expertise with brake repair describe a braking problem to a mechanic or service manager? How about someone without such expertise? Consider also the possible role of a Goodstone service manager. What does experience suggest about the potential behavior of service managers of automobile repair shops? Why might such a manager pressure employees to complete a high daily volume of brake jobs? For example, might a manager's job be on the line, or might there be competition among various Goodstone repair shops? If so, what kind of memoranda might indicate such pressure existed? Note that the store manager perspective produces not only new items of potential evidence but also another potential source of information (i.e., documents). Finally, think about the records of the parts department. What helpful information might you find there?

D. STRENGTHENING GENERALIZATIONS

Unlike historical reconstruction, identifying topics likely to lead to helpful evidence by using the approach of "strengthening generalizations" involves the explicit formulation of generalizations. Was any approach ever more aptly named?

To use this second technique, begin again with an assumption that a factual proposition is correct. Next, convert that proposition to a generalization. Lastly, identify topics by adding either "especially when" or "except when" to a generalization. "Especially whens" tend to add to a proposition's strength whereas "except whens" tend to detract from a proposition's strength. Thus, during theory development questioning you hope that clients can confirm "especially whens" and negate the occurrence of "except whens."

For example, assume that a factual proposition suggesting Goodstone's breach of the duty of reasonable care is that "Goodstone installed the wrong brake discs when it repaired the brakes in Wilson's car." Converting this factual proposition to a generalization produces an assertion such as, "Car mechanics sometimes install the wrong brake discs in a car." This generalization may be "especially true" when

- the mechanic is in a hurry;
- the brake discs that fit one model of car are quite similar to those that fit another;
- the mechanic is inexperienced;
- the mechanic is not closely supervised; or
- the mechanic is under the influence of alcohol or drugs.

On the other hand, the generalization may be true "except when"

- the mechanic is an expert in brake repair;
- the car is owned by an important customer;
- the brake discs come in a clearly marked package; or
- the brake discs had to be specially ordered.

As you can see, "except whens" may be simply the converse of "especially whens." For instance, the mechanic's lack of experience makes it more likely that the mechanic would have installed the wrong brake discs; the mechanic's having expertise makes it more likely that the mechanic would have installed the correct ones. However, you may well identify potential evidence in the context of one thought mode that you would not have identified in the other. For instance, only in the "except when" context did the authors identify the "important customer" item; the authors did not identify "when the customer is unknown to the mechanic" in the "especially when" context. Hence, you may want to think through generalizations with both perspectives in mind.

6. THEORY DEVELOPMENT QUESTIONING TECHNIQUES

This section explores effective theory development questioning techniques. In other words, once you have some idea of the helpful evidence that you hope to uncover, the techniques discussed and illustrated below can help you search for it efficiently and thoroughly. The sections below emphasize how you may use these techniques to uncover helpful evidence.

A. DIRECT INQUIRIES

As in any other interviewing situation, social or professional, the most common way of uncovering information is simply to use a direct inquiry seeking that information. For example, if you want to know whether a new social acquaintance enjoys the game of tennis, you might ask, "Do you like to play tennis?" Similarly, in legal interviews you might ask questions such as:

> "Did you bring with you the letter that Marquis Jackson wrote to you?"

> "Who, in addition to all the king's horses and all the king's men, were at the scene of the accident?"

> "Why didn't you speak to your supervisor personally?"

Answers to direct inquiries such as these may provide all the information you need to gather with respect to an event or topic. If so, you may follow up with additional direct inquiries or move on to other events or topics.

B. THE T–FUNNEL QUESTIONING PATTERN

Particularly if events or topics are important, you'll typically need to seek more information than you are likely to elicit with direct inquiries. To elicit persuasive, factually-rich stories, you can go beyond direct inquiries in two ways:

- You may use open questions to press clients to search their recollections for additional information pertaining to an event or topic. Open questions may produce evidence that you might never have thought to ask about.

- Based on your legal knowledge, you may ask closed questions that identify information that clients would not have been able to recall without the memory stimulus that closed questions often provide.

The "T-funnel technique" is a pattern of information-seeking that relies both on clients' paths of association and your legal judgment to produce persuasive and factually-rich stories.[23] The T-funnel technique's premise is straightforward: Thorough information-gathering rests on a combination of open and closed questions, and efficiency suggests that you employ open questions before barraging clients with closed ones.[24] The diagram below illustrates how the T-funnel technique gets its name.

---

23. Focusing a person on an event more than once can enhance memory. *See* E. Scrivner and M.A. Safer, *Eyewitnesses Show Hyperamnesia For Details About a Violent Event,* 73 J.APPL.PSYCH. 371 (1988).

24. See Chapter 4 for a discussion of the comparative advantages and limitations of open and closed questions.

Open questions form the upper, horizontal portion of the "T;" closed questions form the vertical, lower portion.

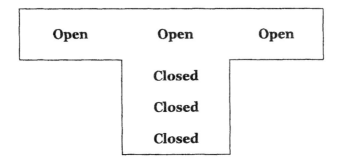

C. T-FUNNEL QUESTIONING TECHNIQUES

Time line questioning and your identification of topics likely to uncover helpful evidence typically identify a variety of events and topics that you want to explore during theory development. For example, assume that on Wilson's behalf in the Wilson/Goodstone matter, you plan to search for evidence that Goodstone's mechanic was under pressure by the manager to finish the brake job on Wilson's car quickly. Your starting point for the search may be a topic ("the mechanic was in a hurry") or an event ("Wilson brought the car in for service"). As the following sub-sections suggest, T-funnels are equally appropriate for events and topics.

1. T-funneling Events

This sub-section illustrates use of the T-funnel technique to explore an event. Assume that one event that Wilson mentioned during time line questioning was bringing his car to Goodstone and authorizing Goodstone to install new brakes. You decide to explore this event during theory development because you believe that you might uncover evidence tending to prove the factual proposition that the mechanic who worked on Wilson's car breached the duty of care by installing the wrong brakes. Potential evidence that you've identified to support this proposition are that the mechanic was inexperienced and/or in a hurry, the mechanic had an unusually large number of cars to work on that day and Goodstone didn't have the necessary parts to complete the work.

When you explore this event through the use of the T-funnel technique, the upper part of the "T" might go as follows:

1. L: Let's go back to the day that you first brought your car to Goodstone and talked to the manager and authorized the brake job. Do you recall that?

2. C: Sure.

3. L: Great. Then please tell me all you can remember about your conversation with the manager. Give me as much

detail as you can remember whether or not you think it's important.

4. C: After I told him that I wanted to replace the two rear tires, he took a look at them and said that the pattern of wear on the tires indicated that I probably needed new brakes. I didn't know anything about brakes and I asked him how much it would cost. He said it would be about $150. I'm pretty cautious when it comes to brakes so I said okay.

5. L: What else was said during this conversation?

6. C: Well, he said he thought he could finish the job before the end of the day but that he wasn't one-hundred percent certain since one of their hoists was not working.

7. L: Okay, that's helpful. What else did you talk about?

8. C: Let's see. I told him that I really needed to have the car back at the end of the day and he said he'd do his best and that he was pretty sure he'd have it for me by 6:00 o'clock.

9. L: You're giving me a good picture of what took place. What else did you and the manager discuss at that time?

10. C: I can't recall anything else.

This is a classic example of horizontal "T" funnel questioning. All questions pertaining to the event—the conversation with the manager—are open. Note that in No. 6, you learn of evidence about the hoist that you might not have thought to ask about on your own, an important benefit of open questions.

Next you move to the lower, vertical portion of the "T."

11. L: Let me ask you just a few more things about what may have taken place during your discussion with the manager. Was anything said about who would actually be working on the brakes?

12. C: No; but they had some sort of a sign that said all Goodstone mechanics were certified or something like that.

13. L: Was anything said about the experience level of the mechanic who would work on your car?

14. C: No, I don't think so.

15. L: Was anything said about parts that would used to complete the work?

16. C: No. He just said they would do a complete check of the brakes.

17. L: How about Goodstone's work load; was anything said about that?

18. C: Not directly. When the manager mentioned that the car might not be finished in one day, he did say they already had a lot of work scheduled.

19. L: Was anything mentioned about the work load of the mechanic who would be doing the brake work?

20.   C: Not that I remember.

21.   L: Did the manager say anything about their having to hurry to get your car finished?

22.   C: No.

23.   L: Did you see or hear anything that gave you the impression they would have to rush to finish your car by 6:00 o'clock?

24.   C: Well, just the fact that the manager said that they had a lot of work scheduled and might not finish gave me that impression.

25.   L: Anything else give you that impression?

26.   C: Not that I recall.

27.   L: Those are the specific questions that I have. Is there anything else that you can remember about the conversation?

28.   C: No.

As you can see, the questions in the lower portion and the upper portion of the "T" both pertain to the same event—the "conversation with the manager." However, the lower-T questions are closed; each reflects your legal judgment about what circumstantial evidence would prove the factual proposition that Goodstone installed the wrong brakes on Wilson's car. By contrast in No. 27 you revert to an open question. Before leaving an important event, you may want to afford clients one more opportunity to recall a hitherto overlooked piece of data.

Clients may initially be uncomfortable with T-funnel questioning because its pattern tends to be alien to social discourse. In social settings, most conversationalists shy away from pressing acquaintances for an abundance of details. Social conversations are not appropriate settings for carrying out interrogations that may make others feel like they are "put on the spot." You could stop a boisterous dinner party crowd dead in its tracks inside of five minutes by pressing for information in T-funnel fashion. However, by continuing to use motivational techniques during theory development, and by explaining your need for information, you can generally assuage any discomfort that clients might express or display.

2.   T-funneling Topics

Next, consider how you can use the T-funnel pattern to probe topics thoroughly. Assume that a topic you want to probe in the Wilson/Goodstone matter is the mechanic's experience. That is, apart from any particular event, you want to probe Wilson's memory for any information tending to prove that the mechanic who installed the brakes was inexperienced. In this context, T-funnel questioning might proceed as follows.

1.   L: When you were dealing with Goodstone, tell me about anything that led you to doubt the experience of the mechanic who worked on your car?

2.   C: I do remember that when I came back to Goodstone after I got out of the hospital, the front desk person I talked to looked up the name of the mechanic and mentioned something about the mechanic having been a probationary employee. But nothing was said directly about the mechanic's lack of experience.

3.   L: Other than this time, what other indications of the mechanic's inexperience did you have?

4.   C: None that I can recall.

5.   L: How about when you first brought your car in to Goodstone?

6.   C: I do remember that while I was talking to the manager, the mechanic who ended up being the one who worked on my car interrupted us a few times to ask questions about a brake job that he was doing on a different car.

7.   L: That could be helpful. How about when you picked up your car the first time, any indication at that time that the mechanic was inexperienced?

8.   C: No.

9.   L: How about when you picked up your car the second time, after you were experiencing problems with it pulling to the side. Any indication of inexperience at that time?

10.   C: No.

Here, Nos. 1 and 3 illustrate open questions in the horizontal portion of the "T." When Wilson appears to be unable to recall additional information (No. 4), you switch in Nos. 5, 7 and 9 to closed questions at the bottom portion of the "T."

The lower-T questioning above illustrates the technique of "taking a topic across a time line." That is, you ask a client to consider a topic with reference to various events that might produce information pertaining to the topic. Alternatively (or additionally), lower-T closed questions might directly seek out circumstantial evidence tending to strengthen a generalization.[25] Consider this example:

1.   L: When you were dealing with Goodstone, did anything happen that led you to doubt the experience of the mechanic who worked on your car?

2.   C: I do remember that when I came back to Goodstone after I got out of the hospital, the front desk person I talked to looked up the name of the mechanic and mentioned something about the mechanic having been a probationary employee. But nothing was said directly about the mechanic's lack of experience.

3.   L: Other than this time, what other indications of the mechanic's inexperience did you have?

25. Of course, you might have identified the evidence through the use of the strate- gies of Historical Reconstruction or Strengthening Generalizations.

4. C: None that I can recall.

5. L: Did you ever have any indication that the mechanic need-
        ed to refer to a manual in order to fix your brakes?

6. C: When I brought my car in the second time and explained
        the problem, the mechanic did ask me to wait a moment
        while he checked some kind of a book.

7. L: How about the mechanic asking others for help; did you
        ever notice the mechanic asking for help from other peo-
        ple?

8. C: No.

9. L: Did you ever notice anything indicating that the mechanic
        might have been a trainee?

10. C: No.

11. L: Can you think of anything you haven't mentioned indicat-
        ing that the mechanic was inexperienced?

12. C: No. I'm pretty sure I've mentioned everything I can re-
        member.

Here, Nos. 1 and 3 repeat the open questions seeking evidence of the
mechanic's inexperience. Again, when the client's memory appears to be
exhausted (No. 4) you switch to closed, lower-T questions (Nos. 5, 7 and
9). In this example, however, the closed questions refer not to events but
directly to potential indicia of inexperience. Finally, with No. 11 you
close this portion of the interview with an open question giving Wilson
one more chance to recall information.

3.   Using "Partial" T-funnels

The T-funnel pattern is not an "all or nothing" technique. You may
decide to probe events or topics only with open, "top of T" questioning.
One reason may be that although you want more information than
clients provide in response to direct inquiries, you don't see the need to
use closed questions to go beyond clients' paths of associations. Or, you
may simply be unable to think of useful closed questions. In such
situations, the flexibility of the T-funnel technique allows you to limit
additional probing of events or topics to open questions.

Assume for example that a client has told you that she left a
meeting early. You want to probe the client's reasons for doing so, but
don't consider the topic worth full T-funnel treatment. Partial T-funnel
questioning of this event may go as follows:

1. L: Paula, why did you leave the meeting before it ended?

2. C: I had an appointment to meet Falconi at 3:00 and I needed
        to leave the meeting at 2:30 to get over to his office on
        time.

3. L: Any other reason you can think of?

4. C: To be honest with you, it wasn't the most productive
        meeting in the world. I didn't think I'd miss anything of
        importance.

5. L: I guess a lot of meetings are like that .... Any other reason you can think of?

6. C: Nope.

7. L: OK, let's move on...

D. ADDITIONAL T-FUNNEL TECHNIQUES

The course of T-funnel questioning, like that of love, is not always smooth. Here are suggestions for handling situations you will frequently encounter.

1. "Park" Information to Avoid Becoming Sidetracked

As questions produce data, either in the upper or the lower portion of a "T," you will often be sorely tempted to ask about that new data before exhausting the initial event or topic which began the "T." If you follow that temptation, you may become sidetracked and neglect to return to the initial event. Instead, resist the temptation and "park" new data until you complete the initial "T." Parking data that emerges through T-funnel questioning is necessary if you are to explore important events and topics fully.

To understand the importance of parking new data, return to the last T-funnel of Wilson, which sought evidence of the mechanic's experience. Recall that in Nos. 5–6, the dialogue went as follows:

5. L: Did you ever have any indication that the mechanic needed to refer to a manual in order to fix your brakes?

6. C: When I brought my car in the second time and explained the problem, the mechanic did ask me to wait a moment while he checked some kind of a book.

At this point, you have not yet completed T-funneling the topic that gave rise to this piece of information, indicia of the mechanic's inexperience. Nevertheless, assume that you continue the interview as follows:

7. L: That's interesting. What do you recall about the mechanic looking at a book?

8. C: I really don't remember much. It was a large black book, in a three ring binder, I think.

9. L: Anything else you remember about the mechanic looking at a book?

10. C: Just that he looked at it for awhile. I was getting pretty frustrated.

11. L: What else can you recall?

12. C: Nothing else.

13. L: Where did he get this book?

14. C: I'm not sure. I think he walked over to the parts department and came back with it.

15. L: How long was he gone?

16. C: Maybe about five minutes.

17. L: Did he bring the book back with him?

18. C: Yes.

19. L: What happened when he came back?

20. C: He looked at the book and asked me a couple of questions about how frequently my car pulled to the left when I applied the brakes.

21. L: Tell me as much as you can about his questions.

22. C: Okay but there isn't much to tell. He asked. . . .

These questions have sidetracked you. Before pursuing all indicia of inexperience that Wilson might be able to recall, you leap at the first bit of bait, the mechanic's referring to a book. Becoming sidetracked like this has two general disadvantages:

- Once sidetracked, you may never return to the topic or event with which you started a T-funnel sequence, here, the mechanic's lack of experience.

- Even if you are careful enough to return to the original T-funnel sequence, sidetracking may so disrupt clients' paths of association that they are unable to recall what they might have remembered in the absence of sidetracking.

Better to "park" new items until completing your intended "T." Then you may if you choose probe parked items with additional T-funnel sequences.

Clients may be disappointed when you park evidence that you have persistently prodded them to recall. Not realizing that you are only parking the evidence temporarily, clients may think it will get lost in a tow-away zone. Hence, when you park evidence you might want to recognize a client's effort and explain that you will return to it. For instance, in lieu of becoming sidetracked in No. 7 above, you might have parked the topic with a statement such as the following:

7.   L: Great. That could be helpful and I'll come back to it in a moment. But for now, let me ask you about any other indications that the mechanic was inexperienced. How about the mechanic asking others for help; did you ever notice the mechanic asking for help from other people?

2. Use T–funnels Cyclically as You Unpark Data

The T–funnel technique is one that you can use to explore any event or topic thoroughly. Thus, when seeking to learn more about items of evidence that you have temporarily parked, you may use T-funnel sequences to probe each. That is, begin exploration with open questions and follow up with closed questions.

Assume for example that instead of becoming sidetracked you parked Wilson's answer in No. 6 above:

6. C: When I brought my car in the second time and explained
        the problem, the mechanic did ask me to wait a moment
        while he checked some kind of a book.

Having completing your intended "T" with regard to "indicia of
inexperience," you now want to explore the mechanic's checking of the
book. The T-funnel for this event may go something like this:

(Upper portion of T, questions only):

L: Now, you mentioned that when you first brought your car back
    to Goodstone and talked to the mechanic, he looked through a
    book. Please tell me everything you remember about this.

L: That's very helpful. Anything else you recall?

* * *

(Lower portion of T, questions only):

L: Where did he get the book?

L: What did the book look like?

L: Did he show you the book?

L: Did he appear to read the book?

L: What if anything did he say about the book?

L: Did he say why he was referring to the book?

L: How long did he look at the book?

* * *

In turn, any topic Wilson mentions in the course of *this* T-funnel
sequence can become the subject of yet *another* T. For example, if Wilson
mentions that, "The book showed two different brake systems for my
car's model and year," you may later start a new T-funnel by asking,
"Tell me all you can remember about the fact that there were two
different brake systems for your car."

Like the images you see when you look in mirrors that face each
other, T-funnel questioning can in theory extend to infinity. Rest assured that in practice this is not so. You need continue questioning only
as long as your legal judgment suggests that the helpful evidence you
search for is important, and a client's memory holds out.

3. *"Kick Start" Clients' Memories through Visualization*

Since open questions typically do little to stimulate clients' recollections, you may want to try to give clients' memories an energy boost
before abandoning open questions and turning to closed ones. Visualization is one method for doing so.

For example, assume that a portion of your interview of Wilson goes
as follows:

1. L: When you got out of the hospital and went back to Goodstone to talk with the mechanic, with whom did you talk?

2. C: A service representative. I don't know his name.

3. L: Tell me everything you can remember about that conversation.

4. C: I don't remember much. I had him look up who worked on my car and when he told me, I asked to talk with that guy. The manager said he wasn't there any more and that he had only been a probationary employee. That was it.

5. L: What else can you remember?

6. C: Nothing else really.

Especially if in your heart of hearts you are a big fan of closed questions, you might pounce on Wilson's lack of recollection the way a vulture may pounce on a just-deceased field mouse, and begin firing closed questions. However, open questions carry benefits that are too valuable to toss away at the first sign of client hesitancy. You can often stimulates clients' memories by asking them to visually re-create in their own minds the settings in which events took place. The re-created scene is most effective if the client can recall the external environment and their own feelings and reactions. Thus, especially if an event is important, you may be able to stimulate a clients' recollections by asking them to form visual images of scenes.

For example, after Wilson's response in No. 6 above you may proceed as follows:

7. L: Perhaps it will help if you take a moment and try to picture the situation in your mind. Think about where the conversation took place.

8. C: It was back in his little cubby where all the service advisors have their individual computers.

9. L: Can you visualize that cubby?

10. C: Sort of.

11. L: Tell me what it looks like.

12. C: It's barely large enough for a desk; there's a door and a glass window looking out on the service area.

13. L: Were you sitting or standing?

14. C: We were both seated; he faced the service area and my back was to it.

15. L: What do you recall about the service advisor?

16. C: She was a rather short woman with dark hair; she was quite friendly. She was easy to talk to.

17. L: All right, if you can see yourself in the room talking to the service advisor, does that help you remember anything else that you talked about?

18. C: . . .

If the "visualization" route doesn't work, you may then resort to closed questions. Even so, you need not completely abandon open questions. A positive response to a closed question may itself jog a client's memory. Thus, if a client's manner suggests that a closed question has re-awakened the client's memory, you may return to open questions and stay with them until the client can recall no more. At that point you may if necessary ask additional closed questions.

4. Press Clients to Search Their Memories

At some point in the series of open questions that constitute the horizontal portion of T-funnels, clients become unable to recall additional evidence. Especially if clients have been able to respond to a number of open questions, you may be inclined to take the first "that's all I can remember" as a signal that to have any hope of uncovering additional evidence you'll have to move to closed questions.

However, the signal may be premature. You may suspect that with additional effort, clients can provide additional information in response to open questions. Thus, rather than retreat to closed questions at once, you might press clients to search their memories further. Consider the following message:

> L: I appreciate how much you've told me about that conversation with the service advisor. Frankly, what occurred during that conversation may be critically important. Keep trying to visualize the conversation, and see if you can recall anything else.

Such a statement may mark the point at which both you as well as clients become uncomfortable with T-funnels, as you press for information in a way that is well beyond what normally occurs during polite social conversations. However, the statement does have the advantage of keeping you in the upper portion of the "T," and in various ways attempts to motivate clients to continue to search their memories. For example, the statement indicates that you expect clients to recall additional evidence, praises them and stresses the significance of the data. Also, it reminds clients to visualize the scene of a conversation.

Clients may respond by becoming frustrated ("I've told you already, that's all I can remember.") or by providing additional evidence ("Come to think of it, there was one more thing . . ."). You certainly need not try to push every client to the point of absolute zero recall. Indeed, if you push too far, clients may provide false information in an effort to meet your expectation that they know more than they have so far revealed. At the end of the day how far to press clients is a matter for your judgment. This section simply reminds you that in the exercise of judgment, you need not accept automatically clients' first pleas of lack of recall.[26]

---

26. Cultural differences can affect what people observe and recollect. *See* RICHARD E. NISBETT, THE GEOGRAPHY OF THOUGHT-HOW ASIANS AND WESTERNERS THINK DIFFERENTLY . . .

5. *Summarize Clients' Responses*

Summarizing clients' previous responses may further aid your attempt to press them to recall further information. Remember that reflecting content is an active listening technique that tends to motivate clients to go on, because the reflection indicates that you have heard and attended to what has been said. Thus, you might have phrased the above message to Wilson as follows:

> L: I appreciate how much you've told me about your conversation with the service representative when you first took your car to Goodstone. Frankly, what occurred during that conversation may be extremely important. So far you've told me that she looked at the two rear tires and indicated that the wear on the tires indicated you probably needed new brakes. She also told you the brake work would probably cost about $150 but that she wasn't one-hundred percent certain the work could be done before the end of the day because one of their hoists was not working and they were waiting for some parts to come in. That is a lot of helpful information. But if you think hard perhaps you can recall some additional matters. Keep trying to visualize your conversation with the representative and see if you can recall anything else.

6. *Use Judgment*

The T-funnel technique is not as rigid in application as it might appear to be on paper. The scope and extent of T-funnel questioning rest on your judgment in individual cases. For example, no T-funnel "rules" exist that can tell you whether to probe one event before another or how extensively to press clients for answers to open questions. T-funnels are a useful method of combining clients' awareness of topics and historical events with your analyses of factual propositions to generate stories that are detailed and persuasive, but they cannot dictate the course of every interview.

That said, do not underestimate the value of the T-funnel technique. Failure to use it effectively, perhaps by switching in midstream to a new event and/or topic and neglecting to return to the original one, is often responsible for the most infamous of all lawyer-client colloquies:

> L: Why didn't you tell me that before you got on the stand?

> C: Because you never asked me.

7. *The Ethics of T-funnel Questioning*

This section considers the ethical propriety of the T-funnel method, in particular the use of closed questions to seek helpful information. To

And Why (2003). THUS, PRESSING CLIENTS FOR FURTHER RECALL MAY HELP THEM RECALL INFOR- MATION THAT CULTURAL EXPERIENCE HAS PREDIS- POSED THEM NOT TO FOCUS ON OR TALK ABOUT.

understand the type of situation that might give rise to ethical concerns, assume that you represent Roberta, a personal injury plaintiff who has revealed to you that she was late for a meeting at the time the accident that is the subject of the lawsuit took place. When you used open, "top of the T" questions to find out whether she could explain why running late didn't affect her driving, Roberta was unable to provide a reasonable explanation. Thereafter, assume that the conversation continues as follows:

1.   L: Roberta, did your being late for this important meeting cause you to drive too fast or not focus on your driving or anything like that?

2.   C: No.

3.   L: That's good to hear, but of course it would help if we can explain why it didn't affect how you drove. Anything you can point to?

4.   C: Not really. I just know it didn't.

5.   L: I realize it's a while ago, but it may be important for us to be able to explain why you were able to drive carefully even though you were running late for an important meeting. If you can put yourself back in the situation, maybe you can remember what was going on?

6.   C: I've tried, but there's just nothing specific that I can think of.

At this point, further open questions would not appear to be productive. Can you then ethically move to the lower portion of the T, using closed questions that constitute possible explanations? For example, might you continue questioning Roberta as follows:

7.   L: Then let me ask you this, Roberta. Did you have your cell phone with you in the car?

8.   C: Yes, I always carry it.

9.   L: Then is it possible that you used the cell phone while you were driving to phone ahead?

10.   C: Of course. I can be such a blockhead, so thanks for reminding me. That's exactly what I did.

11.   L: I'm glad you remembered. Can you tell me about the phone call?

12.   C: Sure. I told them that I was running a bit late. . . .

What is your reaction to No. 9? Do you consider it to be a legitimate effort to uncover information that Roberta may have forgotten, or a thinly-veiled effort to prompt her to invent helpful evidence that she client does not actually recall?

Generally speaking, questions such as No. 9 above are not only valid, but necessary if you are to represent clients in a competent manner.[27] Specific inquiries are memory prompts that often are necessary to enable honest people to recall past events.[28] Had you opted not to ask about a possible cell phone call, you may have missed important factual information.

Nevertheless, some cautions are in order. Clearly, you cannot convert closed questions into leading ones that instruct clients how to answer. For example, No. 9 would constitute an unethical effort to create false testimony had you stated it in this form:

> 9. L: Then we could say that you used your cell phone to phone ahead and you told them that you were running late. That would explain why you continued to drive carefully. Does this make sense to you?[29]

Similarly, you must be alert to indications that clients are making up false testimony rather than honestly recalling what happened. For example, assume that a portion of the dialogue above had gone as follows:

> 9.   L: Then is it possible that you used the cell phone while you were driving to phone ahead?
>
> 10. C: Of course, that's what we can say. Since I carry a cell phone, I'll just say that I phoned ahead and told them that I was running late.

The client's response here plainly suggests that she has used your question as a chance to create false testimony. As a result, you may want to caution her against inventing evidence, and then ask her whether she wants to qualify her previous answer.

E.   BREAK GENERAL DESCRIPTIONS INTO SUB–EVENTS

Clients may provide helpful evidence in the form of verbal shorthand that attaches a conclusory label to what in reality are complex or multiple events. For example, helpful evidence may consist of a

---

27. *See* MODEL RULES OF PROF'L CONDUCT R. 1.1, 1.3; CALIF. RULES OF PROF'L CONDUCT R. 3–110 (Failing to Act Competently).

28. See Chapter 4.

29. For a further discussion of questioning clients at the risk of encouraging or condoning perjury *see* MONROE H. FREEDMAN, LAWYERS' ETHICS IN AN ADVERSARY SYSTEM 59–75 (1975); MONROE H. FREEDMAN & ABBE SMITH, UNDERSTANDING LAWYERS' ETHICS 206–09 (2d ed. 2002). The discussion in these works focuses on the propriety of a lawyer explaining the law to a client as a prelude to asking the clients for facts. A T-funnel inquiry often will not be preceded by an explanation of the facts. But is the likelihood of encouraging perjury really any less

than it would be were a lawyer to explain the law before asking for the facts? Assume you first use open questions to ask Mr. Wilson about indications that the mechanic who repaired his brakes was inexperienced and that Mr. Wilson can recall virtually no such indications. You then follow-up with closed questions to Mr. Wilson such as, "Did you get any indication that the mechanic needed to look at a book or manual to do the work?" or "Did you get any indication that the mechanic needed the advise or help of others to do the work?" Wouldn't Mr. Wilson, like most clients, understand that "yes" answers to these questions with appropriate elaboration would help his case?

"clumped event" that incorporates a variety of sub-events. For instance, a client may say that "We hammered out the Acceleron deal during the August 31 meeting" rather than give a full description of what took place during the meeting. Alternatively, helpful evidence might consist of a "behavior or condition over time," a brief description that applies to numerous events. For instance, a client may say that "My back has hurt ever since the accident" rather than attempt the impossible task of referring to each event during which the client experienced back pain.

These forms of verbal shorthand are a quite natural and useful method of human communication. However, one way to elicit details that enhance the persuasiveness of helpful evidence, is to ask clients to elaborate on verbal shorthand by describing important events giving rise to the conclusory labels. Having identified underlying events, you may use T-funnel questioning to elicit additional helpful evidence.

On some level of course, any boundaries separating an event from a "sub-event" are somewhat artificial. For example, an event underlying the label, "My back hurt all the time," may include the event that "My back was hurting during the company picnic." However, you may subdivide the "company picnic" event even further. For example, you might elicit evidence that at the company picnic, the client's back hurt "during the softball game" and "during the three-legged race." The process of creating sub-events might in theory continue indefinitely. In practice, however, you need not try to reduce all events to their smallest constituent parts. What you hope to accomplish is to obtain facts that are *persuasive*. If you want to persuade a legal audience faced with conflicting accounts about the severity of a client's back pain, the unadorned statement that "my back hurt" will seldom work. A rich description of where, when, and how the client experienced back pain, by contrast, is more likely to be convincing.

1. Techniques for Probing Clumped Events

A clumped event is a series of events cloaked as a single occurrence. For example, assume that you represent The Dolinko Group, an advertising agency, in a breach of contract action against Aranella Corp. Dolinko contends that Aranella agreed to hire Dolinko to conduct an advertising campaign for Aranella's new "Instant Sushi" freeze-dried product. During time line questioning, Feris, a Dolinko Vice–President, tells you, "We made our presentation at a meeting on July 7," and goes on to describe a number of follow-up phone calls to Aranella's general manager. Just what took place during the July 7 meeting may provide important evidence tending to show that the parties ultimately entered into a contract. But since the meeting was lengthy, and undoubtedly consisted of sub-events (e.g., presentation of printed matter, video showing of sample television spot, discussion of costs and fees), you may choose to begin by extracting the sub-events from the clumped "meeting" description before turning to T-funnel questioning.

One basic technique for breaking apart helpful clumped events is the familiar one of eliciting a time line. Just as you ask clients to "start at the beginning" and use open questions to obtain a time line, so too can you elicit a "mini-time line" of a clumped event.

For example, to parse the "advertising presentation" clumped event, you may proceed as follows (questions only):

1. "Think back to the start of the meeting, and try to go step by step and tell me everything you can recall happening."

2. "After you described what campaigns the agency had done previously, what happened next?"

3. "Between the time you discussed costs for the TV ads and before you passed the drawings around, what else happened?"

The mini-time line questioning may uncover sub-events such as "description of previous campaigns," "discussion of costs for TV ads," and "passed drawings around." You may then T-funnel those sub-events that appear likely to lead to helpful evidence.

Of course, clients may be unable to recall the order in which the occurrences comprising a helpful clumped event occurred. For example, a client may say something like, "That meeting happened over two years ago; I really don't remember the order in which things went down." If you are confronted with a response such as this, you may turn to the T-funnel technique to uncover sub-events without regard to their chronology. Your questioning may go something like this:

1. L: I can understand that it's difficult for you to go through what happened during that meeting chronologically. So let's go at it this way. Just tell me as much as you can remember. Don't worry about whether it seems important or trying to put things in any particular order.

2. C: (The client provides a few details.).

3. L: What else happened

4. C: (The client provides a few more details.)

5. L: That's helpful, what else occurred?

6. C: That's all I can remember.

7. L: Did your team and Aranella's representatives talk about the length of the agreement?

8. C: Let's see. I don't think we got into that.

9. L: How about the media through which you would carry out the campaign. Did this subject come up?

10. C: I think we did talk about that a little bit.

11. L: OK, we'll probably come back to that. But one other possibility I can think of that might have been discussed involves a time line for preparing and approving the campaign. Did this topic come up during that meeting?

12. C: Yes, I'm pretty sure it did.

13.   L: Fine. Before we go into some of the things you've mentioned, anything else you can recall being discussed that hasn't come out yet?

14.   C: No.

15.   L: OK, then let's go back to . . .

After the client indicates that she can recall nothing else in response to open questions (No. 6), you use closed questions (Nos. 7, 9, 11) to seek out other topics that may have been discussed. As suggested earlier, you follow the closed questions with an open one that provides a client with another chance to mention a topic that you hadn't thought of (No. 15). With various "sub-events" on the table, you can T-funnel those that you think are likely to lead to additional helpful evidence.

2. Techniques for Probing Conditions and Behaviors over Time

"Conditions and behaviors over time" are another method of talking about a number of discrete events as though they were a single event. For example, clients who say things like, "My back hurt for six months" or "The architectural committee never paid attention to what the neighbors wanted," lump together many discrete happenings into an overall assertion. In other words:

- "My back hurt for six months" consists of chronologically severable occasions when the client experienced back pain.

- "The architectural committee never paid attention to what the neighbors wanted" consists of chronologically severable occasions when the committee ignored neighbors' wishes.

If you can pull helpful concrete events out from this type of verbal shorthand, you then can decide which if any of those events merit T-funnel probing.

Of course, rarely is it possible or desirable to try to identify every moment when a client's back hurt or every architectural committee action that ignored neighbors' wishes. However, identifying even a few sub-events can strengthen clients' stories and help you to uncover additional helpful evidence. To search for sub-events, you might start off with a general question such as, "Can you remember any specific instances when you experienced back pain (or the architectural committee ignored the neighbors)?" Clients may want to beg off the search for concrete events by making statements like, "It was just so often, I can't distinguish one time from another." To press clients to work a bit harder, you might respond with questions such as:

- "Can you remember the first time that you were aware of your back hurting (or the architectural committee ignoring the neighbors)?"

- "Can you remember an occasion when your back pain was at its worst (or the architectural committee's actions most upset the neighbors)?"

Questions such as these can be helpful because they focus clients on periods of time that are most likely to differentiate particular events from an array of largely fungible ones. Thus, the client who initially begged off recalling concrete instances of back pain may say something like, "Now that you mention it, the one time that really sticks out in my memory is the softball game at the company picnic..." In turn, recall of one concrete event may release recollection of others.

A "reverse" technique may also help you uncover events hidden in "conditions and behaviors over time." Instead of asking clients to identify the discrete events that lead to conclusory descriptions, remind clients of events that they've already mentioned and ask whether a condition or behavior arose during those events. For instance, assume that three events in a client's time line are "renting a car," "talking to a witness to the accident on the telephone" and "talking to an insurance claims adjuster." You might remind the client of those events and ask whether the client recalls back pain in connection with any of them.

F. PROBE CONCLUSIONS FOR DETAILS

In everyday conversation, most of us tend to describe events in rather conclusory fashion. For example, we say things like, "The movie was really funny" or "The meeting was really too short to be very productive." At least we talk like that unless we recognize that listeners want us to elaborate, because we realize that habitually launching into detailed descriptions of our experiences will make us very boring indeed.

Clients generally bring social habits such as "the fear of elaboration" with them into legal interviews. But what is acceptable and even desirable in everyday social life tends to hide helpful evidence in dispute situations. Be on the alert for conclusory descriptions and if they relate to important helpful topics, press clients for details. Not only will you often uncover helpful evidence, but also you'll avoid the "filling" problem that can result in a client trying to tell one story and your hearing a different one. "Filling" occurs when you imbue a conclusory description with meanings drawn from your own experiences. To the extent that your experiences differ from those of your clients, you may fail to understand their stories. For example, a client may refer to her adversary as having "agreed" to handle a matter in a particular way during a particular meeting and the client's statement that the adversary "agreed" may strike you as quite helpful. However, the client's understanding of what constitutes words of agreement may differ from yours. If you "fill in" with your understanding, you may fail to ask the client for details relating to what was actually said during the meeting and inadvertently put together a story that fails to reflect what actually happened.

To probe conclusory descriptions, simply ask clients to relate the bases for their conclusions. For example, after a client states, "She agreed that I would handle the Attenborough account," you might ask, "Tell me everything she said that leads you to think that she agreed to your handling the Attenborough account."[30] Or assume that a client indicates that an adversary became very angry and hostile. You might ask, "Tell me everything that happened that indicated she was angry and hostile."

G. PROBE GAPS TO UNCOVER ADDITIONAL EVENTS

As you may recall, a common time line questioning task is to elicit stories that include a chronological account of important events.[31] However, the reality is that time line stories frequently contain gaps. One reason is that clients may not recall events until their memories are stimulated by your more focused theory development questioning. Another is that clients may consciously postpone mentioning events that they consider harmful or embarrassing. Whatever the cause of gaps, however, theory development is a second opportunity to uncover events that clients have not previously mentioned. If you do uncover additional events, you may then decide whether to probe them using the T-funnel method.

Of course, your goal is not simply to put together as complete a story as possible. Rather, the primary purpose of searching for additional events is to uncover helpful evidence. Thus, your search is directed by your legal theories. That is, you try to uncover additional events whose occurrence would further your legal theories. For example, assume that you represent a financial analyst who has been sued for improperly appraising the fair market value of an unsecured promissory note. Thus far, your client has neglected to say anything about contacting independent promissory note brokers and asking them what they would insist on as a discount for purchasing the note. Since having made such contacts would constitute helpful evidence, you might ask whether your client did so.

Effective techniques for searching for possibly omitted events include the following:

- Call previously-disclosed events to clients' attention, and ask if anything happened before or after them. Example: "Can you recall anything else happening after you sent out the dismissal notice?"

- Use the "bookend" technique, reminding clients of events that they have already mentioned and asking if anything took place during the intervening period. Example: "Between the time you

---

30. Clients might perceive questions such as this as challenging their veracity. If you are concerned that a client might have such a reaction, you might want to provide a preparatory explanation explaining the purpose of your inquiry. For a discussion of preparatory explanations, see Chapter 5.

31. See Chapter 6.

sent out the dismissal notice and Ms. Webb came into your office, did anything else happen?''

• Ask about events that are necessary to claims' success. Example: ''Did you file a 'Notice of Claim' in the city clerk's office within 180 days of the accident?'' (Assume that filing such a notice is required before the city can be sued.)

• Ask about ''Normal Course'' events. When describing past happenings, clients may omit mention of routine, repetitive events. Most of us live in worlds dominated by normal course events, such as always getting caught by the same red light on the way to work and routinely checking electronic mail messages when beginning the work day. And, if asked what we do on the way to work or how we spend our work day, we are apt not to mention such events. Often, of course, you are no more interested in hearing about routine events than clients are in mentioning them. However, if the happening of a ''normal course'' event would be helpful evidence, you may try to uncover it. Example: ''Sara, did you do anything after you got into the car and before you started the engine?''

• Ask about events that you have learned about from sources other than clients. Example: ''After our last meeting I talked to Jim Smith, who told me that the company carries out annual employee evaluations. Do you recall talking to Varat about an evaluation of Zolt?''[32]

7. BOLSTERING CREDIBILITY

With helpful evidence in hand, a second frequent theory development questioning task is to pursue evidence bolstering clients' credibility. The need for such information is obvious. In dispute situations, parties often put forward dramatically different accounts of past events. Therefore, evidence bolstering your clients' accounts of those events is often crucial. This section describes common credibility-related topics and suggests questioning techniques for pursuing those topics.

Lawyers often talk about credibility evidence as though it were a unique type of animal. In reality, credibility evidence is simply a form of circumstantial evidence that bears on believability. For instance, the fact that a client has a legitimate reason to recall what took place during a meeting tends to bolster the credibility of the client's account of what took place during the meeting. The reason is that most of us accept the underlying generalization that ''People who have a reason to recall what took place during an event usually accurately report what they say that they observed.'' As with all circumstantial evidence, the probative value

---

32. You may be tempted to conceal your knowledge of an event, perhaps as a test of a client's truthfulness or memory ability. However, this tactic may easily backfire. A client's failure to mention an event that you think took place may only mean that your own knowledge is faulty. On the other hand, you may at least want to delay inquiring about an omitted event that a client may find threatening or embarrassing.

of generalizations such as these is rooted in everyday experience. Thus, if "reason to recall" tends to support clients' credibility, it is because all of us relate and listen to stories regularly and tend to equate accuracy with motivation to recall. Everyday experience also places limits on that tendency; suspect reasons for recall may suggest mendacity.[33]

The subsections below describe common factors that in everyday experience tend to enhance the believability of helpful information. These factors are the results of the same strategies that you can use to identify topics likely to lead to helpful evidence, Historical Reconstruction and Strengthening Generalizations.[34] However, credibility factors remain largely constant from one case to another. For example, no matter what the nature of a factual dispute, clients' ability to recall a reasonable amount of details surrounding an event is likely to bolster their credibility with respect to that event. Thus, you generally need not engage explicitly in Historical Reconstruction or Strengthening Generalizations to identify credibility-related topics. Instead, the list of factors below comprise the topics that are likely to enable you to explore credibility sufficiently in all cases. Again, embarking on theory development questioning with the knowledge of the factors that you intend to pursue is likely to enhance the effectiveness and thoroughness of your questioning.

A. CREDIBILITY ENHANCERS

Each of the factors below constitutes a topic that you might pursue during theory development questioning to test and strengthen the credibility of helpful information that clients provide. Included for each factor is a sample set of T-funnel questions that you might use to search for evidence relating to that factor.[35]

1. Ability to Perceive

"Ability to perceive" is a general factor that tends to buttress an argument that a client's helpful statement is accurate. A T-funnel that you might use to establish that your client was in a good position to observe might go like this:

33. Like all other generalizations, you may strengthen those relating to credibility with "especially whens" and undermine them with "except whens." See Sec. 5, *supra*. For example, "people who remember events accurately often have reasons to recall those events, especially when those reasons exist prior to the time the events take place." To strengthen a client's credibility, you thus try to uncover evidence of "especially whens" such as these.

34. In other words, just as when you search for helpful evidence, searches for credibility evidence implicitly begin with a factual proposition along the lines of, "My client is accurately and honestly describing what occurred." You then may ask yourself, "If this proposition is true, what else also would probably have occurred?" The answers are the credibility-related topics set forth in the text. In other words, "An accurate client would have had a good ability to observe," etc. For further discussion of factual propositions, see Sec. 3, *supra*.

35. For an extensive analysis of factors that tend to detract from the accuracy of perception and memory, *see* ELIZABETH LOFTUS AND JAMES M. DOYLE, EYEWITNESS TESTIMONY: CIVIL AND CRIMINAL (3rd ed., 1997).

Upper-T questions

"How were you able to see (hear) what happened?"

"Anything else that enabled you to see (hear) what happened?"

Lower-T questions

"How far away were you when you saw (heard) that?"

"Was anything interfering with your seeing (hearing) that?"

"Were you feeling well when you saw (heard) that?"

"When you saw (heard) that were you having any problem with your vision (hearing)?"

2. *Reasons to Recall*

People typically have difficulty recalling events that happened weeks or months earlier. The same is true for events that occur routinely. For example, people may not recall the details of a meeting that took place months earlier or was one of many similar meetings. Hence, when clients provide information about the details of "fungible" or "ancient"[36] events, you may try to develop evidence of the accuracy of their recollections with T-funnels such as the following:

Fungible Occurrences

Upper-T questions

"Since this meeting was one of several that addressed the same subject, how are you able to recall that it was at this particular meeting that Jones said that?"

"Any other reason that you remember that it was at this meeting that Jones said that?"

Lower-T questions

"Were you surprised that Jones said that?"

"Was it out of character for Jones to say that?"

"Had Jones ever said anything like that before?"

"Ancient" Occurrences

Upper-T questions

"How are you able to recall that you saw this document before Ms. Howard was hired, since she has been with the company for over three years?"

"Any other reason you remember seeing the document before she was hired?"

---

36. "Ancient" is of course a term of art in this context, simply referring to events that happened sufficiently long ago to raise possible concerns about clients' ability to recall them.

Lower-T questions

> "Was there anything in particular in the document that caught your attention?"

> "Had you ever seen a similar document before that time?"

> "Were you surprised when you saw the document?"

3. Ability to Provide Surrounding Details

Everyday experience suggests that people who have participated in or witnessed occurrences will be able to recall a reasonable number of surrounding details.[37] Thus, you can bolster the believability of clients' accounts of past events by asking them to provide a reasonable amount of surrounding details concerning those events. A sample T-funnel sequence seeking to elicit such details may go as follows:

Upper-T questions

> "Please tell me as much as you can recall about what was said by each of you during this telephone call."

> "Anything else you can remember about the phone call?"

Lower-T questions

> "Approximately what time during the afternoon did the call take place?"

> "Did you call him or did he call you?"

> "Were you speaking on a cell phone or on a land line?"

> "Was anyone in your office when you called?"

> "As far as you could tell, was anyone listening in on the other end of the conversation?"

4. Consistent Actions

Believable stories typically "hang together," meaning that they are consistent from beginning to end. Thus, when clients report what they have done, seen or heard, you may ask them what they did before or afterwards. To the extent that the actions are consistent, they bolster an argument that the clients are credible. Assume for example that a client in an employment discrimination case tells you that he heard his supervisor tell a racially offensive joke and that he was very offended by it. You might then probe for consistent behavior with a T-funnel sequence such as:

---

37. Factfinders tend to believe that ability to recall detail bolsters credibility. *See, e.g.,* STEFAN KRIEGER, RICHARD K. NEUMANN, JR., KATHLEEN MCMANUS AND STEVEN JAMAR, ESSENTIAL LAWYERING SKILLS 57 (1999). Nevertheless, research tends to suggest that accurate recall of details about peripheral matters tends not to relate to accuracy about core aspects of events. See ELIZABETH LOFTUS AND JAMES DOYLE, EYEWITNESS TESTIMONY: CIVIL AND CRIMINAL 4 (3d ed., 1997).

Upper-T questions

"What did you do after you heard your supervisor tell this joke?"

"What else did you do after you heard your supervisor tell the joke?

Lower-T questions

"Did you complain to anyone about your supervisor telling this joke?"

"Did you tell anyone at the company that you heard the supervisor tell this joke?"

"Did you tell any of your friends or family about hearing the joke?"

"Did you make any record of his having told the joke?"[38]

5. *Reasons/Motive to Engage in Conduct*

People in Western cultures generally believe in "cause and effect." That is, events are not random, but explainable by circumstances, mental conditioning and the like. For example, prosecutors almost always try to offer evidence that defendants had a motive to engage in criminal conduct. Similarly, you can support the credibility of clients' stories with evidence that the clients had reasons to have done what they said they did or observed what they say they observed. A T-funnel that you might employ to uncover such information might go as follows:

Upper-T questions

"Can you explain to me why you happened to see the chicken cross the road?" (Such a question is especially likely to be useful when the location of the chicken is an important issue.)

"Any other reason that you happened to see the chicken cross the road?"

Lower-T questions

"Did you think that it was important for you to know about the chicken's whereabouts?

"Had anyone instructed you to keep track of the chicken?"

"Just before you saw the chicken cross the road, were you approached by an older, white-bearded Southern gentleman with the rank of 'Colonel' whose presence scared you?"

---

38. Ultimately you will be concerned not only with the consistency of a client's story but also with the consistency of the collective story of the client and the client's supporting witnesses. This concern emanates from the fact that factfinders often decide cases on the basis of which side presents the most credible overall story. *See* Nancy Pennington and Reid Hastie, The Story Model For Jury Decision Making, in Inside the Juror: The Psychology of Juror Decision Making at 194 et seq. (Reid Hastie ed., 1993); W. Lance Bennett and Martha Feldman, Reconstructing Reality in the Courtroom 7 (1981). *See also* Stefan H. Krieger & Richard K. Neumann Jr., Essential Lawyering Skills, at 145–154 (2d ed. 2003).

6. *Corroboration*

Information from credible sources that supports your clients' versions of events also tends to bolster credibility. A T-funnel pattern of questions seeking evidence of corroborating sources might go as follows:

Upper-T questions

"Are you aware of anything that can corroborate the fact that the meeting took place?"

"Anything else that might substantiate this?"

Lower-T questions

"Do you know of any documents that might refer to this meeting?"

"Do you know of anyone I might talk to who might be able to corroborate the fact that this meeting took place?"

7. *Neutrality/Bias*

Neutrality and its opposite, bias or interest, are familiar factors affecting credibility. As clients tend to be archetypal examples of biased and interested witnesses, you generally will be unable to show that they are neutral with respect to outcomes. However, you may be able to uncover evidence tending to prove that clients' stories are not a product of bias or interest.[39] For example, you might ask questions such as,

Upper-T questions

"Why did you write that particular letter?"

"Any other reason you might have written that letter?"

Lower-T questions

"Was it in your interest to write that letter?"

"Were you aware that writing that letter might place your job in jeopardy?"

"Would an alternative response have furthered your interests even more?"

B. EXPLORING THE CREDIBILITY OF HEARSAY EVIDENCE

As is evident from the existence of the hearsay rule,[40] the legal system generally reflects an attitude that hearsay information lacks trustworthiness. Thus, when clients pass along helpful information that they have received from third party sources, you may want to search for evidence tending to show that the information is accurate.

---

39. One factor that you may use to support an argument that a client is accurate and truthful is that the client's story incorporates harmful information (the subject of a subsequent theory development questioning task, *see* Chapter 8).

40. *See* FED. R. EVID. 801.

The factors that you can rely on to probe the credibility of hearsay information are generally the same as those described above. Of course, clients may have a limited ability to respond to credibility inquiries concerning hearsay declarants. For example, assume that a client's information consists of a hearsay declarant's account of an auto accident that the declarant supposedly witnessed. The client may have no information about whether the declarant was in a position to observe accurately what happened, or had a reason to recall the details of the accident at the time that the declarant spoke to the client. Thus, you'll have to rely on your judgment to ask questions that a client might be able to answer. T-funnel questioning seeking to enhance a hearsay declarant's credibility might go as follows:

Upper-T questions

"Why do you believe that what (the hearsay declarant) says is accurate?"

"Any other reason to believe that what (the hearsay declarant) told you is correct?"

Lower-T questions

"What do you know about (the hearsay declarant's) reliability?"

"Do you know whether (the hearsay declarant) knows either of the drivers that were involved in the accident?"

"Do you know of any source that can corroborate (the hearsay declarant's) version of the accident?"

C. PRESERVING RAPPORT

Depending on the extensiveness and tenor of credibility-related inquiries, some clients may interpret credibility inquiries as indicating distrust or skepticism on your part. If you anticipate such a reaction before theory development questioning begins or see evidence of it in clients' responses during theory development, consider using one of the following strategies:

- *Use a "third party" technique.* The third party technique suggests that the reason for a credibility probe is that a third party (your adversary, an arbitrator, a judge, a jury) may later raise the same concern. For example, assume that you ask, "Can you clarify for me how you were able to overhear the conversation from where you were?" A client may take this question as an indication of your personal distrust in the client's story. In an effort to deflect such a reaction, you might instead ask, "The other side's lawyer may argue that you couldn't overhear the conversation from where you were. If so, what might you be able to say to explain how you were able to hear what was said?"

- *Use a "preparatory explanation."* You may use a preparatory statement to advise clients in advance of theory development questioning that you are likely to ask credibility-related questions, and your reasons for doing so. For example, you may say something along these lines:

> Jean, as we go along I'll no doubt be asking you questions in order to help establish the accuracy of what you tell me. Please understand that this doesn't reflect any personal distrust on my part. But we're in a situation where our opponent may question everything we have to say, so it's important that we be prepared to convince a judge or jury if it gets that far that what we're saying is accurate. Do you have any questions about this?

Chapter 8

THEORY DEVELOPMENT QUESTIONING—UNDERMINING ADVERSARIES' LIKELY CONTENTIONS

1. INTRODUCTION

This chapter describes how you may use the questioning techniques set forth in Chapter 7 to pursue two additional common theory development tasks. These tasks consist of searching for:

- Evidence tending to rebut (diminish the impact of) harmful information that clients have disclosed; and

- Evidence tending to rebut adversaries' likely contentions.

Remember from Chapter 7 that the order in which the book addresses the topics of pursuing helpful evidence and searching for evidence undermining adversaries' contentions in no way suggests that this is an order that you should follow rigidly during theory development questioning. You will often jump back and forth among these tasks as circumstances and your judgment dictate.

2. UNCOVERING EVIDENCE TENDING TO REBUT HARMFUL DISCLOSURES

You can reasonably expect that most information that clients provide to you will support their legal claims. However, clients often make disclosures that you recognize as harmful.[1] For example, a client in an auto accident case may insist that she was driving carefully and within the speed limit, yet admit that at the time of the accident she was running late for an important meeting. Pursuing evidence that may undermine harmful disclosures is a primary theory development task because any information you uncover that tends to vitiate the impact of

---

1. Clients' disclosures can be harmful for a variety of reasons. A disclosure may be so harmful that it negates a factual proposition that you hope to establish. A disclosure might also be harmful in that it supports an adversary's factual contention, undermines a client's credibility, or bolsters an adversary's credibility.

harmful information bears on your preliminary assessments of a client's positions and helps you plan possible strategies for case investigation, settlement and trial.[2]

A useful approach for seeking information that may vitiate the impact of harmful answers is to search for explanations that tend to rebut arguments that adversaries might put forward based on the harmful answers. Assume for example that in a breach of contract case you represent a defendant who claims that "That's my signature on that piece of paper all right, but I really didn't realize what I was agreeing to." In the face of the harmful disclosure ("that's my signature"), you may seek out additional information explaining why the client did not know what he was signing. Similarly, assume that your client in a wrongful termination matter contends that she was fired without good cause, yet admits to having been late to work on a number of occasions. You may seek out information tending to rebut the employer's likely argument that her being late to work was a factor in her termination.

Typically, what you seek to explain away is the inference that an adversary is likely to argue should be drawn from a harmful disclosure.[3] For example, assume that your client Stephanie tells you that she was unaware of problems in her company's shipping department. However, she also reveals that she had previously signed an affidavit on the company's behalf asserting that she was aware of problems in the shipping department. Thus, the harmful evidence is that Stephanie has given inconsistent accounts of the same event, and you can reasonably anticipate that your adversary will use this inconsistency to argue that Stephanie's later account of events is false or mistaken. To counter this inference, you might seek to uncover credible explanations for the changed account. A T-funnel dialogue seeking explanations might go as follows:

Upper-T questions

1. L: Stephanie, you've told me that you never knew about what was going on in the shipping department. But the statement you signed for the company indicates that you realized that something was wrong in that department. If you never knew about what was going on, why did you sign that statement?

2. C: They had typed up the statement and I was afraid that if I didn't sign it they would fire me.

3. L: That's understandable. Any other reason why you signed?

4. C: They said the only way they could ever trust me again was if I signed.

---

2. This section assumes that your adversaries are likely to learn of the harmful information you seek to rebut.

3. For further discussion of explaining away harmful inferences, *see* DAVID A. BIND-

ER, ALBERT J. MOORE & PAUL BERGMAN, DEPOSITION QUESTIONING STRATEGIES AND TECHNIQUES Ch. 7 (2001).

5. L: When you say "they," are you referring to anyone in particular?

6. C: Jeff, the shift manager, said that.

7. L: That's helpful. Can you think of any other reasons that you signed the statement?

8. C: Those were two pretty good ones. I didn't feel right about it, but I signed.

Lower-T questions

9. L: Just to be thorough, let me ask you about a couple of other possibilities. Did Jeff or anyone else promise you anything if you signed the statement?

10. C: I don't remember anything like that. I wish they had.

11. L: Did they indicate that you could keep your job if you signed?

12. C: Well, Jeff said that the only way they could trust me in the future was if I signed. I guess I thought that meant that I'd better sign if I wanted to keep my job.

13. L: Did anyone say anything like the whole incident would be over if you signed?

14. C: Yes.

15. L: This has been very helpful. You were presented with a typed-up statement, and you were afraid that if you didn't sign it they would fire you. You also signed because they said the only way they could ever trust you again was if you signed and because they said the incident would be over with if you signed. Can you think of any other reasons you signed the statement?

16. C: No.[4]

3. UNCOVERING ADVERSARIES' LIKELY CONTENTIONS

The fact-gathering portions of initial client meetings are of course devoted primarily to uncovering and strengthening the probative value of helpful evidence, as well as seeking explanations for harmful disclosures. However, you can further your ability to tentatively assess clients' legal positions and map out provisional case strategies if you have information about adversaries' likely positions. Thus, if earlier phases of interviews, documents, pleadings or other sources haven't already provided you with a good picture of adversaries' likely stances, you might ask clients what they know about their adversaries' likely contentions and supporting evidence.[5]

4. Of course at this point you might well decide to use additional T–funnels to explore matters such as exactly what occurred when they typed up the statement, when they said signing was the only way they could ever trust the client, and why she was afraid. See Chapter 7 on using T–funnels cyclically.

5. If you represent a defendant who has already been served with a complaint, the

Just as you might ask clients for explanations that might vitiate their own harmful disclosures, you can also seek to uncover information rebutting adversaries' likely positions. In this latter situation, however, your search can be twofold:

- Do clients have information undermining the credibility of the evidence on which their adversaries are likely to rely?[6]

- Can clients offer explanations that vitiate the probative value of adversaries' likely evidence?

A. PREPARATORY EXPLANATIONS

Asking clients about adversaries' contentions not only can require them to mentally change gears abruptly, but also creates a risk that some clients will doubt your loyalty. Thus, you might want to preface this part of the questioning with a preparatory statement addressing the following points:

- Your next questions will concern the adversary's likely positions.

- The purpose of the questions is to help you assess the client's legal position.

- You're also interested in finding weaknesses in the adversary's positions.

A preparatory statement along these lines might go something like this:

> Barry, you've given me a lot of helpful information about what went on when Fairplan let you go. What I'd like to talk about now is what they are likely to say about why you were terminated. It helps me a lot to know at the outset as much as I can about what they are likely to say and what facts, if any, they have to back up their position. With that kind of information we can begin to think about how we might respond to their claims. Also the information will help me give you a more meaningful evaluation of where you stand and also it helps me develop some ideas about where we might go from here. The more I know about Fairplan's likely position early on the better position I'll be in to help you.

complaint will of course provide you with some information about the adversary's position. However, that information may be minimal, especially in jurisdictions that authorize "notice pleading." See WRIGHT & MILLER, FEDERAL PRACTICE & PROCEDURE (2002). For example, a complaint in a personal injury case may tell you little more than that the plaintiff alleges that the defendant drove negligently.

6. One way you might identify topics you could use to ask a client about the accuracy of an adversary's evidence is by using the credibility factors set forth in Chapter 7. For a more detailed discussion of how to challenge the accuracy of evidence relied upon by an adversary, *see* BINDER ET AL, *supra* note 3 at 87–100 .

B. QUESTIONING   CLIENTS   ABOUT   ADVERSARIES' CONTENTIONS

To seek out information about adversaries' likely contentions,[7] you can again follow a T-funnel questioning sequence. For example, a T-funnel dialogue eliciting information about what Barry knows about Fariplan's likely stance might go as follows:

Upper-T questions

1. L: What do you think Fairplan will say about why you were let go?

2. C: They'll say the same stuff they said when they let me go. They'll say that I wasn't bringing in enough new customers and that my customer follow-ups were inadequate.

3. L: As far as you know, what other justifications might Fairplan offer?

4. C: None that I know of.

Lower-T questions

5. L: Are they likely to claim you were insubordinate in any way?

6. C: I don't think so.

7. L: How about promptness? Are they likely to claim that coming to work late or turning in work late was a problem?

8. C: I was late with reports a couple of times but I don't think they'll say that had anything to do with their letting me go.

9. L: Okay, I'll come back to this in a minute. Are they likely to talk about your mistreating customers in anyway?

10. C: No. The customers loved me.

In the light of these responses, to more fully flush out the adversary's likely contentions you might then subject answers such as those in Nos. 2 and 8 to further T–funnel inquiry. For example, you might seek explanations as to why Fairplan is unlikely to claim that Barry's being late with reports was a reason for letting him go.[8] Similarly, you might seek to bolster the credibility of the client's response in No. 10.

---

7. You often may have an idea what an adversary will contend from earlier statements made by a client, from documents you have read or from handling cases similar to that of the client's.

8. You might use another T-funnel when probing Barry's assertion that Fairplan is unlikely to claim that his being late with reports was a reason for terminating his employment. For example, an open question that you might use would be, "Why don't you think that Fairplan will say that your being late with reports was a reason for terminating you?" A closed question on this same topic would be, "Might a reason for Fairplan not making an issue of your sometimes being late with reports be that other employees were also often late turning in their reports?"

4. PROBING CLUMPED AND CONCLUSORY RESPONSES

As when they respond to inquiries seeking helpful evidence, clients may provide conclusory or clumped responses to questions seeking to bolster credibility, explain away harmful answers and identify an adversary's likely contentions. For example:

Conclusory Responses to Credibility Inquires

1. L: How far away were you when he said that?
2. C: Not very far.

1. L: Given that you were in several meeting with Smith, why is it you remember that it was at the meeting of the 25th that he agreed to go along?
2. C: Because he was so angry about it. I'd never seen him so angry; everyone was surprised.

Conclusory Responses to Inquiries Seeking Explanations For Harmful Answers

1. L: Roberta, you've told me that at the time of the accident you were late for an important meeting. How is it that being late didn't affect the way you were driving?
2. C: I'd taken care of it.

Conclusory Responses to Adversaries' Contentions

1. Barbara, at this point do you have any idea what arguments First Rate is going to use to say they are not bound by the contract?

2. I think they are going to contend that they agreed to the deal only because we misrepresented our intentions.

When clients provide conclusory answers such as these, you typically need to uncover the concrete information that forms the basis for those answers. Otherwise, you have little chance of evaluating or persuading others of their accuracy. For example:

1. L: How far away were you when he said that?
2. C: Not very far.
3. L: When you say "not very far," what do you mean?
4. C: . . .

1. L: Given that you were in several meeting with Smith, why is it you remember that it was at the meeting of the 25th that he agreed to go along?
2. C: Because he was so angry about it. I'd never seen him so angry; everyone was surprised.

3.   L: When you say that he was so angry, what do you mean?
4.   C: . . .

5.   PROBING CLUMPED EVENTS AND BEHAVIOR OVER TIME RESPONSES

Just as clients may provide conclusory responses to your inquiries about credibility, explanations for harmful evidence and an adversary's likely contentions, so too may their answers consist of clumped events or conclusions about behavior over time. Consider these examples.

Clumped Events

1.   L: How do you think First Air will respond to your claim?
2.   C: They'll probably say that the stabilizer didn't work the way it was supposed to.
3.   L: Why do you think that is what they'll say?
4.   C: Because I was there when they inspected the stabilizer.

Again, one way to parse a clumped event such as "inspection of the stabilizer" effectively is to elicit a "mini-timeline."[9] That is, you might seek a chronology of what took place when they "inspected the stabilizer." You might also use a T-funnel approach, first using open questions to probe the client's recall of what took place during the inspection and then using closed questions to search for additional happenings.

Behavior Over Time

1.   Why do you think that First Rate is going to contend that your company made misrepresentations in order to get them to sign the contract?
2.   Because we've had disputes with them before; they almost always claim that.

As in other circumstances, probing such assertions generally entails asking for concrete examples. For example, in this situation you might ask a question such as, "Can you give me a couple of examples of when First Rate improperly made this kind of contention?"

6.   FILLING GAPS IN STORIES

As you carry out the three theory development tasks described in this chapter, you might ask for or clients may provide narrative accounts of what they did, observed or knew. For example, when you seek to elicit evidence of consistent actions to bolster clients' credibility, they may respond with narrative accounts of a series of events. Like any other narratives, these accounts may contain gaps. For example, the client who was offended by a supervisor's offensive joke may say that, "We got together and decided to talk with the union rep and later we met with her and complained about what happened." Suspecting a gap in the

9. See Chapter 7.

story, you might ask whether anything took place between the time of the employees' get together and the later meeting with the union representative.

7. PRESERVING INFORMATION

Taking notes as interviews progress is the traditional method of preserving information. Notes are essential for conducting interviews effectively. For example, you'll probably need to take notes if you hope to return to parked topics at a later time.[10] Moreover, notes provide a record of information for use as cases progress.[11] However, trying to compile anything close to transcripts of clients' remarks is likely to detract from rapport. Developing personal relationships and building trust and confidence is difficult when your head is buried in a legal pad or a computer keyboard.

"Probe notes" can provide the benefits of note taking without unduly interfering with your ability to focus attention on clients. Taking "probe notes" consists of limiting note taking to words and phrases that relate to significant evidence. For example, you might make a record of key words relating to helpful evidence as well as of information that you decide to "park" for later discussion.

Most clients will undoubtedly expect you to take notes and therefore are unlikely to be put off by your actions. Should a client appear concerned about your taking notes, consider responding with a brief explanation along these lines:

"I'm just making sure I have an accurate record of our discussion. In fact, later perhaps we can go over my notes together, and you can correct anything I've gotten wrong."

Any notes you make should consist of clients' actual words as much as possible. You may tend to instinctively transform clients' expressions into ones that you tend to use, particularly since yours are likely to be more responsive to legal theories. However, when you change words you risk changing stories' meanings. Moreover, using clients' own words is likely to enhance your notes' usefulness for refreshing clients' recollections on the eve of deposition or trial.[12]

Finally, recognize that probe notes will typically not be a sufficient record of what clients have told you. When you conclude client meetings, you almost always should review your notes and write out or dictate a memorandum (usually called a "Memo to File") that spells out more fully than probe notes the details of what you have learned. Moreover,

---

10. For a discussion of parking data, see Chapter 7.

11. Your ability to take and subsequently use probe notes may soon be enhanced by a new Microsoft product called, "ONE-NOTE." See Ben Z. Gottesman, *Microsoft OneNote* 2003 PC Magazine, Oct. 28, 2003 at 102.

12. Note that if you show clients notes in preparing them to testify at deposition or trial, you adversary usually will be entitled to see those notes. *See* Binder et al., *supra* note 3 at 301–302.

update your time line chronologies to reflect the additional information that emerges during theory development questioning.

8.   EXAMPLE: INTEGRATING THE FOUR THEORY DEVELOPMENT TASKS

The following brief example of theory development questioning illustrates many of the principles that Chapters 7 and 8 describe. Beginning with factual propositions suggested by a client's time line story, you inquire into an important event in that story while carrying out the four questioning tasks that these chapters have described.

Assume that you represent Virginia Vega, a programming team leader who was recently fired by Barnes Engineering. After hearing Vega's initial description of her situation and obtaining a time line from her, you conclude that Vega potentially has a cause of action against Barnes for wrongful termination. From what Vega has told you she was fired by her supervisor, Stan Sink, because Sink wanted to promote his good friend Fred Fritz into Vega's position, and not because Vega's work was poor. Your legal theory is that Vega was improperly fired without good cause, and based on her time line story two factual propositions that support this legal theory are that (1) Sink terminated Vega in order to promote Fritz into Vega's position; and (2) Vega's work performance was more than satisfactory. A portion of your theory development questioning proceeds as follows:

1.   L: Virginia, you've given me a very good overview of the various events that occurred prior to your coming here. I'd now like to get into some more details so I'll have a better understanding of where you stand legally. Let me start by asking you to go back to the meeting you had with Sink when he let you go. Tell me everything you can recall about that meeting.

2.   C: I was at my desk when he called me and asked me to come to his office. I went up and knocked on his door and went in. He thanked me for coming and asked me to have a seat, which I did. He then said he had some unpleasant news for me. He told me that he'd just come from an meeting with our department head, Ms. Rodney, and that they had decided that they had to let me go. He said that I'd ignored the company's warnings not to criticize the programmers who worked on my team in public, and he mentioned an incident with one of my programmers, Ms. Baldwin, that had taken place the previous day. He said the decision wasn't an easy one because my work was generally good, but that because of my poor management skills they couldn't keep me on.

3.   L.   I imagine you were stunned.

4.   C: I really was; I was absolutely shocked because I had no idea this was coming and I was totally frustrated by his refusal to discuss the situation. As far as I was concerned

my conversation with Ms. Baldwin was totally proper and justified.

5.   L: Okay, I'll to get back to what happened with Ms. Baldwin in a little bit. But for now let's concentrate on your meeting with Sink. What else happened in this meeting with Sink?

6.   C: He said they would give me a month's severance pay and would have some papers for me to sign, but that they wanted me to leave immediately. He asked that I go back to my office, clean out my desk and leave. He said it would be easiest if I didn't talk to anyone, that I should just take my things and go.

7.   L: What else do you recall?

8.   C: I asked him what was the problem with the way I dealt with Ms. Baldwin but he said he didn't want to get into it. He said the decision had been made and it was best to move on. He said Barnes would give me good references regarding my programming skills and the quality of my work when I applied for another job. He was trying to placate me but he wouldn't look me in the eye. I remember that.

9.   L.   I can understand that he wouldn't. What else happened at this meeting with Sink?

10.   C: Nothing that I remember.

11.   L: Did Sink say anything about Mr. Fritz?

12.   C: No.

13.   L: Did he say anything about talking with anyone other than Ms. Rodney?

14.   C: Not that I remember.

15.   L: Did Sink say anything else about the quality of your work?

16.   C: No. He had never complained about my work.

17.   L: Did Sink say anything about people complaining about your performance in any way?

18.   C: No.

19.   L: Is there anything else you remember about that conversation with Sink?

20.   C: No.

21.   L: Okay, let's go back to a couple of points. Tell me everything that Sink said about discussing the situation with Ms. Rodney.

22.   C: He only said that they had discussed letting me go. He didn't tell me anything else.

23.   L: Did he tell you who as between the two of them initiated the discussion?

24.   C: No. But it probably was Sink since he did say that Ms. Baldwin had come to him about my criticizing her. He just mentioned that but didn't go into any details.

25. L: Did Sink say who actually made the decision to let you go?

26. C: No. But Sink probably would have needed Rodney's permission. I don't think he has the authority to fire people without checking with Rodney or people in H.R.

27. L: Now tell me everything that Sink said about Ms. Baldwin coming to him.

28. C: Nothing other than that she came and complained.

29. L: Did he tell you what she said?

30. C: No.

31. L: Did Sink say when she talked to him?

32. C: No.

33. L: Did he say if she came alone?

34. C: No.

35. L: What else did Sink say about your severance pay?

36. C: Nothing.

37. L: Did Barnes typically give people in your position a month's severance pay?

38. C: No. Usually only two weeks pay.

39. L: Okay. Now please tell me everything Sink said about not talking to anyone else before you left?

40. C: That's all he said.

41. L: Did he say why you shouldn't do that?

42. C: Only that it would be best.

43. L: Did he say why he thought it would be best?

44. C: No. But I assume he was worried about my programmers becoming upset. I get along well with my people and they like me.

45. L: Good; that will be helpful. I'll want to ask you more about that a little later on. But let's talk a bit about Sink's comments about giving you good references. Tell me everything he said about that.

46. C: He said he was sure I would be concerned about that but that I didn't need to worry because he and Ms. Rodney had talked and they had agreed that Barnes would give me good references.

47. L: What else did he say about that?

48. C: Nothing.

49. L: Did he say anything about how they would respond to inquiries about you management abilities?

50. C: No. He just said the references would be good and I needn't worry.

51. L: What did you do after you left Sink's office?

52. C: I went back to my office, made some notes about what had happened, told a couple of my programmers that I had been let go, cleaned out my desk and left.

53. L: That must have been a difficult moment for you. I'll want to come back to your notes and your conversations with the programmers. But before I do that, let me turn to a couple of other matters. Did you ever tell anyone else what happened in Sink's office that day?

54. C: No one other than my husband and my friend Emily.

55. L: Ever tell anyone else at Barnes?

56. C: One of my programmers, Bill Dubey.

57. L: Any one else?

58. C: No.

59. L: Did you ever prepare any other written document or notes about what happened that day in Sink's office?

60. C: No.

61. L: Ever file any complaint with any government agency?

62. C: I thought about doing that but I didn't do it. I just came to see you.

63. L: Ever write a letter to anyone about what happened that day?

64. C: I might have sent an e-mail to my sister; I'm not sure. I can check on that.

65. L: Is there anyone who you haven't told me about who might have knowledge about what happened that day in Sink's office?

66. C: Maybe Ms. Rodney; I don't know.

67. L: Anyone else?

68. C: No.

69. L: Okay, one more thing for now before we get back to your meeting with Mr. Sink. As we go forward, it will help me to get a feel for what the people at Barnes might say about why they were justified in letting you go. What do you think they'll say on that score?

70. C: The only thing I can think of is that I criticized Ms. Baldwin and one other employee in front of other employees.

71. L: I'll want to ask you about those incidents. Anything else they are likely to say as to why they were justified in firing you?

72. C: Not that I know of.

73. L. Are they likely to say your programming was poor in some way?

74. C: I don't think so. Remember Sink said they'd give me good references.

75. L: Are they likely to say you failed to follow instructions?

76. C: Perhaps with respect to Ms. Baldwin because I did criticize her in front of another employee and once before I had been told not to do that. But I only did it this time because Ms. Baldwin asked that her buddy Ms. Garland sit

in when I talked to Ms. Baldwin about her performance evaluation.

77. L: Might they say you were late or that your work was late?

78. C: I don't think so.

79. L: Might they say you were insubordinate in some way?

80. C: No.

81. L: Okay. I want to turn to the incident in which you criticized Ms. Baldwin. Can you tell me a little more about why you criticized Ms. Baldwin in front of Ms. Garland?

Nos. 1–20 illustrate your use of a T-funnel to elicit the details of an important event. Nos. 1–10 illustrate open questions at the top of the T, and in Nos. 11–20 you use closed questions. The closed questions seek additional details of the event, and whether they uncover helpful or harmful evidence depends on Vega's answers. See for example Nos. 11, 13, 15, and 17. This illustration thus demonstrates the point that you often carry out the tasks of pursuing helpful and harmful evidence simultaneously.

Your initial "T" unearths both potentially helpful and potentially harmful evidence. On the helpful side, in No. 2 you learn that Sink refused to discuss the allegedly precipitating event and that he acknowledged that Vega's work was good. No. 4. adds the potentially helpful fact that Vega had no prior indication that her job was in jeopardy. No. 6 unearths the promise of a month's severance pay and Sink's request that Vega not talk with anyone before leaving; these both may prove helpful. Likewise in No. 8 Sink's promise of good references as well as Sink's refusal to look Vega in the eye may help. Nos. 16 and 18 also provide potentially helpful evidence.

On the other hand, Vega's acknowledgement that she criticized Baldwin in front of another employee (No. 4) certainly belongs in the potentially harmful file.

In Nos. 21, 27, 37, 39 and 45, you return to topics that you parked during the initial T-funnel sequence concerning Vega's meeting with Sink. In returning to these topics, you again make use of T-funnels. (See for example Nos. 21–26; 27–34; 39–44). Each of these T-funnels seeks further details that might, depending upon Vega's answers, surface either helpful or harmful evidence. For example Nos. 23 and 25 might have uncovered helpful evidence that Sink made the decision to fire Vega or harmful evidence that Rodney made that decision.

When returning to topics that you parked during the initial "T," you confined yourself to topics concerning the meeting between Sink and Vega. You allowed other parked topics relating to other time periods such as Vega's meeting with Baldwin (No. 5) and Vega's getting along with her programmers (No. 44) to remain parked for the time being.

In Nos. 51–66 you move to the task of searching for evidence that might enhance Vega's credibility with regard to what happened during her meeting with Sink. Nos. 53–64 seek out consistent/corroborating behavior in the form witnesses or documents. Nos. 59–64 illustrate use of a T-funnel to search for documents.

Nos. 69–78 turn to the task of seeking out the adversary's likely contentions. Again, you use a T-funnel to carry out that search.

The example closes with an illustration of how you might begin to look for evidence to undercut a client's harmful admission—i.e. that despite being told not to criticize a junior employee in front of others, Vega did just that in dealing with Ms. Baldwin, and one other employee. Vega's answer may surface evidence tending to explain away her apparently improper behavior.

Chapter 9

GATHERING INFORMATION FOR BUSINESS TRANSACTIONS

* * *

Ms. Milford, your company wants to make a deal to purchase sportswear from the Guangzhou Clothing Cooperative if a way can be found to ensure that no money changes hands until you are satisfied that the clothing they produce meets your specifications. Do I understand your principal concern correctly?

Yes, that's it exactly. Their price is terrific and if they can deliver, it would be a great deal for us.

Okay, what I'd like to do this afternoon is get some preliminary information from you. I'll be interested in matters such as what terms you've already worked out with the Guanghzou representative, how you see the deal with Guanghzou functioning, what role you'd like me to play in helping you put this deal together and things like that. If we have time, I'll probably also get into some more specific details such as where a letter of credit might be established. When we finish today, I can then suggest where we should go from here. Do you have any questions before I start?

No. I'd like to get going, so fire away.

First, why don't you tell me . . . .

* * *

1. INTRODUCTION

This Chapter and the next focus on information-gathering in the context of proposed business deals. This Chapter examines the *topics* you'll typically gather information about when clients' matters involve common private business transactions such as leases, partnerships, and employee agreements.[1] Chapter 10 identifies and illustrates *techniques* for gathering deal-related information effectively.

---

1. Of course the array of potential transactions is vast, encompassing for ex- ample both personal and business agreements and agreements not only between

208

2. DO NOT A "DEAL–KILLER" BE

Experienced transactional clients often think of lawyers as "deal killers."[2] The reason is that lawyers and clients often have different world views with respect to proposed transactions. Clients tend to focus on proposed deals' likely benefits, and are less concerned about what can go wrong in the future. Lawyers, by contrast, often see one of their major transactional roles as protecting clients against downstream risks. Thus, it is not surprising that many business people think that lawyers magnify risks, jeopardize deals by drafting and negotiating too aggressively, and try to kill deals by counseling them not to take risks.[3]

Of course, almost all business ventures entail risk, and businesspeople are often by nature risk-takers. Some risks are financial: a transaction may not produce expected financial benefits. Other risks are psychological: a failed business transaction may harm an individual's or a company's reputation. Still other risks are legal: a non-competition clause in an employment contract may not be enforceable. Client-centeredness suggests that whether or not such risks are worth taking is ultimately for clients to decide. Helping clients evaluate and avoid risks is part of your professional role. However, your primary role is facilitating clients' legitimate business desires. As you gather information and counsel clients with regard to proposed deals, do not let your own sense of risk aversion overwhelm clients' desires to take what they consider to be acceptable business risks.

3. THE TYPICAL PROCESS OF COMPLETING BUSINESS TRANSACTIONS

You may be more familiar with the process by which litigation matters progress from initial interviews through trial than the process by which proposed business deals typically wind their way to completion, since the process of finalizing transactional agreements is largely unencumbered by statutes,[4] court rules and law school attention. However, realizing how deals usually move forward will help you understand what information you usually need to obtain when clients seek your help in connection with proposed deals. Of course, the processes by which transactions get underway and conclude often grow out of cultural protocols. Thus, when your clients or other parties to transactions have

private parties but also between private parties and government entities. The focus on common transactions between private parties keeps these chapters to a manageable scope while furnishing you with a foundation for helping clients in other types of transactional matters.

2. Common types of lawyer behavior that are likely to kill deals are described by M.H. McCormack in The Terrible Truth About Lawyers (1987). See also William A.

Klein & John C. Coffee Jr., Business Organization and Finance: Legal and Economic Principles, 104–09 (1996).

3. See McCormack, *supra* note 2, at 84–91, 111–112, 118–125.

4. Of course, tax rules, corporate codes and the like frequently affect the content of deals. But, by and large, they do not affect the process by which you help a client bring a deal to fruition.

cultural backgrounds that differ from your own, becoming familiar with such protocols can help you produce satisfactory outcomes.[5]

Typically, when proposed deals are other than routine for a client, the process is something like the following.[6] During initial meetings, you gather information of the type described in this chapter. You may need a few meetings (some of which may be by phone) to complete information-gathering. Therefore, an initial meeting might conclude with little more than tentative steps taken toward resolving potential problems and discussing a tentative structure for a proposed transaction.

When you have gathered sufficient data and understand the legal issues that a deal presents, frequently you next prepare a draft agreement (or revise a draft agreement prepared by another party) and send your draft to a client.[7] Afterwards, you and the client meet to review the draft. That meeting may produce a revised draft that you send to the other party. Negotiations may then begin with the other party's lawyer.[8] In preparation for these negotiations, you may again talk to the client and explore negotiation strategy. Strategic planning often encompasses not only the content of agreements' provisions, but also such process concerns as who will be present at negotiations and who will take the lead role in conducting them. The frequent result of negotiations is that you explore further revisions with the client. Eventually, the parties may agree to terms and sign written documents.

Thus, like litigation matters, proposed deals matters cannot be neatly segmented into "interviewing" and "counseling" stages. Clients' need to make tentative decisions may require you to address options before you finish gathering information. Similarly, just when you think information-gathering is complete, negotiations may produce additional problems that require additional investigation. In sum, the ebb and flow of deals typically involve you as interviewer, counselor, drafter and negotiator, sometimes all simultaneously.

---

5. For a detailed discussion of deals-related cultural protocols throughout the world, see TERRI MORRISON, WAYNE A. CONAWAY, GEORGE A. BORDEN, KISS, BOW OR SHAKE HANDS: HOW TO DO BUSINESS IN SIXTY COUNTRIES at (1994).

6. When a client views a deal as routine, the process is quite likely to be more abbreviated. For example, owners of shopping centers routinely enter into lease agreements. Thus, if a shopping center owner comes to you to discuss a proposed lease to a new tenant in an established center, the process will be more attenuated than the one described here. Also, if a client is anxious to conclude a deal quickly, and most of its terms have been worked out before the

client comes to you, the process will be likewise truncated.

7. In complex matters such as mergers and acquisitions, obtaining legal understanding may require considerable legal research.

8. For a discussion of the importance and possible content of such a meeting, see Bill Scott, *Preparing for Negotiations*, in NEGOTIATION: READINGS, EXERCISES AND CASES 60–68 (Roy J. Lewicki, David M. Saunders, & John W. Minton eds., 1999); ROBERT H. MNOOKIN, SCOTT R. PEPPET & ANDREW S. TULUMELLO, BEYOND WINNING: NEGOTIATING TO CREATE VALUE IN DEALS AND DISPUTES 178–204 (2000).

4. INFORMATION GATHERING SIMILARITIES BETWEEN DEALS AND LITIGATION

Most lawyers classify themselves either as "litigators" or "business lawyers," implying that the twain never meet. To some extent, the impression is correct. Rights in litigated matters are highly dependent on which party's version of history a factfinder accepts, whereas historical events often do not control deals' terms. Whatever parties' past dealings, they are generally free to reach any agreement they choose.[9] However, and especially when it comes to the process by which you gather information, litigation and deals matters have important similarities. That is, while the *kind* of information you gather may be very different, the *process* through which you acquire it from your own clients is in many respects similar.[10] Understanding this reality may advance your ability to apply in one field of lawyering the skills you have learned in the other.

Thus, in deals matters as in litigation, you typically begin by trying to preliminarily identify clients' problems.[11] Then, in both contexts a two-pronged approach is an effective way to gather pertinent information. In litigation, the typical first prong consists of eliciting a time line of pertinent events. In deals matters, the first prong typically consists of exploring the topics set forth in Section 6 below, topics that are likely to be important in almost every transaction.

In deals matters, the second prong equivalent to the theory development phase of litigation interviews is transaction-specific information. Thus, second prong inquiries vary according to whether a deal involves lease of a building, formation of a partnership, or something else.

5. GATHERING LEGAL AND NON-LEGAL INFORMATION

This chapter assumes that business clients hire you as something more than scrivener to memorialize final agreements. Even if the parties have agreed to some terms in writing, generally at the time you are consulted deals are typically not yet finalized.[12] But what are clients' expectations concerning your role in concluding deals? Do they want you to restrict your counseling efforts to the legal aspects of a deal? Or do

---

9. However, transactions between parties who have entered into prior transactions with each other are often "path dependent." That is, the terms of the prior deals and the processes by which they were arrived at often heavily influence the process and outcomes of later negotiations.

10. Naturally, the ability to use discovery to gather information about the other party is not present in transactional matters.

11. For a refresher on how to approach this task, see Chapter 5.

12. The Rutter Group is a leading California organization in continuing legal education. Its President, Bill Rutter, has pointed out to the authors that clients sometimes come to lawyers with what they think is simply a "tentative agreement," but which is in fact a fully enforceable contract. For example, a court may construe a "deposit receipt" in the purchase of a house or a "letter of intent" in the purchase of a business to be a binding contract. When clients seek to further negotiate such contracts, the line between litigation and transaction matters is frequently obliterated.

they seek your input with respect to non-legal matters, such as deals' underlying economic wisdom? Understanding the scope of your representation can facilitate your helping clients resolve matters to their satisfaction.[13]

In the abstract, the lines between the "legal" and "non-legal" aspects of business deals tend to blur.[14] Hence, brief examples of each may help you recognize the kind of advice that clients may look to you to provide. When your role focuses on a deal's legal aspects, information-gathering typically concentrates on the following topics:

(a) Proposed deals' validity. For example, if a deal is for an "exclusive dealership," you may have to gather information so that you can determine whether it might violate antitrust laws. Similarly, if a deal is for a tax-free exchange of property, your inquiries might be directed at whether the properties proposed to be exchanged are of "like kind."

(b) Clients' understandings and intentions concerning their rights and obligations. For example, assume that a client seeking to lease space for her retail business tells you initially that she has agreed to pay rent in the amount of "6% of gross sales." You might inquire whether she intends to pay 6% on the gross amount of credit card sales, or to deduct from gross the credit card company's charge.

(c) Clients' expectations concerning what happens in the event of breach. For example, if a proposed deal is an installment sales agreement, you might inquire as to the client's understanding as to whether a single defective shipment constitutes a breach of the entire agreement.[15]

Non-legal inquiries typically focus on practical ways of achieving deals' purposes, and may even extend to their overall soundness.[16] For example, assume that Al Ford consults you about a proposed sales agreement pending with a Chinese production unit. Though he has some business experience, the deal would be Ford's initial entry into the international arena. Ford's concerns include how to have the goods inspected before they are shipped out of China. Though the concern may

---

13. There is no duty to give non-legal advice. However, the ABA Code of Professional Responsibility EC 7–8 states that: "Advice of a lawyer to his client need not be confined to purely legal considerations;" and the ABA Model Rules of Professional Conduct Rule 2.1 states: "In rendering advice, a lawyer may refer not only to law but to other considerations as well, such as moral, economic, social and political factors, that may be relevant to the client's situation." Furthermore, the comment to Rule 2.1 states that technical legal advice may sometimes be inadequate.

14. See Susanna M. Kim, *Dual Identities and Dueling Obligations: Preserving Independence in Corporate Representation*, 68

Tenn. L. Rev. 179 (2001); George Dent, *Lawyers and Trust in Business Alliances*, 58 Bus. Law. 45 (2002).

15. See U.C.C. § 2–612.

16. Be aware that even within the group of clients who are sophisticated businesspeople and who deal with lawyers frequently, some will view your opening a discussion of whether it makes sense to go ahead with a deal as an attempt to substitute your business judgment for theirs, whereas others will welcome such a discussion. See Robert H. Mnookin, Scott R. Peppet & Andrew S. Tulumello, Beyond Winning: Negotiating to Create Value in Deals and Disputes 178–204 (2000).

be "non-legal," Ford might look to you for information about the manufacturing and shipping process. In addition, Ford may be sufficiently uncertain about doing business overseas that he seeks your advice as to whether to go into it. If so, your inquiries are likely to extend into the deal's financial soundness, as well as into a variety of business and personal areas. For example, you may talk to Ford about how much time and energy he is prepared to devote to the new venture, and whether it will unduly detract from his other business and personal endeavors.

As you can see, in transactional matters the topics you need to pursue may grow out of your experience with specific types of transactions as well as out of your knowledge of potentially applicable laws. Even if your experience is limited, however, you may be able to call on the types of resources you won't find in a law library. For example, if you can learn about clients' proposed transactions before initial meetings occur, you may seek advice from a lawyer who has the business experience that you lack. In addition, especially when you are concerned about deals' financial ramifications, you might consult professionals such as bankers, accountants and market analysts. Also, a wealth of practitioner-oriented books discussing particular kinds of deals, such as partnerships and real estate syndicates, are available. If none of these sources are of avail, you may have to associate more experienced counsel or decline representation.[17]

Realizing that information-gathering about proposed deals may embrace both legal and non-legal concerns, turn next to the types of information you routinely gather in proposed deals matters.

6. TOPICS THAT COMMONLY ARISE IN PROPOSED BUSINESS TRANSACTIONS

The following subsections describe topics that you are likely to pursue in almost all proposed deal matters. Even if you are familiar with clients' business practices and the "industries" in which deals arise, you nevertheless usually need to gather information about these topics if you are to negotiate and draft accurate, workable agreements.[18]

A. CLIENTS' OBJECTIVES

Eliciting clients' objectives is a key to counseling clients effectively about proposed deals and negotiating and drafting their final terms. Typically, clients' goals vary between monetary and non-monetary, long-term and short-term.

For example, assume that you represent a retail department store chain that wants to enter into an agreement with a clothing manufactur-

---

17. See, e.g., ABA Code of Professional Responsibility, EC 2–30, EC 6–1, EC 6–3, EC 6–4, DR 6–101, DR 2–110; ABA Model Rules of Professional Conduct, Rule 1.1, Rule 1.16.

18. The discussion assumes that deals are sufficiently large or non-routine to merit individualized analysis.

er. The department store chain hopes to begin a long-term relationship with the manufacturer in order to promote and maintain a particular fashion image. Knowing of this objective, you might prepare a draft that allows the manufacturer considerable leeway in making deliveries and does not treat every failure to comply with design specifications as a breach of the agreement. In the absence of the store's desire to establish a long-term relationship, your draft might look very different.

Clients' objectives may establish that certain terms are "deal break-ers." That is, an aspect of an agreement may be so important to a client's goals that the other party's failure to accede to it will prevent there being an agreement. For instance, a prospective executive may take the position that "if I don't have the final say in scheduling projects, I'm not going to work for them." Hence, knowing if any terms are potential "deal breakers" enables you to draft and negotiate with an eye towards holding deals together.[19]

In addition to inquiring about clients' objectives, seek also to find out about clients' underlying interests. Understanding underlying inter-ests can help you develop multiple alternatives for achieving them, some of which may be more acceptable to the other party than other alterna-tives. For instance, assume that the basis for a client's wanting to bring in a current employee as a partner is the client's desire to retain the employee's services. Knowing that reason may enable you to suggest ways that the client can induce the employee to stay in the business without making the employee a partner.

B. PROPOSED DEALS' CURRENT TERMS AND PRIOR HISTORY

As mentioned above, clients typically consult you at a point when the terms of deals have been at least partially worked out. Therefore, one of your routine inquiries will concern the terms that the parties have thus-far agreed to. In addition, ask about the course of the negotiations leading up to the agreed-to terms, including what terms have been discussed but not yet agreed upon.

Knowing what terms have been agreed upon of course enables you to discuss proposed agreements' legality and soundness, and to identify ambiguities in the parties' understanding.[20] Perhaps less obviously,

---

19. During an initial meeting, clients often are uncertain about their objectives, or think that points are deal-breakers when in fact the other party simply has not made a sweet enough offer. Moreover, during the course of negotiation, in reaction to another party's offers and demands or in response to changes in a client's own situation, a client's stated objectives may change. Thus, during initial meetings *your* objective may not be so much to tie clients down to fixed objectives as it is to understand their pres-ent thinking.

20. As an example of the type of ambi-guity that might exist, assume that a client tells you that "deliveries will be on Thurs-days." Do the parties intend that there be deliveries every Thursday, or only that if there are deliveries, they are to be on Thursday? Also, what constitutes "deliv-ery"—dropping off goods to a common car-rier, or a party's actual receipt? Note, how-ever, that a too-ready willingness to find and eliminate ambiguity may render you a deal-killer. Sometimes parties prefer to leave terms vague and to trust to the future to work problems out. That is, like legisla-

knowing the terms enables you to draft provisions that carry out the parties' understanding. You do not want to kill deals by unwittingly drafting provisions that suggest that you are trying to alter agreed-upon terms in your clients' favor, at least absent clients' desire that you do so.

Understanding the history leading up to proposed deals, including how clients became interested in them and what terms your clients and other parties have discussed but not yet agreed to typically provides you with insight into such issues as parties' objectives and their adversariness or cooperativeness. Thus, the history alerts you to problems that might arise during negotiation and problems that clients may want to have addressed in final agreements.

You may learn when exploring deals' history that parties have intentionally left terms open. It is not unusual for business people intentionally either to omit terms or leave them vague. They may be unable to agree on how to respond to future contingencies. They may nevertheless prefer a deal to none at all and to save for the future decisions on how to handle contingencies when and if they arise. For example, parties to a sales contract may be unable to agree as to what sort of manufacturing defect would constitute a breach. But rather than hold up the deal because of the disagreement, they may prefer to resolve the problem when and if it arises.

Learning what terms have been agreed to or discussed is not necessarily a slam dunk. Clients may be uncertain about what has been discussed and what has actually been agreed upon. The uncertainty may be a product of wishful thinking. For example, a client's statement that "we've agreed to a five year lease" may reflect nothing more than the landlord's willingness to consider a five year lease. Or, the uncertainty may be caused by clients' naive assumptions. For example, a client may state that in calculating gross sales for purposes of determining monthly rent, fees paid to credit card companies are to be deducted from the gross. However, the statement may reflect only the client's assumption and may not be a term to which the landlord has agreed.

C.   TIMETABLES FOR FINALIZING DEALS

With respect to all proposed deals, you typically need to learn by what date your clients or other parties want them finalized. If either is eager to conclude a deal quickly, your ability to identify options and to negotiate changes may well be constrained. Timetables may also alert you to leverage that parties possess. For example, your client's need to complete a deal quickly may provide the other party with leverage.[21] To maintain good client relations, you must agree either to work within clients' timetables or discuss the possibility of changing them.

---

tors, parties may be able to reach consensus only if they agree to vague language and trust that they will be able to work out disputes that may arise in the future satisfactorily.

21. See CHARLES B. CRAVER, EFFECTIVE LEGAL NEGOTIATION AND SETTLEMENT, 11–15 (4th ed. 2001).

That said, recognize that clients' stated deadlines may not be accurate. "I need this concluded by tomorrow" is a phrase that may reflect clients' enthusiasm or anxiety rather than objective reality. Hence, when clients' stated deadlines present a problem for you, or you suspect that deadlines may be flexible, everyone may benefit from your seeking to change them. Similarly when clients report that another party has a deadline, recognize that such a deadline also may not be accurate. An opposing party's stated deadline, for example, may be a negotiation tactic rather than a reality. Or, another party's deadline may provide your client with leverage. For reasons such as these, you often seek information from clients regarding the accuracy of deadlines and the reasons for them.

D. OTHER PARTIES

It takes two to tango, and at least that many to conclude business deals. Information about other parties can often help you finalize deals. Who are the other parties, and what do they do? What objectives do those parties have? What terms, if any, do those parties consider essential? What are the other parties' financial conditions? What is their reputation in the business community? For example, do other parties generally interpret agreements strictly and litigate frequently?

Often, your clients can provide information about such matters. In turn, you can use that information when considering how to word specific clauses and what negotiating approach to employ. For example, knowing that the other side has an urgent need for extrusions that only your client can manufacture quickly in sufficient quantity is likely to affect how favorably to your client you draft the agreement's terms.[22] Moreover, the answer to such questions can help you respond to clients' inquiries about whether they should enter into proposed deals. For example, assume that your questions about the other party's business history reveal that a deal would be that party's first outside its usual line of endeavor. Explicitly discussing that fact may help your client decide whether to go forward with the deal.

In addition to these specific types of questions, almost always ask clients more generally about their relationships with other parties. Have your clients dealt with them previously? If so, how successful have those past dealings been? Clients' answers may reveal their level of trust with other parties, which in turn can help you determine how to word important terms. Also, you may help clients realize that no matter how careful your drafting, the future may be fraught with difficulty. Given that the Ten Commandments seem to exercise little control over many people's behavior, clients need to understand the limits of written agreements. If clients depend on legal documents to insure that other

---

22. ROGER FISHER & WILLIAM URY, GETTING TO YES 41–57 (2d ed., 1997). Whether you intend to approach the negotiation as a problem solver or in a more traditional manner, knowing the other side's needs in going into the deal will often be critical.

parties will perform, they should understand "going in" that making a deal may well be doing little more than "buying a lawsuit."[23]

E. BUSINESS OPERATIONS

Knowing something about how clients' businesses developed and operate is often vital. Particularly when deals are non-routine for clients, understanding businesses' operations and history can shed light on such matters as clients' objectives and deals' timetables. Moreover, that understanding may enable you to identify contingencies to address in final agreements. For instance, assume that a proposed deal calls for a wholesaler to supply your client, a retailer, with goods over a two year period. Knowing how much inventory your client's business needs to have on hand and how long it takes your client to ship an order can help you discuss with the client the wisdom of a provision treating any delay in shipment by the wholesaler as a failure of contractual performance.

What part and how much of a business' operations you need to learn about depends on a number of factors, including the sort of non-legal advice that clients seek, deals' size relative to the businesses, the routineness of deals, and their likely economic impact on clients. For example, if a bank asks you to look over a security agreement in a routine loan transaction, you certainly will not go into the bank's history or its current operations. By contrast, assume that a client wants to purchase an existing business that will involve the client in a new line of endeavor. Now you will probably need to understand how the client's business developed and currently operates, as well as how the "target company" operates.

Recognizing that what information about businesses you need to gather necessarily varies from one deal to another, consider the following items developed by a group of business lawyers to assist in the development of an ABA skills training course.[24]

    A. A description of the current business:

        1. What does the company do, and how and where?

        2. Who are the key employees and what does each do?

        3. What is the company's current financial condition?

        4. Who are the company's primary customers?

        5. Who are the company's primary competitors?

        6. What regulatory agencies commonly oversee the company's activities?

    B. A brief history of the company.

Of course, even these items do not provide complete coverage of all businesses' operations. But they may serve as useful topics that you can pursue in order to learn about companies' business operations.

---

23. The likely merits of your clients' claims should litigation occur will mean little if the other party is insolvent or beyond a court's jurisdiction.

24. See David A. Binder & Carrie Menkel-Meadow, American Bar Association Lawyering Skills Program (1982).

F. HOW DEALS WILL FUNCTION

Two of your principal tasks, which if overused will gain you a reputation as a "deal-killer," are to help clients structure deals so that they mesh with their business operations, and to guard clients against unwanted risks. To accomplish these tasks, you typically must learn how proposed deals will function. For example, if a proposed deal calls for a client to make and deliver special goods, you will need to gather information about what will take place between the time the deal is finalized and the goods are delivered. If necessary, you might even walk through a plant and talk to the employees who will carry out the operations. For example, if a proposed deal will result in additional work for employees, you might seek to learn whether they have the time, staffing and technological capacity to take on the added burdens. Understanding the entire process will help you spot places where difficulties may arise and explore alternative ways the deal might function and what risk allocations, if any, you need to address.

For instance, assume that Barbara brings you a proposed deal calling for her company to manufacture and deliver resistors. In the course of reviewing the deal's functioning, you learn that some of the components that Barbara will need to manufacture the resistors will be purchased overseas. You can then explore problems that might arise in the course of making overseas purchases. The discussion might aid you in advising Barbara how to word a material breach and *force majeure* provisions in order to protect her adequately.[25]

Consider a second example. Jeff proposes to enter into a five-year lease to operate a restaurant in a shopping center. Eliciting information about how the restaurant will function, you learn that it will serve lunch and dinner, and that supplies will normally be delivered in the morning when other shops are open. Noting that the lease provides for unrestricted parking by customers and other tenants in the common areas and that the restaurant does not have access to a delivery dock, you and Jeff might consider altering the parking clause to ensure that deliveries can be received timely (e.g., seeking the establishment of a loading zone).

Descriptions of deals' functioning may not, of course, alert you to all potential pitfalls. However, they might well alert you to unique aspects of clients' situations that you might miss were you to rely only on standard deal-specific checklists. Remember, by their very nature, checklists are meant to apply to whole classes of, say, long term leases and partnership agreements. By contrast, inquiries into deals' functioning of the type set forth in this section delve into clients' specific situations. Thus, while you may well use checklists, supplement them with deal-

---

25. A *force majeure* clause is included in contracts to "protect the parties in the event that a part of the contract cannot be performed due to causes which are outside the control of the parties and could not be avoided by exercise of due care." BLACK'S LAW DICTIONARY (7th ed. 1999). A *force maj-* *eure* clause is not limited to natural events; it may include events specific to the circumstances of the deal. For example, parties may agree that failure to deliver goods due to a third party labor strike does not constitute a breach of the contract.

specific questions such as, "Tell me a little bit about how your restaurant will operate?" and "Can you describe the manufacturing process for me?"

In addition to "walking through" deals and using checklists, you can also often look to experienced clients for information about potential problems that deals might create. That is, you might ask open-ended questions such as, "What potential risks do you see in this deal?" "What have you heard from others who have done business with this manufacturer?" and "What could go wrong in this deal?" No matter the level of your experience, open questions such as these may ferret out problems that you would have missed.

G. DEALS' ECONOMICS

Most clients, even non-profit corporations, view a proposed deal as a way to improve their economic positions. Therefore, the non-legal advice you are called upon to give often concerns deals' economic soundness. In turn, you have to gather information about deals' economics. For example, examining a business' financial statement, projected cash flow and any income and expense projections for a proposed deal will enable you and a client to discuss whether a client's financial projections are realistic.[26]

7. TRANSACTION–SPECIFIC TOPICS

As mentioned above, transaction-specific inquiries in proposed deals matters tend to be much less dominated by substantive legal principles than are theory development questions in litigation matters. The reason is that in deals matters parties are often free to establish whatever obligations they choose. For example, though UCC provisions may allocate the risk of loss of goods according to whether they have been identified in a contract,[27] the parties to an agreement are free to change that allocation if they wish.[28]

Transaction-specific inquiries primarily concern provisions covering obligations and risks typically found in the specific types of deals that clients contemplate. For instance, shopping center leases commonly cover such potential obligations as payment of rent, purchase of insurance and maintenance of the premises. Risks commonly addressed in such leases include what will happen if the tenant defaults, dies or

---

26. This discussion assumes that you have the ability to read and interpret financial statements and documents. If you do not have this ability, you might nonetheless ask for the information with an eye toward having a colleague or a financial professional such as an accountant help you interpret the data. You might also consult books such as DARRELL MULLIS, JUDITH ORLOFF & LARRY BOGRAD, THE ACCOUNTING GAME: BASIC ACCOUNTING FRESH FROM THE LEMONADE STAND

(2000); PETER EISEN, ACCOUNTING THE EASY WAY (1995).

27. See U.C.C. § 2–501.

28. Of course parties are not free to entirely disregard substantive law principles. For example, if two companies plan to form a joint venture and issue stock, various securities regulations have to be complied with and you need to gather information accordingly.

becomes bankrupt,[29] or if the leased premises are destroyed or condemned by the government.[30] Such topics, then, are potential candidates for inquiries in proposed shopping center lease deals.

Similarly, some of the obligations typically addressed in partnership agreements include capital contributions, partners' duties, distribution of profits, and payment of salaries. Risks commonly covered in such agreements include death or disability of a partner, transfer of partnership interests, and management disputes.[31]

Provisions that spell out parties' obligations over the life of an agreement are "operative provisions." They describe what each party must do. "Contingent" or "remedial" provisions address risks. They spell out the parties' rights and duties should problems arise with the operative terms, say because of breach by a party or interference by a third person or an outside force—e.g., a ship carrying goods identified in a contract is lost at sea.

Typically, the terms that you review with clients when inquiring about deals' agreed-upon terms and history are operative terms. But just as typically, you will still need to explore both potential contingent terms and additional operative terms. For example, in a shopping center lease deal the parties may have agreed to one operative term, the amount of the rent, but may not have discussed either the tenant's obligation to purchase insurance (an additional operative provision) or what happens if the tenant merges with another business during the term of a lease (a contingent provision).

Nevertheless, transaction-specific inquiries typically do not embrace all possible provisions. Without written drafts on the table, discussions of all possible provisions that final agreements might contain would be wasteful. You would inevitably discuss many topics that neither party to an agreement considers important. Moreover, subsequent review of drafts with clients would probably repeat much of the discussion. Hence, instead of talking about all possible provisions, make judgments about which topics merit discussion prior to preparing written drafts.[32] You will probably choose to discuss topics when prior discussions with clients suggest that they are important. Absent such indications, you may well

---

29. Contract provisions relating to bankruptcy are often overridden by the Bankruptcy Code. For example, Section 365 of the Bankruptcy Code overrides anti-assignment clauses. See ALLEN MICHEL & ISRAEL SHAKEL, FINANCE AND ACCOUNTING FOR LAWYERS (1996).

30. A compilation of standard provisions for particular types of transactions is beyond the scope of this book. Office form files, formbooks and checklists in books targeted to practitioners are good sources of deal-specific topics. See, e.g., *Commercial Real Property Lease Practice* sec. 2.32 (Cal. CEB, 1976) (commercial real property leas-

es); *Advising California Partnerships* (Cal. CEB, 2nd ed. 1988).

31. For a list of topics commonly covered in partnership agreements, see, e.g., J. RABKIN AND M. JOHNSON, CURRENT LEGAL FORMS WITH TAX ANALYSIS VOL. 1 (1989); ADVISING CALIFORNIA PARTNERSHIPS 2D 149–234 (Cal. CEB 1988).

32. Your judgment may turn out to be incorrect. However, since review of a draft gives a client a second opportunity to discuss most topics you initially choose to omit, your initial exercise of judgment typically does not prevent a client from making important decisions.

skip them until you begin discussing a draft. For example, assume that an important objective of a client seeking to enter into a partnership is to preserve the opportunity to devote time to non-partnership business activities. The client's concern may lead you to have a pre-draft discussion of an "outside activities" provision. But now assume that the client says nothing about wanting to engage in outside activities, and that what the client has said about the way the partnership's business will operate suggests that the client will have little or no time to devote to outside activities. In the latter case, you may not bother to discuss an "outside activities" provision prior to reviewing a draft agreement. [33]

Discussions of potential operative or contingent provisions typically include alternative approaches through which clients' goals might be realized. Return to the example of the partnership client whose objective was to have time to engage in non-partnership activities. Alternative methods of accomplishing this objective include permitting the client total freedom to engage in whatever outside activities the client chooses, or permitting the client to engage only in activities that do not compete with partnership business. Discussion of such alternatives enables you to prepare a draft that reflects a client's preferred approach.

8. PREPARING DRAFT AGREEMENTS

As you have seen, drafts' provisions typically result in part from the information you gather during initial client meetings. How do other provisions find their way into drafts? Usually, they emanate from your knowledge of standard provisions for particular types of agreements, together with your understanding of clients' likely needs. That is, you combine legal and "industry" knowledge with data gathered from clients to predict the choices that clients are likely to find most satisfactory.[34] Those predictions typically produce two kinds of decisions.

First, you decide which obligations and risks, among all those that an agreement might cover, to provide for in an agreement. For example, although partnership agreements may contain a provision concerning capital contributions in the form of property or services, you may choose to omit that provision in a deal where the parties have agreed to contribute cash.

Second, you decide what version of provisions to include in drafts. For example, if in the proposed partnership deal you decide to include a clause concerning "Interest on Capital Contributions," you must further decide whether the clause will provide for the payment of interest or indicate that no interest shall be paid.

---

33. Sometimes, as you know, a client will come to an initial meeting armed with a draft agreement that the other party has prepared. However, in most instances you will not have enough time during the initial meeting to study the agreement carefully enough to review adequately all of its provisions; at least one additional meeting will be necessary. For a discussion of how you might actually review the draft provisions with a client, see Chapter 20.

34. Of course, in thinking about what a client is likely to find satisfactory, you will also consider the needs and desires of the other party: a client does not want you to be a deal-killer.

When drafting business agreements, you almost certainly start with a form or two. Typical sources of forms are office files and standard form books. Realize, however, that forms are not fungible. For example, a form may reflect a buyer's rather than a seller's perspective; you should choose one that adopts a client's point of view. Also, because forms tend to carry language forward from one generation of lawyers to the next, forms may contain language that you do not understand. Rather than parroting language first used in a contract for the purchase of cotton gin parts in the 1800s, be sure you understand the purpose that each clause in a draft serves. If you do not understand language that is commonly included in agreements of the type with which you are involved, be sure to ask someone who does.

In all events, when reviewing drafts with clients, inform them of your drafting decisions and explain that they may want to make different choices.

Chapter 10

TECHNIQUES FOR GATHERING INFORMATION ABOUT PROPOSED BUSINESS TRANSACTIONS

* * *

Ms. Pineda, how much capital have you and Lucero talked about initially putting into the partnership?

We've been talking about $35,000 each.

Why did you choose this figure?

Based on our experience in the retail clothing business, we figure we'll need at least $40,000 in inventory when we open the shop. We figured the expenses of leasing a shop and setting it up plus some advertising costs and initial salaries to be about $20,000. So starting with $70,000 will give us a reserve if we need it.

OK, any other expenses you talked about?

Just how much we could afford to put into it, I guess. We're both very comfortable with this figure.

Did you talk about initial expenses for insurance and advertising?

Oh, yes. That will have to come out of the reserve.

Have you projected your income and expenses for the first year at least?

Here's what we've done . . .

* * *

1. INTRODUCTION

Chapter 9 described topics that typically arise during initial interviews concerning common types of proposed private business transactions. This chapter focuses on techniques for gathering information regarding those topics. To a large extent, the approaches and techniques are similar to those you use in litigation matters. For example, T-funnel questioning is an effective method for exploring clients' wishes about specific terms of agreements. Rather than re-explain those approaches and techniques, this chapter illustrates them in the proposed deals context.

2. PRELIMINARY PROBLEM IDENTIFICATION

As with litigation matters, you may review your understanding of why clients have come to see you by following the introductory portion of initial meetings with preliminary problem identification. Of course, clients usually do not perceive deals as "problems" in the same way that they see disputes as problems. However, clients are nevertheless likely to have several concerns and ideas, and you can approach deals from a client-centered perspective asking about:

(1) Why clients are consulting you;

(2) What concerns they have;

(3) What outcomes they hope to achieve; and

(4) What potential solutions, if any, they have in mind for resolving their concerns.[1]

For example, assume that a new client, Mr. Hernandez, has come to see you. In an initial telephone conversation, Mr. Hernandez told you that he owns several medium-sized shopping centers, and that he has had some meetings with an important potential tenant for one of the centers. The preliminary problem identification portion of the conversation may proceed as follows:

1.   L: Why don't we turn to what brought you in here today. I know we talked about this briefly on the phone, but just to be sure we're on the same page can you tell me about where things stand with the lease now?

2.   C: Gladly. I've had two meetings with the Vice President of Empire Grocery, one of the higher class grocery operations here in town. They're interested in a ten-year lease, and rather than just suggest my standard lease form, I thought maybe I should talk to you first.

3.   L: I'll be glad to try to help you. Perhaps you can begin by telling me why you think that your company's standard form lease may not be adequate.

4.   C: Well, Empire would be an important tenant; the anchor space has been empty for over a year, and I'd really like to fill it. Of course, Empire realizes that, so I'm worried about my bargaining position. We've settled on the rent; that's not a problem. But there are a number of other things that affect the finances that have me concerned. I'm worried about things like who will pay for remodeling the space, when the rent will actually start and things like that.

5.   L: Any other concerns that you have?

---

1. For a refresher on preliminary problem identification see Chapter 5.

6.   C: We haven't settled on what hours they're going to be open. I'd like them open as late as possible, so that might be a problem. Also, if I do offer Empire a better deal than other tenants, I'm concerned about how that might affect those relationships. I guess that's about it.

7.   L: I take it that if you could write your own ticket, you'd like the rent to start as soon as the lease is signed, and have them bear the costs of remodeling. But uppermost in your mind is to secure Empire as a tenant?

8.   C: ...

Here, you find out what brought Mr. Hernandez to your office (No. 1) and seek out his concerns (Nos. 3, 5 and 7). You also make sure that you are clear about Mr. Hernandez's desired outcome (No. 7). Thus, the conversation enables you to learn about the problem from your client's perspective.

Even this brief sample of dialogue touches on some of the topics that Chapter 9 identified as commonly arising in connection with proposed deals. For example, Mr. Hernandez's responses alert you to the likelihood that he is seeking not only legal but also non-legal advice (No. 6). Moreover, you clarify Mr. Hernandez's objectives (No. 7). Naturally, you will explore these and other topics in more detail after preliminarily getting a handle on the scope of Mr. Hernandez's problem.

3. PREPARATORY EXPLANATIONS

As you know, Preparatory Explanations are an effective way of putting clients at ease and promoting their ability to provide the information you seek.[2] In Mr. Hernandez's situation, your Preparatory Explanation may go as follows:

1.   L: A number of your concerns go to the financial aspects of the deal. So what I'd like to do today is to get a general picture of the center and a sense of how it operates. Also, we'll talk a little bit more about Empire and how it operates. I'll also want to know just what terms you and Empire have worked out so far, and any others that you've talked about but haven't resolved. If you feel ready to do so, we can also think about some possible specific lease provisions. Is there anything else you think we ought to cover?

2.   C: No, that sounds like a full menu as is.

3.   L: Great. As we go through matters, I'll try not to go into more details than seem necessary because I realize your time is important and you've dealt with leases many times in the past. But I don't want you to feel rushed. If you have questions or concerns please raise them.

4.   C: I'll do that.

2. See Chapter 5.

5. L: Just one more thing. What lawyers and clients talk about is generally confidential. That means that nothing we talk about will leave the privacy of this office unless you give me express permission to reveal what we've discussed. Now, there are some narrow exceptions to the confidentiality rules. It's unlikely you'll have to be concerned about them, but if at some point I have any concerns along those lines I'll let you know. In the meantime, do you have any questions about confidentiality?

6. C: No I don't.[3]

This explanation is likely to put Mr. Hernandez at ease because you tell him that you're aware of his possible time concerns as well as his experience but also assure him that you are not trying to rush him through the meeting. The explanation is short, and in keeping with his apparent prior experience does not appear to be patronizing.[4]

4. TOPICAL INQUIRIES

Thus far, the approach to gathering information in deals contexts looks much like that in litigation matters. However, in litigation matters this book recommends that you develop clients' stories by combining chronological with theory development topics, with the former typically preceding the latter. However, clients' stories about prior events do not shape deals' operative provisions to nearly the same extent that they do rights and obligations in litigation matters. Hence, moving directly to topical inquiries is typically a more effective approach in deals contexts.

5. ORDER OF INQUIRY

To follow client-centered principles, begin in-depth inquiries with the topics that clients seem to believe are most important. For example, if during preliminary problem identification a client repeatedly mentions his uncertainty about whether or not he should go forward with a deal, you might begin by discussing the client's objectives. On the other hand, if a client repeatedly mentions his anxiety to conclude a deal, you might begin by learning more about the parties' timetable.

If you are uncertain about a client's priorities, consider asking for clarification. For example, as part of a Preparatory Explanation, you might make a statement such as, "I'll be asking you about the terms that have thus far been agreed to and how your business operates....

---

3. Just as you would discuss confidentiality with litigation clients, so too will you want to mention it transactional matters. For a further discussion of confidentiality, see Chapter 5.

4. Recall from Chapter 5 that in litigation matters, preparatory explanations typically alert clients to the differences between time line and theory development questioning. In proposed deals matters, your preparatory explanations can ignore the distinction between time lines and T–funnels prongs set out in Chapters 5 and 6. Clients' legal rights in transactional matters generally are not heavily dependent on the parties' prior dealings and hence your inquiries to a large extent will not be greatly dependent on developing time lines.

Do you have a preference as to which topic you'd prefer to discuss first?"[5]

You may find it difficult to allow clients' interests to control topical order. For example, if Ivan is a new client whose deal relates to a type of business that you know little about, you personally might prefer to start by gathering information about Ivan's business operations. However, unless you feel unable to conduct the interview without having this information, if Ivan is anxious to talk first about provisions on which the parties might have trouble agreeing you should follow his priorities. You almost certainly will be able to inquire about business operations when you discuss those provisions.

If your initial choice of topics grows out of clients' priorities, the order of the remaining topics is of secondary significance. Unless clients' preferences are obvious, you may pursue the remaining topics in whichever order you think best.

6.   USING T–FUNNELS[6]

As you know, the T-funnel technique consists of pursuing topics first with open and then with closed questions. No less than in litigation, this technique is extremely useful in proposed deals contexts.

Consider how you might T-funnel a common proposed deals topic, "the other party." Your client is Serco, a company that hopes to lease a large manufacturing building to the Bictel Corporation for 10 years; Brenda Cassetta is the Serco officer overseeing the deal:

1. L: Now that we've talked about the terms that you and Bictel have worked out thus far, perhaps you can tell me something about Bictel. I find that if I know something about the other party before I start preparing an agreement, I can often phrase things in a way that makes negotiations go more smoothly. What can you tell me about Bictel's objectives in seeking this lease?

2. C: The company makes chemical food additives and it will have to invest in some modifications, particularly in the building's sewer design, to comply with environmental regulations. They don't want to make the investment unless they can amortize the costs over at least 10 years.

3. L: What other objectives might Bictel have?

4. C: They're hoping to make a 15 percent return per year. But there is nothing else specific I can think of.

5. L: Is there any reason in particular that Bictel wants to lease space in that part of town?

5. In most cases, you will not mention each and every topic you intend to pursue during the meeting. Usually, you will want to mention at least a client's objectives, and the terms thus far agreed to. When a client is a new one, you may also want to include the client's business operations, since knowing how a business operates may help you understand all other aspects of a deal and provide advice.

6. For detailed discussion of the T-funnel technique, see Chapter 7.

6. C: Actually, they've leased space in someone else's building for another business division about a half mile away, and I've heard that they're trying to sell a building they own on the other side of town. It looks like they're trying to consolidate their activities down there.

7. L: I know you've been talking about a ten-year lease, but do you think they may be interested in a longer or even more permanent arrangement?

8. C: Actually, in the back of my mind I've thought they may ultimately have some interest in buying the building, so maybe a lease with an option to buy would be the way to go.

9. L: I'll want to ask you more about that in a moment. But first . . .

This dialogue begins a T-funnel pursuit of the other party's objectives. Nos. 1 and 3 are open; Nos. 5 is closed. In No. 1 you also try to motivate Brenda by mentioning an "extrinsic reward."[7] However, in No. 7 you appear to abandon the initial T-funnel (reasons for seeking this location) and move to the topic of a longer lease. Might you have been better off staying with your initial "T" by asking closed questions such as: "Are they interested in providing a better location for their suppliers or customers?" "How about advantages for themselves other than proximity to their other facility?" "Are they trying to get closer access for any other purposes?" Questions such as these are not strictly necessary but they would certainly provide a more thorough inquiry into Bictel's objectives. Uncovering additional objectives could reveal leverage points or problem solving opportunities in upcoming negotiations.[8]

Brenda's response in No. 8 might well have caused you to become sidetracked, as it suggests that what started out as a straight lease may become a lease with an option to buy. However, you "park" the topic and indicate to Brenda that you will return to it, and in the meantime hopefully you will return to the original topic, "Bictel's objectives." Chances are, the topic "Bictel's interest in purchasing the building" will later be the subject of a separate T-funnel dialogue.

Next, consider how you might T-funnel another topic, the lessee's obligation to bear expenses:

1. L: Brenda, you said earlier that Bictel has agreed that the lease will be a triple net lease. I'd like to clarify what costs

---

7. As demonstrated throughout the book, you should routinely incorporate motivational statements into dialogues without waiting for clients to show signs of reluctance. Particularly if they have only infrequently dealt with lawyers in transactional matters, clients may not understand the purpose of your inquiries. In litigation matters, explanations of a topic's relevance may raise difficult ethical concerns, as clients may read an explanation as invitations to tailor their memories to the explanations. In transactional matters, where rights are rarely grounded in disputed versions of past events, explanations are far less likely to prejudice answers.

8. See ROBERT H. MNOOKIN, SCOTT R. PEPPET & ANDREW S. TULUMELLO, BEYOND WINNING: NEGOTIATING TO CREATE VALUE IN DEALS AND DISPUTES, 35–37; 179–181 (2000); CHARLES B. CRAVER, EFFECTIVE LEGAL NEGOTIATION AND SETTLEMENT, 11–15 (4th ed. 2001).

> Bictel will be responsible for during the lease term. Can you tell me what they will be?
>
> 2. C: Taxes, insurance and utilities.
> 3. L: What else?
> 4. C: Nothing; that's it.
> 5. L: How about maintenance costs? Anything there?
> 6. C: Not really. There is no regular maintenance of the building. But if they want some regular cleaning or trash service or anything like that, they'll have to provide it.
> 7. L: Any other costs you expect them to bear?
> 8. C: Well, of course they will be responsible for day to day repairs of things like lights and plumbing. If the transformer breaks down or the roof leaks, we'll take care of those things. But the day to day things are to be their responsibility.
> 9. L: Okay, Bictel will be responsible for day to day repairs. Any other costs whatsoever?
> 10. C: No.
> 11. L: How about the costs of cleaning the building at the end of the term? Who is to bear those?
> 12. C: We hadn't discussed that but we'll want them to bear those as well. We want the place broom clean when they leave.
> 13. L: Off the top of my head that's everything I can think of. Can you think of any costs I've left out?
> 14. C: No.

Here, Nos. 1, 3, 7 and 9 are open questions on the topic of what expenses Bictel will bear. These open questions are interrupted by a closed question, No. 5. However, the effectiveness of the T-funnel technique does not depend on slavish adherence to an ideal order of open followed by closed questions. In addition to No. 5, No. 11 is the only other lower-T closed question, reflecting the fact that there were no other lease costs you could identify. As you do not become sidetracked, but rather stay with the initial topic of the tenant's expenses, you explore the topic thoroughly.

7. ELICITING CHRONOLOGIES

Because you typically gather information in proposed deal settings topically rather than chronologically, time lines are often neither necessary nor useful.[9] Nonetheless, even in deals matters developing a chronology can be helpful. The following subsections illustrate specific instances in which eliciting chronologies of events can be productive.

A. THE TERMS OF PROPOSED DEALS

In simple deals, a straightforward question such as, "What terms have you worked out thus far?" is usually all that is necessary to learn

---

9. For detailed discussion of the time line technique, see Chapter 6.

what terms the parties have already agreed to. In more complex deals, T-funnel questioning may be needed for you to elicit a complete picture of deals' terms. That is, you might ask a number of open questions such as, "Are there any other terms you've agreed to?" followed by closed questions pertaining to the specific deal that is pending.

When the parties have discussed terms a few different times, and those terms have changed, clients may have difficulty remembering just what has been agreed to. Even a T-funnel sequence may not fully jog clients' memories. If clients do have memory difficulties, time line questioning may aid their recall. Examine the following example:

1. C: I know we talked about when and how the deliveries would be made, and about whether the price included shipping costs. But I guess I didn't take good notes, and now I just can't remember if we resolved those things.

2. L: Don, as I mentioned before, we don't want to put something in a draft agreement that you and CIT have not agreed to; they might think we're trying to change the deal. How about a little different approach? Let's go through the three meetings you had with the CIT people one at a time. Tackling things this way sometimes helps people remember more details. Shall we try that?

3. C: Sure. But would it be better just to call up Bauman over at CIT?

4. L: We may end up having to do that. But we don't want them changing the deal on us either, nor do we want to give them the impression that we don't know what we've agreed to. So let's start with the first meeting. Where did that take place?

5. C: It was at their offices.

6. L: Can you picture yourself there and recall the scene?

7. C: Pretty clearly. It was in the afternoon; there were four of us in the room. I was sitting near a door.

8. L: How were you feeling?

9. C: A bit nervous; the deal is really important to us.

10. L: With that picture in your mind, why don't you start at the beginning and take me through the meeting step by step?[10]

11. C: After the usual pleasantries, Bauman asked me to outline our proposal, and I did.

12. L: You've told me about that already, so you needn't do so again. Okay, what happened next?

13. C: . . .

30. L: That was very helpful. What about the second meeting; where and when did that occur?

---

10. Recall that clients often have difficult recalling meetings in chronological order and hence you may need to treat a given meeting as a topic which you then T-funnel. See Chapter 6.

As in litigation matters, breaking "clumps" into sub-events can be a useful technique in deals matters for eliciting details that clients otherwise would be unable to remember. Your asking clients to place themselves at a scene and to remember both their physical and emotional state may further enhance clients' memories.[11]

B. HOW DEALS WILL FUNCTION

Time lines that face forward rather than backward are a useful technique for learning how deals will function. Knowing how a deal will function requires more than knowing that, e.g., "Shirtworld will deliver 12,000 T-shirts printed with the candidate's face and name to the Committee to Elect Dmitri Santorini." If you are to spot potential problem areas and give competent advice, you typically need an overview of how deals will unfold over time. Consider, for example, the dialogue you might have with a representative of Shirtworld:

1.   L: Phil, I know basically what the deal is all about, but it will help me understand problems that might arise along the way if you can walk me through it. Can you start from the point at which the deal is signed, and go step by step through what will happen?

2.   C: Sure, though it's so routine for us by now that we hardly think about it anymore. The very first thing is we order the T-shirts from our overseas supplier, and then we prepare a silkscreen.

3.   L: Do you have to do anything else before you prepare the silkscreen?[12]

4.   C: Well, of course we have to meet with the customer and make sure that the design is one we can work with.

5.   L: In this situation, what do you think that meeting will entail?

6.   C: . . .

9.   L: All right, after the silkscreen is prepared, what will happen next?

A step by step approach such as this may enable you to identify potential problems that may arise in the course of carrying out an agreement. Once problems are identified, you and clients can explore

---

11. Recall from Chapter 9 that sometimes, in addition to learning a proposed deal's terms, you also want to elicit information about the negotiations leading up to those terms. For example, you may want to know what terms the parties have intentionally omitted, and whether the negotiations have been friendly or antagonistic. Time line inquiries are often useful in such situations.

12. If you are knowledgeable about the T-shirt industry, you might realize that a meeting with the customer almost always takes place prior to preparation of the silkscreen. In that case, No. 3 in this dialogue might have been, "Will you meet with someone from the Santorini Campaign Committee before you prepare the silkscreen?" This narrow question is analogous to questions which emanate from your awareness of "normal course" events. See Chapter 7.

whether to address them in final agreements. For example, learning that the T-shirts will be made overseas may prompt discussion of how the agreement might address contingencies such as delays in overseas delivery and possible currency fluctuations.

Finally, through a chronology you learn intimate details of the T-shirt industry that you can lavish upon rapt audiences at social occasions.

C. "QUASI" TIME LINES

While not strictly time lines of events, chronological overviews can help you understand other topics related to proposed deals.

1. Business Operations

Inquiries about business operations typically consist of "here-and-now" topics such as "What does the business do?," "What is your annual volume of sales?" and "Who are your major clients?" However, questions limited to present operations may not provide a true picture of a company. Knowing about companies' pasts can provide insights into such factors as clients' objectives and the problems that deals may create. Eliciting short chronological overviews of businesses' development, therefore, can increase your effectiveness as a counselor.

An open question such as, "Perhaps you can tell me a little about how the company has developed over the years" may be sufficient to elicit all the chronology you need. Sometimes, a client provides too brief a picture—e.g., "We started five years ago and we've been able to treble our gross sales in that period." Such a "quickie time line story"[13] is probably too sketchy to be useful. In such cases, consider a statement such as the following:

> That must be very gratifying. It would give me a little clearer picture of that growth if you could go back to the beginning; tell me how your operations started out, and how they've changed.

You might also consider including a motivational statement in your comments:

> Having a picture of a company's development and the problems you've experienced along the way often helps me understand what you're trying to accomplish with the current deal and spot problems that we might address in the agreement.

While you might ask a few follow-up questions of the "What happened next?" variety, it is unlikely that you will go step by step through a company's entire development. The goal is a general overview of businesses' development, not precise historical narratives.

2. Parties' Past Dealings

Chronologies can also be helpful for learning about parties' past dealings. Again, a single open question may suffice to gather as much

---

13. For a further discussion of "quickie time lines," see Chapter 6.

data as you need: "Tell me something about your past dealings with Kevin." And, if clients' responses are too brief (e.g., "They've been fine."), you can press for further information with the approach described above. For example, you might say something like, "Michael, knowing a little bit more about how past deals with Kevin have worked out will help us think about how to draft the final agreement. For instance, if Kevin in the past has insisted that the absence of a term meant there was no agreement about it, we'll have to be extra cautious when we draft this agreement. Can you think through the past dealings you've had with Kevin and tell me about any big problems that you may have had?"

8. CONCLUSION

Though you largely employ the same techniques in deals and litigation matters, information-gathering in deals matters tends to be more wide-ranging and open. Litigation questioning is generally circumscribed by factual propositions growing out of events that have already taken place.

By contrast, proposed deals matters generally look forward.[14] Hence, inquiries in deals matters tend to be wide-ranging; what "might be" typically raises more possibilities than what "might have been." Most deals can be put together and can unravel in a variety of ways; no single story is controlling. How any deals story unfolds typically depends on how a client *wants* a story to unfold. That is, largely unrestricted by the past, client are generally free to determine where they wish to go, by what route and what risks are worth the trip.[15] Thus, successful information-gathering in deals matters typically features a substantial use of open questions to explore clients' views and expertise on a broad range of possibilities.

---

14. When a proposed transaction involves a repeat deal or a renegotiated deal, your inquiries will typically have to look backward as well as forward. Section 7 above captures this reality.

15. Again, a client's freedom is of course somewhat circumscribed by the other party's needs and desires.

Chapter 11

CONCLUDING CLIENT CONFERENCES

* * *

Ms. Martinez, we've gone about as far as we can today. As we've discussed, by forming a limited liability company you and Richards can insulate yourselves from certain potential liabilities and yet be taxed as individuals. Under current tax law this can be a real advantage since individuals are taxed at a much lower rate than corporations. Do you have any other questions about that?

No. But you did say you'd be able to give me an idea of what your fees are likely to be for this.

Right. My standard fee for setting up a limited liability company is a flat fee of $2500. The fee includes preparing Articles of Organization and an Operating Agreement. Also, I'll file the Articles with the Commissioner of Corporations so the LLC may legally begin operations. I will also prepare the necessary state and federal tax forms. If that fee is agreeable to you, I'll be delighted to undertake this work for you.

Well, it's a little more than I had in mind but I guess we can swing it. Will there be any other costs?

Yes, filing fees, probably not to exceed $200.

So the whole thing should cost less than $3000?

That's right. I understand this may be more than you had in mind, but I think you can see the tax advantages of operating as a limited liability company.

Yeah, I have to keep that in mind. A top of $3000 sounds okay.

Good. As soon as you and Mr. Richards can decide on who the officers and directors will be, I'll need a list of their names and their business addresses. Within a week after I've got that, I'll prepare a draft of the Articles and the Operating Agreement. Then, you can call or come in, and we can go over any questions you or Mr. Richards might have. If everything is satisfactory, I'll file them immediately. We should hear back from the Secretary of State about two weeks after that; then I'll take it from there. When do you think you'll have those names for me?

By the end of the week. We've already been thinking about that, so it shouldn't take long. How long till the company is up and running?

You should be able to start operating in about four-five weeks from when you give me the names. Have you any other questions?

* * *

1. INTRODUCTION

This chapter describes strategies for concluding client conferences productively. Of course, the variations in attorney-client interactions that you may appropriately think of as "conferences" means that a standardized recipe for winding them up effectively is impossible. Thus, the chapter focuses on topics that often are important for you to address during the concluding phase of meetings in which you and clients have addressed significant issues related to their legal problems.

2. SPECIFYING "THE NEXT STEPS"

Social meetings often end on a vague note: "I'll give you a call sometime next week," or, "I'll try to talk to Jeannie and maybe get back to you." On the social level, failure to live up to such vague promises rarely carries serious consequences. In a professional context, however, moving towards satisfactory solutions to clients' problems often depends on shared understandings between you and clients as to the tasks that each of you is to perform. To ensure against breakdowns in communication as to these shared understandings, you may conclude client meetings by addressing (or reviewing) at least the following three matters:

What actions you will undertake, and by when;

What actions clients will undertake, and by when; and

Addressing questions that clients may have.[1]

Identifying actions you will undertake tends to foster clients' confidence that problems will be resolved sooner rather than later.[2] For example, assume that you assure a client that "Within a week after I've got the names, I'll prepare a draft of the Articles of Incorporation and the Operating Agreement. Then, you can call or come in, and we can go over any questions you or Mr. Richards might have. If everything is satisfactory, I'll file them immediately." Such a statement communicates a timetable of concrete steps for moving towards problem resolution, and that you are ready to take them.

Clients should also leave meetings with explicit understanding of their responsibilities, if any. For example, you might remind a client that "I'll be expecting the projected earnings estimates by the end of next

---

1. Of course, one cannot always answer every client question. Often one can do no more than promise a response in the future. Nonetheless, at least address each client question.

2. *Missouri Bar Prentice–Hall Survey* 65–69 & 75 (1963).

week." Even if this is a matter you touched on in mid-conference, a final reminder is often helpful. When clients' tasks are numerous or complex, writing them out improves the chances that clients will follow through. Giving clients specific tasks is also likely to increase their sense of involvement, giving them more confidence in you.[3]

Finally, routinely inviting questions before adjourning meetings is a useful strategy for maintaining rapport and clarifying lingering uncertainties that clients may have.

3. CONCLUDING INITIAL MEETINGS: ESTABLISHING A PROFESSIONAL RELATIONSHIP

The topics described in Section 2 above are generally appropriate at the conclusion of all significant client meetings, including initial ones. The sub-sections below review additional topics that tend to arise primarily during initial client meetings, and that you may find useful to address at the conclusion of such meetings.

A. FORMALIZE AN ATTORNEY–CLIENT RELATIONSHIP

Couples may lead long and happy lives together without ever formally "tying the knot." But your ability to act on behalf of clients depends on formalizing the attorney-client relationship. Hence, before concluding initial meetings, explicitly obtain authority to act on a client's behalf. Make sure to clarify both the scope of your authority and the fee arrangements.

Assuming that clients want you to represent them, common sense and the litigiousness of the American culture suggest that you ask clients to sign written retainer agreements.[4] In a typical scenario, you send retainer agreements to clients some time after they agree to have you represent them. Such agreements often consist of multiple pages. Thus, before adjourning meetings tell clients that they will be sent an agreement and describe generally the agreement's contents and legal significance. Also, ask clients to sign and return an agreement promptly. Clients may find retainer agreements as intimidating or off-putting as other legal documents. Explaining their contents in advance can help you maintain clients' trust and confidence.

B. ESTABLISH A RELATIONSHIP'S PARAMETERS

Having authority to act on a client's behalf leaves open the question of just what it is you have authority to do. Unless you and clients are on

---

3. See Douglas E. Rosenthal, Lawyer and Client: Who's in Charge? 168–69 (1974); S.S. Clawar, You & Your Clients 20 (1988).

4. In general, there is no requirement that your authority to act on a clients' behalf be in writing. See Restatement Third of The Law Governing Lawyers § 14 cmt. c

(1998). Most states, however, require that contingency fee agreements be in writing. Id. at § 38 cmt. b. Also, in certain situations you will need to obtain clients' written informed consent to act on their behalf. See e.g., Model Rules of Prof'l Conduct §§ 1.2 (c), 1.6(a) and 1.7 (b) (2002).

the same wave length, misunderstandings may arise. For example, you may think that a client has authorized you to initiate litigation, whereas a client's understanding is that you are only to conduct preliminary investigation to gauge the client's chance of success should you file suit. Similarly, a client may believe that retaining you to pursue litigation obligates you to pursue an appeal; whereas you intend to agree only to represent the client through the conclusion of trial.

Thus, in addition to establishing your authority to act on a client's behalf, before clients leave your office spell out as clearly as you can your understanding of what they have retained you to do. For example, you may say something like, "Shondell, just so we're together on this, what you're retaining me to do at this point is to research the likelihood that you can exchange your lake side property with the Holmquists for their condo on Walnut Street without having to pay any taxes. After I do that, I'm to get back to you and we'll review the situation further. Am I correct about that?"

C. ESTABLISH A FEE ARRANGEMENT

You should also conclude initial meetings with clear understandings as to fees.[5] Fee discussions often take place near the conclusion of initial meetings, because fee arrangements may depend on the scope of clients' problems and your authority. While the variety of fee arrangements defies setting forth a "typical" fee discussion, the following dialogue may help you verbalize fee arrangements:

1. L: We'll file an answer and thereafter defend this suit vigorously through trial, correct?

2. C: Exactly.

3. L: I'll want to meet with you at least once more before we file any papers with the court to talk more specifically about how I think we ought to proceed. But earlier you asked about my fees, and I think I know enough now to give you a general estimate based on what I know at this point. I'll handle this on an hourly basis; my fee is $225.00 an hour. Some of the work can be handled by Julie, my paralegal assistant, and the hourly rate for her services is $95.00 an hour. I estimate that I'll need to spend about 70 to 100 hours to get ready for a possible trial, though it could go higher if the other side is obstinate and I have to go to court, for example to get court orders requiring them to give me materials that they should turn over voluntarily. My estimate includes taking or attending 3–4 depositions. Other fees will be court costs, costs of the deposition transcripts, and a few other miscellaneous costs for a

---

5. Two areas which typically breed virulent disputes between lawyers and clients are fees and the scope of a lawyer's responsibility. *See* ERIC H. STEELE AND RAYMOND T. NIMMER, LAWYERS, CLIENTS AND PROFESSIONAL REGULATION, 1976 A.B.F.RES.J. 917, 950–56; D.N. Stern and J. Martin, *Mitigating the Risk of Being Sued By Your Former Client*, 51 OKLA.BAR J. 459, 462–63 (1980).

pretrial total of $4,000. If the court decides in our favor, as I suspect it will, we will be able to recoup those costs from the other side. In light of all this, I suggest an initial retainer of $8,500.00; I'll bill you monthly if and when the retainer is used up. Does that sound OK?

4.   C: I guess so. Of course, I wish it weren't that expensive but I guess that's the way things go these days. This is probably a dumb question, but I assume that if the case settles in just a few hours, I'd get the unused part of the retainer back?

5.   L: Of course. You only pay for the time I actually spend. At the same time, remember that if they do take the case to trial, the number of hours I have to spend may go way up. If that starts to happen, I'll let you know. One other thing that I'm ethically required to inform you of is that should you fall too far behind in your payments, I may have to withdraw as your counsel. I'm sure that won't happen, but it's something you should be aware of.[6] Do you have any other questions?

6.   C: No, we seem to have covered everything.

7.   L: Great. Well, you've got your little list there of information I need. And we are going to meet again next Wednesday at 2:00, is that right?

This brief dialogue sets out the specific work you will be undertaking and, based on your stated hourly fee, estimates its cost. In addition, citing "ethical rules" rather than any personal doubt that the client may pay, you explain the consequences of failure to pay your fee. While such a discussion may strike you as "crass," as a professional you are responsible for establishing fee arrangements. [7]

4.   CONCLUDING INITIAL MEETINGS: GIVING A TENTATIVE ASSESSMENT

Needless to say, clients are often anxious to receive assessments of their problems and the parameters of possible solutions as soon as possible. Client expectations of immediate advice are often unrealistic, perhaps founded in false notions about the predictability of legal outcomes. Moreover, initial meetings may well not produce sufficient factual information to enable you to provide realistic assessments or to offer meaningful advice.

However, you may be able to tentatively assess clients' situations. After all, it is unfair, unprofessional and impolite for you to absorb information like a sponge and give nothing back in return. Clients should generally leave initial meetings with some insight into possible

6. For a discussion of when withdrawal of representation is appropriate, see ABA MODEL RULES OF PROF'L CONDUCT RULE 1.16 (2002).

7. *See* MODEL RULES OF PROF'L CONDUCT, Rule 1.5(b) (2002).

resolutions. Unless you really cannot give them, clients are entitled to at least tentative assessments of how things stand.[8]

The issue, then, is how to respond to clients' likely expectations in a way that both inspires their confidence and conveys your need for further information.[9] The suggestions below may prove helpful.

A. ADJOURNING WITHOUT ASSESSING RIGHTS

Clients who want to sue, or who have been sued, usually have an overwhelming "bottom line" interest in knowing whether they are going to "win." "Do I have a good case?" and "Can I get them to tear down the fence?" are questions of the sort that they are likely to ask. While they may not talk about "winning," transactional clients usually have an equal "bottom line" focus. Illustrative questions include, "Will the exchange be tax-free?" and "Do you think they'll grant our license application?"

How might you respond when, because you lack either legal or factual knowledge, you are unable to provide even a tentative assessment? That is, while you believe yourself competent to handle a matter, you are too uncertain of applicable legal rules or of facts to assess realistically a client's position. You can neither reassure clients that their chances are good, nor warn them that they are poor.[10]

In such situations, setting forth the legal parameters in which a client's problem arises and explicitly conveying your desire to provide help may maintain a client's confidence without overstating your analysis.[11] Consider this example.

Your client, Klee, purchased a house from Bussel. A few months later, a wall developed significant cracks, apparently as the result of foundation shifting. Klee does not recall Bussel ever saying anything about problems related to the walls or the foundation. In your judgment,

8. You generally ought to make a tentative assessment even if a client does not think to ask something like, "How do things stand?"

9. Sometimes, even initial meetings conclude with clients making significant decisions. For example, the press of time may compel a client to make a decision based on sketchy data, or an interview may produce sufficient information to permit a decision to be made. The counseling process you might follow to help clients make decisions is the same, whether a decision is made in an initial or a later meeting; for a description of that process, see Chapters 13–20. This chapter assumes that a client is *not* making a significant decision during an initial meeting.

10. For a discussion of how lawyers sometimes manipulate their clients in predicting likely outcomes, see Lynn Mather,

Craig A. McEwen and Richard J. Mainman, Divorce Lawyers at Work 96–98 (Oxford University Press 2001); Gary Bellow, *Turning Solutions into Problems: The Legal Aid Experience*, 34 NLADA Briefcase 106 (1977). For a discussion of the propriety of presenting medical patients with unnecessarily pessimistic prognoses, see M. Siegler, *Pascal's Wager and the Hanging of Crepe*, 293 New Eng. J. of Med. 853 (1975).

11. Obviously, we assume here that you have enough legal knowledge to describe the legal issues that are relevant to a client's problem. If this assumption is incorrect, perhaps you are not competent to handle that problem and should therefore refer the client to another lawyer. ABA Model Rules, *supra* note 4, Rule 1.1. See also Steele and Nimmer, *supra* note 5, at 931–32; ABA Model Code of Prof'l Responsibility, DR 6–101, EC 6–1, EC 6–3.

Klee's ability to recover against Bussel depends on showing that Bussel had actual or constructive notice of wall and/or foundation problems, but said nothing. However, Klee has not provided you with sufficient data for you to assess whether Bussel had such notice. You conclude by telling Klee:

> Cases of this type are governed by the law of misrepresentation. One way to prove misrepresentation is to show that a seller said something that wasn't true.[12] As I understand it, Bussel said nothing about problems with the foundation or cracked walls. However, sellers may also be liable for misrepresentation even when they have said nothing about the condition of property. Sellers have a duty to disclose defective conditions of which they are aware. Thus, your recovering damages probably depends on our ability to show that Bussel was aware of the problems. At this point, I don't have enough information to know whether we'll be able to show that Bussel was aware. We've talked about having a home inspector go through the house and your talking to neighbors about things Bussel had said or repairs he made. When we've gotten that information, I'll be in a better position to let you know how strong your chances are. If it turns out that your chances of recovery are good, we can talk about what action you might take to recover some money.
>
> I really want to help you with this problem. It's very upsetting to buy a house that turns out to have a cracked foundation. I realize that you want to do something as quickly as possible, so I'll ask the home inspector I've worked with before, who really knows houses inside and out, to give this top priority. He'll probably call you tomorrow to arrange the inspection. In the meantime, you'll talk to the Zolts and the Nelsons before the week is out. So we'll work on both fronts at once. All right?

Without predicting the outcome of the factual investigation, this statement hopefully provides enough description of the law of misrepresentation to inspire Klee's confidence that you know the parameters within which a solution might be found. Moreover, it indicates the type of investigation (home inspection; talk to neighbors) that will enable you to provide more specific advice. Also, the statement communicates your integrity. Implicitly, you tell the client that "I know certain things, but I'm willing to be up front about what I don't know." Finally, the explanation helps reassure Klee by articulating explicitly your desire to help.

---

12. For a discussion of the potential ethical problems involved in telling clients what needs to be proved to establish a case, see Monroe H. Freedman, *Professional Responsibility of the Criminal Defense Lawyer: The Three Hardest Questions*, 64 Mich.L. Rev. 1469, 1478–1482 (1966); F. Chilar, *Client Self-Determination: Intervention or Interference*, 14 St. Louis U.L. J. 604, 621–623 (1970). See also the graphic illustration of this problem in Robert Traver, Anatomy of a Murder (St. Martin's Press 1958); the illustrative portions can be found in Andrew Watson, The Lawyer in the Interviewing and Counseling Process 100–108 (1976).

B. ADJOURNING AFTER PROVIDING A TENTATIVE ASSESSMENT OF RIGHTS

When you are comfortable enough to provide tentative assessments, prudence suggests that you also emphasize your need to do additional legal or factual research. Returning to Klee's cracked foundation, assume that the client has given you enough information to predict success in a misrepresentation lawsuit against Bussel. You might couch your assessment in these terms:

> Mr. Klee, based on what you've told me about your conversation with Bussel's former next door neighbor, Gail Glikmann, and on what your contractor friend noticed about the foundation, I think there's a pretty good chance of recovery against Bussel. I do want to caution you, however, that we'll need to have an inspection by a licensed home inspector before I can be more certain.
>
> Also, you asked about your chance of recovery against the real estate agent, Dee Vorsay. Under recent legislation, realtors can be liable if they fail to disclose a significant defect of which they are aware, or could have become aware if they had conducted a reasonably diligent visual inspection. At this point, we don't know very much about what Vorsay knew, and I'm not sure whether the way that courts have interpreted the legislation will allow us to argue that a reasonably diligent visual inspection includes inspection of the foundation. I'll need to do some checking before our next meeting and get back to you on where you might stand with respect to Vorsay.
>
> I intend to do whatever I can to help. When we've nailed down the entire situation, let's talk about how best to proceed.

Here, you tell Klee that "there's a pretty good chance" of recovery against Bussel.[13] However, your prediction is qualified; you remind Klee that you need additional information to make a more certain assessment. Note that this statement, unlike the earlier one, does not provide an overview of the law of misrepresentation. Since you do address the client's probable rights, abandoning the more abstract discussion probably will not undermine the client's confidence.

By contrast, you are unable to make a tentative assessment of Klee's rights against the realtor. Hence, as in the previous subsection you do briefly articulate the controlling parameters, and explicitly express your desire to help.

Despite the qualifications with which you might surround tentative assessments, clients are prone to paying more attention to the assessments than the qualifications. Combined with a psychological phenomenon that many refer to as the "anchoring" effect, your tentative assessments may have greater influence over clients' ultimate decisions than you intend. The "anchoring effect" means that tentative assessments

---

13. When you have enough information to make a more definite assessment, you should generally couch a prediction in terms of numerical probabilities. See Chapter 17.

may create expectations that clients use as the benchmark to which they compare subsequent possible outcomes. Thus, unduly negative tentative assessments may lead clients to accept outcomes that are worse than they could reasonably achieve, simply because those outcomes are better than your tentative assessments. By the same token, unduly glowing initial tentative assessments may lead clients to reject beneficial outcomes simply because they are less than your initial assessments led them to expect. [14]

The anchoring effect need not scare you into refusing to provide tentative assessments. However, realizing that the shelf life of those assessments may be longer than you intend suggests that you be alert to their influence. Stressing the impact of new information on provisional assessments may be one way of countering the anchoring effect.

C. ADJOURNING IN THE FACE OF UNCERTAINTY ABOUT POTENTIAL OPTIONS

Even when you can tentatively assess clients' rights, you may want to conclude initial meetings without exploring possible solutions to their problems. For one thing, you may not know what options are available. More commonly, while you might know about available options, you may lack the facts you need to help clients appraise which option is most likely to be satisfactory.

For example, assume that Phyllis Trimble and Bob Asimow consult with you about their new print shop venture. They want to know "whether we can run the business as a corporation." After some discussion, you recognize that incorporation is a valid option.[15] At the same time, you realize that other options are available which may in the long run be more suited to the clients' needs. For example, they may be better off doing business as a partnership, a limited liability corporation, or a "subchapter-S" corporation. While these options are legally available, you need more information (such as a business plan and projected income) before you can help the clients assess which option might be best. Thus, you want to defer consideration of courses of action until you have more data. You state as follows:

> You initially asked whether you can do business as a corporation. Though we've had just a short time to talk, I can assure you that if you ultimately decide to incorporate you can certainly do so. However, before you decide to do business as a corporation, I think you ought to consider other alternatives that may be a better fit with

14. For a fuller discussion of the anchoring effect, see Russell Korobkin & Chris Gutherie, *Psychology, Economics & Settlement: A New Look At the Role of the Lawyer*, 76 Tex. L. Rev. 101–108 (1997). See also Ian Weinstein, *Don't Believe Everything You Think: Cognitive Bias In Legal Decision Making*, 9 Clin. L. Rev. 783 (2003).

15. Of course, representing parties with conflicting interests would violate your fi-

duciary duties. In this matter, you should give Trimble and Asimow the opportunity to consult with separate counsel. Model Rules of Prof'l Conduct, *supra* note 4, Rule 1.7; Model Code of Prof'l Responsibility, *supra* note 11, DR 5–105, EC 5–14, EC 5–15, EC 5–16; Ronald E. Mallen and Jeffrey M. Smith, Legal Malpractice § 12.2 (5th ed., 2000).

your business, including a limited liability company, a partnership and a sub-chapter S corporation. I'll briefly explain these alternatives and their general plusses and minuses in a moment. But you don't have to decide what to do today. When we have talked more about your business plans and the various choices for structuring your business we can then talk about which structure might be best for you. I'll want you to send me some additional information, and then we can get together and make a final decision. I really want to help you, but for you to make an intelligent choice between these options, we'll need more information than we've been able to gather today. Let's meet again after we get your documents.

As in subsections (A) and (B) above, you lack the information you need to recommend a particular course of action. However, you attempt to instill confidence by assuring the clients of your desire to help, and by identifying the parameters within which a solution is likely to be found.

D. GOOD NEWS, BAD NEWS

Tentative assessments may convey either good news ("I think you've got a real good shot;" "I've just learned that chocolate fudge cake is good for the heart;") or bad news ("Based on what you've told me today, there's some doubt whether Regency will have to agree to your subleasing the property to Explosives Inc."). In either event, you may need to be careful lest clients misinterpret your tentative assessments.

Consider first the happy dilemma of how to convey good news. All too often, clients are prone to hearing only what they want to hear. Therefore, clients may not "hear" a caveat such as, "I'll need to do some research before we can talk about how to proceed with this matter." When clients do fail to hear, they may feel misled and angry if subsequent research alters your assessment.

One way to avoid misplaced confidence is to decline to provide positive assessments unless you are certain of their accuracy. However, such conservatism needlessly frustrates clients and deprives them of assessments that they have a right to hear. Unless you believe clients are incapable of hearing a caveat, emphasizing the tentativeness of assessments seems preferable to following a policy against stating favorable tentative assessments at all. At the same time, unduly stressing caveats may cause clients to wonder whether the news really is good.

With this dilemma in mind, consider the following example. Feinstein wants to sue Archer, the developer of a condominium building, to compel Archer to sell a condo unit to Feinstein. Feinstein contends that Archer refused to sell because of Feinstein's age. You state:

> 1.   L: Ms. Feinstein, your case is covered by a Federal statute forbidding discrimination in the sale of housing. I'm happy to tell you that based on the information you have given me, I think a court is likely to order Archer to sell you the condo on the tentative terms that had been worked out

between Archer and your broker, rather than simply ordering Archer to pay you money damages. However, before we reach a decision about how to best proceed, I want to check the latest court decisions in cases in which courts have been asked to order people like Archer to sell their property. I want to see as best I can what courts have actually been doing most recently in cases like yours. How does that sound to you?

2.   C: So you think I've got a good chance of owning the unit?

3.   L: I think a court will look favorably on your situation and I very much want to help you. But I need to check the latest court decisions before I can tell you just how likely it is that a court will order Archer to sell you the condo. I want to make sure that before you decide to take any action you base your decision on the most up to date information. Does that make sense?

No. 1 conveys both good news and a caveat. Recognizing that the news is good, No. 1 tells Ms. Feinstein that you are happy for her. However, the client's response in No. 2 suggests that she may have heard only the favorable tentative decision, and disregarded the caveat. Thus, No. 3 asks her to confirm that she has heard the caveat. No. 3 is a question rather than a statement. Is it adequately phrased to prevent Feinstein's rose-colored glasses from being too deeply tinted?

Consider next the not-so-happy situation of having to convey bad news. To avoid prematurely dashing clients' hopes, you may (as with good news) contemplate an extreme position of delaying all negative statements until you are certain of their accuracy. After all, who among us does not prefer to postpone, if not avoid, telling clients that their positions appear weak? Again, however, such a cautious approach deprives clients of assessments that they have a right to hear. If prospects seem dim, clients should have the opportunity to know that early on and perhaps discontinue your services.

Clients are unlikely to ignore caveats to negative tentative assessments, since those caveats by definition offer hope. However, you may be prone to "sugar coat" bad news to protect clients' feelings.[16] But if clients are to hear bad news, you must convey it directly. Indeed, consciously using a label such as "bad" may ensure that clients do not distort your message. At the same time, directness and empathy are not incompatible. Thus, when you convey negative tentative assessments, you may also empathize with clients' probable disappointment.

For example, assume that you represent Mr. Pepper, who believes that he was fired illegally by his employer, Data Corp. After talking to Mr. Pepper for an hour, your tentative assessment is that Pepper's chances of regaining his job or recovering damages are poor. Compare these statements:

16. And perhaps to challenge yourself to "get it done?"

Alternative 1

Mr. Pepper, I know you want some idea of what your chances would be if you pursued a wrongful termination claim against Data. Wrongful termination is a relatively volatile area of law; court decisions tend to be conflicting and confusing. This can make it difficult to say where someone in your circumstances is likely to stand. In your situation, many factors are in your favor. You received regular raises, and your annual evaluations were positive. These are things that are important in a case like this. On the other hand, the courts consider strongly how long someone has worked for a company. You were at Data for four years, and while that's a good record, it's probably not long enough to prove an implied agreement that you could remain with Data as long as your work was good. Also, no supervisor ever told you that if you continued to do a good job, your future was secure. I wish I could be more positive at this point but I feel, based on what you've told me, that you have an uphill fight. I'm sorry; I wish I could be more encouraging.

I will be glad to do research and make sure I'm aware of the very latest court decisions. However, I would have to charge you for the time at my regular hourly rate of $225.00 a hour; I'd estimate a fee of about $750.00. I wanted you to hear the down side before you told me to go ahead since you may be throwing good money after bad. What do you think you'd like to do? Have me check further or drop the matter?

Alternative 2

Mr. Pepper, after listening to your story I can't be encouraging. I'd like to say I think things look good but in fact they don't. From what I can see now you probably don't have a case. Two facts probably kill your chances. The first is that you have been with Data for only four years. Courts usually hold that an employee must be with a company for a much longer period of time before they will rule that a company can terminate an employee only for good cause. The second fact is the absence of any statement to you by a supervisor that if you continued to do a good job your future was secure.

I realize my answer is not the one you were looking for. It's a terrible thing to be terminated by a supervisor you do not respect, especially when you've done good work. But I want to be absolutely straight with you, so as not to give you unrealistic expectations.

Now, some facts do cut in your favor, such as your annual promotions and evaluations. Thus, I can research the latest cases to see if there's any basis for a more optimistic prediction. This area of the law is constantly changing, and there may be developments I'm not aware of. However, I would have to charge you for the time at my regular hourly rate; I'd estimate an additional fee of $750.00. I'd be glad to do that research because I'd very much like to help you. What do you think?

While the "bottom lines" might be the same, Alternative 1 seems to "sugar coat" the bad news in a way that Alternative 2 does not. Alternative 1 sandwiches the bad news between favorable factors and willingness to engage in more research. Since some research suggests that people attend more to what they hear first and last than what they hear in between,[17] Alternative 1 may misleadingly soften the negative opinion. By contrast, Alternative 2 puts the negative assessment up front. Also, whereas Alternative 1 vaguely refers to an "uphill fight," Alternative 2 directly tells Pepper that as far as you now know, Pepper probably does not have a good case. Yet, Alternative 2 does not sacrifice empathy for directness. It clearly attempts to convey empathy with the client's probable feelings.[18]

E. ROOKIE NAIVETÉ AND TENTATIVE ASSESSMENTS

Giving even tentative assessments requires that you be somewhat conversant with legal principles and practical options relevant to clients' problems. However, initial meetings typically don't afford you the opportunity to run to the library or the telephone to gain this familiarity. If you are to respond to clients' legitimate desires to know where they stand at the conclusion of initial meetings, you must bring knowledge of legal principles and practical options with you.

"Great in theory," you may say. "But I'm pretty new at this lawyer stuff. How do you expect me to have all this knowledge at my fingertips?"

That concern is a legitimate one. But few attorneys, even very experienced ones, hold themselves out as experts in whatever problems clients may walk in with, and neither should you. A pre-meeting phone conversation with a client, whether involving you, an associate, a secretary, or a paralegal, may alert you to the legal aspects of clients' problems and allow you to research pertinent legal principles and practical options before an initial meeting. Of course, some risk always exists that problems are very different than your initial information suggests. In most instances, however, preliminary information often allows you to do enough research to provide tentative assessments.

---

17. *See*, W.J. McGuire, *Attitudes and Attitude Change, in* 2 THE HANDBOOK OF SOCIAL PSYCHOLOGY, 272–3 (Daneil T. Gilbert, Susan T. Fiske, & Gardner Lindzey eds., 4th ed., 1998).

18. Each alternative assumes that you are familiar enough with the law and the facts to give "bad news." In the absence of such familiarity, you would have to defer giving advice.

Chapter 12

GATHERING INFORMATION FROM ATYPICAL AND DIFFICULT CLIENTS

1. INTRODUCTION

For the most part, client-centeredness assumes a spirit of good faith and cooperation between attorney and client. While clients may be subject to the lapses in memory and emotional travails that beset us all, they are responsive, interested in supplying information and generally honest. However, familiarity with human nature tells you that these assumptions do not describe the entire universe of clients. This chapter examines techniques for interviewing "problem" clients.[1]

2. RELUCTANCE TO DISCUSS PARTICULAR TOPICS

A common exception to the assumption of "good faith and cooperation" concerns clients who are generally open and responsive but who evidence reluctance to discuss particular subjects. With such clients, the directness and breadth of their responses tends to change noticeably when a topic that they find unpleasant or threatening comes along. Rather than remaining open and informative they become evasive and non-communicative. The subsections below examine options for dealing with this common kind of reluctance.

A. SOURCES AND INDICIA OF RELUCTANCE

Consider the following three hypothetical situations:

1. A client's matter involves a potential action for wrongful death based on medical malpractice. The apparent malpractice occurred when the deceased went into hospital for apparently routine surgery. The deceased's condition following the surgery grew pro-

---

1. Chapters 13–18 examine, in part, difficulties you are likely to encounter in counseling clients. For example, Chapter 18 explores, among other matters, how you might proceed when your client cannot make a decision or mispredicts a decision's likely outcome.

gressively worse, and death occurred two weeks later. You are about to question the deceased's surviving spouse about conversations between the deceased and the principal doctor over the two-week period.

2. This client's matter is a civil suit for damages growing out of incidents of sexual molestation. The client is a parent of two young girls who were molested by a man who was their Sunday school teacher as well as a personal friend. You are about to talk to the client about a period of time when the client permitted the molester to live with the client and the children, before the girls revealed the incidents of molestation.

3. This client's matter concerns alleged fraud by a mortgage broker in connection with the sale of a house. Some years earlier the client had purchased a small house and had financed the purchase with a loan from a mortgage loan broker. After making payments for years, the client received a letter from the mortgage company stating that a "balloon payment" was owed, and that unless it were paid the company would foreclose on the house. The client has stated that the broker never said anything about a balloon payment, and you are about to probe the conversations that took place around the time the loan was taken out.

Why might these situations produce client reluctance? In the first example, a surviving spouse will be asked to recall conversations between a recently deceased spouse and an allegedly negligent physician. The surviving spouse may well have to relive the emotional pain that followed the surgery. Recall that "trauma" can inhibit the flow of information.[2] In order to avoid reliving the traumatic experience, the client may be reluctant to recall the details of the conversations.

The ego threat inhibitor may arise in the second example. Asking the client about allowing a person who turned out to be a molester to live in the client's home may threaten the client's ego.[3] The client may well feel guilty and shameful for failing to be more perceptive, and hence may try to avoid discussion of the topic.

Finally, ego threat may also be present in the last example. Fraudulent loan practices may not be as emotionally charged as child molestation. However, the client may well believe that you will regard the client as stupid for not adequately investigating the loan deal, and be reluctant to discuss that part of the transaction.

B. TECHNIQUES FOR RESPONDING TO CLIENT RELUCTANCE

Before thinking about how you might respond when clients evidence a reluctance to provide information, first consider whether in any of the foregoing situations you might have *anticipated* the client's reluctance.

2. For a discussion of the inhibitor of trauma, see Chapter 2.

3. For a discussion of the inhibitor of ego threat, see Chapter 2.

When you feel confident that a topic will create reluctance, you may want to make a preparatory statement designed to motivate a client to participate. Review again the three examples above to explore how reasonable it would be for you to anticipate reluctance.

In the first two examples, the topics by their very nature suggest potential client reluctance. Death of a spouse and molestation of one's children by a close friend are extremely painful subjects. You therefore might anticipate that the clients will be reluctant to talk. But in the last example, is reluctance so easy to predict? If the client feels sheepishly guilty about being taken advantage of, the client may be reluctant to talk. On the other hand, if the client feels outrage because of having been taken advantage of, the client may not want to talk about anything else. Therefore, in the absence of clues that the client is anxious to avoid the topic—e.g., body movements indicating uneasiness; hesitancy to speak; silence; the client's changing the topic—you might reasonably not anticipate client reluctance in the last example.

No matter whether you anticipate reluctance or become aware of it in the course of discussion, your options are to (1) ignore the problem and press on with the topic; (2) postpone consideration of the topic until a future time when greater rapport or some other factor will overcome the client's reluctance; or (3) mention the problem of reluctance and seek to overcome it through discussion. In the abstract, no choice is inherently likely to be better than another. Considering such factors as clients' personalities and your need for immediate discussion of a topic will at least insure that your choices are professionally responsible. Below, consider a few techniques for employing option No. 3, directly raising clients' reluctance.[4]

1. *Motivational Statements*

Motivational statements explicitly recognize or anticipate clients' reluctance and invite them to disregard it. One type of motivational statement consists of two parts. The first part attempts to overcome the inhibiting factor by conveying *empathic understanding* of the clients' anxiety or discomfort. The second part utilizes a *facilitator,* and typically

---

4. Professor Ellmann has argued that the use of techniques to overcome reluctance is manipulative because a client is not first made aware that remaining silent may be a better choice than divulging information. Stephen Ellmann, *Lawyers and Clients*, 34 UCLA. L. REV. 717 (1987). After all, sometimes the resultant data requires you to act against a client's interests. For example, if a client indicates an intent to commit a crime, you may be permitted to disclose this intention to the authorities. See, e.g., ABA Model Rules of Professional Conduct, Rule 1.6 (2002). Professor Ellmann's point that clients are encouraged to divulge information without understanding possible adverse reactions is correct. How-ever, we believe the practice of encouraging clients to reveal information so that you can help them is a time honored one which you should continue. First, until the information is revealed there is no meaningful way to assess whether a revelation is helpful or harmful. Second, Professor Ellmann's point proves too much. All questions are intended to cause clients to reveal information. Surely no one would suggest that each should be preceded by a warning that a response may be harmful; such a result would surely paralyze all lawyer-client dialogue. *See also,* John K. Morris, *Power and Responsibility Among Lawyers and Clients: Comment on Ellmann's "Lawyers and Clients,"* 34 UCLA L. REV. 781 (1987).

points out that benefit the clients are likely to gain by overcoming the inhibitor and discussing a topic openly.[5]

For example, return to the client whose spouse recently died as the result of alleged medical malpractice. Assume that you anticipate the client's reluctance to describe the deceased spouse's deathbed conversations with the physician, and you decide to make a motivational statement in advance. The motivational statement may be along these lines:

> Ms. Bridges, I'd like to turn next to conversations your husband had with his physician after his surgery and before his death. I realize that this may not be easy for you; it may cause you to relive some very painful memories. But I'll be in the best position to help you if you tell me as much as you can recall.

Here you not only acknowledge that the topic will not be easy, but also identify a reason that it may not be easy: "it may cause you to relive some very painful memories." You may have chosen to omit this latter segment, since by including it you run the risk of playing "amateur psychologist." However, since just about everybody would agree that talking about the recent death of a spouse is likely to be painful, there is little risk to such a statement. As for the second, "reward," portion of the statement, it is a generic statement of potential benefit, not keyed in to this or any other client in particular. As such, you may employ this form of remark in most motivational statements.

Consider next the client faced with foreclosure. Assume that you do not anticipate client reluctance to discuss conversations with the mortgage loan broker. But after broaching the subject, you realize that the client seems uneasy and unwilling to talk about it. Since you did not anticipate reluctance, you may be unable to reflect the client's precise feelings. Hence, you might simply try to recognize the client's discomfort with a statement such as,

> "You look uncomfortable. It seems like something is bothering you."

This remark is empathic to a degree; it recognizes the client's discomfort. However, it may suggest criticism and therefore may make the client feel defensive. The client may respond in self-defense: "I don't feel uncomfortable. What makes you say that?" Or, the client's response may be vague: "I guess I'm just uncomfortable talking to a lawyer."

Hence, when clients seem uncomfortable, but you are uncertain of the reason, you may want to try other forms of motivational statements. One alternative is a *normalizing response*. A normalizing response tends not to make clients defensive because it spreads their feelings over a large group of clients. For example, you might say,

> You seem a bit uncomfortable. You know, many people feel there are things they would rather not tell their lawyers. I understand that; after all, we do not know each other very well yet, and I can understand that many people find it difficult to confide in someone

---

5. For a review of facilitators, see Chapter 2.

who is a relative stranger. But only if I have all the information can I fully protect your interests.

Here too, you point out the client's discomfort. But by also stating that many people feel just as the client seems to, you avoid direct criticism. Again, you conclude with a generic statement of reward and a desire to help.

A second form of motivational statement you may use when uncertain of the basis of reluctance is a *request for corrective feedback*. Here, you take personal responsibility for a client's discomfort. A normalizing response puts the focus on the client; a request for corrective feedback places it on you. For example, again in the context of the foreclosure matter, you might say,

> I have the sense there is some difficulty here. Perhaps something I've said has made you uncomfortable, or maybe even something that I've failed to say. Is there anything you want to tell me? I hope you'll let me know if I've said something that makes you feel uncomfortable.

Though clients' reluctance may have nothing to do with what you have said or failed to say, such a remark is likely to convey empathy without putting clients on the defensive. It may even encourage clients to describe the underlying source of concern:

> No, it's nothing you've done. It's just that I think maybe I should have asked about a balloon payment, and I'm feeling kind of dumb.

2. *Confidentiality*

When utilizing motivational statements, you may also want to stress attorney-client confidentiality:

> Remember, unless you tell me you're planning to rob a bank or something like that, everything you tell me is confidential. I cannot and will not divulge anything you say without your express permission.[6]

3. *Changing the Pattern of Questions*

Another option when facing reluctant clients is to change your questioning pattern. If you have been using open questions, try a series of narrower ones; or vice versa.[7] As mentioned in Chapter 4, while open questions do motivate many people to provide narrative-type responses, there are clients for whom this is not true. Even clients who are generally forthcoming in response to open questions may become reluc-

---

6. Hopefully, the humorous reference to bank robbery reminds clients the attorney-client privilege is not unlimited while still providing motivation. For a more complete discussion of confidentiality, see Chapter 5. See also ABA Model Rules, Rule 1.6 and Comments to Rules 1.7 and 1.13.

7. Whether you approach reluctance through open or closed questions, you need to maintain a calm and respectful demeanor. If your tone of voice or body language suggests the topic makes you uncomfortable, the form of your questions will probably have little effect on your client's reticence.

tant to talk about anxiety-producing events. Such clients may respond better to narrow questions which can help ease them into describing anxiety-producing events by eliciting information one step at a time. Narrow questions can remove some of the burden of disclosure by moving into topics "bit by bit."

Assume for example that you represent Charles Brown Inc., which is involved in a proposed deal to sell equipment to Gooddeal Inc. When through an open question you ask Brown to describe his prior relationship with Gooddeal, Brown hesitates and then says, "It's been okay; nothing to really talk about." Sensing reluctance, you choose to ease into the topic through narrow questions such as, "How many times have you dealt with Gooddeal?" "When was the first time?" and "What kind of a deal was that?" Perhaps in response to these specific questions, Brown may gradually reveal what is actually bothering him.[8]

Whether you move from open to closed questions, or the other way round, you may use a motivational statement as well. By way of example, return to the client whose children were molested by a close friend. Assume that your theory is that the church that employed the friend as a Sunday school teacher is liable for damages caused by acts of molestation committed on church property. You are concerned that evidence that the client permitted the molester to live in the client's home may in some way diminish the church's liability. However, you are not aware of any acts of molestation in the client's home. Well into theory development questioning, the client has been quite responsive to your questions. You now begin to question about the period of time the friend lived with the client:

1. L: Now, you indicated there was a period of time when Mr. Johnson came to live with you and the kids. Can you tell me more about that?

2. C: There's not much to tell. He just needed a place to stay; he asked if he could stay with us, so I said OK.

3. L: All right. Please continue.

4. C: That's really all. He stayed about 6 months.

5. L: Why don't you tell me all you can about how he came to live with you, and as much as you can remember about what went on during the period he lived with you.

6. C: Really, there's just not much I can remember. He was a close friend, or so I thought, and he needed a place to stay—that was all.

At this point, you realize that open questions are getting nowhere. Therefore, you change tactics:

---

8. Perhaps, for example, Brown's prior deals with Gooddeal have not gone well and Brown is afraid you will think him a fool for entering into another deal with Gooddeal. Of course, if this is the case it may be very helpful for you to understand why the prior difficulties arose.

7. L: Jean, so far you've been quite open with me and I really appreciate that; I'm sure it's not easy to talk about this with a stranger. I have the feeling there's probably more you can tell me about the period when Mr. Johnson lived with you. Maybe, in the light of what you later found out, you feel uncomfortable talking about allowing him to live with you. Or maybe this part of the story just doesn't seem important. I can understand that. Also many people know things they just feel should remain private; I can understand that as well. But I want to do the very best job I can for you and the girls and if I don't have all the information it's going to be difficult for me to do that. Frankly, one of the hardest things about being a lawyer is learning information from the other side that I should already have been told by a client. Remember, whatever you tell me is confidential except in situations that don't seem to apply to you. So let me ask you this, who first suggested that Mr. Johnson come to live with you.

8. C: He did.

9. L: Do you remember where and when he mentioned it?

10. C: Sometime in the spring, I remember it was around Easter. I had come to pick up the girls after Sunday School, and we just got to talking.

11. L: You're doing fine. Can you tell me as much as you can remember about the conversation?

The statement in No. 7 effectively combines many motivational techniques. You empathize with Jean's feelings, make a normalizing remark, employ the "reward" facilitator, stress confidentiality and change from open to closed questions. Then, with the client seemingly becoming more responsive, No. 11 returns to a more open type of question.[9]

3. RELUCTANCE TO COMMENCE AN INITIAL INTERVIEW

L: Ms. Bryant, how can I help you?

C: I'm just not sure ...

L: Can you tell me a bit about what brought you in here?

C: It's kind of silly, really. A birthday party at a roller rink, I slipped ... I'd just as soon not bother ...

L: Can you tell me a little bit more?

C: It's my husband and friends really, they're pushing me ... I just don't know....

As the foregoing example suggests clients who have set up initial meetings may nevertheless arrive at your office feeling quite reluctant to

9. Though No. 7 seems generally effective, you may have concerns about it. Is the "kitchen sink" approach too lengthy, and perhaps intimidating?

discuss the matters that brought them to see you. For many people, whether it involves beginning a new social relationship, taking a new course or seeing a new doctor, beginnings are difficult. Moreover, as the above example illustrates clients do not necessarily come to see you entirely of their own volition; they are in your office physically, but not mentally.

The following techniques may help you get started.

A. MOTIVATIONAL STATEMENTS AND CLOSED QUESTIONS

The motivational techniques described in the preceding sections are also effective with clients who are reluctant to commence initial interviews. Empathizing with their discomfort, making a normalizing remark and emphasizing confidentiality may help clients get started. Likewise, a shift to closed questions may take the conversational onus off the client at least temporarily. Especially if the questions seek non-threatening, statistical-type information, a client can ease into supplying more important data. For example, with the personal injury client above, you may ask questions such as:

L: At which roller rink did this occur?

L: What time of day did the mishap occur?

L: On what date did this happen?

If you sense that clients' reluctance stems from uncertainty about whether to get enmeshed at all with a lawyer, statements such as, "Only if I have all the information can I adequately protect your interests" may further inhibit client cooperation. Clients may feel that supplying information is a commitment to forging ahead before they have decided to do so. To prevent this reaction, you may want to make a "reward" statement such as, "Only if I first have some basic information can we decide together whether it makes sense for you to become involved with a lawyer."

B. ASKING CLIENTS TO QUESTION YOU

Another motivational approach you can employ when reluctance appears at the outset of a meeting is to ask, "Perhaps you have a question or two you want to ask me?" Asking such a question may ferret out the reason for reluctance. However, be aware that many people are not comfortable asking questions. For example, many law students who have gone through job interviews say they are always uncomfortable when they are asked, "Do you have any questions about our firm?"

A method that may overcome this potential source of discomfort is to follow the general question with a *normalizing question*. In other words, have ready a question of the sort that is likely to have been asked by many past clients, and mention it to the reluctant client as an example of the type of question the client may have. Your remark may go as follows:

Perhaps you have a question or two you want to ask me. For example, clients often want to know whether they are committed to going forward if they talk to me. Well, let me assure you that talking this over with me in no way obligates you to hire me or to go forward with this matter. I'd like to help and perhaps a good place to start is with your questions and concerns.

4. COMMUNICATING WITH AGED AND INFIRM CLIENTS

You may have difficulty getting information from some clients not because of reluctance, but because it is difficult for them to communicate. Common barriers to satisfactory communication include advanced age and medical infirmity. Certainly not every older person will have difficulty recalling and conveying information. But when the situation does arise, you want to be prepared to surmount it.

One skill you need to draw upon to interview and counsel clients with such difficulties is patience. What initially seems clients' marginal ability to respond may be little more than a relaxed style of speech. Moreover, elderly and infirm clients may want to talk more about their physical condition, the medical care they need and its expense rather than their legal situation. In such circumstances, you may afford them leeway to talk as you listen empathically before redirecting them to more relevant concerns. Furthermore, age and the side effects of medication tend to slow memory. You may therefore wait longer than usual for aged and infirm clients to respond. Also, you may reassure them that if a "senior moment" prevents them from remembering information until after they have left your office they are welcome to contact you. But when clients have genuine difficulty understanding and responding, you will need more than patience.

One simple technique is to ask closed questions. Clients who have difficulty communicating are more likely to respond to closed questions than open ones. However, you must be careful. The more difficulty that clients are having, the more likely are you to ask questions that are leading. Clients' responses to open questions may in turn mislead you if they simply agree to incorrect information rather than point out your mistakes.

Another technique is to speak to aged and infirm clients in surroundings comfortable to them. Thus, you may urge such clients to come to your office with a close relative or friend. Or, you may hold the major portion of an interview in clients' homes. Estate planning lawyers often interview clients in the presence of a client's personal physician.

If none of these techniques succeed, you'll need to consider whether you can represent a client without someone first having been appointed as a conservator or a guardian ad litem.[10]

---

10. *See* RESTATEMENT THIRD OF THE LAW GOVERNING LAWYERS § 14 cmt. d. Special considerations may also apply to gathering information from children. *See* Nancy W.

5. RAMBLING CLIENTS

L: Mr. Weldon if you could write your own ticket in this matter how would you like this situation to turn out?

C: I'm glad you asked me that because I've given it a lot of thought. I mean a lot of thought. I guess I've spent weeks thinking about this. I'd like several things to happen. I'm not sure I can have them all but I'd really like to have each of them if it doesn't turn out to be too expensive. Money, of course, is a concern to me. I don't have all the money in the world and I know that lawsuits are really expensive. I don't want to lose any more money. God only knows, I've already lost a fortune. I mean a fortune for someone in my circumstances and I want to get back all the money this has cost me. I mean I want all of it; every damn penny that this has cost me. I guess the biggest item is what I had to spend to remedy the problems with the lack of adequate retaining walls. I don't have an exact figure today but I have most of the bills at home and I know I've spent more than $75,000 dollars on these walls and that doesn't take into account the other $10,000 I put into getting the house back in shape after the mud slide. That slide was just ruinous. I mean there was mud in most of the house including the living room, the den, the dining room and the kitchen. It took almost two months to get the house back in shape and we had to live in a motel for at least a month. And of course, there is all the aggravation that this caused both me and my wife, especially my wife. For days she couldn't sleep or eat; she had to see our doctor several times and take a bunch of pills. She is still after me over the whole thing; it's just awful. Also there is all the landscaping we lost and had to replace and the trip to New York that we had to cancel. I had to have an architect draw plans for the retaining walls, get permits to put them it and hire a contractor. It almost a year just to get this done. There was so much hassle and frustration along the way that I really can't begin to tell you about it. It was unbelievable. My brother in-law is a broker and he says he has never seen anything like it. Of course, I'd like to see this guy punished. He knew damn well that the hill hadn't been properly graded. He told me that the hill was in perfect shape and dummy that I am I believed him. My brother in-law told me to have a geologist look at it but I was too stupid to listen. I remember him telling me, "Bob you've got to get a geologist." But I'd already had a contractor look at the house and he said it was fine. That Harvey Yellin is a crook and should be punished just like any other crook. I can't

Perry and Larry L. Teply, *Interviewing, Counseling, and In–Court Examination of Children: Practical Approaches for Attorneys,* 18 CREIGHTON L. REV. 1369 (1985) as well as RESTATEMENT THIRD OF THE LAW GOV- ERNING LAWYERS § 14 Cmt. d. For an additional discussion of dealing with clients you suspect may be mentally infirm, see Chapter 21.

tell you how much I hate that bastard. I really can't; night after night I wake up thinking about the bastard. Even after it happened the way he treated my wife when she called him was just unforgivable. He yelled at her and swore and she ended up crying. I just couldn't calm her down. I finally called him and we had it out and I mean we had it out. I told him just what I thought and he didn't like it either but it certainly made me feel a little bit better. Any how this is how I'd like this to turn out. I want cold hard cash in my pocket and him in jail that would be the ticket I'd like to write.

Perhaps every lawyer's worst fear are rambling clients, clients who view questions as licenses to speak almost endlessly about whatever comes to mind.

Clients, of course, may ramble for a variety of reasons. Clients may ramble because topics relate to emotionally charged or threatening occurrences, or because of a "greater need" to discuss their own subjects. Or because of underlying personality factors, clients may have difficulty sticking to topics.

Your initial decision in the face of a rambling response is likely to be whether to ignore or respond to the rambling behavior. For instance, assume that a client responds as in the above example. Would your tendency be to ignore his rambling, to interrupt him and try to get him more focused, or to attempt to confine him in the future to relevant responses? Obviously no formula points to an unerringly correct approach. Your judgment in individual cases must inevitably depend on such factors as time pressures, overall rapport, the degree to which rambling responses provide relevant information and the extent of the rambling. You may well decide to ignore rambling. Indeed, even when clients' responses consist of little more than rambling you may choose to ignore it, perhaps on the theory that they will eventually wear down and respond to ensuing inquiries.

When you decide to confront rambling clients, the following approaches may help. First, you may respond by empathizing with the clients' concerns as evidenced in the rambling statements. Often, clients will ramble continuously about the same limited subject matter. Yet, aware that the clients' responses have little or nothing to do with your questions, you may repeatedly fail to respond to what the clients say. The conversation resembles two ships passing in the night: you ask questions that are not answered, clients make statements that you ignore. By simply empathizing with clients' concerns, you may satisfy their need to be heard and thereby diminish their tendency to ramble.

For example, consider this dialogue from a videotaped sample lawyer-client interview prepared in England.[11] In this demonstration, the

11. Videotape: Solicitor/Client Relationship—Video 1, (The Law Society, Ellis & Barton Productions Ltd., 1984).

client has come to see a solicitor about a divorce. The lawyer is questioning the client about the husband's earnings:

1. L: And before he was made redundant [laid off], you think he was earning a hundred and twenty pounds a week?

2. C: Yes.

3. L: Now, whose name is the rent book in?

4. C: Um, I think it's in both our names, but the rent gets paid from my husband's bank account on a standing order. And the thing is it hasn't gone through the last couple of months because we've had these letters from the council saying we're in arrears but all he does is throw them in the bin. And what I reckon is that he's going to take the car and sell it without telling me, and that's not on because it was my Mum's money what we used . . .

5. L: Yes, yes . . . hold on. The rent book is in both your names and your husband's been paying the rent, until recently, at any rate.

6. C: Yeah, but I don't reckon he's going to pay the arrears, and if he sells the car . . .

7. L: Right. Yes, well, if we're going to make quite sure that you are able to keep the flat, Mrs. Albert . . .

In this exchange, the client is clearly concerned about her car. Perhaps because the lawyer never acknowledges the concern, the client keeps returning to it. Consider the possible benefit of an empathic response by the lawyer such as:

> Mrs. Albert, I know how concerned you are that your husband not sell a car that belongs to both of you and that was bought with money that your mother gave you. I'd like to talk to you about that a bit later on. For the moment, however, let's concentrate on an even more pressing concern, making sure you and your children can stay in your flat. Now, in that regard . . .

Here, the lawyer explicitly acknowledges that the lawyer has heard the client's concern. Moreover, the empathic response includes "reward" facilitators—if the client bears with the lawyer now, the lawyer will satisfy the client later, and by sticking with the lawyer's topic, the client will have her most pressing concern addressed. Though brief, this sort of response can greatly reduce a client's impetus to ramble. Note that following the empathic response, the lawyer simply proceeds with the interview.

If rambling persists despite your empathic response, you may employ a series of closed questions. Their limited focus of inquiry offers clients less opportunity to ramble. Once you get a client back on a non-rambling track, you may even revert to a more open questioning pattern.

Another approach, which you can use when speaking with talkative clients who you anticipate are likely to get off track, is to alert the client in advance to your possible need to interrupt. To apologize in advance, you might make a comment along the following lines.

> I want to apologize in advance for any interruptions I may make in our conversation if I find we're getting off track. I don't like to interrupt but I find that in many instances it helps us use our time together more effectively.

Such an apology is usually well received. Typical client responses are, "You're right; I'm just so upset it's hard to stop myself" and "I know I'm a real talker, so go ahead and speak up when you need me to stop."

A final approach is to (1) interrupt clients in mid-stream, (2) explicitly point out that they are talking about a subject that is different from the one you have asked about and (3) secure their agreement to focus on your topic. Because this approach can offend clients, you typically will employ it only in situations involving continued or severe rambling. Nonetheless the approach is one that you may need to use in situations that involve prolonged or severe rambling. The following example illustrates this approach.

> L: After you told Ferguson that he needed to research his deals more carefully, what happened next?
>
> C: He brought in three more dead deals. It made me think of the decision to hire him. We never should have done that. We didn't interview enough candidates because we were desperate to find someone. Gosh we were desperate. I don't think we called all the references and not everyone interviewed him. I know I didn't. Of course, it wasn't my decision. Jennifer Suplee was....
>
> L: (Interrupting) Dorothy, let me interrupt you. I think we need to be a bit more focused here. I'm trying to learn what happened just after you told Ferguson that he needed to research his deals more carefully; this is something that is important for me to learn about in deciding how we should reply to his complaint. However, you're telling me about what went on before Ferguson was hired. For instance you're talking about not calling all his references and not fully interviewing him before he was hired. These matters may be important and we can come back to them. But for now let's focus on what happened next after you told Ferguson that he needed to research his deals more carefully. Is that okay?

Here, when you interrupt you first clearly identify the topic on which you seek information. Next, you try to motivate Dorothy to focus on your topic by explaining that the topic is important to you. Next you make clear exactly in what respect Dorothy's response talks about a topic different from the one you have asked about. Indeed you go so far as to specifically identify the subjects that she has talked about: "[Y]ou're talking about not calling all his references and not fully interviewing him before he was hired." You then try to motivate Dorothy by acknowledging that her information may be important. Finally you seek her agreement to concentrate of your subject. When such interventions produce your desired result, you might further motivate clients with a comment such as the following.

> Dorothy, that was great. You've focused your answer on what happened after you told Ferguson that he needed to research his deals more carefully. I really appreciate your keeping your attention focused on that topic.

With clients who are severe ramblers, you may need to use this "interruption" approach more than once before you can focus clients on the information you seek to elicit. And of course in some situations you may never fully succeed in doing so and thus may end up having to deal with clients who ramble repeatedly.

6. CLIENTS WHO ARE HOSTILE, ANGRY AND EXPLOSIVE

Clients' inner pressures may escalate to the point that they explode into fits of anger, hurt or hostility. With some clients, fits take the form of tears; with others, they take the form of complaints, threats or accusations. Though you may think such fits are confined to inherently emotional matters such as child custody disputes, in fact outbursts are possible in virtually any type of matter.

For example, assume that a client with whom you have enjoyed good rapport in the past owns a commercial building and seeks assistance about how to evict a tenant who is several months behind in rent. During the discussion, you learn that recently the client received a notice from the bankruptcy court that the tenant, Rowe, has sought protection from creditors pursuant to Chapter 11.[12] The dialogue then goes as follows:

1.   L: That's going to present some complications that we need to talk about. Once a debtor seeks the protection of the bankruptcy court, the court automatically halts any lawsuit against the debtor. Before we can evict Rowe, we'll need permission of the bankruptcy court, which may not be granted.

2.   C: What does that mean? When will I be able to get my back rent, and when will I be able to get this deadbeat out?

3.   L: That's hard to say. We'll need to file two actions. First, we'll have to go to the bankruptcy court and get its permission to sue Rowe. Then, we have to file an unlawful detainer action against Rowe in state court ...

4.   C: WHAT THE HELL IS ALL THIS? WHO IS BEING PROTECTED ANYWAY? HE'S GOT MY MONEY, HE'S ON MY PROPERTY, AND THE BEST YOU CAN DO IS

12. See 11 U.S.C. § 101 et seq. (1988).

TELL ME IT'S HARD TO SAY. I'VE HAD IT WITH THIS FUCKIN' LEGAL SYSTEM. A FEW MONTHS AGO SOME OTHER TENANTS JUST ABOUT DESTROYED ONE OF MY BUILDINGS, THESE GODDAMN PUNKS SCRAWL GRAFFITI ALL OVER THE WALLS AND THE COPS AND COURTS DON'T DO A DAMN THING!

Here, the conversation was proceeding along smoothly when, out of the blue, something you said triggered the client to do his best impression of Mt. Vesuvius. Such eruptions are likely to leave you wondering, "Where on earth did that come from? Should I have seen it coming? What do I do now? Why did I go to law school anyway?"

Realize that you need not feel guilty for failing to predict sudden outbursts. After all, geologists have spent entire careers trying to predict earthquakes and volcanic eruptions, often without success. Sporadic and intense human behavior is often no easier to predict than seismic waves.

If you often cannot predict sudden outbursts, you can at least anticipate that some clients will suffer sudden losses of control. Clients may, with some justification, feel that problems are undeserved, unfair, outrageously expensive, difficult to escape and a "no-win" situation. Recognizing that it is very normal and understandable that clients may sometimes lose control should help you realize your need to try to respond to outbursts with skill and compassion.

First, recognize that at times clients may give off cues that an eruption is imminent. If you realize that a client is tired and on edge, you might initiate a short break. For example, perhaps you and a client have spent a good deal of time pouring over a complex document, and you notice the client becoming impatient and cranky. You might say, "We've been at this awhile. I know I'm getting worn down. How about a short breather?"

If an outburst occurs without warning, active listening is a powerful skill for responding with compassion. You may not be able to immediately take away clients' hurt and anger, but you can let them know that you understand and accept how upset they feel. For example, following the client's outburst in No. 4 above, you might have said, "I can understand your outrage. The bankruptcy laws seem to protect only the tenant at the expense of the owner."[13]

Another tactic is to allow clients a "cooling off" period following an emotional outburst. It is often unrealistic to expect that active listening responses will instantly defuse clients' anger and allow you to continue on as if nothing had happened. Offer clients a chance to relax, perhaps with a soft drink or fruit juice.

13. You need not, and probably could not, respond to all the ills apparently besetting the client. It is generally enough to respond to the immediate source of the client's complaint.

Finally, help clients recover from outbursts by offering a face-saving, "normalizing" response. After an outburst, clients may feel sheepish, embarrassed or ashamed. As a result, they may try to make light of their discomfort. For example, the client above might say, "Well, my friends always say I have a short fuse." Control the impulse to tease back: "Short? More like invisible!" Instead, offer a response that generalizes and normalizes a client's feelings: "All of us blow up once in a while when we face seemingly outrageous situations," or "I know that many owners faced with your situation feel like they're being screwed over by the legal system." Then, re-affirm your desire to help: "When you feel ready, we can talk some more. I want to help you find the best route to make the best of a bad situation."

Working with hostile, angry clients is neither easy nor pleasant. However, most clients respond to coping skills such as active listening, cooling off periods, normalizing replies, and affirmations of your desire to help.[14]

7. FABRICATION

One of the more vexing problems is talking to clients who you strongly suspect of lying.[15] Lying may be active or passive: clients may either supply false information, or withhold accurate information.[16] Obviously the line between clients who may be mistaken and who may be lying, or those who are simply reluctant to supply information and those who consciously withhold it, is not a bright one. The matter is one of degree, rooted in clients' conscious intent. You have to rely on your judgment as to which side of the line clients' conduct falls.

A. COMMON CAUSES AND INDICIA OF FABRICATION

Typically, the inhibitors of ego threat and case threat are the root cause of fabrication. Clients may lie in the belief (probably often correct) that truthful information will hurt their cause. They also may lie because they are ashamed or guilty about what really happened, or because they believe you would not respect them if you knew the true facts. Such feelings are not limited to clients: How freely do you share information that casts you in a negative light?

---

14. For detailed discussion of these as well as other techniques for coping with angry, hostile and explosive clients, see Robert M. Bramson, *A Hostile–Aggressive Trio: German Tanks, Snipers and Exploders, in* COPING WITH DIFFICULT PEOPLE 8–37 (Robert M. Bramson, ed., Anchor Press/Doubleday 1981); J.E. Groves, M.D., *Taking Care of the Hateful Patient*, 298 NEW ENG.J.MED. 883–887 (1978) (coping with "entitled demanders").

15. In considering the issue of whether a client is lying, recognize what psychological studies repeatedly show, namely that

what people honestly think they perceive may be due in part to their self interest in having events come out a certain way. *See, e.g.,* ELIZABETH F. LOFTUS AND JAMES M. DOYLE, EYEWITNESS TESTIMONY: CIVIL AND CRIMINAL § 3.08 (1987). While this phenomenon is of concern to lawyers, it is not one that involves fabrication. The client reports what she or he honestly believes to be true, though the client is in fact mistaken.

16. Although this problem perhaps arises more frequently in litigation than in deals matters, the problem is certainly not unknown in the latter area.

The bases upon which you might detect fabrication are the stuff of the literature of cross-examination, a full discussion of which is beyond the scope of this book.[17] Generally, inconsistencies are one clue to possible fabrication. A client's statement to you conflicts with what the client previously told somebody else; bad luck if the somebody else is a police officer. Or, a story may have internal inconsistencies—one portion does not square with another. For example, a client states at one point that he was driving late at night; at another point, he states that his car lights were not on.

Implausibilities also suggest fabrication. For example, in an actual case, a client testified, "James is fine now, but when I took his temperature, it was so high that it broke the thermometer." Common sense and experience suggest that the story is implausible. Not only are extremely high temperatures usually fatal, but also they rarely result in broken thermometers.

On other occasions, a story may appear implausible because it conflicts in some way with a more believable story. For example, assume that a client tells you that a 6–month–old child's broken leg was caused by the child falling off a sofa onto a carpeted floor. The story may conflict with the medical expert, who concludes that the X-rays indicate a spiral fracture of the leg, and that spiral fractures can be caused only by a great deal of rotational force, not by a fall from a sofa.

These are some of the more common factors that are likely to lead you to suspect fabrication. Below, consider potential responses you might make.

B. RESPONDING TO SUSPECTED FABRICATION

Even an indirect suggestion that you suspect clients of lying can severely damage your attorney-client relationships. Therefore, first be reasonably confident of your diagnosis of fabrication. Movies have fostered an image of streetwise lawyers who can unerringly spot a lie and immediately force people to "come clean" with a statement such as: "Come on, nobody would believe that. I haven't believed something like that since I was 3 years old. Now, tell me what really happened." Most of us, however, are not blessed with such blinding certainty. Better to eliminate other possible explanations before leaping to the conclusion that clients are lying. After all, it may be that the third party, supposedly neutral witness, is mistaken, not your client. Perhaps the doctor in the spiral fracture case above misread the X-rays or picked up the wrong X-rays. Perhaps the client has made an honest mistake. You should at least consider such possibilities before you employ any of the following techniques.

1. Prevention

Hopefully, one benefit of a client-centered approach itself is reduced likelihood of fabrication. The more rapport you have with clients, the

---

17. *See, e.g.,* Francis Lewis Wellman, The Art of Cross Examination (1931); Albert J. Moore, Paul Bergman & David A. Binder, Trial Advocacy Chapter 13 (1996).

less likely that they will lie. But in particular, three other strategies may help to prevent fabrication. One is "topic avoidance." If you delay discussion of critical points that are most likely to lead to fabrication until after you have had a chance to build rapport, you may reduce the chance that clients will lie. Many criminal defense attorneys employ this technique, intentionally postponing discussion of what happened prior to an arrest until one or two meetings with their clients have taken place.[18]

A second strategy is "disclosure." By disclosing data already in your possession that is especially case or ego threatening, you lessen the risk that clients will deny its existence. This device is one frequently used by parents of young children. Assume that a father enters a room and finds an overturned beaker of milk in the middle of the living room rug moments after the father saw his six-year-old daughter Melinda playing in the living room. The father might confront Melinda with a question such as, "Melinda, did you spill the milk?" But that question is prone to elicit a defensive, deceitful response from Melinda. Instead, the father might say, "Melinda, it seems you've spilt that milk you were drinking. Why don't you tell me what happened." This remark discloses that the father already knows "the worst" and is likely to elicit a more honest response provided the father's tone of voice and body language indicate that he is not threatening punishment.

You too will frequently be aware of negative information concerning clients. Perhaps you will know that a client seeking advice about a business venture has previously declared bankruptcy. Or, that a doctor who is a defendant in a wrongful death case has previously been discharged from the staffs of two hospitals. In each case, a question which puts the onus on the client to be the first to reveal the information may elicit an evasive, misleading or dishonest reply. Instead, a remark such as, "I understand you have had some problems in a couple of hospitals in the past. Can you tell me something about that?" may ease the client towards a full and forthright reply.

A "war story" is a third strategy you may employ to prevent fabrication. A war story is simply a tale drawn from your prior experience.[19] Sometimes, you tell a war story simply to entertain or impress clients with the depth of your experience. In this instance, you may tell a war story to illustrate the pitfalls of dishonesty. For example, assume that you represent the owner of a restaurant who is applying for a liquor license. You are aware that the client has two "silent partners" ("Suds" McCalla and "Bugsy" Berenson) who are said to have ties to organized crime. Such information, if true, would in all likelihood prevent issuance of the liquor license. If you fear that the client will lie when asked about connections with Suds and Bugsy, you may tell a war story as follows:

---

18. Experienced criminal law specialists have mentioned this point to the authors on numerous occasions. However, texts and articles tend to be either silent on this point, or are perhaps contradictory. For an example of the latter, *see* F. LEE. BAILEY & HENRY

B. ROTHBLATT, FUNDAMENTALS OF CRIMINAL ADVOCACY 45 (1974).

19. If you are a newcomer to the legal profession, you may consider substituting an event that another attorney encountered and told you about for one of your own.

I've handled a number of cases in which clients have sought liquor licenses, and issues concerning an applicant's associates arise frequently. Unfortunately, sometimes clients do not level with me completely, and information is concealed which, had I known about it earlier, could have been easily met and overcome. For instance, a couple of years ago a client of mine was seeking a liquor license, and there was some question about whether she had sold liquor to a minor in another state. When I asked her about it before we went before the Board, she assured me that she had never been licensed anywhere, that there must be some confusion. Then the Board came up with a record showing she had been licensed. As it turned out, she had signed the application in the other state simply to help out a friend; she never took an active role in the liquor business and had I known about it we could have explained what happened and she would have gotten her license. As it was, the license was denied, and by the time we could petition again, the business opportunity dried up.

For the next few minutes I'll be asking you for information about your business operations because these applications for liquor licenses are pretty thorough. As we go through the application, be sure to tell me everything so if there's any problem in the offing we can try to think of ways to solve it.

Here, you tell a war story aimed at impressing the client with the need to be accurate. The message is that even if the information may be in some way negative, you may nevertheless produce a successful result. Thus, the war story is also motivational.[20]

2. *Confrontation*

When despite your best preventative efforts you are convinced that clients are lying, and you want to uncover the actual facts, you must confront them.[21] Available confrontational techniques range from indirect to direct, the latter consisting of explicit statements of disbelief. Consider here four confrontational techniques, beginning with the most indirect.

a. *Request Clarification*

Requests for clarification phrase confrontation in terms of your own confusion, rather than clients' misstatements. The approach provides a useful way of checking out whether your suspicion of fabrication is correct by providing clients with an opportunity to explain away the inconsistencies or implausibilities that concern you. To use this ap-

---

20. You could also combine disclosure with a war story. For example, here, after telling the war story, you might have disclosed that you knew about Suds and Bugsy.

21. For a brief discussion of whether or not a lawyer will always want to obtain all the facts, see M.H. Freedman, *Professional Responsibility of the Criminal Defense Lawyer: The Three Hardest Questions*, 64 MICH.L. REV. 1469, 1471–72 (1966).

proach, explicitly point out what troubles you, and ask clients for clarification. For example, you might state,

> I'm a bit confused. You've told me that minimum pricing was discussed at the meeting; but your own employee's memo summarizing the meeting makes no mention of that. Can you clarify this point for me?

* * *

> I'm a little confused. According to the accident report, you told the officer you were going home at the time of the incident. But just a short time earlier, you told me that you were on your way to a doctor's appointment. Could you explain this difference for me?

These requests for clarification do not overtly indicate your disbelief, and they explicitly provide clients with an opportunity to explain. The first client may explain, "The employee had to leave the meeting for about 20 minutes to talk to the shop foreperson. Thinking back on it, that's when we talked about minimum pricing." The second may respond, "I was going home after the doctor's office and I guess I was nervous and just left out the part about the doctor."[22]

Of course, clients' explanations may not eliminate your suspicions. For example, do you find the second client's explanation persuasive or unconvincing? If you find it unconvincing, you'll in essence be in the same position that you were in before the explanation. That is, you'll be back to square one, faced with a new or perhaps continuing suspicion of fabrication. When that is the situation, you may then use an approach in any of the sub-sections below.

b. The Omniscient Third Party

Another method of probing suspected fabrication while attempting to preserve rapport involves ascribing your need to broach a possible untruth to a non-present yet powerful and critically important third party. The third party is, of course, not present at your conversation and therefore is in no position to dispute the position you ascribe to it. Potential third party "whipping people" include opposing counsel, a judge, or even "law firm policy."

For example, you may take the role of opposing counsel, and ask clients why their version of events is more likely to be believed than their adversaries' versions. By stressing that "this is what our opponent is going to say," you confront clients without personally indicating your disbelief. The tactic may impel clients either to provide explanations (which you can then investigate), or to admit that their original stories were not entirely accurate.

Assume for instance that you represent a salesperson sued by a former employer for unlawfully taking that employer's customer list and

---

22. For a more detailed discussion of how you might deal with inconsistent or implausible statements, see David A. Binder, Albert J. Moore & Paul Bergman, Deposition Questioning Strategies and Techniques, 101– 114 (2001).

using it on behalf of a new employer. The salesperson's story, which you find unbelievable, is that the salesperson did not take the customer list but has developed the customers on the salesperson's own. You may confront the client with the adversary's likely story as follows:

> Pat, let's look at what the attorney for A. Co. (the former employer) is going to say. They will say that you worked for them for 14 years; that you were given monthly customer lists; that you agreed to turn over all customer lists to A. Co. if you left employment; that after you left you called on exactly the same customers you did when you worked for A. Co., and that you even showed one of these customers that you still had the A. Co. list. How are we going to overcome this story?

A somewhat difficult variation of this technique is for you to ask clients to help you figure out what story an adversary is likely to present, and how to refute it. To establish an adversary's story, you typically need to work with clients by suggesting some possibilities. If clients have difficulty refuting an adversary's story, they may understand the weakness of their own stories, and perhaps tell more truthful ones. On the other hand, if clients too readily refute an adversary's story, you may point out that the adversary is unlikely to rely on such an easily refuted story. Then, continue to work with clients to develop a story that an adversary is more likely to tell. You may continue this process until you and clients arrive at more realistic versions. When clients cannot refute an adversary's ultimate story, they may tell more truthful versions.[23]

A third variation of this technique is conduct a mock cross examination by assuming the role of opposing counsel and questioning clients in the way that opposing counsel might at deposition or trial. You might preface such an approach with an explanation along these lines. "What I want to do now is help you see how Jean's lawyer is likely to question you during the deposition. This will help us see what we're up against. So what I'm going to do is play the role of Jean's lawyer and ask you the kinds of questions she might ask you." Often, until a role play exercise such as this forces clients to confront a story in a dynamic setting, clients do not face up to the obvious weaknesses in their stories.

3. *Silence*

Alone or following the use of other techniques, silence can be a powerful indication of disbelief. Though you say little or nothing, your body language conveys your lack of belief and your expectation that clients will tell the truth. You need not have Shakespearian training to carry out this technique. Direct eye contact, a facial expression that is

---

23. Of course, continually asking clients for explanations you find satisfactory is fraught with the danger that clients will try to come up explanations that you find adequate rather than with explanations that constitute the truth. On the other hand, recognize that your role is that of a zealous advocate and that you have a professional obligation to help clients recall what actually happened. Indeed, it may be appropriate for you to use closed questions to seek out possible explanations such as, "Does seeing the document now refresh your recollection as to who was at the meeting?"

both serious and indicative of disbelief, and perhaps a few shakes of the head are often more than sufficient.[24]

4. *Direct Verbal Confrontation*

Direct confrontation involves starkly telling clients that (a) a story is not believable and (b) why you disbelieve it. Consider this example:

> Mr. Thomas, I simply do not believe what you are telling me. According to you, your brother failed to repay the $100,000 when it was due and you did not realize it until over a year later. People whose brothers owe them $100,000 by a certain date don't forget such a date for a whole year. I'd like the truth.

Directly confronting clients is difficult. Clients may get angry, accuse you of misdeeds, and terminate the relationship. Thus, you should make such a statement only if you are quite certain that clients have indeed lied. Keep in mind, however, that the statement's purpose is to help clients tell the truth. Therefore, your own conduct should be consistent with this goal. Your demeanor when making the statement, for example, should indicate your concern and desire to help. And, you might include a motivational statement, such as advising clients that telling the truth is likely to be in their best interests. In addition, you may let clients know that you will continue to accept them even if they admit to having lied. Thus, in the debt example above, you might have preceded the confrontational statement with a motivational statement as follows:

> Mr. Thomas, I'd like to help you, and I think that perhaps I can help you, but only if you are honest with me. Unfortunately, in my experience clients sometimes are less than totally honest. I'm used to that, and if it turns out that's occurred here it will in no way interfere with my willingness to help you. But frankly, I simply do not believe . . .

Do not expect positive results, if any there are, to occur instantly. Clients may need time before realizing that admitting to fabrication and telling a truthful story is in their best interests. Perhaps more meetings will have to take place before clients "come clean." You may even have to repeat the motivational and confrontational statements. But short of terminating the attorney-client relationship, this is about as forceful as you can be when confronting a possibly fabricated story.

Ultimately if clients stick with their stories and your suspicions continue, you will have to consider whether to withdraw as counsel.[25]

---

24. Nevertheless, you may find this technique difficult to learn and employ. Most of us are not comfortable staring at another human being and waiting until the other speaks.

25. For a discussion of when a lawyer may withdraw, see ABA MODEL RULES, *supra*

note 6, Rules 1.2, 1.16, and 3.3 and Comments thereto; MODEL CODE OF PROF'L RESPONSIBILITY, EC 2–32, DR 2–110, DR 7–102 (1980).

Part Four

DECISION–MAKING

Part Four (Chapters 13 through 21) explores the process of helping clients decide how best to resolve their problems. Chapter 13 offers a guide to exercising judgment concerning the types of decisions that clients should have the opportunity to make and provides an overview of how to carry out your counselling role, including a discussion of how and when to offer your opinion or attempt to intervene in clients' decisions. Chapter 14 sets forth a four step approach for carrying out the counselling process. Chapters 15 through 18 examine issues that commonly arise during counselling and suggest client–centered strategies and techniques for addressing them. Chapters 19 and 20 illustrate the use of counselling strategies and techniques in the contrasting contexts of litigation and proposed business transactions. Finally, Chapter 21 briefly addresses issues that may arise when you consider referring clients to mental health professionals.

Chapter 13

PRINCIPLES UNDERLYING
EFFECTIVE COUNSELING

---

* * *

From what you tell me, Mr. Rodale, your objective is to get DataCo's auditing department operating efficiently as quickly as possible. Is that right?

Exactly. We've got to decide quickly whether it makes sense to let Ms. Jensen go as soon as possible.

Well, from what you've said, it seems clear that DataCo has every legal right to terminate Ms. Jensen. She has repeatedly ignored warnings about getting her work done on time and, given the problems that her repeated tardiness has caused, there is certainly good reason to fire her. What you need to do, however, is determine whether you want to go ahead and terminate her or whether you want to follow some other course of action, such as suspending her or having her agree to resign in exchange for some kind of a severance package. From what you said so far, it does not appear as though the decision is going to be an easy one. Terminating Ms. Jensen seems to have a number of possible downsides attached to it, such as lowering morale in the audit division. Am I correct?

Yes; that will certainly be one result.

Well, in that light, what I think we should do is to try to take a look at each of your options and try to figure out which one, on balance, will probably best accomplish your overall objective. Why don't we start by focusing on outright termination?

* * *

Ms. Biggs, has our discussion given you a picture of what options the partnership could follow in setting up a bank account and the pros and cons of each?

Yes, but I'm somewhat conflicted. On the one hand, I want to make sure that once the partnership is going David won't be able to make bank withdrawals of more than $3500. On the other hand, I can see that asking for this kind of protective provision in our written agreement may really poison the negotiations and our future relationship. What do you think I should do?

* * *

1. INTRODUCTION

Numerous decisions usually have to be made as clients' matters move toward resolution. A decision may involve ultimate resolution of a client's principal problem: Should a settlement offer be accepted? Should a contract be signed, despite its failure to include an exclusive dealing provision? Often, however, decisions involve subsidiary considerations: Should discovery be undertaken immediately? Should the draft of a proposed agreement include an arbitration clause? Who should prepare the draft—you or the other party?

This chapter explores issues that arise when you counsel and advise clients with respect to both ultimate and intermediate decisions.[1] Those issues include:

　a.　Who, as between you and clients, should generally have the final say?

　b.　What decisions regarding the handling of a matter should you explore with clients?

　c.　With respect to decisions that require client consultation,

　　1.　What information should you elicit from clients before decisions are made?

　　2.　What information should you make available to clients before decisions are made?

　　3.　When should you provide opinions as to what decision should be made?

　　4.　What criteria should you use in arriving at opinions as to what decision should be made?

　　5.　Are you responsible for ensuring that clients fully understand the ramifications of their decisions?

　　6.　Under what circumstances might you suggest that clients' decisions are wrong?

These are the questions that are central to your understanding of counseling, the process by which you help clients decide what courses of action to adopt in order to resolve problems. This chapter describes the essential client-centered principles that govern that process.

---

1. Your obligation to counsel and advise is a reminder that you should not on your own represent a client whose matter requires expertise or experience that you do not have. See ABA MODEL RULES OF PROFESSIONAL CONDUCT Rule 1.1 (2002) [hereinafter MODEL RULES]. Otherwise, you might end up like Louis Arthur Dodrill, a lawyer who was disciplined after admitting to a bankruptcy judge that he knew "nothing whatever about bankruptcy," was "thoroughly incompetent in bankruptcy court," and "had no business being there." Dodrill v. Executive Director, 824 S.W.2d 383 (Ark. 1992). You have to at least admire Mr. Dodrill's honesty.

2. CLIENTS ARE PRIMARY DECISION–MAKERS

A central tenet of client-centeredness is that you should generally afford clients the opportunity to make decisions. Clients should have primary decision-making power in part because of the simple truth that *problems are theirs, not yours.* After all, clients and not you have to live with decisions' immediate and long term consequences. For example, deciding to take depositions may result in a client, not you, expending thousands of dollars.[2] Similarly, clients will receive the benefits or suffer the losses attendant to decisions to hire an expert, leave an arbitration clause out of an agreement, or accept a settlement offer. Given that clients bear the brunt of decisions' consequences, clients presumptively should have the opportunity to determine what courses of action to take.

A second reason for clients having primary decision-making power is that decisions should be made on the basis of what choices are most likely to *provide clients with maximum satisfaction.* Presumptively, clients are better able than you to assess which potential decisions are most likely to prove satisfactory. For one thing, as you recall from Chapter 1, resolving problems typically requires consideration of non-legal consequences, as to which clients are likely to possess more expertise than you. Moreover, even if both you and a client agree precisely on a decision's likely consequences, you and a client will not necessarily weigh those consequences equally in making the decision. The relative importance of decisions' consequences depends largely on values that often vary from one person to another, and autonomy notions assign primary importance to clients' values.

The following example illustrates the interplay between decisions and subjective personal values. Assume that you represent Stephanie Kimmel, who has sued Badger Outlets for wrongful termination of employment. The case has been pending for over a year, and Badger has made a settlement offer of $35,000. So far as the legal consequences go, your opinion is that if the case were to proceed to trial, Kimmel would be likely to recover at least $65,000. At the same time, trial is still six months away, and there is a small chance, perhaps 20%, that at trial Kimmel will recover nothing. Should she accept the offer?

Your personal opinion may be that Kimmel should accept the offer. From your legal, "objective" standpoint, accepting the offer makes sense because Kimmel gets money at once that she needs, and she avoids the risk of losing altogether. However, *Kimmel* may assess the likely consequences differently. For example, she may attach little value to the offer because $35,000 would not allow her to improve her life style substantially. Moreover, non-legal consequences may be of equal or greater concern to Kimmel. For example, Kimmel may decide to reject the offer because she is angry and wants to air her grievances in a public

---

2. Contingency fee lawyers sometimes advance (as the Rules permit them to) clients' litigation expenses. *See* MODEL RULES, note 1 *supra*, Rule 1.8(e). Even in those situations the cost of depositions affect clients' financial interests because the lawyers' costs will be deducted from any recovery that the clients receive.

courtroom, even at the risk of losing. Kimmel's state of mind might also be a relevant factor. For instance, if the pendency of the case makes her anxious and restless, she may choose to settle to gain peace of mind. Whatever Kimmel's bottom line, she like all clients may value likely consequences differently than do you, and therefore should have the opportunity to make the decision.[3]

Clients' subjective assessments of likely consequences lie at the heart of determining maximum client satisfaction in transactional matters as well. Assume that you represent George Martino, the owner of several shopping centers, including a new mid-sized center. On Martino's behalf, you are negotiating a proposed lease with SafeBet Markets. Under the lease, SafeBet would become an anchor tenant in the new center. Per Martino's instructions, during negotiations with SafeBet you have repeatedly asked SafeBet's lawyer to agree to a lease provision obligating SafeBet to pay a pro-rata share of the maintenance costs for the upkeep of the center's common areas. Such a provision is typical in commercial leases in your area. During a prior negotiating session, SafeBet's lawyer told you that a common areas clause is unacceptable to SafeBet. Tomorrow you are scheduled to have your final negotiation meeting with SafeBet's lawyer. In your opinion, there is only a small possibility that SafeBet will accede to the common areas provision. The decision to be made is whether or not to continue to insist on that provision.

One likely consequence of continued insistence on the provision is that SafeBet will break off negotiations, and as a result Martino will not acquire income from the lease. How important is it to Martino to obtain rent? If immediate additional income is important, or if Safebet's tenancy will encourage other potential tenants to lease space, the alternative of dropping the common areas clause will seem attractive.

However, if Martino's dropping the demand for a common areas provision becomes generally known, his bargaining position in future lease deals might be harmed. Future potential tenants might assume that if Martino did not require a common areas provision in a lease with SafeBet, he probably is in some way desperate for tenants. As a consequence, such tenants might be more willing to push Martino for concessions, making future lease negotiations difficult. How important is it to Martino to avoid this risk? If he believes that the absence of such a clause in SafeBet's lease will become generally known and therefore influence future deals, Martino may conclude that maintaining the demand is of great importance.

While Martino might have to evaluate many other potential consequences before making a final decision about whether to drop the demand for a common areas provision, what should be clear is that an

3. A standard by which clients make decisions based on maximum satisfaction does not prevent your bringing to a client's attention such important considerations as the interests of third persons, of society as a whole, or of your own interests. Moreover, sometimes you may express disagreement with a decision even though you think it likely to provide maximum client satisfaction. See Sec. 5 *infra*.

assessment of what choice is likely to produce maximum satisfaction for Martino requires Martino's subjective evaluation of the importance of the decision's likely ramifications.

Thus, in neither litigation nor transactional matters can you determine what decisions are likely to lead to maximum client satisfaction through reference to external standards or your own values. Sensible choices about important decisions should take account of decisions' likely economic, social, psychological and moral ramifications *and* their relative importance. While you may help clients identify decisions' likely ramifications, only clients can determine their relative importance.

As the above examples also suggest, the subjective factor of "risk aversion" often has a substantial impact on clients' decisions. This point was made succinctly nearly three centuries ago:

> Price and probability are not enough in determining what something is worth. Although the facts are the same for everyone, 'the utility...is dependent on the particular circumstances of the person making the estimate.... There is no reason to assume that ... the risks anticipated by each [individual] must be deemed equal in value.' To each his own.[4]

Thus, when choosing a course of action, neither you nor a client can do more than predict *likely* consequences. Every decision entails a risk that predicted consequences may not occur. So, if Martino abandons the common areas provision, it does not follow automatically that SafeBet will sign the lease; or that if the lease is signed, Martino will receive the projected net income; or that Martino's future negotiating position will be damaged if he decides not to insist on the provision with SafeBet. These consequences are, to paraphrase Charles Dickens' *A Christmas Carol*, shadows of what *may* be, not what *will* be. Hence, by conceding to SafeBet, Martino indicates a willingness to risk a weakened bargaining position with future tenants. A different Martino, aware of precisely the same potential consequence, might not be willing to take this risk, and as a result might not concede to SafeBet. The fact that two clients can make the same predictions about consequences, yet make different decisions depending on their willingness to run risks, is a strong factor in favor of clients being the primary decision-makers.

Moreover, even if you could become fully conversant with clients' value and preference structures, you perhaps ought not be trusted to make important decisions because of potential conflicts of interest. When it comes time to make decisions, your interests and those of a client frequently are adverse. For instance, in making decisions about what provisions to include in a deal, lawyers often want to include a great many more contingency provisions than do clients.[5] Lawyers often want

4. Peter Bernstein, Against the Gods: The Remarkable Story of Risk 103 (1996) (quoting Daniel Bernoulli, Exposition of a New Theory on the Measurement of Risk (1738)).

5. *See e.g.*, Donald C. Langevoort & Robert K. Rasmussen, *Skewing the Results: The Role of Lawyers in Transmitting Legal Rules*, 5 S. Cal. Interdisc. L. J. 375 (1997) (examining economic, social, and psycholog-

clients to agree to contingency provisions not only to protect the clients but also to make sure that if a contingency ultimately does arise, the lawyer cannot be sued for malpractice.[6] Clients on the other hand are often more interested in making deals than in being fully protected if an agreement should ultimately break down. Clients often predict that insistence on a contingency provision may kill the deal and they are therefore willing to drop the provision and take the risk that the contingency will not arise.[7]

That lawyers and clients often have conflicting interests suggests once again that decisions ought to remain in a client's hands. Even if you could determine a client's values and preferences, the temptation to decide the matter in a way that advances your personal interests is reason to allow a client to make the ultimate choice.[8]

3. A STANDARD FOR CLIENT DECISION-MAKING: "SUBSTANTIAL LEGAL OR NON-LEGAL IMPACTS"

An emphasis on clients as primary decision-makers may suggest that clients should have the opportunity to make each and every decision. Some commentators, in fact, have urged such a position.[9]

However, a "client makes all decisions" position is unworkable and, in fact, inconsistent with client-centeredness. If clients were to make all decisions, you would have to inform them of each time a decision were necessary and engage them in discussions of potential options and consequences. As even simple matters may require scores of decisions

ical reasons for overstatement of risks to clients); *see also* John S. Dzienkowski & Robert J Peroni, *The Decline in Lawyer Independence: Lawyer Equity Investments in Clients*, 81 Tex. L. Rev. 405, 432–33 (2002) (discussing the decision-making effect that financial investment in clients has on their lawyers, and suggesting that it solves some of the disparate goal problems usually found in this sort of agency dilemma).

6. More cynical commentators may suggest that lawyers' insistence on covering "all possible contingencies" also arises from lawyers interests in higher legal fees. *See* Deborah L. Rhode, In the Interests of Justice: Reforming the Legal Profession 84–85 (2000). Such a cynical attitude would never apply to readers of this book, of course.

7. For an interesting description of this phenomenon, see the Los Angeles Times' description of the negotiations between the San Diego Padres and Bruce Hurst. Los Angeles Times, Part III at 1 (Dec. 9, 1988).

8. Other common examples of potential lawyer-client decision-making conflicts include whether to accept an offer, whether to

take depositions, and whether to call a witness to testify. In each of these instances, what may be financially beneficial or convenient for a lawyer may conflict with what is financially, economically or psychologically best for a client. The unfortunate reality is that all too often lawyers do put self interest before clients' interests. See, e.g., Lisa Lerman, *Lying to Clients*, 138 U. Pa. L. Rev. 659 (1990) (reporting on lawyers' dishonesty to clients to mask divergent and self-serving activity); Kevin McMunigal, *Rethinking Attorney Conflict of Interest Doctrine*, 5 Geo. J Legal Ethics 823, 823 (1992) ("The subject of attorney conflict of interest in recent years has 'dramatically increased in importance and in the frequency with which it is litigated.' ").

9. *See* Alex J. Hurder, *Negotiating the Lawyer–Client Relationship: A Search for Equality and Collaboration*, 44 Buff. L. Rev. 71 (1996) (calling for negotiation between lawyer and client in making all decisions); Mark Spiegel, *Lawyering and Client Decisionmaking: Informed Consent and the Legal Profession*, 128 U. Pa. L. Rev. 41, 65–67 (1979) (noting, but expressing disagreement with, such commentary).

(including such seemingly picayune matters as whether to send documents by regular or overnight mail), total client decision-making would force you to be in nearly continuous communication with clients. Undoubtedly, most clients would not have the time, the desire or the financial resources to hire you under these conditions. And even if they did, you would undoubtedly soon regard practicing law under such conditions as a sentence to a career of virtually continuous communication with a small number of clients.

Moreover, insistence on client consultation on each decision would deprive clients of the option of leaving certain decisions to the lawyer. As a consequence, such insistence would be inconsistent with client-centered decision making.[10]

If consultation about every decision is unacceptable, how might you decide what decisions to call to clients' attention, and which to make on your own? In the past, some authorities attempted to draw a distinction between matters' "substantive" and "procedural" aspects. They suggested that lawyers should review with clients decisions affecting the objectives of representation, but need not do so with respect to decisions that only affect the means by which the objectives are secured. Some courts continue to echo this ends-means distinction.[11]

However, in practice a distinction based on means-end reasoning is unworkable. One reason is that decisions about "means" may be so important that most clients would reasonably expect to make them. For example, the economic consequences attached to a decision about whether to pursue discovery vigorously or cautiously may be so large that a client should be the one to make it.

Moreover, what you regard as a "means" may for a client be an "end." Assume for instance that you represent a client charged with burglary, and a decision arises about whether or not to call the client's sister as an alibi witness. You believe that the sister will make an excellent and helpful witness, but the client insists that she not be called because in the client's view testifying will cause the sister undue stress.[12] For you, the decision involves a means to an end, but for the client not calling the sister as a witness is itself an objective. Because personal values can so often affect a conclusion about whether decisions involve ends or means, the distinction will often be of little help to your thinking about whether decisions are for you or clients to make.

---

10. See also section 5 *infra*.

11. For a discussion of this distinction, see Mark Spiegel, *The New Model Rules of Professional Conduct: Lawyer–Client Decision Making and the Role of Rules in Structuring the Lawyer–Client Dialogue*, 1980 AM. B. FOUND. RES. J. 1003, 1003–04; Mark Spiegel, *Lawyering and Client Decisionmaking: Informed Consent and the Legal Profession*, 128 U. PA. L. REV. 41, 65–67 (1979); David B. Wilkins, *Do Clients Have Ethical Obligations to Lawyers? Some Les-*

sons *from the Diversity Wars*, 11 GEO. J. LEGAL ETHICS 855, 875 (1998).

12. Recall the traditional song "Long Black Veil," where a man accused of murder refuses to disclose his alibi: "I was in the arms of my best friend's wife." As a result, he is convicted and executed. For versions of this haunting song, see JOHNNY CASH, *The Long Black Veil*, on ORANGE BLOSSOM SPECIAL (Sony Records 2002); DAVE MATTHEWS BAND, *The Long Black Veil*, on LISTENER SUPPORTED (RCA Records 1999).

Asking clients early on to indicate what kinds of decisions they want to be consulted about is a potential approach to the issue of when you need to consult clients.[13] However, this "informed consent" approach too is typically inadequate. For one thing, you cannot expect meaningful advanced directives from inexperienced clients. Such clients cannot realistically anticipate which upcoming choices will warrant consultation and input and which will not. [14]

Moreover, except in the most routine of matters, advance directives are unlikely to be workable even with experienced clients. Changes in clients' circumstances, unanticipated reactions from adversaries and the difficulty of predicting in advance what categories of decisions will be appropriate for client decision-making are among the factors that detract from the viability of the informed consent approach.

A better approach to the question of when to involve clients in decision-making is to acknowledge explicitly that "bright line" approaches represented by the "ends-means" and "informed consent" tests simply are inadequate guidelines. In their place is what you may call the "substantial impact" standard. If this standard lacks the comfort of bright line approaches, it is a realistic one that honors the values of client-centeredness while providing "safe harbors" for appropriate lawyer decision-making. Explicitly stated, the "reasonable lawyer" standard is as follows:

> Lawyers should provide clients with the opportunity to make decisions whenever a reasonably prudent and diligent lawyer would or should know that a pending decision is likely to have a *substantial legal or non-legal impact on clients.*

The "substantial impact" standard requires that you comport with professional norms with respect to decision-making. For example, you need to be aware of and comply with ethical rules governing decision-making.[15] Similarly, you should be familiar with the kinds of decisions that competent lawyers generally afford clients the opportunity to make. In that regard, the "substantial impact" standard probably reflects the behavior of most practicing lawyers. That is, undoubtedly most practitioners do afford clients the opportunity to make decisions that are likely to substantially affect clients' legal or non-legal concerns. For example, litigators often consult clients about such matters as granting continuances, filing motions, taking depositions, and pursuing negotiation strategy. Indeed, a lawyer might even consult a client as to the wisdom of asking a question on cross examination in circumstances where the impact of a critical admission might be undercut by an explanation, and the lawyer believes that the client may know whether the witness will give that explanation. Likewise, when substantial impact decisions arise

---

13. See Richard. A. Epstein, *Medical Malpractice: The Case for Contract*, 1976 AM. BAR. FOUND. RES. J. 87,199–28.

14. For an exploration of this "informed consent" problem in the doctor-patient relationship, see, e.g., JESSICA W. BERG ET AL.,

INFORMED CONSENT: LEGAL THEORY AND CLINICAL PRACTICE 167–186 (2d ed. 2001).

15. See, for example, MODEL RULES, *supra* note 1, Rules 1.2, 1.4.

in transactional matters, lawyers commonly discuss with clients such issues as whether to ask corporate officers to personally guarantee payments that the corporation will be obligated to make under the terms of proposed deals, whether a seller of a factory will agree to clean up environmental contamination prior to closing, and which of various options for restructuring companies' debts best suit their needs.[16]

The "substantial impact" standard also requires consideration of what you know about individual clients. That is, you may know from prior dealings or conversations that a decision that would not have a substantial impact on most clients will substantially affect a particular client. If so, the standard requires that you afford that client an opportunity to make the decision. The reverse is also true: prior dealings with a client may allow you to make decisions with respect to matters that have substantial impacts, even though the standard would in most circumstances require consultation. For example, if a client has authorized you to use your discretion with respect to how many depositions to take, you may not need to consult the client each time you notice a deposition unless you have reason to think that the client may want to reconsider the earlier authorization.

Like any norm grounded in reasonableness rather than bright-line rules, the "reasonable lawyer" standard cannot claim to offer a simple calculus neatly resolving all decision-making issues. Rather, the standard leaves room for practical decision-making. This should hardly be surprising; much about the practice of law calls for you to exercise practical judgment of the type set forth in the standard.[17] Moreover, the standard

---

16. Some data is emerging concerning the kinds of decisions lawyers typically examine with their clients. One comprehensive study involved nearly seven hundred public defenders from five different jurisdictions. Rodney J. Uphoff & Peter B. Wood, *The Allocation of Decisionmaking Between Defense Counsel and Criminal Defendants: An Empirical Study of Attorney–Client Decisionmaking*, 47 U. KAN. L. REV. 1 (1998). The survey inquired into the beliefs and practices of defense attorneys regarding decisionmaking on twelve strategic decisions that repeatedly confront them. *Id.* at 30–31. Most respondents strongly agreed than only four of the twelve should involve client consent: (1) to waive a jury trial; (2) to accept a plea bargain; (3) to waive a preliminary hearing; and (4) whether the client will testify at trial. *Id.* at 33. The majority of the respondents advocated a lawyer-centered approach to decision-making, but a substantial minority advocated client-centeredness. *Id.* at 38. The two factors identified by the highest percentage of respondents as justifying limiting client participation were the client's general low intelligence and concern that the client will make a poor decision. Other anticipated factors like workload, time constraints, and client mistrust were not as significant to the lawyers. *Id.* at 52–55. Another study, researching lawyers who work on civil rights and poverty issues, suggests that lawyers' views on lawyer-client decisionmaking vary substantially by the practice settings in which they work. Ann Southworth, *Lawyer-Client Decisionmaking in Civil Rights and Poverty Practice: An Empirical Study of Lawyer's Norms*, 9 GEO. J. LEGAL ETHICS 1101, 1105 (1996). Aspects of an attorney's workplace affecting these views include the sources of payment and resource constraints, the sophistication and expectations of their clients, the extent to which ongoing relationships with clients are maintained, the types of service they perform, and the specific political and social agenda. *Id.* at 1124–1131. *See generally* David B. Wilkins, *Do Clients Have Ethical Obligations to Lawyers? Some Lessons from the Diversity Wars*, 11 GEO. J. LEGAL ETHICS 855 (1998) (discussing the growing involvement of corporate clients in the minutiae of legal decision-making).

17. Many complex lawyering activities require the exercise of practical judgment, which does not allow for strict, well-defined processes and algorithms. *See* Mark Neal

is client-centered. It focuses on the likely impacts on individual clients, rather than on fuzzy distinctions between "ends" and "means."

For an example of how you might apply the "substantial impact" standard in practice, assume that you represent Gower "Tower of Power" Bower, a financially independent professional basketball player nearing the end of his career with the Smeltics. Gower is in the "option" (last) year of his current contract; you are negotiating an extension with the Smeltics. Gower's primary goal is a three year contract that would allow him to continue to receive his salary for three years even if he were injured or let go. (The Smeltics, he knows, have a history of not re-signing former stars to save money once they are somewhat past their prime.) Gower would like a raise in his $1,800,000 per year salary, but is willing to forgo an increase in favor of a three-year deal. He is anxious to conclude the negotiations as quickly as possible, since a career-ending injury is always a possibility.

Early in the negotiations, the Smeltics' attorney asks that Gower consent to a thorough physical examination. Should you or Gower make this auxiliary decision? The standard allocates the decision to Gower if its consequences are likely to have a substantial impact on him. Here, the outcome of the physical might well determine whether the team makes a multiyear offer. Thus the decision is likely to have a substantial impact, and the decision is one for Gower to have the opportunity to make.

The Smeltics' attorney next reminds you that the team's usual policy is not to negotiate in midseason. However, the team is willing to negotiate with Gower if a new contract can be signed within two weeks. You understand that if Gower does sign quickly, he will probably not be eligible to benefit financially from royalties from a cable TV contract that you expect the Smeltics to conclude after the season concludes. If he were to sign a new contract *after* the Smeltics signed a cable TV contract, Gower would probably receive a salary bonus in the range of $50,000 to $75,000. The standard would probably permit you to decide whether to open negotiations immediately. Given that a three year deal is worth at least $3.6 million more than a one year deal, the decision is not likely to have a substantial impact on him.[18]

Analyzing the likely impact of a decision in light of Gower's actual situation and his preferences, rather than using vague distinctions such as "ends" and "means," seems to be the best way to allocate decision-making responsibility. And, since it looks to the likely impact on clients,

Aaronson, *Thinking Like a Fox: Four Over-lapping Domains of Good Lawyering*, 9 Clinical L. Rev. 1 (2002) (defining the elements of practical judgment); Alexander Scherr, *Lawyers and Decisions: A Model of Practical Judgment*, 47 Vill. L. Rev. 161 (2002) (developing a model for consistency of lawyering tasks generally).

18. This is to say that the standard might not *require* you to consult with Gower about the decision. You might of course choose to do so and make a decisional pass to Gower.

the standard comfortably satisfies rules governing your duty to allow clients to make decisions.[19]

4. THE "SUBSTANTIAL IMPACT" STANDARD AND LAWYERING TACTICS

This section considers the issue of whether the substantial impact standard may unduly interfere with your exercise of professional judgment about tactics. For example, if a decision to pursue a certain line of questioning on cross examination is likely to have a substantial impact, are you therefore obligated to consult the client regarding cross examination questioning strategy?

Most clients, recognizing their own lack of expertise, undoubtedly assume that you will make such decisions and do not expect to be consulted about them. Think, by analogy, of the look you'd give a plumber who asked you what size pipe fitting you thought should be used under your bathroom sink. The customer's act of hiring the plumber signals the customer's desire for the plumber to make those decisions which are in the plumber's traditional domain. Similarly, a client's decision to hire you is tacit willingness for you to make lawyering tactics decisions free from consultation. Thus, such matters as how you cross examine, write briefs, or phrase contingency clauses are generally for you alone to decide, even though they may have a substantial impact. They involve primarily the exercise of the skills and crafts that are the special domain of lawyers.

However, "lawyering tactics" are often not a sufficient excuse for failure to consult clients. When decisions are likely to have an influence beyond that normally associated with the exercise of lawyering skills and crafts, the "substantial impact" standard requires that you consult with a client. For example, consider these situations:

(a) A witness you are considering calling on behalf of your client is the client's boss.

(b) You are considering phrasing a contingency clause in a purposely vague manner because you do not think the other party will agree to the precise language your client desires, and the vague wording may at a future date be interpreted in your client's favor.

(c) You are considering whether to remove an action from state to federal court.

(d) You are considering whether to defend an action vigorously, as opposed to passively countering the plaintiff's moves.

You probably should consult the client in each of these situations. The decisions carry effects beyond those normally associated with the use of professional skills and crafts.

---

19. *See, e.g.,* MODEL RULES, *supra* note 1, Rules 1.2, 1.4.

Thus, in (a), developing a case-in-chief may usually be a matter entirely for your professional judgment. But calling a client's boss raises sensitive issues beyond those normally associated with direct examination. Hence, the need for client consultation.

Similarly, in (b), the question of how to phrase the contingency clause is not simply one of professional craft, but of risk aversion and of a client's willingness to live with uncertainty. That decision too does not involve primarily the craft of legal writing, but may have a substantial impact on the client's position in the event the contingency arises. Hence, the need for consultation.

In (c), whether an action is tried in state or federal court is likely to have many effects, such as what evidentiary rules apply, what the composition of the jury may be, and when the action may come to trial. Again, even though the decision rests in part on the exercise of professional judgment, the potential impacts suggest the need for client consultation.

Finally in (d), costs to a client may be very different depending on how vigorously a suit is defended. Costs of course are the type of impact which very much suggest the need for client consultation.

Again, determining the impact of the exercise of professional skills and craft maybe difficult. However, leaving all decisions that may be characterized as involving lawyering tactics in attorneys' hands alone is inconsistent with client-centeredness. As the four examples above demonstrate, many lawyering tactics decisions require client consultation.[20]

5. YOUR ROLE IN THE COUNSELING AND ADVISING PROCESS

This section provides an overview of the counseling process, the process through which you and clients sort through possibilities and arrive at decisions.[21] The remaining chapters of this book elaborate on the important components of this process and provide strategies and

---

20. The fact that a decision requires client consultation does not mean that the consultation is necessarily lengthy. As you will see in Sec. 5 *infra,* the extent of the counseling obligation varies, depending on, among other factors, the complexity of the decision. Hence, if you think that the decision to remove a case to federal court, for example, is so apparent that it lacks complexity, you might satisfy your obligation with a statement such as, "We have the opportunity to remove this case to federal court, where it will come to trial a year or more sooner than if we stayed in state court. You've said you want to get to trial as soon as possible. I see no added costs or other disadvantages of removing the case. Do you see any problem with our removing it?"

21. Counseling conversations do not necessarily precede all decisions. For example, you may represent experienced, "repeat player" clients who want you to carry out their decisions rather than have you participate in making them. For instance, a sophisticated property owner may simply want you to draw up a lease rather than become involved in a process of reviewing with you the transaction's financial soundness. Similarly, a credit manager of a large company is unlikely to seek your opinion as to whether to institute suit against a debtor. The credit manager is likely to make such a decision and expect you to carry it out.

techniques for carrying them out effectively. The remainder of this chapter summarizes the major components of the counseling process:

- Exploring alternative courses of action and their likely consequences. Consideration of alternatives and their likely consequences allows clients to make informed decisions about which choice is most likely to provide maximum satisfaction. So far as reasonably possible, your role includes assisting clients to evaluate alternatives and likely consequences free from distorting biases.[22]

- When appropriate, providing advice as to the choices you believe to be in clients' best interests and the reasons you think that those choices will maximize client satisfaction. The advice-giving function may also include intervening in clients' decisions with which you disagree.

A. EXPLORE ALTERNATIVES AND CONSEQUENCES

By definition, every decision encompasses at least two possible choices. For example, a decision as to whether to accept a settlement offer encompasses at least "accept" and "don't accept." Of course, many important decisions may encompass more than two choices. The choices when a client has to respond to a settlement offer, for example, may include (a) accept, (b) don't accept but make a counter-offer, and (c) don't accept and don't make a counter-offer. When they have the opportunity to make decisions, your obligation is to make clients aware of reasonable alternatives and the likely consequences of each possible choice.[23]

When courts and professional bodies such as the American Bar Association refer to lawyers' legal obligations with respect to counseling, they speak principally in terms of disclosure of information that lawyers (experts) must provide to clients (non-experts). However, clients generally have a reasonable opportunity to make decisions only if you elicit information from them as well as provide it to them. Succinctly stated, counseling must typically be a two-way street.

1. *Information to Elicit from Clients*

The subsections below set forth the types of information you typically try to elicit from clients during counseling discussions.

---

22. *See* Russell Korobkin & Chris Guthrie, *Psychology, Economics and Settlement: A New Look at the Role of the Lawyer*, 76 Tex. L. Rev. 77, 129–30 (1997). *See also* Chapter 18.

23. *See* Model Rules, *supra* note 1, Rules 1.4, 1.2. Engaging clients in counseling dialogues is not only ethically required but also an important method of protecting yourself from malpractice claims. *See* 1 Ronald E. Mallen & Jeffrey M. Smith, Legal

Malpractice 274–75 (5th ed. 2000). A reality of modern legal practice is that when decisions go sour, clients often blame (and sue) their lawyers for failing to advise them adequately of the options and risks involved in pivotal decisions. *See id.* at 278–79. Engaging in and documenting counseling dialogues as recommended in this chapter can help protect you from specious malpractice claims. *See id.* at 279.

a. Clients' Objectives

The best measure of decisions' quality is the extent to which they satisfy your clients' objectives. Thus, clients should evaluate alternatives in the context of relevant objectives. To the extent that those objectives are not already "on the table," you may want to clarify them at the outset of counseling discussions. For example, you might start off a discussion with a comment such as, "It's been awhile since we talked about what kind of business relationship you hope to have with the defendant after this case is over. Can you give me your current thinking on this before deciding whether to pursue discovery aggressively?"

b. Potential Solutions

Ask clients for their thoughts about potential solutions. Clients may well be able to identify workable alternatives that would not occur to you, in part because clients may have "industry experience" that you lack and because clients' proposals often reflect their unique non-legal concerns. Even if clients' proposals aren't fully workable from a legal standpoint, you often can combine aspects of their proposals with your ideas to end up with more satisfactory solutions. Thus, during counseling sessions you may often ask questions such as, "What possible lease terms do you have in mind?"

c. Potential Consequences

What is true for alternatives is also typically accurate for consequences—clients' experiences and non-legal concerns may enable them to anticipate consequences that you would have overlooked. Thus, whether you or clients identify alternatives, you should generally ask questions such as, "What do you see as the likely effects of including an insurance-funded buyout provision in the partnership agreement?"

d. Bases for Clients' Predictions

Assertions about likely consequences typically rest on predictions. For example, consider this brief exchange:

L: What do you see as the likely consequences of asking Johnson for a personal loan guarantee?

C: I think that Johnson will walk away from the deal if we even propose that.

Here, the client's perceived consequence is a prediction about Johnson's behavior. And the accuracy of predictions such as these can be a factor that clients may need to consider before making decisions. To help clients evaluate predictions' accuracy, you may ask clients to indicate the bases of their predictions. For instance, you might ask the client above, "What is your basis for saying that Johnson will walk away from the deal if we ask for a personal guarantee?" The prediction may be based on the client's past dealings with Johnson or other similarly strong indicators of Johnson's likely reaction, or it may be based on little more than a hunch or on what the client has heard about how others have reacted to similar requests. Clients' predictions may also be distorted by persistent psychological habits known as "heuristics and biases"[24] that researchers often refer to as "psychological traps"[25] or "cognitive illusions."[26] Thus, by ferreting out clients' bases for predicting consequences, you can help them make more informed and hopefully more satisfactory decisions.[27]

e. Questions and Concerns

Finally, remind clients that you welcome questions and want to know about any concerns relevant to the alternatives and consequences. Encouraging clients to raise current concerns and questions increases the likelihood of arriving at satisfactory problem resolutions.

2. Information to Provide to Clients

Since counseling is a two way street, here are essential topics that you typically communicate to clients.

a. Potential Solutions

Suggesting alternatives is often your most important counseling role. In many situations you are likely to be aware of sensible alternatives that clients would have neither the legal experience nor knowledge to know about. For example, in a litigation matter you may suggest pursuing injunctive relief or punitive damages, potential solutions of which a client may be unaware. And in a business transaction, you might know of tax reasons for structuring a deal in one form rather than another.

Often, alternatives that you suggest do not simply grow out of your knowledge of "the law." Rather, you also draw upon your professional experience, awareness of human behavior and "industry knowledge." For example, you may through your practice with real estate matters be able to offer for a client's consideration various rent-fixing formulas that are used in connection with the leasing of commercial buildings. Similarly, your experience in the criminal justice system may allow you to propose a diversion alternative that, by including a particular type of community service, permits a client to avoid a jail sentence.

Finally, your ability to identify additional solutions may simply be a product not of greater knowledge, but of greater emotional distance from a problem.

---

24. See e.g., MAX H. BAZERMAN, JUDGMENT IN MANAGERIAL DECISION MAKING (5th ed. 2002); JOHN S. HAMMOND ET AL., SMART CHOICES: A PRACTICAL GUIDE TO MAKING BETTER DECISIONS (1999); Amos Tversky & Daniel Kahneman, Judgment Under Uncertainty: Heuristics and Biases, in JUDGMENT UNDER UNCERTAINTY: HEURISTICS AND BIASES 3–20 (Daniel Kahneman et al. eds. 1982).

25. See JOHN S. HAMMOND ET AL., SMART CHOICES: A PRACTICAL GUIDE TO MAKING BETTER DECISIONS 189–216 (1999).

26. See Chris Guthrie et al., Inside the Judicial Mind, 86 CORNELL L. REV. 777, 780 (2001). These habits which serve as both limitations on and shortcuts in decision making stem from the theory of "bounded rationality," first introduced by Nobel Prize winner Herbert A. Simon. See HERBERT A. SIMON, MODELS OF MAN (1957).

27. For a discussion of how you might respond to clients' cognitive illusions in the context of decision-making, see Chapter 18.

b. Potential Consequences

Identifying consequences (both legal and to the extent you can predict, non-legal as well) goes hand-in-hand with identifying alternatives. In other words, at appropriate points in counseling discussions you talk to clients about what you view as options' likely consequences. For example, if you suggest the possibility of naming a corporate trustee to a client for whom you are drafting an inter vivos trust, you might either at the same time or later in the conversation advise the client that corporate trustees charge fees while individual trustees who are a testator's personal friend often do not, and that a court is likely to hold a corporate trustee to a higher standard of care than an individual trustee (legal consequences).[28] You might also mention that trust beneficiaries often have difficulty convincing corporate trustees to exercise discretion, compared to individual trustees who know the trust beneficiaries personally (a non-legal consequence).[29]

c. Advice

Providing advice about decisions that clients ought to make is a traditional counseling role for attorneys. Advice-giving can be consistent with a client-centered approach, so long as it is preceded by a counseling process that affords clients a reasonable opportunity to consider alternatives and consequences.[30]

B. PROVIDE AN OPPORTUNITY TO EVALUATE OPTIONS AND CONSEQUENCES

At bottom, counseling is the process of identifying and evaluating options and likely alternatives. Of course, counseling is a fluid process that may vary greatly in its particulars from one client to another. For example, one client may want to have all reasonable options "on the table" before evaluating any of them, while another client may prefer to focus first on a single option and move on to others only if evaluation suggests that others may be more satisfactory. As you know, which solutions are "best" often rest largely on subjective factors unique to each client. Value preferences, degree of risk aversion, and beliefs about which consequences are most important are some factors that you may help clients think through before choosing a "best" solution.

---

28. See, e.g., Estate of Beach, 542 P.2d 994, 998 (Cal. 1975) (holding that a bank serving as a trustee could be held to a higher standard of care than a non-professional trustee).

29. If you realize that either clients' or your predictions about likely consequences are incorrect, you may (if circumstances allow) suggest re-visiting previously-made decisions. To take an obvious example, a client may decide to conduct business as a general rather than a limited partnership to take advantage of certain tax advantages. If the rules change and those advantages no longer exist, you may advise the client to re-consider the decision. Possibly unreliable predictions about matters less compelling than changes in substantive rules may also lead you to suggest reconsideration of decisions. For example, perhaps a client chose to do business as a general rather than a limited partnership to satisfy the desires of a major investor. Should that investor cease to be involved in the business, you might suggest that the client reconsider the decision.

30. For further discussion of advice-giving, see Section D *infra* and Chapter 18.

For example, in the Gower–Smeltics matter, assume that two of the options that Gower and you have identified are opening negotiations immediately on a three-year contract at the same salary and forgoing negotiations until after the basketball season concludes. Assume further that among the likely consequences identified by you and Gower are the following: if Gower waits until after the season to negotiate a contract, "plus" consequences include the possibility that as a free agent open to competitive bidding from different teams, he will be offered an increased salary, and enhanced post-career opportunities resulting from the added publicity the competitive negotiations produce. On the "down" side, delay in signing a new contract subjects Gower to the risk that an injury will reduce or end his career before he can sign a new contract, and may hurt his post-career opportunities if the delay suggests that he is disloyal to the team and its fans.

During the process of evaluating the options, you need to afford Gower the opportunity to weigh the likely consequences. Which consequences seem most likely to occur, and which are most important to Gower? How risk averse is Gower? What are his personal values on the questions of franchise loyalty, his family's financial security, standing up to the team ownership, and the like? Only through engaging in a process by which he has an opportunity to compare and assess such factors can Gower make a decision that is most likely to satisfy him and his family.

C. AFFORD CLIENTS A REASONABLE OPPORTUNITY TO EVALUATE ALTERNATIVES AND CONSEQUENCES

How far does the obligation to discuss alternatives and consequences with clients extend? This question covers at least two issues. First, should you counsel clients with respect to every conceivable alternative and consequence? Second, how much understanding of alternatives and consequences should clients possess for you to have provided adequate counseling?

Answers to these questions ultimately rest on professional judgment in the context of individual clients and their problems. In general, however, the following standard articulates the extent of your counseling obligation:

> In your role as a counselor, provide clients with a reasonable opportunity to understand and evaluate those alternatives and consequences that similarly-situated clients would consider pivotal to the decision at hand.

Consider what this standard entails.

1. *"Pivotal Alternatives and Consequences"*

Limiting your obligation to identifying and evaluating "pivotal" alternatives and consequences recognizes that it is virtually impossible to explore all possible alternatives and likely consequences. "Pivotal" alternatives and consequences are those that might alter or change clients' decisions, and are reasonably foreseeable or likely to occur.

For example, assume that a client based in the United States is negotiating a purchase of knives from a Chinese manufacturer, and that the manufacturer insists on payment upon delivery of the knives to a carrier in Shanghai. The client is willing to agree to this arrangement provided a way can be found to inspect the goods before they are shipped. However, the client has no offices in China and knows no one in China who could inspect the goods on the client's behalf. Accordingly, the client is considering abandoning the deal. An opportunity to have the goods inspected by a reputable Chinese inspection company would obviously be a "pivotal option" because it would make or break the client's decision to go ahead with the deal and is an alternative that most clients would probably want to consider. By contrast, the option of arranging for the client to play every state lottery game every day until the client wins enough money to pay for a private inspector to fly to China would not make the cut, based on your judgment that such an option is just plain silly.

2. "Similarly–Situated Clients"

The extent of your counseling obligation is measured not by a mythical "average" or "reasonable" client. Rather, your obligation is to make clients aware of the alternatives and consequences that "reasonable and similarly-situated" clients would want to know about. In other words, how extensively you counsel depends on such factors as:

- the economic or psychological significance of a decision;
- the probable importance of a decision to a matter's outcome;
- a client's experience, knowledge, personal values and concerns
- a client's cultural identity, which may produce alternatives and consequences that are pivotal primarily for people who share that cultural identity.

Of course, each client is not a "tabula rasa." Your judgment about what alternatives or consequences are pivotal to a particular client will necessarily and legitimately be influenced by your past experiences with comparable clients.

3. "Reasonable Opportunity to Understand and Evaluate"

Since clients' actual levels of understanding are beyond your ken, the standard refers to the process that should precede decision-making. Your counseling responsibility is to afford clients a reasonable opportunity to *understand* and to *evaluate* options. Pursuant to this standard, you provide adequate counseling even if you cannot be fully certain that clients do have fully understood and evaluated their options. So long as you have offered them a reasonable opportunity to do so, you have satisfied your obligations as a professional counselor. The prevailing ethical and doctrinal authority is consistent with this conception.[31]

---

31. According to the Model Rules, lawyers must obtain "informed consent" to a   proposed course of action, defined in the Rules as "agreement ... after the lawyer

The primary justifications for a process standard rather than one based on clients' actual awareness is that the latter is frequently impossible to gauge accurately or even to attain at all. For instance, assume that you represent Garvey, a homeowner who purchased defective kitchen cabinets from the Highs Big Box Home Improvement Store. When his dispute with Highs failed to resolve informally, you filed suit to recover the cost of his cabinets and of the contractor's time required to remedy the defects. As trial approaches, Highs makes a settlement offer that you explore thoroughly with Garvey. You explain that the settlement offer is probably at least as good an outcome as Garvey is likely to obtain through a trial. Aware of the tensions that the dispute has created for Garvey and his family, you also advise Garvey that a likely consequence of refusing the offer and going to trial is that the trial will greatly exacerbate those tensions. Garvey participates in the counseling discussions and has no trouble understanding what you have said. Nevertheless, Garvey persists in what you consider an unsupportable belief that a jury will find Highs' conduct to be outrageous and award him far more than Highs has offered.[32] Moreover, Garvey denies that trial will be any more stressful than what he and his family have lived with so far.

This summary raises doubts that Garvey fully understands and appreciates the alternatives and their likely consequences. His desire to go to trial does not reflect a difference in values so much as it does a misunderstanding of how a group of neutral jurors will react to what happened. Moreover, no matter how clear and rational Garvey's thinking, he may never be able to anticipate in advance the additional stress of going to trial. Thus, were the counseling standard to demand actual client understanding, you would have cause to doubt whether you have achieved it in Garvey's case. However, you satisfy the process standard if you have afforded Garvey a reasonable opportunity to evaluate the options and likely consequences.

As you can no doubt appreciate, what a "reasonable opportunity" consists of depends on the unique facts of individual settings. Common situational factors that may help you feel comfortable that you have provided a "reasonable opportunity" include:

- A decision's likely impact. The greater a decision's potential legal or non-legal impact, the greater the amount of time and effort you

has communicated adequate information and explanation about the material risks of and reasonably available alternatives to the proposed course of conduct." MODEL RULES, *supra* note 1, RULE 1.0(e). Rule 1.4 further requires that lawyers "reasonably consult with the client about the means by which the client's objectives are to be accomplished" (Rule 1.4(a)(2)) and "keep the client reasonably informed about the status

of the matter" (Rule 1.4(a)(3)). The "law of lawyering" (which tends to encompass the malpractice) standards echo this "reasonable opportunity" conception. *See, e.g.,* RESTATEMENT THIRD OF THE LAW GOVERNING LAWYERS § 20 (2000).

32. Garvey's seemingly distorted thinking may be due to the cognitive illusions known as "hindsight" or "self serving" bias. See Chapter 18.

may need to devote to counseling under a "reasonableness" standard.

- A decision's complexity. A reasonable opportunity may require a greater counseling effort when discussions involve complex legal doctrine or factually complicated alternatives and consequences.

- Clients' backgrounds. Such factors as clients' legal sophistication and experience and clients' levels of emotional involvement can affect what constitutes a reasonable opportunity.

- Time available for deciding. Counseling discussions may have to be curtailed when decisions must be made quickly.

- Clients' willingness to participate and pay. You cannot lock your office door and force clients to participate in counseling discussions. Still less can you force them to pay for your time if they are willing to make decisions despite greatly truncated counseling.

Recognize, however, that a reduced counseling effort may be unreasonable if a client faced with an important and complex problem wants to but is unable to explore alternatives and consequences only because the client cannot pay your full hourly fee.

D. PROVIDING ADVICE

When decision-making is at hand, clients may ask for your advice in a variety of ways. For example, clients may say such things as:

- "I'm leaning towards accepting the settlement offer. Do you think that's what I ought to do?"

- "I just don't know what to do. What do you recommend? What do think I should do?"

A radical interpretation of the client-centered approach might lead you to reject all such requests for advice in order to avoid influencing decisions. However, such an extreme interpretation demeans clients' ability to make independent judgments, deprives clients of the opportunity to get advice from a person who has professional expertise and emotional distance from problems, and directly frustrates clients' expectations. Client-centeredness does not require you to hide from giving advice. Far from it. Client-centeredness encompasses the notion that as a matter of autonomy, clients who seek your help are entitled to ask for and receive advice.

What client-centeredness does entail is that you generally respond to requests for advice only after you have counseled clients sufficiently to be familiar with their objectives, concerns and values. Having this information makes it more likely that any advice you may give will reflect clients' best interests and values. For example, assume that Cathy Gilliger consults you about terminating an employee who has become a problem at her company. The options you have discussed consist of firing the employee and asking the employee to resign upon several months' severance pay. When evaluating these options, the consequences that

Gilliger deemed most important were (1) supporting the supervisor who gave the employee a poor evaluation; and (2) avoiding a lawsuit by the employee. Gilliger asks for your opinion about what she ought to do. Given the values and concerns that Gilliger expressed, you would probably advise her that the severance pay option seems the better course. You might say something like, "In my opinion, given what you have told me about what you want to achieve, you'd be better off with the severance pay option, since it would both support the supervisor and minimize the risk of a lawsuit."[33] You may personally feel that it is wrong to "pay off" an employee simply to avoid a lawsuit, but your opinion should reflect the client's values, not yours.

While clients' objectives, concerns and values may emerge during any phase of your representation (e.g., during time line or theory development questioning), a counseling discussion of those matters in the context of the decision at hand may be necessary before you can feel confident that you understand a client's position. Hence, a sensible approach is to provide opinions only after you have counseled clients with respect to specific decisions that need to be made.

In a variant of the situation described above, clients' questions and actions may suggest that they want you to advise them as to what you *personally* would choose to do were you in their situations. For example, clients may say such things as:

"What would you do if you were in my shoes?"

"I'm leaning towards disinheriting my three sons. Is that what you would do?"

Again, respect for client autonomy and independence means that providing opinions about what you would do were you the decision-maker is consistent with the values of client-centeredness. When you do provide such opinions, including the experiences or reasons underlying them reminds clients that their decisions may reasonably differ from yours. For instance, you may accompany opinions with comments such as:

I've never personally been faced with having to decide whether to accept a settlement offer, especially in a situation that I've felt so strongly that I've been wronged. But frankly, I think that at this point I'd feel that I made my point and I'd want to get on with my life. So I'd probably take their offer, but I can understand if you come to a different conclusion.[34]

To the extent that you can refer to the experiences of other clients in similar situations, you may refer to decisions that they've found

33. On the other hand, had Gilliger emphasized her desire to "make an example of the employee to all others, no matter what the cost," you might well have suggested the option of firing the employee.

34. In some instances, you may have difficulty determining whether a client is asking for advice based on the client's values or yours. For a discussion of how you might make this determination and of techniques for offering advice based on your personal values, see Chapter 18.

satisfactory. For example, in the above situation your comments might go along these lines:

> I've represented a few clients whose situations were somewhat similar to yours, and talked to other attorneys too. Most of my clients and those of the attorneys I've talked to have decided to accept settlement offers that are as reasonable as this one, and at least personally I've never had a client contact me after a case has been settled and tell me that they regret their decision.

Clients may request your personal opinion because they want moral support for decisions they've more or less already made. In such situations, your response may again combine your moral stances with the reasons or experiences underlying them. For example, a conversation may go as follows:

> C: So at this point, I'm leaning strongly towards disinheriting the lot of them. Do you personally think that's the right thing to do?

> L: That's a tough judgment to make, and I certainly won't try to talk you out of your plans. I'm a "blood is thicker than water" type, so I'd have a really hard time disinheriting my children. At the same time, I'm fortunate that my family relationships haven't been as troubled as yours. I suppose that if I were in your situation, I might well make the same decision that you have.

As the above discussion implies, offering advice in the absence of clients' requesting it is generally inconsistent with the values of client-centeredness. Offering unsolicited advice fulfills one traditional image of lawyers as advice givers, an image that depicts them as telling clients what to do. ("If I'm going to be your lawyer, I'll expect you to follow my advice. Now here's what we're going to do first...") An attorney who regards counseling as presenting clients with "fait accompli" has no need even to review with clients options and likely consequences. Needless to say, the only noteworthy aspect of this approach is that it manages to violate just about every tenet of client-centered counseling, and a few rules of professional conduct to boot.

Taking a somewhat more nuanced approach with regard to giving unsolicited advice, you might review options and consequences and then advise clients as to what decisions they ought to make and why. For example, you might say something along these lines:

> To sum up then, Mr. Garvey, basically what you have to decide is whether to accept or reject High's settlement offer. We've talked about the plusses and minuses of each option. I'll be frank with you, I think you ought to accept the offer. If it were me, that's the decision I'd make. But of course, the decision is up to you. Are you prepared to make a decision now, or do you want to mull it over for a day or two?

Here, unsolicited advice follows discussions that presumably comply with the counseling standard of giving clients a reasonable opportunity to decide. However, many clients are apt to resent unsolicited advice and view it as paternalistic and demeaning, even if you do first engage in a counseling process. Moreover, clients are likely to interpret unsolicited advice as meaning that you and not they are the primary decision-makers. Regardless of their legal sophistication, many clients think themselves quite capable of making decisions. Thus, giving unsolicited advice to clients is likely to impair rapport, weaken client confidence in you, and reduce client participation in the problem-solving process.

Apart from whether clients resent unsolicited advice, providing it generally violates client-centered norms.[35] Client-centeredness presumes that clients are capable of acting autonomously. Unsolicited advice suggests that clients cannot recognize their own best interests and thereby overrides client autonomy. Finally, satisfactory decisions generally reflect both legal and non-legal concerns, and clients are the experts when it comes to recognizing and evaluating non-legal concerns. Typically, then, unsolicited advice is inconsistent with client-centered lawyering.

E. INTERVENING IN CLIENTS' DECISIONS

Client-centeredness regards clients as moral agents whose decisions you are normally bound to respect, even if you would have made different ones. At the same time, this client-centered position assumes that clients are prepared to make reasonable and morally acceptable choices. However, these assumptions are certainly less than universally correct. For example, you may consider some decisions to be morally wrong, and others to be wrong because they conflict with clients' expressed values or goals or are contrary to a rational assessment of their best interests. The sections below explore the propriety from a client-centered standpoint of expressing your disagreement with clients' decisions in such circumstances.[36]

1. Decisions That Substantially Contravene Clients' Stated Objectives

Being a lawyer does not provide you with a license to refuse to implement or even to try to talk clients out of all decisions with which you disagree. Indeed, client-centeredness insists that clients have the privilege to make lousy decisions that "give up the store" if they so choose. Nevertheless, client-centeredness need not be a straitjacket that prevents you from asking clients to reconsider decisions that you regard

35. For an argument that client-centeredness is inappropriate when lawyers deal with collectives of poor clients. *See* William H. Simon, *The Dark Secret of Progressive Lawyering: A Comment on Poverty Law Scholarship in the Post–Modern, Post–Reagan Era*, 48 MIAMI L. REV. 1099, 1106 (1994) ("lawyers have a legitimate interest in expressing their values in their work.... [N]ot all lawyer power and influence should be seen as illegitimate domination").

36. This section focuses generally on when you might intervene. See Chapter 18 for a more detailed discussion of when intervention is appropriate as well as for a discussion of specific techniques you might employ once you decide to intervene.

as substantially contrary to their best interests as they've defined them. This section considers how you might react to clients' decisions that you regard as substantially contrary to their stated objectives. Consider the following situations:

- A tax client's expressed objectives are to minimize taxes and maximize financial gain. Yet, the client decides not to hire an appraiser to evaluate the market value of a contaminated parcel of real property that the client has inherited, even though you are very confident that an appraisal will produce tax savings that substantially outweigh the costs of the appraisal.

- A divorce client indicates that a principal objective is financial protection for herself and her children. However, the client is prepared to accept a weak financial settlement from her spouse "just to get this mess behind me as soon as possible."

- You represent a neighborhood association in a low income area and are attempting to convince state officials not to re-open a landfill on nearby vacant land. The association's long-term objectives are to safeguard health and protect property values. However, the association's leaders are prepared to accept the state's offer to make small cash payments to a select group of nearby residents and limit the amount of garbage that can be dumped into the landfill each month, though you believe that the offer does nothing to assuage the association's long-term concerns.

In each of these examples, the clients' decisions seem not only ill-advised but also inconsistent with their expressed objectives. In each case, therefore, you might at least seek to have the clients reconsider their decisions. For techniques for so doing, please see Chapter 18.

2. Decisions That Contravene Your Moral Beliefs

Another reason that you may find yourself in disagreement with clients' decisions is that they contravene your moral beliefs. Again, just as you should usually afford clients latitude to make decisions that conflict with your view of their best interests, respect for clients' autonomy suggests that you generally allow clients to make decisions consistent with their own moral compasses. Yet, client-centeredness need not cause you to wholly abandon your moral commitments. When clients opt for courses of action that you believe are morally repugnant (though lawful), self-respect for your own autonomy may make it appropriate for you ask them to reconsider their decisions. Professional rules encourage you to do so,[37] and your conception of your role as a professional may require you to do so.[38]

37. *See* MODEL RULES, *supra* note 1, RULES 2.1, cmt. 2.

38. While client-centeredness encourages you to respect clients' personal values and discourages you from imposing your own values, recognize that values are typically *preferences*, not absolute moral commitments. Moreover, few adhere to the relativist idea that moral values are simply personal and cannot be the subject of principled disagreement. Your moral vision permits you to make grounded choices about

Consider an example of a situation in which a client's decision may present deep moral concerns for you, and how you might intervene. Assume that you are outside counsel for Norne Company, a large multinational energy supplier whose stock is publicly traded. You have been asked to review a sophisticated, seemingly legal accounting and management plan by which assets of the company are traded to and from separate shell corporations, resulting in significant overstating of the company's profits. The favorable profit reports, you understand, will lead to inflated stock prices and investor overconfidence in Norne securities. (Indeed, this is the entire purpose of the plan.) Your legal judgment is that the scheme is lawful, but you also recognize that at some point down the road the company's true worth will be revealed, the stock price will fall dramatically, and investors and retirees will lose millions of dollars.[39] When your client indicates that the company has decided to go forward with the plan, may you advise the company's executives that you consider it ill-advised and morally improper and ask them to reconsider?[40]

A "yes" response is consistent with client-centeredness and professional autonomy. Your interest in furthering what you perceive as society's interests through your law practice allows you to raise your moral concerns. You can do so by first recognizing the legitimacy of the company's legal position, and of the short term commitment to an increased stock price. Proceeding to the moral dimension, you may point out the risks of harm to employees who hold company stock in their retirement plans and to outside investors who may not know of or understand the ploy. You may also raise concerns about broader social harms caused by corporate actions that many people are likely to perceive as underhanded and manipulative. Should the executives refuse to alter their plans your choice would be between continuing as outside counsel and perhaps helping the client to limit the plan's future scope, or withdrawing as counsel if ethical rules permit you to do so, which in this case they seem to do.[41]

Consider a second example that may raise moral concerns. Assume that you represent Magic Properties, a large development company. Magic owns a factory leased to Community Corp., a corporation initially financed by the Small Business Administration. Community employs and retrains approximately 100 low income wage earners. Bob Lynn, Magic's Vice President for property management, has consulted you because

right and wrong, and client-centeredness does not take that option away from you. *See* Paul R. Tremblay, *Shared Norms, Bad Lawyers, and the Virtues of Casuistry*, 36 U.S.F. L. Rev. 659 (2002).

39. The Norne hypothetical is loosely based on the account of the Enron fiasco in Deborah L. Rhode & Paul D. Paton, *Lawyers, Ethics, and Enron*, 8 Stan. J.L. Bus. & Fin. 9 (2002). (Enron was a major power company that collapsed virtually overnight

as a result of the company's fraudulent business practices and false financial reporting.)

40. Of course, when the action that a client proposes to take is illegal or even runs the risk of being found illegal, you must point such illegality out to the client. *See* Model Rules, *supra* note 359, Rule 1.2(d).

41. *See* Model Rules, *supra* note 1, Rule 1.16.

Community has fallen behind in its rent. Though Community pays rent each month, its payments are invariably late and incomplete. Thus, although the lease calls for a monthly rent of $5,000, Community commonly remits no more than $3,500. At present, Community is $15,000 in arrears in its rent. You have reviewed Magic's options and their likely consequences with Lynn, and he has decided to institute suit to terminate Community's lease and recover past due rent. Magic will then be able to re-let the factory at substantially higher rent. Lynn has indicated that Magic is not greatly concerned about the $15,000 arrearage, but in the interests of its employees and shareholders wants to make the factory more profitable.

You have no doubt that Lynn's prediction about Magic's ability to gain more income from the property is correct. Hence, his decision is neither logically nor legally "wrong." However, in your view his decision is morally wrong. Even with Community paying only $3500 per month, Magic derives a positive cash flow from the factory. You believe that Magic's desire for additional income from the factory is outweighed by the good that Community accomplishes by employing and retraining low income workers. In these circumstances, may you suggest to Lynn that he reconsider his choice?

Again, a "yes" response is consistent with client centeredness and professional autonomy. You can recognize the legitimacy of Lynn's values by saying something like, "Maximizing Magic's profits and protecting its shareholders are important considerations." Then, you can ask Lynn to consider how Community promotes the social good, how his decision is likely to affect Community, and whether Community's interests in this instance ought to trump Magic's. However, if Lynn rejects your position, you should allow his views to prevail unless you either intend to ask Lynn to seek other counsel or to withdraw if ethical rules permit you to do so.[42]

While moral tensions arise frequently in law practice,[43] your intervention because of moral disagreement is apt to be somewhat infrequent. One reason is simply that palpable costs attend to assuming moral superiority over clients. No one wants to be known as a "moral know it all" or a "goody two-shoes."[44] Second, moral tensions arrive in shades of gray, and individuals are very seldom openly or admittedly immoral. A client who suggests a scheme that you consider immoral will undoubtedly offer a reasoned defense based on assumed facts which you cannot be sure are wrong. You may discuss your concerns, but unless you are completely certain that the harm and the unfairness that you perceive are unable to be justified, your reluctant choice will often be to go along with clients' decisions.

---

42. MODEL CODE, *supra* note 2, at DR 2–110(B) & (C); MODEL RULES, *supra* note 1, Rule 1.16.

43. *See* DEBORAH L. RHODE, IN THE INTERESTS OF JUSTICE: REFORMING THE LEGAL PROFESSION (2000)

44. *See* SIMON BLACKBURN, BEING GOOD: AN INTRODUCTION TO ETHICS 72 (2000).

3. *Other Lawyer–Client Value Conflicts*

a. *Risk–Aversion*

The common stereotype of lawyers as nay-sayers who want to throw cold water on all sorts of clever plans[45] suggests that you and clients may often differ as to how they should proceed in the face of an uncertain future. From your perspective, clients about to enter into deals or to precipitate litigation often resemble high school lovers who are determined to wed: They unduly minimize the risk that something will go wrong. But from clients' perspectives, you may be too ready to recommend against decisions because uncertain contingencies may ultimately sour it.

In part, clients' desires to press forward in the face of uncertainty may reflect mis-prediction of likely outcomes. For example, the high school lovers may erroneously believe that few marriages end in divorce or may believe that the high rate of divorce simply does not apply to them.[46] But often, clients recognize the same risks that you do but disagree about whether they are worth taking. In such situations, client-centeredness suggests that clients' attitudes towards risk and not yours should prevail.[47]

For example, assume that your client is Jerry Bilt, Vice President of Landview Corp., which is negotiating to buy several acres of land from Donner Development Co. Landview plans to construct a housing tract on the land. Donner refuses to include in the proposed sales agreement a clause protecting Landview should all or part of the land, because of soil conditions or otherwise, prove unbuildable. Bilt, relying on a study conducted by a Landview soils engineer, is anxious to purchase the land and begin construction. You might point out the advisability of a review by an independent soils engineer and Landview's lack of recourse should all or part of the land prove unbuildable. But if Bilt has confidence in Landview's own soils engineer, perhaps because of his prior experience with the engineer, and wants to proceed with the purchase, you should honor his decision. The risk is what many lawyers and business people would consider a common business risk. Unless Bilt has grossly mis-

---

45. *See* Langevoort & Rasmussen, *supra* note 5, at 375; MARK MCCORMICK, THE TERRIBLE TRUTH ABOUT LAWYERS 111–12 (1987).

46. *See* MAX H. BAZERMAN, JUDGMENT IN MANAGERIAL DECISION MAKING 19 (5th ed. 2002) (explaining that failure to recognize base rates has many unfortunate implications). Often failure to rationally assess the probability of risk also involves the salience of such incidences in one's memory. Cass R. Sunstein, *What's Available? Social Influences and Behavioral Economics*, 97 Nw. U. L. REV. 1295, 1297 (2003). Thus, events that come to mind easily appear more frequent than cases that occur at the same or even a higher rate. *Id.* at 1301. For example, the parents of the high school lovers may also be high school sweethearts and still married. For a further discussion of perhaps intervening in clients decisions when their decisions appear to be heavily influenced by the "availability heuristic," see Chapter 17.

47. If your client is impaired and incapable of appreciating risks, you have an opportunity and perhaps an obligation to be more directive. *See* MODEL RULES, *supra* note 2, RULE 1.14.

predicted the likelihood that the land will be unbuildable, the risk is Landview's to take.[48]

b. Interference with Professional Skills

Lawyer and client autonomy clash most directly when clients' decisions conflict with lawyers' standards of professional practice. For example, a litigation client may want to refuse an adversary's first request for a continuance, when your usual practice may be to grant such requests. Or, a client may desire to make a legal argument in a trial brief which you think extremely tenuous and not worth making. Similarly, a transactional client may want to accept language that you consider vague and poorly drafted. In each case, acceding to the client's request seems to compromise your professional standards, and may harm your reputation within the bar and thus affect your ability to gain and represent future clients. For example, if the poorly drafted agreement winds up in litigation and becomes known to other lawyers and potential clients, you may lose future business and suffer embarrassment.

If attorneys were nothing more than "hired guns," the short answer to such conflicts would be that since the clients' desires are neither illegal nor immoral, you are powerless to raise your disagreement. However, you have a professional interest independent from that of clients in how you conduct your practice. In matters which are not "pivotal" to clients' aims and which raise such concerns, you need not remain unquestioningly silent. If you want to resist clients' wishes, however, remember that clients may have legitimate reasons for asking you to engage in conduct that you regard as compromising your professional standards. Thus, even as you politely request that clients reconsider their decisions, recognize the legitimacy of their values:

> Your not wanting to give them a continuance is perfectly understandable; it keeps maximum pressure on them. My problem with that response is that I almost always grant a continuance to an adversary when the adversary's lawyer is in trial and cannot answer within the statutory time. Frankly, I expect and almost always receive the same courtesy from other attorneys. Thus, while I agree with your views, I think we should grant the continuance this one time and at the same time let them know we will insist that they

---

48. In many cases, you may find it difficult to determine whether your disagreement with a client's decision emanates from a client's having mispredicted likely consequences or from a client's being less risk-averse than you. You may tend to combine the two criteria, believing that "the reason the client wants to go ahead is because the client is mispredicting the consequences." Because misprediction may result in your explicitly telling a client that you believe the client is wrong, do not treat disagreement as a problem of misprediction without solid evidence. For example, unless you have some expertise in soils engineering, or unless Bilt's statements indicate that he has misunderstood the report of Landview's soils engineer, you probably should not regard his desire to go forward with the purchase as a problem of misprediction. In this same spirit, some researchers have concluded that lawyers systematically overstate risk, either because of their role training or (more cynically) because of their self-interest, as greater risks tend to correlate with greater fees. See Langevoort & Rasmussen, *supra* note 5.

comply with time limits in the future. Will that be acceptable to you?

F.   REFUSING TO IMPLEMENT CLIENTS' CHOICES

You may advise clients that decisions mis-predict outcomes, conflict with their stated values, may be immoral, do not take sufficient account of risks, or conflict with your professional standards. If clients hold fast to decisions despite your counseling efforts, how might you respond?

Your immediate reaction might be, "Well, I'll just withdraw." Even after thinking about the effect of that choice on your pocketbook and your career, you may hold to that reaction. However, the ethical rules in your jurisdiction may constrain your ability to withdraw. While jurisdictions that follow the Model Rules tend to allow great latitude to lawyers who cannot abide clients' courses of conduct,[49] you will have to consult the rules in your state if you find yourself in such a predicament.

---

49.   For a discussion of when withdrawal may be proper, see MODEL RULES, *supra* note 1, Rule 1.16. For example, Rule 1.16 (b)(4) permits termination of the attorney-client relationship by the lawyer, even if doing so may cause "material adverse effect on the interests of the client," if "the client insists upon taking action that the lawyer considers repugnant or with which the lawyer has a fundamental disagreement."

Chapter 14

IMPLEMENTING AN EFFECTIVE COUNSELING PROCESS

* * *

Bob, we've created quite a list of the advantages of insisting upon personal guarantees from Metal Beams' officers. But let's think for a moment about the possible negatives. An obvious one is that it increases the chances that Metal Beams won't go for the deal. Do you think that is a serious risk?

I just don't know. Metal's president, Marsh, has been around a long time and he may be really offended if we start talking about personal guarantees. It's hard to know how he'll react.

So a negative of asking for the guarantees is that we run a somewhat undefined risk of offending Marsh at the outset.

I guess that's right, but, on the other hand, if we don't have the guarantees the size of our financial risk is pretty big and the board may be unhappy.

Okay. On the con side of forgoing the personal guarantees is both an increased financial risk and the risk of making the board unhappy. But let's think for just a moment about other possible problems with asking Metal's officers to sign personal guarantees.

It might cause them to look elsewhere for future deals. We know they have other projects in mind and if things go well with this deal, we'd like to have a shot at those other projects as well.

How likely is it that if you insist on guarantees in this deal, it will influence Metal Beams in the future?

Well, knowing Marsh, I think there is some chance of that.

Okay; anything else you can think of?

* * *

1. INTRODUCTION

The counseling approach described in Chapter 13 consists of four steps:

1. Clarifying clients' objectives;

2. Identifying alternative solutions;

3. Identifying the likely consequences of each alternative; and

4. Helping clients decide which alternative is most likely to be satisfactory.

This chapter explores techniques for effectively implementing this four step approach. The discussion explains techniques for implementing the client-centered counseling approach across a wide spectrum of types of clients and legal matters involving both litigation and transactions. Chapters 15 through 18 recognize the limits of a "one size fits all" approach to counseling techniques. Those chapters suggest refinements that can help you adapt counseling meetings according to the unique circumstances of individual clients and decisions.[1]

2. THE IMPORTANCE OF NEUTRALITY

Taking clients through the decision-making process typically affords you with numerous opportunities to communicate your preferred decisions without explicitly telling clients what you think they ought to do. The words you choose, the way in which you order discussions, even your body language may convey messages about what you want clients to do. For example, if each time a client mentions a possible advantage of option A, you mention a possible disadvantage, the client may perceive you as arguing against option A. However, effective counseling usually requires the appearance of neutrality. That is, in most situations try to convey a message that you have no favorites among available alternatives.[2]

A generally neutral stance is consistent with the client-centered approach, which regards clients as problems' owners who presumptively are autonomous and capable of making decisions in accordance with their best interests. Instrumentally, neutrality encourages clients to disclose all relevant information, especially when you counsel clients who by nature or cultural conditioning defer to experts and authority figures.[3] If your behavior indicates that you favor a particular solution,

---

1. For example, they consider techniques for counseling clients who seem unwilling to think through options in an organized or systematic way, or who are reluctant to make decisions, or who make decisions based upon unrealistic predictions (or, at least, predictions different from yours).

2. You are neutral only with respect to specific options. As the book's emphasis on the value of rapport makes clear, you certainly need not be neutral with respect to broader matters such as your interest in clients and your willingness to help resolve their problems. And, as you recall, you may

not be neutral when a client's decision raises moral concerns. See Chapter 18.

3. Clients' cultural backgrounds may incline them to defer to professionals as authority figures. See Chapter 2. See also, Paul R. Tremblay, *Interviewing and Counseling Across Cultures: Heuristics and Biases,* 9 CLINICAL L. REV. 373 (2002); Susan Bryant, *The Five Habits: Building Cross-Cultural Competence in Lawyers,* 8 CLINICAL L. REV. 33, 74 n.138 (2001) (revealing how a student from the Ivory Coast explained that the lawyers in his country are "the fixer[s]" who would solve the problem as the lawyer saw fit); Devon W. Carbado, *(E)Racing the Fourth Amendment,* 100 MICH. L. REV. 946,

such clients will often be unwilling or perhaps unable to think through alternatives and consequences themselves, and they might be reluctant to verbalize those that they do identify. As a result, such clients will not participate actively in the resolution of their problems.[4]

Accordingly, strive to maintain impartiality throughout the counseling process.[5] If you do not, clients may not hear what you have to say and may fail to express their own thoughts fully. Either circumstance may prevent clients from having a reasonable opportunity to consider pertinent alternatives and consequences.

3.   COUNSELING PLANS

Just as teachers commonly prepare lesson plans before entering classrooms, you might prepare counseling plans before embarking on important counseling conversations. Counseling plans should not dictate the order in which you address subjects during such conversations any more than lesson plans anticipate exactly what happens in classrooms. Rather, counseling plans promote thorough counseling conversations by providing visual reminders of points you want to cover. Moreover, the process of preparing counseling plans can help you organize your thoughts and make the ensuing conversations more productive and efficient.

You can develop helpful counseling plans by simply outlining your thoughts regarding clients' objectives, the alternatives for trying to achieve those objectives, and the consequences that you think are likely to occur and others that you want to inquire into with clients. Depending on your graphics skills, you may format the outlines as charts that you and clients refer to during counseling conversations. If you do intend to refer to counseling plans when talking to clients, include blank lines (or other means) that make them easy to update with new ideas that clients (or you) later identify.

4.   PROVIDE PREPARATORY EXPLANATIONS

As you may recall, preparatory explanations are useful throughout the interviewing and counseling process to alert clients to what to expect during ensuing discussions. Preparatory explanations tend to build rapport and to encourage clients' full involvement in the subjects under

---

1001 N.229 (2002) ("[F]OR MANY ASIAN AMERICANS, WITHHOLDING CONSENT FROM AN AUTHORITY FIGURE IS CONTRARY TO CULTURAL NORMS."); LESTER W. KISS, *REVIVING THE CRIMINAL JURY IN JAPAN*, 62 Law & Contemp. Probs. 261, 283 (1999) (EXPLAINING THAT JAPANESE CULTURAL CHARACTERISTICS SUCH AS THE HIERARCHICAL NATURE OF SOCIETY, THE HIGH LEVEL OF TRUST IN AUTHORITY FIGURES, AND THE DESIRE TO MAINTAIN HARMONY ARE OBSTACLES TO AN EFFECTIVE JURY SYSTEM IN JAPAN).

4. Neutrality is also an aspect of "defensive lawyering" by which you seek to minimize the likelihood that clients can prevail in malpractice actions against you when decisions that they later claim you imposed on them do not work out as they hoped.

5. Some scholars have pointed out that consistently maintaining such an appearance may be impossible. *See* THOMAS L. SHAFFER AND JAMES R. ELKINS, LEGAL INTERVIEWING AND COUNSELING IN A NUTSHELL 239 (3d ed. 1997); William H. Simon, *Lawyer Advice and Client Autonomy: Mrs. Jones's Case*, 50 MD. L. REV. 213, 225 (1991).

discussion.[6] In the decision-making context, you may employ preparatory explanations to direct clients' attention to the decisions that need to be made and the general factors that clients need to consider. Such an explanation may go as follows:

1. L: Jan, next you need to decide who you want to appoint as the guardian for your children should something happen to you. What we can do is talk about the two kinds of guardians for which the law provides, what sorts of qualities you are looking for in a guardian, and possible candidates. Maybe you already have someone in mind. Even if you do, I'll ask you to consider all possible candidates and the pros and cons of each. This will give you a solid basis for whatever decision you ultimately make. Does that make sense?

2. C: Sure, although I'm pretty sure that James and Kim are the people I want.

3. L: Great; it sounds like you've already given some thought to this issue. So let's start by talking about . . . .

Though brief, your explanation identifies the decision (naming a guardian) and advises Jan that she will need to think about objectives (qualities of a guardian) and alternatives (possible candidates), and that the discussion may review a number of consequences (pros and cons). This description gives even a relatively inexperienced client a preview of what to expect. Of course, a single description of the process may not be adequate, and you may have to re-explain it as you approach the various steps.

In the above dialog you encourage Jan to think about options and consequences even though she appears to have reached a tentative decision. Counseling in the face of clients' preliminary decisions is consistent with neutrality. Your purpose is not to undermine their tentative decisions, but to make sure that they have reasonable opportunities to make satisfactory choices.[7] Most likely, Jan will understand your statement in No. 1, "Even if you do, . . ." as indicating that you accept any choice that she ultimately makes.[8]

5. CLARIFYING CLIENTS' OBJECTIVES

You should normally open decision-making discussions by clarifying clients' objectives with respect to the decisions that need to be made. Clarifying objectives at the outset is often helpful for at least three reasons:

6. For discussion of the purposes of preparatory explanations, see Chapter 5.

7. Remember that your obligation under the counseling standard is to provide clients with a reasonable opportunity to consider pivotal alternatives and consequences. See Chapter 13.

8. A short reminder of the counseling process may be more than adequate when you represent clients who you have previously counseled. For example, a statement such as "Let's turn now to the pros and cons of the different options" may suffice.

- Options often do not become apparent until after clients realize and verbalize pertinent objectives. For example, a litigation client may not recognize that alternative dispute resolution is a viable option until after the client realizes that "ability to do business with the adversary in the future" is one of the client's objectives.

- Clients' initial objectives may change as cases progress. For example, either the general economic climate or a client's personal circumstances may have changed since you first discussed objectives. Updating clients' previously-identified objectives is sensible whenever you think that a change in those objectives is reasonably possible.[9]

- Decisions often involve subsidiary issues to which previously-identified objectives do not necessarily apply. For example, during an initial meeting you may learn that a corporate client's overall goal is to raise capital to build a new plant through a public sale of stock. This objective alone will not resolve a number of subsidiary issues that are likely to arise along the way, such as which underwriter to work with and whether to issue both preferred and common stock. Giving clients a reasonable opportunity to make decisions such as these would begin with a discussion of the client's objectives with respect to these subsidiary issues. For example, you might ask the client, "What criteria are you thinking about for choosing an underwriter?"

Commencing counseling by exploring clients' goals is inherent in a client-centered approach. By starting with clients' objectives, you avoid treating problems solely as legal matters, and you continue to identify problems from clients' perspectives.

An effective way to begin clarifying clients' objectives is to employ open questions. The following example is illustrative:

1. L: Claire, the next thing we have to talk about is which underwriter you want to handle the offering. Have you talked this over with the Board?

2. C: No, I wanted to meet with you before I go to the Board.

3. L: I'll be glad to give whatever help I can. Why don't you start by telling me what you're trying to accomplish by choosing one underwriter rather than another.

4. C: Obviously, a major objective will be selecting an underwriter that will give us the best price. Given where our stock is selling now, my thinking is to get a guarantee of at least $24.00 a share. Also, given the competitive nature of the industry, speed is absolutely essential; I'd want an underwriter who will guarantee to complete the offering within 60 days.

---

9. The key words here are "reasonably possible." Every client meeting does not necessitate a review of objectives. Repeatedly asking clients about new objectives may imply a subtle criticism: "What's wrong with you? Your objectives never change."

5.   L: Given what you've told me about the competition you're facing, I understand why that is so important. Any additional objectives I should know about?

6.   C: Well, in recent years I've become increasingly concerned about interference from institutional investors. I'd like to use a firm that will be able to target sales to individual investors.

7.   L: All right. Anything else?

8.   C: I think that's about it.

9.   L: Fine. Let's think about some underwriters who might meet these specifications. . . .

Here, the open question in No. 3 alerts Claire to talk about objectives. If you sense that clients may be reluctant to discuss objectives, you might motivate them to do so by including in your alert a "reward" statement such as, "When objectives are clear, most clients that I've worked with find it easier to come up with solutions that make the most sense."

Nos. 3, 5 and 7 are open questions consistent with the upper part of a T-funnel questioning sequence. However, when the client concludes identifying objectives, you do not turn in No. 9 to lower-T narrow questions searching for "other possible objectives." Instead, you move on to a discussion of options. Unless clients fail to mention objectives that you think most similarly-situated clients would have mentioned, the ones that clients do identify are normally sufficient to start the counseling process. If other, probably secondary, objectives are lurking, they invariably emerge in the course of counseling conversations. In this case, however, were you an experienced securities lawyer, you might have recognized that maintaining a relationship with a previously-used underwriter might have been one of Claire's objectives. If so, you might have substituted a closed question for No. 9 such as, "If I recall, you used Merrill Shearson for your previous offerings. Is it important that you continue to do business with them?"[10]

6.   IDENTIFYING ALTERNATIVES

With clients' objectives out in the open, you can engage clients in discussions of alternative potential solutions. Typically, the most sensible approach is for you to take the lead in presenting options. For example, assume that a client has consulted you concerning what to do about a "problem employee." You might begin this phase of the discussion by saying something like, "Jim, the options I see are to fire Mr. Frankel, to transfer him to a different department, or to give him what we call a 'golden handshake.' "

Clients may well be frustrated if you open up discussions of alternatives by asking about solutions that they have in mind. For one thing, some clients may doubt your competence, reacting internally by thinking

10. For a review of the T-funnel approach see Chapter 7.

something like, "Why the heck are you asking me for suggestions? Isn't that what I hired you for?" For another, when you do finally voice your thoughts, clients may feel that you are "playing games." They may well wonder why you held back if you had possible solutions in mind all along.[11]

Of course, clients' greater familiarity with problems' contexts may enable them to identify options that would not occur to you. Therefore, after mentioning alternatives that you consider reasonable, be sure to invite clients to contribute additional ideas.[12] For example, you might say to Jim, "These are the alternatives I see. You might have some others in mind and I'd like to hear them. Feel free to mention any possibility that has occurred to you because in the end the decision has to be one that you're comfortable with."

That said, circumstances are certain to arise when it makes sense for you to offer clients the first opportunity to propose options. A common such circumstance arises when clients' backgrounds and experiences suggest that they are likely to be ready sources of reasonable options. Assume for example that a client whose company develops computer software programs is about to hire a programmer in order to diversify the company's software products, and consults you with respect to drafting a contract of employment. In view of your client's business experience, you might well ask the client to lead off a discussion of options concerning crucial contract terms. For example, you might say something like, "What do you have in mind as far as whether we should include a non-competition clause in the agreement, and if we have one what terms would you like to see?"[13]

Another example of situations in which it may make sense for you to ask clients to lead off a discussion of potential solutions arises when clients identify with cultures that differ from your own and with which you have had little prior experience. Clients' differing cultural experiences may produce potential solutions that are unlike those you would identify. For example, many years ago legal realist Karl Llewellyn and anthropologist E. Adamson Hoebel studied Cheyenne legal customs by eliciting "trouble stories."[14] By asking members of the Cheyenne to recount concrete disputes and how they had been resolved, Llewellyn and Hoebel aimed at "the development of a social science instrument for

---

11. Clients may in earlier discussions have identified an option or two. For example, Jim might have suggested the possibility of firing the employee. In such instances, you might show "recognition" by identifying an option as one a client first mentioned: "Jim, as you mentioned earlier, one option is to fire Mr. Frankel. The others I see are ..."

12. Similarly, clients who are overly-deferential to authority figures may not mention an option unless you specifically invite them to do so. The upshot of your failing to

invite options may be that perfectly sensible options never come to light, and that the client does not fully pay attention to those you identify.

13. Whether you start with your alternatives or those of a client, you discharge your role as a client-centered counselor. Under both approaches, you actively involve a client in the process of exploring potential solutions.

14. See KARL LLEWELLYN AND E. ADAMSON HOEBEL, THE CHEYENNE WAY (1941).

the recording and interpretation"[15] of the Cheyenne legal system. In much the same way, consider asking clients to describe disputes similar to their own that have occurred within their culture, including how those disputes were resolved. If clients can describe such "trouble stories," their accounts may suggest solutions that you would not have otherwise identified.[16]

At the same time, consider the possibility that clients from other cultures may have little idea about what solutions are viable in the American legal system and as a consequence may select options that are not available.[17] When you recognize that clients are unfamiliar with our system, your best approach may be to start with options you see as available. Doing so may reduce the risk that you will end up frustrating clients by asking them for their input and then telling them that the options they have selected are not viable.

Whether you or clients begin the identification of options, resist the temptation to try to awe clients with your legal acumen by prefacing the discussion of options with a grand discourse on legal theories and issues that underlie the options you have selected. For example, in an estate planning matter, forgo the opportunity to expand on the intricacies of the Rule Against Perpetuities, and in a litigation matter on the chances that a hearsay statement will qualify as a "declaration against interest." Unless clients indicate a desire for such information, prefatory lectures either connected or unconnected to particular options will most often serve only to mystify, frustrate and confuse. Save the legal analysis for your law professor friends, who unaccountably really do seem to like this kind of stuff.

7. IDENTIFYING CONSEQUENCES

With potential options on the table, you may turn counseling conversations to thinking through likely legal and non-legal consequences. For example, if a decision concerns whether to include a buy-out provision in a proposed agreement, your discussions of this option will focus on both the legal effects of buyout provisions and non-legal factors such as whether having a buy-out provision will increase the client's sense of security or cause the other party to have doubts about the proposed agreement.

A. THE NECESSITY TO PREDICT

Assessing consequences involves predictions about future events. That is, your counseling task is not merely to help clients understand

---

15. *Id.* at viii.

16. For a rich analysis of problem resolutions of the Hopi tribe, see Pat Sekaquaptewa, *Evolving the Hopi Common Law,* 9 KAN. J. OF LAW AND PUB. POLICY 761 (2000).

17. *See* Gary Bellow, *Turning Solutions into Problems: The Legal Aid Experience,* 34 NLADA BRIEFCASE 106 (1977). When you represent clients who come from a country other than the United States, gathering information about the legal system with which they are familiar can help you gain a better understanding of their expectations. See Susan Bryant, *The Five Habits: Building Cross–Cultural Competence in Lawyers,* 8 CLINICAL L. REV. 33, 74 (2001).

options' likely consequences, but also to assess the chances that those consequences will in fact occur.

Predictions are, by and large, statements of probability. Scientists generally ascertain probability by observing the same phenomena over time and measuring outcomes. For example, by observing the effects of a general anesthetic on a population of patients over time, medical researchers can predict that allergic reactions will occur in a given percentage of cases. The data (experience) collected in arriving at an overall percentage can be called a data base.

The predictions that you and your clients make almost always center on the behavior of a variety of actors such as adversaries, judges and juries, government officials, and consumers, for which accurate data bases typically are not available. Human behavior as it relates to legal problems is so complex and factually varied, and so little studied empirically, that it does not lend itself to mathematical or statistical analysis.[18] For example, one cannot predict with certainty that an impeached witness will not be believed, or that an owner of property will be so put off by a "lowball" offer that the owner will cease negotiations. Any data bases that you and clients may have individually acquired for predicting future consequences have usually been arrived at by highly selective and intuitive processes in which seeming similarities tend to mask important differences, and thus introduce uncertainty into data bases.[19]

However, those imperfect data bases are often all that you and your clients will have available for making predictions. The question, then, is on whose data bases should predictions be made—yours or your clients'?

B. PREDICTING LEGAL CONSEQUENCES

Predicting legal consequences is the essence of providing legal advice. That is, responsibility for predicting legal consequences rests primarily on you. Clients generally expect you to have a better data base for predicting such matters as how a jury is likely to rule, what legal consequences attach to doing business as a corporation rather than a sole proprietorship, how acquiring a trademark might protect a company's product, and whether a corporation's omission of information from a securities prospectus might subject the corporate officers to criminal or civil liability.[20]

---

18. Some aspects of behavior that are of interest to lawyers are relatively predictable. *See generally* Symposium, *Probability and Inference in the Law of Evidence*, 66 B.U. L. Rev. 377 (1986). But much of the prognostication that clients expect lawyers to engage in remains dependent on some degree of subjective analysis. *See, e.g.*, Paul Brest & Linda Hamilton Krieger, *Lawyers as Problem Solvers*, 72 Temp. L. Rev. 811, 821–23 (1999).

19. Researchers have developed a literature about common fallacies in human reasoning processes that they often refer to as "cognitive illusions." Predictions about likely consequences may reflect cognitive illusions rather than rational judgments. For a discussion of common cognitive illusions and how you might try to counteract them, see Chapter 18.

20. Occasionally you may seek clients' predictions about legal consequences. Clients with legal problems often consult friends and business acquaintances who have had similar problems. Clients sometimes find the experiences of their lay peers

C. PREDICTING NON–LEGAL CONSEQUENCES

Non-legal consequences, as you know, consist of the likely economic, social, psychological, political and moral ramifications that may flow from adopting particular solutions. And just as you generally have the better data base for predicting legal consequences, clients often have the better data base for predicting non-legal ones. Clients often know better than you the likely economic effects on their companies when employees have to take time away from their regular duties to participate in discovery and prepare for trial; the likely social effects of suing a defendant who has a high-profile, exemplary reputation in the community; and the likely psychological effects of accepting settlement offers after having previously stated to friends that they would go "all the way to trial." Therefore, you typically rely on clients to predict non-legal consequences.[21]

At the same time, your own experiences may enable you to predict (or at least inquire about) common non-legal consequences. For example, when it comes to recognizing how the business operations of a retail merchant whose rent is tied to the Consumer Price Index might be affected by fluctuations in the Index, or psychological consequences such as the potential degree of stress that a long trial can create, you may contribute valuable insights to clients' thinking about non-legal consequences.

Similarly, clients may be so tied up with their own concerns that they fail to recognize that one or more of their possible alternatives may have a substantial positive or negative impact on third parties or society in general. In such situations, you may well want to call such possibilities to their attention. For example, a client faced with enormous financial concerns may recognize that the option of resurrecting his business by closing one of his stores may cause severe financial harm to the employees and their families but not think about how selecting that option may also cause substantial financial harm to other businesses in the community and perhaps damage to the client's general reputation beyond that which will result from letting his employees go.

D. ORGANIZING THE DISCUSSION OF CONSEQUENCES

The subsections below examine techniques for counseling clients with respect to likely consequences.

very persuasive, and tend to consider those experiences a foolproof data base from which to predict their own legal outcomes. On occasion, clients may (privately, at least) disbelieve legal predictions that you make that conflict with friends' experiences in similar matters. Thus, when clients appear to be skeptical about your legal predictions, you may want to find out if they have contrary ones and their bases. If you think clients' predictions are based on wrong or too-limited data bases, you may at least

discuss why your predictions differ from theirs. (Of course, you may also learn in the process that *your* prediction needs to be amended.) For a further discussion of dealing with clients' reliance on the experiences of others, see Chapter 17.

21. This point underscores the statement in Chapter 13 that counseling is a two way street and that information must flow from the client to you as well as in the other direction.

1. *Review Options Separately*

Many people have difficulty making decisions simply because without assistance they cannot focus on discrete options and their attendant advantages and disadvantages. Just as simultaneous input from competing sources can immobilize a robot, so are clients often immobilized by inability to attach discrete consequences to specific options. Thus, an effective strategy for analyzing options and their consequences is to focus on options separately.

2. *Ask Clients to Choose a Starting Place*

To maintain a client-centered approach, ask clients which option they want to discuss first. For instance, you might say, "Peter, it appears that our options are either to demand reinstatement plus back pay, or to offer to resign on the condition of a suitable severance package. Which of these do you prefer to discuss first?"

This approach builds on the advantages of neutrality, as you leave to clients the choice of which option to discuss first. The technique also tends to encourage clients to participate actively in counseling discussions.

3. *Adopt the Role of Information Seeker*

After clients select an option, you may continue to place them in the figurative limelight by asking them to identify what they see as the pros and cons of the chosen option. Again, beginning with clients' ideas preserves neutrality: you avoid implicitly discarding an option by mentioning sixteen "cons" as opposed to one "pro." Also, you continue to encourage clients' full participation. If you begin by describing the pros and cons that you see, clients may unwittingly be content with your description on the ground that "you're the expert."[22]

You can seek clients' thoughts about consequences in one of three ways. You can ask them only about advantages, about both advantages and disadvantages, or only about disadvantages. For example, if the option that a client selects first is whether to include an arbitration clause in a proposed agreement, your choice of questions includes:

     1. "Why don't you start by telling me what advantages you see of including an arbitration clause?"

     2. "Great. What are the pros and cons you see of including such a clause?"

     3. "Okay, maybe we should begin with your outlining what problems you see in including an arbitration provision."

---

22. Remember this is a general approach, not a recipe to follow slavishly. For example, if a client is extremely naïve, nervous, or unfamiliar with the legal system, you might well consider beginning the discussion of pros and cons yourself. Similarly, if a client indicates interest in legal consequences, or if you think legal consequences will predominate in a client's thinking, you may begin by predicting legal outcomes. For a discussion of how you might do this, see Chapter 17.

Normally, question No. 1 is the most sensible choice. Clients usually prefer the options that they choose to discuss first. Therefore, to ask clients to talk about advantages first is generally to see matters from their perspectives. By the same token, if a client has previously expressed concern about an alternative, you may ask the client to begin by describing its potential downsides. For example, if initially the client above had said, "I'm not sure about arbitration; the last time we were in arbitration we got burned," starting with question No. 3 may make sense. However, in neither instance does question No. 2 make sense. It asks the client to focus on two things at the same time, pros and cons. As a consequence No. 2 reduces the chances that the client will focus thoroughly on each of them.

The familiar T-funnel questioning pattern is well suited to fully eliciting clients' ideas about likely consequences. Open questions uncover the consequences that clients can identify on their own, and closed questions seek clients' reactions to possibilities that you raise.[23] Pursuant to the counseling standard,[24] the consequences that you mention through closed questions should be ones that similarly-situated clients are likely to consider pivotal.

Consider this example of using T-funnel questioning to elicit a client's thoughts about likely consequences. Assume that your client, Doug, is exploring who he should appoint in his will as guardian for his children, ages seven and five. Doug's alternatives are his sister, Helen, and his brother, Bob. The option Doug has selected to discuss first is his sister.

1. L: Doug, what are the advantages you see in appointing Helen?

2. C: Well, she will be able to spend more time with the children and also the children know her better.

3. L: OK. Those are important points. What other advantages do you see?

4. C: I think it'll be less of an economic imposition on her than it would be on Bob.

5. L: That's also important. What else do you see as a positive reason for naming Helen?

6. C: She's more interested in education than Bob is, so I think she'd be more concerned about their school work.

7. L: I understand your making education a top priority. To summarize, then, it seems that the factors in favor of Helen are that she will probably spend more time with the children than Bob, is closer to them, is financially better

23. Using closed questions to suggest additional possible consequences does not require you to make predictions about the likely consequences of a client's decision. Rather their use takes advantage of your expertise and experience to initiate a dis- cussion of consequences a client at least ought to consider. For a discussion of how you might meld in the consequences you foresee, see Section 6 *infra*.

24. See Chapter 13.

off and will be more concerned with their schooling. I can see that you've given this a lot of careful thought. What other advantages do you see?

8.   C: That's about it.

9.   L: Okay. Here are some other factors that you may want to consider. Any differences as far as ability to manage the children's assets might be concerned?

10.   C: Well, Helen's not so great with money matters, but her husband has a lot of experience in that area.

11.   L: All right. How about in terms of allowing the children to maintain their current friends and contacts?

12.   C: Well. . . .

Nos. 1, 5, and 7 are open questions giving Doug the opportunity to list all the reasons he can think of to choose Helen, the first option he wanted to talk about. No. 3 gives recognition, and No. 7 provides recognition, includes an active listening response and employs the familiar summary technique.

Nos. 9 and 11 demonstrate the turn to closed questions. Choosing consequences commonly relevant to selecting a guardian (friendships and money management ability), you search for other consequences that Doug might want to evaluate. Note that the closed questions do not specifically seek pros or cons. That is, No. 9 identifies the topic "managing assets." It does not ask, for example, "Would ability to manage assets be a pro of choosing Helen?" The latter type of question may suggest that Helen is a better money manager, rendering it non-neutral.

Since the closed questions do not specifically seek pros or cons, clients' responses may be unclear as to how they regard a consequence. For example, Doug's response in No. 10 leaves it unclear as to whether he considers Helen's being not so great with money matters a con of choosing Helen. If you are uncertain, you may ask a clarifying question that converts an ambiguous response into a pro or con. In this context, your might ask Doug something like, "Do you think that we need to think of money management skills as a con of choosing Helen?"

4. *The Cross over Phenomenon*

Despite the seeming orderliness of a T-funnel approach, rarely will it be possible or desirable to systematically run through each alternative individually, taking up pros and then cons. Rather, clients tend to "cross over" from one alternative to another. And, within a single alternative, they often jump back and forth between "pros" and "cons."

Several factors account for clients' tendency to cross over. Comparing pros and cons naturally leads people to cross over. For instance, examine Doug's response in No. 6, "Well, she is more interested in education than my brother is and I think she'd be more concerned about their school work." Doug is thinking about both his brother and his sister. And, as is often the case, the pro of one alternative is the con of another, and vice versa. The pro for the sister (attention to children's education) is simultaneously the con for the brother (less attention to children's education). Hence, the very asking of questions concerning advantages and disadvantages invites clients to make comparisons and to cross over.

Similarly, your organizational efforts notwithstanding, clients tend to stray back and forth on the "pros v. cons" ledger within the context of a single alternative. Many clients state a downside of an alternative almost in the same breath as they state an upside. For instance, Doug may say, "Helen will look after the kids' education, but I've got to say that she's not the world's best disciplinarian." A plus of Helen is offset immediately by a minus. Of course, Doug can cross over even further by also shifting to the "Bob" option: "Helen will look after the kids' education, but I've got to say that compared to Bob, she's not the world's best disciplinarian."

When clients cross over from one option to another, your follow-up question may stay on the original side of the ledger (e.g., "pros of Option A," if that is the point with which you began). Alternatively, you may ask about the side to which the client has crossed over (e.g., "cons of Option B"). Maintain neutrality when making your decision. That is, focus on the option that appears to be uppermost in a client's mind, not simply on the option you favor. And if you do return to the original side of the ledger, you may further a neutral stance by expressly acknowledging through active listening the consequences that a client mentioned during the cross over. Whichever choice you make, the key to helping clients arrive at satisfactory decisions is continuing to tie consequences to specific options.

For an example of how you might respond to cross over, assume that you represent a commercial shopping center developer, Montoya Realty. On Montoya's behalf, you have been negotiating a lease with Exotic Electronics under which Exotic will rent four thousand square feet in a corner shopping mall from Montoya for five years. All but one of the terms of the proposed lease have been agreed to. The exception is that the officers of Exotic have refused to sign personal guarantees unless Montoya modifies the rent requirements. At present the proposed lease calls for Exotic to pay an amount equal to 5% of Exotic's yearly gross sales, but in no event less than $5,500 per month. Exotic's officers, however, are willing to sign personal guarantees only if the minimum monthly provision is reduced to $4,500. You are now consulting with Alfredo Gomez, the Montoya vice president who manages the shopping center. Both you and Gomez agree that the only way to get the personal guarantees is to accede to Exotic's demand to reduce the minimum monthly rent. The options you have identified together are: (1) Insist on the guarantees and reduce the rent; (2) Drop the demand for guarantees and go ahead with the deal at the $5,500 monthly rent figure; or (3) Terminate negotiations with Exotic and lease the space to Radio Hut, which is willing to lease the property at $4,000 minimum monthly rental as against 7% of gross sales. A portion of the counseling session goes as follows:

1. L: Alfredo, which of these options shall we discuss first?

2. C: Let's talk about insisting on the guarantees. That's what I prefer.

3. L: Just so we're on the same page, by this arrangement you get the Exotic officers' personal guarantees, and in return you accept their proposal to reduce the minimum monthly rent to $4,500. What do you see as the advantages of going that route?

4. C: Well, signing guarantees gives Exotic a strong incentive to make sure the business turns a profit. I know that a difference of $1000 a month may not be that much, but if you think in terms of a 5 year lease, there is a real incentive for them to pay attention to the operation. And since most of our money comes from the percentage of gross, I want a tenant whose top management will pay attention to what is going on. If we take Radio Hut I just don't think we'll get that.[25]

5. L: Okay; so forgoing the added monthly rent is worth it because you expect to make that up through the percent of gross. Also, you've mentioned a downside of Radio Hut— their attention to operations may not be as great so your actual income may be less even though the monthly minimum is higher. Before we talk more about Radio Hut, do you see any other advantages to going with Exotic and guarantees?

6. C: It's also the kind of customers that Exotic will attract to the center. The quality of Exotic's merchandise is better than Radio Hut's and therefore the kind of customers they will attract will have more money to spend in all the stores.

7. L: That sounds like an advantage not of the guarantee necessarily, but of signing Exotic over Radio Hut. But that's important for us to identify. Let me stay with that for a while. From what you're saying, you think that another pro of having Exotic is that they'll attract customers with more money than will Radio Hut and that means there is another negative in Radio Hut's column.

8. C: We have to be careful though. Radio Hut has a big name; it's certainly better known than Exotic's. So Radio Hut overall may attract more customers.

9. L: That's a plus for Radio. Do you see others?

---

25. Gomez here makes a prediction about Radio Hut's top management. Recall from Chapter 13 that ascertaining clients' bases for making predictions is often an important part of the counseling process. Thus, you might follow up Gomez's statement with an inquiry about his basis for making the prediction. For further discussion of how you might do this, see Chapter 18.

10. C: There probably is less worry about whether they are giving us correct figures regarding gross sales. Radio is a national company; they use standardized accounting procedures. If things get tough, they are probably less likely to fudge.

11. L: So another pro for Radio is that their sales figures are likely to be more reliable, and hence it will be easier to know if the percentage rent figures are correct.

12. C: Exactly.

13. L: Anything else working in Radio's favor?

14. C: Not that I can see at the moment.

15. L: How about going ahead with Exotic without any personal guarantees? What advantages there?

16. C: It's hard to think of any. A promise of a bigger minimum is important only if they do poorly and I don't think that is going to happen. If I did, we wouldn't be talking with them. To me the guarantees are the key. That gets top management focused on this store and that's exactly what is likely to make the operation quite profitable.

17. L: So without a guarantee, there's lack of management incentive.

18. C: Right.

19. L: Well, then, let's see if I can summarize where we are. It seems like you are saying now that the option of Exotic without the guarantees is off the table. If that's the case— and we can discuss it more if you wish—then we're down to two competing options: Exotic with the guarantee or Radio Hut with its greater percentage of gross sales terms. Does that make sense?

20. C: That does seem to be what I've been saying, but I'm not ready to drop the option of Exotic without the guarantee totally just yet. Can we keep that in the mix for a bit?

   [*The dialogue moves to a later point in the meeting.*]

41. L: Anything else you can think of that would be a negative of making a deal with Radio Hut?

42. C: I think that's it.

43. L: Okay, now that we've talked about each of the options, let's make sure that we've considered all the possible consequences of each. Maybe we can start by finishing up the option of insisting on personal guarantees from Exotic's officers. As far as the "pros" of that option go, so far we listed your belief that top management will pay close attention to business operations. Now, another one that may be so obvious that you didn't bother to mention it is that personal guarantees offer extra protection should Exotic itself default on the rent. Would you agree?

44. C: Sure.

45. L: All right. Now let me ask you some additional questions about potential advantages of insisting on guarantees. Should Montoya decide to sell the shopping center during the term of Exotic's lease, would having guarantees make a sale more attractive?

46. C: Given the size of the center and the variety of tenants and lease provisions, I don't think so.

47. L: Would having guarantees in this instance help your negotiating stance with respect to other prospective tenants?

48. C: Probably it would—that's a point I hadn't considered.

49. L: OK, we'll list that as another pro. How about. . . .

   [The dialogue continues with your use of "lower T" (closed) questions to explore additional consequences of insisting on the guarantee from Exotic, and resumes a few minutes later.]

61. L: Now let's turn for a moment to possible downsides of insisting on personal guarantees from Exotic. So far, we don't seem to have anything down. Can you think of any?

62. C: Not right off; I guess that's why I kind of favor this option.

63. L: And maybe that's the option you'll end up with. But just to make sure, let me play devil's advocate and ask you a couple of questions. Might insisting on guarantees negatively affect your long-term relationship with Exotic?

64. C: Well . . .

This dialogue illustrates the kinds of structural choices you may make when discussing options and consequences. No. 1 asks Gomez which option he wants to discuss first, and No. 3 pursues the advantages of his chosen option. No. 5 stays with the topic of advantages of the initial option, even though Gomez concluded No. 4 with a negative of a different option. This choice to stay with Gomez's initially favored option does not violate neutrality principles since No. 5 first acknowledges Gomez's cross-over (". . . you've mentioned a downside of Radio Hut. . . .").

No. 7, by contrast, does move the conversation away from Gomez's first option, personal guarantees, to a general comparison between Exotic and Radio Hut. Crossing over to a different option seems to be a reasonable choice, since Gomez has twice steered the conversation in that direction. Arguably, this switching indicates that Gomez is focused on the larger question of Exotic versus Radio. From the standpoints both of neutrality and successfully communicating with Gomez, therefore, following Gomez's lead is sensible.

Having switched to the advantages of Radio Hut in No. 9, you stay with this topic until in No. 14 Gomez indicates that he can think of no more advantages. In Nos. 8 and 10 Gomez identifies pros favoring Radio Hut, which Nos. 9 and 11 acknowledge. However, in acknowledging these pros, you do not cross over to mention Gomez's implied negatives of selecting Exotic. That choice too seems reasonable. You need not mechanically acknowledge clients' every change of reference from one option to another. Acknowledging the "pro" consequence that Gomez does mention, the likelihood that Radio Hut will attract more customers than Exotic, sufficiently maintains impartiality.

No. 15 introduces the third alternative into the discussion (waiving a request for personal guarantees from Exotic) even though you and Gomez have not fully discussed the first two alternatives. This tactic too is consistent with neutrality, because you give Gomez a chance to discuss each option before committing (or eliminating) too quickly to an option already on the table. Also, discussing the advantages of demanding the guarantee from Exotic implicitly raises the disadvantages of not doing so. Thus, putting that option forward squarely for Gomez's evaluation makes sense.

No. 19 summarizes what has transpired thus far and risks dismissing, albeit tentatively, one of the three options. While you don't want to foreclose options prematurely, your open and non-dogmatic approach suggests that you have efficiently simplified Gomez's task.

Nos. 41 through 43 mark the transition to lower-T systematic review of each option. No. 43 summarizes the previously identified advantages of one option, and then asks about possible additional advantages of that option. Nos. 45 and 47 continue in that same vein. No. 61 turns to the "cons" of the same option. However, since no "cons" emerged in the earlier conversation, you begin the search for cons with an open question. When still no cons emerge, you turn to a closed question (No. 63). No. 63 maintains neutrality by indicating that inquiries about possible disadvantages do not imply rejection of the option. You then raise a specific possible disadvantage. In similarly thorough fashion, you would T-funnel the pros and cons of the remaining option.

Finally, compare Nos. 45 and 47 in the dialogue above with Nos. 9 and 11 in the earlier "Doug" dialogue in sub-section 3 above. In Nos. 9 and 11, you simply identify a category and ask which way it cuts. In Nos. 45 and 47, by contrast, you subtly suggest two reasons that having guarantees might be a pro. Thus, you are somewhat less neutral with Gomez than you were with Doug. On the other hand, Gomez's response in No. 46 is clear that he does not regard the lack of guarantees as a con, whereas Doug's response in No. 10 is more ambiguous. Hence, somewhat non-neutral questions such as Nos. 45 and 47 may be more likely to produce unambiguous responses than neutral questions such as Nos. 9 and 11. In the abstract, then, you have a choice as to which form of closed question to use. Realize that, in some circumstances, suggesting that a factor is a pro or a con may bias a response by indicating your own preference. In Gomez's case, given the substantial discussion of consequences which preceded the questions, Nos. 45 and 47 appear not to be overly suggestive.

5. *Discuss Consequences You Foresee*

Discussions of likely consequences usually include advising clients of the potential legal and non-legal consequences that you foresee. If, as will often be the case, you first ask clients to predict consequences, you might then either (1) integrate the consequences you foresee into the discussion, or (2) wait until clients conclude and supplement their lists with your own.

Deciding between these two approaches itself requires you to predict likely consequences of each approach. The "pros" of "integrating" include more equal participation in a discussion by you and clients, and greater opportunities to have on one plate, as it were, all the consequences relating to particular options. Also, since clients' evaluations of options typically rest heavily on what the legal consequences are likely to be, postponing legal predictions is unrealistic. For example, a client generally cannot evaluate the merits of a settlement offer without knowing the likely outcome of trial. Hence, when you ask clients to discuss the pros or cons of accepting a settlement offer, you will almost certainly integrate your prediction of the likely outcome of trial into the discussions.[26]

The downsides of integrating include the risk of influencing clients' decisions by jumping in quickly with your own predictions and giving an impression that clients' predictions are not very important. These cons seem particularly apt to occur if your predictions require lengthy explanation.

The advantages of delaying your predictions until after clients are "predicted out" are pretty much the converse of the cons stated above. Delaying your own predictions indicates serious interest in clients' ideas. Also, when both you and clients see the same consequences, allowing clients to state them may promote their confidence that they can play important problem-solving roles. The main "con" of delay is the danger that your later discussion of consequences makes clients feel "sandbagged." That is, clients may feel manipulated if you implicitly brush off their earlier attempts at prediction with lengthy catalogues of your own.

On balance, you are generally better off following the integrationist approach. Not only does it make you and clients joint partners in searches for solutions, but also you are likely to find it a more natural conversational style. Especially since a discussion of consequences is likely to be rather frenetic, with much crossing over among alternatives and consequences, steadfastly delaying your predictions is likely to sound artificial. If your overall approach is consistent with client-centeredness, interspersing your predictions with those of clients is unlikely to run roughshod over client autonomy.

---

26. The implicit message of law school notwithstanding, remember as noted in Chapter 1 that many client decisions are *not* dominated by legal consequences. For example, neither Doug's selection of a guardian nor Gomez's choice of tenants hinges primarily on legal consequences.

For a clearer sense of how you might integrate your predictions into discussions of consequences, return to the discussion with Doug, the client who is attempting to choose a guardian for his young children. Doug's options, you will recall, are his sister, Helen, and his brother, Bob. Assume that one legal consequence of Doug's selecting Bob is that Bob, a nonresident, would have to post a bond. (The dialogue picks up with a repeat of No. 11 from above.)

11. L: How about in terms of allowing the children to maintain their current friends and contacts?

12. C: Well, again, Helen seems best on this one. She lives close to us; the kids could go to the same school. Bob, on the other hand, lives out of state. The kids, however, seem to like Bob more, even though they know Helen better. It's tough; maybe the move wouldn't be too upsetting.

13. L: Perhaps in the long run the children might feel more comfortable with Bob?

14. C: That's a real possibility. He's further away but they relate better to him. Maybe I've been trying to avoid facing this fact.

15. L: Doug, I sense this is isn't an easy choice to make, and I'm glad we are taking the time to go through it. Your conclusion, however, is that while a pro of choosing Helen is that the children could maintain their current contacts, an even stronger pro is that in the long term the children will feel more comfortable dealing with Bob. Is that right?

16. C: I think that's right.

17. L: There is one legal point I should throw in here; I'm not sure how important it is to you. It concerns the necessity to post a bond. Because your brother lives out of state, the court is probably going to require him to post a bond if he is appointed guardian. It's to ensure that if he were to mismanage the kids' money or run off with it, the kids won't be left empty handed.

18. C: What exactly is a bond?

19. L: It's the same as an insurance policy; what happens is that for a premium an insurance company issues a policy that says in effect that if the guardian takes or mismanages the children's money, the insurance company will pay.

20. C: Well, I trust my brother. Does he have to post a bond?

21. L: I'm afraid it's quite likely. Under our state's law, you can waive bond for a resident, but with nonresidents judges have discretion to require bonds and they usually do. That distinction may not make sense but that's the way things are. A bond would cost about one and one half percent of the total value of the property. The bond premium would be paid out of the money you left to the children.

22. C: So it would cost about $6,000 a year, right?

23. L: Correct. Therefore a disadvantage of appointing your brother would be the extra cost of about $6,000 each year. Correspondingly, an advantage of choosing your sister is that it would save about $6,000 a year.

24. C: Are there other legal requirements that might make a difference?

25. L: Not really. Whoever is guardian would have to hire a lawyer to file an account with the court once a year. An account is a written statement outlining what income the children received during the year from their property and what expenses the guardian incurred. It is a simple document and probably could be prepared for about $1,000 or $1,500 a year. It would be required of whoever was appointed as guardian. I guess, however, I should ask you if it would be a problem for your brother to hire a local lawyer given that he lives out of state?

26. C: I don't think so, so long as he doesn't have to come here. Would he have to do that?

27. L: No, it could all be done by mail or computer. Okay; with the legalities of posting bond and filing an accounting in mind, let's go back to the practical pros and cons. What else do you see as a pro. . . .

No. 11 is a question exploring consequences that Doug foresees. No. 13 is an appropriate attempt to clarify Doug's ambiguous response in No. 12. The first sentence of No. 15 is an active listening response to Doug's apparent discomfort; the second sentence notes that each alternative has a pro and that the pro favoring Bob is the stronger. This clarification is likely to help Doug sort out his apparent discomfort. That you do not go further in No. 15 and note a cross over to cons seems okay. Again, only unthinking rigidity would require you to verbally note each lurking cross over.

No. 17 is a shift from Doug's predictions to yours, integrating your forecasts into the discussion. You insert the prediction at a point where Doug is discussing a related topic—i.e., the children living out of state. Because the insertion is "naturally" connected to a topic already under discussion, Doug is likely to view the insertion as neutral.[27] Arguably, switching from Doug's prediction (that the children will be happier with Bob) to a con of selecting Bob (the expense of a bond) may lead Doug to think that you are rejecting his position. However, the previous active listening response and the comment, "I'm not sure how important this is" should help to eliminate any inference of rejection.

No. 18, "What exactly is a bond?," is a reminder that even a common term may constitute legal jargon.[28] Fortunately, Doug's ques-

---

27. Of course, a dry transcript does not permit a full assessment of neutrality, especially since non-verbal cues such as body language and facial expressions often undercut verbal messages. For instance, hold-ing your nose while continuing to ask a client for pros of an option probably suggests rejection of the client's input.

28. Jargon in this context refers to the many legal abstractions to which your

tion spurred an explanation (No. 19). In No. 25, by contrast, you anticipate the need to explain what an "account" is without forcing Doug to ask.

No. 23 summarizes with a cross over. Nos. 25 and 27 continue to integrate legal with non-legal predictions. Finally, No. 27 summarizes the legal aspects of guardianship and then returns to Doug's forecasts.

This sample is, of course, not a model for every situation. However, it should help you begin to understand how you and clients can work together when exploring likely consequences.

6. *Identify Downstream Consequences*

A common general consequence of decisions is the likelihood that they will foreclose or leave open future possibilities. For example, assume that a decision involves whether to retain a particularly highly qualified expert witness before discovery gets underway. The client may want to postpone retaining an expert as long as possible in the hope that it will never become necessary to spend the money to do so. However, you may conclude that failing to retain the expert before beginning discovery will greatly restrict your capacity to figure out what witnesses to depose, the order in which to depose them, and the topics to pursue.[29]

Even clients with a good capacity to predict likely consequences may well overlook the degree to which decisions are likely to circumscribe or leave open the possibility of future decisions. Thus, an important contribution you can often make to the counseling process is to point out that a "pro" of an option is that it leaves open future possibilities, while a "con" is that it is likely to foreclose future possibilities. For example, to the client faced with whether to authorize you to retain an expert immediately, you may say something such as, "Greta, I understand that waiting to retain an expert can save you money in the short term. However, I think that we need to retain the expert now. The judge is going to want us to commit to a discovery plan pretty quickly, and we need the expert's help to prepare an effective plan. In other words, the expert can really help with such important issues as the topics to pursue during discovery and whom to depose. I'm recommending this because I think that it's in your best long-term interests."

7. *Chart Alternatives and Consequences*

Making written charts of options' advantages and disadvantages generally helps clients to arrive at satisfactory decisions. Charts are particularly helpful when situations are complex or decision-making may

training and experience gives content, but which are often meaningless to clients. For example, think about how you might explain what the following terms mean: "cause of action," "trust," "deposition," and "security interest." If you have difficulty, it is because these terms refer more to concepts than to physical realities. You must be able to understand and communicate the underlying meaning of such terms if you are to counsel effectively.

29. A "decision tree" is the common name for an outline of the downstream consequences that alternative decisions are likely to entail.

take place some time after discussions of options and consequences.[30] While you might organize a chart in any number of ways, the example below illustrates one simple way in the context of the Montoya–Exotic hypothetical. As you recall, in that hypothetical Alfredo Gomez was considering three options: 1. Reducing the monthly rent to $4,500 and obtaining personal guarantees; 2. Keeping the monthly minimum at $5,500 and waiving the guarantees; and 3. Leasing the space to Radio Hut rather than to Exotic. In this situation, you might prepare a chart as follows:[31]

Exotic Guarantees		Exotic Waive Guarantees		Radio Hut	
Pro	Con	Pro	Con	Pro	Con

Writing down consequences as they emerge is often essential because discussions of alternatives and consequences are often characterized by "cross-overs" between options, advantages and disadvantages. Without written records, both you and clients will have difficulty remembering what territory has already been covered. Also, seeing consequences in writing may stimulate both you and clients to recall additional ones.

Moreover, charts are valuable because few clients can hold in their minds all of the pros and cons of a variety of alternatives. Psychological studies tend to show that most people can hold no more than seven facts in their minds at one time.[32] Hence, written records drawing together various options and their respective pros and cons can help clients get full and balanced views before making final determinations.

When decisions rest on only two viable options, charts such as the one depicted above readily help clients compare options to each other. In such situations, a "pro" of one consequence is likely to be a "con" of the other, producing two rather neat columns and facilitating a weighing of options. When clients have to weigh three or more viable options, however, pros and cons are unlikely to be mirror images. For example, a consequence may be a "con" compared to one option but a "pro" compared to another one. In such situations, intelligible charts can usually do no more than indicate the advantages and disadvantages of options considered individually, leaving comparisons to clients.

---

30. Charts are also an aspect of "defensive lawyering." Keeping copies of charts in your files can help you respond to clients who later claim that you didn't provide them with an adequate opportunity to consider options and alternatives.

31. For another method of preparing a counseling chart, see Robert Dinerstein, *Client–Centered Counseling: Reappraisal and Refinement*, 32 Ariz. L. Rev. 501 (1990).

32. *See* George A. Miller, *The Magic Number Seven, Plus or Minus Two: Some Limits on Our Capacity for Processing Information*, 63 Psych. Rev. 81 (1956); Herbert A. Simon, *How Big Is a Chunk?*, 183 Science 482 (1974).

8. MAKING DECISIONS

At some stage in counseling conversations, discussions of alternatives and consequences typically result in decisions. Having had what they (and you) consider a reasonable opportunity to decide, clients may simply announce their decisions: "Based on what we've been talking about, it really makes sense to accept the settlement offer. That's what I want to do." Other times, you may ask clients for their decisions, and those decisions will come forth readily:

> L: Doug, we've gotten everything out. If you're ready to make a decision now, who do you want to name as your first choice of guardian, Helen or Bob?

> C: All things considered, I guess I'll go with. . . .

However, counseling conversations do not always produce decisions quite this smoothly. Sometimes you may have to re-review options and consequences, perhaps asking clients to think carefully about how likely consequences really are and how much importance they carry. Referring to charts and summarizing their contents will often help you carry out re-reviews:

> Alfredo, you seem a little uncertain now as to whether you really want to insist on personal guarantees from Exotic's officers. It may help if we review what we've talked about here today. Let's look over this chart, and see if it helps. . . .

Other times, clients may need (and have the luxury of) additional time to think it over. In such situations, you may give clients a chart and a handshake and ask them to "call me in the morning."

Other complicating factors are that clients may ask for your opinion about what to do, or may make decisions in which you feel a need to intervene. Similarly, clients may be affected by one or more "psychological traps" that tend to lead clients to make decisions that appear to them to be satisfactory but seem to be based on mispredictions of one sort or another. Chapter 18 explores strategies for responding to these situations.

Chapter 15

CLARIFYING CLIENTS' OBJECTIVES

---

* * *

Peiguo, I'm glad I caught you in. I've just spoken with the lawyer for Genesco; they're quite interested in your proposal. Genesco's lawyer indicated, however, that they probably couldn't go for an all cash purchase. The lawyer wanted to know whether you'd have any interest in part cash and part stock. The lawyer says that Genesco is doing quite well and that if you're interested at all in stock you can look at Genesco's books.

I don't know. I was originally thinking about cash. You know I had that real estate deal with Han Properties cooking. But last week Han told me they are not sure they can get the necessary financing. So I really don't know what to say.

Okay, Peiguo, let's assume for a moment that things don't work out with Han. In what way would that affect your need for cash from the deal with Genesco?

* * *

1. INTRODUCTION

The four step counseling process introduced in Chapter 13 begins with embarking on the decision-making process with clients' relevant objectives in mind. The underlying hypothesis is that you increase the likelihood that clients will make satisfactory decisions if you afford them an opportunity to evaluate options in the light of relevant objectives. This chapter examines issues that may arise when you seek to clarify clients' objectives and explores techniques that can help you to overcome those problems.

2. VAGUE OR UNCERTAIN OBJECTIVES

To the extent that objectives are definite and unambiguous, they are more likely to help clients make satisfactory decisions. Yet clients may have trouble articulating objectives in a way that promotes effective decision-making. That is, they may refer to objectives in a way that is vague or uncertain. Consider these examples:

An Estate Planning Matter

L: What objectives seem most important to you in thinking about the qualities of a guardian for your kids?

C: I'm not really sure; I guess I just want someone who will take really good care of them.

A Litigation Matter

L: Before reviewing ABC's settlement offer in more detail, it may help you to think about what you've been trying to accomplish by maintaining this lawsuit. What would you say have been your most important goals?

C: Nothing really complicated, I guess. They really tried to screw us, and all I know is I want to make them pay for everything I've been put through.

In both of these examples, you use open questions to afford the clients a chance to talk about what is uppermost in their minds. They respond, however, by articulating their goals in a vague, uncertain way that is unlikely to promote their ability to think through options effectively. For example, the estate planning client hasn't identified any qualities suggesting that one person rather than another is better suited to be named as guardian. Similarly, the litigation client hasn't suggested any criteria for evaluating the attractiveness of the settlement offer.

In such situations, consider following up with open questions that allow clients to clarify and concretize their goals. For example you may mention goals that you think similarly-situated clients would likely have. You may use one or more closed questions to do so efficiently. As usual, you may follow your questioning with an open one asking for any ideas that your questioning may have stirred up. For example:

An Estate Planning Matter

L: What objectives seem most important to you in thinking about the qualities of a guardian for your kids?

C: I'm not really sure; I guess I just want someone who will take really good care of them.

L: What kinds of things are you thinking about when you say "take really good care of them?"

C: I guess at the most basic level someone who wants them and will love them. And of course see to their education and religious upbringing.

L: I thought that these were the kinds of things you had in mind. Before we get down to specific possible guardians, any other general thoughts about the kind of care you want for your kids?

A Litigation Matter

L: Before reviewing ABC's settlement offer in more detail, it may help you to think about what you've been trying to accomplish by maintaining this lawsuit. What would you say have been your most important goals?

C: Nothing really complicated, I guess. They really tried to screw us, and all I know is I want to make them pay for everything I've been put through.

L: When you say "pay for everything," what do you have in mind?

C: They've caused us no end of trouble and I want to be sure that if we agree to settle that it's all taken into account.

L: I think I have a pretty good idea of the difficulties you encountered, but just so that we're not overlooking anything can you give me some specifics?

3. INCOMPLETE OBJECTIVES

As Chapter 14 suggests, at the outset of counseling conversations you can ordinarily be content with the objectives that clients mention in response to open questions. Beginning counseling conversations with a litany of closed questions seeking all possible objectives is rarely helpful, because clients often cannot realize that they have additional objectives until they confront decisions that make those objectives relevant. For example, assume that you represent a client who is interested in operating his business as a partnership rather than as a sole proprietorship. Here, the client's objectives are likely to relate to the operation of the business and the advantages of working with a partner. The client may well have additional objectives, such as having a method of resolving disputes quickly and cheaply. If so, however, those objectives will no doubt emerge later in the discussion, such as when you discuss the advisability of an arbitration clause.

That said, you may want to augment clients' ideas about objectives when they neglect to mention ones that almost any similarly-situated client would almost surely have in mind. In such situations, you may again use a closed question or two to verify that clients do have those objectives in mind. The main reason to take this step is that if you regard an objective as one that all clients have in mind, you are likely to proceed on this assumption even when a particular client omits mention of it. Thus, asking clients about common objectives that they don't mention on their own is a client-centered strategy through which you avoid treating a particular client as though that client were like every other client.

For example, assume that Marcy is an estate planning client who needs to name a guardian for her children. In response to open questions concerning the qualities that Marcy seeks in a guardian, she indicates that the guardian should be someone who (1) the children already know and are comfortable with, and (2) is capable of managing the money that that will be left to the guardian to care for the children. Here, you might follow up with closed questions identifying widely accepted objectives for clients selecting guardians. Thus, your conversation with Marcy might continue as follows:

L: Just thinking about this in more detail for a moment, do you have any religious preferences when it comes to choosing a guardian?

C: Yes, I would like the guardian to be someone who generally shares my religious views and practices.

L: How about educational background, is that important to you in choosing a guardian?

C: Not really. I didn't go to college myself and while I hope my kids will I just don't think that's a factor that I'd even consider.

L: That's fine. How about a guardian's interest in sports teams, how important is that?

C: Now there you've mentioned a big one. No New York Yankee fan will ever serve as a guardian of my kids.

L: That shouldn't be a problem. By the way, now that we've talked about a few specifics, any other important objectives you may have in mind?

C: . . .

4. UPDATING CLIENTS' OBJECTIVES

As you know, the "Preliminary Problem Identification" phase of initial client meetings is a time when you typically first learn about clients' objectives.[1] Nevertheless, as stressed in Chapter 14, a discussion of objectives in the context of decision-making is often helpful because earlier objectives may have changed or those objectives may not be applicable to a decision at hand. When you do revisit earlier objectives,

---

1. See Chapter 5.

acknowledge the earlier discussions before addressing clients' current thinking.

Consider this example. Assume that you have been advising "Felice" on legal aspects of her take-out food business, "Broccoli Heaven." Felice first came to see you when she was about to start up a sit-down operation. Her objective was to expand the business while remaining focused on take-out by bringing in "Clara" to manage the sit-down side of things. You and Felice reviewed different options for operating the expanded business, including making Clara a partner, forming a corporation with Felice and Clara as shareholders, and Felice continuing to do business as a sole proprietor with Clara as an employee. Felice decided on the latter option because she had never worked with Clara before, but told Clara that in six months' time she would consider giving Clara an ownership interest in the business. That time having passed, Felice returns to your office.

1.   L: Good to catch up with you about how things are going, Felice, so let's turn to the business at hand. If I recall correctly, your initial plan was for Clara to manage the sit-down business while you focused entirely on the take-out side. Is that still your goal?

2.   C: Actually, I've been thinking a lot about this. I'm glad that I didn't just rush into a full partnership or anything like that, because I realize that we're not always totally in synch as to how to run the business. She's done well, don't get me wrong, but her way of doing things is sometimes different from mine and I guess I've found out that it's more important than I thought it would be to have things done my way. Does that make me sound like an egomaniac?

3.   L: Not at all. I understand that maintaining the business' reputation is very important to its success.

4.   C: Exactly. Clara is a good businesswoman and good to work with and I still want her to be responsible for the sit-down service. It's just that however we arrange things, I don't want to lose all control over that part of the business. You know, I'd like to have some oversight on what she does.

5.   L: We can probably arrange for you to have some control over the sit-down business even if you decide to go with a partnership or a corporation rather than remaining as a sole proprietor with Clara as an employee. Before we talk about these options, has your thinking changed in any other way since you expanded the business and started working with Clara?

6.   C: No. Overall, things have gone really well and I'm very happy with how successful the sit-down operation has been without hurting the take-out side.

7.   L: That's great. So now let's look at the options we've been talking about...

Here, you begin in No. 1 by referring to Felice's initial objective and asking whether her thinking has changed in any way during the preceding months. Before leaving this part of the discussion, in No. 5 you also give Felice a chance to mention other possible changes in her overall objectives. As you turn in No. 7 to a discussion of options, Felice's newly-stated goal of maintaining some control over the sit-down operation will be an important part of whatever decision she makes.

Chapter 1 pointed out that the four step counseling approach is not intended as a rigid process that you must follow in lock-step fashion, but rather is one that you frequently modify in the course of counseling conversations. For example, in No. 6 above, Felice indicates that she has no other primary objectives. Assume then that after discussing options and consequences Felice decides to accede to Clara's wishes by making her a full partner. When you turn to the issue of capital accounts (the amount of money that each partner agrees to contribute to and keep in the business to cover unexpected expenses), Felice says, "I'd like for the partnership agreement to end up saying that no more than $25,000 has to be kept in the partnership account—hopefully less if Clara agrees. I don't think we need a big cash reserve, and I'd like to have money available for outside investments." Felice here has identified a new objective, one whose relevance she might not have identified at the outset of the discussion. In this way, counseling conversations often go back and forth between objectives, options and consequences.

5. ILLEGAL OR "IMMORAL" OBJECTIVES

As a client-centered lawyer, you are an agent whose primary role is to help clients attain their objectives. A corollary of this principle is that on occasion you may find yourself working to accomplish objectives that you personally do not think are in clients' best interests. However, across a wide spectrum of situations, your personal beliefs are unlikely to prevent you from furthering client objectives with which you disagree. That is, despite reservations you may have, you can take the steps necessary to accomplish your clients' aims. Moreover, you need not proceed without voicing your concerns. As you and clients discuss alternatives and likely consequences, you can air any concerns that you may have about their aims. Hence at the end of the day you can usually carry out clients' chosen options without losing a great deal of sleep. For example:

- A transactional client's objective may be to expand an existing business. You may think that the business is already over-extended or that expansion is imprudent in the then-existing economic climate. You may advise the client of likely pitfalls (negative consequences), but undoubtedly can do the legal work necessary to carry out the expansion plans if the client decides to go forward despite the potential pitfalls and pursue the plan to expand.

- A manufacturer's objective may be to file a lawsuit seeking damages from a supplier who failed to deliver raw materials on time. Though the lawsuit is legally meritorious, your judgment is that suing the supplier is a mistake because regardless of the outcome, in the long run the client stands to lose by alienating the supplier. Again, you may certainly advise the client of the likelihood of negative consequences, but probably you will have few qualms about representing the client in the lawsuit if the client decides to take the risks you've identified and press forward with the suit.

More troubling for you may be those clients who seek your help to accomplish objectives that are illegal or that you believe to be morally wrong. As in the earlier situations you may seek to alter clients' desires to pursue illegal or "immoral" ends while discussing likely consequences. For example, you might point out that a likely downside of a transactional client's "immoral" objective is that it will result in a popular backlash that will endanger the client's long term business goals. Should clients persist in their desired options, however, you may need to give careful thought to your willingness or ability to continue as their lawyer.

For example, consider the following circumstances:

- **"IMMORAL" OBJECTIVE I**: A developer's objective is for you to obtain approval to build houses on land that is contaminated and poses a serious health risk to future residents. Your judgment is that the developer can legally proceed by carrying out only the minimal remediation required by an impotent local government agency. However, you have serious moral concerns about the project because of the level of risk to the health of future residents. You might point out that likely negative consequences of going ahead with the project include a poor public image, unsold houses and huge damage awards. Nevertheless, the developer may decide to go ahead with no more than the minimal remediation of the contamination than the local agency has required.

- **"IMMORAL" OBJECTIVE II**: The objective of a tenant who has failed to pay rent for over three months is for you to use all procedural means of defending an eviction action in order to live rent-free as long as possible. Your moral concerns grow out of your realization that the landlords are an elderly couple who depend on rental income from the property to meet monthly expenses. After discussing with you possible, though from the client's standpoint less desirable alternatives, the client may insist that you mount a vigorous procedural defense.

- **ILLEGAL OBJECTIVE**: A manufacturer's objective is to limit the number of workers for whom the manufacturer has to provide employee benefits by having you draft agreements by which certain workers acknowledge that they are independent contractors. Your judgment is that the agreements are illegal because the workers are employees as defined by state law. Nevertheless, after refusing options for restructuring the workers' job descriptions so that they genuinely are independent contractors, the manufacturer insists that you draft agreements for the workers' signatures.

In each of these situations, clients ask for your help to accomplish objectives that you believe to be immoral or that are flatly illegal. For a discussion of how you might respond in such situations, see Chapter 18.

Chapter 16

IDENTIFYING ALTERNATIVES

---

* * *

Linda, the studio is definitely interested in your script. You've told me that you don't want just to sell your script, but you also want to make sure that the contract you end up signing gives you some power to make sure that the movie is faithful to what you've written. I know this is your first script, but perhaps you have some ideas about what kind of control might give you the protection you want?

Up to this point, I've always done writing for other people. So I'm not too sure how to go about this. I assume that the studio won't want to give me veto power over the movie?

You've got that right. Generally there are two areas in which control might be exercised by a writer. One is casting approval, the other is review of the screenwriter's script. I'd say we have two options when it comes to casting approval. One is for you to have the right to participate in the casting process; the other is for you to approve a final list from which the leads will be chosen. I think that the studio might be open to either possibility. With respect to supervision of the final cut, it's almost unheard of for a first-time author to get final cut approval. But given the extraordinary success of your novel, I think that asking for final cut approval will at least produce a counter-offer. Do you have any other possibilities in mind when it comes to control?

* * *

1. INTRODUCTION

Suggesting possible solutions is among your primary counseling functions. Of course, clients' expectations with respect to solutions that you put forth are likely to vary widely depending on such factors as their experience and legal sophistication. At one end of the spectrum, clients may want you to do little more than effectuate solutions that they have already decided upon. At the other end, clients may look to you entirely for possible solutions. This chapter focuses on what may be the most common scenario, with you perhaps taking the lead in suggesting solutions but (as in the example above) also soliciting clients' thoughts about additional potential solutions.

2. TWO BASES OF EXPERTISE

Your ability to identify potential solutions typically rests on two principal foundations. You begin to build both of these foundations in law school, by analyzing legal principles and encountering concrete situations to which lawyers and judges have applied those principles. You will no doubt continue to expand your knowledge and skills in both of these areas throughout your legal career.

One foundation, primarily legal in nature, consists of your knowledge of legal rules and procedures and the types of solutions that lawyers commonly use to solve problems similar to those facing your clients. For example, solving a commercial lease problem might depend in part on your knowledge that one way to resolve a dispute over how to determine rent in a lease agreement is to adjust the amount of future rent according to changes in the Consumer Price Index.

The second foundation, primarily factual in nature, grows out of your knowledge of clients' individual characteristics and the particular industries and the surrounding circumstances in which clients find themselves. While two clients may have what appear to be very similar legal problems, you may suggest a solution to one client that you do not suggest to the other because of differences in their characteristics and circumstances. For example, assume that you represent two employers who are about to hire new employees. You may suggest a long-term employment contract to one client but not to the other, because of differences in the industries in which they do business and the prospective employees' competing opportunities for employment.

Later sections of this chapter illustrate how you might combine "legal" and "factual" familiarity to develop potential solutions.

3. IDENTIFY "PIVOTAL" ALTERNATIVES

Many problems have a number of potential reasonable solutions. For example, among the potential solutions to most litigation problems are trial, mini-trial, arbitration, mediation, and settlement. Within the "settlement" option you might identify still further options, such as whether damages in a torts case should be paid out as a lump sum or in the form of an annuity. Similarly, among the potential solutions for a transactional problem involving a client's need for capital are public and non-public stock offerings, public and non-public bond offerings, and loans from a variety of institutional and individual sources.

Effective counseling does not require that you routinely try to dazzle clients by trotting out all possible reasonable alternatives. Instead, common sense and the counseling standard described in Chapter 13 suggest that your task is to provide clients with a "reasonable opportunity" to consider those alternatives that "similarly-situated clients" would be likely to find pivotal.[1] This standard calls on you to apply your knowledge of legal rules and processes to each client's individual circumstances to formulate a limited number of realistic alternatives that clients are likely to consider satisfactory. For example, while a "living trust" may be a common estate planning tool that many clients find pivotal, a living trust would probably not be a realistic alternative for a client whose estate is too small to require probate.

As usual, you must exercise professional judgment when deciding how many and which alternatives to include in counseling conversations. Unfortunately, rules such as "present clients with no fewer than three and no more than five alternatives" and "always mention punitive damages to potential plaintiffs" simply don't exist.[2] Moreover, circumstances vary so widely from one client to another that a finite list of circumstances that almost always affect the identification of alternatives is impossible to compose. However, among the circumstances that commonly affect either how many alternatives you might mention or what alternatives are realistic are the following:

- Time constraints. When decisions have to be made quickly, you may well focus on no more than two or three realistic options that your experience suggests are most likely to be effective and satisfactory.

- Clients' backgrounds, resources and desires. How much patience and interest in the counseling process does a client have? Is a client willing to pay for your time for an elaborate review of several possible alternatives?

- Clients' abilities to carry out alternatives. For example, a procedure for handling employee grievances that might be realistic for a large company may be completely unrealistic for a smaller "mom and pop" business. Similarly, a proposed settlement of a dispute concerning the alleged violation of a non-competition agreement may not make sense if your client has no ability to monitor the alleged violator's activities.

- Other parties' positions and interests. What is realistic typically depends not only on your assessments of your clients' circumstances, but also those of clients' associates and family members, as well as the likely reactions of opposing parties and counsel, judges and juries and the like.

4. PROFESSIONAL SATISFACTION

You may well find that developing satisfactory alternatives is one of the most creative and satisfying aspects of law practice, in many ways the essence of effective lawyering.[3] Assessing situations and crafting

---

1. See Chapter 13.

2. However, a good general rule of thumb is that the level of potential confusion increases with the number of alternatives presented.

3. For example, in an Internet survey conducted by one of the authors, the great majority of practicing lawyers who responded indicated that the source of their greatest satisfaction as lawyers was developing

solutions that respond to clients' legal and non-legal concerns is often intellectually challenging as well as exhilarating and immensely gratifying. While an ability to craft effective solutions undeniably is partly a product of wisdom that develops over time, an expanding literature seeks to identify the characteristics of expertise and translate them into skills that novices can learn and use.[4] Whatever methods you use to fashion alternatives by applying knowledge of legal rules and processes to real-world settings, crafting solutions is the area where you can often be of most assistance to your clients.

5. DEVELOP FAMILIARITY WITH RELEVANT "INDUSTRIES"

While developing options may be the aspect of law practice that you find to be the most intellectually challenging, creative and satisfying, you are unlikely to glean much of what you need to know to craft potential solutions out of law school textbooks. As suggested above, developing realistic alternatives typically requires familiarity with the contexts (the "industries") in which problems arise. Imagine, for instance, that you are working with the following three clients. One is a supplier of industrial gloves and similar safety equipment who is being threatened with eviction from a warehouse in an industrial park, and who seeks advice about restructuring the rent called for in the lease. The second is an elementary school principal who seeks advice about formulating appropriate disciplinary rules and procedures. The third is a married couple who want to draft wills for the purpose of naming a guardian for their two young children. (You are, you'll be happy to know, a bit of a Renaissance lawyer.) In each case, your ability to formulate potential solutions requires knowledge of the clients' non-legal worlds, including:

   a.   General operation of the "industries" touching upon the clients' problems. For the industrial supplier, relevant industries include warehouse and industrial parks operations; for the principal, elementary school education and discipline; for the parent, child-rearing practices and guardianship functions.

   b.   How each client specifically operates within these industries. For example, how the glove and safety equipment supplier and the industrial park operator conduct their businesses; the role of students' parents in the existing disciplinary system; and what

effective solutions to clients' problems. See *Paul Bergman, The Movie Lawyers' Guide to Redemptive Legal Practice*, 48 UCLA L. REV. 1393, 1403–1405 (2001). *See also* Patrick Schiltz, *On Being a Happy, Healthy, and Ethical Member of an Unhappy, Unhealthy, and Unethical Profession*, 52 VAND. L. REV. 871, 929 (1999). ("What many lawyers find most gratifying about practicing

law is having ordinary people show up at their offices with problems, and then seeing the lives of those people improved in tangible ways as a direct result of their lawyer's (sic) efforts.")

   4.   *See, e.g.*, Gary L. Blasi, *What Lawyers Know: Lawyering Expertise, Cognitive Science and the Function of Theory*, 45 J. LEGAL EDUC. 313 (1995).

child-rearing practices the couple follows and plans to follow in the future.

c. Generally-available alternative solutions in the particular problem area. For the industrial supplier, you will need to be familiar with commonly-used industrial park or commercial rent provisions; for the principal, codes of conduct and disciplinary procedures that schools have developed; for the married couple, standard guardianship provisions.

Now look at two of these clients more closely. Assume that Swapco is the tenant that has leased a warehouse in an industrial park. Swapco shares a loading dock with another tenant. The owner is pressuring Swapco for back rent and has threatened to begin eviction proceedings. Melinda, Swapco's president, admits to being behind in the rent. At the same time, she complains that the owner has failed to provide tenants with security protection and has not provided Swapco with adequate dock access, and that under these conditions Swapco cannot make a profit. She has purposefully withheld rent in the hope of pressuring the owner into resolving these problems.

In this situation, standard options for Swapco include taking its chances at trial should the owner commence eviction proceedings; paying the back rent; renegotiating the agreement; or moving voluntarily to a new location, perhaps pursuant to a negotiated agreement in which the owner forgives all or part of the back rent.

However, familiarity with the three areas noted above can help you to identify additional potential solutions. Assume that Melinda is willing to have Swapco remain a tenant if the security and docking problems can be resolved. Your knowledge of (a) warehouse operations and security systems generally, (b) Swapco's security problems and the industrial park's particular security operation, and (c) alternative security systems available on the market might enable you to formulate creative proposals for solving Swapco's security problems. Likewise, your knowledge of (a) warehouse loading and unloading procedures and traffic patterns in industrial parks generally, (b) Swapco's receiving and delivery procedures, and (c) typical lease provisions concerning dock access might enable you to develop proposals concerning additional loading docks and access routes, and staggered delivery hours (e.g., setting specific hours for Swapco and its dock-mate to load and unload). Finally, your knowledge of (a) rent calculations in industrial parks and of accounting procedures, (b) Swapco's financial condition, and (c) typical commercial and industrial rent formulas might enable you to devise alternative rental formulas (e.g., lower monthly minimum rent combined with a percentage of net or gross income) that might protect Swapco while it is having economic difficulty and also protect the landlord once the industrial park problems are solved and Swapco becomes more profitable.

As for the parents who want to nominate a guardian, assume that their first choice for guardian is the husband's brother and his wife, who themselves have a toddler. With respect to housing, the clients' objectives include allowing their children to have as "normal" a home life as possible after the clients' deaths. A standard option in this situation is for the clients' children to move into the guardians' home.

Here again, awareness of the relevant "industries" may enable you to develop additional options for this couple. For example, familiarity with (a) the housing "industry," (b) the clients' and the proposed guardians' current housing arrangements and financial conditions, and (c) generally-available provisions relating to housing of wards might enable you to suggest that the guardians enlarge either the guardians' or the clients' home using funds from the clients' estate, or selling both the guardians' and the clients' homes and buying a larger home.[5]

In both the Swapco and the guardianship matters, note that (as is frequently the case) the various options are neither compelled nor forbidden by legal rules.[6] All are allowable; their usefulness depends on the extent to which they help the clients meet their objectives. Your ability to identify such options does not come from knowledge of legal rules. Rather, your ability emerges from familiarity with the broad situational contexts within which the clients' problems arise, the clients' particular methods of operation within the situational backdrops, and the range of realistic options that might resolve them.

Thus, no matter how extensive your knowledge of legal principles, you are not prepared to counsel unless you are familiar with the "industries" relevant to a problem. Many years ago, one way that newly-minted lawyers gained such experience was through mentors. While the economics of the modern practice of law have tended to relegate mentors to the endangered species list,[7] other sources of experience thrive. Sometimes, you can pick up necessary familiarity from clients. For example, Melinda can probably tell you about Swapco's security practices and, indeed, may even know something about alternative security systems. Practitioner literature and formbooks may provide information about particular industries. Other times, of course, you may need to consult an expert, even to find out what the relevant "industries" are. The expert may be another lawyer who specializes in a particular field.

---

5. More than one counseling session may be needed for all of these alternatives to emerge. For instance, based on an initial discussion with the will client, you may prepare and send out for review a draft will that contains "standard" guardianship provisions. Then, reviewing the draft with the client in a later meeting, you may point out alternative ways of accomplishing the goals of the guardianship.

6. Of course, in some matters legal principles will torpedo or limit particular options. For example, if a non-competition clause attempts to bar an employee from pursuing her or his occupation for 20 years, such a clause would probably be invalid. However, rarely will legal principles *mandate* particular options.

7. *See, e.g.,* Deborah H. Rhode, In the Interests of Justice: Reforming the Legal Profession 38 (2000). The mentoring function has been revived in some circles through an organization, modeled after a similar English practice, known as "The Inns of Court." *See* Allen K. Harris, *The Professionalism Crisis—The 'Z' Words and Other Rambo Tactics: The Conference of Chief Justices' Solution*, 53 S.C. L. Rev. 549 (2002); Nora C. Porter, *Enriched by Colleagues: How Lawyers are Learning from Each Other and Enjoying Social Camaraderie through Membership in the American Inns of Court*, 24 Pa. Lawyer 20 (2002).

Gathering information from a variety of sources combined with familiarity with how the real world operates is the catalyst for many of the alternatives you identify, and is necessary for you to be a competent counselor.[8]

A sample dialogue can illustrate how you might incorporate industry knowledge into counseling conversations. Assume that you are talking with Melinda, Swapco's president, about the possibility of renegotiating the lease to include provisions requiring the owner to provide Swapco with adequate access to its loading dock. The dialogue might proceed as follows:

1. L: Melinda, let's see if together we can develop some ideas that I can suggest to the owner to take care of the dock access problem. I know from previous experience working with industrial park matters that most owners don't like to commit themselves to specific rules regarding loading dock access. It's difficult to set up rules that don't prejudice some tenants, and it's also difficult to monitor specific parking and access rules. But if I can learn a bit more about your particular situation, maybe we can come up with a good solution. So please tell me a little more about your loading dock situation.

2. C: As you know, I'm one of the smaller operations in the park. Most of our customers are small companies and even individuals, who come in throughout the day in cars and pickup trucks to pick up merchandise. Our edge on our competitors is that we deal in smaller quantities and give personal service. But a lot of the time customers can't get in and out of our dock because large lorries waiting to get into Maxwell Industries' warehouse just to the east of us line up and block access to our dock. Once these big rigs get lined up, it's impossible to get them to move; the line is just too long and trucks can't back up. I know we've lost a lot of business because smaller customers especially just don't like the hassle.

3. L: That's got to be really frustrating. When I visited your warehouse last week, I probably came in like your customers, off of Hanley and then turned on to Bolas where the dock is located. I noticed that Logan Street also accesses the industrial park. Could your customers reach you by entering on Logan?

4. C: Sure, but they'd have the same problem reaching my dock. The line of trucks on Bolas would still prevent access.

5. L: How many trucks does it take to block off your access?

6. C: Well, when four large rigs are in line, which isn't at all unusual, our access is pretty much cut off. Sometimes as

---

8. This discussion should demonstrate that gaps in substantive knowledge are not the only cause of the sense of inadequacy that often pervades newly-admitted lawyers. Gaining familiarity with relevant industries, not doing additional legal research, may be the method by which you can overcome such feelings.

many as seven or eight trucks line up, and the line doesn't move for fifteen or twenty minutes.

7. L: Could the trucks line up on Logan, and not proceed to a warehouse until space was free on Bolas?

8. C: That might be an idea, but I think the police will hassle the truckers if they were to wait out there—I'll have to think about that a bit more.

9. L: If the lorries lined up on Hanley, would that disrupt traffic there?

10. C: No, the trucks could be angled in such a way on Hanley that they stay within the industrial park and then move on to Bolas once there is space available.

11. L: Okay, so that's one possibility we might work with. Can you think of any others?

12. C: Not really.

13. L: Well, let me try one other. Suppose lines were painted on Bolas such that the trucks waiting to go to Maxwell's were instructed to leave a space in front of your dock. Would truckers pay attention to such lines?

14. C: I'd like to think about that. You know, we might even be able to do the painting. I remember seeing that done someplace.

No. 1 refers to your existing experience in industrial park matters, mercifully saving you as a reader from having to wade through a lengthy (but perhaps fascinating) recital of industrial park practices. Though you probably learned something about Swapco's operations during earlier information-gathering, in No. 1 you seek additional information specifically related to its dock access problems. In No. 3 you make an active listening response, and take advantage of what you have learned about Swapco's operations to suggest one possible option. When Melinda nixes that suggestion, you elicit more information about the specifics of Swapco's operations in No. 5, and in No. 7 suggest a second alternative. No. 9 again seeks information. In No. 11 you confirm an option suggested by Melinda in No. 10 and then ask her an open question seeking other possible options. When Melinda cannot add to the list, No. 13 suggests a third option (perhaps based on awareness that municipalities often paint lines across intersections to signal that they must remain clear) that Melinda embellishes upon in No. 14. Later, you and Melinda can review the pros and cons of the options outlined in Nos. 7, 10 and 13.

6. BRIEFLY DESCRIBE ALTERNATIVES AND OUTCOMES THAT ARE LIKELY TO BE UNFAMILIAR TO CLIENTS

In many counseling interactions, the odds are high that you will suggest alternatives that may be unfamiliar to clients. Rather than expecting (often erroneously) that puzzled clients will interrupt you to ask you what such alternatives entail, consider providing brief descriptions as well as a summary of unfamiliar alternatives' principal likely consequences when you first mention the alternatives.

For example, assume that you mention the following alternatives to clients with minimal experience with legal affairs:

> 1. "One option is to enter into a prospective purchaser agreement with the Environmental Protection Agency."[9]

> 2. "We could consider including a non-competition clause in the partnership agreement."

> 3. "One option is to give Mr. Frankel what we call a 'golden handshake.'"

Bare bones descriptions such as these would likely be unfamiliar to such clients. If so, clients may well become distracted by trying to figure out the meanings of unfamiliar options. Moreover, when it comes time later to analyze and compare options, clients may well choose to discuss an unfamiliar option first not because it seems the most satisfactory, but simply because they want to know what it means. An exchange such as this is likely to result:

> L: Which option would you like to discuss first?

> C: You said something about a prospective purchaser agreement. I'm not really sure what that is, so let's talk about that one first.

Rather than create the possibility of distraction and risk altering the direction of conversations about alternatives, simply provide brief descriptions of unfamiliar options. Unless you are certain that clients are familiar with options, err on the side of providing brief descriptions. Even if you are mistaken and clients are familiar with a term, the likely result is that you will boost their self-esteem. Thus, if you advise a client of the option of a prospective purchaser agreement, your "default" position would be to briefly review what such an agreement entails. For example, you might begin with a statement such as, "As you may already be aware, a prospective purchaser agreement involves ..."

Moreover, effective descriptions of alternatives often include mention of their likely legal outcomes, at least when those outcomes are reasonably predictable. For example, consider one of the most common decisions that litigation clients have to make, whether to accept or refuse a settlement offer. Compare the following descriptions:

---

9. A company intending to purchase contaminated property can reduce future liability for any cleanup activities by entering into a prospective purchaser agreement with the government. The company will typically agree to perform some limited cleanup tasks and/or pay some amount of money in return for a release from liability and contribution protection. See UNITED STATES ENVIRONMENTAL PROTECTION AGENCY, GUIDANCE ON SETTLEMENTS WITH PROSPECTIVE PURCHASERS OF CONTAMINATED PROPERTY (May 24, 1995).

A.

"Marguerite, we have two options before us that we need to talk about today. One is to resolve this lawsuit by accepting the settlement offer I received yesterday from Fred's lawyer. The other is to reject that offer and proceed to trial. We'll compare each of these in as much detail as you need. Which would you prefer to start with?"

B.

"Marguerite, we have two options before us that we need to talk about today. One is to resolve the case by accepting the settlement offer I received yesterday from Fred's lawyer. That offer, in a nutshell, asks your company to pay Fred $350,000 and provide him a letter saying something to the effect that he did nothing wrong. We can talk more about this later, but I just want you to know at the outset what they have in mind. Now, your other choice is to reject that offer and proceed to trial. The trial would begin in about a month, and my best overall prediction is that at trial Fred has a better than 50–50 chance of getting a judgment in the $450,000 range. Again, we can talk more about that and compare these options in more detail. Which of these options would you prefer to talk about first?"

Statement "B" is likely to be far more helpful to Marguerite than Statement "A." Statement "B" quickly and briefly highlights the qualitative implications of each choice, facilitating her ability to compare their principal differences. Fuller review of subsidiary factual details such as when the $350,000 would need to be paid, the contents of the letter, how long the trial would take and the cost of the trial can await later discussion. Similarly, your summary provides only the most likely result of trial. Often, options have a range of possible legal outcomes and clients may need to know about them before making decisions. For example, when predictions about trial outcomes hinge on the admissibility of important items of evidence, counseling conversations may review the chances of admissibility. At the outset, however, you may sensibly limit descriptions to options' most likely legal outcomes.[10]

7. FRAME OPTIONS NEUTRALLY

As you know, maintaining neutrality is often vital to promoting client autonomy.[11] What may be dismaying, then, is how easily you can influence clients' responses without intentionally doing so.

Social scientists have long known that the way in which a question is asked can influence an answer. Perhaps the best known example is that of the "Kinsey Reports," which were an empirical investigation into

---

10. If clients ask for more details about options' likely consequences, you can of course respond immediately to their concerns.

11. See Chapter 14.

American sexual mores.[12] Questions asking people *if* they engaged in oral sex or homosexual activity were far less likely to uncover the extent of the behavior than questions asking people *how often* they engaged in the activity. The second type of question implies that the questioner expects that the respondent has engaged in the sexual activity and thus will not think ill of the respondent for confirming it.

Similarly, current cognitive psychology research into a phenomenon often called the "framing effect" demonstrates that people are likely to take risks when options are framed as gains and less likely to take risks when those same options are framed as losses.[13] For instance, assume that in the Swapco scenario, Swapco's current monthly rent is $4,000. Melinda hopes to renegotiate the rent down to $3,000; the owner offers to reduce it to $3,500. As Melinda's attorney, you might describe the owner's offer in one of these two ways:

    a. "By accepting the owner's offer, you gain $500 a month off your current rent."

    b. "By accepting the owner's offer, you lose $500 a month off our original proposal."

Research suggests that Melinda is more likely to accede to the owner's offer phrased as it is in "a." That is, Melinda is less likely to risk losing the settlement offer when she is told what she stands to gain rather than what she stands to lose.[14]

One effective means of maintaining neutrality in the face of research suggesting that anything you say may affect clients' thinking is to describe the same choice as both a gain and a loss. With Melinda, for example, you would make *both* of the statements above: "By accepting the owner's offer, you gain $500 a month off your current rent, though that's a loss of $500 a month as against our original proposal."[15] Additionally, to maintain a neutral stance you might indicate that the option produces "less than what we hoped to end up with when we filed the lawsuit, but certainly more than we can expect to receive if we go to trial."

12. ALFRED C. KINSEY ET AL., SEXUAL BEHAVIOR IN THE HUMAN MALE (1948).

13. *See, e.g.,* MAX H. BAZERMAN, JUDGMENT IN MANAGERIAL DECISION MAKING 49–52 (5th ed. 2002); Daniel Kahneman, *Reference Points, Anchors, Norms, and Mixed Feelings*, 51 ORGANIZATIONAL BEHAV. & HUM. DECISION PROCESSES 296, 297–98 (1992); Amos Tversky & Daniel Kahneman, *Rational Choice and The Framing of Decisions*, 59 J. BUS. 251, 255 (1986); Amos Tversky & Daniel Kahneman, *The Framing of Decisions and the Psychology of Choice*, 211 SCIENCE 453 (1981). Other terms for the "framing effect" include "presentation format" and "representational structure." For a description of numerous studies identifying and analyzing the impact of representational structures on reasoning, see Jeffrey J. Rachlinski, *The Uncertain Psychological Case for Paternalism*, 97 Nw. L. REV. 1165, 1206–1219 (2003).

14. See Russell Korobkin & Chris Guthrie, *Psychological Barriers to Litigation Settlement: An Experimental Approach*, 97 MICH. L. REV. 107 (1994) (plaintiffs tend to be risk-taking overall; defendants tend to be risk-averse overall).

15. *See* John M. A. DiPippa, *How Prospect Theory Can Improve Legal Counseling*, 24 U. ARK. LITTLE ROCK L. REV. 81, 104 (2001) ; Jeffrey J. Rachlinski, *Gains, Losses, and the Psychology of Litigation*, 70 So. CAL. L. REV. 113, 171–72 (1996).

8. EVALUATE CLIENTS' IMMEDIATE REJECTION OF ALTERNATIVES

One situation that commonly arises when you describe alternatives is that clients may immediately reject them. For example, imagine that part of the Swapco dialogue had proceeded as follows:

> 7. L: Could the trucks line up on Logan and not proceed to a warehouse until space was free on Bolas?
>
> 8. C: I think the police will hassle the truckers if they wait out there—that'll never work.[16]

Client-centeredness does not mandate that you automatically acquiesce in the client's rejection and consign the rejected alternative to the Graveyard of Unwanted Options. Of course, a client's clear rejection accompanied by valid reasons may well deserve your respect and acquiescence. For example, assume that when you suggest a particular person as a possible guardian, the client responds, "I've thought about him, but honestly he would not give the children any religious training whatsoever, and there is no way I could accept him." This client has evidently considered the option, knows a critical likely consequence, and finds it personally unacceptable. Arguably the client has had a "reasonable opportunity" to consider the alternative, and you may let well enough alone.

However, automatic acquiescence in clients' rejections is not always consistent with client-centered lawyering. Clients may reject alternatives out of hand for reasons that in your estimation have little or nothing to do with their potential for being satisfactory. Reasons that clients may do so include:

- Clients may mis-predict options' likely outcomes. For example, a transactional client may reject including a "non-competition clause" in a draft employment agreement because of what you consider a mistaken belief that its inclusion will lead the other party to terminate negotiations.[17]

- Clients may fail to understand what options actually entail. For example, a litigation client may reject mediation in the mistaken

16. Of course, instead of rejecting an alternative as soon as you identify it, a client may reject it when you try to examine its pros and cons during Step Three. In most situations, however, how you respond does not depend on when a client happens to reject an alternative.

17. Mis-prediction is common, and often results from what cognitive scientists often refer to as "cognitive illusions." Among these illusions are the "availability heuristic," which means that a person's judgment about how likely an event is correlates to how vivid a similar event is in that person's

mind, regardless of how common the event really is. Another cognitive illusion is the "self-serving bias," which tends to make us discount information detracting from positive self-images. *See, e.g.*, Richard Birke & Craig R. Fox, *Psychological Principles in Negotiating Civil Settlements*, 4 HARV. NEGO. L. REV. 1, 2 (1999). A third cognitive illusion is known as "reactive devaluation," which posits that "people tend to devalue proposals solely because they have been offered by an adversary." Korobkin & Guthrie, note 14 *supra*, at 150. For further discussion of cognitive illusions, see Chapter 18.

belief that the mediator will issue a ruling and that it will be binding.

- Clients may wear rose-colored glasses and reject options because they are convinced that far better solutions are just around the corner. For example, a litigation client may reject what you consider a very good and very final settlement offer in the mistakenly optimistic belief that "they are sure to sweeten the deal if we turn the offer down."[18]

From the standpoint of the counseling standard, clients who hastily reject options for such reasons arguably have not had a "reasonable opportunity" to make decisions. At the least, compliance with the standard suggests that at some point in counseling conversations you give clients the opportunity to reconsider hastily-rejected reasonable alternatives. How and when you do so is a matter of judgment, depending in part on your assessment of the reason for the rejection. For example:

- If you are not sure of a client's reason for hastily rejecting a reasonable option, it makes sense to try to clarify rather than guess at the reason: "You've said you don't want to even consider the Logan Street option. It might help me think of other possible solutions if you tell me what bothers you about the Logan Street option."

- You may realize that rejection grows out of a client's failure to understand an option. If so, you might when you deem it appropriate offer a clarification. For instance, assume that a client says something like, "Mediation? No way. I'm not going to let some stranger decide what happens." You might then explain mediation in more detail. When you do so, an effective rapport-building technique is to take on yourself the onus for the lack of understanding: "I'm sorry for not explaining the mediation option more clearly. Very briefly, what happens in a mediation is this ..."

- You may realize that a client has immediately rejected a reasonable option in the unwarranted belief that far better ones are in the offing. For instance, a client may say something like, "Accept that ridiculous, lowball offer? We can't help but do much better at trial." Here, you might wait until other options have been discussed and discarded before resurrecting the hastily-rejected one.

9. RECAST CLIENTS' INADEQUATE ALTERNATIVES

The above sections review issues that may arise when you suggest solutions to clients. Now think about issues from the opposite perspective, clients proposing alternatives to you. Your client-centered attitude

---

18. This reaction is common when clients are faced with situations in which each option is perceived to be a "loser." For a discussion of techniques useful in helping clients faced with "lose-lose" situations, see Chapter 18.

and skills may occasionally be sorely tested by the impracticality or unavailability of suggested alternatives. For example, a tenant-client whose objective is to enter into a sublease may propose filing suit to compel the landlord to consent to the sublease, even though the landlord has not yet rejected a proposed subtenant. Or, an employer whose objective is to enter into an employment contract with Ramseyer may ask you to "include a non-competition clause that will tie Ramseyer to my company forever." Lastly, a client who wants her entire estate to go to a charity may insist that a no-contest clause is the best way to discourage a will contest by her disinherited child. Assuming the impropriety or inadequacy of each of the suggestions, how might you respond?

Generally, you best serve clients by taking inadequate proposals off the table rather quickly.[19] To do so effectively, respond empathically and then explain the reason for your rejection:

1. L: Mr. Even, those are my suggested options. Have you thought of any additional ones?

2. C: After all the troubles I've had dealing with the landlord, I really want to take the bull by the horns and sue before the landlord tells me that I can't sublease to the subtenant I locate.

3. L: The landlord has caused you enormous aggravation, and I can understand your desire to sue. Unfortunately, were we to file suit now, before you've even proposed a subtenant, the landlord would have it thrown out in a heartbeat and the court might require you to pay the landlord's legal fees. So I don't think filing suit is an option you should consider. If we could do it, I'd recommend differently. But unfortunately we cannot.

At the same time, recognize that clients' suggestions often reflect legitimate objectives. When that is so, after making an empathic response to indicate that you understand their objectives, look for other solutions. Depending on who has greater "expertise," you might either suggest a different option that responds to their objectives, or ask clients to think of other possibilities. For example, in Mr. Even's case you might continue with No. 3 as follows:

3. However, it's clearly very important that you be able to sublease the property. Can you think of anything we can offer to the landlord to persuade her to accept whoever you come forward with as a subtenant?

In the above example, you ask for the client's suggestions. However, when you have greater expertise, you typically suggest the options. For example, you may respond to the client who wants to disinherit a child as follows:

---

19. Be wary, however, of rejecting a client's proposed alternative out of hand. What strikes you at first as fanciful may simply reflect a client's greater imagination or willingness to take risks.

Given the circumstances you've described, I can understand why you want your property to go to the Environmental Federation, and your desire to prevent a will contest. But simply putting a no contest clause in your will may not prevent your child from contesting it. If you leave everything to charity, the child has nothing to lose by contesting the will. And the legal fees your executor will incur if your child does contest will reduce the amount that goes to the charity. Therefore, one option to consider is to leave the child enough in your will to make the child reluctant to contest the will. We can talk about that in a bit. But before we do, do you see any other ways of perhaps preventing a contest?

10. ADDING ADDITIONAL OPTIONS AS THE COUNSELING PROCESS CONTINUES

As stated earlier, while effective counseling conversations often comprise the components of the four steps described in Chapter 13, counseling conversations are in reality often cyclical. That is, discussions may bounce back and forth among objectives, options, consequences and even tentative decisions until clients decide what to do. Thus, counseling discussions may often ultimately encompass options that are not yet on the table at the time that you and clients first begin to discuss consequences.

The upshot of this reality is that effective counseling doesn't require you to identify options at the earliest possible moment. One or two realistic options are usually more than enough to get counseling discussions under way. Indeed, having too many alternatives on the table at one time may overload clients' circuits and hinder rather than facilitate their thinking.[20] As counseling discussions go on, you and clients may be better prepared to consider options that neither of you envisioned at the outset.

For example, assume that you represent a civil defendant who is considering whether to offer a negotiated settlement prior to trial. The client's interest in resolving the matter quickly may lead to the initial alternatives of (a) offering a cash payment of $50,000; and (b) offering a cash substitute, a two-acre parcel of real estate the client owns that has a market value of approximately $50,000, but in which the client has a basis of only $35,000. As you and the client examine the consequences of these alternatives, the client may realize that an unwelcome consequence of giving up the real estate is forgoing its future appreciation. As a result, protecting future appreciation may become a new goal which leads to identification of additional alternatives. For example, a new alternative might be an offer which consists partly of cash and partly of some other non-cash asset.

---

20. *See* JOHN S. HAMMOND, RALPH L. KEE- NEY & HOWARD RAIFFA, SMART CHOICES: A PRAC- TICAL GUIDE TO MAKING BETTER DECISIONS (1999); Stephen Ellmann, *Lawyers and Clients*, 34 UCLA. L. REV. 717, 730 (1987).

11. THE IMPACT OF CHANGED CIRCUMSTANCES

Counseling is dynamic not only in the sense that conversations often bounce around among objectives, options and consequences, but also in the sense that problems often take on new complexions as matters progress. As you know, new circumstances may arise because the outside world changes, or because of changes in clients' attitudes or perceptions. Thus, the commercial office building owner who initially insisted on an extremely lessor-oriented lease may become more accommodating as changed economic conditions leave the building half occupied. Similarly, the client who was totally committed to defending a suit vigorously when it was first served may, many months later, develop the attitude that the suit is not worth defending. Thus, until decisions have been finally implemented, clients may voice objectives which require re-analysis of decisions you had thought were behind you.[21]

Such re-analyses may entail return trips to the drawing board for new potential solutions followed by examination of their likely consequences. An alternative that emerges during re-analysis may even be one that a client has previously rejected. The dialogue may go something as follows:

1. L: Willie, I sent you the draft of the will and asked you to look it over. I'll go over it with you, but first do you have any questions?

2. C: Well, like I wanted, the will leaves everything to the Federation. But seeing it written out has made me more uncomfortable about leaving so much money to the Federation and disinheriting Eddie completely.

3. L: What has made you uncomfortable?

4. C: Well, I'm still worried about his gambling, and I'm afraid that he'll throw everything away. But I read recently that a lot of big charities spend almost as much money on fundraising as they do on their work. Plus I read that last week the Federation has put a lot of effort into something about spotted owls, and that's just not a big deal to me. So I'm just not too sure anymore.

5. L: You've really given this a lot of thought. You might remember that when we first talked I mentioned the possibility of your leaving some of your money to Eddie in trust, but after we talked about it you decided to disinherit him instead. Now that you have some concerns about the charity, perhaps we should think about a trust for Eddie again. We can certainly include limitations on how much money Eddie can get and how he can spend it. Does that make sense?

6. C: Yes. I'm a bit hazy on what you said before, so . . .

---

21. *See* DONALD G. GIFFORD, LEGAL NEGOTI-
ATION: THEORY AND APPLICATIONS 192 (1989).

Chapter 17

IDENTIFYING CONSEQUENCES

---

* * *

Linda, as you well know, even though you're the author of the best-seller that's being made into the film, it would be unusual for the studio to grant you final cut approval. However, we might include a provision along those lines in our proposed agreement. I know you've been talking to others and thinking about this, so why don't we start off with any advantages you see to asking for final cut approval?.

I guess the main thing is nothing ventured, nothing gained. If we don't ask for it we'll for sure never get it. And this book really was a labor of love. But since more people might associate my name with the movie rather than with the book, I'd really like to have some say in the finished product.

Fair enough. Final cut approval definitely is a way of protecting your name and reputation. Any other advantages we should think about?

Well, this may sound a bit grandiose at this point, but I'm working on another book that I think also has cinematic possibilities. So if I can help make the first film successful, I'd think that should make it easier to sell my next book and film rights and have as much creative control as possible.

Hopefully you'll have a string of successful books and movies. These are certainly good reasons to seek final cut approval, but we should consider downsides. Any you can think of?

I guess my biggest fear is that as a first time author I don't want to come across as overly demanding and unrealistic. I've heard that once you get a bad image it's hard to shake.

That's a valid concern, but maybe we can address it by how we present your proposal. Anything else that might concern you?

This probably isn't much of a reason, but if I have final cut approval and the movie bombs for some reason, I go down with everyone else. If I don't have it, I can always have an out by claiming I could have made the movie a lot better.

* * *

347

1. INTRODUCTION

This chapter discusses additional strategies and techniques you may use when exploring options' likely consequences.

2. RESPONDING TO CONSEQUENCES THAT CLIENTS FORESEE

The two subsections below briefly discuss issues that commonly arise when clients identify consequences.

A. CONVERT CONSEQUENCES INTO PROS OR CONS

As you recall, the counseling standard calls for clients to have a reasonable opportunity to understand alternatives' likely pros and cons. However, clients may refer to consequences in ways that leave you uncertain as to whether the clients view them as pros or cons. In such instances, you can help clients evaluate options by asking them explicitly to label consequences as either pros or cons. Consider the following examples.

Example No. 1

L: So you'd first like to talk about the option of going to trial?

C: Yeah. And from what I hear, going to trial means this thing won't be resolved for a long time.

L: That's possible, and it's certainly likely that going to trial will be a much slower way of resolving this thing as compared to accepting their the settlement proposal. But just so we're clear on this, do you regard keeping this matter unresolved for some time an advantage or a disadvantage of trial?

Example No. 2

L: What do you see as the advantages of requesting a variance from the zoning board?

C: Primarily, I can start the business in the location that I think is best. Another thing to think about is that the local homeowners' association will probably get involved if I ask for a variance.

L: You think the homeowners' association might oppose the request?

C: Yes.

L: So a downside of seeking a variance is having to deal with the homeowners' association.

In each case you eliminate potential uncertainty by clearly establishing consequences as pros or cons.

B. INQUIRE INTO CLIENTS' DATA BASES

Assessing alternatives' likely pros and cons generally requires clients to make predictions. For example, the client in the illustration above predicts that the homeowners' association will "probably get involved if I ask for a variance." The likelihood that such predictions will come to pass depends in part on the soundness of clients' data bases for making them. Thus, to help clients assess the validity of their predictions, you may often choose to probe the data bases on which clients rely. The next two sections examines two common problems that may arise when you inquire into clients' data bases.

3. PROBE THE ADEQUACY OF CLIENTS' DATA BASES

Consider the following dialogue:

1.   L: Mr. Derian, do you see any disadvantages of coming back to Woods with a proposal for a five-year employment contract?

2.   C: I'm afraid that if we do that, she'll break off negotiations and look elsewhere.

Here, Derian predicts how Woods is likely to react to a possible employment contract proposal. To help Derian think about how much weight this prediction deserves, you may at some point in the counseling conversation probe into the sources of this prediction. For example, should you decide to probe the data base underlying the above prediction immediately, your conversation with Derian may continue as follows:

3.   L: Woods' breaking off negotiations is certainly not what we want to happen. But why do you think that's what Woods will do?

4.   C: Just my general sense, I guess. I've been in the high-tech industry for a while now, and in most of the companies I'm aware of, the entrepreneurial types who run them don't like to tie themselves down to long-term contracts.

5.   L: And five years is considered a long-term contract?

6.   C: Things change so fast in this business that anything over a year is considered long-term.

7.   L: Do you know whether Woods has the same attitude towards long-term contracts as other entrepreneurs in the field?

8.   C: I assume so.

9.   L: Now you've met with Woods and I of course haven't. Was there anything about what she said or how Woods said it

> that leads you to think that proposing a five-year contract
> will lead Woods to break off negotiations as opposed to
> countering?
>
> 10. C: Nothing specific, just a hunch. I haven't really spent much
>   time with Woods.
>
> 11. L: Can you think of any way of finding out more about how
>   Woods is likely to respond to a five-year proposal?
>
> 12. C: Not really.

Here, when you inquire in No. 3 into Derian's data base, Derian responds in terms of industry practice generally (No. 4). Then you follow up by asking whether the "entrepreneurial type" generalization applies to Woods (No. 7) and Derian's basis for thinking that Woods is likely to break off negotiations (No. 9). However, realize that clients may perceive such questions as challenging their knowledge and predictive abilities. Therefore, when you inquire into clients' data bases and the extent to which you do so has to depend on such factors as the seeming importance of the prediction to the ultimate decision, how close in time the client is to making such a decision, the element of trust you've established in the lawyer-client relationship and your estimate of the likely quality of clients' data bases. To soften any sense that you are intruding into clients' private domains, you might phrase a data base inquiry such as No. 3 above in this way:

> 3. Woods' breaking off negotiations is certainly not what we want
>   to happen. To help you decide how much weight you want to
>   give the possibility that Woods will react in this way, can you
>   tell me why you think that's a risk?

Phrased as a way of helping Derian to make a more satisfactory decision, No. 3 lessens the risk that Derian will perceive the question as a challenge.

In this example, you learn that Derian's data base is limited to general beliefs about high tech entrepreneurs, and that Derian has little or no specific data on the precise issue as to whether or not Woods will break off negotiations. Therefore, you might want to consider strategies that might produce additional data that Derian needs in order to have a reasonable opportunity to make a decision. One strategy consists of helping clients think about avenues for obtaining more information. For instance you might talk about your contacting (or asking Derian to contact) other sources to check on the accuracy of Derian's assertions about industry norms and Woods specifically. However, depending on factors such as the amount of time and money a client is willing to devote to a decision and the importance of the prediction to the decision, an alternate strategy that you might pursue is to inform a client of a prediction's shakiness. For example, assuming in the Woods matter that you decide not to suggest contacting outside sources at least at this stage of the conversation, your statement conveying the shakiness of the prediction may go as follows:

13.   L: We'll list that one possible disadvantage of proposing a five-year contract is that Woods might break off the negotiations. However, we'll put an asterisk next to it to remind ourselves that we don't have much hard evidence at this point to support the prediction. Would you agree with that?

4. RESPOND TO DATA BASES EMANATING FROM COGNITIVE ILLUSIONS

In the Derian/Woods example above, at the end of the discussion you remain uncertain about the sufficiency of Derian's data base underlying the prediction about Woods' reaction to a contract proposal. In other situations, clients may refer to data bases that you regard as problematic. A common reason that data bases are problematic is that people often base predictions on one or more of what researchers have come to call "cognitive illusions." Cognitive illusions (sometimes also called "cognitive distortions") are heuristics (mental shortcuts) that tend to produce illogical conclusions.[1] Chapter 18 describes a number of common cognitive illusions and explores strategies for responding when clients rely on them in the context of decision-making. The reality, however, is that clients may make assertions that suggest the presence of cognitive illusions at any point in the interviewing and counseling process.[2] Hence, by way of illustration, this section examines the cognitive illusion often referred to as the "availability heuristic" in the context of predicting alternatives' likely consequences.[3]

The "availability heuristic" refers to the tendency of us all to generalize from scant data. For example, we may generalize from one badly-prepared meal that "pork chops are greasy." Similarly, we may generalize from seeing one film that "modern romantic comedies are really dumb." Thus, it should hardly surprise you that clients may predict consequences based on a single case that the client read about in a newspaper or heard described at a dinner gathering. Influenced by the

---

1. Amos Tversky & Daniel Kahneman, *Judgment Under Uncertainty: Heuristics and Biases, in* Judgment Under Uncertainty: Heuristics and Biases 3 (Daniel Kahneman 1982); Massimo Piattelli-Palmarini , Inevitable Illusions: How Mistakes of Reason Rule Our Minds 66–67 (1994) (summarizing experiments demonstrating that "doctors, generals, politicians and engineers are as likely as others to believe that two often-related conditions are more likely to appear together than either separately, even when making judgments in their own area of expertise").

2. Indeed, the first thing a client says after an introductory handshake may suggest that the client labors under the influence of a cognitive illusion. For example,

nearly the first thing out of a client's mouth may be that "I'm upset because the city intends to take my property by eminent domain and has made an offer that totally ignores how unique and special a piece of property it is." Such an assertion suggests the possible presence of the "endowment effect," which leads people to overvalue their possessions. For discussion of the endowment effect, see Russell Korobkin & Thomas S. Ulen, *Law and Behavioral Science: Removing the Rationality Assumption From Law and Economics*, 88 Cal. L. Rev. 1051, 1113 (2000).

3. "Overgeneralization" is another term in common use for what this section refers to as the "availability heuristic."

availability heuristics, clients all too often focus almost exclusively on the predictive power of vivid but not necessarily representative prior events.[4]

Here's an example. Assume that you represent Doreen, who hired you to challenge her deceased widowed father's will. That will left most of the father's estate to his much younger housekeeper. As trial nears, the housekeeper's lawyer offers to settle the matter for a small but not insulting share of the estate. When you meet with Doreen, you advise her that the chances of doing significantly better by going to trial are low. However, Doreen regards settlement as disadvantageous. When you inquire into her reason for wanting to reject the settlement offer, Doreen tells you about a co-worker who around a year earlier had refused a settlement offer in a similar case and gone to trial. The trial resulted in the will's invalidation and the co-worker receiving the entire estate. Based on the co-worker's case, Doreen believes that it is a mistake to accept the settlement offer. Doreen's reasoning seems to reflect the influence of the availability heuristic, since the fact that Doreen's co-worker prevailed in her lawsuit does not mean that most will contests are successful or that the circumstances that resulted in the co-worker's success exist in Doreen's case.

Counseling clients such as Doreen, who appears to be relying on questionable data bases, raises a host of admittedly difficult issues. For one thing, you are likely to find it difficult to have clients recognize weaknesses in their reasoning, as the "cognitive illusion" literature suggests that the availability heuristic and other forms of problematic reasoning are powerful and difficult to overcome.[5] Moreover, delving into weaknesses in clients' reasoning processes risks damaging rapport. Clients can easily interpret questions about data bases as a challenge to their acumen and/or an implicit attempt to usurp their right to make their own decisions. Clients are particularly likely to draw such inferences when your inquiries follow immediately on the heels of clients' statements expressing significant confidence in their predictions. Finally, the timing of inquiries also bears consideration; clients' attitudes towards inquiries as challenging and demeaning or helpful may vary according to the level of trust and rapport that you have established.

---

4. For further discussion of the availability heuristic, see MAX H. BAZERMAN, JUDGMENT IN MANAGERIAL DECISION MAKING 14–18 (5th ed. 2002); Russell Korobkin & Thomas S. Ulen, note 2 *supra*, at 1087–1090; Cass R. Sunstein, *What's Available? Social Influences and Behavioral Economics*, 97 NW. U. L. REV. 1295, 1297 (2003). The classic work in the field is Amos Tversky and Daniel Kahneman, *Availability: A Heuristic for Judging Frequency and Probability, in* JUDGMENT UNDER UNCERTAINTY: HEURISTICS AND BIASES 166–168 (Daniel Kahneman et al. eds., 1982).

5. For a discussion of the likelihood that "cognitive illusions" exert powerful influence see Daniel Kahneman & Amos Tversky, *Choices, Values and Frames* 39 AM. PSYCHOLOGIST 341, 343 (1984); Russell Korobkin & Chris Guthrie, *Psychology, Economics and Settlement: A New Look At The Role of The Lawyer* 76 TEXAS L. REV. 77, 121 (1997). ("Framing effects are remarkably persistent even after the experimental subjects have the effect explained to them.").

Assume that at some stage of a counseling conversation you choose to respond to what you perceive as a cognitive illusion arising from clients' use of the availability heuristic. Among the strategies you might pursue are the following:

- Inquire into clients' knowledge of the example on which they rely. A potential benefit of this strategy is that if your questioning of Doreen helps her realize that the co-worker's case is different in important ways from hers, or that she is unfamiliar with the specifics of the co-worker's case, she may on her own decide to give it little weight when deciding whether to accept or reject the settlement offer. A potential risk of this strategy is that to the extent the prior example and that of a client is similar in important ways, the result may be that the client attaches even greater weight to the prior example. The risk grows out of the reality that the outcome of one case is almost always a problematic predictor. The risk is especially great if your professional experience suggests that the prior case on which a client relies was probably an aberration or simply a random outcome that is unlikely to repeat itself in your clients' cases.

- Point out to clients that no matter how similar two cases are, over-generalizing from an "N of 1" is inherently risky and often misleading. A potential benefit of this strategy is that your explicitness makes it less likely that what you say will strengthen the attraction of an illogical heuristic. On the other hand, a potential risk is that you may put yourself directly at loggerheads with clients who simply do not see the same error in reasoning that you do.

The dialogue below illustrates how you might carry out the first strategy, exploring the similarities and differences in the cases of Doreen and her friend.

1.   L: Doreen, it sounds like your friend got a great result in her case, and of course my goal here is for you to be just as satisfied with the outcome of your case. With that in mind, before we come to any final decision about the settlement offer I think it may help for you to consider how similar our case is to your friend's case. Is this OK with you?

2.   C: I've talked to her a lot about her case and they sure seem alike to me. We even talked about the two cases and I think we should reject the settlement offer.

3.   L: If the two cases really are very similar, it might make sense to turn down the settlement. And if that's what you still want to do after we've discussed this for a little bit then of course I'll go ahead and do that. But since I don't know much about your friend's case, you can help by giving me as much information as you can. I want to make sure that we are together on this and you can help me by telling me what you see about the two cases that makes them similar. Can you do this?

4.   C: Sure. (In response to this and a couple of "what else" type of open questions, Doreen brings out a few facts about the co-worker's case that gives it a facial similarity to hers.)

. . .

9.   L: As you know, there's no jury in these kinds of cases. Do you know who the judge was in your friend's case?

10.   C: No, we didn't get down to that level of detail.

11.   L: Unfortunately, that can be important. Many local judges were reassigned a few months ago, after your friend's case was decided, and frankly the judge who will probably preside over our case is not particularly sympathetic to overturning wills. So this is one difference we may want to take into account. One other question I have, do you know anything about the mental impairment that your friend's parent had at the time the will was signed?

12.   C: My friend said that he had real problems.

13.   L: Did your friend say whether they called an expert witness, and what the expert said about the mental impairment?

14.   C: She said something about that, but I honestly can't remember now.

15.   L: (further questioning uncovers a couple of additional differences and areas as to which Doreen is uncertain about similarities in the friend's case)

. . .

21.   L: Doreen, now that we've had this discussion, one possibility is that you can find out a bit more information from your friend about what happened in her case. Is that something you can do?

22.   C: I don't know. I suppose I could.

23.   L: Also, at this point do you think it makes sense to at least consider some of the advantages of accepting the settlement offer, so that you can have them in mind as you talk to your friend?

24.   C: I guess it can't hurt.

No. 1 is an active listening response that together with No. 3 explicitly acknowledges the legitimacy of Doreen's position. When seeking to have clients re-examine their predictions, such acknowledgements may be particularly important in that they allow you to start the conversation on the client's side and not on the attack. No. 1 also assures Doreen that your goal is to produce a satisfactory outcome and seeks her approval to examine her friend's case in more detail. No. 2 illustrates a common reality: Doreen appears to be strongly wedded to her position. No. 3 reflects client-centeredness: you reassure Doreen that if she maintains her position you will implement her decision to go to trial. No. 3 also tries to motivate Doreen to talk in more detail about her friend's case by explaining that her responses will help you. After Doreen responds to your open questions by describing a few similarities, your T-funnel narrow inquiries in Nos. 11, 13, and 15 reveal possible areas of difference that may weaken the predictive value of the friend's case. Nos. 21 and 23 illustrate how you might use clients' recognition of differences to help them think about whether potential weaknesses in their data bases suggest that they might re-evaluate their initial predictions. In both instances you ask Doreen if she is willing to take a step that may lead to a re-evaluation of her original prediction. An alternative approach might be to suggest explicitly that in light of the differences Doreen ought to reconsider her prediction. Realize, however, that the likely success of either of these approaches is uncertain, given the reality that clients often are extremely wedded to predictions derived from cognitive illusions.

The dialogue below illustrates how you might carry out a second strategy for attempting to counter the availability heuristic. Here you explicitly point out to clients that no matter how similar two cases are, relying on an "N of 1" is inherently risky and often misleading.

1. L: Doreen, it sounds like your friend got a great result in her case, and of course my goal here is for you to be just as satisfied with the outcome of your case. With that in mind, it may well be that what happened in your case is very similar to what happened to your friend. I don't know, we haven't really talked about your friend's case in any detail. But my concern is that we not put too much weight on the outcome of that case. I have to point out to you that your friend's case is only one of many similar kinds of cases, and the outcomes have varied widely. I think that we should really be talking about what's likely to happen in your case without giving your friend's case more weight than it may deserve given that it is only a single case. What do you think?

2. C: I don't know. I've spent lots of time talking to my friend, I think our cases really are alike, and I'm confident I'll win just like she did.

3. L: You may well be correct. But before you reach a final decision, think of this. Think of two very similar houses for sale in your neighborhood. What they ultimately sell for may be very different because of important differences that you don't see until you look at the houses more closely or just because some buyers are willing to pay more than others. In the same way, there will undoubtedly be differences between your case and your friend's case, and even if there weren't any differences we'll have a different judge than your friend had. So I really do think the way to go is to look at your case in more detail—at your house, so to speak. That's the best advice I can give you.

4. C: I feel like you're really trying to talk me out of something here.

5. L: I suppose to some degree I am. I'm not trying to tell you what to do, I'm just suggesting what I believe you need to

think about before making a final decision. We both want you to end up with as much money as possible. If your final decision is to reject the settlement offer and go to trial, I'll have no trouble with that but I want you to have a clear and realistic understanding of all the risks involved.

6.   C: I'm thinking that I'll still want to go to trial, but I guess I'll listen to what you have to say.

Again, No. 1 is an active listening response that also assures Doreen that your goal is to produce a satisfactory outcome and acknowledges that the cases may be quite similar. Unlike in the first dialogue, however, in No. 1 you also warn Doreen against relying on a single past occurrence. Finally, you conclude No. 1 by seeking Doreen's permission to discuss the merits of her case in more detail. As in the first dialogue, in No. 2 Doreen appears to be strongly wedded to her position. In No. 3 you acknowledge the legitimacy of the client's position and use an analogy to try to persuade the client to keep an open mind before making a decision. No. 5 includes an active listening response acknowledging Doreen's sense that you are pressuring her to abandon what she considers a correct decision. At the same time, No. 5 is also client-centered. You explicitly tell Doreen that you share her goal of getting as much money as possible, and that if she decides to reject the settlement offer you will support her position. You also indicate that your comments are intended to help her get a clear picture of the risks involved.

As with the first strategy, the results of your efforts to encourage and persuade clients to abandon judgments based on cognitive illusions will often be uncertain.[6]

5.   HELPING CLIENTS RECOGNIZE NON–LEGAL CONSEQUENCES

Helping clients evaluate options includes focusing attention on their likely non-legal consequences. In part you can accomplish this task with open questions such as, "Besides retaining the opportunity to do better at trial, how would refusing the settlement offer affect other aspects of your life?"

However, open questions do not necessarily bring to clients' minds all the important non-legal consequences they may want a chance to consider. Thus, to stimulate clients' thinking about non-legal consequences, you may also employ closed, "lower-T" questions to search for additional potential consequences. The following subsections briefly explore common bases of questions aimed at non-legal consequences.

A.   "INDUSTRY KNOWLEDGE"

Just as knowledge of the industries in which problems are situated often suggests options, so too is such knowledge commonly the basis of

---

6. More research is undoubtedly needed to determine how lawyers might best counsel clients who judgments appear to be influenced by cognitive illusions. See Russell Korobkin & Chris Guthrie, note 5 *supra*, at 120–21.

closed questions seeking additional potential consequences. Though clients may in general be more expert than you when it comes to predicting economic, social and psychological consequences, using your industry knowledge often enables you to help clients recognize consequences that they do not foresee in response to your open questions.

For example, assume that in the earlier example, Derian is a computer programmer and analyst, and Woods is the president of an architectural company that uses computers to generate building plans. Woods has offered Derian an employment contract that is terminable by either party "at will." In the course of discussing that offer, Derian has suggested countering with the alternative of a five-year contract.

In response to open questions about non-legal consequences, Derian states that the potential "pros" of a five-year contract are job security at a very good salary (economic and psychological consequences) and the opportunity to develop contacts with people who are very knowledgeable about Woods' state-of-the-art software design (social and economic consequences). The only potential "con" Derian foresees, based on Derian's conversations with former associates of Woods, is that Woods may respond by breaking off negotiations (uncertain negative economic, social and psychological consequences).

Use of knowledge pertaining to the computer industry may serve as the basis of closed questions prompting Derian's recognition of additional social, economic and psychological pros or cons to seeking a five year contract. In the economic realm, for example, you might ask how being in building design work for five years might affect Derian's future employability. Within this topic, you might ask how working for Woods for five years might affect Derian's ability to (1) handle different computer languages, (2) work in areas other than computer-aided design, (3) develop and market new applications, and (4) stay abreast of changes in hardware and software design. Such topics would become the basis of closed questions searching for industry-specific economic pros and cons that Derian may not have otherwise considered.

B. EVERYDAY EXPERIENCE

Everyday experience can also serve as a good source of closed questions searching for additional potential non-legal consequences. At times, "knowledge of an industry" and everyday experience may overlap and lead you to identify similar potential consequences. However, the latter often enables you to identify consequences that the former does not.

For example, assume that you represent Whittington, a stockbroker who is charged with a securities-related offense that even upon conviction is unlikely to result in loss of license. Whittington thinks that he has done nothing wrong but has been offered a plea bargain, and must decide whether to accept it or proceed toward trial. Everyday experience may enable you to ask Whittington about potential consequences of accepting the plea bargain, such as (a) the likely attitudes of Whittington's clients, family members, co-workers and friends (economic and social consequences); (b) the likely effect on Whittington's self-esteem (a psychological consequence); and (c) Whittington's potential sense of regret in future years if Whittington pleads guilty rather than pressing for complete acquittal (a psychological consequence). In the absence of closed questions, Whittington will likely miss the opportunity to identify and examine a number of potentially important non-legal consequences.

C. EFFECTS ON OTHER PERSONS

Non-legal consequences may involve the effects of clients' actions on third parties or even society as a whole. For example, assume that you represent an owner of retail stores with branches in different parts of the city. The owner is considering closing one or two branches that are underperforming the others. You think that a significant non-legal consequence is the negative impact the closures will have on the neighborhoods in which they are located, and that your client ought to at least consider this impact before going ahead with the closures. To give the client a chance to do so, you may ask a narrow question such as, "Do you think that closing those branches will adversely affect the surrounding neighborhoods?"

Clients may genuinely appreciate or brush off discussion of potential negative effects on third parties that their decisions may cause. If the latter situation results and you foresee serious harms to outside interests, you may have to evaluate your willingness to continue to represent the client. For a further discussion of this issue, see Chapter 18.

6. ARTICULATING LEGAL CONSEQUENCES YOU FORESEE

As you know, predicting legal consequences is almost always your responsibility. And as set forth earlier,[7] you can facilitate client understanding by briefly highlighting an option's most likely legal consequences when you first mention the option. For example, if "go to trial" is an option, you might immediately point out that the most probable result is "severing the partnership with you and the defendant each receiving half the book value." The following subsections explore additional techniques for discussing legal consequences.

A. DESCRIBE SUB–PREDICTIONS

Predictions about legal outcomes are often amalgams of sub-predictions. For example, one basis of a prediction that a jury will rule in your client's favor may be a sub-prediction that "we can demonstrate to the jurors that the plaintiff had plenty of opportunities to mitigate damages but failed to do so." Making explicit sub-predictions such as these can help clients evaluate the likelihood that predicted legal consequences will ensue and hence the satisfactoriness of alternative solutions.

7. See Chapter 13.

In litigation matters, legal sub-predictions typically concern one or more of the following factors:

- How a judge or jury is likely to resolve disputed issues of fact;
- Whether important evidence is likely to be admissible;
- How a court (trial or appellate) is likely to resolve unsettled questions of law; and
- How a trial judge is likely to exercise discretion.

With respect to the first factor, litigation matters typically center on disputed accounts of historical events. Hekyll claims that he had an oral agreement with Jekyll; Jekyll denies it. The State claims that Yeazell robbed a bank; Yeazell asserts an alibi. Marks claims that he became disabled as a result of being struck by a car driven by Spencer; Spencer contends that Marks' injuries are greatly exaggerated and that whatever physical limitations Marks has pre-existed the collision. When you talk about a trial's likely outcome, then, you might describe your sub-prediction as to how a judge or jury is likely to resolve factual questions.[8]

With respect to the second factor, sub-predictions may also involve your judgment as to what legal ruling a judge is likely to make in an area where the law is unclear. For example, assume that you represent the owner of a shopping mall who has been sued by a political interest group for illegally limiting the group's alleged First Amendment right to distribute leaflets near the mall. If you regard the application of the First Amendment to the largely uncontested facts as unclear, your prediction as to the legal outcome may rest on a variety of sub-predictions, such as the current political makeup of the judges who sit on your jurisdiction's highest court.[9]

Finally, outcomes often rest on discretion. That is, legal rules often do no more than establish wide parameters, leaving to judges and even to juries a decision as to what constitutes a fair outcome in a specific situation. For example, a convicted defendant may be sent to prison or placed on probation. Likewise, a probate judge may have wide discretion as to how large a family allowance to award a decedent's family. Finally, a judge (or jury) has discretion to decide what damages are appropriate to award an injured civil litigant by way of punitive damages. In each of these cases, a prediction would involve a sub-prediction as to how discretion is likely to be exercised.

---

8. This portion of the conversation can be especially difficult when you think that a judge or jury is likely to discredit much of a client's testimony. Saying something along the lines of "That's just not a believable story" tends to communicate your personal distrust of a client and may damage rapport beyond repair. To indicate factual weaknesses while retaining rapport, you might focus on how other relevant parties are likely to react to a client's story. For example, you might say something along these lines: "Based on the documents that were in your files, the defendant is likely to argue that you knew about the inventory problems at least four years earlier than that, and frankly we don't seem to have a very good response to that argument." See also the discussion in Chapter 12 regarding dealing with a client's apparent fabrication.

9. Here, the frequent challenge is to say something meaningful without launching into a "verbal law review article." Detailed legal analyses are more likely to obfuscate than enlighten.

Predictions about legal outcomes in transactional matters also often rest on sub-predictions. The sub-predictions tend to fall largely into the second and third categories above, since factual issues usually have not ripened into disputes in transactional contexts. For example, since every provision of a proposed agreement is a potential gleam in a litigator's eye, you may need to predict whether a court will uphold a non-competition clause in an employment agreement. In turn, that prediction may rest on a sub-prediction about how a court is likely to interpret its language, a sub-prediction falling into the second category. And, in a matter in which a client seeks a liquor license for a restaurant located in a primarily residential area, you may need to predict whether the Alcoholic Beverage Control Board will issue the license. Since the Board is likely to have discretion, the prediction falls primarily into the third category.

When the likelihood of government agency review of transactional matters is uncertain, you may find it necessary to make additional sub-predictions. To the extent that you predict the outcome of agency review, the sub-predictions mirror those above. But in addition, you may need to make sub-predictions about the likelihood of agency review itself. For example, assume that a client is concerned about whether an exchange of property will qualify as an IRS 1031 Tax Deferred Exchange. If the client wants to claim that the exchange is tax free, you may need to make the usual sub-predictions about what conclusion an audit will reach and what consequences will ensue if the IRS finds that the exchange was taxable. But in addition, you may have to make sub-predictions about whether in the first place the IRS is likely to audit the return, and when.

B. STATE PREDICTIONS AS NUMERICAL PROBABILITIES WHEN PRACTICAL

In daily life, we are generally content to use vague language when making predictions. For example, we may say that "I think we'll have a pretty long wait at that restaurant at this hour." Carrying these same habits over into legal contexts, you may tend to make statements such as, "We've got a pretty good shot at a not guilty verdict," or "I don't think a copyright violation claim will hold up."

However, vague terminology such as this is more likely to create misimpressions than to inform. If you tell a client that she has a "pretty good shot" at winning, she may think she has a 90% chance of success. Meanwhile you, knowing in your own mind that the case was somewhat of an uphill fight from the outset, meant that she had a 60% chance of winning. Hence, without suggesting more certainty than you really feel, you can enhance client understanding by characterizing legal outcomes as numerical probabilities. You may use either percentage estimates (e.g., "30–40%") or numerical frequencies (e.g., "4 out of 10"), though some studies indicate that the latter tends to promote clearer understanding.[10] Consider these illustrations:

     1. "There's a small chance that if we go to trial, you'll recover punitive damages." vs. "There's a small chance, about 1 in 10, that if we go to trial you'll recover punitive damages."

     2. "I'm reasonably certain that the Board will approve the request for a variance," vs. "I'm about 90% certain that the Board will approve the request for a variance."

Whether in litigation or transactional contexts, percentage estimates are more tangible than vague assertions and therefore are more likely to be helpful to clients. This is so because clients tend to draw wildly different meanings from terms such as "a good chance."[11] Unless you reduce a discussion to specific figures, chances are excellent that clients will misunderstand the prediction you had in mind. (At least they will 64% of the time!)[12] There are two caveats to keep in mind, however.

- Refer to percentages only if you can reasonably estimate what they are. If you practice in an area regularly, you may have an ample enough data base to offer reasonably reliable percentages.[13] On the other hand, issues may be uncommon, the facts may be quite murky or you may not have a sufficient track record to believe that you can talk in terms of percentages. In such situations, percentages may falsely imply more expertise or certainty than you truly possess. In those cases, prudence suggests that you rely on more indefinite statements such as, "I think you have a pretty good case, but I can't be any more precise than that."[14]

- Some clients may find percentages less meaningful than descriptive prose. Clients come from a variety of backgrounds and have different learning styles. If you recognize that a client is inadequately processing numerical information, by all means try to couch predictions in other terms. As the professional, it's your task to adapt to clients' needs rather than the other way round.

10. See Jeffrey J. Rachlinski, *The Uncertain Psychological Case for Paternalism*, 97 Nw. U. L. Rev. 1165, 1208 (2003).

11. For example, our experience suggests that client estimates of the phrase "good chance" can range from a 40 percent chance to a 90 percent chance.

12. Of course, you should take care to never understate or overstate your actual estimate. For a discussion of the practice of some lawyers in consciously overstating the risk of failing to settle, see Gary Bellow, *Turning Solutions Into Problems: The Legal Aid Experience*, 34 NLADA Briefcase 106, 109 (1977).

13. Referring to a "range within a range" is a means of maintaining the advantages of percentages without conveying more certainty than you believe warranted. For example, when referring to the chance

that proposing a non-competition clause will lead Varat to cut off negotiations entirely, you might say that "the chances of that happening are small, no more than 10–20%." As long as you do not opt for too much elasticity ("the chances of that are somewhere between 10 and 90%"), the "range within a range" approach is likely to convey more accurately your actual prediction than vague terms such as "pretty good."

14. Admittedly, the use of indefinite language such as "pretty good case" runs the risk that clients will misinterpret your meaning. In general, however, that risk may be preferable to using percentages in a way that implies more confidence than you possess.

C. IDENTIFY RANGES OF OUTCOMES

To further enhance clients' ability to evaluate options, consider describing a range of possible results rather than simply the only one that you consider the "most likely" to occur. For example, assume that you tell a client that "The most likely result of going to trial is that your opponent will get a judgment in the neighborhood of $100,000. I'd say the chances of that result are about 8 in 10." At the same time, you usually should put boundary limits on the client's potential liability by saying something like, "There's a small chance, say 1 in 10, that the judgment could be as high as $150,000 and about the same chance that it might be as low as $25,000." Providing such boundaries tends to assist clients to see the full scope of possible outcomes and thus helps insure that they have a reasonable opportunity to decide. To try to ensure that clients understand these predictions as more than simply a collection of random numbers, remember to go over the sub-predictions that form the bases for your estimates. For example, you might add that "the $150,000 figure is based on the possibility that the judge will hold your company responsible for the loss of the Di Fiori account, but as I said before I think the chance of that is only about 5–10%."

Providing clients with ranges of possible results is as useful in transactional as in litigation matters. For example, you might tell a builder whose application for a building permit is subject to an environmental impact report that "the most likely outcome, about a 9 in 10 chance, I'd say, is that the city will require you to pay for widening the street. The best likely result is that the city will share the street widening costs with you, but there's no more than a 1 in 10 chance of that happening because of recent budget cuts. Of course the worst possibility is that the city will deny you a building permit altogether, but I'm happy to tell you that I think there's virtually no chance of that happening."

D. CHARACTERIZE LEGAL PREDICTIONS AS ADVANTAGES AND DISADVANTAGES

In elementary school, you no doubt learned that to add or subtract fractions you have to first convert them all to the same denominator. In much the same way, you can help clients evaluate options by converting legal predictions into advantages or disadvantages. That is, in addition to describing ranges of possible outcomes, label those outcomes as advantages ("pros") or disadvantages ("cons"). For example, you might say that "a disadvantage of going to trial rather than accepting the settlement offer is that there's an 8 in 10 chance that the plaintiff will get a judgment in the neighborhood of $100,000. On the other hand, an advantage of the trial option is that you would retain about a 2 in 10 chance that the judgment will be for as little as $25,000."[15]

---

15. Describing outcomes as advantages or disadvantages may lead clients to perceive outcomes as gains or losses. Such perceptions sometimes create "cognitive illu-sions" that may bias clients' judgments. For further discussion of this cognitive illusion see the discussion in Chapter 16 regarding the "framing effect."

The dialogues below illustrate how you might help clients to evaluate options by describing consequences in terms of percentages and advantages or disadvantages as well as the sub-predictions on which your estimates are based.

Example No. 1—Transactional Matter

Your client is a builder who is considering the options of (a) applying for a permit to build an office complex in a highly developed downtown area; and (b) applying for a permit to build the complex in a less congested suburban area. In your estimate, the "most likely" outcome of option (a) is that the builder will receive a permit subject to having to pay for street widening and excess parking. The "best likely" outcome is that the city will grant the permit without restrictions; and the "worst likely" is that the city will deny the permit. You might discuss these consequences as follows:

1. L: One advantage of going ahead with the downtown application is that you retain a slim chance, no more than 2 in 10, that the city will grant the permit without restriction. A disadvantage is that you take a very small risk, I'd say 1 in 10 or less, of having the city deny the permit altogether, and you will have wasted time and money. However, as I told you earlier, the most likely result is that the city will grant the permit, but it will require you to pay for street widening and to provide traffic monitors at peak times as well as excess parking. I think the chances are at least 7 or 8 in 10 that the city will impose these requirements.

2. C: Why do you think they'll impose all those requirements? This office complex will be a great asset to the community, and I'd be surprised if the city would want to create all these roadblocks.

3. L: I know how much care you've put into the planning of this project and you're right, it would be a great asset to the city. But as you know, in recent times the Planning Office has been under pressure from homeowner and consumer groups to manage growth. Based on the street widening and excess parking requirements that have been imposed on other applications in the central downtown district, I think it likely that the same requirements will be applied to your project. Now, what I want you to think about is whether you see having to fulfill these conditions as an advantage or a disadvantage of putting the building downtown, compared to the possibility of building in the 'burbs free of these requirements.

4. C: Frankly, while these requirements would increase costs on the front end, both might end up as advantages. Wider streets and more parking may enhance the overall attractiveness of the building and allow us to charge higher rents. On balance, I really don't see the requirement as a

real disadvantage. Also, there's some chance as you said that the city won't require any improvements at all, so that's another advantage of going ahead downtown because it will give me time to think about whether I'd want to propose these improvements on my own.

5. L: Right. But just to be sure you've thought through this, let's not forget that a disadvantage of going ahead with the downtown site is the small chance, no more than 1 in 10 I think, that the city will deny the permit and cost you valuable time and money. If you decide to build in the 'burbs, an advantage is that there's virtually no risk of that. But of course going the 'burbs route has the disadvantage of giving up your 2 in 10 chance that the city will approve your downtown application without imposing any conditions.

6. C: Well, outright denial of the permit is a disadvantage for sure. But on balance, this is the only possible disadvantage that really concerns me and from what you've said, it's a longshot. So at this point I'm strongly leaning towards pursuing the downtown site.

In this dialogue, No. 1 characterizes the "best likely" and "worst likely" outcomes as a pro and a con respectively. When you mention the most likely result, the client, in No. 2, questions the basis of the prediction. In No. 3 you make an active listening response and a sub-prediction, explaining the rule and the past actions of the Planning Office that give rise to the prediction. In No. 4, the client characterizes the "most likely" result as an advantage, and then "crosses over" to the other option. In No. 5, you point out how the options mirror each other. That is, an advantage of one option is a disadvantage of another. Here, for example, Option "b" carries no risk of disapproval, but gives up the chance that the downtown site (Option "a") will be approved without restriction.

Example No. 2—Litigation Matter

Your client, Asimow, has brought suit for fraud in the sale of a house. The complaint alleges that the sellers concealed defects in the property, and seeks damages in the amount of $90,000, and punitive damages in an unspecified amount. After some of the usual pretrial skirmishes and discovery proceedings have taken place, the defendant offers to settle for $35,000. Asimow's options are to (1) accept the offer; (2) make a counter-offer; or (3) proceed to trial. You believe that the "most likely" result of trial (a 70–75% chance) is that Asimow will recover $53,000 in general damages and nothing by way of punitive damages. You believe there is only a 10% chance of the "best likely" result, $90,000 and again little chance that Asimow will be awarded punitive damages. On the downside, you believe that there is a very small chance-about 5–10%-of the "worst" likely result, Asimow recovering nothing. As to settlement, the most likely result of Asimow's accepting the offer is of course the 100% chance that Asimow will realize

$35,000. Should Asimow reject the offer, the "worst likely" result is a small chance, about 10–15%, that the other side will reduce or withdraw its offer and Asimow will go to trial and recover nothing. The "best likely" result of rejection is about a 30% chance that another, higher offer will be made before trial, perhaps as high as $45,000.

A sample dialogue may help you think about how to discuss consequences such as these with clients:

1.   L: Why don't we turn to the bottom line question before us: whether to accept their settlement offer, make a counter-offer or proceed toward trial. Which option do you want to talk about first?

2.   C: Trial, definitely.

3.   L: I guess that doesn't surprise me. I know how anxious you are to testify about what happened, so we need to consider that option very carefully. I've reviewed the case thoroughly. As I've told you, the most likely outcome of trial, about a 70% chance, is that you'll recover $53,000. That's not a figure I picked out of the air—it covers repair of the cracked foundation and structural problems in the house related to it. At the same time, I think there is virtually no chance that you'll be awarded punitive damages.

4.   C: But I really got screwed. Why wouldn't I get at least some punitive damages?

5.   L: You did get a raw deal, and I'd love to tell you that there's a good chance of getting punitive damages at trial. But I can't tell you that. Remember that punitive damages are generally designed to punish defendants who have substantially victimized other people. Jurors have lots of discretion in awarding them, subject of course to review by the judge. In this case, because we admit that the sellers gave you ready access to the house, and you hired a home inspection service to prepare a report prior to the sale, I think it unlikely that you'll get punitive damages. I'm very confident that you'll get around $53,000, but not punitive damages.

6.   C: And why only the $53,000 figure?

7.   L: That's my best estimate of how the jurors are likely to resolve the conflicts in the experts' testimony. Our expert will testify to the cracks in the foundation, and their likely cause. Their expert will testify that there's nothing wrong with the foundation but frankly I think the jurors will accept the opinions of our expert based on her background and the extensive testing she did. I'm basing the $53,000 figure primarily on that factor. The other damages relate to problems with the roof and the front and back yard. Our expert's testimony cannot tie those problems to the foundation, and I think there is little evidence that the sellers were aware of those problems. That's why I place the chance of recovering $90,000 at only about 10%.

8. C: Well, I must say it's not as good as I hoped for.

9. L: I understand your disappointment. But let's talk more about trial—what do you see as the advantages of proceeding to trial?

10. C: Well, it sounds like I'll get more money than they're offering. And at trial I could do even better than $53,000, right?

11. L: That is another possible advantage, that you retain the 10% chance that you'll recover as much as $90,000.

12. C: One thing about settlement, it puts money in my pocket much sooner. So I guess that's an advantage of settling. Aside from the delay, is there any other reason why I shouldn't go to trial?

13. L: A disadvantage of trial we have to keep in mind is that you could come away empty-handed. Lawyers always remind clients that trial is never a sure thing. However, given the strength of our expert, I'd say the chance of losing is slight-maybe 10–15%.

14. C: That doesn't sound too bad.

15. L: Do you see any disadvantages to proceeding to trial?

16. C: Not really; just the delay in getting the money but I want to get more if I can.

17. L: That leads me to the option of making a counter offer. . . .

Abundantly willing to follow the counseling model, in No. 1 you ask Asimow which option she prefers discussing. In No. 3 you make an active listening response, then remind Asimow of the likely outcome of trial, the option Asimow chose to discuss first. (Remember, you probably would have mentioned the most likely outcome when you initially mentioned the trial option during Step Two.) Sub-predictions are the subject of Nos. 5 through 7. The sub-predictions involve the trier's exercise of discretion (No. 5) and factual uncertainty (No. 7). In No. 9 you empathize with Asimow's disappointment, and ask what she sees as the advantages of the trial option. When Asimow in No. 10 mentions the chance of getting more money, in No. 11 you restate that chance in percentage terms as an advantage. In No. 12 Asimow crosses over, both to disadvantages and to the settlement option. You partially cross over by describing a disadvantage of trial in No. 13. In No. 15, you inquire about disadvantages Asimow may see. In No. 16 Asimow indicates that she sees no further disadvantages and returns to her desire for a greater financial recovery. You respond by turning to an alternative that might accomplish this objective, making a counter offer.

Chapter 18

FINAL DECISION–MAKING

* * *

I really appreciate all the time you've spent with me going over this, but I still can't decide between taking what they've offered and going to trial. What do you think I ought to do?

* * *

I don't want to talk about whether to accept their offer; just turn it down.

* * *

1. INTRODUCTION

Once clients have had a reasonable opportunity to identify alternatives and likely consequences, the time for decision-making is often at hand. In actuality, your decision-making role may be no more than engaging clients in discussions of options and consequences. As these discussions unfold, clients may well settle on the solutions they find most satisfying. Thus, clients will often simply tell you what they've decided to do without your even asking, and counseling conversations can move seamlessly on to implementation of those decisions or other topics.

However, decision-making may become a focus of counseling conversations in a variety of circumstances. For example:

- Clients may be reluctant to make decisions following even extensive discussions of options and likely consequences.

- Clients may make decisions that you believe are antithetical to their best interests or to your moral beliefs.

- Clients may make hasty decisions without adequate consideration or discussion.

Any of these circumstances may result in your taking an active role in the decision-making process. This chapter explores strategies and techniques for responding in situations such as these in ways that are consistent with client-centeredness.

2. CLIENTS REQUEST YOUR OPINION

Though counseling conversations may provide clients with a "reasonable opportunity" to discuss options and likely consequences, clients may nevertheless be reluctant to make decisions without first hearing what you think they ought to do.[1] Responding to clients' requests for your opinions is consistent with a client-centered approach. After all, client-centeredness is an attitude of seeing the world from clients' perspectives, and when those perspectives include seeking your advice you ought to provide it. Thus, the issue is not *whether* you give advice but rather *how* you provide it.[2] The strategies described below can help you think through how to respond to requests for advice that clients may make during or following discussions of options and consequences.

A. GIVING ADVICE BASED ON CLIENTS' VALUES

When clients request your opinions, client-centeredness suggests that you respond based on your best understanding of each client's unique mix of values and attitudes towards the consequences at stake. Your responses should include the bases for your advice, which typically comprise explanations of why your solution is likely to produce a satisfactory result and comport with the clients' values and attitudes. This approach encourages clients to disagree with your recommendations should they conclude that you have misunderstood their beliefs and attitudes or failed to evaluate the consequences in the same way the clients do. A dialogue conveying your opinion in a way that is consistent with this approach may go as follows:

L: Next, Diana, let's come back to the question we've been talking about, whether to insist on a personal guarantee from Lease Corporation's officers.

C: I know we've gone round and round on this, but I just can't decide. What do you think I ought to do?

L: Well, I agree that it's time to cut bait on this one. In the abstract, either choice might make sense, so primarily my advice grows out of what you've said as we've talked. I know your accountant has advised you to get personal guarantees, and I don't want to come between your and her. However, and you can tell me if I'm wrong, as we've talked your primary objective has been for this deal to go through, and you feel that Lease Corporation itself is financially pretty solid. You've also been worried that insisting on personal guarantees might sour this deal and spoil future business opportunities. Frankly, I read

---

1. For example, clients may request your opinion because they are unable to decide what option to choose or because they want a second opinion before going forward with a decision they have pretty well decided upon.

2. As you may recall from Chapter 15, we define advice-giving broadly to include both advising of consequences and advising which option a client might choose. The discussion in this section is limited to the latter meaning.

the situation with Lease Corporation pretty much the same as you do, and given your primary objective my advice would be that you do not insist on personal guarantees. Does this make sense to you?

Your response to Diana is consistent with the above suggestions. You identify what you understand to be Diana's principal concerns and attitudes, and explain why you think that going forward without personal guarantees is a satisfactory outcome. Thus, you give advice in a way that is client-centered and that gives Diana a chance to assess the wisdom of your choice.

B. GIVING ADVICE BASED ON YOUR PERSONAL VALUES

Though client-centeredness generally entails giving advice based on your perception of clients' values and attitudes, clients may want to know what you personally would do. For example, they may ask questions such as, "What would you do if you were in my shoes?" or "What would you do if you were me?" When it is apparent that clients seek advice based on your personal values, expressing your opinions is consistent with client-centeredness because you satisfy clients' legitimate requests for relevant information.[3]

As when you give opinions based on your understanding of clients' values, provide not only your opinions but also their bases. Including the values and attitudes underlying your opinions allows clients to compare their attitudes and values to yours and thus helps them decide how much weight to give your opinions.

For example, assume that you represent an employer who has to decide which form of non-competition clause to include in a contract proposal to a prospective employee, Huber. One option is a very restrictive clause that has about an 80% chance of being held invalid; the other option is a less restrictive provision that is almost certainly valid. At the same time, the latter provision would give Huber far more opportunity to seek other employment should Huber cease working for your client after signing the contract. The client asks, "Which clause would you personally choose if you were in this situation?" You might respond as follows:

> That's pretty difficult to say—I've never been in this exact situation. But in my experience people often go along with what they agree to. Also, I'm pretty willing to take risks, and here I'd want to discourage Huber from going elsewhere so I'd be willing to take the risk that Huber will live up to the agreement rather than try to defy it and risk being sued. So based on that, I'd choose the more restrictive language. Now you may feel differently, in which case you might not want to do what I would do.

---

3. The situation here is one in which the client asks for your opinion after first having engaged in a discussion of the likely pros and cons of alternatives. Section C below concerns how you might respond when clients ask for your opinion before such a discussion has taken place.

You may be uncertain from the context of clients' questions whether they are seeking opinions based on their values or yours. For instance, what if a client asks, "What would *you* do?" or, "I want to do what's right. Do you think I'm doing the right thing?" These questions are ambiguous with respect to whose values should underlie your opinion. Thus, before answering you may first clear up the ambiguity with a question such as,

> I'm happy to answer that. But just so I'm clear, do you want to know what I'd personally do, given who I am and what's important to me, or what decision seems best suited to your own values and concerns as I understand them?

C. RESPONDING TO CLIENTS' PREMATURE REQUESTS FOR YOUR OPINION

Clients may ask for your opinion before you have had a chance to engage them in counseling conversations that provide a "reasonable opportunity to decide."[4] As a result, you may not be able to give advice based on their values and concerns with respect to the decisions that need to be made simply because you are unsure what those values and concerns may be. Thus, an effective way to respond to premature requests for your opinion is to suggest deferral. Consider the example below:

> L: Next, Diana, let's talk about whether to insist on a personal guarantee from Lease Corporation's officers.
>
> C: You probably deal with these issues all the time; what do you suggest?
>
> L: I wish I could give you a simple answer, but what might be best for some clients may not be what's best for you. For example, you may be more or less willing to take risks than other clients. Can we do this? Let's briefly go through the pros and cons of each option and maybe you'll be able to figure out what makes most sense in your particular situation. If you're still uncertain, hopefully I'll have a better sense about what to recommend. Does that sound OK?
>
> C: Sure.

Here, Diana is willing to engage in a counseling conversation. However, clients may not always be so pliant. For example, after your explanation above, instead of "Sure," Diana might have said something like:

> C: That sounds like it'll take some time, and frankly I don't want to devote the time or money to it. You're the lawyer, and I'm sure you've come across these situations lots of times. I'll go along with what you think is best.

4. See Chapter 13.

This time, Diana refuses your invitation for a counseling conversation and again asks for your opinion. Should you accede to her wishes and suggest "what you think is best?" Generally, the answer is "Yes." Again, a client-centered approach comprises respecting clients wishes. Moreover, refusing to accede places you in something of an adversarial relationship with your own clients. As above, however, the key is to explain the bases for your recommendations. As before, the strategy is client-centered because you give clients an opportunity to evaluate how closely your reasoning comports with their attitudes and concerns. For example, after Diana repeats her request for your opinion you may say something along these lines:

> I can't always be sure I know what's best. But here's my thinking in your situation. This is the second time they've approached you about this deal, so it seems to me like they are anxious to make the deal. If that's the case, they may be willing to go for personal guarantees and that would give you a lot of protection. What do you say we ask for personal guarantees and see how they respond? Does this approach make sense to you?

3. RESPONDING TO CLIENTS WHO ARE UNABLE TO DECIDE

Aware of potential alternatives and their likely consequences, clients may nonetheless have difficulty making important decisions. The subsections below provide a menu[5] of strategies and techniques that you may employ to help clients break decisional "logjams" even as you remain client-centered.[6]

A. ACKNOWLEDGE CONFLICTING FEELINGS

As do relatives, likely consequences as you know come in two general varieties: good ones (advantageous) and bad ones (disadvantageous). As a result, clients often have to accept bad consequences in order to receive good ones, or forgo some good consequences in order to obtain others. For example, assume that a client is to decide whether to authorize an environmental study on industrial property that the client wants to sell. A potential "good" consequence of the study is that it will demonstrate that the land is free from contamination, increasing its market value. "Bad" consequences include the cost of the study and the possibility that it will reveal the presence of contaminants that the client may have to eliminate or reveal.

Situations such as these can produce conflicting feelings that result in indecision. "Active listening" responses that explicitly acknowledge

---

5. As the term "menu" implies, you may pick and choose from the strategies as your judgment dictates. Which strategy you use and how many you try is entirely up to you. You of course may choose to combine some strategies.

6. Not included in the discussion is the well-worn strategy of delay. Advising clients to "take some time to think it over" may often be a useful strategy, but the discussion assumes that the time for decision is at hand.

such feelings may "unblock" clients' thinking and enable them to make decisions.[7] The following examples illustrate how you might acknowledge the conflicting feelings that mixed bags of consequences often generate.

WIN-LOSE CONFLICTS: Conversations about options that have both good and bad consequences may go something like this:

C: This is not an easy choice to make. Like we've discussed, I like the security of a five-year lease, but this business changes so fast that I hate to lock us in to this location for that long a time. On the other hand, if I don't accept the five year lease, and the location does well, I could face a significant rent increase in less than two years. Yuk!!

L: You're exactly right; the choice is not an easy one. The extended lease gives you security, and that's important. At the same time, that security may entail costs down the line. So as the old song goes, you can't have one without the other, and you're going to have to decide whether the security of a five year lease is worth the risk of locking yourself in down the road. But at least no matter which way you go, you will end up with something that you do want.

Analysis: Reflecting back the client's discomfort with having to choose between conflicting consequences may put the client in a position to make a decision. You further that possibility by pointing out that though a decision may produce a loss it will also certainly create some gain.[8]

LOSE-LOSE CONFLICTS: When you deliver "bad news," clients may be blocked by the realization that any option they choose carries negative consequences. The resulting conversations may go something like this.

C: If I settle now, I get practically nothing. Their offer is pretty insulting. But you tell me that trial involves delays and lots of expenses, and you can't assure me that I'll win even if I hold out for a trial. Either way, I'm feeling ripped off. I don't like this one bit.

L: That's very understandable. Neither choice is all that appealing. I wish I could give you better news, but the settlement offer is what it is, and the trial chances aren't good either. I guess you'll have to accept that you'll be pretty unhappy no matter which way you go.

Analysis: Here, your statement reflects back the client's feelings that both options are flawed. Again, your acknowledging the client's frustration may enable the client to make a decision.

7. See Stephen Ellmann, *Lawyer and Client,* 34 UCLA L. REV. 717 (1987)

8. See Russell Korobkin & Chris Guthrie, *Psychology, Economics, and Settlement:*

A New Look At the Role of The Lawyer, 76 TEXAS L. REV. at 115 (1997).

Win-Win Conflicts: Even "good news" may arouse conflicting feelings when clients have to give up on some "goods" in order to obtain others. The resulting conversations may go something like this.

C: If we proceed to trial, you're pretty confident that I'll end up with no less than $40,000 and maybe as much as $70,000; that's great. At the same time, their settlement offer of $50,000 is pretty darn appealing too. I had no idea that my case was worth anything near this when I first came to see you. So I just don't know what to do.

L: I'm glad that whichever way you go, you'll feel like you came out of this a winner. That's a great position to be in, so you just have to decide which way you want to go.

Analysis: Here, your feedback echoes the client's feeling that both options are favorable. Your validating the client's beliefs may produce a decision.

Active listening responses such as those in these three examples may not make the conflicts any less real or painful. However, capturing clients' conflicting feelings in a few words may provide the clarity that enables them to make decisions.

B. "VALUE–RATE" CONSEQUENCES

Affording clients a "reasonable opportunity to decide" means that the consequences that clients regard as significant are likely to be already on the table before you call on clients to make decisions. However, if clients remain indecisive, you may promote decision-making by asking them to "value-rate" those consequences. That is, you may seek clients' attitudes as to how strongly they value those consequences.[9]

Asking clients to value-rate consequences is especially appropriate when, as is often true, the process of identifying likely consequences consists primarily of compiling lists of "good" and "bad" consequences. In and of themselves, such lists do not necessarily indicate clients' value-ratings. For example, assume that a "good" consequence of accepting a settlement offer is that a client will receive $25,000 immediately. A "bad" consequence of accepting the offer is that the client forgoes trial, the most likely result of which is that the client will be awarded $40,000. What this information alone does not tell you is the client's value judgments with respect to these consequences. That is, the client may strongly value the chance to receive $25,000 immediately and be only mildly disappointed at giving up a good chance to recover a larger sum in the future. Asking clients to signal explicitly how strongly they care about consequences may provide the clarification that in turn enables them to make decisions.[10]

---

9. See Peter Toll Hoffman, *Valuation of Cases for Settlement: Theory and Practice,* 1991 J. Disp. Resol. 1.

10. An alternative strategy would be to ask the client what he or she sees as the specific pros and cons of having $25,000

A straightforward technique for seeking clients' value ratings is to ask questions such as:

> Looking over the list of likely consequences we've made, does any one stand out in your mind as being especially important, either as a consequence you want to see happen or one you want to prevent from happening?

In response, the client in the above example may say something like, "I sure do like the idea of getting a good chunk of money immediately." If so, you may link that preference to the decision: "If that's what is most important to you, it sounds to me like what you would find most satisfactory is to accept the settlement offer. Are you comfortable with that?"

Asking clients to attach numerical ratings to consequences is a somewhat more rigorous approach to seeking clients' value ratings. Though numbers imply greater precision than words, you needn't pretend that their use eliminates subjectivity or uncertainty. Rather, the advantages of numerical ratings are their familiarity and their ability to reduce consequences that may be very different in kind from one another to a common calculus. That is, clients' indecision may be a result of the difficulty of comparing the value of an "apple" to that of an "orange."[11] For example, the client trying to decide whether to accept the settlement offer may be unable to decide between the "economic" advantage of receiving $25,000 immediately and the "psychic" advantage of "forcing those weasels to go to trial." Attaching a numerical rating to each advantage creates a common scale that may make clients comfortable enough to make decisions.[12]

For an illustration of how you might ask clients to use numbers to indicate value-ratings, assume that Rosett, a homebuyer, sued the sellers for fraudulently concealing defects. The sellers have offered to settle for $35,000. You have told Rosett that if the case goes to trial, the most likely result is a 70–75 percent chance that Rosett will receive a judgment in the range of $50,000 as general damages but nothing by way of punitive damages.[13] Small chances (5–10 percent) exist that Rosett will get a judgment as high as $90,000 or as little as zero because judgment will be for the sellers.[14] Rosett has to decide whether to accept the settlement offer or push towards trial.

---

immediately or proceeding to trial. This strategy too, however, may still leave the client undecided and bring you back to using a value-rating approach.

11. Having to evaluate consequences of different types tends to complicate the decision-making task.

12. Researchers known as "decision theorists" promote the effectiveness of using numerical ratings to promote effective decision-making. See JOHN S. HAMMOND,

RALPH L. KEENEY & HOWARD RAIFFA, SMART CHOICES: A PRACTICAL GUIDE TO MAKING BETTER DECISIONS (1999).

13. Again to simplify the discussion, we omit mention of attorney's fees and other costs. In an actual discussion, you would work through the calculations necessary to convert "gross" figures to "net."

14. Note that in situations when a client may come away completely empty-handed, the worst likely and the worst possible outcomes overlap completely.

Assume that your conversation with Rosett thus far has produced the following lists of likely consequences:

"Goods" (Advantages of accepting the settlement offer): Assured money; money comes soon; enough funds to repair almost half of the defects; stress ends; no more missed work; no risk of losing and getting nothing; no risk of the sellers walking out of court smiling after they win.

The converse of these consequences would be "bads" of rejecting the settlement offer and going to trial. That is, the "trial" option entails giving up a sure, speedy receipt of money and maintains the stress of involvement in litigation.

"Bads" (Disadvantages of accepting the settlement offer): Guilty feelings for caving in; lose 70–75 percent chance of getting about $50,000; lose a 5–10 percent chance of getting $90,000; forfeit chance of vindication at trial; lose opportunity to tell the story in public; worry that later on will continually fret over whether trial would have produced a better result.

The converse of these consequences would be "goods" of rejecting the settlement offer and going to trial. That is, the "trial" option preserves a 70–75 percent chance of receiving abut $50,000 and a 5–10 percent chance of receiving as much as $90,000.

As you can see, and as will often be true, these consequences are a motley mix of apples and oranges. That is, one consequence ("stress") is a psychological consequence while another (receiving $35,000 immediately) is an economic consequence. Thus, to help Rosett overcome indecisiveness you might ask a question such as:

Let's try this. We've got a list of consequences here. Let's first look at the ones that we've identified as advantages of accepting the settlement offer.[15] Using a scale of 1–10, with 1 indicating that a consequence is less important to you and 10 indicating that a consequence is very important to you, just give me a number to put next to each of them. Don't worry about trying to be too exact, we're not trying to be scientific or anything. I don't think numbers have magic powers, but I have found that doing this can help clients clarify their thinking and make decisions that they feel confident about.

Rosett may respond by attaching the following ratings to the advantages of accepting the settlement offer:

Avoiding the stress of trial: 2 (Weakish importance)

Receiving funds quickly to do about half the needed repairs: 8 (Important consequence)

Smile on a baby's face: Priceless (Parody of current credit card ad)

15. Alternatively, you might ask Rosett to identify the list of consequences to be rated.

In the same way, you might ask Rosett to attach numbers to other consequences. If at the end of the discussion "8" is the highest number that Rosett attaches to a consequence, that may indicate that accepting the settlement offer is the decision that Rosett finds most satisfactory. If on the other hand Rosett also attaches an "8" to a disadvantage of accepting the settlement off (e.g., "guilty feeling for caving in"), you might suggest that Rosett "cross out" the equal and opposite consequences and look to the value-ratings of other consequences.[16]

While by no means a sure thing, taking clients through a discussion of value-ratings along these lines may enable them to overcome indecisiveness and choose satisfactory resolutions.[17]

A final strategy for seeking clients' value ratings is to ask about their "level of regret." That is, focus on "goods" that clients may have to give up and ask them how much regret they would feel if that that "good" were to materialize. For example, you might ask Rosett, "On a scale of 1–10, how badly would you feel about accepting the settlement offer if you knew for sure that if the case went to trial you'd receive about $90,000?" Explicitly indicating their level of regret is another way that clients can value-rate consequences.[18]

C. INVOLVE CLIENTS' TRUSTED ASSOCIATES IN DECISION–MAKING

Your prototypical counseling conversations may be one-on-one with clients. However, talking to trusted associates can often help clients overcome their indecisiveness. For example, in many cultures a longstanding custom is to share the making of important decisions with family members.[19] Thus, when time permits you may suggest to clients that they talk over decisions with trusted family members, a business colleague or a friend. You may suggest that clients talk to such trusted associates on their own, outside of your presence. Alternatively, you may invite clients to bring such associates with them to a joint meeting.[20] In

---

16. See HAMMOND ET AL., *supra* note 12, at 94–103 (describing "even swaps").

17. If you or your client feel that the use of numbers or a ten point scale seems inappropriate for some reason or confusing, you can ask clients to rate consequences through the use of a 5 point scale and asterisks, stars, or checkmarks. For instance, you might suggest that a client use a 5 star system with 5 stars being the most important.

18. For what it's worth, there exists a strong psychological phenomenon that minimizes regret, making decisions already made look better in hindsight, especially when, as here, one will never know how the risks would have played out in fact. *See* for example Tom Gilovich, Victoria H. Medvec & S. Chen, *Commission, Omission and Dissonance Reduction: Coping With Regret in*

the Three Doors Problem, 21(2) PERS. SOC. PSYCHOL. BULL. at 182–190 (1995); Tom Gilovich and Victoria H. Medvec, *The Experience of Regret: What, When and Why*, 102 PSYCHOL. REV. 379–395 (1993).

19. *See, e.g.,* DERALD W. SUE & DAVID SUE, COUNSELING THE CULTURALLY DIFFERENT: THEORY AND PRACTICE (1999).

20. Of course, a risk of involving nonclients is that the privilege for lawyer-client communications may cease to apply. This risk can be a considerable one in situations where an adversary is likely to depose the third person or call such person as a witness at trial. At the very least, therefore, you have to advise clients of the possible risks. In some instances, you may want to secure a clients' written acknowledgement of the risks or even written consent to the involvement of "outsiders." If the third per-

either situation, involving what some refer to as a "moral community"[21] in decision-making can help clients overcome indecisiveness.[22] When clients indicate a desire to review a decision with another person, you probably want to give them a copy of whatever written list of alternatives and pros and cons you have created during your counseling sessions. Such a document will help clients bring to the attention of the outside person a summary of the various matters that you and they have discussed.

A situation in which the "trusted associate" strategy may be contra-indicated occurs when have reason to believe that an associate is likely to overcome clients' autonomy. If you have reason to suspect that "trusted associates" may wield excessive control over clients' decision-making, you may at least explore with clients in advance their thoughts about sharing the decision-making process and remind them that decisions are ultimately theirs to make.[23]

The following example illustrates how you might broach with clients the involvement of trusted associates in decision-making. Assume that your estate planning client Jeanne Flynn is unable to decide whether she wants an "inter vivos trust" or a simple will. You might proceed as follows:

> L: Jeanne, I appreciate how thoughtful you are about all the considerations we've discussed. It's probably because you are giving it so much thought that you're having such a hard time deciding, as you see the advantages and disadvantages of each choice. So here's an idea. We can put this off to another meeting, and in the meantime, if you'd like to you can talk this over with someone who you are close to and trust, though not someone who will inherit from you. If you want to talk with someone before we meet again, you can take with you a copy of the list of advantages and disadvantages we've written down and show the person what we've been talking about. Or, if you want to bring someone with you and meet with me again to discuss this situation, that would be fine.

> C: I can do this legally, talk with someone else? You don't mind?

son's presence is necessary to your representation of the client, then the resulting conversations will be privileged. *See* Craig S. Lerner, *Conspirator's Privilege and Innocent's Refuge: A New Approach to Joint Defense Arguments,* 77 NOTRE DAME L. REV. 1449 (2002). Some commentators have argued that the "necessity" exception to the loss of privilege is satisfied in cultures where important decisions are only made with the family present. *See* Jeffrey A. Parness, *The Presence of Family Members and Others During Attorney–Client Communications: Himmel's Other Dilemma,* 25 LOY. U. CHI. L.J. 481 (1994).

21. Amelia J. Uelman, *Can a Religious Person Be a Big Firm Litigator?,* 26 FORD-HAM URB. L.J. 1069 (1999).

22. An advantage of joint meetings is that your presence may ensure that "nothing gets lost in the translation."

23. You should also note here the wisdom of Model Rule 1.8(f)(2), and its Comments [11] and [12], which permit a lawyer to receive payment from a third person for representation, but only if the lawyer's independent professional judgment on behalf of the client is not impaired in any way. A relative or friend may pay the client's legal fees, but cannot control the lawyering process in any way.

L: You certainly can and I don't mind at all. From a legal stand-point, the only thing to remember is that if this person meets with me and you it's possible that what any of us says during that meeting won't be confidential. What that means is that if later on for some reason a lawsuit were filed concerning your will, you or the person you brought with you might have to divulge what was said in our meeting. If this possibility is a concern to you please feel free to ask me about it.

C: If you don't mind, I would like to talk this over with my godfather Hiram. He's always been there for me. Could I take a day or so and speak with him? Maybe he'd help me decide. He always jokes that I'm "the waffle" because I always take forever to make up my mind.

L: You can absolutely do that. I think talking to your uncle is not a problem since he is not one of the people you are considering leaving money to.

But remember, you can also ask him to come here with you, so I can join in and maybe clarify any questions that come up. It's your call. If you think it will help for us all to talk, let me know and I'm happy to set up a convenient time.

C: Oh, I definitely think it will help if we're all together. I didn't think lawyers did this kind of thing.

L: Sure we do, especially if we've read through "Lawyers As Counselors."

A dialogue such as this may provide clients with an avenue for sorting through conflicting feelings and arriving at satisfactory decisions. This particular dialogue is somewhat truncated for purposes of illustration. In an actual case, you might explain the effect on the lawyer-client privilege in somewhat more detail and also talk about confidentiality as it applies to Jeanne's telling Hiram what you've said and showing him your list of pros and cons. In addition, you might want to clarify Jeanne's relationship with Hiram. If your sense is that Hiram is a very strong-willed person who may well override Jeanne's autonomy, you can at least talk to Jeanne about her need to be personally comfortable with whatever decision she makes.

D. OFFERING UNSOLICITED ADVICE

Indecisive clients do not necessarily ask for your advice. However, offering unsolicited opinions in an effort to break decisional logjams can be consistent with client-centered lawyering. Hearing your opinions may help clients to make decisions, even if they do not follow your advice.

The propriety of offering unsolicited opinions follows from the simple truth that indecisive clients do not have a choice between "decision" and "no decision." In most instances, non-decisions are themselves decisions. Thus, refusing to intervene when clients are unable to decide does not preserve client autonomy, but rather may produce default decisions with which clients are unhappy. For example, assume that a client has to decide whether or not to authorize you to take a series of depositions. The client's inability to decide is the equivalent of a decision not to take the depositions. Similarly, in a transactional context a client may be undecided about whether to propose including an arbitration clause in a contract. Indecision is the equivalent to there being no arbitration clause.

Offering unsolicited advice to break decisional logjams is typically a two-step process. First, enhance a client's willingness to listen to your opinion by pointing out explicitly that a non-decision is by default a decision:

> Joe, we've got to submit our contract proposal by 5:00 tonight. I know we've talked about this at length, and if you can't decide whether to include an arbitration clause in the proposed contract, that's the same as saying that we won't put one in.

Then, state your opinion, again making reference to your understanding of the client's values and solicit the client's response:

> Since we can't escape making a decision of one sort or the other, let me give you my advice. As we talked, whenever I pointed out that some people promote arbitration as a relatively inexpensive and quick way to resolve disputes, you have mentioned that you've worked with this company before and that you never had a problem with them. Also you've said that you're not sure how they will react to an arbitration proposal but you have no reason to believe they would be offended such a clause. Also you told me that you realize that if a problem should arise arbitration can reduce the costs of resolving disputes. And, I agree that arbitration does have this advantage. Therefore it seems to me that we should go ahead and include that clause in the proposed contract. Maybe I've misheard you but in light of all that you've said does that make sense to include the clause in the proposal?

As you see, your statement in this context differs little from when clients ask for your opinion. Your advice is tailored to clients' articulated values and attitudes, and you invite their response.

4. INTERVENING IN CLIENTS' DECISIONS

While client-centeredness puts clients at the center of the decisional universe, you need not automatically accept all decisions that clients make. The discussion below explores the question of when you may appropriately question or voice disagreement with clients' decisions. In extreme circumstances, you may go even further and discontinue representing clients who insist on adhering to decisions with which you disagree.[24]

---

24. This discussion takes place in the context of situations in which clients have actually reached a conclusion about what solution to adopt before you attempt to intervene. Of course in some instances you may find it makes sense to intervene in a

A. MISPREDICTION

Client-centeredness starts from the perspective that lawyers should generally trust well-counseled clients to select sensible solutions that that maximize their satisfaction. However, you may on occasion strongly believe that clients' decisions are not likely to maximize their satisfaction and indeed be antithetical to their best interests. Often, the reason for your belief will stem from your perception that clients have identified consequences or reached decisions on the basis of erroneous predictions. That is, they have predicted the likelihood of future occurrences based on data or assumptions that from a logical perspective do not justify their predictions. For example, a plaintiff may predict how a defendant corporation will react to a proposed settlement offer knowing virtually nothing about the person in the defendant corporation who will evaluate the offer.[25] This section explores some common sources of misprediction and discusses strategies you might adopt to help clients recognize that their predictions may be faulty.

1. *Potentially Insufficient Data Bases*

A frequent source of misprediction is simply that clients predict outcomes without an adequate basis for doing so. One way this may come to your attention is when clients lack a sound response to a question such as, "Why do you think they'll react like that?" Alternatively, your experience and knowledge may suggest strongly that clients' predictions are erroneous.

Assume for example that Barry, a litigation client, decides against taking depositions. When you ask Barry to explain the decision, he responds by saying that the adversary "will appreciate that we're not trying to run up fees and so will make us a better settlement offer." However, your prior dealings with the adversary's lawyers have convinced you they will view the failure to take depositions as an indication of weakness and so refuse to negotiate seriously. In such a situation, effective representation suggests that you indicate to Barry the problems you see with his prediction. Doing so does not interfere with client autonomy, but rather seeks to assure that clients make decisions based on realistic predictions.

When calling seeming mispredictions to clients' attention, one way to preserve rapport is to explicitly and empathically acknowledge the

clients decision making process before a client actually reaches a decision. For example, early on in a counseling session a client may identify a possible alternative that you know to be illegal. In such a circumstance you probably will immediately intervene by calling the client's attention to the illegality. However, to promote clarity of discussion, we have focused this discussion of intervention into clients decision making in the post decision context. What we say about intervention in this context is equally applicable to the pre-decision contexts.

25. Of course, the client's prediction might be based on some other data such as how the corporation has responded to similar offers in the past. But this example assumes that the client's prediction is focused on how a particular corporate officer is likely to respond. For the difficulties involved in predicting likely corporate responses see Timothy F. Malloy, *Regulating by Incentives: Myths, Models and Micromarkets*, 80 Tex. L. Rev. 531, at (2002).

soundness of their objectives. Then, advise clients of what you regard as more likely consequences, and the reasons for your beliefs. Finally, offer clients an opportunity to re-evaluate the situation.[26] Since "how" you say something can be as important as "what" you say, match your demeanor to your words. Pounding your desk to emphasize the errors of clients' ways or threatening to play recorded versions of "West's Dicennial Digests" until clients change their minds are inappropriate methods of persuasion.

For example, to call the misprediction about the consequences of not taking depositions to Barry's attention, you might say something like,

> Your desire to keep pretrial costs low and to communicate your willingness to settle on reasonable terms are good ideas. I have mentioned these points to Minton's attorney a number of times, and perhaps they'll eventually come around. But I have to tell you that in my view it is highly unlikely that not taking depositions will induce Minton to make an acceptable settlement offer. My experience suggests that if anything, Minton may take a harder line because his lawyers will see our doing nothing further as an indication that we believe we have a weak case and realize that we will be less prepared to go to trial if the case doesn't settle. As a consequence, probably they are going to push Minton to take an even more aggressive stance. You may know Minton better than I, but I've had some past dealings with the lawyers representing Minton; they are competitive, tough people who often urge clients to adopt hard line positions. With these lawyers representing Minton, I don't believe forgoing depositions will accomplish what you want.

> Now, if you decide at the end of the day that you don't want to go ahead with depositions, then of course that is certainly what we'll do. But given what I've told you, does it seem worthwhile to talk about the possibility of taking depositions a bit more?

This statement empathizes with Barry's ultimate objective, points out why you believe that the decision is unlikely to further it, and invites Barry to reconsider.[27] At the same time, you reassure Barry that the decision is his to make and that you will abide by it.[28]

26. In some instances, of course, you may not have a basis for making predictions that are different from those made by a client. Rather, your intervention will be based on your observation that a client lacks the information necessary for making a sound prediction. In these instances, you will limit your intervention to calling such an absence to the client's attention and then asking the client to reconsider the decision.

27. The statement does nothing more than invite the consideration of other options, because presumably none of the options are likely to accomplish the client's ultimate objective. Had there been such an option, the statement could have referred to it.

28. Should clients such as Barry stick with decisions that you regard as based on mispredictions, you may ask clients to acknowledge in writing that you reviewed with them the risks that the decisions would not achieve their desired aims. Such "defensive lawyering" unfortunately may be necessary in an era in which clients are all too ready to blame lawyers for failing to achieve the clients' objectives when the clients' own choices were the real culprits. The risk of course is that your tactic may damage rapport.

Recognize that intervening in decisions that you find troubling is no guarantee that clients will change their minds and come around to your way of thinking. In the end you may sometimes find yourself implementing decisions that you do not think are in clients' best interests.

2. *Mispredictions and "Cognitive Illusions"*

Continuing social science research suggests that lawyers and clients may arrive at different decisions because of the biasing effects of "cognitive illusions." Either lawyers or clients might be susceptible to the influence of heuristics[29] that from a strictly rational perspective cause them to reach illogical conclusions.[30] Nonetheless, to the extent that you as the lawyer are less susceptible to the influence of such heuristics than your clients,[31] you may be able to take steps to help serve clients' needs. This section describes some of the most common cognitive illusions. Section 3 below provides suggestions for how you might respond when you become aware that they have become significant factors in clients' thinking.[32]

Understand at the outset, however, that what constitutes a cognitive illusion may be in the eye of the beholder. Decisions are generally thought to be "rational" when they are consistent with "expected value analysis," an outcome that focuses on whether decisions maximize

---

29. Heuristics are simply "rules of thumb," or short cuts to decision-making that everyday living ingrains in us. For example, "loudness" may be a heuristic that you might use when deciding whether to go to a certain restaurant. See Daniel Kahneman & Amos Tversky, *On the Psychology of Prediction*, 80 PSYCHOL. REV. 237 (1973).

30. Daniel Kahneman and Amos Tversky pioneered the study of cognitive illusions and are the scions of all who have followed and created what is now a vast literature. To begin near the beginning, see Daniel Kahneman and Amos Tversky, *Prospect Theory: An Analysis of Decision Under Risk*, 47 ECONOMETRICA 263 (1979). Cognitive illusions have also been termed "Cognitive Biases" and/or "Cognitive Fallacies." See generally MAX H. BAZERMAN, JUDGMENT IN MANAGERIAL DECISION MAKING 5th Ed. (2002) (explaining cognitive fallacies). Other sources include CHOICES, VALUES AND FRAMES (Daniel Kaheman and Amos Tversky eds., 2000); Philip E. Tetlock and Barbara A. Mellers, *The Great Rationality Debate*, 13 PSYCHOLOGICAL SCIENCE 94 (2002).

31. Some studies indicate that lawyers are less susceptible than clients to cognitive illusions. See e.g. Russell Korobkin and Chris Guthrie, *supra* note 8 at 113. ("Our lawyer subjects were affected to nearly the same degree as our litigant subject by the

framing, anchoring and equity-seeking variables tested.") However, other studies suggest that lawyers make many of the same cognitive mistakes as do lay people. See e.g., Jeffrey J. Rachlinski, *The Uncertain Psychological Case for Paternalism*, 97 Nw. U. L. REV. 1165, 1217 (2003).

32. As the use of the phrase "significant factor in clients' thinking" implies, you certainly need not try to offset the impact of cognitive illusions at the first indication that clients' thinking reflects their impact. In the course of counseling conversations, clients may well make statements that are consistent with the presence of a cognitive illusion. For example, a client who is thinking about whether to accept a settlement offer may say something like, "One reason that maybe I should refuse the offer and go to trial is that I've already put over $10,000 into this case and I don't want to see it go to waste." Such a statement is consistent with the "sunk costs" cognitive illusion, described below. However, whether you respond to the illusion is a matter of judgment. If the client is "free associating" through a variety of factors, you may reasonably decide not to address the "sunk costs" illusion. On the other hand, if the discussion suggests that the illusion is a significant factor in the client's thinking, you may want to address it using one of the strategies described below.

clients' economic positions.[33] As you would expect, lawyers tend to prefer decisions that are in this sense rational.[34] However, clients' failure to make decisions that conform to expected value analysis does not necessarily indicate that clients are irrational or subject to the influence of cognitive illusions. Rather, clients' "irrational" decisions may simply reflect different sets of values. For example, a client may accept a settlement offer out of sympathy for an adverse party, even though the offer fails to maximize the client's financial position.[35]

The subsections below examine cognitive illusions that commonly arise in the course of attorney-client counseling.

a. The Sunk Costs Phenomenon

The sunk costs phenomenon is the equivalent of the old phrase, "throwing good money after bad." That is, having already committed money or other resources to a project, clients may continue to do so rather than face up to the reality that they cannot recoup their investment.[36] The sunk cost phenomenon distorts the decision-making process because clients focus on what they've already invested rather than on the likely consequences of the currently available options.

For example, assume that Johnson has spent considerable time and money trying to put together a business deal. Based on the investment of time and money he has already expended on the deal, Johnson may decide to continue trying to put the deal together even if from a rational perspective Johnson's time would be better spent on an alternative deal with better prospects. What may have happened is that the "sunk costs" phenomenon has led Johnson to focus on what he has previously expended with the thought that those past expenditures increase the likelihood of ultimate success.[37] Similarly, a litigation client may reject a settlement offer because it fails to cover moneys already spent, even though rationally the offer has a higher economic value to the client than the most likely outcome of trial.

b. The Gambler's Fallacy

This illusion involves misconceptions of chance. For example, poker players may believe that having been dealt five weak hands in a row increases the odds that the next hand will be strong. Rationally, such a

---

33. For a discussion of what many agree are the six principles of rational decision-making, see Scott Plous, The Psychology of Judgment and Decision Making 81–82 (1993). The principles include ordering of alternatives, dominance, cancellation, transitivity, continuity and invariance.

34. See Korobkin & Guthrie, *supra* note 8, at 137.

35. For a discussion of how you should respond when clients express values that differ from yours, see Sec. 5 *infra*.

36. *See* Hammond, et al., *supra* note 12, at 195. See Max H. Bazerman, *supra* note 30,

at 76–78; Russell Korobkin and Thomas S. Ulen, *Law and Behavioral Science: Removing the Rationality Assumption From Law and Economics*, 88 Cal. L. Rev. 1051, 1124–1125 (2000).

37. Of course, Johnson's prior expenditures may have placed him in a better position to conclude the deal than when he started. On the other hand, those expenditures may have no connection with the probability of his ultimately concluding the proposed deal.

belief is incorrect. Each deal of cards is independent from every other deal, so as a result the cards in the previous five deals have no effect on the likely result of the sixth hand. In other words, at the beginning of each deal, the odds of obtaining a strong hand are no different from what they were on each of the prior occasions.[38]

Clients too may engage in this kind of thinking. For example, a litigation client may say something like, "We've lost these kinds of cases four times in a row. We're bound to win this one."

c. The Endowment Effect[39]

Research strongly indicates that people tend to place a greater economic value on items they own than on those that they do not.[40] As a result, people tend to want more for their property than they would be willing to pay for it if they had to purchase it on the open market. Because people under this illusion tend to believe that their property has special value, they therefore tend to reject offers that the market might see as fair.[41] Thus, the endowment effect may cause a property owner to refuse an offer that reflects the property's fair market value, even if that same owner would not make a higher offer were the owner seeking to purchase the same property. Similarly, a litigant's distorted sense of the value of a case might lead the litigant to refuse a settlement offer that the litigant would think fair were the litigant to view the worth of the case from a juror's neutral perspective.[42]

The effect of the endowment illusion seems to vary depending on the context. Thus "experimenters have ... found that the endowment effect is more robust for entitlements with no close market substitutes than for goods that have close substitutes or are themselves readily purchasable."[43]

d. The Overconfidence Phenomenon

People who know the odds of a particular event coming to pass nevertheless tend to predict without any evidence for doing so that they will beat the odds. For instance, a person may believe that "good things are more likely to happen to me than to the average person and bad things are less likely than average to happen to me."[44] And most people believe that they are above average drivers, which by definition cannot be accurate.

---

38. See BAZERMAN, *supra* note 30, at 20–23.

39. This illusion is sometimes referred to as the "Status Quo Bias" although that bias is perhaps slightly broader than the endowment bias. See Russell Korobkin, *The Endowment Effect and Legal Analysis*, 97 Nw. U. L. R. 1227 at 1236 (2003).

40. See Korobkin, *supra* note 39; Korobkin & Ulen, *supra* note 36 at 1108.

41. People are not necessarily "irrational" when they attach special values to their own goods. For example, regardless of what

"the market" thinks that a piece of land is worth, the owners of the land who raised their children on it may quite rationally be unwilling to part with it simply for the "fair market price" because the land has a psychological "added value" for its owners that the market would not recognize.

42. See Korobkin & Ulen, *supra* note 36, at 1108.

43. Korobkin, *supra* note 39, at 1238.

44. See Korobkin & Ulen, *supra* note 36 at 1091.

The relevance of this cognitive illusion to clients faced with making decisions is readily apparent. A litigation client, for example, may be inclined to reject a settlement offer in the belief that a judge will uphold the legality of a non-competition clause, despite your informing the client that judges regularly invalidate such clauses. Similarly, a client seeking to rent space to open a new restaurant may want to agree to unfavorable terms in the belief that her restaurant will do much better business than previous restaurants in the same site.

e. *Self–Serving Bias*

Closely related to the overconfidence phenomenon is "self-serving bias," which tends to lead decision-makers to put unwarranted stock in the rightness of their causes and the strengths of their claims.[45] For example, two individuals with opposing views on the wisdom of capital punishment may examine identical statistics and both think that the statistics support their attitudes. Similarly, fans of opposing teams may watch the same game yet be convinced that the referees unduly favored the opponent. This cognitive function operates to inflate decision-makers' perceptions of why the facts of a case necessarily cut in their favor.[46] Thus, since this form of bias also tends to lead decision-makers to interpret ambiguous cues or evidence as confirming their views, this psychological force is sometimes called the "confirming evidence trap."[47]

f. *The Anchoring Effect*

This cognitive illusion refers to decision makers' tendency to allow information to which they have previously been exposed to "anchor" their expectations. Typically, the phenomenon grows out of the "power of numbers," which often leads people to see a relationship between numbers and reality even though the numbers are in fact irrelevant. For example, professional accountants asked to estimate the extent of fraud among business executives gave very different answers depending on whether the question asked whether fraud occurs in "more than ten out of a thousand companies" or in "more than two hundred out of two thousand companies." The higher anchor of "two hundred" produced far higher estimates of the extent of fraud, even though the numbers of ten and two hundred were irrelevant to the actual extent of fraud.[48]

45. See Korobkin & Ulen, *supra* note 36 at 1091.

46. *See id.* Researchers demonstrated this point with the following experiment. Groups of undergraduates were assigned randomly to groups, and given identical folders with information about a lawsuit pending before a judge. Their task was to estimate the amount of damages the judge would order (liability was conceded). One group was randomly assigned to pretend to be the plaintiff; the other, the defendant. Based on this random assignment, and with no other investment in the case, the plaintiff group estimated the worth of the case substantially higher than did the defendant group. In a control variation, the two groups were not told that they were to identify with a party until just before the end of the evaluation process. In that variation, the differences between the groups was not significant.

47. Hammond, et al., *supra* note 12, at 198.

48. See Korobkin & Ulen, *supra* note 36 at 1100.

The anchoring effect may apply in an array of common legal settings. For example, a personal injury client's expectations of the ultimate settlement figure (or the outcome of trial) may be different depending on whether the adversary's initial settlement offer is $50,000 or $250,000. Similarly, a property owner's expectations about the length of a lease that a prospective tenant may ultimately agree to may be influenced by whether the tenant initially proposes a one year or a five year lease.

3. *De–Biasing Strategies*

Cognitive illusions such as those described above tend to be so ingrained in decision-makers' thinking that they operate on the subconscious level. While cognitive illusions may also influence your own thinking, awareness of their existence may render you less susceptible to them than many of your clients.[49] This section describes potential de-biasing strategies you may employ when you become aware that cognitive illusions are affecting significant aspects of clients' decision-making processes.

Research studies permit a "tentative conclusion that, at least in some circumstances, lawyers taking an active role in their client's litigation decision-making processes *probably* can affect the extent to which psychological factors … motivate litigants' ultimate decisions."[50] However, the general effectiveness of de-biasing strategies is uncertain.[51] For example, in some contexts use of de-biasing strategies can lead to worse outcomes.[52] Moreover, their effectiveness is likely to be highly context-dependent. That is, a de-biasing strategy that may be effective in one context may impede good judgment in others.[53] And clients may persist with seemingly "irrational" decisions that are in fact completely rational because their values are broader than simply economic interests. For instance, clients who highly value achieving peaceful resolutions of disputes may opt for settlements that seem less than optimal from the perspective of the comparison of a settlement offer to a likely trial verdict. In all such situations, client-centeredness dictates that clients' values should generally prevail.

a. *Lawyer as Educator*

The "Lawyer as Educator" strategy is one that you may use in an effort to de-bias cognitive illusions such as Sunk Costs and the Gambler's Fallacy.[54] Through the use of this strategy, you attempt to alter clients' thinking by explaining the cognitive illusions that you think are

---

49. See Korobkin & Guthrie, *supra* note 8, at 87.

50. *Id.* at 120 (italics in original).

51. Experienced researchers agree that cognitive reasoning is a complex topic, and certainty about superior and inferior reasoning methods is impossible. See, e.g. Jeffrey J. Rachlinski, *supra* note 31 at 1207–1214.

52. *Id.* at 1222. (Study showing that de-biasing the self-serving bias in a litigation context produced lowered settlement amounts for the de-biased litigants.)

53. *Id.* at 1210.

54. The term is borrowed from Korobkin and Guthrie, *supra* note 8 at 115.

leading to irrational decisions. For example, you might tell a client whose thinking reflects the "sunk costs" phenomenon something along these lines:

> Where you seem to be going is rejecting the settlement offer. A major factor in your thinking seems to be that going to trial gives you a chance to recoup all the money you've spent on this case already. Now, if proceeding to trial is your final decision of course that's what we'll do. But first let me mention a common factor that may be affecting your thinking. It's sometimes referred to as sunk costs, but the label really doesn't matter. The basic idea is that people sometimes focus too much on money and time they've already put into a case. They believe they have to keep going given all the time, money and effort they've put into a case. What you've already put into this case has brought us to where we are now. We can't change what's already happened. Instead, you should be thinking about what's likely to work out best for the future given where the case stands at this point. Now from that standpoint, let's compare the settlement offer to what's likely to happen at trial. As I've said, I think if this case goes to trial I think. . . .

Here, you educate the client by briefly describing the sunk costs illusion, and then suggest that the client focus more "rationally" on comparing the proposed settlement with the probable outcome of trial.

You can adapt the "lawyer as educator" strategy to each client's particular situation. In the example below you use the strategy with a client who appears to be a victim of the gambler's fallacy.

> Sarah, I realize that the presence of homeless people on the side-walks of the streets surrounding the mall that your company manages may be damaging to the ambience that you are trying to maintain. But asking your security personnel to prevent them from keeping their shopping carts on the surrounding sidewalks is only likely to create legal problems for you. Your management company has tried to do something like this a couple of times in the past two to three years in your downtown mall, and each time a civil liberties group got a court order upholding the rights of the homeless. Your company even had to pay some damages and court costs. What you've been suggesting is that this time the outcome will be different. You don't think you'll lose three times in a row, because a judge is bound to realize that enjoining your past efforts to deal with homeless people has made the problem worse. Unfortunately, I have to tell you that I don't think the outcome will be different this time. What you seem to be thinking is that the third time will be a charm, that having lost twice in the past you're bound to win this time. But the most important factor is that the basic First Amendment principle that led to the prior court orders hasn't changed a bit. Your chances of winning this time are no better than they were before. I have to tell you that if you start this policy again, you will almost certainly lose again.

b. Consider the Other Side

A second potential de-biasing strategy is entitled "Consider the Other Side." This strategy may be effective with clients operating under such illusions as the "endowment effect," the "overconfidence" bias, and/or the "self serving bias." As you recall, these illusions tend to lead clients to see their positions in an overly favorable light. Use of the "Consider The Other Side" strategy may help clients reconsider their predictions from a more realistic perspective.[55]

As the title suggests, this strategy entails explicitly asking clients to consider problems from their adversaries' perspectives. Use of the strategy may run some risk that clients will see you as overly sympathetic to the other side. Therefore, when you use this strategy assure clients of your loyalty and desire to help them achieve satisfactory results.[56]

The following example illustrates how you might use the "consider the other side strategy" with a client who appears to be influenced by the endowment bias.

1. L: Bob, at this point you seem inclined to lease the property only if Emerson agrees to pay $3.00 a square foot. You've said several times that they don't really understand how unique the Broadway property really is. Now, I think you should make a deal only if it provides what you consider to be a satisfactory return. On the other hand, I do want you to fully consider this matter before you make a final decision. So let's just for the moment look at the property from Emerson's perspective to try to understand how likely it is that Emerson will consider Broadway as special. We know they've looked at other possible downtown locations, so as compared to those locations what might Emerson see as particularly outstanding about the Broadway property?

2. C: The greater amount of foot traffic we get as compared to those other locations.

3. L: That certainly could be important. Anything else that stands out in your mind as unique about Broadway?

4. C: The way I maintain the common areas. I take special pride in that.

5. L: Great, I'll add that to my list here. Anything else you can think of?

6. C: Not really.

---

55. Obviously the ultimate success of this strategy will depend strongly on a client's ability to get out of his or her "own shoes."

56. See Charles Lord, Mark R. Lepper & Elizabeth Preston, *Considering the Opposite: A Corrective Strategy for Social Judgment*, 47 J. Personality & Soc. Psychol. 1231 (1984).

7. L: Then let's go back to your point about foot traffic. Looking at it from Emerson's perspective, how important is the amount of foot traffic likely to be to Emerson?

8. C: Somewhat, but from what I understand most of their customers come into their stores in response to sales promotions and Emerson's reputation.

9. L: If you were in Emerson's position, then, would you be willing to pay a premium for rent based on the amount of foot traffic that the Broadway location generates?

10. C: Well, maybe not.

11. L: And what about maintenance of the common areas? How big a part is that likely to play in Emerson's thinking?

12. C: I think that can be important because I know that Emerson depends on its reputation and is seeking to expand into new areas of the city, and I think that Emerson would view our common areas as a definite plus.

13. L: So from Emerson's perspective the way you maintain the common areas might help justify the amount of rent you are seeking?

14. C: I do.

15. L: That's fine. What that suggests is that we try to get Emerson's people to realize the comparative value of the way we maintain the common areas, and downplay the level of foot traffic. Does that make sense?

16. C: Makes sense. Here's one idea on that . . .

Here you combine your suggestion that Bob look at the deal from Emerson's perspective with a motivational statement that doing so may produce support for the uniqueness of the property. At the same time you assure Bob of your allegiance.[57] Using the T-funnel technique, you then elicit information about the factors that Bob sees as making the property unique and then turn to whether Emerson will view the factors in the same way that Bob does.[58]

57. In contrast to the statement used in the lawyer as educator example, here you say nothing about the possibility that a cognitive illusion may be playing a role. Here you say nothing such as "a common factor that may be affecting your thinking is what is called the endowment effect." Whether such an omission is or is not a good idea is not clear. See Lord et. al. *supra* note 56.

58. Our colleague Kenneth Klee points out that transactional clients often encounter negotiation difficulties because their lawyers do not help them see the advantages of thinking about the other side's perspective at the negotiation planning stage.

In this next, example, your client Mary appears to be influenced by the overconfidence and self serving illusions:

1. L: Mary, you've said several times that you feel Tolliver was totally unjustified in firing you and that the jury is certain to see things in your favor, so you're leaning toward rejecting their settlement offer and proceeding to trial. Now, I think we can present a strong case and if that's your decision I'm with you all the way. But if it's OK with you I'd like us to do a final check before we reject the offer. Let's look at the case that Tolliver will present, because that's what the jury will see. That'll help us understand what we'll be up against at trial and how we're planning to respond. Is this okay?

2. C: OK, but as I say I don't see how we can lose.

3. L: Well, one thing Tolliver will rely on is that, as you admit, on that day that your boss, Katherine, asked Tulsi to work overtime, you called Katherine a sorry excuse for a supervisor and said she was too lazy to do her own work.

4. C: No question that's what I said. I said it because it was true.

5. L: And that will be one of our arguments. But one thing Tolliver is likely to argue is that your comments caused others to stop working and spend time talking about whether or not Katherine was being fair to Tulsi. Do you agree they will make that argument?

6. C: Sure. But that's not my fault. I can't help what others do.

7. L: That's a response we can make, but remember that you'd previously been told that if you had criticisms of Katherine you should take them to her boss, Mr. Fairchild?

8. C: But it was after 4:00 and Tulsi had to leave by 5:00 to be able to pick up her daughter. I didn't have time to talk with Fairchild.

9. L: Still, they'll argue that you should have talked to Katherine privately in her office, not in front of other workers.

10. C: I guess that's a point.

11. L: Is there anything we can say about why you didn't go to Katherine in her office rather than in front of your co-workers?

12. C: Not really; I guess I just lost it.

13. L: You were really frustrated. This isn't to criticize you, but just to help us evaluate where we stand by looking at the case from Tolliver's perspective. Let's turn briefly to one other issue . . .

Here, you attempt to preserve rapport and client confidence by agreeing that Mary has a strong case and expressing your willingness to carry out her final decision. Your motivational statement helps Mary to understand what she has to gain by examining her adversary's perspective. The remainder of the conversation elicits likely arguments and responses, hopefully helping Mary evaluate her case more realistically. Even if Mary may at the end of the day rejects the settlement offer, at least you have done your best to reduce the likelihood that her decision is a product of a cognitive illusion.

B. "IMMORAL" DECISIONS

To this point, the chapter has examined situations in which clients' mispredictions may make it appropriate for you to intervene in decision-making. Separate sets of issues arise when you have moral qualms with clients' decisions. In such situations, you cannot justify intervention on the rationale that decisions conflict with clients' objectives and best interests. Rather, raising moral concerns rests on the concept that like clients, you too are an autonomous individual whose values and broader social concerns deserve respect.[59] At the same time, as an agent you cannot be a "moral know-it-all" who tries to bend all clients to your moral visions. Formal ethical rules offer little guidance on how to navigate between moral blindness and moral domination.[60] This section explores how you might conduct effective "moral dialogues" in the context of client-centeredness.[61]

Generally, among the principles you can follow to conduct effective "moral dialogues" are the following:

- Point out that while you have some concerns, final calls are for clients to make and you will implement the clients' decisions.[62]

    Example: "I'd like to talk a little more about having these workers sign agreements acknowledging that they are independent contractors rather than employees. Of course if you contin-

---

59. See William H. Simon, *Ethical Discretion in Lawyering*, 101 Harv. L. Rev. 1083 (1988). This understanding of your right as a professional to your own moral integrity is a growing subject of discussion in legal ethics literature. *See, e.g.,* David Luban, Lawyers and Justice: An Ethical Study (1988); Deborah L. Rhode, In the Interests of Justice: Reforming the Legal Profession (2000); William H. Simon, The Practice of Justice: A Theory of Lawyer's Ethics (1998).

60. Rule 1.2 of the Model Rules of Professional Responsibility provides a general overview of lawyer/client decision-making roles but has little to say about moral disputes.

61. The conducting of "moral dialogues" has been promoted by Tom Shaffer, among others. *See, e.g.,* Thomas L. Shaffer, *The Ethics of Radical Individualism*, 65 Tex. L. Rev. 963 (1987).

62. On some occasions your moral disagreement may be so strong that you seek to withdraw.

ue to think that that's the best way to go then of course I'll prepare the documents accordingly."[63]

- Avoid use of the term "moral." Its use may exacerbate tensions rather than promote client openness.

    Example: In the hypothetical above, avoid making a statement such as, "Frankly, I have some moral concerns about your wanting to have these workers sign agreements acknowledging that they are independent contractors rather than employees." Instead, you might say something like, "If I understand this right, having the workers acknowledge that they are independent contractors rather than employees leaves them unprotected in a lot of important ways. I worry about the unfairness of the plan to the workers. Can we talk a bit about that?"

- Acknowledge the legitimacy of clients' objectives.[64]

    Example: "So long as we structure the agreements and the work assignments properly, you are certainly within your legal rights to establish these workers as independent contractors."

Adherence to these principles enhances the likelihood that clients will "hear" what you have to say and thus consider your views seriously.

For example, assume that you represent Ari, the owner of a shopping center, who has filed suit against Diana, the owner of an adjoining shopping center. The suit claims that Diana damaged Ari's business by erecting a fence along the property line that divides the two shopping centers, cutting off car access from one of the city's main commercial thoroughfares into Ari's center. Since filing the suit, Diana has offered to tear down the fence, which was built because troublemakers attracted to a bar in Ari's center were harassing customers and employees in Diana's center. (The businesses in Diana's center cater largely to senior citizens.) Diana asks that after the fence is torn down, Ari share in the cost of a private security service for both shopping centers. Ari has tentatively decided to reject Diana's offer, knowing that with the small rents of the traditional shops in Diana's center, the costs of a prolonged suit will probably compel her to sell the center. Ari hopes to buy it, evict the present tenants, and convert the center to an extension of his more upscale concept.

Assume further that you agree that Ari's prediction is likely to be correct: prolonging the suit may well force Diana to sell. However, Ari's decision is inimical to your values. The fence, though perhaps improper, was at least erected for understandable motives. Moreover, as Diana's

---

63. As many writers have noted, frequently a moral dialogue demonstrates that our clients are as interested in doing what's right as we are. You cannot assume that clients always want to maximize their interests at the expense of fairness or respect for others. *See, e.g.,* Roy Stuckey, *Understanding Casablanca: A Values-Based Approach* to Legal Negotiations, 5 CLINICAL L. REV. 211 (1998); Stephen Ellman, *Symposium: Case Studies in Legal Ethics: Truth and Consequences,* 69 FORDHAM L. REV. 895 (2000).

64. Again, this principle assumes of course that clients' goals are in fact legitimate.

shopping center is one of the few in the city that caters to elderly customers; you want Diana's center to continue to operate. In these circumstances, you might say to Ari something along these lines:

> Ari, I fully understand your desire to maximize the profitability of your center. Your goal of buying Diana's center is an important and legally legitimate one. But I worry about what it might mean for that neighborhood. Her offer to share the costs of the security service now that she has removed the fence seems a fair one to me. Your plan seems like it will lead her to go out of business, and that would hurt a lot of older folks who come to her stores. Have you thought about the harm that this strategy you are proposing will create for Diana and her elderly customers?

This statement recognizes the legitimacy of Ari's values, and without using the term "moral" conveys your disagreement with his tentative decision and expresses competing values.[65]

As when you probe cognitive illusions, intervening in decisions that you disagree with is no guarantee that clients will change their minds and come around to your way of thinking. Thus, unless you intend to withdraw as counsel, you may find yourself implementing decisions that you disagree with.[66]

5. ACCEPTING DIFFERENCES IN RISK AVERSION & VALUES

This section briefly examines three common situations in which client-centeredness suggests that you should not intervene in decisions with which you disagree.

A. RISK AVERSION

"Risk Aversion" refers to people's willingness to take risks. You may prefer a bird in the hand to two in the bush; a client may opt to pass on the one in the hope of getting the two. Thus, you may find yourself in disagreement with clients' decisions not because clients' mis-predict outcomes but rather because clients are more or less willing than you to take risks. For example, clients may well understand that a decision has a low chance of accomplishing their objectives but choose to run the risk. Moreover, clients may tend to be particularly risk averse when a decision may produce a "catastrophic" result, even if the likelihood of that result coming to pass is relatively small.[67] In such situations, you effectively

---

65. If Ari persists in his plans, notwithstanding the harm that will befall Diana and her customers, you would have to decide whether you would withdraw as his attorney, assuming you could properly do so. For whatever it's worth, the authors would withdraw in this case. The Model Rules would permit doing so under these circumstances. *See* MODEL RULES PROF'L CONDUCT R. 1.16(b)(4)(2002)(termination of rep-

resentation permitted if "the client insists upon taking action . . . with which the lawyer has a fundamental disagreement").

66. For a discussion of the principles and ethics rules governing withdrawing as counsel, see Comment to ABA Model Rules of Prof'l Conduct 1.16.

67. For example, a client may be willing to "roll the dice" on the outcome of trial when the worst possible outcome is a fine of

discharge your duty to give clients a "reasonable opportunity to decide" by thoroughly exploring potential outcomes and the likelihood of their occurring.

For example, return to Barry, the litigation client who has decided not to take depositions. Assume that you have pointed out that Barry lacks an adequate database for predicting that his adversary Minton will be so impressed with that decision that Minton is likely to increase a settlement offer. Nevertheless, Barry continues to believe that not taking depositions is the best approach. To clarify the basis of Barry's decision, you may say something along these lines:

> If you recognize that refusing to take depositions has only a slight chance of inducing Minton to make a reasonable settlement offer, and decide to take the risk that we'll be less prepared for trial, that is fine; you are entitled to do so. My main concern is that you not decide against depositions based on what seems to me an erroneous assumption about how Minton will react. Just so we're clear, you're prepared to take that risk? If you are, I'll certainly go along with it.

An affirmative response suggests that Barry understands the riskiness of the decision and opts to take that risk. You have thus afforded Barry a reasonable opportunity to decide, and in your role as counselor you can do little more.[68]

B. VALUE DIFFERENCES

Value conflicts are a second common source of disagreement between attorneys and clients. Such conflicts may relate to matters of substance, e.g., you think it in a client's best interests to maximize monetary recovery whereas the client proposes to accept less money in order to promote a future relationship. Or, value conflicts may relate to matters of procedure, such as whether or not to employ an aggressive style of negotiation.[69] In either event, when such conflicts do arise, client-centeredness dictates that you generally accede to your clients' values.

$200. However, that same client may be anxious to settle prior to trial when the trial's worst possible outcome is a lengthy prison sentence. For a discussion of factors that affect risk averseness, see Paul Slovik, Baruch Fischhoff, Sarah Lichtenstein, *Facts Versus Fears: Understanding Perceived Risk* at 463, in JUDGMENT UNDER UNCERTAINTY: HEURISTICS AND BIASES (Daniel Kahneman, Paul Slovic, Amos Tversky, eds., 1982)

68. A practical reality is that even client-centered lawyers sometimes do recommend that clients reconsider "mispredicted" decisions. However, do so only when you think that clients' decisions are grossly ill-conceived and likely to create substantial harm to their interests. Moreover, before suggesting that a risk is not worth taking, be confident that you have a sufficient basis

in law and practical experience for doing so. Finally, on those occasions when you do ask clients to reconsider, preface your remarks by assuring clients that you have their best interests in mind and discuss the harms that you foresee and why you think that they are likely to occur. (For a research study indicating that lawyers' recommendations tend to have an effect on client decision-making, see Korobkin & Guthrie, *supra* note 8, at 117–129).

69. For an example of possible differences in negotiation strategy that Americans might take account of when negotiating joint venture agreements in China, see Edward R.J. Neunuebel, *Foreign Direct Invest Vehicles in China* in DOING BUSINESS IN CHINA (Li Yong & Jonathan Reuvid eds., 4th ed. 2000)

For example, assume that you represent a plaintiff who wants to settle for much less than the plaintiff is likely to recover at trial because the defendant promptly apologized and had a sympathetic excuse for behaving carelessly.[70] Perhaps you disagree with the client's desire to settle "on the cheap." However, the client appears to value fairness and taking responsibility over maximizing financial gain. If so, accept the client's decision. You thereby allow clients to decide on the basis of those values that provide maximum satisfaction.[71] Similar considerations militate in favor of your accepting the decision of a client who is an injured consumer to accept a settlement that creates an injunction that favors future consumers over the client's personal financial interests.

C. CULTURAL DIFFERENCES

Value conflicts may stem from divergent cultural norms. Traditional American cultural norms tend to put more faith in the importance of "objective facts" than do the cultural norms of many other countries.[72] This reality may create conflicts when you represent clients who identify with cultures from other countries. For example, assume that you represent a U.S. resident who grew up in a foreign country who plans to manufacture and export tools to the client's country of origin. In discussing upcoming negotiations with your client, you indicate that you plan to stress the importance of fixed costs for justifying the products' wholesale prices. The client, however, may respond by telling you that retail merchants in the client's country of origin are unlikely to be impressed by statements based on objective facts such as fixed costs. Rather, the client suggests that given the importance that people in the client's country of origin place on making people more productive, you should emphasize the tools' capacity to increase productivity. Your client's knowledge of values in his home country should trump your sense of the usefulness of stressing fixed costs.[73]

6. THE BORDERLAND OF INTERVENTION

On the borderland of intervention lie situations when clients' proposed decisions contravene your views as to what is in the bests interests of third parties or society as a whole, but seem neither immoral in most peoples' eyes nor illegal nor based on mis-prediction. Commentators who adhere to what has been termed a "contextual" approach to client counseling suggest that lawyers have an ethical obligation to advise clients about what the lawyers think would be fair and congruent with

---

70. Korobkin & Ulen, *supra* note 36, at 111.

71. This proposition assumes, of course, that prior to the actual decision the counseling process has brought to the client's attention the fact that the client is surrendering some likely economic gain and that the client has had a chance to think about the consequences of such a surrender. For a

further discussion of exploring consequences, see Chapter 19.

72. See Terri Morrison, Wayne A. Conaway and George A. Borden, Kiss, Bow Or Shake Hands: How To Do Business In Sixty Countries at xii (1994).

73. For a more comprehensive discussion of cultural differences that may result in value differences, see Chapter 2.

the best interests of society, the extent of the obligation depending on the contexts in which problems arise.[74] These commentators suggest that clients can benefit from such advice, "even in contexts where their decision is not clearly immoral or illegal."[75] If clients refuse to accede to their lawyers' views of what is right and just, the lawyers should discontinue their representation.[76]

Talking to clients about how their decisions may harm innocent third parties or even society as a whole can be compatible with client-centeredness.[77] After all, client-centeredness contemplates that lawyers talk to clients about non-legal consequences and the potential consequences of proposed decisions for third parties.[78] However, what the contextualists and other "moral activists" frequently fail to acknowledge is that what initially appear to involve disputes about values often boil down to factual conflicts. For example, assume that you represent a client who asks you to seek a variance from a rule that limits the discharge of emissions that the client's plant is allowed to produce. A contextualist might urge you to try to convince your client that the plan contravenes society's interest in a clean environment. The client, however, is unlikely to argue that "My value is to foul the environment." Rather, the client is more likely to point out how the variance will in the long run promote a clean environment or will promote other useful social goals, such as creating jobs. Even if you are unconvinced by the client's claims, you are unlikely to be so sure that the client is wrong that you are willing to send the client packing. Thus, the obvious unjustness of clients' positions that pervades so much of the moral activists' writings tends not to represent reality.

Another downside of the moral activists' approach is that followed to its logical conclusion, lawyers will represent clients only in situations in which the clients' moral values are largely congruent with those of their lawyers. That result may itself not be in the best interests of society. For one thing, society may be better off when lawyers represent clients whose values they may disagree with. That enhances the possibility that clients will at least hear about the unjustness that their decisions might produce, perhaps leading them to abandon or at least modify their decisions. Moreover, reasonable compromise may be less likely when not only clients but also their lawyers adhere to the same moral point of view.

Thus, while you should not act as a "hired gun" who is willing to carry out a client's bidding no matter what its harmful consequences, neither is it realistic or in society's best interests for you to be a "moral know it all" who can always be certain that clients' decisions are wrong

---

74. A frequent spokesperson for the contextualist approach is Deborah L. Rhode. See, e.g., DEBORAH L. RHODE, IN THE INTERESTS OF JUSTICE (2000).

75. See DEBORAH L. RHODE, *Ethics in Counseling*, 30 PEPPERDINE L. REV. 602, 608 (2003).

76. *Id.* at 607.

77. See Paul R. Tremblay, *Client-Centered Counseling and Moral Activism*, 30 PEPPERDINE L. REV. 615, 616–617 (2003).

78. See Chapters 14 and 17.

because they contravene your sense of what is fair and just. As a client-centered lawyer you are free to express your misgivings about clients' proposed decisions, whatever the source of those misgivings may be. At the same time, drawing moral lines in the sand will rarely be possible or wise.

7. COUNSELING "MY MIND IS MADE UP" CLIENTS

If indecisive clients are at one end of a continuum, clients who are certain of what they want to do even before discussions of options and consequences take place are at the other. For example, an estate planning client may state after brief discussion of her family situation and general financial condition that "I know just what I want to do, and that's leave everything to my youngest daughter. Can you write that up for me?" Or, a litigation client may dismiss your inquiry about taking depositions out of hand, saying something like "I've heard enough people talk about depositions that I know I have no desire to get involved with them. Whatever you do, no depositions."

If you know enough to realize that clients' pre-formed conclusions involve mis-prediction or "immorality," you may respond as set forth above. But what if you lack the data base for reaching such conclusions? Indeed, what if you think that clients' pre-formed choices are reasonable? Do you have an obligation to ensure that all decisions that are for clients to make are preceded by counseling dialogues?

The ABA Model Rules of Professional Conduct encourage lawyers to initiate decision-making dialogues and to exert their best efforts to ensure that clients are aware of relevant considerations before making decisions.[79] However, the Rules certainly do not mandate you to force clients to engage in counseling conversations before implementing their decisions. Moreover, as a standard that requires you to give clients a "reasonable opportunity to make decisions" suggests, whether and how much counseling you need to do depends on the circumstances of individual cases. For example:

- After minimal discussion about her family background and financial condition, a client previously unknown to you asks you to "write up a will leaving everything to my youngest daughter and call me when it's ready to sign." Prudent regard for ethical rules and your own career suggests that you decline the client's request until further counseling has occurred. With so little information, you are not even in a position to evaluate the client's legal capacity to make a will.

- In the same situation, sufficient counseling has occurred for you to be confident that the client has the legal capacity to make a will and that her wishes are legitimate. At the same time, the client expressly declines to hear about other options. Here, you might

---

79. Model Rules Prof'l Conduct R. 1.4 Cmt. [5], [6].

draft the will and prepare a letter for the client's signature acknowledging that she refused your request to talk about options other than a will.[80]

- A business client who you have previously represented in collection cases faxes you documents on a new similar matter, and notes on the fax cover sheet that you are to "handle per the usual." Assuming that nothing seems out of the ordinary, you may reasonably decide to go forward on the new matter in the absence of a counseling dialogue.

- In the same situation, the new collection matter is different in significant ways from those you have previously worked on for the same client. For instance, perhaps the new matter involves significantly more money, or collection procedures have changed substantially since you last handled a matter for this client. Such circumstances suggest that you contact the client for a review of options and consequences.

When you do feel the need to initiate counseling dialogues with clients who seemingly have their minds made up in advance, you may do so directly or obliquely. With a direct approach, you explicitly seek clients' verbal agreement to participate in counseling. You may enhance the chances of agreement by empathizing with clients' stated desires, acknowledging their right to make the final decisions, and citing rules laid down by an "absent third party."

For example, assume that you represent McGee, the litigation client who does not want even to discuss the adversary's offer of settlement. When you tell McGee about the offer, McGee responds, "That's not at all what I had in mind. I'm not letting those bastards get off this easy, and I don't even want to talk about it." While you do not think that McGee's rejection is necessarily wrong, you do believe the offer is significant enough that McGee ought to consider it seriously. Using a direct approach, you might tell McGee something like this:

> I understand your wanting to punish them for the injuries you've suffered. And after we discuss their offer a bit, you, of course, have the final word and can reject it. But this offer is a significant improvement over their previous one, and I think you owe it to yourself at least to consider it. Also, to fulfill my obligation as a lawyer I want to discuss with you some of the consequences of accepting and not accepting this offer before you reach your final decision. Can we talk about it a bit either now or sometime soon?

This statement empathizes with McGee's desires, emphasizes McGee's right to have the final say, and supports the need for a dialogue

---

80. Lawyers may write "CYA" letters such as this in an effort to avoid malpractice claims. *See* Mark C. Suchman, *Working Without a Net: The Sociology of Legal Ethics in Corporate Litigation,* 67 Fordham L. Rev. 837 (1998). A downside of this practice is that you may drive a wedge in your relationship with clients. A "note to the file" recounting your efforts may be an adequate alternative.

by mentioning an obligation created by an "absent third party."[81] Your goal is McGee's agreement to discuss the decision.

Using an oblique approach, you simply sashay into counseling dialogues without asking clients to agree to do so. While some may find this technique manipulative, it is nothing more than an attempt to carry out your ethical responsibilities. Moreover, that clients may have preconceived decisions in mind does not mean that they are dead set against discussion.

In the oblique approach, you again empathize with clients' objectives and emphasize that they have the final word. However, instead of seeking explicit agreement, you simply proceed to counseling by asking some questions. For example, return to the will client, Littleton, who states, "I know just what I want to do, and that's leave everything to my youngest daughter. Can you write that up for me?" You might respond:

> You must be very close to her. I'm glad to tell you that you are perfectly free to leave all your property to one child if that is what you wish. And, of course, you have the final say in how to leave your property. But tell me a little bit about what led you to this decision.

This statement opens up discussion of the decision without Littleton's agreement to do so. However, at least until Littleton objects, assuming that she has absolutely no interest in counseling seems incorrect.

---

81. In other situations, "law firm policies" or "my supervisor's practice," among other sources, can serve as "absent third parties."

Chapter 19

THE COUNSELING MODEL
AND LITIGATION

1. INTRODUCTION

This chapter explores how you might apply the counseling principles explored in Chapters 13 to 18 to typical decisions that arise in the course of litigation. Using a hypothetical case, the chapter explores decision-making at three different stages of a lawsuit. Admittedly, the hypothetical oversimplifies reality. For example, a few short pages of text cannot capture the judgments that you make continuously throughout counseling conversations and the vagaries inherent in all social interactions. However, examining counseling "snapshots" as a case unfolds over time may further your understanding of how common variables such as changed circumstances, decisions' apparent importance and clients' emotional involvement affect whether you have afforded clients a reasonable opportunity to make important decisions.[1]

2. A CASE STUDY: VITISSIAN v. LINUS HAULING CO. AND INDUSTRIAL RESOURCES CORP.

George Vitissian is a 48–year–old married man with two children. Until having recently been fired, he was President of Linus Hauling Co., a rubbish disposal company that is a division of Industrial Resources Corp. Linus's business consists of picking up and disposing of solid waste. For approximately a year before coming to Linus, George had been a Vice President of one of Linus's competitors, Dumpright. In his capacity as a Dumpright VP, George had consulted you on several occasions about contract and labor matters.

George came to see you shortly after he was sacked by Linus. His sacking was supposedly due to his poor management and a corresponding drop in Linus's revenues. However, George believes that he was fired in retaliation for actions he took after he learned that Linus was regularly engaged in secretly dumping Class II (toxic waste) materials into Class I landfills authorized only for non-toxic materials. George

---

1. See Chapter 13.

reported his discovery to Industrial Resources' President and said that he intended to cease the practice immediately. Resources' President said that Linus had done nothing wrong and that if George couldn't be a team player he'd be better off working elsewhere. A few days later, George was let go.

George is a college graduate who majored in engineering; he is articulate, self-assured and comfortable in his dealings with you. George belongs to a number of environmental organizations and one of his primary goals when he became President of Linus was to become a leader in the movement for greater cooperation between industrialists and environmentalists. Thus, he was angry and embarrassed to learn that Linus was engaged in illegal dumping, and to realize that despite Linus's carefully-crafted image of concern for the environment its primary response to his disclosure of illegal dumping was to fire him. After his termination, because George and his wife needed two incomes, George took a lower-salaried job as a Vice President with another Linus competitor, Cleanfill Co. However, George's primary regret is that since Cleanfill is a much smaller company than Linus, George is no longer in a position to have a major influence on corporations' environmental practices. Thus, George's primary goal is to regain his position as President of Linus.

Assume that under the law in your jurisdiction, dumping Class II materials into Class I landfills is unlawful, and that proof that George was fired for disclosing an illegal business practice would establish the tort of wrongful termination.

3.   "SNAPSHOT 1": WHETHER TO FILE SUIT

During an initial telephone conversation, George summarized what had happened and agreed to mail you copies of various documents substantiating Linus's illegal dumping of Class II materials. You agreed to meet with George after looking over the documents to talk over the options that might be available to him. The primary options that you have thought of include:

- George might file a lawsuit based on wrongful termination, seeking reinstatement as well as general and punitive damages. George could also seek injunctive relief in the form of a court order that Linus cease its illegal dumping practices.

- George might instead file an administrative claim with the state Unlawful Employment Practices Agency (UEPA), which is charged with resolving claims of employment discrimination (including claims of retaliatory firing). The UEPA has the power to order that Industrial Resources and Linus reinstate George, but unlike a judge does not also have the power to award compensatory and punitive damages.

- George might seek reinstatement through voluntary alternative dispute resolution processes such as negotiation, arbitration and mediation.[2]

The documents that George sent you make you confident that you can prove that Linus was engaged in illegal dumping. The crux of the case from your standpoint is whether you can also prove that George's firing was in retaliation for his plans to cease the illegal dumping. If so, you have an excellent chance of recovering both actual and substantial punitive damages as well as obtaining a court order requiring Linus to cease its illegal dumping. At the same time, your inquiries have revealed that local judges are reluctant to order reinstatement, believing that in general it is unwise to force employees on reluctant employers. By contrast, the UEPA would almost certainly order reinstatement if George's firing was illegal. However, you have learned that the UEPA is backlogged and that months are likely to go by before the UEPA investigates George's case. Moreover, the agency is subject to political pressure, and it frequently clears disputes off its docket after months of inaction by simply advising complainants to go to court. Overall, your personal belief is that filing a lawsuit offers George the best chance to protect his legal rights and punish Industrial Resources and Linus for their reprehensible behavior.

George has come to your office to talk about where he should go from here. After you and he exchange introductory pleasantries, the conversation proceeds as follows:

1. L: George, I've been thinking about your problem with an eye to what seem to me are your three main objectives: getting your job back, recovering lost salary and halting Linus's illegal dumping. Do I have those right?

2. C: I'd only add that if I can't get my job back, I want those bastards to pay for what they've put me through. Pardon my French.

3. L: No, no; you needn't apologize. I understand how angry you are. What I'd like to do is go through what I see as your primary options. The one option that responds to all of your objectives is litigation—you know, going to court. Only a court can compel Linus to rehire you and to stop its dumping practices, plus award damages. Within the litigation option we have at least two ways to go. We could file the complaint and pursue it aggressively, including immediately undertaking extensive investigation. Alternatively, we could take a slower approach, filing the complaint and indicating our willingness to resolve the dispute before both sides have to devote time and resources to the case. Filing the formal complaint might pressure Linus into talking with us. An alternative to litigation is to file a complaint with the Unlawful Employment Practices Agency. As you probably know from your own experience, the

2. For a summary of alternative dispute resolution processes, see JACQUELINE M. NO-LAN-HALEY, ALTERNATIVE DISPUTE RESOLUTION IN A NUTSHELL (2001); STEPHEN J. WARE, ALTERNATIVE DISPUTE RESOLUTION (2001).

UEPA can't award damages or order Linus to halt illegal dumping; but it can order you reinstated. Finally, we can approach Linus and see if they are interested in negotiating a settlement. Here, too, there are at least a couple of possibilities. I could prepare a complaint and mail it to Linus's counsel, indicating that it will be filed and served unless they open meaningful negotiations immediately. Or, we can indicate our interest in negotiations without sending a complaint. So those are your options, in a nutshell.

4.   C: Well, negotiation alone probably is a waste of time. I tried to talk to them when I was getting the ax, but no one paid any attention. Let's forget about that. I do have some interest in the UEPA. I know it can be a waste of time, but I've heard of cases in which it ordered reinstatement.

5.   L: OK, let's forget about negotiation. Since you mentioned that you do have some interest in the UEPA, maybe we should talk about that first. Does that make sense?

6.   C: Sure. One reason that I'm intrigued by the idea of filing a complaint with the UEPA is that I assume that would be less expensive than suing. Especially since I'm not earning as much now, that's an important factor.

7.   L: That's certainly true. Of course, if the UEPA just sits on it and tells you in a few months that if you want anything done you have to go to court then you'd be back to where you are right now except time will have gone by. So apart from the possibility of saving money, and that's certainly an important factor, is anything else about the UEPA option appealing to you?

8.   C: The main thing is that it offers me a way to get my job back without looking like I'm just another greedy, unhappy ex-employee seeing how much money I can make from being fired. My main goal is to get back into a position where I can be a leader in solving environmental problems. As President of Linus I can do that and the UEPA route gives me that chance.

9.   L: On paper, you're certainly right. And if you decide that the UEPA is the way to go that's fine with me. I can help you with the paperwork and maybe try to move things along if you'd like me to stay involved. But to be honest with you, what I know about the UEPA suggests that all you'll accomplish is you'll waste a few months while your complaint sits in its files. As for litigation, that's probably the best way to take your anger out on these people. You have a very good chance of hitting them where it hurts the most, in the pocketbook.

10.   C: You think we'd win if we took it to court?

11.   L: With the documents you've got, together with your testimony, I think the chances are good, probably at least 80%, that we'll be able to prove that illegal dumping was going on. We'd still have to prove the connection between the

dumping and your firing, and as to that issue it's simply too early for me to say. Proving what was in their mind isn't easy, but I think that the timing of your firing and your conversation with the President of Resources is strong evidence by itself that you were fired illegally. Of course, we'll have to do some investigation. That will cost you some money, which is why I mentioned the possibility of filing the lawsuit to show we mean business, but not diving into investigation right away in the hope that they might reinstate you to get rid of the case and keep what they've been doing out of the papers.

12. C: If we do it that way, how much is it likely to cost?

13. L: It's partly out of our control, because it depends on how aggressive Linus is. I'd ask for a retainer of $5000, that would cover my services for 20 hours. Of course, if this settles earlier you wouldn't even have to spend all of that. But if Linus takes a hard line approach and litigates this seriously, it will cost considerably more in attorney's fees and other costs.

14. C: I'm not liking this—it's starting to sound as expensive as I was afraid it would be. Any other downsides that I should know about?

15. L: Probably the biggest thing I have to mention is that even if we win a lawsuit, and as I told you while it's still early I'm very optimistic about that, the chance that a judge will order your reinstatement is small, say about 20%. Judges in this area especially are just reluctant to order re-hiring. On the other hand, if we win you can recover substantial damages including perhaps punitive damages and also obtain an order for Linus and Resources to cease illegal dumping.

16. C: It's not an easy decision, is it?

17. L: No, and of course you can take some more time to think about it. Just to be thorough, can you see any options beyond the ones we've talked about?

18. C: One thought I've been mulling over is to contact someone I know in the mayor's office and getting the word out about the illegal dumping. I'm not sure that will work, because trash companies seem to have a lot of political clout. Also, I've been thinking about approaching someone in the media with my story. What do you think about those things?

19. L: We can certainly talk about both of those possibilities. Whichever one you want to start with, tell me more about what you have in mind and how it ties in to your objectives of getting reinstated and reimbursed for what you've been through.

20. C: I'd love to go to the media with this . . .

Here, you begin by clarifying George's objectives (No. 1). You then identify options (No. 3) and later ask George about possible additional ones (No. 17). In between, the discussion touches on consequences of the litigation and UEPA options. As this organization suggests, client-centered counseling does not require you to exhaust all possible options before opening a discussion of consequences. The order in which you address these topics in particular matters is entirely for your judgment. Similarly, you and George would undoubtedly discuss additional consequences of the litigation and UEPA options after discussing the "media" and "political pressure" options.

Consider the wisdom of No. 5. Here, you readily acquiesce in George's immediate rejection of negotiation. However, further discussion of negotiation would seem vital to ensuring that George has a reasonable opportunity to decide. His rejection of negotiation may be a case of misprediction based on an inadequate data base.[3] Perhaps George was so emotionally involved when he attempted to talk with people at Linus and Resources that his approach to negotiation did not fully test their receptivity. Moreover, a potential disadvantage of litigation that is likely to emerge later in the conversation is that once the claim of illegal dumping becomes a matter of public record, George's leverage for achieving a settlement may be substantially diminished.[4] Both of these reasons militate in favor of your resuscitating the negotiation option before George makes a final decision.

Other counseling techniques that this dialogue illustrates include:

- You take the lead in suggesting available options (No. 3). Your rather lengthy statement and its complexity (mentioning two variations of the litigation option) may be too complex for some clients, but perhaps appropriate here in view of George's experience and comfort level.

- You look to George to choose the option he wants to discuss first (Nos. 5 and 19).

- Using percentage terms, you predict how a judge or jury is likely to resolve a specific factual dispute (No. 11).[5]

- You empathize with George's anger (No. 3).

- You attempt to respond immediately and directly to George's questions (e.g., No. 15).

- You attempt to estimate the downsides of investigation should George choose to litigate (No. 9).

At the same time, other aspects of the conversation may frustrate rather than facilitate George's ability to make a satisfactory decision.

---

3. For further discussion of misprediction, see Chapter 18.

4. In some circumstances, however, threatening to "go public" with information about illegal activity in order to exact a settlement may constitute extortion. See 31A AM. JUR. 2d, *Extortion, Blackmail and Threats* § 26 (2003).

5. Though you do not indicate the most likely outcome of trial, given your lack of information about the reason that George was fired, your omission is perhaps understandable.

One potential problem is that when George mentions his interest in the UEPA, you quickly respond negatively (Nos. 7 and 9). These responses may reflect your personal preference for litigation and seem especially inappropriate at this early stage in the conversation.

A second troublesome aspect of the conversation is that when George mentions additional options (No. 18), you immediately turn the conversation to whichever of those options George wants to talk about first. You may have served George better by "parking" those options until you and George had gone through the litigation and UEPA options more thoroughly. Some jumping back and forth among options and consequences is natural. Here, however, the immediate switch to the new options combined with your negative reactions to filing a complaint with the UEPA seem to constitute subtle methods of removing the UEPA as a potential option.

4. "SNAPSHOT 2": WHETHER TO TAKE A DEPOSITION

Assume that after you fully explored possible solutions with George, he decided to proceed by suing Linus and Resources.[6] However, since he has only moderate savings, he has asked you to proceed judiciously and to notify him as your time approaches twenty hours.

You have now filed suit on George's behalf; the suit seeks George's reinstatement, an injunction against illegal dumping, and compensatory and punitive damages. Linus moved to dismiss, and when the motion was denied, filed an answer denying George's claims. The case is in the discovery phase.

You decided first to undertake brief discovery to cement the factual proposition, "Linus dumped Class II materials into Class I dumpsites during the nine months that George worked for Linus,"[7] and to that end deposed Linus's principal dispatcher, Alison Anderson. During Anderson's deposition, the name of Ken Karst came up repeatedly, and you believe he might provide important evidence of illegal dumping. However, it also came out in Anderson's deposition that Karst is a substantial customer both of Cleanfill and Linus. Recognizing that involving Karst in George's lawsuit against Linus may have an adverse impact on George's job with Cleanfill, you decide to consult with George over the phone about taking Karst's deposition:

> 1. L: George, I'd like to talk to you about deposing Ken Karst. Last week I took Alison Anderson's deposition. Things went well; she was clearly trying to protect Linus, but I think I got some good evidence of illegal dumping activities. I'm calling because in her testimony, Anderson mentioned Karst's name a couple of times. My belief is that Karst will be able to verify that Linus officials offered to

---

6. For convenience, the text refers to the defendants only as "Linus."

7. For more on factual propositions, see Chapter 7.

dump Class II materials into Class I fills. However, from what Anderson said, I surmise that Karst is a substantial customer both of Linus and Cleanfill. I'm worried that taking his deposition will involve Karst in your lawsuit. If Karst resents that, he might retaliate by taking his business away from Cleanfill, and that might hurt your position. That's potentially a big disadvantage of taking Karst's deposition, and so I thought I'd better talk to you before going ahead with it.

2.   C: Thanks, I appreciate the call. How important do you think his testimony will be?

3.   L: As someone who is outside the company, I'd say it's likely to be important. As I told you earlier we have about a 80% chance of proving that illegal dumping was taking place. I think an outsider's evidence would really cement our position and allow us to focus the rest of our efforts on showing that you were fired in retaliation for planning to do things legally.

4.   C: Besides taking his deposition, what else could we do?

5.   L: Well, we always have the option to do nothing right now, or I could try to talk to Karst informally right now. Another possibility is that we could find some other outsider, not a customer of Cleanfill, who might know about Linus's illegal dumping practices. Do you know anyone?

6.   C: No. Of course I know a lot of people who I dealt with when I was at Linus, but nobody offhand who knows anything about the illegal dumping.

7.   L: Let's keep the possibility of someone else in the back of our minds. You might think of any friends you have at Linus who might put you on to someone. Meanwhile, can you think of any other options?

8.   C: I can't. It seems to me that whether you talk to Karst informally or take his deposition, he may get angry because it's not his affair. What do you think?

9.   L: Not knowing anything about Karst, it's difficult to say if there's any advantage in proceeding in one way rather than the other. I was hoping you might be able to give me some insights.

10.   C: From what I know of him, he's a pretty touchy guy. I've heard talk that he's got a real temper. If we can avoid it, I'd like to leave Karst alone.

11.   L: Here's one thought. Do you know Karst well enough to talk to him and ask if he'd be willing to talk to me informally rather than have me take his deposition?

12.   C: I know him slightly but I'd feel uncomfortable talking to him about my situation. I know it might help the case for me to talk to him, but I'm worried about what might happen. I'm still new at Cleanfill, and I just don't know what to do. What do you think?

13. L: At this point I'm not sure either. But you're closer to the situation than I am. So on a scale from one to five with five being the highest, how important is to you at this time to avoid the risk of upsetting Karst?

14. C: Pretty high.

15. L: Say a three or four?

16. C: I'd say a four.

17. L: Okay, how important is it for you at this point to know whether Karst knows about the illegal dumping?

18. C: Not that important now, given what's in the documents I sent you. Maybe it's a two.

19. L: I guess for now we should put involving Karst on the back burner.

No. 1 brings George up to date[8] and explains what decision is called for and why. In identifying the option of taking Karst's deposition you provide a brief summary of the pros and possible cons of taking the deposition. However, in elucidating the cons you assume, without checking with George, that Karst might dislike being deposed and strike back by taking business from Cleanfill, thereby hurting George. Just as you want to make sure that clients have adequate data bases for making predictions, you need to make sure that you too have adequate data bases. George presumably knows Karst better than you do and hence you might have more sensibly asked George if he thought that taking Karst's deposition might have had such consequences. As the conversation develops your assumptions appear to be correct. Nonetheless, it might have been preferable to have at least verified your assumptions with George before continuing the discussion.

Ordinarily you might have put other options on the table before moving to a discussion of pros and cons. However, you initially called George specifically to talk about taking the deposition, and the disadvantage you mention in No. 1 motivated the call. Hence, this part of your approach responds to the realities of everyday conversation and seems acceptable.

In Nos. 5, 7 and 11, you mention additional options and ask George if he can add any. No. 5 also includes what you may think of as a "search for an option." That is, deposing an outsider other than Karst is an option only if you or George are aware of such an outsider. When neither of you can identify someone, this option is temporarily shelved.

With respect to likely consequences, your conversation does identify potential advantages of speaking to Karst (No. 3). However, you do not identify, nor press George to identify, additional pros and cons. Furthermore, you do not attempt to distinguish between the pros and cons of talking with Karst as compared to the pros and cons of taking his deposition. Instead, you seem content to rely on George's potentially

8. See Chapter 5.

superficial data base (No. 10) to conclude that the potential disadvantage that motivated your phone call is likely to occur.

With respect to decision-making, you use the "rating technique" to facilitate George's decision-making ability.[9] In Nos. 13, 15, 17 and 21, you ask George to assign degrees of importance to potential consequences.

Despite George's prior legal experience, and the fact that you can probably revisit the option later in the case, the adequacy of the counseling here is dubious. The decision may in fact become final if neither of you can identify another outsider who knows of illegal dumping and if Karst becomes unavailable. Moreover, you neither address nor invite George to address the important subject of potential advantages of taking Karst's deposition now. For example, might having his testimony alter Linus's bargaining position? In combination with the other shortcomings identified in the analysis above, you may not have provided George with a reasonable opportunity to decide whether to depose Karst.

5. "SNAPSHOT 3": WHETHER TO SETTLE

George's case against Linus progressed swimmingly. You deposed an "outsider" other than Karst who provided strong evidence that Linus was engaged in illegal dumping. In addition, you located company memos suggesting that George was fired in retaliation for making noise about illegal dumping. Though trial is still some months away, you regard the case as very strong. In quiet moments, you mentally plan the dynamite opening statement you will be able to deliver.

Your thoughts of qualifying for the Opening Statement Hall of Fame suddenly vanished when George excitedly phoned a couple of days ago to say that he had just been hired to run Best Disposal, a waste disposal company in another state. He therefore no longer is interested in regaining his job at Linus. George is excited about the new job and does not want the personal and professional disruption that preparing and returning for trial would cause. George wants you to settle the case for as much as you can, both to compensate him for the suffering he endured and to make Linus pay for its illegal actions. You asked George to come in and see you, and the discussion goes as follows:

1. L: George, I must say you're looking and sounding better than at any time since I've known you. Congratulations on the new position—I'm delighted for you.

2. C: Thanks, the whole family is excited. They're especially looking forward to enjoying some nice, cold winters finally.

3. L: I know you've got a lot to do, so let's get right down to business. When we spoke on the phone, you said that you didn't want to go to trial and wanted to settle for as much as we can get. Do you still feel that way?

9. See Chapter 18.

4.   C: Definitely. I want to concentrate all my energy on the new position.

5.   L: OK. The main thing we have to think about is the timing. But first, let me ask you something that might have an impact on which way you decide to go. Does anyone at Linus know about the new job?

6.   C: Not that I know of, but I suppose it's bound to come out sooner or later. It's a pretty small network of companies and word of my accepting the position with Best Disposal is bound to get back to Linus rather quickly.

7.   L: The reason this can be important is that once people at Linus find out that you've taken a new position out of state, our leverage will probably go down. Linus's counsel will believe that you are no longer interested in being rehired and will probably figure that you won't be anxious to disrupt your new position by preparing for and going through a trial. With that in mind, let's talk about the two options I see: (1) begin negotiating with Linus at once, or (2) sit tight for a few months until the mandatory settlement conference. The judge will hold that conference in a few months, about a month before the trial is scheduled, and this is a time when parties normally talk settlement. But before we discuss these, do you see any other alternatives?

8.   C: No. But let me ask you, do you think I should ask Best Disposal to try to keep word of my new job from leaking out?

9.   L: You know, George, I just don't think you ought to worry about that. You've already got a lot going on in your life and this would be another thing to worry about and you'd probably ultimately be unsuccessful in keeping your new job quiet. If Linus finds out and it costs you a few dollars, so be it. At least that's my reaction. So let's focus on the two options we do have. Which one do you want to talk about first—negotiating now or waiting until the mandatory settlement conference?

10.   C: I think you're right about my not trying to keep the new job a secret. I can't imagine how I'd do that anyway. So let's talk about trying to settle right away. That way we could put all this behind us and maybe we can get it done with before Linus hears about the new job. Unless you have to tell them?

11.   L: Frankly, it may come out when Linus's counsel wonders why we're dropping the demand for reinstatement. I'm not going to lie to her if she asks. To help us figure out which option makes most sense for you, we'll make a little chart; you know how fond I am of them. And first off, we'll note the two advantages of trying to settle now that you mentioned. One, if Linus comes up with a figure that you're willing to accept, you'll be able to put the whole case behind you sooner. Two, the earlier we settle, the less

chance Linus has to find out about the new job. Any other advantages that strike you?

12. C: Well, maybe the sooner we offer to settle the more they'll offer. After all, we're probably saving them some money by settling earlier.

13. L: I agree. You may have heard the term "sunk costs," and this refers to the fact that parties sometimes continue to litigate even when it's not in their best interests to do so, just because they've already invested so much time and money in a case. So settling earlier rather than later can reduce the chances of Linus behaving that way. OK, we've got some good reasons to open settlement negotiations early, so we should consider possible disadvantages.

14. C: I really can't think of any.

15. L: Well, one that I can think of is that opening negotiations now may lead Linus's counsel to smell a rat. After all, we have no particular reason to negotiate now, and so Linus's attorney may wonder why you're so anxious to settle. Even if Linus doesn't know about the other job, asking to settle may lead Linus to think that our case is weak. So I think we should note that a disadvantage of opening settlement talks now is that you might get a lowball offer.

16. C: OK, is there anything else I have to gain by waiting until the mandatory to talk settlement?

17. L: There's this: waiting requires no further activity on your part. They've already taken your deposition, and you've gone through all the files. I realize that you can't entirely close the matter in your mind. But at least as far as your daily life is concerned, I don't think you'll have to do anything more. And that would allow us to talk settlement at a more natural time and lead them to think that the case is likely to go to trial. Even if they know you don't want to be rehired, they may still be plenty worried about the actual and punitive damages. Any other pros you can think of in waiting until the mandatory settlement conference to bring up settlement?

18. C: No. This has been helpful, and I appreciate that there may be some advantages to waiting. But the more we talk, the more convinced I become that I want you to try to settle this now, and if the money is reasonable, I want to get out. I don't care about every last nickel at this point. I'm willing to give up some money. I want to recover at least what I've got into this case, plus my salary differential for the time I was at Cleanfill. Is that reasonable?

19. L: That's certainly reasonable. But just so you can feel comfortable with your decision, let me tell you what I think would happen if the case were to go to trial. In terms of money, the salary differential by the time of trial will be about $125,000. I'd say the chances of that verdict are quite good, in the range of 80–90%. As for punitive damages, some of these company memos about why they need

to fire you are pretty inflammatory. I'd say the chances are at least fifty-fifty that you'll be awarded punitive damages. How much those punitive damages will be is really hard for me to predict until I have a chance to see who is on the jury but they could be equal to or greater than the $125,000.

20. C: The punitive damages sound good and they ought to have to pay them given what they've done and how they treated me. However, if I can recover your fees and my costs, plus the $125,000 I'd be happy.

21. L: I think that's something I could negotiate towards now. Of course, if Linus doesn't come back with that, we'll have to talk again. Are you comfortable with this?

22. C: Yes.

23. L: By the way, one thing we haven't talked about because it doesn't affect you directly is the injunction claim. I know of your genuine concern for the environment. How do you feel about giving up the injunction claim? Are you concerned about how it might effect others in the community?

24. C: I've thought of that, and have already arranged to turn over information to the local authorities. Hopefully they'll pursue Linus.

25. L: Do you have any personal friends, or maybe people you left behind at Linus, who you may feel you've let down by dropping the suit?

26. C: Not really. I'm sure they expect me to do what's best for me and my family in the long run.

27. L: Any other ramifications that you can see that we haven't talked about?

28. C: Not that I can see.

29. L: Okay, I'll get in touch with Linus's attorney and keep you up to date on how things are going. And again, congratulations on the new job.

30. C: Great; I'll look forward to hearing from you.

Here, changed circumstances create a new set of objectives, which in turn lead to a counseling conversation about options and consequences. The conversation focuses on a decision about whether to attempt to negotiate a settlement now or later.

In No. 3 you make sure that George's objectives remain unchanged. Then after exploring the potential viability of a "negotiate now" option (No. 5) you identify that option and that of waiting to the mandatory settlement conference. Then in No. 7 you ask George if he can think of other alternatives. You do not describe what each option entails, but given George's experience such an explanation is surely unnecessary. Moreover, you demonstrate neutrality by asking George which option he prefers to discuss first (No. 9). However, at the beginning of No. 9, you summarily dispose of a related option of asking Best Disposal not to disclose George's employment without bothering to investigate the likelihood that such an approach might help preserve George's leverage. Doing so is inconsistent with client-centered lawyering since you arrogate the decision to yourself without having any basis for determining the likely effectiveness or consequences of talking with Best Disposal.

Nevertheless, Nos. 11–17 demonstrate a rather full discussion of likely consequences, leading to the decision (No. 18).[10] Together with George's background and the length of time he has lived with the lawsuit, your discussion with George seemingly provides him with a reasonable opportunity to consider pertinent alternatives and consequences.

With No. 18, the conversation turns from the timing of settlement discussions to the settlement that George considers satisfactory. George proposes an amount that in essence does nothing more than make him "whole." That is, on the assumption that Linus acted illegally, George is satisfied to receive what he would have gotten had he remained with Linus until starting his job with Best Disposal, including being reimbursed for court costs and attorney's fees.

In No. 18, George indicates what kind of settlement will make him happy. In No. 19 you convert George's settlement formula into concrete monetary terms ($125,000) and explain the monetary recovery that is likely to occur should his case go to trial. Your doing so helps ensure that George can meaningfully understand and compare the pecuniary consequences of settlement with the likely financial consequences of going to trial. So doing helps make sure that George has a reasonable opportunity to decide and provides him with a basis for believing that he made an informed decision.

Since George's settlement proposal is based on an assessment of his needs and values rather than on misprediction, your judgment (No. 21) not to question George's decision as to the amount he is willing to accept seems sound.

Also in No. 21, rather than insisting that George give you his bottom line before you begin negotiations, you indicate that his chosen figure is something that you could "negotiate toward." You may of course during negotiations ask for a higher figure and George will no doubt accept more if you can get it. (No. 30)[11]

10. The discussion of consequences, though thorough, is not as extensive as it might be. For example, you do not ask George about whether negotiating now has any disadvantages.

11. For a discussion about the wisdom of obtaining bottom lines from clients before beginning to negotiate on their behalf, see Jacqueline M. Nolan-Haley, Alternative Dispute Resolution in a Nutshell 31–34 (2001). Also recognize that many clients may not want to give you a bottom line. Consider this comment the authors received from a CEO of a subsidiary of a NYSE company. "It's hard to imagine a circumstance early in litigation that would cause me to reveal my bottom line to anybody—my own lawyer included. Several reasons—I probably would not have enough information to have arrived at a 'bottom line,' I wouldn't trust the lawyer to grind hard enough even if I knew my bottom line (no advantage to me in sharing this information with anybody) and I wouldn't trust the lawyer to not attempt to add some success fee to my bill if they negotiated a particu-

Finally, the conversation reviews legal and non-legal concerns that "similarly situated clients" might consider pertinent to the settlement discussion. Falling into the former category is the injunction claim (No. 23); in the latter are potential effects of settling on friends or former colleagues at Linus (No. 25). Moreover, note that in asking George about likely consequences, you draw his attention to the likely effect on third persons. Thus in No. 23 you ask "How do you feel about giving up the injunction claim? Are you concerned about how it might effect others in the community?" However, George never fully responds to your questions. Rather he talks about turning documents over to local authorities but there is no discussion about how likely it is that doing so will adequately protect the community. Should you have continued to explore the likely adequacy of George's solution? Certainly George's resolution is not illegal. But in your eyes would it be immoral should it be likely that local authorities will do nothing about the situation? If your answer is yes, and George insisted on settling without pursuing an injunction, would you withdraw as his counsel?

Finally, before leaving this part of the conversation, you offer George a chance to mention non-legal concerns that you may not have thought of (No. 27).

larly good deal for me (either as hidden hours or through a direct ask). In fact, the only way a lawyer (mine or the other guy's) will have an idea of my 'bottom line' is when I walk away from failed settlement negotiations! Even then, they'll never be sure it all wasn't part of the game, if I've done my job. I think we all have a role to play in this drama called litigation and I don't believe that sharing all of the client's inner thoughts necessarily enhances the attorney's ability to execute their role. In fact. I'd never be certain I got the best deal possible if I started out divulging my 'bottom line'."

Chapter 20

COUNSELING "DEALS" CLIENTS

---

* * *

Miriam, today we are going to go over the buy-sell agreement I've prepared for the company. Did you have a chance to read through the copy I mailed to you?

I spent almost two hours with it. It looks terrific. You've really thought of everything. I'm quite pleased but I do have a couple of questions.

I'm glad you're happy. Why don't we start with your questions?

* * *

1. THE SCOPE OF THIS CHAPTER

This chapter explores the counseling model in the context of proposed deals.[1] It assumes that, as suggested in Chapter 9, you and a client have had one or more meetings leading to your producing a draft document which you have sent to the client for review. You now meet to review the draft. Such post-draft meetings typically entail counseling conversations in which you explain drafts' provisions, give clients the opportunity to consider alternative provisions, and encourage clients to decide which alternative is most likely to be satisfactory.[2] Of course, subsequent negotiations may require further counseling dialogues and new decisions including deals' overall wisdom.[3]

This chapter explores the counseling model through the use of illustrative case studies. Of course, such illustrations cannot capture the richness and complexity of counseling actual clients. Nonetheless, the

---

1. Although this discussion occurs in the context of reviewing proposed commercial agreements, the discussion is equally applicable to discussion of settlement agreements in litigation. Likewise, except for those parts of the discussion which focus on negotiation, the discussion also applies to the review of documents in the estate planning context.

2. As pointed out in Chapter 9, a similar, though typically more attenuated, dialogue often takes place before preparation of a draft. However, the most significant counseling usually takes place after a draft has been prepared.

3. For the most part, how you counsel is independent of which party's lawyer drafts a proposed agreement. However, for ease of understanding, this chapter assumes you are the drafter.

illustrations may further your understanding of how you might adapt your counseling according to such variables as clients' knowledge, experience, risk aversion, willingness to pay and the time available. Whether matters involve litigation or transactions, your "bottom line" remains affording clients a reasonable opportunity to make important decisions.

Counseling about deals generally has two dimensions: discussing the adequacy of individual provisions of draft agreements and discussing the underlying wisdom of the deals themselves. The first case study, "PSD Corporation," explores counseling with respect to individual provisions. The second, "Snacks Sixth Avenue," examines how counseling principles apply to discussions of deals' wisdom.

2. CASE STUDY NO. 1: PSD CORPORATION

Your client is PSD Corporation, whose representative is Andrea Paul, PSD's president. Ms. Paul has worked with lawyers in the past but does not think of herself as legally sophisticated. PSD is a small corporation that develops and markets software programs. PSD has been your client for the past two years and you are familiar with its operations, officers and directors.

In an initial meeting pertaining to a proposed new deal, Andrea told you that PSD is developing a software program for use by lawyers. The program is one that lawyers, aided by paralegals, can use to track evidence and documents during the discovery phases of a lawsuit. Although other evidence programs are available, Andrea believes that PSD's program will be considerably more sophisticated than any now on the market. PSD has been working on its program for about five months and anticipates that it will take at least eighteen to twenty months to complete the program and the documentation. The initial marketing phase will then take another six months. PSD is very excited about the project and wants to retain the services of its lead programmer, Rhonda Fleming, until the programming and the initial marketing phases are complete. Andrea has talked with Fleming about Fleming's committing herself to the project for that twenty-four-month period, and Fleming has indicated interest provided that she is given a free hand in developing the program and is adequately compensated. No specific terms of compensation have been discussed, but Fleming's current salary is $65,000 per year. Fleming has indicated that before she commits herself to any formal agreement, she wants a lawyer to look it over.

During the initial meeting, you also described alternative approaches that PSD might use to tie Fleming to PSD for the duration of the project—i.e., at least twenty-four months. Among the options you reviewed were signing Fleming to an employment contract which provided a salary increase, giving Fleming some equity interest in PSD, and giving Fleming some equity interest in any income PSD derived from the marketing of the evidence program. After you and Andrea batted the various options around, Andrea decided that PSD did not want, for various reasons, to give Fleming an equity position in PSD, although it might be willing to give her interest in income PSD derived from the program. Andrea's favored approach was an employment contract with a salary increase.[4] At the discussion's conclusion, Andrea said she thought PSD should offer Fleming a salary increase to $75,000 per year.

Four days after meeting with Andrea, you prepared a draft agreement and mailed it to her.[5] Your cover letter asked Andrea to read the agreement and to then set up a meeting so that the two of you could discuss it. Today you are meeting with Andrea to review the agreement. The proposed agreement is twenty pages in length and contains clauses regarding the following:

(1) Identification of the parties,

(2) The contract term and Fleming's duties,

(3) Fleming's compensation, including provisions providing incentives and covering inflation,

(4) PSD's ownership of all program codes and copyrights developed by Fleming while working on the project,

(5) Fleming's limits on outside computer activities during the duration of the project,

(6) Unfair competition by Fleming after termination (e.g., trade secrets and customer lists, and customer lists clauses),

(7) PSD's right to terminate Fleming's employment under various circumstances,

(8) Fleming's rights should PSD breach the agreement,

(9) PSD's and Fleming's obligation to arbitrate any disputes,

(10) PSD's obligation to indemnify Fleming with respect to lawsuits concerning the inadequacy of the program,

(11) Notices required to each party, and

(12) Choice of Law.[6]

3. PREPARING TO REVIEW AN AGREEMENT

Preparing to meet with clients to discuss a draft agreement usually requires you to make three determinations: (a) Which provisions it makes sense to discuss; (b) Which omitted or alternative versions of provisions it makes sense to discuss,[7] and (c) In what order to discuss the provisions. Consider briefly each of these tasks.

4. Obviously you would have used the counseling model to help your client reach this decision. In the interest of time, however, we have omitted the dialogue leading to it.

5. As you recall from Chapter 9, followups to initial meetings normally are preceded by your sending clients a draft agreement to review.

6. For a discussion and exploration of provisions commonly found in employment agreements see J. Rabkin & M. Johnson, 5 Current Legal Forms With Tax Analysis (1989); Advising California Employers 215 et seq. (Cal. CEB 1981).

7. Note that for the most part you face these same issues even if the agreement is one which has been drafted by the other side. As to task (b), while you may not

A. DECIDING WHICH PROVISIONS TO DISCUSS

Typically, providing clients with a reasonable opportunity to decide if a draft's provisions are satisfactory does not require that you review with them each of its provisions. One reason is that the sheer length of many agreements defies individual consideration of each of their provisions. But in addition, some operative and contingent terms may be so apparent or unimportant in the context of a particular deal that no client review seems warranted. For example, in the PSD matter, consider the clauses pertaining to the agreement's duration (two years) and the giving of required notices. The first may be so plain to Andrea, and the second so unimportant, that absent questions from Andrea, you would plan not to review them with her.[8]

Similarly, certain contingency provisions may come into play only under circumstances you think extremely remote. For example, many commercial leases contain provisions governing the parties' rights in the event that a portion of the leased premises is condemned through eminent domain.[9] Assume that a client desires to lease a warehouse for a year; that the landlord's twelve page proposed lease contains an eminent domain provision; and that you put the chance that a governmental agency will exercise its eminent domain powers over the leased premises during the term of the lease at less than 5%. Here, too, absent a client's questions or a provision that you consider extremely unfavorable, you may plan not to review the provision.

Often, however, determinations of whether to review provisions with clients are not so obvious. When preparing to review drafts, you may have to evaluate such factors as provisions' apparent importance, their interaction with other provisions, clients' prior opportunity to review them, clients' prior experience, their willingness to pay for your time, and the time available for discussion. When in doubt, try to involve clients in the decision-making process. Consider the following dialogue:

1. L: Andrea, let's turn our attention to the agreement I sent you. Have you had a chance to go over it?

2. C: I spent about an hour last night looking through it, and it's just the kind of thing I had in mind. I'm particularly glad you put in the provision about arbitration. I've been

know whether the other party has "consciously" chosen to omit a provision, in looking over the other party's draft you still need to think about whether to inform a client about the possibility of including a provision the other party has omitted.

8. Be warned, however, that even a provision apparently so benign as one requiring that notices of breach "be given within 10 days" may in a particular context merit individual review. A client may not have thought through whether, given the client's business practices, a 10–day notice period provides adequate time to discover a problem and report it. This problem, for example, might be particularly acute in the PSD matter should Fleming start to use PSD's customer lists and PSD not learn of such use soon after Fleming begins to use them. Other seemingly "boilerplate" provisions that you may in some contexts want to review with clients include the following: Should notices be written or oral? Is notice by electronic mail adequate? To whom should notices be sent?

9. See, e.g. *Commercial Real Property Lease Practice* §§ 3.98–3.109 (Cal. CEB 1976).

involved in arbitrations many times, and I really think that's the way for a company like PSD to go. If problems arise, we want to stay out of court.[10]

3.   L: Good. As I recall, PSD has never used employment contracts but you're familiar with them, correct?

4.   C: Right. We used them with consultants when I was with FastPro.

5.   L: Well, does it make sense then to limit ourselves to talking over those provisions about which you have questions or concerns and those on which I feel I need your input?

6.   C: Absolutely. I'm counting on you to know what's important and what's not. As I said, I've looked at this thing and if our discussion skips something that I want to know about I'll ask you. If we go over everything, it's going to take too much time. I really don't want to devote more than an hour or so to this. I think we can skip the stuff regarding her rights if we fire her and in fact all the clauses starting with number 6. I'm willing to leave those things to you.

7.   L: I appreciate that; I think I monitor our hourly charges as closely as you do so I guess we can skip number 6 and those after it. Which of the remaining provisions would you like to talk about?

8.   C: My only interests are numbers 2 and 5; the ones on compensation and our rights to terminate her.

9.   L: Good, those are on my list too; so we'll talk about those. Any others?

10. C: No.

11. L: Okay, let's turn to number 2.

Here, in No. 8, Andrea indicates that she wants to talk only about two provisions and expressly states that she has no interest in talking about what might happen should PSD terminate Fleming. Does your acceding to Andrea's "waiver" in Nos. 6 and 8 deprive her of a reasonable opportunity to explore the termination provision as well as the agreement's other ten provisions? Ought you for example treat the situation as one in which the client has already reached a decision?[11]

Without knowing more about Andrea, her objectives, the nature of the deal, and the details of the parties' prior discussions, and actually reading the draft, you have an inadequate basis to answer these questions. For example, without knowing the specific terms of the various provisions, the time Andrea has devoted to reviewing the provisions and Andrea's prior experience with them, no conclusion about your obligation to discuss the post-termination provisions with her is possible.

10. Without an express indication or knowledge from past dealings that a client understands arbitration, you would have to take the initiative to discuss the clause with her. Clients often think they understand provisions when in fact they do not. For example, a client may have a general sense of what arbitration is, yet not understand its bypassing of a jury and its finality.

11. See Chapter 18 .

But recognize that should you fail to ask Andrea to consider those provisions you may not only deprive Andrea of a reasonable opportunity to consider an important factor, but may also open you up to a malpractice claim should matters turn out different from what she expected.[12]

Nonetheless, the dialogue may help you understand how preliminary discussions with clients can help you develop information from which to judge which provisions to discuss.[13] Of course, any judgment must be a preliminary one since subsequent discussions may lead to greater or lesser review than you or clients initially contemplated.

B. ALERTING CLIENTS TO OMITTED OR ALTERNATIVE VERSIONS OF PROVISIONS

As you know, rarely during pre-draft information-gathering do you discuss every potential provision. As a result, you often have to rely on your own judgment, rather than on any overt discussions with clients, when deciding what provisions to include in draft agreements.[14] The upshot is that almost every draft omits provisions that potentially might be included in a final agreement. For example, the PSD draft omits common provisions such as PSD's right to terminate the agreement in the event of merger, and Fleming's obligation to mitigate damages in the event of PSD's breach.[15]

Similarly, almost any provision included in a draft typically results from your choice among possible alternative versions of the provision. For example, one common alternative to the cash salary provision in the PSD draft is compensation in addition to cash, such as a car or an expense account. Therefore, before meeting clients to review drafts, you must decide which if any of the omitted or alternative versions of a provision they should know about.

By and large, the factors to consider when determining which omitted or alternative versions of provisions to review with clients are the same as those you think about in the context of included provisions. That is, given clients' experience, objectives, the type of deal, and the parties' prior discussions, you evaluate factors such as the seeming importance of omitted or alternative versions of provisions, clients' prior

---

12. For example if PSD does terminate Fleming and her rights at that time turn out to be greater than Andrea believed they would be, you might be open to a malpractice claim by PSD. For a discussion of how you might go about discussing individual contractual provisions with a client, see sec. 4(A) *infra.*

13. Inquiries such as that just illustrated, of course, will sometimes give you little help. Clients sometimes respond by telling you they have been too busy to read anything and wish to discuss only a very limited number of provisions. Such responses often put you face to face with a client

whose mind is mostly made up and who wants to rely on you for most of the decision making. In such circumstances if you believe your client may not have had a reasonable opportunity to explore all the important decisions, you might try some of the approaches described in Chapter 18.

14. For discussion of the factors you typically rely on when deciding on which provisions to include in a draft, see the discussion of "Preparing Draft Agreements" in Chapter 9.

15. For sources of common employment agreement provisions, see note 6 *supra.*

experience, their willingness to pay, and the time available for discussion.

In addition, factoring in clients' reactions to included provisions can help you decide whether to mention omitted or alternative versions of provisions. For example, assume that Clause 5 of the PSD draft agreement obligates PSD to employ Fleming for two years. If Andrea were to indicate that the two-year term could be a problem if PSD were to abandon the evidence tracking system project, you probably would then suggest alternative versions of Clause 5, such as one giving PSD the right to terminate the agreement in such an event.

When you do decide to mention omitted or alternative versions of provisions, you may say something like the following:

> Andrea, while we're looking at the compensation clause, let me mention an additional possibility since you seem to think that the amount of the salary might not be a sufficient inducement to Fleming. We might include a provision giving her the use of a company car, or an expense account, or perhaps a bonus. I can explain how this kind of provision might work and what the tax consequences would be, if you are interested. Do you want to talk about these ideas?

As this statement suggests, you typically mention omitted or alternative versions of provisions in connection with the included provisions to which they are most closely tied. This practice facilitates clients' understanding the impact of adding omitted provisions or adopting alternative ones.[16]

C. ORDER OF REVIEW OF PROVISIONS

As noted in Chapter 5, you typically begin follow-up meetings by asking clients about their current concerns. Through clients' responses, you are likely to learn whether any of a draft's terms are particularly worrisome. When counseling clients about agreements you ought to give priority to any provisions that they mention as a concern. When clients do not mention special concerns, you may organize reviews in a manner that you think most effective and efficient. For example, you may go through provisions in numerical order or according to their importance.

D. USE "TERM SHEETS"

Having preliminarily decided which of a proposed agreement's terms you want to review with a client, consider providing the client with a "term sheet" to facilitate the client's active participation in a counseling

---

16. Making a list of consciously omitted provisions will help you remember to mention the provisions at pertinent times. Note, however, that retaining this kind of list in your file might provide evidence of malpractice—the list would provide evidence that the excluded provisions were intentionally omitted from the document. To undercut any such argument, your file should also contain an indication that you gave the client a reasonable opportunity to consider whether to include each of the omitted provisions in the agreement.

discussion. A term sheet is simply a short outline of the important provisions that you intend to review in the order in which you plan to review them. While a term sheet is not a substitute for review of agreements' specific language, a term sheet can help clients understand what issues you consider most significant.

4. TOPICS TO EXPLORE WHEN COUNSELING ABOUT DEALS' INDIVIDUAL PROVISIONS

Law schools pay scant attention to how you might counsel clients with respect to the adequacy of provisions typically found in proposed deals. Nor do practitioner-oriented works typically tell you what subjects you need to cover in order to explore provisions' adequacy.[17] This section is an attempt to fill this void. It describes the topics that typically are relevant to clients' decisions about the adequacy of provisions. Subsection (D) focuses on how you might incorporate these topics into counseling conversations.

A. PROVISIONS' MEANING

No matter how concise and attentive to laypeople's vocabulary a draft is, clients frequently find various provisions confusing. Yet, to avoid embarrassment, clients may not reveal their lack of understanding. Hence, any doubt in your own mind about whether clients understand provisions should prompt you to explain them.

Because it is often the abstract quality of provisions that confuses clients,[18] a useful way of explaining provisions is to offer concrete examples of how they would work in practice. For example, assume that you have decided to review paragraph 9 of the proposed agreement between PSD and Fleming with Andrea. That provision reads as follows:

> PSD shall, to the maximum extent permitted by law, indemnify and hold Fleming harmless against expenses, including costs, reasonable attorneys' fees, judgments, fines, settlements, and other amounts actually and reasonably incurred in connection with any action or proceeding brought against Fleming by any third person arising by reason of Fleming's employment by PSD. PSD shall advance to Fleming any expenses to be incurred in defending any such proceeding to the maximum extent permitted by law.[19]

---

17. Practitioner-oriented works often do a splendid job of setting out the potential content of a myriad of provisions for use in various types of deals. However, to our knowledge they say little or nothing about how to walk clients through the subjects that must be examined before a client has a reasonable opportunity to determine a provision's adequacy.

18. *See, e.g.,* G.E. Myers and M.T. Myers, The Dynamics of Human Communication: A Laboratory Approach 124–5 (5th ed. 1988). *Cf.* J.B. White, *The Invisible Dis-*

course of the Law: Reflections on Legal Literacy and General Education, 54 Col. L. Rev. 143 (1983).

19. Recognize that the clauses used in this and other illustrations are not intended as "models." Our focus is on the counseling process rather than the specific language of potential provisions. For the most part, in actual practice, provisions tend to be more precisely (if not more confusingly) worded than this text's illustrative provisions.

To explain this provision, you might proceed as follows:

L: Andrea, let's look at paragraph 9 for a minute. In essence, this clause provides that should someone sue Rhonda personally as the result of her work for PSD, possibly because of a claim about some defect in the software, PSD will pay for her legal defense and also will pay any judgment entered against her by a court. Also, if she settles any such suit and the settlement is a reasonable one, PSD will also pay that.

Absent questions from Andrea, this statement probably adequately explains the meaning of paragraph 9. The contingency seems a remote one, and Andrea is apparently experienced. Of course, you might have given a more detailed explanation. For example, you could have pointed out that Fleming might be sued for reasons other than defects in the software and clarified what a "reasonable" settlement might be and how it would be determined whether a settlement was in fact "reasonable." But on balance, the concrete examples in the explanation in all likelihood give Andrea a reasonable opportunity to understand the provision.

Note that the explanation takes it as a given that *some* version of indemnity clause is appropriate and does not include a legal justification for the provision. For example, you do not launch into an explanation of the law's "default position" with respect to indemnity. That is, you do not explain what indemnity obligation PSD might have in the absence of an indemnity clause. Unless provisions are legally controversial, or clients' questions indicate that they want to know what they missed out on by not attending law school, choosing not to explore the role of indemnity provisions seems valid. Clients tend to be more interested in provisions' "bottom lines"—what they mean—than in whatever legal justifications underlie their use.

B. PROVISIONS' ADEQUACY FROM CLIENTS' PERSPECTIVES

After explaining provisions, the next step in the review process typically involves helping clients assess their adequacy. Generally, provisions provide benefits for one party and impose burdens on the other. You seek, therefore, to help clients predict whether provisions' benefits are adequate, or their burdens too steep.

For example, on the benefits side, you might help Andrea predict whether tying Fleming to PSD for two years is likely to allow PSD sufficient time to develop and market its software program. Similarly, you might ask her whether the restrictions on Fleming's outside computer activities adequately ensure that Fleming's time and energy will be mainly directed toward PSD's project.

On the burdens side, you might help Andrea assess whether PSD can live with the contingency provision requiring PSD to indemnify Fleming. In another case, you might ask whether a client who is about to lease space in a small commercial shopping center can comply with a provision that requires remaining open twelve hours a day. Clients often fail to evaluate carefully their ability to comply with potentially burdensome contract requirements, particularly when they are contingent on future occurrences. You therefore often need to encourage clients to think through the adequacy of contingency provisions that impose burdens.

Inquiries into clauses' adequacy can be quite straightforward. Consider the following examples.

Is The Protection Adequate?

1. L: Andrea, paragraph 1 requires Fleming to work full time for PSD on the evidence program for two years. You need to think about whether PSD will need Fleming for more than two years. Realistically, is the project going to be finished and in the market place within that time?

2. C: I really think eighteen months should do it, so I'm quite comfortable with two years.

* * *

12. L: Great. How about paragraph 8? What this paragraph means is that should Fleming quit before the two-year period expires, she could not develop programs in the legal field for another company or freelance for herself for six months plus a period of time equal to that remaining on her contract. Will this restriction give PSD adequate protection from competition by Fleming should she leave before the end of the contract?

13. C: I think so. We have a couple of other people working for Fleming on the project. I think we'd be all right.

Nos. 1 and 12 combine the tasks of explaining a provision's meaning and inquiring about its adequacy. Since each provision is intended to provide PSD with benefits, the questions encourage Andrea to assess the protection they provide.

Are The Burdens Bearable?

1. L: Andrea, let's talk about paragraph 2. This paragraph commits PSD to pay Fleming an annual salary of $75,000 plus periodic bonuses of $5,000 if certain aspects of the source code are completed by July 1, January 1 and April 2. Is PSD going to have any problem at all meeting those financial requirements?

2. C: I'm sure we won't.

3. L: Good because paragraph 6 says that if PSD breaches the agreement in any way, Fleming can at her option terminate the contract. So, if PSD were not to pay Fleming's salary or give her the incentive payments called for by paragraph 2, Fleming would be free to walk away from PSD.

4.   C: What happens if we are a few days late with a payment?

5.   L: Well, the provision says that any failure on PSD's part must be material. A couple of days shouldn't be a problem, but if payments get much later than that, especially the monthly salary payments, or if PSD were continually late, then that might constitute a "material" breach giving Fleming a right to end the contract. Do you have any reason to think that PSD is going to have any difficulty complying with its obligations under paragraph 2?

6.   C: No. We are in good financial shape. I just don't see a problem.

Your review of the provisions that impose burdens on PSD again both explains the provisions and assesses their adequacy. Would you accept Andrea's conclusion in No. 6 without any questions?

Clients' Dissatisfaction With Provisions

In the examples above, the client was pleased with the draft agreement. Alas, that will not always be so. Matching objectives against provisions' consequences may reveal that clients are dissatisfied with provisions. Such dissatisfaction typically requires you or clients to try to develop better alternatives. Indeed, dissatisfaction may produce entirely new objectives as well. Consider this dialogue:

1.   L: Andrea, next let's look briefly at paragraph 5. In essence it says that PSD can fire Fleming if she fails to perform in any way or in any way breaches the agreement. Is this adequate to meet your needs?

2.   C: The one problem I see is that it may not go far enough. We don't want to be stuck with Fleming if for some reason we decide to abandon the evidence software project.

3.   L: Do you anticipate that PSD might want to do that?

4.   C: Not really, but in this business that is always a possibility. For example, someone may beat us to market.

5.   L: I see your point. If you want to, we could add a clause saying that if PSD chooses to sell or abandon the evidence tracking project during the two-year period, PSD shall have the right to cancel the contract after some reasonable notice to Fleming. Would that give you what you need?

6.   C: I think it would; it would only be fair to give her some notice.

7.   L: Assuming we add this provision, how do you think Fleming will react?

8.   C: . . .

Here, Andrea is dissatisfied with the draft of paragraph 5. That dissatisfaction is the catalyst for her mentioning a new objective (No. 2). Aware of that objective, you mention another alternative (No. 5), the consequences of which you then begin to explore (No. 7).

C. PROVISIONS' ADEQUACY FROM OTHER PARTIES' PERSPECTIVES

Part of assessing provisions' adequacy is evaluating their likely effect on other parties, both in terms of negotiating final agreements and the parties' long-term relationships. For example, a provision may give your client all the protection in the world, but insisting on such protection may offend the other side or cause it to walk away from the deal.[20] If such important risks exist, they are for clients to take or avoid. Thus, even when clients are satisfied with provisions, the reasonable opportunity standard often requires that you inquire about their potential effect on future negotiations and relationships,[21] and when appropriate raise the possibility of altering them.[22]

For example, assume that you are exploring paragraph 8 with Andrea:

1. L: Andrea, we're agreed that paragraph 8's language prohibiting Fleming from engaging in any other computer programming work during the two years of the contract meets PSD's objective that Fleming devote full attention to PSD's project. However, just to be safe, let's take a minute to talk about Fleming's likely response. Before we submit the draft to her let's at least consider how she might react to it and whether it might anger her in some way. After all, there's no point alienating Fleming if we can avoid it.[23]

2. C: I agree, so long as we don't give up anything we need.

3. L: I understand. What problems, if any, is Fleming likely to have with a requirement that she not do any outside work?[24]

4. C: Well, I think she does do some programming with a couple of other people on weekends. She might not want to give that up.

5. L: What does that work entail?

20. *See* M.H. McCormack, The Terrible Truth About Lawyers 111–112, 84–87 (1987). Even if you succeed in winning such one-sided provisions, you may find later that this was a pyrrhic victory. *See id.* at 142–145 ("lopsided deals don't last").

21. If the proposed agreement being reviewed has been drawn by the other side, the comments in this section apply to any revisions you suggest be sent back to the other side.

22. Some lawyers believe you need not explore this topic on a paragraph by paragraph basis. They say that so long as a client has read an agreement, you can simply ask a client if the client believes that any of the provisions are likely to harm the negotiations or the parties' ultimate relationship. Such an inquiry may cause a client to identify potentially troublesome provisions. But it is highly unlikely that the question will cause a client's mind to run through each of the agreement's paragraphs. The client's response therefore will be based on less than a complete review.

23. Whenever you ask a client to think about the other party's likely reaction, make sure the client understands that he or she, rather than the other party, is your primary concern. If you begin to examine this subject without prior explanation, a client might doubt your loyalty.

24. Lawyers sometimes examine the other party's perspective through role playing, with a client playing the other party. Thanks to Bill Rutter of the Rutter Group for pointing this out.

6.   C: I'm not sure but it has something to do with education of school children.

7.   L: Okay; so Fleming may have some objection to giving up that work. Do you think we should leave the provision as it is or make some changes in it, such as to allow her to spend a limited time, say on weekends, working on outside projects?

8.   C: I'm not sure we ought to do that. Lots of us have started spending some weekend time at the office, and especially as we get close to marketing the program, I'd hate for her contract to say that she has a right not to work on weekends.

9.   L: Can you see any alternative that would allow her to continue with some outside work and still protect PSD?

10.   C: I can't think of anything. Besides, the way the clause reads now allows us to start at a strong place; if she wants to change it let her bring it up. Don't forget she is getting a big raise in this deal from her current salary.

11.   L: Certainly the raise means that PSD ought to have first call on her activities. But since you've said that Fleming's current activities are not a problem for you, how about itemizing the specific outside work Fleming is now doing, and providing that she can continue to do that work? That provision might help us in negotiations by allowing us to point out that the agreement is drafted with both parties' interests in mind.

12.   C: It sounds fine now, but the outside work may become a problem down the road.

13.   L: How likely is that?

14.   C: I really can't say.

15.   L: All right, one negative of allowing her to continue with her present activities is that there's an undefined risk that those activities may conflict with your future needs. Do you see any other cons?

16.   C: Well, ...

This conversation demonstrates that examining provisions from other parties' perspectives can involve each step of the counseling process. No. 1 includes an inquiry into Andrea's objectives. The conflict that emerges between Andrea's objective and the impact of the provision leads you to examine possible alternatives (Nos. 7 and 11) and their likely consequences (No. 10; Nos. 12–15).

No. 11 illustrates the inevitable relationship between examining provisions from other parties' perspectives and negotiation strategy. In No. 10, Andrea takes a traditional stance toward negotiation, stating that standing by the draft may be advantageous as it allows PSD to "start at a strong place." In response, you set forth an alternative that might meet both PSD's and Fleming's needs (No. 11); Nos. 12–15 begin to examine the consequences of this "problem solving" approach.[25]

D. AN ILLUSTRATIVE "DEALS COUNSELING" CONVERSATION

This section illustrates how you might carry out the four step approach to counseling set forth in Chapter 13 when talking to transactional clients about the provisions in proposed agreements. As in litigation matters, the touchstone is to afford clients with reasonable opportunities to make decisions about "pivotal" matters.

For a change of pace, assume that your client is Fleming rather than PSD. Last week you met with Fleming for the first time and gathered basic information about her proposed deal with PSD. You learned that PSD has offered Fleming a two-year employment contract at an annual salary of $75,000. Fleming, who is 29, has been a computer programmer for seven years and has done work on PSD's evidence tracking program since coming to the company six months ago. Fleming is quite happy with the financial terms of PSD's offer, but she has never signed a formal contract of any kind and has not tried to read through the details of PSD's proposal. Accordingly, at the conclusion of the meeting, you and Fleming agreed that you both would review the proposed agreement and then meet to discuss it. The discussion focuses on paragraph 4, which reads as follows:

> During her employment by PSD Fleming shall devote her full energies, interests, abilities, and productive time to the performance of her duties under this agreement and shall not, without PSD's prior written consent, engage in any computer activities or services of any kind for herself or any other person or entity which services are designed to produce financial benefit for Fleming or any other person or entity.

The dialogue is as follows:

1.   L: Rhonda, it's nice to see you again. Any new developments since we last met?

---

25. For discussion of traditional and problem-solving approaches to negotiation, see, e.g., CHARLES B. CRAVER, EFFECTIVE LEGAL NEGOTIATION AND SETTLEMENT (4th ed. 2001); RUSSELL KOROBKIN, THE THEORY AND PRACTICE OF NEGOTIATION (2002); STEPHEN B. GOLDBERG, FRANK E. A. SANDER, NANCY H. ROGERS, DISPUTE RESOLUTION: NEGOTIATION, MEDIATION AND OTHER PROCESSES 20–121 (1999); Note that many lawyers have traditionally regarded negotiation strategy as strictly a matter of "professional craft," and thus not a matter requiring client consultation. However, as the text suggests, a client may not have a reasonable opportunity to choose an alternative unless the client is aware of its potential impact on negotiation strategy. Indeed, whenever a provision places a burden on the other party that the other party has not agreed to, the provision's potential impact on future negotiations is a consequence that you should typically discuss with a client. In addition to asking a client to assess a provision's potential impact on negotiations, client-centeredness also suggests that you often consult a client with regard to other issues of negotiation strategy. Such issues might include whether in general to take a "cooperative" or "competitive" approach to the negotiations; whether you or the client should conduct the negotiation; and if it is you, whether the client should be present. Remember, a client may know the other party far better than you do. For further discussion of counseling dialogues with respect to negotiation, see DONALD GIFFORD, LEGAL NEGOTIATIONS: THEORY AND APPLICATIONS 55–72; 184–200 (1989).

2.   C: Not at all.

3.   L: I've gone over PSD's draft and I think I understand what PSD is proposing. Have you had a chance to go through the agreement since we last met?

4.   C: I read through it, but frankly I'm not sure I understand it all. I understand that it's for two years and I would get $75,000 a year plus a cost of living raise in the second year. Also, I understand the fringe benefits stuff. But all that stuff about what happens if I leave and things like that is somewhat confusing.

5.   L: As I recall you've never been involved in a contract such as this, so I can see why you may have some questions. What we will do today is go through what I see as the significant provisions, and I hope that by the time we're through you'll have a good picture of what's involved. But before I get started, are there any particular clauses you'd like to talk about?

6.   C: Well, I'm not sure I understand paragraph 4. Does it mean that I can't do any other programming work while I'm working for PSD?

7.   L: It does seem to say that, and we will certainly talk about that one. Are there other provisions that particularly concern you?

8.   C: Not specifically.

9.   L: OK, then why don't we start with paragraph 4. What it says is that while you work for PSD you can't, without PSD's written consent, engage in any outside computer work with the intent of making money for you or anyone else. In other words, you can't do any programming that will immediately or eventually bring you money. From what you've said, these restrictions present problems. Why don't you tell me what they are?

10.   C: At home on the weekends, I've been working on a program with a couple of friends. It's a tutorial program for use by high school students in helping them learn economics. We've made quite a bit of progress on it and should have a prototype done in four to six months. Our plan is to market the program as soon as we beta test the prototype. Also, once in awhile I get a chance to do some independent consulting work which I do on weekends to pick up some extra money. So if I couldn't do these things, then I'm not sure I'd want to sign the contract even though it gives me a $10,000 raise.

11.   L: You want to keep your opportunities for additional income open.

12.   C: Exactly; I don't want to compete with PSD, and I understand they are entitled to a full week's work. But what I do on the weekends or at night at home or at PSD is my own business.

13. L: There are a number of ways we might try to work this situation out. Let me list some for you and then see if you have some other ideas. You might try to get PSD to agree that you can continue with your current activities, perhaps suggesting a cap on the amount of time you can devote to them. After all, you've been doing this kind of work right along and they are obviously happy with you. Or, since stopping those activities will cost you money, you might ask for a bigger raise than $10,000. With respect to either option, you might approach Andrea informally or we might go back to them in a more formal way by revising this paragraph. Do you see any other possibilities?

14. C: Not really, unless I just go ahead and sign. What do you think I should do? I'm not sure how to handle this situation.

15. L: I can understand why you'd like some advice on this, and I want to give you all the help I can. Signing the agreement as it stands is an option we can talk about. But before I can give you an opinion about what option might be best, we'll need to talk some more so that I can be sure that I fully understand your underlying interests as well as those of the company. Let's talk a bit about each of these approaches and try to figure out the possible advantages and disadvantages of each. After we've done that it may become clear how you should proceed. Let me list the choices on this piece of paper so we can keep track of the possible pros and cons. Let's start with the possibility of their agreeing to your keeping on with your current activities. What do you see as positive about such an approach?

16. C: That seems like the most friendly approach; certainly it's less antagonistic than asking for more salary. The company's pretty new and I'm uncomfortable asking for more money, especially since they are already offering me a $10,000 raise.

17. L: So going back to them about maintaining the status quo has the advantage of keeping matters on a friendly and informal basis and avoids the discomfort you may feel about asking for more money. What other advantages do you see for seeking to keep up your current outside activities?

18. C: It's better than asking for more salary because I don't have to try and figure out how much more would be fair and because I really want to continue my outside work. I really like the tutorial project. I want to continue working on it because I think it's a valuable idea. Also, the consulting lets me work on various projects and keeps me from going stale.

19. L: I can see you really want to maintain your outside activities. A real disadvantage to asking for more money and giving up all your outside work would be the loss of

variety in your work life. Any other advantages you see to keeping the outside work?

20. C: It's an approach that I feel comfortable with. In fact, as I think about this matter, I really don't want to ask them for more money. They're being generous, and I wouldn't feel comfortable asking for more money. They'll just get pissed and things will get messy. I just don't want to risk that.

21. L: Well, you know PSD better than I do, so maybe we should drop that idea. So let's talk about how to approach PSD. What about a formal approach of redrafting the agreement to provide that you can continue working on the tutorial program and do consulting on the weekends and presenting that redraft to them? What advantages might that have over your just going to Andrea informally?

22. C: None that I see. It presents the same problems. If I bring this up, then the whole thing is likely to become unraveled. I like the idea of the $10,000 annual raise, I like the company. It's not that I'm afraid PSD may back away from the deal. They need me more than I need them. The problem is that once Andrea finds out about my extra work she'll always be looking over my shoulder to make sure I'm working on the PSD project. If that happens, a great work situation will go down the tubes. Instead of being able to work independently, someone will always be checking on what I'm doing. I wish this damn language weren't in here. If it weren't I could just sign this thing and get on with my life.

      Maybe, I should just sign the agreement and continue with my present practice. They don't know what I'm doing now and they are not likely to find out. What happens if I sign, continue with my work and then they find out?

23. L: That probably would give PSD the right under paragraph 5 to terminate your contract. Now, the agreement contains an arbitration clause. Therefore, you'd have to file an arbitration claim if you believe that PSD had improperly terminated you. [*Explanation of arbitration provision omitted*] There is a small possibility, say ten percent or so, that an arbitrator might find the clause invalid because it placed an unreasonable restriction on your activities. If an arbitrator were to hold that, then if PSD fires you and you file an arbitration claim, you'd have a right to damages under paragraph 6. You would be entitled to any difference in salary between what you were being paid by PSD and your new job. You would, of course, have to try to get a new job and I guess from what you've told me that wouldn't be a problem. But as I said, the chances that an arbitrator would find the clause invalid and therefore rule in your favor are quiet slim.

24. C: I just don't think PSD will fire me even if they find out about my extra work. They need me; that's why they're

offering me the $10,000 raise. The longer I work on the project the more they'll need me. Unless it's illegal or something, I'd just as soon sign the deal as it is and take my chances. That way I get the raise and there is no hassle about extra work. What do you think about that?

25. L: I'm not sure you should run the risk. In my experience people are best off facing problems before they arise. Why run the risk? If they fire you in the middle of the contract, where will that leave you?

26. C: I'm great at what I do. I'd find another job quickly. Maybe not at $75,000 a year but certainly close to what I'm making now. And furthermore, I'm sure they are not going to fire me. They really need me. The more I think about this the more I realize that the best thing to do is sign the agreement and not worry about this paragraph.

27. L: Rhonda, if you do that and they fire you, at best you'll have to sue them if you want to enforce the contract. If it were me I wouldn't put myself in that situation. I'd face the situation now and rest easy at night.

28. C: I know this possible arbitration claim bothers you but unless there are some other serious problems with this agreement, I'm just going to let sleeping dogs lie and sign. Really, I feel comfortable with that.

29. L: Okay. As long as you understand what the risk is, I guess I can't say anything else. Let's see if there are other problems; perhaps there won't be. Why don't we start with paragraph 1. What this says is . . . .

Nos. 1 and 2 properly start the follow-up meeting by inquiring about new developments and reporting on your actions.[26] In No. 3 you ask Rhonda whether she has read the agreement. This question is clearly appropriate. Through the response in No. 4, you learn that Rhonda has not read the agreement thoroughly and seems uncertain about the meaning of many of its provisions. Hence, affording her a reasonable opportunity to decide probably requires you to conduct a thorough review, and your comment in No. 5 reflecting your decision to review each clause seems correct.[27]

No. 5 is a brief Preparatory Explanation of your intent to review the provisions. The explanation may defuse any uncertainty on Rhonda's part about what the conference will entail. Nos. 5 and 7 ask Rhonda to identify troublesome provisions. As you recall, the beginning of conferences is a good time to give clients an opportunity to express concerns.[28] As Rhonda expresses concern only about paragraph 4 (No. 6), you sensibly start your review with that paragraph (No. 9).

26. *See* Chapter 5.

27. This assessment assumes no problems of time, money or client willingness to review the document.

28. *See* Chapter 5.

As suggested in the earlier subsections, No. 9 starts the review by briefly explaining the clause's likely legal effect without getting caught up in legal abstractions. You also inquire as to its adequacy by asking whether it creates an undue burden. The active listening response (No. 11) encourages Rhonda to identify additional burdens. In describing the burdens she sees (Nos. 10 and 12), Rhonda is concurrently outlining her objectives with respect to paragraph 4. Thus Nos. 9 and 11 simultaneously uncover burdens and identify objectives. Your move in No. 13 to potential alternatives cuts off discussion of further objectives that Rhonda might have. Might you have asked an additional question such as, "Are there any other difficulties you have with paragraph 4?"

No. 13 begins the discussion of alternatives by identifying possible alternatives you see. Given Rhonda's apparent inexperience with employment contracts, starting with alternatives you see seems appropriate.[29] You propose that PSD either permit her to continue her current activities or compensate her for giving them up. You also indicate that PSD might be approached either formally or informally. Certainly the alternatives are not the only ones that you might have mentioned. For example, another alternative is for Rhonda to be free to do her own work on weekends. However, you cannot mention all possible alternatives[30] and your choices seem to cover the basic approaches. Note also that you explain each alternative, and maintain neutrality between them. Finally, you ask Rhonda if she sees any additional options.

In No. 14, Rhonda indicates that she sees an additional option—to sign the agreement as it stands. She then asks for your opinion about which option to follow. In No. 15 you acknowledge the viability of her suggested option. Then, since any opinion you give should be based on Rhonda's values,[31] you tell her that you will need to talk further before giving her any advice. To ameliorate possible disappointment, you include an active listening remark ("I can understand . . .") and expressly articulate your desire to help. Moreover, by telling Rhonda that "it may become clear how you should proceed," you leave open the possibility that she may be able to make the decision herself.

As you can see, the dialogue in Nos. 13–15 fails to comport fully with the counseling model. After Rhonda contributes a new option (No. 14), you fail to ask her if she sees any others. Also, at the conclusion of No. 15 you instruct Rhonda to start with the "status quo" option, rather than asking her which option she prefers to discuss first. Remembering that paragraph 4 is the one of most concern to Rhonda, you might conclude that these shortcomings deny her a reasonable opportunity to explore all pivotal and pertinent options. However, with five options already on the table, and Rhonda expressing uncertainty, perhaps your decision not to troll for additional ones is sensible. On the other hand, your starting with one of your own options is more questionable.

29. *See* Chapter 14.
30. *See* Chapter 16.

31. *See* the discussion of "Providing Advice" in Chapter 13.

Perhaps you have ceased to be neutral and have shown a personal preference for one option.[32]

With Nos. 15–19 you move the conversation to a discussion of options' likely consequences. No. 15 asks Rhonda about the pros of the "status quo" option. Although her mention in No. 16 of not asking for more money crosses over to a con of a different option, No. 17 keeps Rhonda focused on the pros of the status quo option. Moreover, Nos. 17 and 19 both incorporate active listening responses; the former reflects content, the latter reflects both content and feelings. No. 17 "converts" the consequences Rhonda identifies to advantages. No. 19 acknowledges Rhonda's cross over by converting it to disadvantages,[33] but returns Rhonda to the pro side of the ledger by searching for additional advantages.

In No. 20, Rhonda rejects the "ask PSD for more money" option. She gives two reasons for doing so: (1) her own discomfort and (2) not wanting to risk messing up the deal. In No. 21, you accept her decision. However, given Rhonda's relative inexperience, how confident can you be that Rhonda has an adequate data base to predict correctly that "things will get messy"? For that matter, "messiness" is a vague term; further discussion might reveal that PSD would seriously consider a counter-proposal. Hence, No. 21 may too readily accept Rhonda's rejection. Given Rhonda's concern over paragraph 4, affording her a reasonable opportunity to consider the option might at least have prompted you to inquire about the adequacy of her data base.[34] Consider this approach:

> Rhonda, I can tell that you want to avoid angering PSD and that this is an important goal. But before you decide not to ask for more money in exchange for giving up the outside activities, we should think about whether doing so really will create hard feelings on PSD's part. Why do you feel they would get angry if we make this counter-offer?

This comment might cause Rhonda to examine her data base and reconsider her decision.[35] Alternatively, she might stick with her decision, reasoning that though she has little or no data base for predicting that a demand for a bigger raise will create hostility, she nevertheless does not want to take the risk. With misprediction put to the side, and no question of immorality, the issue becomes one of whose sense of risk aversion prevails. And as you know, absent special circumstances,[36] you should not push clients to take risks that they choose not to take.[37]

---

32. Such a preference is at least understandable from a psychological standpoint. You may feel you have been of no help if the client simply signs the proposed draft. However, ethical rules demand that you put a client's interests above your own. See ABA Model Rules of Professional Conduct Rule 1.7(b); ABA Model Code of Professional Responsibility, EC 5–1, EC 5–2.

33. *See* Chapter 17.

34. *See* Chapter 14.

35. Even if her decision does not change, you have at least afforded her a reasonable opportunity to consider the matter.

36. Such circumstances include a client's choice raising moral concerns and a situation where a client is likely to incur a major loss for little gain.

37. *See* Chapter 18. The situation here is the opposite of what you will usually encounter in the deals setting. The more

Return for a moment to No. 21. Here you turn to the alternative of presenting PSD with a revised draft that permits Rhonda to continue her current outside activities, and ask her what advantages she sees. In No. 22, Rhonda indicates dissatisfaction with any approach that discloses her outside activities to PSD. Stating that PSD is not aware of her extra work, Rhonda returns to her previously-broached option of signing the agreement as is. After brief discussion, Rhonda chooses this option (No. 28), and you concur with her choice (No. 29).

The conversation above incorporates many of the counseling techniques that this book has explored. In addition to those techniques just discussed you also convert the chance that an arbitrator will invalidate the restriction to percentage terms and explain what result would ensue were she to prevail (No. 23). Moreover, if Rhonda's question at the end of No. 24 can fairly be interpreted as a request for your personal opinion, you do give her the benefit of that opinion (No. 25).[38] However in doing so it is not clear that you give Rhonda an adequate explanation of why you would not take the risk.[39]

Yet, the dialogue manages to miss most of the underlying concerns of client-centered counseling. Perhaps as a result, Rhonda's choice may be both immoral and based on mispredictions. Rhonda decides that the "sign as is" option is most likely to achieve her objective of continuing her outside work on the basis of a number of predictions: that she will not be found out; that if she is, she will not be fired; and that if she is fired, she will quickly land a comparable job somewhere else. Yet, despite Rhonda's apparent inexperience with how PSD might react to counterproposals, you question none of these dubious predictions. Instead, you meekly assume that her data base for making each is adequate.

Your failure to question Rhonda's data bases also means that potential "cons" go unexamined. You neither ask Rhonda in open fashion what downsides she might see, nor do you use closed questions to raise possible downsides. For example, you might have asked, "Will needing to hide your outside activities be a daily source of worry for you?" and "Would future job opportunities be hurt if you are fired by PSD?" Moreover, you fail to mention a potential negative legal consequence. If Rhonda does develop a successful program with her partners and PSD finds out about it, PSD might claim a proprietary interest in such a product.

Additionally, you allow Rhonda to make what is arguably an immoral choice without so much as a whimper. Rhonda intends to sign the agreement and ignore its restriction on outside activities. Even though there is a 10% chance that an arbitrator would hold the restriction invalid, Rhonda's proposed course of action is deceptive. Engaging Rhon-

---

typical situation is represented by Nos. 25–29 in the Rhonda dialogue—the client wants to take a risk which you believe is not warranted.

38. *See* Chapter 18. As there suggested, perhaps it would have been better had you first asked a question to find out whether Rhonda wanted your personal opinion.

39. Again see Chapter 18.

da in a discussion of this moral concern may well be necessary if she is to have a reasonable opportunity to consider the "pivotal" consequences of her choice.[40] For example, you might have said, "I realize that the outside activities are very important to you, and I appreciate your desire for diversity. But I have some concern over your signing the agreement intending not to comply with paragraph 4. How do you feel about that?"[41]

Finally, recognize that instead of engaging Rhonda in a fuller counseling dialogue, you attempt to dissuade her from her intended path by trying to convince her that the risks (of being found out and fired) are not worth taking. When Rhonda asks for your opinion about whether she should sign, without clarifying her question you interpret it as one seeking to know what you personally would do, and you respond that she should not run the risk (No. 25). However, Rhonda clearly views the risks as minimal (No. 26). Against this backdrop, your pushing her not to run the risks (No. 27) seems a blatant attempt to substitute your sense of risk aversion for hers.[42]

Despite your urging, Rhonda refuses to go along with your advice (No. 28). Thus, to reduce your exposure in the event of a possible future claim by Rhonda that you provided inadequate counseling, you might prepare a "Memo to the File" summarizing the discussion and Rhonda's ultimate decision.

In the end, then, the conversation probably does not provide Rhonda with a reasonable opportunity to make a decision about paragraph 4. Admittedly, you need not slavishly follow every step of the counseling model when reviewing agreements. But here, given (a) the importance of paragraph 4 to Rhonda; (b) her inexperience; (c) the paucity of hard data that PSD would react negatively to an alternative proposal; and (d) Rhonda's contemplated deception and its attendant risks, the number and the severity of the deviations from the model are unwise.

On the other hand, you at least do attend to the topics you typically need to explore when counseling a client about an individual provision. You explain its meaning (No. 9) and explore its adequacy and that of

---

40. In addition, you will want to consider withdrawing should Rhonda insist on going ahead with her choice.

41. Some lawyers would have no qualms about allowing Rhonda to sign the agreement despite her stated intention to disobey its restriction on outside activities. They might find justification for such a position in the notion that when a promisor agrees to a contract, the promisor does no more than promise to perform or in the alternative pay damages. Here, however, it appears that Rhonda wants to sign the agreement as it is but has no intent to perform her promise. See, for example, her comments in the second paragraph of No. 22. Accordingly, Rhonda's position seems morally questionable and is certainly legally problematic. Making a promise without the intent to perform it constitutes deceit. See WILLIAM PROSSER & PAGE KEETON, THE LAW OF TORTS 763 (5th ed., 1984). Moreover such a breach by Rhonda might create a risk of her losing her rights to compensation, including her right to compensation based on profits from the marketing of the program assuming she decides to seek this additional form of compensation. In such a case, Rhonda might have the right to sue you for failing to point out that her promising not to work on other projects without the intent to keep such promise could result in her losing substantial compensation.

42. See Chapter 18.

potential alternatives from Rhonda's perspective (Nos. 9–27). The one topic that gets rather short shrift is examining a provision from the other party's perspective. But the reason for that is understandable. When the other party prepares a draft, you need to examine that party's perspective only when a client wants to offer an alternative. Here, Rhonda's accepting PSD's version of paragraph 4 largely obviated the necessity to explore PSD's likely reaction.

5. COUNSELING CLIENTS ABOUT DEALS' OVERALL WISDOM

The discussion above focused on counseling clients about proposed deals' individual terms. This section turns to what many call "Go/No Go" questions.[43] That is, what counseling strategies are appropriate when clients seek advice about deals' overall wisdom.

Of course, client-centered counseling principles apply equally to both types of decisions. No matter if the question is "Should I sign this lease" or "Is this the right time to bring in a partner?" or some other global sort of question, you examine alternatives and consequences in light of the client's objectives. This section examines how variables such as clients' backgrounds and circumstances might lead you to apply the general counseling approach to the "Go/No Go" context.

A. CASE STUDY NO. 2: SNACKS SIXTH AVENUE

You represent Josef Thrush. For the last three years, Josef has been running a catering business out of his house, mostly catering birthday and anniversary parties in people's homes. You represented him in connection with the initial licensing of his catering business, and you have consulted with him from time to time as problems arose regarding employees, payments from customers, and the like.

A couple of weeks ago, you got a phone call from a very excited Josef. He told you that for some time he had been thinking of stopping the catering business in favor of opening up a restaurant. By having a restaurant, he hopes to realize a more steady income. While he realizes that a restaurant might not be immediately profitable, he thinks that a restaurant in the appropriate site soon would be profitable, and would offer a great potential for growth.

The site Josef has located is the Sixth Avenue Shopping Center, a block-long collection of upscale shops. A restaurant site is currently vacant in the Center, and Josef has begun lease negotiations with Arthur Crenshaw, the Center's manager. Josef believes that the people who tend to patronize the Center's shops will be attracted to his style of cuisine. Josef's discussions with Crenshaw resulted in Crenshaw giving Josef a written lease proposal. After telling you all this, Josef said that he is

---

43. This term is borrowed from James C. Freund although used in a slightly different way from that used by Mr. Freund. *See* J.C. FREUND, LAWYERING: A REALISTIC APPROACH TO LEGAL PRACTICE 268 (1979).

anxious to get started, but he asked you to look over the lease proposal "just to make sure I'm not signing my life away." He mailed it to your office and made an appointment to meet with you two days later so that you could review the lease with him.

Based on the phone conversation and review of the lease, you understand the parties' preliminary agreement to be as follows: Josef and Crenshaw have agreed to a five-year lease for rent of $108,000 per year ($9,000 per month) minimum, as against 7% of gross annual sales. The lease term would start in two months from signing, giving Josef time to make modest capital improvements. The lease is "net, net, net," meaning that Josef would have to pay for repairs, real property taxes and assessments, and fire insurance. In addition, Josef would be obligated to pay a pro-rata share for maintenance of the Center's common areas. From what Josef told you, you know that for last year the taxes for the restaurant location were $3,600, and the maintenance cost was $400 per month.

B.   SHOULD JOSEF ENTER INTO THE LEASE?: "GO/NO GO"

You are now meeting with Josef to review the lease proposal. He remains very anxious to open a restaurant in the Center. However, from your prior dealings with Josef, you realize that while he is excellent at planning and preparing menus, he is not always as careful in making business decisions as he might be. On a couple of occasions that you can remember, Josef has made quick decisions that he has regretted in hindsight. Hence, you think it important for Josef to have a chance to consider whether it makes sense for him to open up his restaurant in the Sixth Avenue Center at all. This portion of the conversation goes as follows:

1.   L: Josef, I've looked at the lease, and there's a couple of ways we can go here. Either we can just go through the lease and make sure you are comfortable with specific provisions, or we can spend a few minutes first talking about whether this deal makes sense for you at all.

2.   C: Well, I'm pretty committed to it. But if you think it's a big mistake, I guess I should know about that.

3.   L: I'm not suggesting that at all; in fact, I don't have enough information to begin to make that judgment. I'm sure you've given it a lot of thought, so it might be helpful if you and I took a few minutes to look at the forest before we focus on the trees.

4.   C: The trees? Does the lease say I'm paying for those too? I wouldn't be surprised—it seems like I have to pay for everything else in that Center.

5.   L: Hopefully, your restaurant will be a smash and it'll be worth it. But it does sound like you have some concerns about the financial commitment you'd be making by signing this lease, so maybe we ought to talk briefly about it. I understand your thinking that a restaurant can provide

steadier income than a catering business and also that it might provide a greater opportunity for growth. But tell me, have you explored other possible sites for the restaurant?

6.   C: No, I figured you'd ask that. I assume there's lots of other places around town where I could open my restaurant, but this one just seems perfect. The clientele and the types of businesses that the Center has will fit in perfectly with my restaurant operation. Also, it's in a growing market, and the location would be very convenient for me and my employees. I don't really want to look elsewhere.

7.   L: You've obviously thought carefully about the advantages of this location. Are there any other pros you can think of?

8.   C: The parking is good. Also, most of the shops are open late, and people are usually around there after dark. That's important because I want to have both a dinner and a lunch crowd.

9.   L: It sounds like an ideal spot. Any other advantages?

10.   C: No. What else could I ask for?

11.   L: Let's look at it from the other side—any disadvantages that you see?

12.   C: No, only I wish the rent weren't so high.

13.   L: Is there any room to negotiate further on that?

14.   C: I don't think so. Crenshaw was definite; standard rent in the center is $3.00 a square foot minimum, against a percentage of gross. And given what I've seen in other restaurant leases recently, 7% is a pretty standard percentage for restaurants in the area.

15.   L: So the options really are to accept this deal or to keep the catering business going until some other opportunity comes along?

16.   C: Yes, but I'm not really interested in looking elsewhere. Also, my goal when I began catering was to go into a restaurant, and I just feel the time is right.

17.   L: Then let's talk about what you see as the major potential drawback, the cost of the lease. For the first year at least, the minimum cost is $116,400. That includes rent, real property taxes and common areas maintenance, assuming the latter two don't increase. And if your annual gross is higher than $108,000, 7% of the excess belongs to the Center. So what we should do is approximate as closely as we can your other likely operating expenses, compare expenses to expected income, and see what the bottom line might look like. Have you projected income and expenses?

18.   C: Yes. I was given access to the books of the restaurant that used to be in that location. It was making money and would still be in operation if the owner hadn't died. Over the last two years, it grossed about $290,000 per year; expenses averaged around $210,000. I'm going to put

about $20,000 into modernizing the place, and together with my style of cuisine, I figure I can do at least $420,000 gross the first year, and $470,000 the second year. That's based on an average price per meal of around $5.50 for lunch and $9.50 for dinner. I know what other restaurants in the area are charging and these prices are reasonable. If I do 160–180 meals a day, I'll reach that gross.

19. L: How about the expenses side?

20. C: Because I pay my employees very well and need a couple more people than the old restaurant, and also to take care of unexpected expenses, I added 35% to the expenses of the old restaurant; that amounts to about $280,000. Plus if I'm serving more meals, my food costs will be higher, say $40,000. So I'm looking at about $320,000 in expenses the first year.

21. L: Have you calculated the number of seatings for both lunch and dinner?

22. C: I really didn't get that specific.

23. L: I think that might be worthwhile; it's one of the biggest differences between being a caterer and running a restaurant. When you cater a party you know in advance how many meals you'll be serving but in the restaurant business the most realistic way to think about likely income is in terms of number of meals per day. How many square feet of seating are available and how many customers can you serve at one time?

24. C: The entire restaurant is 3,000 square feet; the layout gives me about 1,500 square feet for seating. It'll hold around 60–70 people at once.

25. L: All right. How many meals a day do you figure to serve at lunch, and how many at dinner?

26. C: At lunch, I can probably count on two seatings. At least for the first year, let's figure one seating for dinner.

27. L: Working through those figures it seems like your income projections are based on two full seatings at lunch and a full seating at dinner almost every day. Is that realistic?

28. C: I guess I didn't get down to that level of detail. I mainly made my projections based on the old restaurant, and assuming I could do better.

29. L: Unfortunately, the books can't tell us how many meals the restaurant served. Perhaps it would be worthwhile to think through the likelihood that you can serve this many meals per day, especially in the opening months. Also, I'm wondering about your cost projections. Your costs may be different from those you encounter in the catering business and from those incurred by the former tenant. Have you actually worked through all of your costs?

30. C: I pretty much relied on cost figures from my business. I guess I haven't really worked the numbers.

31. L: I'm certainly not an expert on food and restaurant costs, but it does seem to me that you ought to work through the numbers a bit more. Costs for things like utilities and insurance are likely to differ from those in your catering business. Can you work the numbers through by yourself, or would you be better off going through those with your accountant?

32. C: I'll think about that. But I'm glad we're doing this. I guess I liked the location so much that I got carried away. I can see that it makes sense to do some more specific projections on both the income and expense side.

33. L: Why don't you do that, and then we can talk further. If the deal makes economic sense, and probably it will, then there are some other factors to think about, such as how much time you'll need to devote to the restaurant and whether your time commitment is going to take you away from other things you are now able to do.

34. C: I've thought about those things. I'm pretty comfortable with the time commitment. I've got a great chef who wants to continue working with me and take on more responsibility. She'll be able to share a great deal of the supervision, so I should have enough free time.[44]

35. L: So going with the restaurant is not a disadvantage in terms of time?

36. C: No. It's actually an advantage because I should have more time on the weekends. The restaurant would be closed on Sundays as was the previous one; I hate having to work Sundays, but in the catering business, that's a big day.

37. L: Sundays free sounds great. Okay, at this point here's what I suggest. You sit down either with or without your accountant and run more specific projections. Call Crenshaw, let him know of your continued interest and see if he'll commit to holding the site open for you for a week or so. Then, if the finances make sense, we can get back together and go through some of the specific provisions in the lease. There's a few other financial matters we'll want to try to control in connection with potential increased costs under the lease. For example, as the lease now reads, increased property taxes will be passed on to you. And under current tax laws, if the center is sold, its assessed value will undoubtedly go up. We can talk about adding a clause to the lease to protect you from some kinds of tax increases. We can also talk about the wording of specific provisions once you decide the deal as a whole makes sense. Does that seem okay?

44. This comment suggests that as is undoubtedly usually the case in the restaurant business, the chef's role in Josef's decision is critical. Hence, before Josef makes a final decision to "Go," you would want to delve into the terms of any deal between Josef and the chef, the desirability of providing the chef with financial incentives to stay, and what might happen if the chef leaves.

38. C: Sounds good to me. I appreciate the advice—I didn't really think about actual seatings, but I can see that I have to. When can we meet again?

39. L: Just about any time you like . . .

As you can see, Josef has experience in the food service industry. Thus, he is somewhat familiar with food costs and the expenses of meal preparation, as well as with how to price meals to customers. But his experience is as a caterer and not a restaurateur. At the same time, he may be a bit impetuous. He has found a location that apparently will enable him to realize his goal of operating a restaurant and he does not want to consider other possible locations. Thus his mind is partially made up. In the light of these individual circumstances, do you give Josef a reasonable opportunity to decide whether to go forward with the deal?

This question is germane only because Josef agrees to talk about the practical viability of the deal. Josef initially asked you only to "look over" the lease proposal and therefore was perhaps interested in nothing more than your views on its individual provisions. Because business people often resent your giving what they see as business advice,[45] you sensibly ask whether Josef wants to talk about whether the deal makes sense (No. 1). Josef's mild acquiescence (No. 2) opens the door to the Go/No Go discussion.[46]

The "objectives" portion of the discussion is quite truncated. In No. 5 you make but passing reference to Josef's overall objectives and make no effort to update them. Surely a question or two about new or changed objectives would have been appropriate. On the other hand, perhaps your limited exploration is sufficient as only "a couple of days" have gone by since Josef explained his objectives to you.

Turning to options, apart from the question at the end of No. 5, you concur in Josef's limiting the alternatives to opening a restaurant in the Sixth Avenue site. The brief mention of staying in the catering business (No. 15) is not supported by any examination of its consequences. Moreover, you mention but do not push Josef to explore alternative locations for the restaurant (Nos. 5–6). Finally, you fail to mention other possibilities, such as a shorter lease with renewal options or your client's distributing "Josef's Gourmet Cuisine" in pre-packaged form in upscale food stores and markets.

You and Josef then explore a number of likely consequences, particularly financial ones. In Nos. 7 and 9, you convert Josef's reasons for wanting to open a restaurant in the center to advantages and search for additional ones.

45. *See* Chapter 9.

46. The timing of a "Go–No Go" discussion often varies from that depicted in this example. For example, such a discussion may follow, or be interspersed with, a discussion of a deal's individual provisions. Among the reasons for clients belatedly wanting to discuss a deal's underlying wisdom are dissatisfaction with an individual provision that becomes manifest only after discussion of that provision, negotiating demands made by the other party, and changed circumstances in the client's life.

In No. 11 you begin the search for disadvantages. Though Josef sees none (No. 10), his concern about the high rent sets the agenda for the rest of the discussion. First, you check the data base for his assertion that the rent is fixed (No. 13). Then, in Nos. 17–32 you help Josef focus on the possibility that the deal may not "pencil out." As this portion of the conversation illustrates, consideration of a single consequence may be quite extensive. You first elicit the data base for Josef's financial predictions. (Nos. 18–22) Then, in Nos. 23–29, you bring to bear your knowledge of restaurant financing and accounting procedures to suggest that Josef needs more financial information to make a better informed prediction of the deal's likely financial consequences. From experience, you know that the restaurant industry typically calculates gross sales in terms of numbers of seatings per day.[47]

Moreover, you also briefly explore potential non-financial consequences, such as time commitment (Nos. 33–36).

At the end of the day, Josef recognizes that his calculations may be both incomplete and overly optimistic and decides that, either on his own or with his accountant; he will make more precise calculations before going further. Hence, the "Go/No Go" discussion never reaches the decision stage.

Despite the truncated search for goals, the focus on a single alternative and consideration of a limited set of consequences, you seem to give Josef a reasonable opportunity to explore the "Go/No Go" decision. You do not immediately acquiesce in his predilection to enter into the lease. Securing his permission to expand the scope of the discussion allows you to begin to educate Josef about the likely financial consequences of leasing the restaurant.

In this context, initially focusing almost entirely on the financial viability of the single option enhances, rather than detracts from, Josef's opportunity to decide whether to go ahead with the lease deal. The limited focus results in Josef's realizing that he lacks the data to predict whether going forward is likely to allow him to achieve his goal of having a steadier income.

Of course, the limited focus would have been more troublesome had Josef had adequate financial and marketing data. Had the data been adequate to show that the deal was financially viable, or had Josef wanted to take the risk of not getting more precise data, allowing Josef to enter into the lease without giving him the opportunity to examine other alternatives and consequences might well have fallen below the "reasonable opportunity" standard. For example, had Josef decided to open the restaurant without having an opportunity to consider such matters as whether the restaurant would have to remain open on Sundays for Josef to make as much as a restauranteur as he does as a caterer, or without your reviewing the chef's commitment to the restau-

---

47. *See* D.A. Dyer, So You Want to Start a Restaurant? 37–39 (Rev. ed. 1981).

rant, Josef probably would not have had a reasonable opportunity to make the "Go/No Go" decision.[48]

At the same time, the dialogue is not completely decision-free. In addition to deciding to make more financial calculations, Josef decides to hold off further negotiations until he has more financial data. Also, Josef accepts your suggestion in No. 37 that he call Crenshaw and seek a commitment to hold the site open. Neither decision is subjected to a counseling dialogue. As to the former, you do not examine the consequences of delay. And as to the latter, you do not give Josef the opportunity to consider and evaluate other possible options, such as saying nothing to Crenshaw or purchasing an option for a longer period than a "week or so."

Consider, therefore, whether the lack of a counseling dialogue about holding off negotiations and what to tell Crenshaw is appropriate. Arguably these decisions are rather insignificant. The delay may be no more than a week and talking with Crenshaw appears to be a simple matter. Moreover, Josef is somewhat experienced and familiar with Crenshaw. You make your suggestions explicit and give him the opportunity to voice disagreement. You might reasonably expect that Josef would be aware of and would raise negative consequences if there were any.

However, the decisions may be quite important. For example, the financial analysis may take longer than "a week or so," and the delay may result in someone else leasing the restaurant site. Moreover, the opportunity you give Josef to voice disagreement may mean little if he is unaware of or blind to any potential downsides. For example, he may have no idea whether other people are interested in the space. Balanced against these risks, reasonable opportunity may dictate spending a few moments on potential consequences such as: "Do you see any problems with a delay?" or "Do you know if anyone else is interested in the space?"

---

48. Remember that the standard only requires you to afford Josef the *reasonable opportunity* to consider the pertinent and pivotal alternatives and consequences. There is no requirement that you insist that Josef consider these matters if he does not want to do so. *See* Chapter 13.

Chapter 21

REFERRING CLIENTS TO MENTAL HEALTH PROFESSIONALS

1. INTRODUCTION

This chapter explores the process of referring clients to mental health professionals. Generally, such referrals are either *case-related* or *client-related*. Generally, you make *case-related* referrals when clients' mental health issues directly relate to case outcomes. For example, mental impairment growing out of an automobile accident may directly relate to a personal injury plaintiff's claim for damages. *Client-related* referrals, by contrast, arise when you think that mental health professionals may be able to help clients who display psychological symptoms such as severe stress or depression, even though those symptoms do not directly bear on the merits of legal claims.[1] After describing strategies for making referrals effectively and empathically in each of these situations, this chapter examines common circumstances that may incline you to refer clients to mental health professionals.

2. STRATEGIES FOR MAKING REFERRALS

This section sets forth a few strategies you can follow to make it more likely that clients will act on your suggestions that they consult mental health professionals. These strategies also tend to facilitate empathy, so that referrals are less likely to damage rapport. In general, these strategies are the same whether referrals are case-related or client-related.

A. PRE–REFERRAL PROCESSES

Clients are more likely to accept suggestions that they consult mental health professionals if you refer them to a specific person (or

---

1. Since clients' mental functioning is almost always likely to have some bearing on case outcomes, the line between case-related and client-related referrals may at times be difficult to discern. However, the distinction can affect a number of types of decisions you and clients may make. For example, retaining a mental health profes- sional as an "expert witness" means that formal discovery rules regulate an adversary's access to information known to the expert. Whether you and a client decide to retain a mental health professional as an expert, then, may depend on your judgment as to whether a referral is case-related or client-related.

office) who is immediately available and whose general procedures you can describe. Therefore, if possible, do the following before making referrals.

Your first consideration is identifying an appropriate mental health professional who is willing to accept a referral. The field of mental health professionals is vast, encompassing formally-trained people such as psychiatrists, psychologists, social workers, crisis center counselors, drug and alcohol counselors, and marriage and family counselors. The offices in which such professionals work are also varied, ranging from traditional private practice to government-funded community mental health centers, university mental health clinics, and crisis centers. Depending on clients' backgrounds, economic status and cultural backgrounds, you may also refer clients to spiritual leaders, community elders and others who may lack formal degrees or certificates.

Thus, even if you are confident that a client needs the services of a mental health professional, you may be uncertain about what sort of mental health professional might best provide assistance. In such situations, consider seeking advice from other sources, such as another lawyer. Local or state psychological, psychiatric, or social work associations also might be of assistance. Often, clients or their close confidantes can also suggest possible sources of assistance.[2]

When you have obtained the name of a specific person or agency, contact the professional and verify that counseling is currently available including, if possible, specific dates and times. Additionally, obtain a description of what the counseling process will entail and the counselor's likely fee so that you can subsequently communicate this information to a client.[3]

B. DISCUSSING REFERRALS WITH CLIENTS

With a potential referral in hand, consider using the following strategies to help clients understand the need to talk to a mental health professional.

2. When you make a case-related referral, you typically consider a mental health professional's suitability as an expert witness. Once you retain a mental health professional as an expert, your adversary's ability to discover the professional's opinions is circumscribed by formal discovery rules. The most notable of such rules is the "work product" privilege set forth in Rule 26(b)(3) of the Federal Rules of Civil Procedure and in many states' discovery rules, which often insulate the opinions of non-testifying experts from discovery.

3. Because the process of finding a qualified mental health professional may be-

come lengthy, you may think that a client, not you, should have the burden of making the search. However, placing the burden on a client would make it far less likely that a client will actually end up talking to a mental health professional. And, if the professional's intervention is at all successful, the time you spend preparing to make a referral is likely to be far less than the time you would otherwise have spent listening to a client repeatedly unload his or her day-to-day living problems on you. What if a client declines a referral? As the client did not authorize your search, you will probably be unable to bill for your time.

1. Client–Related Referrals

When referring clients to mental health professionals, explain what aspects of their current situations indicate a need for referral. When referrals are client-related, your explanations will commonly touch on what appear to you to be symptoms indicating emotional turmoil. For example, an explanation might point out that a client appears to be under a great deal of stress and seems to be spending an undue amount of time dwelling on day-to-day problems.

Maintain rapport by empathizing with clients' current situations and dilemmas. At the same time, point out that you lack the time and expertise to discuss and help resolve the problems.

Try to "normalize" a client's situation by explaining that people with legal difficulties frequently experience stress, and that many people benefit from counseling. In outlining the potential benefits, point out that in addition to reducing stress, a counselor may be able to help the client make decisions and may be able to refer the client to other specialized sources of help in the community (e.g., vocational guidance, day-care centers, rehabilitation programs, self-help programs).

When clients' reactions suggest that they are uncomfortable with the thought of consulting a mental health professional, empathize with that discomfort. Remember that clients' cultural backgrounds may incline them to have negative attitudes towards seeking mental health help. Explicitly talking to clients about the cultural origins of their discomfort may help them overcome such negative attitudes.

Finally, explain what mental health counseling will entail. Indicate that you can arrange a specific first appointment at a time convenient for the client and also indicate the counselor's likely fee.

To consider how you might go about making client-related referrals to mental health professionals, review the following two examples

Case No. 1

Susan Peters is a 37–year old woman with two children. She has initiated divorce proceedings after ten years of marriage. Her husband is not interested in seeking custody of the children. He gives all his time and attention to work and never really wanted children. She wants a divorce and an opportunity to start a new life. However, her children are upset about the divorce, and one of the children, Dennis, is currently in trouble at school for fighting and truancy. Her husband's parents are calling her daily and haranguing her. Her babysitter has just quit, and she has no one to watch the children while she is at work. She doesn't know whether or not to quit her job, or to try to find another babysitter. Further, she cannot decide what items of personal property she is willing to allow her husband to keep. She talks about her problems incessantly and almost to the exclusion of everything else. She cries often.

She keeps calling you under the pretext of discussing the case, but then quickly switches to a discussion of day-to-day problems. You have tried to be empathic, but really do not have the time or the expertise to advise her how to handle her child's school problem or whether or not to keep working. You sense that with mental health counseling, Ms. Peters might be able to resolve her day-to-day problems, as well as her problems with the property settlement agreement.

1. L: Susan, it seems you're facing a lot of problems you weren't really expecting. Dennis is having problems at school, your in-laws are hassling you, and now the babysitter has quit. All of these problems seem to be causing you a great deal of stress. Many clients in similar situations have also been quite upset and didn't know where to turn for help. You've called me a number of times and I only wish I could be of help in some way. Unfortunately, I really don't have the time or training to help you with these problems, but I do know of some professionals who do. Many clients have benefited from counseling, and I think it could be helpful for you to talk to someone now.

2. C: I don't think I'm that sick. You know, I don't think there's anything wrong with me. It's just his parents are impossible and won't leave me alone, and now the school is calling about Dennis. I just don't know what to do with all of this, and I just can't decide what property I should have.

3. L: You're right. You really do have too many things happening at one time. It's a lot to cope with, and it's very normal to experience a great deal of stress in the face of problems like these. I wish I could offer some helpful suggestions, but I can't. However, Dr. Mathison at the Reed Clinic on Broadway, near 6th, has counseled a number of people going through divorces. I think she could help you make some of the decisions you're facing, and also help with Dennis and your in-laws. She specializes in counseling families and children; that's why I thought she'd be the right person for you to talk to. I'm pretty sure I can call and arrange an appointment for you. Shall I go ahead?

4. C: I don't know. I think I should handle these problems myself.

5. L: I can understand how you might want to handle this alone. Many people feel reluctant to seek help from a counselor. I guess I've also seen how upset you've been in the last few weeks and really think that you could benefit from some outside advice and support. Dr. Mathison would probably meet with you for one hour per week and you could discuss some of your personal concerns. In addition, she could contact Dennis' teacher and the school counselor. I think she would be quite helpful. Would you like me to call for an appointment for you?

6. C: I guess so, but how much will this cost?

7.   L: I can't tell you for sure. If your insurance company provides coverage for mental health counseling, Dr. Mathison will help you get reimbursed for your sessions with her. If not, she will arrange a payment plan with you or help you identify other people who can assist you. The most important thing is for you to meet with her and once you discuss your problems and concerns I'm confident she will find ways to help you.

Analysis

In general, you adequately follow the suggested guidelines. In Nos. 1 and 3, you articulate those aspects of Ms. Peters' situation that indicate the need for a referral. You express empathy for her dilemma, but also indicate that you lack both the time and expertise to provide help for her many problems. In No. 3, you point out that it is quite normal to experience stress, and that counseling can be beneficial. In No. 5, you empathize with Ms. Peters' discomfort about seeking counseling. Additionally, in Nos. 3, 5 and 7, you point out the ready availability of counseling, and explain briefly what the counseling will entail. However, perhaps in No. 3 or No. 5 you might have explained the likely cost of visiting Dr. Mathison.

Assume that Ms. Peters remains adamant that she is not interested in seeing Dr. Mathison or any other counselor. Would you then intervene and try to convince her to see a counselor? Examine the following possibilities:

Alternative 1: Susan, I think you're making a mistake. You've got so many problems now, and the way to straighten them out is to see someone like Dr. Mathison. I'm going to call and arrange an appointment for you.

Alternative 2: Susan, I'm disappointed to hear you're not interested. You have a lot of problems right now, and you're under a lot of stress. Many clients have been helped by counseling, and I think you could benefit from it also. If you change your mind, please call and I'll go ahead and make an appointment for you.

Alternative 3: O.K., Susan. I wanted to make the suggestion, but certainly you are free to make your own decision. I'd like to give you this paper with Dr. Mathison's phone number and address so if you change your mind you can call her and set up an appointment. I've already spoken with her and I know she can give you an appointment on Tuesday, Wednesday or Thursday afternoons.

Client autonomy may be less of a concern when the issue is whether clients should see a mental health professional than it is when clients select a course of action for resolving case related problems. After all, the usual purpose of referring clients to a mental health professional is to help them achieve autonomy. Nevertheless, some clients may find Alternative 1 offensive. For other clients, Alternatives 2 and 3 may be too weak to be effective. In the end, you must make your own judgment, informed by your assessment of clients' needs and your attitude towards client autonomy, about how to respond when clients refuse referral to a mental health professional.

Case No. 2

Bernard Sossin was arrested for embezzling funds from the insurance company with which he was employed. Although he has told his wife, Rhoda, about the arrest and the loss of his job, he has been unable to break the news to his children, Ruth and Adam. Without income, his debts are mounting. He is determined not to go into bankruptcy, at least until after his trial, which is set for 90 days hence. In addition to the concern he feels about telling his children, Mr. Sossin is worried about what to say to his social acquaintances and how to handle his financial situation. He is considering withdrawing his children from private school. He would like to get a temporary job but has no idea how to do so. He is especially uncertain of how to explain why he now needs a job. He is mulling his problems over continually and has started to drink. He calls you at least twice a week, supposedly to talk about the case. However, Mr. Sossin always turns the conversation to the subjects of his children, his lack of a job, and his worries about facing his friends. You have decided to end this meeting with Mr. Sossin by recommending he seek counseling to help him cope with his problems.

1. L: Bernie, there is something I'd like to discuss with you. You've called me a number of times this past week to discuss your concerns about your family, your job situation, and what to tell your friends. You seem to want to talk about these problems a lot, and they seem to be causing you a lot of stress at this time. I'd like to help with these problems, but they're really out of my area of expertise. It's not just the job, or what to tell the kids, we've been over that. Right now the real problem, as I see it, is all the stress you're under. You've got all of this plus the worry of the trial, so I can understand why you're so preoccupied with your problems. I'd like to make a suggestion. There is a Dr. Bolberg who has an office in this building. He has counseled a number of people with problems similar to yours, and I think he can help you.

2. C: Look, you know how I feel about shrinks. No way. I know I've been drinking a little too much, but what do you expect? I'll stop being such a pain in the ass, but you gotta admit I'm really in a mess.

3. L: Hey, I was pretty sure you wouldn't like the idea of seeing a counselor, but there's really nothing wrong with doing it. One doesn't have to be sick to need some help. You've got enough problems for two or three people to handle, and counselors often know about resources that I'm not at all aware of. Do yourself a favor, let me call Dr. Bolberg and arrange an appointment. It can't hurt and it might help.

4.   C: I fail to see how lying on a couch and going on and on about my mother is going to help me now.

5.   L: Listen, you've been watching too much T.V. I'm not talking about five years of intensive psychoanalysis. Dr. Bolberg will meet with you once or twice a week and talk to you directly about the problems you raised with me. I think he'll be able to help you feel a lot better in a short period of time. Unless you say no, I'd really like to give him a call. I think it would help.

Analysis

In reviewing the foregoing example, consider the following:

1.   In No. 1, do you do an adequate job of pointing out the factors indicating that a referral may be helpful? Why or why not?

2.   In No. 3, are you empathic about Bernard's discomfort about seeing a counselor? Why or why not?

3.   Do you do an adequate job of explaining what the counseling will entail? Why or why not?

4.   What other things might you have said to facilitate this referral?[4]

2. *Case–Related Referrals*

When discussing case-related referrals, your explanations are likely to emphasize the relevance of mental health issues to cases' outcomes. For example, here you discuss a case-related referral with Mr. Beckworth, an electrical engineer whose job requires sustained attention and the ability to make quick decisions. Mr. Beckworth was rear-ended on a freeway. Since the accident he has had memory problems, has difficulty learning new information, has problems retaining information, and is easily distracted. He shows increasing irritability and is distraught about his future ability to provide for his family.

L: Mr. Beckworth, as you know what we are seeking to recover in your case is damages for all the injuries you've suffered. Those damages can include compensation for any brain injuries that the accident caused. To help us evaluate that situation and get a treatment plan going, I'd like to refer you to Dr. Sanna Franklin for an evaluation. She's a very good neuropsychologist, and specializes in the effects of brain injuries on people's behavior. You hit your head on the steering wheel during the accident, and that may explain the cognitive and emotional problems you've been experiencing.

---

4. You can often make clients feel comfortable with a referral by saying something like, "With your permission, I can give the counselor a brief overview of your legal situation and the other issues that are causing you a lot of stress right now. Then when you have your first meeting the counselor will be up to speed and able to help you more quickly."

C: How can a doctor figure this stuff out? An x-ray won't show all the changes that have happened in my brain since that damned accident!

L: You're probably right about that, and that's why it's so important for you to see Dr. Franklin. She has evaluated many people who have had head injuries in car accidents. Unfortunately, car accidents are very common. The good news is that they have developed some standardized tests of things like memory and attention, as well as personality tests that can give us some very specific and helpful information. It could make a big difference in the amount of money you get in damages. Also, seeing Dr. Franklin can help you get the treatment you need to get better. It may also help your family better understand what is going on with you. I know you want help for you and your family. Dr. Franklin is certified to do this kind of evaluation and I would like you to see her as soon as possible. She has an appointment available on Thursday, the 28th at 10:00. It will take about two hours for the first appointment.

C: It sounds like it will cost a lot of money. Can't my family doctor do this? He's covered on my insurance plan.

L: I understand and want to be sensitive to your concerns about expenses. Dr. Franklin will discuss the fee arrangement and will also bill your insurance whenever possible. You need to see someone with specialized training. A referral to someone without it would be a total waste of your time and money. I'm confident it's worth it for you. The evaluation will give us specific information that can help us determine such things as the size of the settlement we should ask for, and what kind of treatment can best aid in your recovery. The insurance company may claim that you had these problems before the accident, or you're just faking symptoms to get a bigger settlement. We absolutely need this information to get you the best settlement and treatment possible.

Here, you focus on the case-related reasons for the referral and the potential benefits. You are generally empathic, and acknowledge Mr. Beckworth's concern about expenses. You also rely on the facilitator of "external reward," explaining the importance of the evaluation to a satisfactory case outcome.

3. ARCHETYPAL SITUATIONS INVOLVING CASE–RELATED REFERRALS

Case-related referrals can arise whenever mental health professionals' evaluations and opinions are likely to play a formal role in case outcomes. While anything approaching a compete list of legal problems likely to require case-related referrals is not possible, the two examples that this section briefly describes may help you recognize the appropriateness of referrals in other settings.

Brain damage which may accompany personal injuries is a frequent reason for making case-related referrals. Consider these scenarios:

Case No. 1

Mrs. Sugarman, age 72, was shopping for a birthday present for her grandson. She was walking down an aisle of a toy store and didn't notice the small plastic beads that had been spilled on the floor. She slipped and hit her head on a shelf and blacked out. She reports feeling confused and forgetful ever since the accident. She reports she doesn't feel like her "old self," and often can't find the right word for what she's trying to say. She says she used to be very active and independent but now she's afraid to even go to the market alone.

Case No. 2

Jeremy, age 14, was enjoying the premiere of the latest kung fu action film at a new theater in his local shopping mall. He reports he was sitting in his seat, totally engrossed in the film, when a speaker fell off the wall and hit him on the side of the head. He was stunned for a while and then felt a little disoriented when he walked home with friends. He thought everything was fine but now finds he's easily distracted at school, and gets low grades on tests no matter how hard he studies. He used to be a very motivated student with a strong B average. Now his grades are dropping and he could care less. His parents think the head injury is responsible for his low grades and want to sue the movie theater.

In each scenario, changes in behavior and the level of the clients' anxiety suggest that head injuries may have caused brain damage. Thus, a referral to a neurologist, a psychiatrist, or a neuropsychologist would be appropriate. When you talk to a professional to whom you are considering making a case-related referral, consider asking the professional to address such questions as:

Has the client suffered brain damage?

Is the brain damage a result of the incident that is the subject of the pending litigation?

What are the plaintiff's functional deficits?

What will be the short and long-term effects of the injury?

How will these short and long term effects affect earning capacity?

Is rehabilitation possible? If so, what rehabilitation services does the patient require?

Who else is damaged by the plaintiff's deficits (spouse, children, parents, etc.)?

To what extent is the plaintiff aware of the losses sustained?

What is and will be the nature of the plaintiff's mental and physical suffering?

Is the client malingering?

Are the client's problems organic or psychological?[5]

Questions such as these generally ensure that a professional's evaluation responds to the case-related issues that prompted the referral.

Child custody disputes are a second common scenario in which lawyers make case-related referrals to mental health professionals.[6] In such settings, spouses contesting for custody of their children often challenge each other's mental health and argue that their spouses' mental health problems detract from their parenting ability.

Referrals to mental health professionals in child custody cases are especially likely to arouse deep feelings of shame, embarrassment, inadequacy and loss of control. These feelings increase when a client's family or cultural background stigmatizes the seeking of help for emotional problems. Thus, you may need to exercise patience, demonstrate a good deal of empathy and explain the importance of mental health evaluations on custody issues before clients are willing to seek help.[7]

4. ARCHETYPAL SITUATIONS INVOLVING CLIENT–RELATED REFERRALS

As with case-related referrals, a list of situations that typically produce client-related referrals is impossible to compile. Indeed, almost any state of affairs resulting in legal problems has the potential to cause clients to experience such symptoms as stress, anxiety and depression that in no way directly relate to case outcomes. For example, prolonged negotiations may cause severe stress to a client seeking to enter into a long-term lease. Similarly, a client who has consulted you with respect to legal issues arising in connection with the estate of a recently-deceased parent may be depressed about the parent's death and angry about the perceived greed of other family members.

Because clients often react emotionally to situations creating legal problems, not every display of emotion justifies a client-related referral. However, when clients report and appear to you to be under an abnormal amount of stress or appear unusually depressed, referral to mental health professional may be appropriate. For example, consider these scenarios:

- Sal Hepatica is going through bankruptcy. Sal has been either late for or has forgotten about a number of appointments. Moreover, Sal has failed to collect needed information and often makes such

---

5. See S. Essig, W. Mittenberg, R. Petersen, S. Strauman, & J. Cooper, *Practices in Forensic Neuropsychology: Perspectives of Neuropsychologists and Trial Attorneys*, 16 ARCHIVES OF CLINICAL NEUROPSYCHOLOGY, 279 (2001).

6. The stress of their families' breaking up also often results in client-related referrals. However, clients may be reluctant to consult mental health professionals for help in coping with divorces and child custody disputes, fearing that doing so will only provide additional ammunition to their spouses.

7. For a description of clients' common psychological reactions to divorce as well as a description of how the psychological impact of divorce affects family lawyers see G. Benjamin, M. Reid & J. Gollan, *Psychological Aspects of Divorce*, WASHINGTON FAMILY LAW DESKBOOK, 2000.

remarks as, "I just can't seem to get going these days. It's easier to stay in bed than have to deal with bankruptcy and my friends."

- Mary Poppins has sued her former business partner. For many years, Ms. Poppin's business was extremely successful in providing nannies for child care. However, Ms. Poppins took steps to dissolve the partnership when an audit revealed that her partner had been skimming funds for years. She also learned that many of the nannies she placed did not have proper work documents, and criminal proceedings are possible. As a result, she is extremely angry. She frequently responds to your requests for information with angry outbursts directed at her ex-partner, and repeatedly dwells on the same incidents despite your best efforts to show empathy and explain your need for information.

Each of these scenarios depicts a client for whom a referral to a mental health professional seems appropriate. The clients' emotional problems are beyond your ability to respond to, and without help from a trained professional these clients seem unable to provide the information you need to accomplish the purpose for which they sought legal assistance. Thus, you may consider following the strategies described above to encourage the clients to seek the help of a mental health professional.[8]

5. CONCLUSION

Suggesting that clients consult a mental health professional is often difficult. You may feel that merely mentioning the subject will cause clients to become angry or at least uncooperative, and rupture the lawyer-client relationship. Admittedly, the referral process outlined above is no guarantee that ruptures in the lawyer-client relationship will never occur. However, referrals are often necessary. You can advance your ability to make referrals successfully if you get to know and build a track record with a small group of referral sources that you can count on to handle both client and case related referrals. This chapter offers the suggestions above as a useful starting point for thinking about when and how and to whom to make referrals. You may be surprised to find that many clients will appreciate your efforts to help them find assistance for the many problems and concerns they unexpectedly experience while seeking help with their legal situations.

8. The motivator of "external reward" is not of apparent use when you make client-related referrals, because mental health issues do not directly influence case outcomes. Nevertheless, you may use a form of "external reward" by pointing out that a satisfactory outcome is possible only if a client is able to participate fully in the attorney-client relationship.

*

Index

References are to Pages

ACTIVE LISTENING
See also, Motivation
Generally, 48–49
Amount of, 63, 123
Angry clients, responding to, 261
Clients' data bases, probing, 353–356
Compared with passive listening, 48–49
Content, reflecting, 28, 49
Counseling, use of during, 319, 338, 354, 356, 364, 366, 371, 373, 433
Decision-making, facilitating, 371–373
Difficulties in mastering, 57–62
Distractors, 44
Feelings, responding to, 11, 28, 41–42, 49–55
Hostile clients, use in responding to, 99–100
Identifying content and feeling, 42–44
Importance of, 41, 49, 135
Non-empathic responses, 55–59
Passive listening techniques, 44
Preliminary problem identification, use during, 90–99
Proposed deals, use during, 433
Rambling clients, responding to, 257, 258
Rapport, facilitating, 28, 88, 91, 135; see also, Rapport
T-funnel, use during, 178
Time line phase, use during, 123, 126, 135, 138, 140

ADVANTAGES
See Consequences

ADVERSARY'S CONTENTIONS
Rebutting, 194–196
Uncovering, 196–198

ADVICE GIVING
See also, Counseling Process
Attorney personal values, based upon, 272, 369–370
Business advice, see Proposed Deals
Clients' requests for, 289, 368–371
Clients' values, based on, 10–11, 38, 289, 368–369
Consistency with client-centeredness, 285, 289
Counseling process, preceded by, 289
Immoral decisions, 391–393

ADVICE GIVING—Cont'd
Knowledge, need for legal and non-legal, 332
Legal parameters, identifying, 239
Predictions, based on, 307
Premature requests for, 370
Tentative, 238, 241, 248
Unrequested, 291–292, 378–379
Written charts, use of, 320

AGED CLIENTS, 255

AGREEMENTS
See Proposed Deals

ALTERNATIVES
See generally, Chapter 16
Change in objectives, effect on, 346
Changed circumstances, impact of, 346
Clients, conflicting feelings towards,
Lose-lose, 372
Win-lose, 372
Win-win, 373
Clients identifying, 9–10, 87–88, 91–99, 283, 304, 305
Counseling plan, inclusion in, 301
Cross over phenomenon, 311, 315
Cultural experience, suggested by, 305
Framing Effect, see Consequences
How many to identify, 332–333, 345
Inadequate, responding to, 342–345
Industry knowledge to identify, 284, 334–338
Information to obtain, 282
Information to provide, 284
Initial client conference, identifying during, 88
Lawyer identifying, 157, 284, 304, 306, 332, 345, 405
Legal meanings, explaining, 319, 338–340, 412
Neutrality in framing, 300
Order of review, clients deciding, 309
Pivotal alternatives, 286, 332–333
Predictions, based on, 307
Preparatory explanations, use of, 301
Reasonable opportunity to evaluate, 285
Rejection by client, reacting to, 342–343
Reviewing separately, advantages of, 309
Uncertainty about, 242

ALTERNATIVES—Cont'd
Unfamiliar, describing, 319, 338–340

ALTRUISTIC APPEALS, 30

ANCHORING EFFECT
See Cognitive Illusions

ANGRY CLIENTS
See Hostile Clients

ATTORNEY–CLIENT RELATIONSHIP
Activity and new information, effect on, 109–111
Authority, attorney's, 236
Conflicting interests, 274
Fee agreements, 237
Formalizing, 236
Illegal or immoral objectives, responding to, 328
Mental health professional, effect of referral on, 445
Substantial impact standard for decision-making, 276
Scope, clarifying, 236
Value conflicts, 296, 328
Withdrawal, see Ethics

ATTORNEY ROLE
See also, Counseling; Advice Giving
Alternatives, suggesting, 284, 304
Autonomy, retaining, 293, 294, 295, 297
Breaks, providing, 261
Client perception of, 21–23
Consequences, predicting, 307
Counseling obligation, extent of, 275, 282
Decision-making
Intervening in, 292–295
Which decisions to make, 276, 286
Defining, 3–4
Downstream consequences, explaining, 320
Eliciting information from clients, 116–119, 211–212, 282
Extent of counseling, 275, 282
Fabrication
Responding to, 265
Techniques for preventing, 264
Fees, establishing, 237
Identifying alternatives and consequences, see generally, Chapters 13, 14
Improper objectives, responding to, 328
Informed consent standard, problems with, 277
Neutrality, see Neutrality
Next steps, specifying, 235
Non-legal consequences, predicting, 308, 317
Objectives
Clarifying vague, 323
Suggesting, 304, 325
Predicting consequences, 307, 308, 317
Professional relationship, establishing, 236
Professional skills, decisions based on, 280, 297
Proposed deals, 209

ATTORNEY ROLE—Cont'd
Providing information to clients, 284
Psychological counseling, role distinguished from, 58
Rambling clients, interrupting, 260
Reasonable opportunity to decide, providing, 286
Referrals to mental health professionals, see generally, Chapter 21
Reluctance of clients
Anticipating, 248
Responding to, 249
Retainer agreements, 236
Scope, clarifying, 236
Substantial impact standard for decision-making, 275
Value preferences of attorney, voicing, 291, 328
Written charts, preparing, 236, 320

ATTORNEY VALUES
See also, Advice Giving
Basis for decisions, 369
Conflict with client choices, 36–38, 274, 328
Cultural differences, 32, 34–40
Difficulty in active listening and helping client, 57–58
Risk aversion, 296

AUTONOMY OF CLIENTS, 4–5, 290, 292, 300

AUTONOMY OF LAWYERS, 293, 294, 295, 297

BACKWARDS REASONING, 160

BAD NEWS, 243, 372

"BEFORE AND AFTER" EVENTS
Defined, 164
Sources of,
Inferences, 164, 200
Witnesses, 165
Time line phase, eliciting during, 183–184

CARTOON, 41

CASE THREAT
Avoidance of, 20–21, 262
Defined, 20–21
Fabrication, result of, 262
Omitted events, 20, 185
Theory development, 197

CHECKLISTS, 218

CHEYENNE "TROUBLE STORIES," 305

CHRONOLOGICAL NARRATIVE
See Time Line Phase; Time Line Stories

CIRCUMSTANTIAL EVIDENCE
See also, Credibility
At trial, using, 162
Before and after events, 164–165
Defined, 161–162

CIRCUMSTANTIAL EVIDENCE—Cont'd
Factual propositions, using to establish, 161–162
Historical reconstruction, developing through, 163
Premise, use with, 171–172

CLIENT–CENTERED APPROACH
Advantages of, 3–8
Advice giving by attorney, 10–11, 285, 289
Assumptions underlying, 3–8, 247, 272
Attributes of, 8–11
Clients as primary decision makers, 272
Clients' objectives, seeking, 303
Comparison to traditional conception, 4, 291
Cultural differences, responding to, 38–40
Defined, 3
Fabrication, reducing, 263
Intervention in decisions, 292, 295
Neutrality, consistent with, 300
Proposed deals, 209
Risks, 7–8, 296

CLIENT CONFERENCES
See also, Follow–Up Meetings; Initial Client Conference,
Actions attorney will take, identifying, 235
Actions client will take, identifying, 235
Adversary's contentions, see generally, Chapter 8
Business transactions, 208–233
Concluding, See generally, Chapter 11
Documents, requesting client to bring, 81
Fees, establishing, 237–238
Formalizing relationship, 236
Greeting clients, 82–83
Icebreaking, 83–86
Preparatory explanations, 103–106, 120–126, 192–193, 197, 226
Preparing for initial conference, 81
Reluctance of clients, responding to, see generally, Chapter 12
Specifying next steps, 235
Telephone, initial conference by, 81
Tentative advice, 101–103, 238, 241

CLIENT CONFIDENCE
Bolstering, 235, 236, 239
Client expectations, responding to, 239
Desire to help, conveying, 239, 240, 241, 243, 268
Initial conference, concluding, 239
Reporting activity and data as bolstering, 109

CLIENT RELUCTANCE
Affect on counseling obligation, 289
Anticipating, 248
Responding to, see generally, Chapter 12
Sources of, 247
Time line development, 143–144
To commence an interview, 253
To discuss particular topics,
Anticipating, 248

CLIENT RELUCTANCE—Cont'd
To discuss particular topics—Cont'd
Indicia of, 247
Motivational statements, 248
Responding to, 118, 248

CLIENT TRUST, DEVELOPING, 20, 27, 28, 41, 90, 201, 236, 350, 352

CLIENT VALUES
Bases for lawyers' advice, 10, 368–369, 386
Culturally based, 32, 34

CLOSED QUESTIONS
See also, Yes–No Questions
Accuracy and completeness, effect on, 75, 130
Advantages of, 71–72, 130, 228
Aged and infirm clients, use with, 255
Credibility evidence, eliciting, 188–193
Defined, 67
Details, eliciting, 71, 228
Disadvantages of, 72–74
Identifying consequences, 357, 435
Motivation, effect on, 71–72, 252, 254
Omitted events, eliciting, 129
Omitted objective, eliciting, 304
Rapport, harming, 72–73
Use during
Proposed deals, 228–229
T–funnel, 168–169, 172, 228–229
Theory development, 168
Time line phase, 130–131
Use in communicating with,
Aged clients, 255
Client reluctance, 252
Rambling clients, 258

CLUMPED EVENTS
Breaking into sub-events, 115–116, 180–182, 199–200, 231
Defined, 115
Illustrations of, 115–116, 182–183, 199, 231
Overcoming client tendency towards, 115, 182
Reasons for, 115, 182, 231
T–funnels, 180–183

COGNITIVE ILLUSIONS
Anchoring effect, 241, 385
Availability heuristic, 351–356
Data bases emanating from, 351–352
De-biasing strategies, 353–356
Distorting effect of, 284
Endowment effect, 384
Framing effect, 341
Gamblers' fallacy, 383
Overconfidence phenomenon, 384
Responding to data bases emanating from, 351–356
Self-serving bias, 385
Sunk costs phenomenon, 383

CONCLUDING CLIENT CONFERENCES
See generally, Chapter 11

CONCLUSIONS
See also, Clumped Events; Conditions and Behaviors Over Time
Defined, 184
Details,
Contradiction between, 189–190
Probing for, 185

CONDITIONS AND BEHAVIORS OVER TIME
Defined, 183
Eliciting discrete events, 133, 183–184, 200
T-funnels, 200

CONFIDENTIALITY
Insurance-retained counsel, 107
Overcoming reluctance, 251, 253
Preparatory explanation, discussion during, 106–107

CONFLICT OF INTEREST
Decision-making, 274

CONFRONTATION
See Fabrication

CONSEQUENCES
See also, Decision–Making; see generally, Chapter 17
Acknowledging conflicting feelings, 371–373
Advantages and disadvantages, seeking, 309
Clients identifying, 283, 348
Clients' understanding of, 287, 319
Counseling plan, inclusion in, 301
Counseling process, see Counseling Process
Cross over, 311, 319, 320, 321, 366, 434
Data bases for predictions, 349–356, 380–382
Downstream consequences, 320
Everyday experience, role in identifying, 357
Identifying, 358–366
Industry knowledge, using to identify, 356
Non-legal, clients as having better data bases, 5–7, 308
Lawyer identifying, 285, 317, 408
Predictions, based on, 306, 308, 317, 349–356
Reasonable opportunity to evaluate, 285
Range of outcomes, identifying, 362
Sub-predictions, 358–360
Legal consequences, predicting, 358–368
Mis-predicting, 296, 380–382; see also, Cognitive Illusions
Non-legal, 306, 308, 356–358
Numerical probabilities, use of, 360–368, 405
Organizing discussion of, 308
Pivotal consequences, 285, 297
Predictions, based on, 283, 295, 306, 307, 349–356
Process for exploring, 308

CONSEQUENCES—Cont'd
Pros and cons, converting to, 348
Rating technique, 373, 409
Risks, see Risks
T-funnels, use of to uncover, 310, 354
Third persons, effects on, 358
Value rating of, 373, 376
Written chart of, 320

CORRECTIVE FEEDBACK, 251

COUNSELING PROCESS
See also, Attorney Role; Consequences, Mental Health Professionals
Advice giving, consistency with client-centeredness, 289
Alternatives, identifying, 304
Clients' minds made up, 302, 397–399, 405, 419–420
Clients' values, advice based on, 289
Consequences, exploring, 306, 308, 317, 354
Cross over phenomenon, 311, 319
Cultural differences, 395
Cyclical nature of, 12, 322, 328, 345
Deal's overall wisdom, 437
De-biasing strategies, see Cognitive Illusions
Decision-making, see Decision–Making
Defined, 271
Foundations for, 332
Four steps of, 300
Immoral decisions, see Immoral Decisions
Integrating pros and cons, 317, 408
Intervening in decisions, 379–399
Litigation clients, examples regarding
Whether to file suit, 401–406
Whether to take depositions, 406–409
Whether to settle, 409–414
Neutrality, maintaining, 300, 302, 309, 312, 315, 316
Objectives, clarifying, 302, 323–330
Opportunity to decide, 285, 323
Overview of, 281, 300
Plan for, developing, 301
Premature requests for advice, responding to, 370
Preparatory explanations, see Preparatory Explanations
Primary decision-makers, clients as, 272
Proposed deals, see generally, Chapter 20
Rapport, maintaining during, 317
Reasonable opportunity to decide standard, 287
Risk-aversion, 393–394
Similarly-situated clients, obligation measured by, 287
Standards for extent of counseling obligation, 286
What alternatives to suggest, 286
What decisions to discuss, 285
T-funnels, use during, 310
Time demands, 289, 322
Transactional matters, see Proposed Deals
Two-way street, 282

COUNSELING PROCESS—Cont'd
Value differences, 394–395
Written charts, use of, 236, 320

CREDIBILITY
Circumstantial evidence, effect upon, 162
Conditions and behaviors over time, effect upon, 163, 183
Contradictions, effect upon, 189
Details, effect upon, 189, 200
Doubting clients', 192, 268
Evidence relating to, 150 n.1
Experience, effect upon, 159–160
Factors affecting, 186–192
Implausibility, effect on, 263
Inquiries regarding, 186–191
Omitted events, 200
Theory development phase, exploring during, 186–191

CROSS OVER PHENOMENON, 311, 319, 320, 321, 366, 434

CULTURAL DIFFERENCES
Accepting clients' cultural values, 395
Affect on counseling obligation, 287
Alternatives, clients' suggesting, 305
Decision-making, 395
Dimensions of, 34–38
High context/High content communication, 35
Long term/Short term orientation, 35
Masculinity/Femininity, 35
Neutrality re options, need for, 300
Observing and recollecting, 177 n.26
Power distance, 35
Proposed deals, 209–210
Responding to, 38–40
Time line development, 120
Uncertainty avoidance, 35

DATA BASES
See Consequences

DEAL–KILLER, 209, 214–215

DE-BIASING STRATEGIES
See Cognitive Illusions

DECISION–MAKING
See also, Attorney Role; see generally, Chapter 18
Active listening, use of during, 371–373
Autonomy of clients, 4–5
Alternatives, seeking during, 283
Borderland of intervention, 395–396
Clients' conflicting feelings,
Lose-lose, 372
Win-lose, 372
Win-win, 373
Clients' minds made up, 302, 397–399, 405
Clients unable to decide, 368–378
Conflicting interests, 274
Cultural differences, 395
Decisions for clients, standard for, 275
Draft agreements, 417–437

DECISION–MAKING—Cont'd
"Ends" vs. "means", 276
Feelings, acknowledging to facilitate, 371–372
Immoral decisions, see Immoral Decisions
Implementing decisions, see Implementing Decisions
Intervening in, 292, 379–399
Lawyering skills decisions, 280, 297
Mis-predictions, 296, 380–382, 405
Neutrality during, 300
Objectives, clarifying, 283, 302, 326
Preparatory explanations, use of during, 301
Risks, 7–8, 296, 393–394
Subsidiary decisions, 303
"Substantive" vs. "Procedural", 276
Third persons, use of to facilitate, 376–377
Values,
Attorney, see Attorney Values
Clients', 272, 291, 368–369, 386
Role of in decision making, 272
Written charts, using, 236, 320

DETAILS
Accuracy, effect upon, 189
Credibility, effect upon, 189
Eliciting, 133, 149, 184
Events, as gateway to, 181, 184
Factual propositions, using to prove, 156–157
Persuasiveness of, 189
T-funnels, eliciting through, 189
Theory development, eliciting during, 149, 181, 184
Time lines, use during, 133

DIFFICULT CLIENTS
Aged or infirm clients, 255
Angry and hostile clients, 99–101, 260
Fabricating clients, 262
Rambling clients, 99–101, 256
Reluctant clients, 247

DIRECT EVIDENCE
Defined, 161–162
Factual propositions, use to prove, 161–162

DISADVANTAGES
See Consequences

DISTRACTORS, 44

DOCUMENTS
Adversary's position, 196
Availability of, 134
Client's responsibility to obtain, 134
Credibility evidence, 120, 148
Historical reconstruction, 148, 165
Information, source of, 120, 135, 142
Multiple perspectives, 165
Potential evidence, identifying as, 134, 142, 148
Proposed deals, 210, 221–222
Recollection, use to enhance, 120, 134, 142, 148

DOCUMENTS—Cont'd
T-funnel to uncover, 207
Time line phase, use during, 134–135, 142, 148

DOWNSTREAM CONSEQUENCES, 320

EFFECTS ON THIRD PERSONS
See Consequences

EGO THREAT
Avoidance of, 19–20
Client reluctance, cause of, 248
Credibility inquiries, 186–192
Defined, 19
Fabrication, as cause of, 262
Omitted events, 118
Theory development phase, 192

ELEMENTS
Abstract nature of, 153
Defined, 153
Factual propositions, restating as, 163–164
Illustrations, 153
Trial, establishing at, 153

EMPATHIC UNDERSTANDING
See also, Active Listening
Bad news, conveying with, 244
Communicating through active listening, 42, 135
Defined, 48
Follow-up meeting, showing during, 110
Illustrations of, 95–99, 135
Importance in attorney-client relationship, 48–49
Non-empathic responses, 55–57
Note taking, 121–122
Open questions, 128
Rambling clients, 256, 258
Reference to mental health professional, 447
Reluctance of clients, responding to, see generally, Chapter 12
Time line questioning, use during, 121, 135

ENDOWMENT EFFECT
See Cognitive Illusions

"ESPECIALLY WHENS," 166, 187

ETHICS
See also, Attorney Values
Counseling standard, applying, 277
Difficult clients, see generally, Chapter 12
Fabrication, 179, 268
Intervening in decisions, 293
Questioning techniques, 75, 178–179
Withdrawal, 268, 298

ETIQUETTE BARRIER, 24

"EXCEPT WHENS," 166, 187

EXPERIENCE
See also, Filling
Cultural, 120

EXPERIENCE—Cont'd
Everyday, use of, 159, 186, 356–357
Historical reconstruction, 163
Potential evidence, use to develop, 159–161
Time line stories, use to elicit, 115–116

FABRICATION, 180, 262–268

FACILITATORS
Defined, 18
Summary list, 31
Types of, 27–31

FACTUAL PROPOSITIONS
Adversary's, 150, 196–198
Affirmative stories, 158
Defendants', 158
Defined, 23, 154
Details as linking events to, 154, 181
Developing, 154
Events, effect on importance of, 180–181
Illustrations, 155–158
Industry knowledge, need for, 157, 356–357
Multiple, 156–157
Need to develop, 154
Number of, 157
Omitted events, identifying possible, 200
Plaintiffs', 157–158
Potential evidence, developing from, 154, 164
Proving, 155, 164
Use of, 164

FEELINGS
See also, Active Listening; Motivation
Acknowledging to facilitate decisions, 371–372
Client-centered approach to, 11
Conflicting, 61–62, 372–373
Defined, 42
Illustrations of, 42–44

FEES
Agreement for, 237–238
Discussing, 238
Preparatory explanation, discussion during, 105
Specifying, attorney's responsibility for, 238

FILLING IN
Avoidance of, 184
Clumped events, 181–183
Conclusions, 184
Defined, 75–76, 184
Illustrations, 77, 184–185

FOLLOW–UP MEETINGS
Beginning, 108
Changed concerns and objectives, 108
Lawyer's interim activity, 109
New information, 109–110
Order of discussion, 111

GAPS
Filling in to mask, 75
Inferences affected by, 130

GAPS—Cont'd
Preparing chronologies to identify, 148
Probing to uncover additional events, 185, 200
Time line stories, 132, 138, 140, 185

FULFILLING EXPECTATIONS
Defined, 29
Illustration, 29
T-funnels, use during, 177

GAMBLERS FALLACY
See Cognitive Illusions

GENERALIZATIONS, 163–164

GOOD NEWS, 243

GREATER NEED
Defined, 26
Overcoming, 26
Rambling, produced by, 99–101, 257

HARMFUL EVIDENCE, 21, 150, 194–197, 199–200, 206–207

HELP, CONVEYING DESIRE TO, 239, 240, 241, 243, 268

HELPFUL EVIDENCE
See generally, Chapter 7; pps. 196, 201

HISTORICAL RECONSTRUCTION
"Before and after" events, 164
Defined, 163
Illustration of, 164
Multiple perspectives, 165
Potential evidence, use to develop, 162, 171

HOSTILE CLIENTS, 99–101, 260

ICEBREAKING, 83–86

IMMORAL DECISIONS, 295, 298, 328–330, 391–393, 395–399, 414, 434–436
See also, Moral Values

INDUSTRY KNOWLEDGE
Client knowledge, 221
Defined, 157
Need for, 160
Non-legal consequences, 356
Proposed deals, 212–213, 221
Use of,
    Alternative solutions, 334–338
    Draft agreements, 212–213, 221
    Factual propositions, developing, 157, 160–161
    Potential consequences, identifying, 356–357
    Potential evidence, developing, 157, 160–161

INFERENCE DRAWING
"Before and after" events, 164–165
Chronological order of events, 118
Specific evidence, 162

INFIRM CLIENTS, 255

INFORMED CONSENT STANDARD, INADEQUACY OF, 277

INHIBITORS
Avoidance through,
    Leading questions, 74–75
    Open questions, 68
Defined, 18
Summary list, 31
Types of, 19–26

INITIAL CLIENT CONFERENCES
    See also, Client Conferences; Advice-giving
Client expectations regarding, 238
Concluding, See generally, Chapter 11
Difficult clients, 99
Establishing professional relationship, 236
Information gathering prior to, 81
Objectives, focus on, 87
Potential solutions, outlining during, 238
Preliminary problem identification, 86–101
Preparatory explanations, use of, 103–106, 197–198
Reluctance of clients, responding to, see generally, Chapter 12
Specifying next steps, 235
Tentative legal assessments,
    Giving, 101–103, 238
    Not giving, 239

INTERVENING IN DECISIONS, 292–295, 379–399

JACK AND THE BEANSTALK, 113

KICK STARTING A CLIENT'S MEMORY, 175

LEADING QUESTIONS
Advantages of, 74
Defined, 67–68
Disadvantages of, 75
Ethical propriety of, 75, 180
Information, effect on accuracy and completeness of, 75
Inhibitors, using to overcome, 74–75

LEGAL CONSEQUENCES
See Consequences

LEGAL THEORIES
Abstract nature of, 153
Defined, 153
Elements, converting to, 154
Explaining to client, 180 n.29
Factual propositions, converting to, 154
Illustrations, 153
Plaintiffs', 157
Time line story, suggested by, 150, 152

MEMORY
Aged clients, 255
Empathy for client difficulty, 177, 255
Forms of questions as affecting, 68–75
Multiple time line stories, 142–143
Probe notes, 135–136

MEMORY—Cont'd
Promoting through,
Chronological order, 117
Client's own words, using, 117
Clumped events, breaking up, 115, 180–181
Details, eliciting, 172
Documents, 134
Expectancy, 29
Note taking, 135–136
Pressing clients, 177
Summary technique, 131–132, 178
T-funnel, 172, 180
Time line phase, 117
Topical search, 156–157
Visualization, 175–177

MENTAL HEALTH PROFESSIONALS
Case related referrals, 451–452
Typical situations involving, 452–454
Client related referrals, 447–451
Typical situations involving, 454–455
Discussing referrals with clients, 446–452
Pre-referral actions, 446–447
Referral strategies, 445–452

MINIMAL PROMPTS, 46–47

MIS–PREDICTIONS
Cognitive illusions, see Cognitive Illusions
Data bases, insufficient, 380–382, 405

MORAL VALUES
Advice-giving, 291
Clients', respect for, 292, 293
Intervening, justifying based on, 293–295
"Moral community," 377
Moral "know it all," 295, 396
Objectives, 328

MOTIVATION
See also, Facilitators; Inhibitors
Attorney-client dialogues, 18–19
Closed questions producing, 71, 254
Confidence in lawyer, 109–110
Generally, 16–18
Intercultural communications, 32–40
Needs, 16–18
Normalizing remarks, use of, 254
Promoting through,
Active listening, see generally, Chapter 3; 249
Closed questions, 71–72, 252, 254, 258
Confidentiality, reminder of, 251
Corrective feedback requests, 251
Neutrality, 300
Normalizing responses, 250, 253, 254
Open questions, 68–69, 177
Questioning pattern, changing, 251
Reward statements, 177, 250, 253, 254, 258
War story, 264
Reluctance of clients, use in responding to, 249, 254

MOTIVATION—Cont'd
T-funnel, 175–176
Theory development questioning, 175–177
Time line phase, 118

MULTIPLE PERSPECTIVES, 165

NARROW QUESTIONS
See Closed Questions

NEUTRALITY, MAINTAINING, 300, 302, 309, 312, 315, 316

NON–LEGAL CONCERNS
Awareness of, 90, 211–212
Changes in, 108–109, 111
Client-centered approach, 5
Client initial agenda, 87–89
New information, effect on, 108–109, 111
Preliminary problem identification, eliciting during, 88–89, 96–97
Prominence of, 5
Proposed deals, 211–212

NON–LEGAL CONSEQUENCES
See also, Consequences
Counseling process, addressing during, 306
Identifying, 5–7
Importance to client, 5–7
Predicting, 308
Types of, 4

NORMAL COURSE EVENTS, 160, 231 n.12

NORMALIZING RESPONSES, 250, 253, 254, 262

NOTE TAKING
Explanation of, 121, 135–136
Probe notes, 135–136
Rapport, effect on, 121–122
Theory development phase, 201
Time line phase, 121, 135–136

OBJECTIVES
Alternatives suggested by, 303
Changed, 326
Clarifying, 213–214, 228, 302, 326, 404
Decisions inconsistent with as basis to intervene, 292
Eliciting information concerning, 283, 302
Illegal or immoral, 328
Incomplete, 325
New information, effect on, 108–110
Omitted by client, suggesting, 304
Open questions to elicit, 303
Other party's, 228
Overall objectives, 213–214, 224–225
Preliminary problem identification, eliciting during, 87–88, 91–99, 224–225
Preparatory explanation, identifying during, 302
Proposed deals, 213–214, 225
Reward statement, using, 228
Seeking clients', 283, 302, 326
Specific objectives, 224
T-funnels, use of to elicit, 228, 304

OBJECTIVES—Cont'd
Updating, 302, 326
Vague, techniques to clarify, 323

OMITTED EVENTS, 115, 118, 129, 130, 185–186

OPEN QUESTIONS
Accuracy and completeness, effect on, 68–70, 97, 128, 168–169
Advantages of, 68–69, 128–129, 168–169
Clarifying or identifying objectives, 303, 324
Consequences, reviewing, 310
Disadvantages of, 70–71
Inefficiency of, 70
Inhibitors, avoiding by using, 68–69, 97, 128
Motivation, effect on, 68–69
Objectives, clarifying, 303, 324
Preliminary problem identification, 91–94, 95–98
Proposed deals, information gathering, see Chapter 10
T-funnel technique, 168–169, 229
Theory development, 168–169
Time line phase, 128–130, 230
Use in responding to client reluctance to discuss a particular topic, 251

OVERCONFIDENCE PHENOMENON
See Cognitive Illusions

"PARKING" DATA
Defined, 173
Explaining, 173, 228
Note taking, need for, 201
Returning to, 174–175
Sidetracking, 174, 228
    Use during, T-funnels, 173, 228
    Topical search, 228

PARKING ON DATES
Not included

PASSIVE LISTENING TECHNIQUES, 44

PERCEIVED IRRELEVANCY, 25–26

PERSONALITY CONFLICTS, 31–32

POTENTIAL EVIDENCE
    See also, Factual Propositions Amount of, 157
Categories of, 158–166
Choosing what to pursue, 151–158
Developing through using,
    Experience, 160
    Factual propositions, 154–159
    Historical reconstruction, 163
    Multiple perspectives, 165
    Narrowing generalizations, 165–166
    T-funnels, 170
    Theory development, 154–159
Documents, 134
Identification of, need for, 166
Omitted events, identifying potential, 200
Probative value, 154

POTENTIAL EVIDENCE—Cont'd
Sources, identifying, 158–166
Topical searches, as basis for topics, 170–171

PREDICTIONS
    See also, Consequences Bases of, obtaining, 283
Cognitive illusions, impact on, see Cognitive Illusions
Need for, 283, 306, 317
T-funnels, use of to explore, 354

PRELIMINARY PROBLEM IDENTIFICATION
Beginning with, importance of, 89–91, 224
Client perspective or initial agenda, 87–91, 95, 224
Concerns, eliciting during, 88–89, 224
Concluding, 93
Defined, 87–89
Empathy, providing during, 90
Four main topics, 87–89
Illustrations and analysis of, 94–99, 224–225
Non-legal concerns, 89, 225
Objectives, eliciting during, 87–89, 95–98, 224–225
Premature diagnosis, avoiding, 89
Process described, 91–95, 224–225
Proposed deals, 211
Rapport, effect on, 90
Structural guide, use of, 93, 101–103, 224–225
Telephone conversation, prior to, 81–82
Tentative nature of diagnosis, 101–103

PREMATURE DIAGNOSIS, 77–78

PREPARATORY EXPLANATIONS
Advantages of, 104, 225, 301
Confidentiality statements, 106–107
Content of, 104–106, 120–121, 197, 225–226
Credibility inquiries, 192
Decision-making, preceded by, 301
Illustrations and analysis of, 120–122, 225–226, 302
Length of, 107, 121
Proposed deals, 225–226
Rapport, aiding, 192
Time line questioning, 120–126
Use when,
    Draft agreement review, 225–226
    Making decisions, 301
    Time line phase, 120–121

PROPOSED DEALS
Adequacy of provisions, 423–425
Alternative approaches, 214
Client priorities, effect on topical inquiries, 213–214, 226
Contingencies, 218, 220
Deal-killer, 209, 214
Draft agreements,

PROPOSED DEALS—Cont'd
Draft agreements—Cont'd
Discussions with client before preparing, 210, 222
Forms, using, 222
Preparing, 210, 221–222, 417
Reviewing with clients, 210, 417–420
Experience, attorney's, 213
Finalizing, 215
Information to gather,
Alternative approaches, 214
Business operations, 217
Chronology, 215
Client priorities regarding topics, 213–214, 226
Deal-specific data, 219–220
Economics, 219
General data, 210
How deal will function, 218, 231
Legal and non-legal concerns, 211–212
Negotiating history, 214–215
Objectives, 213–214
Obligations, 212
Other party, 216, 426–428
Potential terms, 218
Prior dealings, 215, 216, 232–233
Priorities, clients', 226
Risks, 218–220
Terms, potential, 218–230
Terms agreed to, 229–230
Timetable, 215
Legal consequences of, 220
Litigation, compared to, 211
Objectives, both parties', 214, 216
Obligations, assigning, 212
Omitted provisions, discussing, 420–421
Overall wisdom of, 437
Progression, 209, 213
Provisions,
Contingent provisions, 220–221
Counseling concerning adequacy,
Meaning of, explaining, 220–221, 420–421
Operative provisions, 220–221
Remedial provisions, 220
Risks, evaluating, 219–220, 273
Substantial impact standard, 277
Term sheets, use of, 421
T-funnel questioning, use of, 223, 227, 230
Time line questioning, 229
Timetable for, 215
Transaction-specific topics, 219
Walking through a deal, 219

QUASI TIME LINES, 232

QUESTIONS
See also, Closed Questions; Leading Questions; Open Questions; Yes No Questions
Changing pattern of, 251
Client questions, inviting, 236, 254, 284
Generally, 65–66, 168–172

RAMBLING CLIENTS, 256

RAPPORT
Active listening, as facilitating, 28, 88, 91, 135
Adversary's position, discussing, 391
Client expectations, responding to, 238–239
Client reluctance to discuss topics, 118
Closed questions, effect on, 68, 72–73, 95
Credibility inquiries, 192
Data bases, inquiring into, 350
Fabrication, preventing, 263
Facilitating, 32, 33, 40, 41, 64, 66, 72, 81, 87, 91, 100, 135, 145, 249, 260, 264, 266, 281
Inviting questions, 236
Mental health referrals, 445
Note taking, 136
Open questions, effect on, 68, 90
Preliminary problem identification, 90
Pre-meeting communications, 81
Preparatory explanations, 104, 122, 301
Rambling clients, 95, 257
Theory development, 167–168
Time line phase, 118, 127
Unsolicited advice, 292

REASONABLE OPPORTUNITY TO DECIDE STANDARD, 286, 300, 303, 342, 350, 362, 367, 368, 370, 373, 394, 397, 405, 409, 413, 415, 418, 423, 432, 436, 442, 444

RECOGNITION
Defined, 30
Illustrations, 140
Open questions, use of to provide, 68
T-funnels, use during, 177

REFERRALS TO MENTAL HEALTH PROFESSIONALS
See, Mental Health Professionals; see generally, Chapter 21

REWARD
Client reluctance, overcoming 250, 253, 254
Defined, 31
Objectives, eliciting, 304
Motivation, providing, 177, 228, 253, 258
Rambling clients, 256, 258

RISKS
Aversion to, 7, 10, 19, 209, 274, 281, 285, 296, 393, 416, 434, 436
Avoiding, 209
Business risks, 209, 219
Conflicting attorney-client values, 273
Decision-making, impact on, 7–8, 296
Defined, 393
Evaluating, 209
Information about, proposed deals, 209, 273
Opportunity to evaluate, 285
Responding to clients' attitudes towards, 393–394

ROLE EXPECTATIONS
Dealing with, 22–23, 104–105

ROLE EXPECTATIONS—Cont'd
Defined, 21–22

SELF–SERVING BIAS
See Cognitive Illusions

SILENCE
Listening technique, 45–46
Responding to fabrication with, 267

SIMILARLY–SITUATED CLIENTS, 287, 324, 325

SNAPSHOTS (LITIGATION), 401–414

SOLUTIONS
See Alternatives

STEREOTYPING, RISKS OF, 32–34, 36

STORIES
See also, Time Line Stories
Adversary's, 114, 148; see generally, Chapter 8
At trial, 113–114

STRENGTHENING GENERALIZATIONS, 161, 162, 165–166

SUBSTANTIAL IMPACT STANDARD
Defined, 275
Impact on lawyers' tactics, 280

SUMMARY TECHNIQUE
Advantages of, 131
Illustrations of, 310, 316
T-funnels, 178
Time line phase, 131–132

SUNK COSTS
See Cognitive illusions

TACTICAL CHOICES, IMPACT OF COUNSELING STANDARD ON, 280

TELEPHONE CALLS
Follow-up meeting by, 108
Preliminary information gathering by, 81–82
Preliminary problem identification, 81–82, 91, 94–95
Prior to initial conference, 81

TENTATIVE LEGAL ASSESSMENTS
Additional information, need for, 242, 246
Bad news,
  Conveying, 243, 245
  Sugar coating, 244, 246
Caveats, conveying, 241, 243
Empathy, conveying with bad news, 244, 246
Expectations of client, effect on, 241, 243
Good news, conveying, 243
Illustrations of, 239, 241, 242, 243, 246
Inability to give, 239
Initial conference, concluding with, 238

T–FUNNELS
Adversaries' likely contentions, 198, 207, 389
Clarification during, 184
Client discomfort, 197–198
Clumped events, breaking up, 180–181, 200
Conditions and behaviors over time, 163, 183
Consequences, use of to explore, 310, 354
Counseling, use during,
  Clarifying objectives, 304
  Discussing consequences, 310
Credibility inquiries, 187–192
Cross over during, 311
Cyclical use of, 174
Defined, 167–168
Diagram of, 168
Documents, 207
Ethical considerations, 178
Events,
  Clumped events, breaking up, 168–170
  Discrete, focus on, 168
  Previously discussed, 168
Illustrations, 168–175, 206
Importance of judgment, 170, 175, 178
Judgment, need for, 178
Kick starting client's memory, 175–176
Objectives, use of to obtain, 304
"Parking" data, 173–175, 206
Partial "T's," 172
Previously discussed events, 168
Proposed deals, use in information gathering, 223, 227–230
Questioning techniques, 168
Rebutting harmful evidence, 195, 207
Summary technique, 178
Topics, 170–172
Tornadoes distinguished, see "Wizard of Oz"
Visualization technique, 175

THEORY DEVELOPMENT
See also, Credibility; T–Funnels; Topical Searches, 166
"Before, during and after," 164
Beginning, 167
Client discomfort, 192
Co-authored time lines, 141–142
Conclusions, probing for detail, 184
Credibility inquiries, 186–191
Defined, 149
Details, search for, 149–150
Documents, 165, 196, 207
"Especially whens," 166
"Except whens," 166
Events,
  Clumped, breaking up, 179–180
  Discrete, focus on, 168
  Omitted, 115, 118, 129, 185–186
  Selecting to pursue, 168
Filling gaps, time line stories, 159
Legal theories, need for, 152–153
Multiple factual propositions, need for, 156

THEORY DEVELOPMENT—Cont'd

Omitted events, probing for, 115, 118, 129, 185–186

Order of questioning, 168

Potential evidence, developing questions from, 149–150, 166

Preparing for, 166

Probe notes, 201

Probing gaps for additional events, 185

Questioning techniques, 166–167

Time line phase,
    As basis for, 118–119
    Shift from, 118

Topical searches, 170

When to begin, 133–134, 149

"THIRD PARTY" TECHNIQUE, 192, 266

THIRD PERSONS, FACILITATING DECI-SION–MAKING BY USING, 376–377

TIME LINE PHASE

See generally, Chapter 6; see also, Time Line Stories

Advantages of, 116–119

"Ancient" events, probing, 148

Chronological gaps, 132–133, 138

Clarifying stories, 130

Closed questions, use during, 130–131

Clumped events, 115–116, 182

Cultural influence on, 120

Defined, 112–113

Detail, seeking during, 133–134

Difficult clients, 143–148

Documents, use of during, 134–135

Earlier events, probing for, 126–127

Examples of, 137, 230

Expanding "quickie" time line stories, 127–128

Gaps, 132

Illustrations of,
    Active listening, 125, 126
    Closed questions, 130–131
    Clumped event, eliciting mini-time line, 115–116, 182

Inability to provide, 143–148

Note taking, 135–136

Open questions, 129–130

Summary technique, 131–132

Memory, stimulating, 117–119

Multiple sub-stories, 142–143

Normal course events, 129

Note taking during, 135–136

Omitted events, 115, 118, 129

Open questions, use during, 128–130, 230

Perceived irrelevancy, avoidance of, 136

Preparatory explanation, 120–126

Proposed deals, use in, 226, 229–233

Purposes of, 113–114, 229–230

Quasi-time lines, 232

TIME LINE PHASE—Cont'd

Starting at the beginning, 126–127

Summary technique, 131–132

Theory development, bridging into, 118–119

Updating, 148

TIME LINE STORIES

See also, Time Line Phase

Accuracy of, 117

Attributes of, 114–116

Beginning of, 126–127

Chronological gaps, 132–133, 138

Clarifying, 130–131

Clumped events, 115–116

Co-authored, 141–142

Completeness of, 112, 117, 119

Conclusions, 116, 128

Conditions and behaviors over time, 183

Courtroom perspective, 117

Cultural influences on, 120

Defined, 115–116

Evaluating, 117, 128, 141, 148

Expanding, 127

Factual propositions, developing from, 118

Illustrations, 137–141

Inferences drawn from,
    Chronological order, 118
    Length of intervals between events, 131

Intervals between events, 131

Legal theories, suggested by, 116, 117, 133–134

Length of, 141

Multiple sub-stories, 142–143

Omitted events, 115, 118, 129

Quickie stories, 127, 232

Sequence of events, 114, 118

Updating, 148

TOPICAL SEARCHES

Client discomfort, 118, 170, 192

Combining topics, 178, 221, 226

Defined, 150–151

Efficiency, 167

Illustrations, 168–170

Omitted events, uncovering, 164–165

Order of inquiry, 167

Parking data during, 173

Probing uncovered events, 184–185

Proposed deals, 208, 211, 212–221

Recall, promoting, 167

Specificity of, 184

Time line, using during, 119, 133

TRANSACTIONS

See Proposed Deals

TRAUMA

Client reluctance, cause of, 24–25, 248

Defined, 24

VALUE RATING OF CONSEQUENCES, 373, 376

VISUALIZATION
Defined, 175
Illustrations, 175–177, 231

WAR STORIES, USE OF, 21, 264

WITHDRAWAL, 268, 298

YES–NO QUESTIONS, 72

†